Leicester Abbey

Essays to celebrate 150 years of

The Leicestershire Archaeological and Historical Society

1855   2005

Leicester Abbey

medieval history, archaeology
and manuscript studies

EDITED BY

Joanna Story, Jill Bourne and Richard Buckley

LEICESTER

The Leicestershire Archaeological and Historical Society

ISBN 0-9542388-1-8 / 978-0-9542388-1-0

Designed at The Red Gull Press and 4word Ltd
Printed and bound in Great Britain by 4word Ltd, Bristol

First published 2006

Contents

vii Abbreviations

viii Acknowledgements

Joanna Story   ix Introduction

Richard Buckley   1 The archaeology of Leicester Abbey
with Steve Jones, Peter Liddle,
Michael Derrick and James Meek

David Dawson   69 An incense-boat cover from Leicester Abbey

Anthony Squires   75 The landscape of Leicester Abbey's home
demesne lands to the Dissolution

Richard Buckley   95 Leicester Abbey after the Dissolution
with Steve Jones, Paul Courtney and David Smith

Geoffrey Martin   119 Henry Knighton and Leicester Abbey

Teresa Webber   127 The books of Leicester Abbey

Michael Gullick   147 The binding descriptions in the library
catalogue from Leicester Abbey

Michael Gullick   173 Summary catalogue of surviving manuscripts
and Teresa Webber   from Leicester Abbey

David Postles   193 On the outside looking in: the Abbey's
urban property in Leicester

Anthony Roe   217 Abbot Sadyngton of Leicester Abbey and
onychomancy: an episode of clerical
divination in the fifteenth century

David Crouch   225 Early charters and patrons of Leicester Abbey

289 Bibliography

295 Index of Manuscripts

Rory Naismith   297 Index of Medieval People and Places

311 General Index

Abbreviations

Bodl.	Bodleian Library
BL	British Library
CBMLC	Corpus of British Medieval Library Catalogues
CCCM	Corpus Christianorum, Continuatio Medievalis
f. / ff.	folio / folios
fl.	*floruit*
JBAA	*Journal of the British Archaeological Association*
PL	*Patrologia Cursus Completus, Series Latina,* ed. J.-P. Migne, 221 vols. (Paris 1844–65)
LCMS	Leicester City Museums Service
ODNB	*Oxford Dictionary of National Biography,* ed. H. C. G. Matthew and B. Harrison (Oxford 2004), cited *sub nomen*
ROLLR	Record Office for Leicestershire, Leicester and Rutland
TLAAS	*Transactions of the Leicestershire Archaeological and Architectural Society* (1866–1912/13)
TLAHS	*Transactions of the Leicestershire Archaeological and Historical Society* (1955–)
TLAS	*Transactions of the Leicestershire Archaeological Society* (1921/22–1954)
TNA	The National Archives (formerly, The Public Record Office (PRO))
ULAS	University of Leicester Archaeological Services
VCH	*Victoria County History*

Dating conventions

s.	*saeculum* (century)
s. xii in.	early twelfth century
s. xii med.	mid twelfth century
s. xii ex.	late twelfth century
s. xii^1	first half of the twelfth century
s. xii^2	second half of the twelfth century
s. xii$^2_4$	second quarter of the twelfth century
s. xii$^1_3$	first third of the twelfth century

Acknowledgments

The publication of this book has been made possible through the sponsorship of The Leicestershire Archaeological and Historical Society, in celebration of its 150th anniversary in 2005. We are particularly grateful also to The Aurelius Trust which gave a generous grant to support the purchase and publication of plates of Leicester Abbey manuscripts, most of which are reproduced here for the first time. It is all too often the case that plates of pages from medieval manuscripts are reproduced only when they are illuminated and 'special'; we felt strongly that it was important to reproduce here images from a wide range of books surviving from the abbey's library to illustrate the 'typical' variety of book of different dates, styles and decoration owned by a medieval English Augustinian monastery.

Plates are reproduced by kind permission of The President and Fellows of Queens' College Cambridge (ch. 6, figs. 3 and 5; ch. 7, fig. 3; ch. 8 figs. 1–2); The Master and Fellows of Trinity College Cambridge (colour plate E; ch. 6, figs. 4, 6–8; ch. 8 figs. 3–11); The Master and Fellows of Pembroke College, Cambridge (ch. 7, fig. 2); The Bodleian Library, University of Oxford (ch. 8, figs. 12–15 and 21); The Trustees of the National Library of Scotland (ch. 6, fig. 2); The Chatsworth Settlement Trustees (colour plate B and ch. 1, fig. 8; © The Devonshire Collection, Chatsworth); The Lincolnshire Archives and the Diocese of Lincoln (ch. 10, fig. 1); Tate, London 2005 (cover and ch. 1, fig. 11); The Record Office for Leicestershire, Leicester and Rutland (colour plate C); The Victoria and Albert Museum (ch. 2, fig. 2).

We are grateful also to the following for permission to reproduce other images: John Finnie for his 'reconstruction' painting of the abbey (colour plate A); Web Aviation 2003 (ch. 1, fig. 1); Anthony Squires (ch. 3, figs. 2, 6–9, 11); Anne Tarver (ch. 3, figs. 4 and 5); James Meek (ch. 9, fig. 1). Thanks also to Indexing Specialists (UK) Ltd for the General Index, and Rory Naismith for the Index of Medieval People and Places. The Leicester City Museum Service (LCMS) and the Record Office for Leicestershire, Leicester and Rutland (ROLLR) have helped often with enquiries by authors and editors of the volume. Finally, the editors would like to thank Michael Gullick for his overview of the production and design of the book and his careful editorial guidance. Who better than a scholar of medieval book production to oversee the publication of such a volume.

J. S., J. B. and R. B.

Introduction

Joanna Story

In the mid-fifteenth century, a small paper manuscript was copied at Glastonbury Abbey, beginning with the abbey's accounts and completed by a miscellany of prose and verse items in Latin and English.[1] One of these is a burlesque Latin poem written in deliberately bad 'schoolboy' Latin that follows a relentless rhythm, ignores grammatical convention and twists vernacular words into Latin-sounding ones; it survives in a number of other copies made in England, Ireland and on the continent and parodies the drunken lifestyle of a monastic house. As such, it is part of a long satirical tradition that used the medium of poetry to poke fun at establishment figures, and to elevate the wit and linguistic dexterity of the poet. The abbot sits down to drink at a feast and invites the other brethren to partake because, if they are left out, 'they will give us a hard time in the chapter house'. But the prior contradicts the abbot, and a drunken row ensues when a canon of the house joins in the debate. The unhappy poet is left, without a drink, to deal with a vomiting abbot, a puking prior and questions from the bishop.

The Glastonbury copy of this popular poem is particularly interesting because it provides both the longest version of it (some 62 stanzas) and also because it attributes the drunken spectacle to the abbot, prior and canons of Leicester Abbey. The poem begins:

> Quondam fuit factus festus,
> et vocatus ad commestus,
> Abbas, Prior de Leycestrus,
> cum totus familia.[2]

The name of Leicester fits the rhythm of the verse and, since the residents of Leicester Abbey were Augustinian canons (rather than Benedictine monks or Franciscan friars) as the narrative demands, most scholars have assumed that the Glastonbury manuscript preserves the most reliable version of the poem.[3] The consequential aspersions cast on the morals of the community at Leicester Abbey have been critically overlooked in favour of the interest in the poem as an example

---

1. The poem, 'Satryicum in Abbates', is item VIII in Cambridge, Trinity College 0.9.38, ff. 14r–16v. See, A. G. Rigg, *A Glastonbury miscellany of the fifteenth century: a descriptive index of Trinity College, Cambridge MS 0.9.38* (Oxford 1968), 32, 46–7; H. Walther, ed. *Initia carminum ac versuum medii aevi posterioris latinorum* (Göttingen 1959), no. 16347; W. Meyer, ed. '*Quondam fuit factus festus*, ein Gedicht in Spottlatein', *Nachrichten von der königlichen Gesellschaft der Wissenschaten zu Göttingen*. Philologisch-historische Klasse (Göttingen 1908), 406–29; F. J. E. Raby, *A history of secular Latin poetry in the middle ages*, 2 vols (Oxford 1957), ii, 307–8.

2. Loosely translated (to retain the regular Victorine sequence):
> Once a feast was fabricated,
> To the banquet were invited,
> Abbot and the Prior of Leicester
> and their whole community.

3. See for example, G. G. Coulton, *Europe's apprenticeship: a survey of medieval Latin with examples* (London 1940), 258–9.

of late medieval English wit and the contemporary popularity of drinking songs and anti-clerical satire. It bears comparison, however, with another humorous Latin poem linked to Leicester, copied into a late thirteenth- or early fourteenth-century manuscript that was part of the abbey's library (Gullick and Webber, below, pp. 190–1, no. 23). This second poem seems to have been written by one of the canons of Leicester Abbey, who, rather than scorning his superiors, mocks a group of the abbey's tenants who had dared to bring to the king's court a series of complaints against their monastic landlords.[4] The poem is especially notable because it comments on a series of events that occurred in or soon after 1296 that are documented elsewhere, in the royal court rolls; it also confirms that, when it came to witty Latin verse, the Leicester canons could give as good as they could got – especially when their social inferiors were the target.

The Glastonbury manuscript of the drinking poem dates to *c.* 1450, and the choice of Leicester Abbey as the poem's target undoubtedly reflects the contemporary fame of Leicester's powerful and rich Augustinian house; but it need not preserve a genuine memory of that monastery as a place with a binge-drinking discipline problem. As noted already, the poem survives in other manuscripts copied both in England and on the Continent; these indicate that the poem could have been composed as early as the thirteenth century and thus that it circulated widely for some time before being copied by the Glastonbury scribe. It is very likely an English composition but its barbed attack on Leicester may simply be because 'Leycestrus' conveniently fits the scansion of the verse; indeed the next best copy of the poem (in an Irish manuscript) fingers Gloucester rather than Leicester as the house of degenerate drunkenness.[5]

The Glastonbury scribe's laugh at Leicester was a taunt in the manner of the football terraces of today; a generic parody of monastic gluttony and indiscipline rather than an informed accusation levelled at a rival monastic house. Nevertheless, there may have been genuine reasons for the Glastonbury scribe to ridicule Leicester at the time the poem was copied; in 1440, the bishop of Lincoln had made a formal visitation to Leicester Abbey to investigate – not accusations of drunken excess – but charges of sorcery that had been made against the unpopular Abbot Sadyngton by members of his own community (Roe, below, pp. 217–24).

The Sadyngton story and the Glastonbury drinking poem provide rare allusions to the less salubrious reputation of Leicester Abbey in the mid fifteenth century. A lot more evidence survives, however, for the more sober and serious side of the social and cultural history of the Abbey in the late middle ages. Particularly important in this respect is the evidence preserved in two manuscripts from Leicester Abbey that date to the later fifteenth century, now Oxford, Bodl. Laud misc. 623 and Laud misc. 625 (Gullick and Webber, below, pp. 183–6, nos. 16 and 17). The first of these contains a catalogue of the books in the abbey's library that was compiled by a Leicester canon called William Charyte, who became precentor and then, by 1463, the abbey's prior. Charyte's catalogue is of national importance since it is unparalleled among British medieval library catalogues in its comprehensive coverage of the contents and bindings of the abbey's manuscripts; as such, it provides important insights into the intellectual culture and possessions of a rich, late medieval English Augustinian house as well as clues to the physical layout of the library at Leicester (Webber, below, pp. 127–46 and Gullick, below, pp. 147–72).

4. R. H. Hilton, 'A thirteenth-century poem on disputed villein services', *English Historical Review* 56 (1941), 90–7, reprinted in his *Class conflict and the crisis of feudalism: essays in medieval social history* (London 1985), 108–13.

5. BL, Harley 913 (s. xiv in.) which also contains a well-known Middle English verse collection known as the 'Kildare Poems'; W. Heuser, ed. *Die Kildare Gedichte*, Bonner Beiträge zur Anglistik 14 (Bonn 1904) and A. M. Lucas, ed. *Anglo-Irish poems of the middle ages* (Dublin 1995).

Charyte was also responsible for copying the second of the Leicester Laudian manuscripts, known from its title in the library catalogue as the 'novum Rentale' or 'new Rental' (Oxford, Bodl. Laud misc. 625; Gullick and Webber, below, pp. 185–6, no. 17). The book is a link to the abbey's medieval archive that was largely destroyed after dispersal at the Dissolution; it provides a summary of the abbey's property, as was known to Charyte in the late fifteenth century. Crucially, it preserves digests of the abbey's medieval cartularies (collections of charters), now lost, including summaries of rentals made in 1254, 1341 and 1408 as well as relevant material from the archives of the bishop of Lincoln and the earls of Leicester (Crouch, below, pp. 225–87).

The rentals preserved by Charyte are a rich source for the local history of the town of Leicester and its environs from the mid thirteenth to mid fifteenth centuries (fig. 1). Through the rentals we can reconstruct some of the medieval streetscape of Leicester and its suburban settlements, and investigate the economic and tenurial relationship between the inhabitants of the town (including women) and the abbey over time (Postles, below, pp. 193–215). We know, for example, that in 1341 in the parish of St Leonard's, Diana Squirt lived in a tenement sandwiched between that of William le Palycere and another rented by Roger de Sybbesdon, and for this she owed the abbey an annual rent of a cock, a hen, and 2 shillings. Alice de Barnseby owed the abbey 6d for a tenement, once held by John Pistor, located on the east side of the oven in the parish of St Martin; her neighbour in 'Hot Place' was John Turvey who paid 12d the abbey for the tenement once held by Simon de Okam. Details such as these, preserved for taxation purposes, are an important source of medieval social history; 'Geryn's Rental' (from which these examples come) provides a snapshot of Leicester communities on the eve of the Black Death. Barely eight years later, in 1349, the Black Death reached Leicester and killed, according to Henry Knighton, more than 380 inhabitants of the parish of St Leonard's and around 400 of those living near St Martin's – including, undoubtedly, some of those whose names, professions and homes are preserved in the rental.[6]

Other types of historical source further illuminate the connections between local and national affairs. Especially important for medieval Leicester is the Chronicle written in the late fourteenth century by Henry Knighton, a local man, scholar, canon of Leicester from c. 1370–c. 1396, and confidante of the high nobility (especially the household of the Duke of Lancaster). Through his contemporary account of national affairs, we can begin to understand how a monastic community such as Leicester was informed about the high politics and economic concerns of the nation, and assess the importance of monastic writers such as Knighton to the interpretation and dissemination of such events to contemporary audiences as well as to posterity (Martin, below, pp. 119–25). These sorts of contacts with the secular elite are also revealed in the charters that record the transfer of land and privileges between benefactors and the abbey. The abbey's charters often describe in some detail the topography of the local landscape as well as privileges that were attached by tradition or ownership to particular places (Squires, below, pp. 75–94). Importantly also, they link the abbey and its immediate environs to the wider world of the secular and ecclesiastical nobility, and the politics of medieval piety and patronage. The ninety-four charters calendared in this volume (Crouch, below, pp. 225–87) date from the foundation of the abbey in 1138/9 to c. 1250 and many are printed here for the first time, offering a new resource for students of both local and national, political and ecclesiastical history.

6. A. Hamilton Thompson, *The Abbey of St Mary of the Meadow, Leicester* (Leicester 1949), 29–30; G. H. Martin, ed. *Knighton's Chronicle*, Oxford Medieval Texts (Oxford 1985), 98–9.

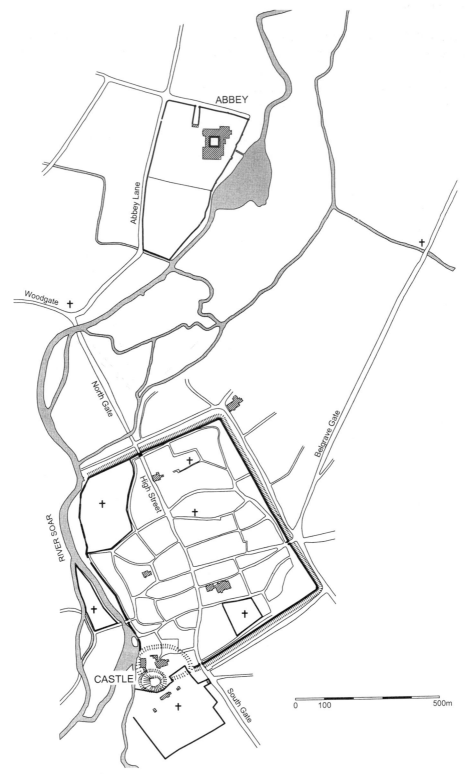

Fig. 1. Map of medieval Leicester and the Abbey of St Mary of the Meadows

The largess of the abbey's noble patrons accounts for the quantity of rural and urban property accumulated by the abbey (Postles, below, pp. 193–45; Squires, below, pp. 75–94) as well as the quality of its library (Webber, below, pp. 127–46; Gullick and Webber, below, pp. 173–92), its material possessions (Dawson, below, pp. 69–74) and the physical fabric of the church and its associated monastic and estate buildings (colour plate A). The wealth of the medieval abbey was recorded at its Dissolution in 1538 – exactly four hundred years after its foundation – and the abbey's buildings and site were described by the Crown's Commissioners (Buckley et al. below p. 67). That document is complemented by a detailed plan of the abbey's grounds drawn up in the early seventeenth century for the new secular owners of the property, preserving details of the lands that had been controlled directly by the abbey ('in demesne') and the extent of the estate that had come into royal hands in the sixteenth century (colour plate B; the 'William Senior Leicester Abbey map'). However, the post-Dissolution history and archaeology of the abbey has been a relatively neglected subject, in part because of the total destruction of the abbey buildings, save only for the gatehouse that was to become the core of a grand late-sixteenth-century mansion, known later as Cavendish House. This building receives detailed architectural and archaeological analysis for the first time in this volume (Buckley et al. below, pp. 95–118).

From its inception in 1855, the Leicestershire Archaeological Society (later the Archaeological and Architectural Society, then the Archaeological and Historical Society) has been actively involved in the exploration of the site of Leicester Abbey. Much of what is known about the physical form of the abbey comes from excavations in the nineteenth and earlier twentieth centuries that were sponsored by the Society, and the public presentation of these excavations has shaped the way in which the abbey is remembered in the modern city. The account below of recent excavations at the site show just how much these earlier campaigns missed and how much more there is to learn about the archaeology of English medieval monasticism from future excavation there (Buckley et al. below, pp. 1–67).

Buckley's survey of the early history of excavation of the site as reported in the Society's *Transactions* and local newspapers demonstrates how the Society and the archaeology of Leicester Abbey grew up together. It is entirely appropriate, therefore, that in its 150th anniversary year, the Society should choose to sponsor the publication of a new volume dedicated to the medieval history, archaeology and manuscripts of Leicester Abbey. Not since the appearance in 1949 of A. Hamilton Thompson's seminal book, *The Abbey of St Mary of the Meadows, Leicester* – also published by the Society – has the abbey been subject to the detailed scrutiny of an academic monograph. We hope that this book serves as a fitting tribute to the longevity of the Leicestershire Archaeological and Historical Society, and (more importantly perhaps) that it stimulates further research into the rich history and material remains of one of the least known but most important medieval monasteries in the English Midlands.

The Archaeology of Leicester Abbey

Richard Buckley

with Steve Jones, Peter Liddle, Michael Derrick and James Meek
and contributions from Deborah Sawday, Angela Monckton, Jennifer Browning
and Tony Gouldwell

Medieval Leicester Abbey survives today only as the precinct walls and as fragments of monastic barns; all other buildings of one of the wealthiest Augustinian abbeys in the country were swept away shortly after the Dissolution. Some structures survived beyond the sixteenth century, including the monastic gatehouse that was reused as the core of the mansion of the Hastings and Cavendish families, but even these had disappeared by the last quarter of the eighteenth century. Hence, it is only by excavations undertaken since the mid-nineteenth century that the layout of the abbey church and its claustral buildings has been identified. W. K. Bedingfield conducted major excavations on the site in 1929–32 as part of the process of turning the abbey grounds into a public park (fig. 1), extending the Abbey Park that had opened in 1882. His work enabled the construction of low walls in 1934 to mark out the plans of the principal buildings as a means of improving public understanding and enjoyment of the site. Unfortunately his fieldwork was never published in detail and few records have survived, mainly survey-plans of walls uncovered in the course of the works.

Since then the site of the Abbey has remained rather sterile with no public interpretation of the archaeological remains, rendering it largely unknown to and ignored by the visiting public. To counteract this, Leicester City Council embarked in 1997 on a programme of research in connection with a Heritage Lottery Fund (HLF) application for the 'Abbey Park Restoration and Development Project'. This included, amongst other things, a review of the current state of archaeological knowledge of the abbey, a geophysical survey of the abbey grounds, and a survey of the precinct walls.[1] The studies identified a series of research objectives to ensure that any future proposals for the display and interpretation of the site will be based on accurate and up-to-date archaeological data. Although the HLF application was postponed, it was decided to continue with

Acknowledgements: The project has involved many people in fieldwork and in preparation of specialist reports: P. Liddle (interpretation of the Bedingfield excavation plans); D. Smith (interpretation of Cavendish House); P. Seary and J. Sturgess (precinct walls survey); P. Courtney (post-Dissolution history); M. Derrick, J. Meek, S. Jones (field work reports and many of the plans reproduced in this paper); D. Sawday (pottery and tile); A. Monckton (environmental remains); J. Browning (animal bone); T. Gouldwell (fish remains). The excavations were directed by R. Buckley with S. Jones, with on-site supervision by N. Finn, J. Meek, and P. Liddle, assisted by R. Kipling, M. Derrick, J. Thomas, J. Tate, J. Coward, L. Hunt, A. Hyam, M. Parker and staff of the School of Archaeology and Ancient History, in particular M. Palmer, D. O'Sullivan, N. Christie, S. James, D. Mattingly, T. Hopkinson, I. Reeds, R. Thomas and M. Gillings. Particular thanks are due to J. Meek for

taking over in 2002 and to S. Jones for his work on the kitchen. I am grateful to A. Stevenson and R. Jenkins of the ROLLR for their assistance in tracing sources and to staff of Leicester City Council for their support and encouragement and for allowing us to undertake the excavation, in particular D. Pick, D. Jarvis, S. Marbrook, B. Dayaram, J. Selman, R. Everiss and R. Welburn. Finally, I should like to thank M. Palmer, N. Christie and N. Finn for their helpful comments on this paper and to P. Courtney and P. Liddle for their support, encouragement and advice.

1. R. Buckley, 'Abbey Park, Leicester: an archaeological desk-based assessment', unpubl. ULAS report 97/12 (1997); Geophysical Surveys of Bradford, 'Geophysical survey of Leicester Abbey', unpubl. report (1997); P. Seary and J. Sturgess, 'Survey of the precinct walls of Leicester Abbey', unpubl. ULAS report 97–12 (1997).

a limited programme of fieldwork within this research framework as a training exercise for under-graduate students of the School of Archaeology and Ancient History at the University of Leicester. The site has statutory protection as a Scheduled Ancient Monument and is under no threat, so the overriding objective of the fieldwork has been to ensure that damage to buried archaeological remains is minimised. Hence, the excavation strategy was to assess the nature, extent, sequence and dating of archaeological deposits through limited, sample investigation only. At the time of writing, six seasons of work at the site in 2000–5 have included excavation, geophysical and stand-ing building survey. The results of the excavations have been documented in a series of fieldwork reports lodged with the Leicester City Sites and Monuments Record and summarised in 'Archaeology in Leicestershire and Rutland' in the Society's annual *Transactions*. This paper sum-marises our present state of knowledge of the site, along with a review of earlier excavations, details of more recent investigations and a consideration of the standing buildings.

Archaeological investigations at Leicester Abbey

The eighteenth and nineteenth centuries

The church and conventual buildings of the Augustinian abbey were demolished soon after the Dissolution, leaving little trace above ground to indicate where they had once stood. In the early seventeenth century, Arthur Barfoot, the Countess of Devonshire's gardener, carried out the first

Fig. 1. Aerial photograph of the site of Leicester Abbey, taken during the 2003 season of excavations viewing to the south-west

recorded excavations on the site. John Nichols, the antiquarian scholar of Leicestershire, quoted Samuel Carte who had spoken to John Hasloe, the grandson of Barfoot, who claimed that his grandfather had dug on the site of the abbey church in search of relics. He had found several stone coffins, 'the cavities of which did not lie uppermost but were inverted over the bodies' and bones which he believed to be those of Cardinal Wolsey. The Countess would not have them disturbed and ordered that they should be covered up again.[2] The impetus for such work was no doubt the promise of treasure; Throsby noted that, 'it has been a received opinion in Leicester that there was buried with him [Wolsey] a considerable quantity of riches, which has caused the inhabitants of that place, at various times, to dig for them'.[3] Others had nobler motives; Mr Browne Willis had a great veneration for Wolsey as the founder of Christ Church College, Oxford, and wrote to Dr Chartlett in 1716 offering to bear the costs of reburying Wolsey there.[4] In 1747, a labourer digging on the supposed location of the high altar of the chapel, found a human skull and several human bones and supposed, from their location, that they were those of Wolsey.[5]

In 1845, James Thompson, editor of the *Leicester Chronicle* (and founding member of the Leicestershire Architectural and Archaeological Society), wrote to the British Archaeological Association informing them of his excavations within the Abbey Grounds, undertaken in 1844–45 'in the hope of discovering the abbey church'.[6] In Thompson's collection of finds at Leicester City Museum Service (LCMS), there is the handle of a jug found at the abbey in 1845.[7] In a paper read in May 1854, Thompson noted that 'even a century after the Dissolution, the very site of the church had become conjectural', and that 'it is necessary to be premised that no vestige of the abbey church, cloisters or domestic offices remains at the present day above the surface of the ground'.[8] In the same volume of *Transactions*, the text of the Crown Commissioners' Survey of 1538/9, the 'Scytuacion of the late monasterye of Leicester', was published in full, demonstrating a clear awareness of the layout of the principal monastic buildings, if not their precise position within the precinct.[9] Thompson had little to inform his excavation strategy, so he commenced with a trench in the centre of the gardens, which revealed decayed wood, human and other bones, together with 'a drain, a leaden pipe, and the tusk and jaw of an animal'.[10] He also investigated an area known as 'The Laundry' as there had been frequent discoveries of encaustic tiles there. Several days' work revealed an area of flooring composed entirely of encaustic tiles; Thompson thus expanded the trench (60 × 4–5 feet) and declared that the pavement was part of the nave floor of the abbey church.[11] Work stopped pending permission from Lord Dysart to proceed, but the 'enquiry was not fortunate enough to meet his lordship's notice' and nothing further was done.[12] A contemporary commentator, J. Burtt, writing in the Society's *Transactions*, observed that Thompson's excavations 'seem to have gone but a very small step towards removing the existing state of uncertainty'.[13]

2. J. Nichols, *The history and antiquities of the county of Leicester*, 4 vols in 8 (London 1795–1815), i pt. 2, 273; J. Throsby, *Select views in Leicestershire* (Leicester 1789), 287.

3. Throsby, *Select views*, 286.

4. Nichols *Leicester*, i pt. 2, 274.

5. W. Jackson, 'History and description of Leicester Abbey', *Journal of the Royal Institute of British Architects*, 3rd ser. 1 (1894), 129–34 and 166–70 at 168; J. Thompson, *Leicester Abbey: a historical paper* (1856), 18. Thompson states this event took place in 1787 (according to the *Cambridge Chronicle*).

6. J. Thompson, 'Proceedings of the central committee', *JBAA* 1 (1846), 237–62 at 245.

7. J. Thompson, 'On Leicester Abbey and its ancient remains', *JBAA* 6 (1851), 116–22. The jug handle is LCMS acc. no. A115.1951.

8. J. Burtt, 'Contributions to the history of Leicester Abbey', *TLAAS* 4 (1878), 32–6.

9. See appendix below, 67, reprinted from L. Fox, *Leicester Abbey: history and description* (Leicester 1938; 2nd edn. 1949), 14–15 (TNA, SC 12/10/11), previously printed in *The Archaeological Journal* 27 (1870), 204–6 and *TLAAS* 4 (1878), 33–4.

10. Thompson, *Leicester Abbey: an historical paper*, 19.

11. Ibid. 19.

12. Ibid.

13. Burtt, 'Contributions', *TLAAS* 4 (1856), 33.

In 1854, the brothers George and Thomas Nevinson began excavations at the site and both subsequently became committee members of the Leicestershire Architectural and Archaeological Society when it was formed in 1855.[14] In 1855, Thomas Nevinson exhibited several ornamental bricks from Leicester Abbey garden, thought to have been used for the borders of flowerbeds.[15] These bricks, patterned with a Tudor rose and stem, were later identified as dating to the period of Cavendish House, c. 1590.[16] In the first volume of *Transactions*, we are told that 'some curious Roman ampullae' found by Mr Goddard in the Abbey Grounds were also exhibited.[17]

Further excavations were undertaken in the later 1850s under the auspices of the Archaeological Society. At a meeting of the Society on 25 February 1856, George Nevinson exhibited some encaustic tiles and fragments of stained glass found at the abbey and, 'read an interesting paper on the supposed site of the monastic church which he purposed to continue at a future meeting'.[18] Nevinson's talk was reported in the *Leicester Chronicle* on 1 March 1856, noting that his talk was illustrated with, 'a plan prepared by Mr Millican and a rough plan of his own'.[19] At a meeting of the Society on 26 April 1856, Nevinson reported that the foundations of some old walls had been exposed to view, although 'at present it was impossible to assign them to any particular buildings of the abbey'.[20] His remarks were illustrated by two plans made by Millican (later reused in the excavations of the early 1920s). Several trenches were cut, including one 60 × 4–5 feet in an area called 'The Laundry' which revealed part of a tiled floor. The account of this trench is identical to one described by Thompson the same year, referring to work he had done ten years earlier; it is uncertain whether these accounts reflect two similar trenches or a single excavation. It is clear, though, that Nevinson was less certain than Thompson that the church had been discovered. At the same meeting, Mr G. C. Bellairs exhibited an ancient stirrup, said to have been found near Leicester Abbey (and which is still on display in the Jewry Wall Museum).

The annual report of 1858 notes the Society's excavations in the grounds of Leicester Abbey, conducted 'with a view to the discovery of the position and some remains of the Church and Monastic buildings, have not hitherto been attended with success, but will be resumed in the ensuing Autumn'.[21] On 30 August 1858, Thompson exhibited a papal bulla of Innocent III (1193–1216) found in the Abbey Grounds and shown to him originally by Mr Warner (presumably the proprietor of Warner's Nursery which occupied the site).[22] The same year, an iron key was found near the abbey ruins.[23] The British Archaeological Association visited the site in August 1863, suggesting that excavations continued in the 1860s; on 26 September 1864, Thomas North exhibited a number of coins from 'recent excavations at Leicester Abbey'.[24] These excavations included a number of trenches (close to the present cricket oval) that appear on the extant tracing of the 1930s excavations. From the finds recovered in this area, it is possible that the features uncovered, which included 'tanks', have no connection with the abbey but relate entirely to an earlier phase of activity at the site. The newspaper article of 25 August 1923 notes that the late dates

---

14. *Leicester Chronicle*, 13.1.1855.

15. 'Meeting on April 30th 1855', *TLAAS* 1 (1866), 18–19 at 19.

16. ROLLR L1914.2 (Cable Collection 2, 157, an unidentified newspaper article of 25.8.1923 recording the discovery of similar bricks in 1919).

17. 'Meeting on September 10th 1855', *TLAAS* 1 (1866), 40–61 at 42.

18. 'Meeting on February 25th 1856', *TLAAS* 1 (1866), 72–3 at 72.

19. A newspaper article of 25.8.1923 noted that Nevinson's paper does not appear in *Transactions*; ROLLR L1914.2 (Cable Collection 2, 157).

20. 'Meeting on April 26th 1858', *TLAAS* 1 (1866), 167–70 at 169.

21. 'Annual General Meeting, July 28th 1858', *TLAAS* 1 (1866), 173–212 at 78–9.

22. LCMS acc. no. A241.1951.

23. LCMS acc. no. A6.1860.

24. 'Nineteenth Annual Meeting, Leicester 1862', *JBAA* 19 (1863), 30–56 at 49; 'Meeting on September 26th 1864', *TLAAS* 2 (1870), 346–76 at 346.

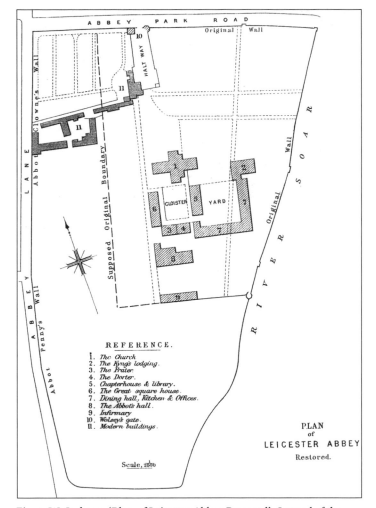

Fig. 2. W. Jackson, 'Plan of Leicester Abbey Restored', *Journal of the Royal Institute of British Architects*, 3rd ser. 1 (1894), plate opposite p. 168

of the Roman coins fit in with 'Mr Bushe-Fox's recent statement that the tanks we have unearthed are Late Roman work'.[25]

Other archaeological finds were made in the vicinity of the abbey during extensive excavation works associated with the flood relief scheme and the creation of Abbey Park in 1879–82. In 1879, Captain Whitby exhibited at the Society's meeting fragments of pottery from the bases of two jars (one with a potter's mark), discovered in the Abbey Meadow.[26] Whitby had observed a 'working party' in the Abbey Meadow (probably engaged in work on the extensive flood defences that was well underway by November 1879).[27] He noted that there was comparatively little topsoil on the surface and immediately underneath was:

> marley clay, then sand and gravel, then solid clay, under which lies a deposit of

25. ROLLR L914.2; Cable Collection 2, 157.

26. 'Meeting on November 24th 1879', *TLAAS* 5 (1882), 218–31 at 219.

27. T. Williamson, 'The history of Abbey Park' in 'Abbey Park restoration management plan' III, Leicester City Council unpubl. report (1997), 10.

fine sand and black mud, and under the black mud I saw the bones of animals.
The horse (skull perfect), boar tusks (gnawing teeth perfect), and in the sand
above, I saw the skull of a man . . . near to this skull, but 8 or 9 feet deeper,
under the deposits named, in mud and clay, were two pieces of pottery, which I
believe to be Roman.

Further Roman finds found in Abbey Meadow were exhibited in September 1880 and September
1881, and a possible lead sheath and a medieval pitcher from Abbey Meadows were accessioned by
the Museum in the 1880s.[28] Later, Nevinson gave the Society a collection of tiles and 'other interesting relics from Leicester Abbey'.[29]

In 1894, William Jackson prepared a plan of the abbey precinct, including the conjectured position
of the church and claustral buildings (fig. 2).[30] His work was based on the Crown Commissioners'
Survey and the results of the Nevinson brothers' excavations, although much uncertainty remained
regarding not only the location of the church and claustral ranges within the precinct but also the
position of individual buildings relative to one another. This was of course entirely understandable as
the Commissioners' Survey refers only occasionally to compass points to assist with the positioning
of buildings and courtyards. Hence – with the benefit of hindsight – we can see that the main group
of buildings is incorrectly arranged on Jackson's plan which shows them too far south.

The twentieth century

In 1903, the Secretary of the Society reported a proposal to 'lay out a portion of the Old Leicester
Abbey grounds for building purposes'. The Society expressed its hope that the owner of the estate
would preserve the boundary walls and 'arrange for the ground to be carefully examined before
the site is laid out for building'.[31] This plan, however, came to nothing and the site remained under
cultivation until ownership passed to the city in 1925.

On 27 February 1923, the *Daily Express* reported that 'the Leicester Corporation and the
Archaeological Society have decided to make an excavation in Leicester Abbey'. The *Express* made
much of the lost tomb of Cardinal Wolsey, unsurprisingly perhaps since the official opening of
Tutankhamen's Tomb had taken place on 18 February, just a week earlier. 'It is believed', the article
continues, 'that there is a beautiful sepulchre which was covered up by the Countess of Devonshire
before the Civil War'. The lure of Wolsey's tomb is unlikely to have been the major motive behind
the Archaeological and Historical Society's programme of investigation, but there is little doubt
that enthusiasm for the project was fired by the spectacular finds in the Valley of the Kings that had
captured the imagination of the world's press. The *Leicester Mercury* of 26 February 1923 reported
that the Society was seeking funds for the work and by March £200 had been donated to cover the
cost of the work, to be undertaken by at least six labourers 'at present unemployed'.[32] A preliminary
survey was carried out on 19 March 1923 by T. H. Fosbrooke and the brothers W. K. and R.
Bedingfield, and excavations commenced on 9 April 1923 at the spot where the Nevinsons had discovered some foundations.[33] It was later reported that, 'acting upon certain clues, amongst which
was a plan left by Nevinson who did some work in the sixties, work was commenced under the
supervision of Mr T. H. Fosbrooke FSA, about two-hundred yards to the south-east of Councillor

28. 'Meeting on November 29th 1880', *TLAAS* 5 (1882),
296–300 at 296; LCMS acc. no 8.yd.1907 and yg.1452.1885.

29. 'Meeting on June 1st 1896', *TLAAS* 8 (1889), 198–200, at 199.

30. Jackson, 'History and description'.

31. 'Annual General Meeting, January 26th 1903', *TLAAS* 9

(1904–5), 220–222 at 222.

32. *Leicester Mail* (5.3.1923), with further speculation about the
location of Wolsey's grave.

33. *Leicester Mercury* (20.3.1923).

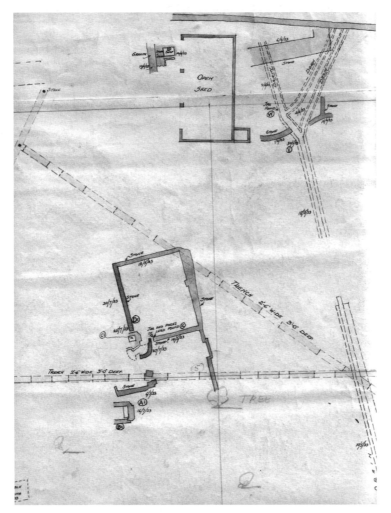

Fig. 3. Part of the plan of the 1923 excavations showing the southern part of the kitchen and associated drains. (Not to scale)

Whittle's residence, the abbey farm'.[34] Fosbrooke, 'explored by trench and probe large areas of the Abbey Grounds, principally in the area of what is now the cricket oval . . . but found only fragmentary remains, few of which seemed to be of the monastic period of occupation'.[35]

A plan from this period survives in the LCMS collections (fig. 3) showing a series of trenches identified by letter codes and dates, together with plans of buildings discovered, colour coded to indicate their period. No accompanying notes survive, but detailed contemporary newspaper accounts permit (to some extent at least) descriptions of excavations to be correlated with the plan.[36] For example, the *Leicester Mercury* recorded on 9 April 1923 that two walls, one 1 foot 9in thick and another 3 feet 2in thick with an angle in it, had been discovered along with a number of

34. *The Illustrated Leicester Chronicle* (21.4.1923).

35. W. K. Bedingfield, 'Presidential address 1930–31', *Transactions of the Leicester Literary and Philosophical Society* 32 (1931),

5–24 at 19.

36. Compiled by Joyce Brown for the 1923 excavations; Leicester City Museum file.

Swithland slate slabs and a few fragments of medieval glazed earthenware.[37] The next day's paper recorded the discovery of two further wall-angles and a length of wall foundation 39 feet 4in running southwards; reports on consecutive days recorded discoveries of a brick wall, more slates, tiles and ditches, and a wall with a stone base and a top of brick.[38] The *Mercury* articles acknowledged the difficulties of interpreting the remains, adding that, 'speculation must be deferred till a sufficient area of foundations has been laid bare'. Some moulded stone was also recovered, together with several ceramic tiles 'which bear a great resemblance to the Roman roof tiles, in that they have the remains of flanges on one edge and on the opposite side bear crossed comb markings'. These sound like Roman box flue tiles, combed to provide a key for mortar and which, when broken, appear to have one or more flanges. As Bedingfield later noted, these investigations added weight to the nineteenth-century theory that there is also a Roman site within the abbey precinct.[39]

A small plan of the discoveries was published in the *Leicester Mercury* on 14 April 1923. On 17 April, the prominent medievalist A. Hamilton Thompson visited the site and suggested that work should be done to the north.[40] A buttress uncovered by Nevinson in the 1854–6 excavations was again uncovered and another red brick enclosure was found, followed by two stone walls each about 20 feet long and joined almost at right angles, as well as two other walls running transversely, one over 3 feet thick.[41] Next, a wall *c.* 30 feet long running east–west was found varying in thickness from one to two and a half feet with more paving. They also began digging at an 'old watergate' in the abbey precinct wall, and discovered an 'old water tank' and an area of wrought stone with a chamfered edge.[42]

Around this time, plans were drawn up of the excavations and structures uncovered.[43] The next discovery comprised several fragments of encaustic tiles found at the end of a long wall, with projections at the outer side and paving (5 × 12–15 feet) with slabs with a chamfered edge on one side.[44] A new area to the west was excavated but uncovered only two or three sections of wall, and at this stage it was felt that almost all of the walls shown on Nevinson's plan had been uncovered.[45] The next discovery recorded by the local press was a human skeleton without signs of a coffin.[46] Another new area in the east was tackled, yielding a wall 100 feet long but 'of as yet indeterminate width'. A well-made drain about 2 feet square was discovered with fragments of brick and tile, followed by another wall and objects such as a medieval drinking cup and a pot base.[47] Two more drains were uncovered (one with slab flooring and slate capping), and finally on 2 June the discovery of a wall 16 feet long with a curve eastwards was recorded.[48] This is the last detailed press notice of the excavations, though the extant plan dates the opening of the last trench to 27 July 1923; it was later reported that work continued until 1925, terminating in July of that year with the death of Fosbrooke.[49]

At the time, the excavations were considered to be rather limited, partly because of the shortage of funds but also because the site remained under cultivation and, 'could not be interfered with without doing damage'.[50] The extant plan, however, suggests that a fairly significant area was examined – by modern standards at least – to the south of what we now know to be the main claustral ranges.

37. *Leicester Mercury* (9.4.1923).

38. *Leicester Mercury* (10.4.1923), (11.4.1923) and (12.4.1923); *Leicester Mail* (13.4.1923).

39. Bedingfield, 'Presidential address', 19.

40. *Leicester Mercury* (18.4.1923).

41. *Leicester Mercury* (19.4.1923) and (21.4.1923) which includes a photograph of some of the findings; *Leicester Mail* (20.4.1923).

42. *Leicester Mail* (24.4.1923); *Leicester Mercury* (24.4.1923) and (26.4.1923).

43. LCMS acc. no. A179.1974 1–3.

44. *Leicester Mercury* and *Leicester Mail* (27.4.1923).

45. *Leicester Mail* (5.5.1923).

46. *Leicester Mercury* (8.5.1923).

47. *Leicester Mercury* (12.5.1923) and (15.5.1923).

48. *Leicester Mercury* (18.5.1923) and (2.6.1923).

49. Bedingfield, 'Presidential address', 19; *Leicester Mail* (27.11.1930).

50. *Leicester Mercury* (25.8.1927).

Colour plate A: John Finnie, 'Leicester Abbey in the later middle ages', a reconstruction based on excavation and documentary evidence

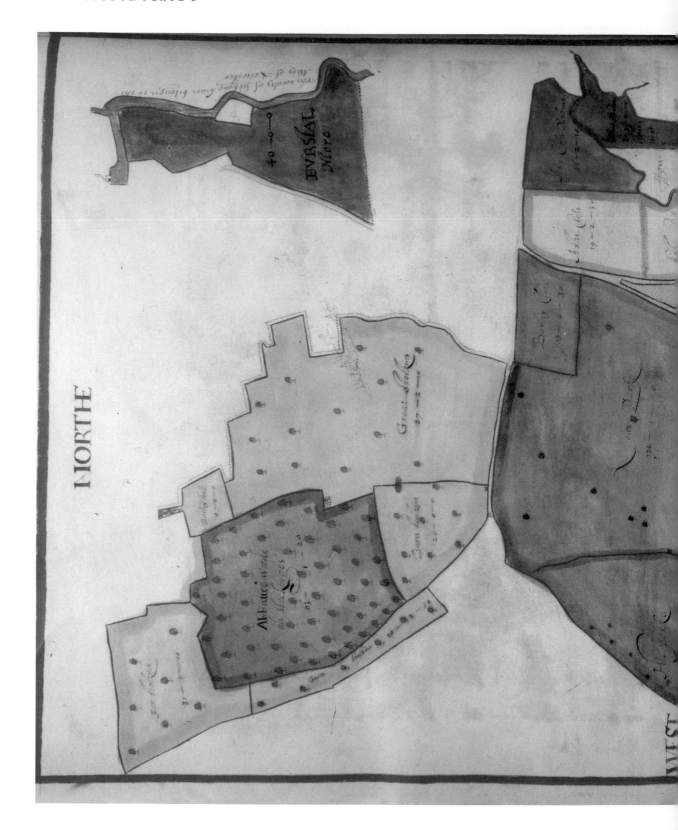

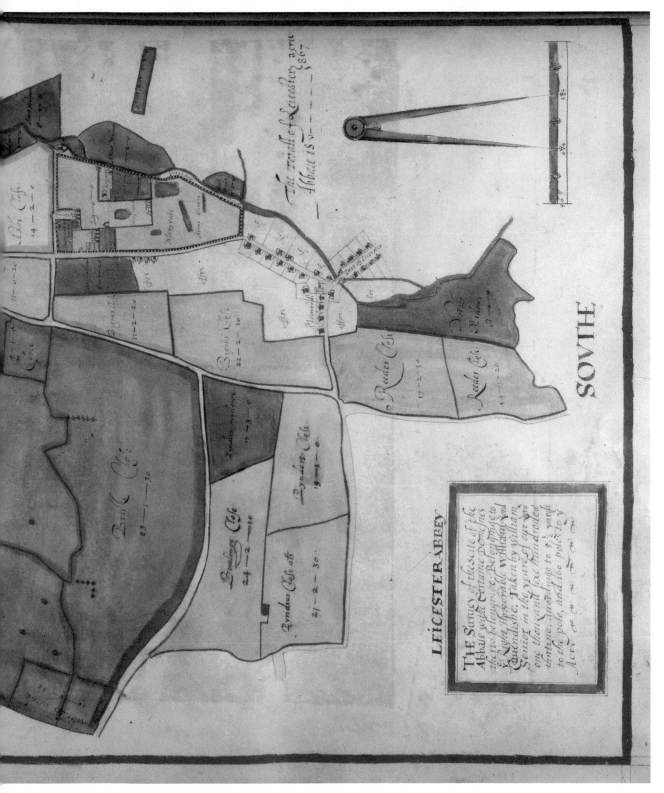

Colour plate B: William Senior, 'A survey of the site of Leicester Abbey' (1613) (reduced)

Colour plate C: James Fish, 'Map of Beaumont Leys' (1686)
(detail), showing the abbey precinct and the remains of
Cavendish House (south view)

Colour plate D: The hinged lid of a thirteenth-century Limoges enamel incense-
boat, found in the sacristy at Leicester Abbey in 1930 (slightly enlarged)

Colour plate E: Cambridge, Trinity College B.16.5, f. 1r (actual size)

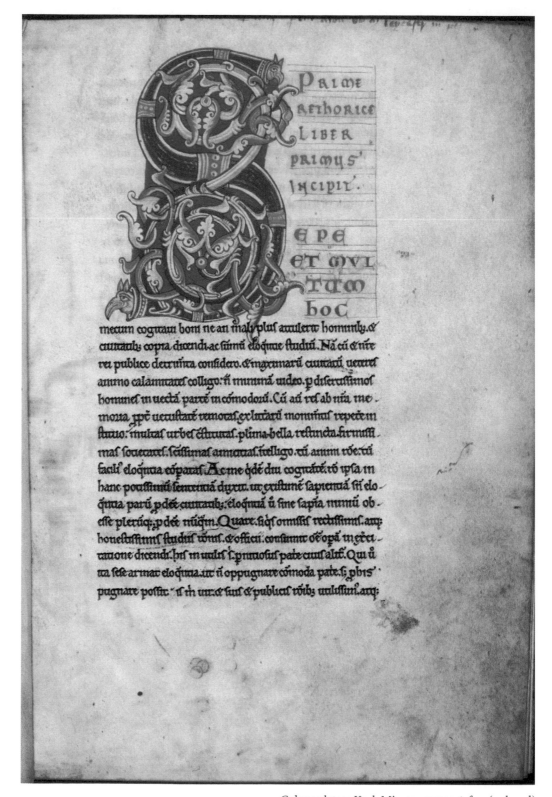

PALME
RETHORICE
LIBER
PRIMUS
INCIPIT.

EPE
ET MVL
TVM
hoc

mecum cogitam boni ne an mali plus attulerit hominib; &
ciuitatib; copia dicendi. ac summi eloquiae studiū. Nā cū &ñre
rei publice detrimita considero. & maximarū ciuitatū uetere
animo calamitates colligo: ñ minimā uideo. p diserússimos
homines in uectā parté in cōmodoru. Cū aū res ab ñra me.
moria. ipé uetustate remotas. ex litarū monimis repete in
stituo: multas urbes ēstiuctas. plima bella restincta. firmissi
mas societares. sciñimas amicitias. itelligo. tū animi rōe: tū
facili eloquitia cōparas. Ac me qdē diu cogitāté: ró ipsa in
hanc potissimū senteniā dixit. ut existimé sapientiā ñ elo
quitia parū pdee ciuitatib; eloquiā ū sine sapia nimiū ob
esse pleruñq; pdee nūcqm. Quare. siqs omissis rectissimis. atq
honestissimis studiis rōnis. & officii. consūmit oé opā in exer
citatione dicendi. his in utilis. s primiosus pae ciuis alit. Qui ū
ita sese armat eloquitia. itt ñ oppugnare cōmoda pae. s; pbis
pugnare possit: is mi uir. & suis & publicis rōib; utilissimi. atq;

Colour plate F: York Minster, XVI.M.6, f. 1r (reduced)

In 1925 the Earl of Dysart offered the abbey grounds as a gift to Leicester City Council and the Deed of Gift for 32 acres of land was signed on 31 December 1925. Shortly afterwards, the committee of the Leicestershire Archaeological and Historical Society formed a sub-committee, 'to consider the question of excavations at Leicester Abbey' and an Excavation Committee was constituted in 1926.[51] Bedingfield was co-opted with George Farnham and H. C. Snow to the Abbey Grounds Sub-Committee, and charged with considering options for making use of the site for the public benefit.[52] By June 1927, excavation work had been in progress for a few weeks and the *Leicester Mercury* reported that 'workmen have been excavating on the site which is believed to have been the burial ground . . . the skeleton of a giant was found and not many yards away, the remains of a dwarf were also discovered'.[53] A *Mercury* report on 24 August 1927 suggests that these works were not necessarily of an archaeological nature but were connected with the initial clearance of the site in preparation for laying it out as a public park. This involved the felling of trees, grubbing out of roots and the clearance of land that was described as 'a veritable jungle of weeds'. A report the following day bemoaned the fact that previous archaeological work on the site had been so limited and made a plea to the chairman of the Parks Committee, saying 'if Councillor Toone wants to make the historic addition to the Abbey Park a real attraction to the city . . . he must turn some of his spare labour to the work of digging in the grounds. A little excavation would probably disclose some rare architectural treasures that could be exhibited as real ruins of the abbey'.[54]

Newspaper reports between October 1927 and January 1928 chart the developing plans for the park which was to include a cricket oval surrounded by lime trees, a children's play area, a rose garden, tennis courts and a bridge across to Abbey Park. The precinct walls were to be repaired and a new entrance with a pair of gate turrets would be created in the north wall on the site of the original entrance – the one remaining original turret being restored – but there would be no attempt at 'resuscitation' of the abbey ruins.[55] By 'abbey ruins' it seems clear that the upstanding remains of Cavendish House continued to be referred to in this way, just as they had been in the nineteenth century. A plan published early the following year shows the proposed layout of the new park, with a bowling-green, hard tennis courts and grass courts on the site of what is now known to be that of the church and claustral ranges.[56] Later that year, the final plans for the park, with a proposed budget of £49,000, were passed by the City Council despite opposition from some councillors on the grounds of cost.

One morning, 'during the fertile moments of the early shave', Bedingfield says that it occurred to him that the very deep trenching required to kill the pervasive weeds on the site was not dissimilar to archaeological trenching; the Committee accepted his idea to combine the works and asked him to select the area which would yield the best results.[57] A plan of the proposed scheme published in 1928 indicates that extensive excavations were in progress on the site.[58] Much of the work was carried out using unemployed and untrained 'Distressed Labour'.[59] In January 1929, it was reported that the church as far as the transepts had been uncovered and in the following month,

51. C. J. Billson, 'The open fields of Leicester', *TLAS* 14 (1925–6) 3–29 at 13; A. Hamilton Thompson, 'The Leicestershire Archaeological Society in the present century', *TLAS* 21 (1940–1), 122–48 at 135.

52. Bedingfield, 'Presidential address', 19; *Leicester Mail* (27.10.1927).

53. *Leicester Mercury* (22.6.1927).

54. *Leicester Mercury* (25.8.1927).

55. *Leicester Mail* (27.10.1927).

56. The original survives in the LCMS collections. The plan is a

bird's eye view by P. H. Grundy of Bedingfield and Grundy Architects. The layout is similar to what was eventually put into effect, the most notable differences being that the bridge over the Soar is shown with a gate tower at either end and tennis courts, a sunken rose garden and an old English garden are on the site of the abbey ruins. See also, *Leicester Mail* 3.1.1928.

57. Bedingfield, 'Presidential Address', 20.

58. *Leicester Mercury* 26.8.1928.

59. Williamson, 'History of Abbey Park', 24.

Fig. 4. A stone coffin discovered during the 1929–32 excavations. The inset is of
W. K. Bedingfield

Bedingfield reported that foundations thought to be the north and south aisles of the abbey church and the north and west side of the cloister had been found.[60] In April 1929, two stone coffins (fig. 4) were unearthed at the 'end of the old cloister' within the cloister garth that Bedingfield believed to be of monastic date rather than of Saxon origin as others had suggested.[61] He argued that 'continuation of the excavation work would probably reveal the old hospital and the Chapter House'. One of the burials discovered in the eastern cloister alley was wrapped in a vestment of rich embroidery.[62] A coffin lid bearing an inscription together with worked stones, part of a Norman column and some tiles were also found.[63] After locating the corner of the nave of the abbey church, a huge area was stripped of some '10,000 cubic yards of soil' to reveal the rest of the abbey church and the claustral ranges.[64] Other significant finds included the papal bulla of Innocent III and the lid of a Limoges enamel incense boat.[65] Bedingfield produced his plan of the abbey 'based on foundations disclosed up to September 1930' and the Crown Commissioners' Survey of 1538/9 (figs. 5 and 6).[66] The excavations seem to have been largely completed by the beginning of 1931, although an article in the *Daily Sketch* for 27 November 1931 suggests that some work was still underway.

Bedingfield's vision was that the church and claustral buildings should be 'indicated in the turf

60. *Leicester Mail* (15.1.1929); *Leicester Mercury* (2.2.1929).

61. *Leicester Mercury* (16.4.1929).

62. *Leicester Mail* (22.7.1929); Acc. no. A234.1951.

63. LCMS acc. nos. A876.1951 and A875.1951. The inscription reads PAV[..]AT.OV[.]. A newspaper report notes that it was found 'to the east and south of the angle formed by the choir and east cloister where the Chapter House ought to be and it is a few yards from the site of the burials found recently in the cloister walk itself'; *Leicester Mail* (16.8.1929) and (17.8.1927). This may suggest that it is the coffin of an abbot, perhaps Paul, 1186–1204/5, or another senior member of the community.

64. Bedingfield, 'Presidential address', 20.

65. LCMS acc. no. A241.1951. *Leicester Mail* (15.1.1930) and *Leicester Mercury* (15.1.1930), with a photograph of the bulla (LCMS acc. no. A135.1951); *Leicester Mail* (19.2.1930). For the incense boat, see D. Dawson, 'An incense-boat cover from Leicester Abbey', below pp. 69–74.

66. The original pencil-drawn site plan survives as ROLLR DE6218/1 (thanks to R. Jenkins for drawing it to my attention), together with a draft of the published plan (ROLLR DE6218/3); a tracing of it is in the archives at the Jewry Wall Museum.

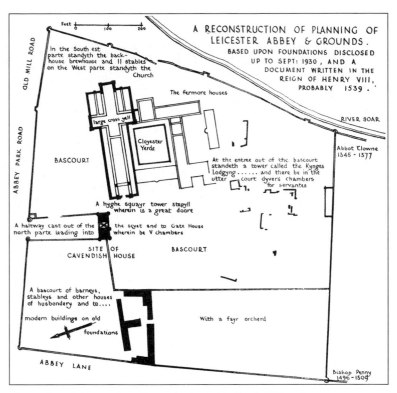

Fig. 5. Plan of the north enclosure by W. K. Bedingfield (1930)

Fig. 6. Plan of the abbey by W. K. Bedingfield (1930)

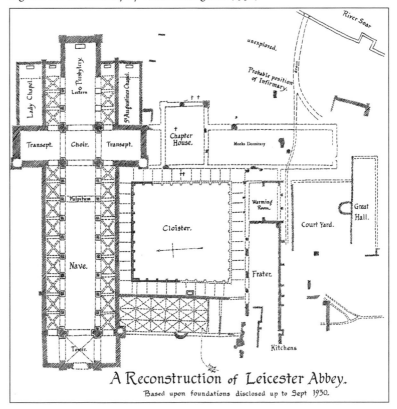

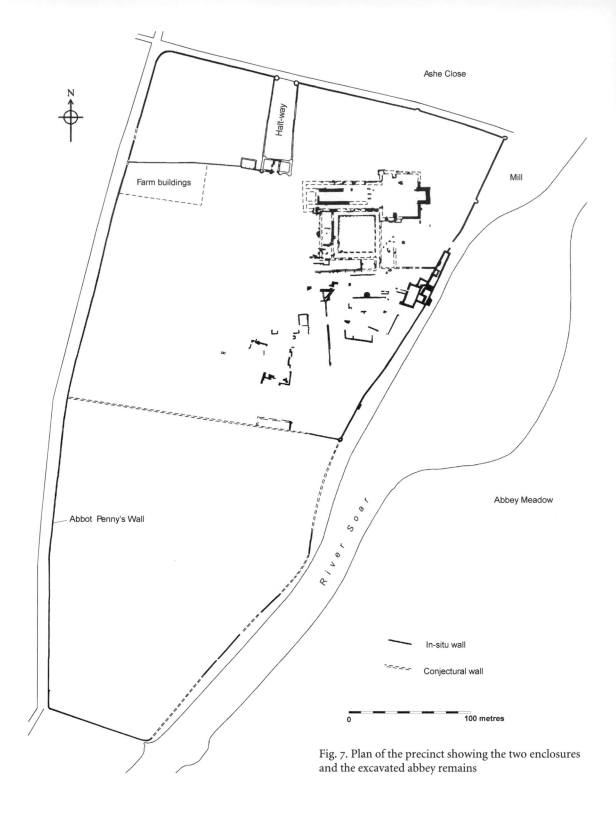

N

Ashe Close

Mill

Halt-way

Farm buildings

Abbot Penny's Wall

River Soar

Abbey Meadow

In-situ wall

Conjectural wall

0   100 metres

Fig. 7. Plan of the precinct showing the two enclosures and the excavated abbey remains

and [with] dwarf embankments in such a manner that the visitor may see at a glance the glories that are passed'.[67] He further proposed a cross on the site of the altar, a cenotaph to Wolsey and a display cabinet near the main entrance. At the time of the official opening of the Abbey Grounds on 21 April 1932, no decision had been taken concerning the future of the excavated remains of the site. Shortly afterwards, however, the plans of the principal buildings were laid out with low walls to form a centrepiece for the new Abbey Grounds. These walls, in most places, comprised an earth core with an outer skin of mortared granite placed in the approximate position of the underlying robber trenches, although in some places, as recent restoration works on the south wall of the church have shown, the core is composed of genuine medieval masonry.[68] Work on laying out the abbey plan continued until at least 1934, as shown by the recent find of a bottle built into one of the reconstructed church walls, containing a message from the workmen dated 1934 and a motor car hubcap of a similar date from the backfill of one of Bedingfield's trenches in the vicinity of the kitchen.[69]

The scheme for the Abbey Grounds also included restoration of the precinct walls, the provision of new gates and the restoration of Cavendish House to serve as the park-keeper's residence, with a cloakroom and changing room for the tennis courts. In May 1932, Bedingfield was asked by the Parks Committee to write a 'booklet recording the history of the Abbey with a plan indicating the principal items of interest'.[70] This report was written eventually by Levi Fox, incorporating Bedingfield's plan of the excavated remains.[71]

Description of the site

The visible medieval remains of Leicester Abbey comprise the precinct walls and parts of the monastic barns. The lines of the foundations of the church and most of the claustral buildings are laid out on the ground with low walls, based on the results of the 1930s excavations. The west range of Cavendish house survives largely intact, together with the ruined principal façade of its south range. Archaeological excavation has made a considerable contribution to our understanding of the medieval abbey, amplified by careful analysis of the standing buildings on the site and the documentary and pictorial sources.

Precinct walls

The precinct walls enclosing the medieval abbey survive remarkably well. There are two main enclosures: a northern one containing the abbey ruins and Cavendish House and a southern one that contains no visible archaeological features (fig. 7). Nichols recorded three large walled closes, east-southeast of Cavendish House, furnished with gates, in which fishponds, terraces and walks could still be seen, used chiefly as orchards, 'being well stocked with cherries &c'.[72] He noted that 'only a small part of the old house is preserved for any useful purpose; a low building with a leaded roof, the remainder being merely a mass of ruins'. Nichols quoted in full a detailed description of the abbey precinct walls by a Mr Bickerstaffe, which includes much important detail, if a little confused in parts. Extracts from this are incorporated into the description that follows, which is based on a visual inspection of the walls in 1997 and information contained within the statutory listing description.

67. Bedingfield, 'Presidential address', 24.

68. S. Jones, forthcoming.

69. The hubcap is from a Dunlop Magna wheel of 1934-7, as used on the Morris Minor and Morris 8 models (identified by R. Bird of the Morris Register and S. Laing of the motor museum at Gaydon, Northants, as a 1934 example – it was fixed by a screw rather than a nut).

70. ROLLR CM28/7, 164.

71. L. Fox, *Leicester Abbey: history and description* (Leicester 1938, 2nd edn. 1949, 3rd edn. 1971).

72. Nichols, *Leicester*, i pt. 2, 293.

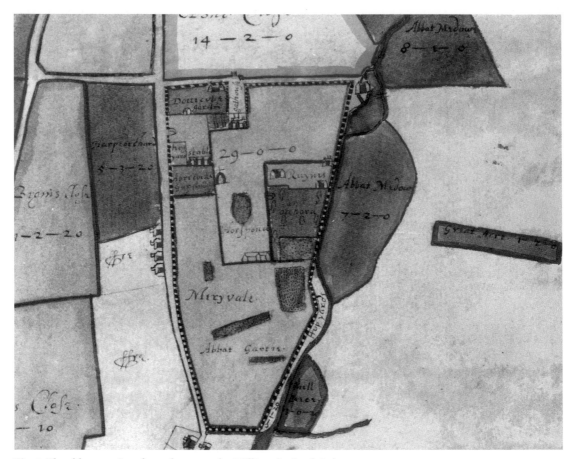

Fig. 8. The abbey precinct from the survey by William Senior (1613)

1. Northern enclosure

This seems to be the earlier of the two enclosures; stone walls form the east, north and west boundaries and fragments of the south wall divide it from the southern enclosure. The enclosure was probably furnished with polygonal projecting towers at the corners, together with interval towers of varying form, at least on the north and east sides. The entrance to the enclosure was from the north, via an outer gateway with flanking polygonal towers leading via a 'halt-way' to the main abbey gatehouse on the site of Cavendish House.[73]

The survey of 1613, prepared by William Senior for William Cavendish, the new owner of the site (colour plate B / fig. 8), shows that by this time the northern enclosure contained a dovecote garden (in the north-west corner), a gatehouse (presumably the Hastings mansion, later Cavendish House), a 'hog yard' and stables (on the site of the present farm buildings), 'apricocks garden', and 'ruynes' on the site of the church and claustral buildings, an orchard and a 'horse pond'. In the southern part of the precinct was the Abbot's Garden, whilst along the river bank, just outside the east wall of the southern enclosure, was a hopyard. This is likely to be post-

73. The term 'halt-way' was used in the Crown Commissioners' Survey of 1538–9, in relation to the parallel walls lead- ing from the outer to the inner gateway: presumably traffic waited here before entering the inner precinct.

medieval in date as hopped beer only began to overtake the more traditional ale early in the six-teenth century, although it had appeared by the late fifteenth century in many high-status house-holds.[74] Many of the other features, however, could be of medieval origin; certainly many of the field names which appear on the Senior map are the same as those listed on the particulars of sale to William Parr just thirteen years after the Dissolution.[75] Some of the walls that subdivide the precinct on this map could be medieval, although they could relate to the mansion of the late six-teenth or early seventeenth century.

The perimeter walls, as built, were probably in coursed Dane Hills sandstone with a rubble core, but have been refaced with granite rubble or granite and sandstone rubble over much of their length. There is also some evidence for patching with narrow-section brick, which, from its form and rich terracotta or dark grey reduction-fired colour, could be early sixteenth century in date. Only in a few places do fragments of original facing survive. These boundary walls have been attributed to Abbot Cloune (1345–78) but there is no firm evidence for this; it is equally possible that they are of the twelfth or thirteenth century.

West wall

This is made mostly of pink, uncoursed granite rubble, but with some stretches of granite and sandstone rubble and patched repairs of brick, slate, tile and cobbles. Most of the granite facing and curved granite coping to the top of the wall appear to belong to the 1930s restoration. Later re-facing or re-building has destroyed any evidence of polygonal corner or interval towers. Just inside the west wall are the remains of monastic farm buildings with access via modern gates (see below).

North wall

The junction of the north and west walls is marked by a smooth curve; the fabric is mostly granite rub-ble, probably the result of later rebuilding. Occasionally, there are stretches of coursed sandstone that could be remnants of medieval facing, including one patch that ends abruptly c. 1.8m from the corner. This may indicate the location of a lost corner tower, although sandstone masonry on the interior of the curve, high in the wall may argue against this interpretation. The section of the north wall which lies east of the main gateway has been substantially rebuilt along its entire length, the exterior elevation refaced mostly with pink granite rubble, with occasional small patches of coursed sandstone and areas of earlier, mixed rubble. The interior face is rather more confused, consisting of sandstone and granite rubble with patching in brick, tile, slate and cobbles as a result of many different repairs. The only fea-ture of particular note in this stretch of the north wall is a projecting semi-circular interval tower, mainly refaced in granite rubble but with yellow oolitic limestone quoins. This appears three-sided internally and therefore may originally have been octagonal in form, although there is no surviving evidence that it ever projected beyond the inner face of the boundary wall.

At the north-east angle of the boundary wall is a corner tower, partly of Dane Hills sandstone, but mostly of recent granite rubble; little can be dated unequivocally to the medieval period, although some rough courses of sandstone masonry at its base could be original. Again, this may have been octagonal in plan but modern refacing has caused it to appear semi-circular. Nichols

74. C. Dyer, *Standards of living in the later middle ages* (Cambridge 1989), 58.

75. Augmentation Office, particulars for grants; William Parr, Marquess of Northampton, 4 Edw VI. Section 3; W. G. D. Fletcher, ed. 'Some unpublished documents relating to Leicestershire, pre-served in the Public Record Office', *Associated Architectural Societies Reports and Papers* 23.1 (1895), 213–52 at 240–2; see also below, 96.

Fig. 9. The entrance to the abbey, looking south from what is now Abbey Road, from Throsby,
History and antiquities, plate following p. 283

referred to the tower, describing it as 'six square . . . with an equilateral window frame . . . looking
north-east', which 'once afforded a pleasing prospect, at an easy distance, of the elegant church
tower of St. Margaret'.[76] The ground level inside this tower is over a metre higher than outside.

Outer gateway and halt-way walls

The present main entrance to the abbey grounds from Abbey Park Road is apparently on the same
site as the medieval outer gateway; from pictorial evidence it probably comprised two polygonal
towers with timber gates between them. One or both towers may have served as porters' lodges controlling access to the 'halt-way' that led to the main gate of the abbey, on the site of Cavendish House.

Pridden's engraving of 1786 shows a pair of polygonal projecting towers some distance apart, the
intervening space spanned by a length of wall in the centre of which is a taller section of wall with a
circular archway closed by a pair of substantial boarded gates.[77] Newton's engraving of 1787 for
Throsby (fig. 9) depicts a similar arrangement, although here the towers are cylindrical, possibly
two stories in height, and the gates have iron strapping. Throsby noted that the 'grand and ancient
entrance . . . is still entire and I rather think that the very gates are those used at the Dissolution'.[78]

Only the easternmost turret survived intact into the twentieth century and was extensively
restored, raised in height and crenellated as part of the works to convert the site into a public park
in the 1930s. At the same time, the western turret was entirely rebuilt to match its opposite number
and it is possible that remnants of original fabric were incorporated. Today, both turrets have
square-headed doorways facing inwards to the passageway, the jambs of which may be reset

76. Nichols, *Leicester*, i pt. 2, 294. To see St Margaret's Church,
the window must in fact face south or south east.

77. Nichols, *Leicester*, i pt. 2, pl. XVIII.

78. J. Throsby, *The history and antiquities of the ancient town of
Leicester* (Leicester 1791), 288.

medieval work, although the lintel of the west tower door is a modern restoration. The west and east towers have matching square-headed windows on the south-east and south-west facets respectively, with traces of others on the north facets, now destroyed. The eastern tower has evidence for a blocked doorway with a semi-circular sandstone arch in its east facet. Neither tower shows any evidence for a plinth course. Internally, the eastern turret is an irregular octagon in plan, as a result of a fireplace in the south wall, and is constructed of uncoursed sandstone and rubble to a height of around 2.8m, but coursed sandstone ashlar thereafter. The fireplace may be contemporary with the turret. It has an oblong chamfered lintel, covered with graffiti of some antiquity, including inscriptions in cartouches, a pair of concentric circles and several dates including 1725 and 1738. Above the fireplace is a relieving arch of rough, irregular sandstone voussoirs. The low height of the fireplace lintel (0.6m above ground) indicates that the floor level has been raised considerably.

The halt-way walls are marked by three large fragments, one of which is bonded into the south-east corner of the eastern gate turret. These have been largely refaced or rebuilt in granite and sandstone rubble with occasional brick and slate, but there are small patches of coursed sandstone. At their southern ends, the halt-way walls kink slightly before connecting with the south and west ranges of Cavendish House. Recent excavations suggest that this may be the result of a later modification, perhaps early in the seventeenth century when much of the façade of the house was remodelled. Two stones on the west face of the east wall inscribed 'J. Kirby' and 'A. Kirby' also suggest rebuilding and consolidation. Pictorial evidence suggests that the halt-way walls were originally crenellated, consistent with the 'fortified' character of the main gateway itself, comprising a large rectangular structure with polygonal turrets and crenellated parapets (see below, 28).

East and south walls

The eastern precinct wall has undergone less radical restoration work than the northern and western walls, and is of particular interest as a number of architectural details of probable medieval date survive. Apart from interval towers and wall facings, these include features relating to a group of monastic buildings (probably the infirmary) that were constructed against its inner face, and are known from the 1930s excavations. Other details may relate to post-Dissolution changes made in connection with the layout of the gardens of the late sixteenth-century mansion. The dating of the various phases of the wall is difficult, because of extensive vegetation cover and later restoration works, particularly in the 1930s, which used similar materials.

Early maps and mid-nineteenth-century photographs show that the River Soar originally flowed much closer to the eastern precinct wall than it does now. The present course is a result of flood relief works in 1879–80 when the channel was widened and deepened and smaller channels to the east were filled in. The William Senior map of 1613 (colour plate B, fig. 8) shows the abbey mill was located immediately adjacent to the north-east corner of the northern enclosure; it was demolished apparently in the later eighteenth century.[79]

The first stretch of boundary wall running to the south of the north-east corner tower is mainly rubble-work (granite and sandstone), but with some re-used blocks of sandstone ashlar and some flat blocks of sandstone laid in random courses. In this area, the ground inside the enclosure is *c.* 2m higher than outside, with the result that the wall leans considerably and has been propped with a buttress. Whether this difference in ground level reflects the medieval topography in any way is uncertain, but it is not a recent creation (such as spoil from the 1930s excavations) as it appears in a

79. Nichols, *Leicester*, i pt. 2, 294.

photograph dated 1909.[80] A heavily restored semi-octagonal interval tower stands *c.* 42m from the north-east corner. The lower facets of the tower are plain and vertical and are composed of rough, coursed sandstone in the lower 2.5m of the tower, but above this the facets step out from two very bold convex mouldings to support a projecting parapet. The bottom few courses of this parapet are sandstone and may contain some original material. The rest of the parapet is granite rubble and of the form described above. The moulding is reminiscent of the machicolations of late medieval castle architecture (although it lacks the necessary holes) and forms one of the pseudo-military features that characterise the east wall. The tower's form may be medieval, but preserved through piecemeal repairs so that little of the material need be original.

This tower appears on an engraving of 1794 in Nichols, a sketch by Flower of about 1820–30 (fig. 10) and on J. M. W. Turner's watercolour of Leicester Abbey (fig. 11).[81] To the south was another interval tower which appears on the 1909 photograph and which was described by Nichols as, 'a square dome, standing, like the other, not two yards from the river forward from the wall with two loopholes south east and one on each side'.[82] Today, the wall is breached at this point with an entrance into the Abbey Grounds from the river-side walk.

Fig. 10. A drawing by John Flower of one of the towers on the eastern precinct wall, overlooking the River Soar (*c.* 1820–30)

The stretch of the east wall south of this gateway offers the best opportunity for studying the fabric to recover stratigraphic sequences and address questions about the nature and use of the walls of the northern enclosure in the periods immediately before and after the Dissolution. On its exterior are some of the best-preserved fragments of apparently original medieval facing, comprising a double-chamfered plinth course at the base and drip mouldings towards the top of the wall. Some 30m south of the breach is the outlet of the abbey's main drain, indicated by a double-chamfered arch of regular sandstone voussoirs visible on both sides of the wall. This appears to have been uncovered during Bedingfield's excavations and was subject to more detailed investigation in 2005 (below, 64).

The inside face of this stretch of wall was related structurally to a small complex of buildings located during the 1930s excavations, interpreted as the infirmary on the basis of evidence from the Crown Commissioners' Survey and by analogy with other monastic layouts. Several buildings abutted the inner face of the precinct wall, using it to form their own eastern walls, while another appears to have intruded into the thickness of the wall. What at first sight seems to be an interval

80. ROLLR Henton Collection, 1252.

81. Nichols, *Leicester*, ii pt. 1, pl. XIX, following p. 294 and ROLLR Flower Sketchbook vol. i, 914.2. Turner's watercolour of Leicester Abbey (present location unknown) is no. 856 in, A. Wilton, *The life and works of J. M. W. Turner* (London 1979) (not illustrated); the intaglio etching of it by W. R. Smith is W. G. Rawlinson, *The engraved works of J. M. W. Turner R.A.* 2 vols (London 1908–13), no. 280.

82. Nichols, *Leicester*, i pt. 2, 294.

Fig. 11. J. M. W. Turner, 'View of Leicester Abbey', engraved by W. R. Smith, showing the eastern precinct wall and the ruins of Cavendish House in the background, from *Picturesque views of England and Wales* (1834)

tower at the southern end of this stretch is more likely to have formed part of this complex of buildings. It originally projected into the course of the Soar and was described by Nichols as 'arched on each side to humour the course of the river'.[83] Today, the tower has been much rebuilt and only the arch on the southern (upstream) side together with a cutwater appears to be original work. This structure was probably a garderobe for the monastic infirmary, as suggested, delicately, by Nichols. 'Some connoisseurs', he said, 'have seriously considered these domes [i.e. interval towers] as fortifications. One of them juts from the wall resting on an arch, a few yards upon Soar, calculated I will venture to say to give their daily cates [dainty food] a watery grave'.[84]

A thick mat of ivy obscures a small recess on the interior face of this section of wall, and very likely covers similar features further along this side of the wall. The section of the east wall extending to the south-eastern corner of the northern enclosure has been subject to many phases of rebuilding, but it contains a number of recognisable features, some of a pseudo-military nature. These include three sandstone-cased arrow slots, facing outwards, with wide splays behind, numerous putlog holes and the remains of another possible rectangular interval tower (extensively rebuilt or refaced in mixed rubble). It includes on its inner face two small vaulted compartments, the partition between which has broken off but is unlikely to have extended far beyond the inner line of the wall. The vault and partition are ruinous and are composed of unfaced rubble set in very coarse pink mortar. A small parapet runs above the vault together with a wall-walk that extends for a short distance along the wall on each side. The tower is pierced by four small, rectangular apertures, two on the east wall and one each on the north and south walls, lined with small, sub-rectangular blocks of granite or sandstone.

83. Ibid.   84. Ibid.

Fig. 12. 'View of Leicester, taken within the Abbey Wall' (1796), probably made from within the north precinct of the abbey and showings its southern wall and two surviving medieval buildings, from Nichols, *Leicester*, ii, pl. 19

A small, sub-circular tower stands in the south-eastern corner of the northern enclosure, refaced or rebuilt in granite; it is depicted in Flower's sketchbook and other nineteenth-century illustrations.[85] The southern and eastern walls each contain doorways *c*. 2m high, with chamfered dressed-sandstone gothic arches of two equal segments and chamfered jambs. The latter are rebated on the inside as if to accommodate a door. The interior of the tower is lit by arrow slits on its northern and southern sides. Near the southernmost point of the tower is a short rubble projection that starts a section of the east wall of the southern enclosure, now demolished (see below, 21). It is difficult to determine whether the architectural features of this tower are a result of modern rebuilding or genuine work of the medieval or post-medieval periods, although nineteenth-century engravings suggest that they are genuine, if reset.

The doorways lead into a small walled garden in the south-east corner of the northern enclosure. On the 1613 William Senior map, this garden occupies the southern part of a walled enclosure containing 'ruynes' and an orchard. An engraving of 1796 (fig. 12) appears to be a view southwards from within the northern enclosure and depicts a wall with gateway that is probably the south wall of the northern enclosure, flanked by a pair of two-storey stone buildings substantially intact, one of which has mullioned windows in its end wall and a chimney. At least one of these buildings appears on the Senior map and it is possible that they represent medieval structures that survived the Dissolution, perhaps corrodians' (pensioners') houses, of which there could have been many. The foundations of the easternmost building were uncovered in 1923 and appear on the surviving excavation plan.[86]

85. ROLLR Flower Sketchbook vol. i, 914.2.   86. See below, fig. 16.

The pseudo-military features apparent in this area, including arrow slits, wall-walks, parapets and interval towers, along with obvious re-facing and rebuilding, suggests a phase of restoration and remodelling at a late period in the history of the site. It is conceivable that they are garden features, perhaps of the seventeenth-century Cavendish House period, intended to enhance the appearance of the existing medieval 'romantic ruins' and provide seating with prospects through to the abbey meadows.

At its western-most point the tower joins a short section of wall made of mixed rubble and granite; if extrapolated westwards in a straight line it would meet the west wall at or near the straight joint between the west wall of the northern enclosure and Abbot Penny's brick wall (see below, 21–4). It may preserve the part of the line of the south wall of the northern enclosure but it is unlikely that much of its present fabric is medieval. It is, however, shown on Senior's map as the south wall of an orchard and perhaps was built in the late sixteenth or early seventeenth century. It contains another Gothic archway rather different from those in the tower, with pointed chamfered stops at its base and an irregular arch, made perhaps of re-used voussoirs from an earlier four-centred arch. A short return to the north, at the western end of this fragment of wall, might be part of the west wall of the orchard. Nothing else survives of the south wall of the northern enclosure; it was probably demolished when the southern enclosure was added in the late fifteenth or early sixteenth century.

2. Southern enclosure

The addition of the southern enclosure in the late fifteenth or early sixteenth century was apparently a result of two building campaigns; the boundary comprises fragments of granite rubble walling on the eastern side and part of the south, and a brick wall known as 'Abbot Penny's Wall' on the west and part of the south sides. The 1613 Senior map labels the interior of the enclosure 'Meryvale' and 'Abbat Guerne' with other features which could be fishponds (colour plate B, fig. 8). A 'hop yard' runs along the east wall adjacent to the river.

The granite rubble wall forming the eastern and part of the southern boundary of the precinct survives in a very fragmentary state and bears no significant architectural features. It is clear that this wall was in a similar state in the early nineteenth century, and Nichols refers to the 'many breaches, even to the surface of the earth'.[87] Abbot Penny's wall, however, is a remarkable survival from the late medieval period.

Abbot Penny's wall

This red-brick wall forms part of the south and west boundaries of the Abbey Grounds and is constructed of bricks measuring 9 × 2¼ × 4 inches, laid in English Bond (alternating courses of headers and stretchers). The wall stands on a sandstone plinth, 0.75m high, with a chamfered brick course above that is an original feature, and has an overall height of about 2m (excluding the modern blue brick copings). Internally, sandstone and brick buttresses (0.6m wide) also seem to be original, since a chamfered brick course matches that present above the plinth on the remainder of the wall. The wall has been pierced by two modern gateways and at least one earlier opening has been bricked up.

At the south-west angle, the wall is chamfered with sandstone quoins and stands c. 2.5m high.

87. Nichols, *Leicester*, i pt. 2, 294.

Fig. 13. Nichols, *Leicester*, iii, pl. 17 (left) and the statue niche as it is today (right)

Here, an eroded sandstone niche of decorated or perpendicular form with an ornate canopy above held a statue, presumably of the Virgin (fig. 13). The niche is hexagonal in plan, the front three facets project beyond the face of the wall, and it has an elaborate vaulted canopy including secondary and tertiary ribs. The front three facets of the canopy appear to have been ogival although the two front pendants are now missing, as are two small, engaged pilasters that bounded the niche on either side. The front of the base of the niche also projects, supported by what appears to have been a 'cyma reversa' moulding. The niche may be in its original position, or it may have been removed from a position in which its vaulted canopy was more readily visible.

The wall is best known for its elaborate diaper patterns (fig. 14) in contrasting blue bricks, mostly laid as headers ('flared headers'), but supplemented with stretchers as necessary. These were first drawn by Norris B. Robertson in April 1913 and redrawn in January 1939 by P. M. Watson.[88] There are at least forty-four patterns or symbols, at least eight of which are on the internal face of the wall. These include heraldic symbols, lozenge, chequer, chevron and cross-patterns, and recognisable symbols, including a portcullis of Tudor type and a chalice set on a paten. In addition, there are three sets of Gothic black-letter initials. The designs are not evenly spread along the length of the wall, nor are the different categories of design evenly dispersed; similar sets of

88. ROLLR DE2897/8. The designs have been surveyed recently by Neil Finn using modern equipment.

Fig. 14. Abbot Penny's wall (*c.* 1500), showing the 'mr' and 'ihc' symbols in flared headers

designs cluster in short stretches of the wall. This variation may be the result of different builds or of different teams of workers. It suggests that the symbols built into the wall may not have resulted from one single, coherent programme.

The exterior face of the southernmost section of the wall contains nineteen highly varied designs, many of which recur in the sections further north. These include geometrical designs, heraldic imagery, crucifixes, downward-pointing 'arrows', diaper patterns, and patterns based on chevrons. They are more dispersed to the south than to the north. Two modern gateways have been cut through this section of wall, the southernmost of which may have obliterated a motif completely, whilst the northern has truncated a triangular motif on its southern side, and is wide enough potentially to have obliterated at least two others. About 4m north of the northern gate there is a blocked opening which interrupts the chamfered brick plinth, shown by two plain brick jambs without stone quoins, surviving to a height of 0.7m. The top of the opening has been destroyed.

Further north is a second blocked opening with a four-centred brick arch, 1.07 × 1.39m, with the eroded remains of a sandstone coat of arms above it (fig. 14). This is almost certainly a niche as on the interior face of the wall is a brick buttress that appears to be original. Nichols refers to this as a 'single blank escutcheon', although the remainder of his description is rather confused and it is not entirely clear whether he thought that it was a niche or a blocked doorway.[89] However, the concentration of patterns and initials of religious significance flanking this feature suggest that it was a statue niche.

89. Nichols, *Leicester*, i pt. 2, 293.

The niche opening is flanked by four blue-brick designs to the south and one to the north; these are overtly symbolic and different to other designs. The first (from the south) is a large 'I'-shape with two equal-armed crosses on either side. The second is a pair of Gothic letters 'IP', interpreted as the initials of Abbot John Penny. The third has been interpreted as a chalice resting on a paten and therefore of liturgical significance; the fourth is interpreted as 'ihs' for 'Christ' (fig. 14 right).[90] This reference to the name of Christ is matched by the fifth design, the letters 'mr' (fig. 14 left), which is an abbreviation for 'Mary'. These last two 'inscriptions', on either side of the arch, use blue bricks inserted into the wall, some at an angle of 45 degrees (cutting through the coursed red bricks) to produce the angled strokes of the letters. This technique is not found elsewhere in the wall.

The wall has been attributed to Abbot John Penny, and dated *c.* 1500. The reasons for this are twofold. First, John Leyland in his itinerary, compiled between 1535–43, says 'This Peny made the new bricke work in Leicester Abbay, and much of the bricke waulles'. Second, one of the motifs in the wall – the letters IP – is thought to represent his initials, suggesting that it was built in his lifetime. Penny was abbot between 1496 and 1507/8, although in 1505 when Penny was appointed bishop of Bangor (a see with small revenues that were not easy to collect) he was permitted to continue to hold Leicester Abbey 'in commendam' until 1507/8 when he was succeeded there by Richard Pexall.[91]

The 1613 Senior map (colour plate B, fig. 8) labels a field to the west of the abbey precinct as 'Brick Close' and it is tempting to suggest that this was the site of the clay pits and brick kilns associated with brick production for this wall and other buildings within the abbey precincts. Other early brick buildings in the county also seem to have had brick-works located close to the construction site. At Kirby Muxloe Castle (1480–84), there are no references to payments for transportation of bricks, while areas of burning, soil marks and scatters of brick to the south of Cropston reservoir have been interpreted as the brick-yard for Bradgate House (*c.* 1490).[92]

3. Discussion

The northern enclosure of the precinct seems to be the earlier of the two enclosing the principal monastic buildings, with a wall constructed of dressed sandstone with a rubble core. It has been suggested that Abbot William Cloune, 1345–77/8, was responsible for building the boundary wall on the north and east sides of the precinct, enlarging the original site of the abbey grounds, together with the construction of the gatehouse and the Abbot's Hall.[93] Recent excavations on the site of the gatehouse, however, have suggested an earlier and smaller precursor that could have been associated with an earlier line of the northern precinct wall further south than at present (see below, 28). If correct, the early precinct may have had a gatehouse with projecting external bastion, comprising parallel walls terminating with circular or polygonal towers which later became enclosed by the enlarged north precinct wall, forming the 'halt-way' referred to by the 1538/9 Crown Commissioners' Survey. A bastion of that type gives the impression of an outer defensive work and raises the question of whether the precinct walls were considered to be primarily defen-

90. H. Blake, G. Egan, J. Hurst and E. New, 'From popular devotion to resistance and revival in England: the cult of the holy name of Jesus and the Reformation' in *The archaeology of Reformation 1480–1580*, ed. D. Gaimster and R. Gilchrist, Society for Post Medieval Archaeology Monograph 1 (Leeds 2003), 175–203 at 179.

91. A. Hamilton Thompson, *The Abbey of St Mary of the Meadows, Leicester* (Leicester 1949), 73.

92. A. McWhirr, 'Brickmaking in Leicestershire before 1710', *TLAHS* 71 (1997), 37–59 at 43.

93. Jackson, 'History and description', 5.

sive or an expression of the grand status of the abbey. Both interpretations may be true; the precinct walls may have started out as defensive structures, but became more symbolic from the fourteenth century onwards. A similar pattern may be evident in the boundaries of the Newarke precinct in Leicester where the Newarke Gateway of about 1400, and the Turret Gateway built *c.* 20 years later exhibit pseudo-military architecture: crenellated, with turrets, loopholes, and (in the case of the latter) a portcullis slot. Elsewhere, as in Coventry for example, civic pride appears to have overtaken defence as the motivation for the construction of the town defences by the late fourteenth century.[94]

Another problem raised by the abbey precinct is that the main entrance is located as far as possible from the town, and faces away from it. Its location could have been a symbolic gesture, creating not only a clear distinction between the spiritual and temporal and an assertion of the independence of the abbey from the town, but also an expression of pride and status by presenting the main entrance to travellers coming to Leicester from the north. Other Augustinian establishments in Leicester also dominated routes into the town, the Austin Friars outside the West Gate and the Newarke Collegiate enclosure outside the south gate.

The enclosed southern precinct, added by the end of the fifteenth century with its overt Christian symbols and brick construction – a fashionable new building material in fifteenth-century Leicestershire – displays similar connotations of status and power. It is no coincidence that this long stretch of wall runs along the route from the town to the abbey's main gate; its visual symbols and sophisticated building material provided an overt statement of the spiritual significance and temporal power of the site to visitors from the town. Geophysical survey within the southern precinct has confirmed the position of fishponds suggested on the 1613 Senior map although no evidence has emerged so far to indicate that this area was used for anything other than agricultural purposes.

Leicester Abbey's excavated remains
Although no site notebooks survive from the 1929–31 excavations, a pencil-drawn plan labelled 'Aug & Sept 1930' is in the ROLLR and appears to be the original composite plan of the results of the work.[95] Fragments of wall are marked by dashed lines, and the lines of drains, patches of tile flooring and modern sheds are shown, together with the position of some burials. This is the surveyor's field plan, probably produced using a theodolite or plane table, and includes by a number of base lines and hand-written measurements, together with a few notes indicating areas which had not been explored, areas which remained un-surveyed and the position of a modern shed and a former shed. The plan shows that robber trenches were not recognised as such, and no attempt was made to link fragments of walls. A further plan drawn by Bedingfield's colleague, P. H. Grundy, dated 1930, illustrates the development of the interpretation of the results of the excavations.[96] Here, the 1538/9 Crown Commissioners' Survey has been used to identify individual buildings, marked by descriptive extracts from the text on the plan, together with arrows indicating the sequence of the narrative that may represent the commissioners' route through the maze of buildings.

In the LCMS collections is a traced copy of the original site plan, updated in pencil to incorporate additional discoveries from 1931; this did not, however, record the results of work known by recent

94. I. Soden, *Coventry: the hidden history* (Stroud 2005), 228.
95. ROLLR DE6218/1.
96. ROLLR DE6218/3.

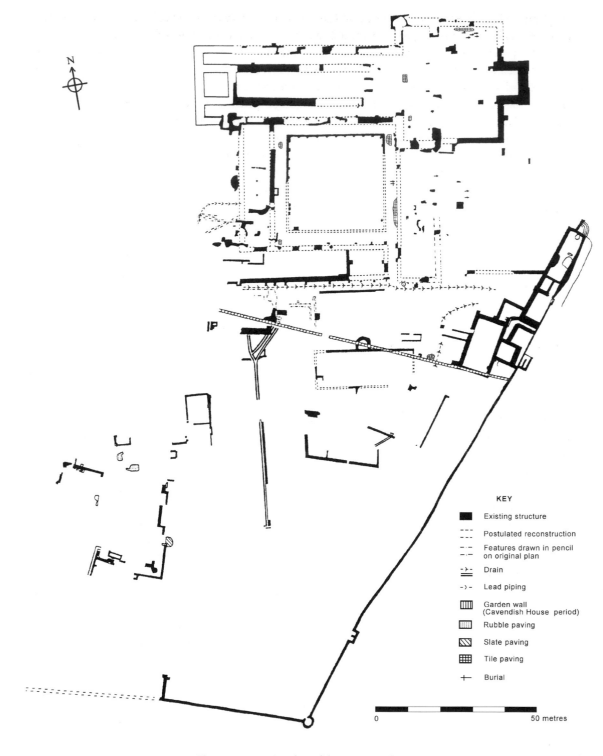

KEY

■ Existing structure

- - - Postulated reconstruction

- · - Features drawn in pencil
       on original plan

-·▶·- Drain

-·)·- Lead piping

Garden wall
(Cavendish House period)

Rubble paving

Slate paving

Tile paving

+ Burial

0   50 metres

Fig. 15. Composite plan of the 1923–5 and 1929–32 excavations (after Liddle 1995)

excavations to have been undertaken next to Cavendish House. In the same collection, a second plan shows the wall lines that Bedingfield proposed laying out, including a range of buildings constructed against the precinct wall and now interpreted as the infirmary, and the footprint of what was believed to be the monastic gatehouse.[97] In the event, only the walls discovered by 1930 were laid out on the ground; interestingly, later published plans of the site also exclude the range of probable infirmary buildings, perhaps because it was thought that they represented later structures on the site.

Essentially, the wall lines on the interpretative plans were created by linking up the clearly identifiable fragments of masonry discovered and by reference to comparative monastic site plans. For the most part, what is laid out on the ground today is an intelligent interpretation of the results of the excavation. Areas with the most uncertainty are where the walls had been largely robbed of their stone, particularly the east range including the chapter house. As discussed above, recent restoration work has indicated that many of the laid-out walls are nothing more than a crust of masonry above an earth core, presumably in places where the underlying masonry had been extensively robbed. A photograph of the church area dated September 1930 shows isolated stretches of walling standing proud of a levelled surface. Another photograph from November 1930 shows that the walls of the north cloister walk stood c. 1m above the levelled surface. In all cases the rough masonry suggests these are the rubble core of walls or foundation material rather than faced superstructure. Hence some of the reconstructed walls incorporates genuine masonry, as has proved to be the case for the south wall of the church where a substantial stretch of the rubble core has been revealed during consolidation in 2005, corresponding with a definite wall line shown on the original site plan.

Interpretation of the excavated plan

A composite plan was prepared by Liddle in 1995 (fig. 15) using all of these sources, but principally the tracing of Bedingfield's plan, his plan for the proposed layout of the walls on the ground and plans of the 1923–5 excavations in the museum records.[98] This shows the actual evidence of structural remains encountered in the excavations upon which Bedingfield based his interpretative reconstruction plan.[99] Interpreting such a plan is not straightforward since many walls have been heavily robbed and their lines were not recognised during excavation. In addition, there has been a tendency to assume that the remains are all medieval and of one constructional phase, whereas in fact they represent a palimpsest of occupation over a long period of time. It must be remembered that the abbey was in existence for c. 400 years and underwent many changes during that time. Similarly, the post-Dissolution mansion and associated gardens were in occupation for more than a century and the succeeding tenant farm/market garden for a further 300 years. Nevertheless, Bedingfield was able to identify the principal monastic buildings grouped around the cloister by reference to comparative Augustinian monastic plans and by analysing the 1538/9 Crown Commissioners' Survey. The Survey describes, with reasonable clarity, seven main elements:

1. A gatehouse with lodgings and an enclosed area in front
2. A courtyard with farm buildings
3. An inner court with the bake-house, brew-house and two stables on one side, and on another access to the church (4); access to a yard with guest facilities (5)

97. On tracing paper, labelled 72.1959/4.

98. P. Liddle, 'The abbeys and priories of Leicestershire and Rutland' *TLAHS* 69 (1995), 1–21, figs. 6 and 7. The interpretation of

the layout of the monastic buildings in this section incorporates and expands upon the 'Leicester Abbey' section of this article.

99. Bedingfield, 'Presidential address', pl. 3.

4. The church and claustral ranges (the west range comprising chambers, the south range the refectory and the east range the dormitory and, by implication, the chapter house and library)

5. An adjoining yard surrounded by a hall and chambers, apparently guest facilities including a tower called the King's Lodging and a great dining chamber (with bay window) linked to the kitchen and officials' quarters

6. The infirmary houses

7. An outer court with servants' quarters

1. The Gatehouse

Recent excavations on the site of Cavendish House have demonstrated that this is the site of the medieval gatehouse and that it was examined in the 1930s, although the results were not recorded on the plan that has survived until today. Re-examination of one of Bedingfield's plans detailing the proposed layout of reconstructed walls, indicates that he also believed the gatehouse to be at this location. Element 2 seems to be represented by the existing barns and farm buildings west of Cavendish House which may incorporate fabric from the medieval home farm. The results of the excavation of the gatehouse and a survey of the agricultural buildings are considered in more detail below.

Excavations were undertaken by ULAS in 2000–4 on the south side of the surviving ruined north façade of Cavendish House to clarify the plan and phasing of the post-Dissolution mansion and its suspected medieval precursor, the abbey gatehouse.[100] The work was evaluative and restricted in the main to the removal of modern overburden and intrusions, in order to reveal the uppermost significant archaeological deposits. Such deposits were then subject only to limited sample excavation sufficient to establish their nature, extent and dating, the overriding principal being to minimise unnecessary damage to remains which were not otherwise under any threat. The seasonal nature of the work meant that it was possible only to open up comparatively small trenches each year (fig. 16). Although inferior to open-area excavation, the strategy satisfied reasonably well the differing requirements of student training and research, although it put some limitations on the interpretation of the results.

It was clear during the excavation work that the site had been previously trenched, probably in the 1930s. Despite this, evidence survived for further walls and robbed foundations giving increased resolution to the plan of this building in the medieval and post-medieval periods.[101]

Phase 1: twelfth or thirteenth century? (fig. 17)

The earliest structure identified is interpreted tentatively as a gatehouse of the simplest form, comprising a central north–south gate hall *c.* 2.5m (8.3 feet) wide at its narrowest point, flanked on either side by small rooms that functioned perhaps as porters' lodges. Evidence for the north wall of this building consisted of an east–west robber trench [87 and 1144], the substantial proportions

100. R. Buckley and A. Butler, 'Leicester Abbey', *TLAHS* 75 (2001), 129–30; R. Buckley and M. Derrick, 'An archaeological evaluation at Leicester Abbey: first season 2000', unpubl. ULAS report 2001–074 (2001); J. Meek and R. Buckley, 'An archaeological evaluation at Leicester Abbey: second season, Summer 2001', unpubl. ULAS report 2002–010 (2002); J. Meek and R. Buckley, 'Leicester Abbey' *TLAHS* 76 (2002), 81–5; S. Jones and R. Buckley, ed. 'An archaeological evaluation at Leicester Abbey: third season, summer 2002', unpubl. ULAS report 2004–65 (2004a); S. Jones and R.

Buckley, ed. 'An archaeological evaluation at Leicester Abbey: fourth season, summer 2003', unpubl. ULAS report 2004–78 (2004b) S. Jones and R. Buckley, 'Leicester Abbey' in R. Buckley and S. George, ed. 'Archaeology in Leicestershire and Rutland 2003' *TLAHS* 78 (2004), 143–78 at 143. See further, Buckley et al 'Leicester Abbey after the Dissolution', below pp. 95–118.

101. In the text, archaeological context numbers are indicated by square brackets.

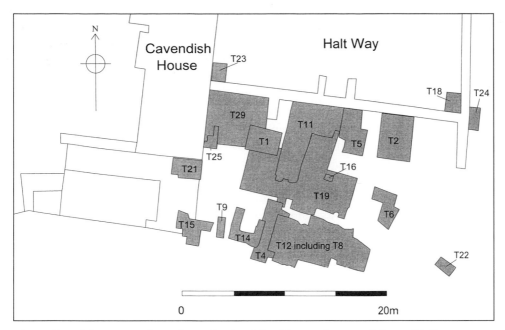

Fig. 16. Plan of the excavated trenches at the site of the abbey gatehouse and Cavendish House (2000–4)

Fig. 17. Plan of Phases 1 and 2 of the abbey gatehouse

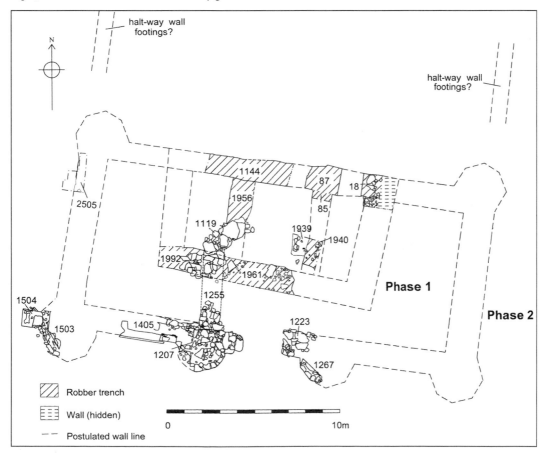

of which (1.13–1.3m wide) are consistent with monastic-period construction. The robbing of this wall dates to Phase 4 and is discussed in more detail below (p. 110). At its eastern end, a small fragment of the granite and sandstone footings of this wall survived [18]. Under the wall of the Phase 3 cellar (see below, p. 105), these footings turned southwards, providing information about the position of the east wall; evidence for the south wall [1992] of the building was found in the 2002 season. The foundations of this south wall (of unbonded sandstone rubble) survived in an extremely fragmentary state to the west of the gate hall, considerably truncated by a modern service trench and by what was probably an excavation trench of the 1920s–30s that had also destroyed all evidence for the stratigraphic relationships of the remains of the south wall with surrounding layers.

A robber trench running east to west [1961] (4.13m long × 1.6m wide) provides evidence for the continuation of this wall to the east. A small section was excavated across this feature, indicating that it was at least 1m in depth. The suggested position of the west wall of this early gatehouse is extrapolated from the symmetry of the gate hall; its projected line would coincide with an internal north–south wall of the Phase 3 and 4 gatehouse (see below, pp. 104–10), although it has not proved possible to determine whether surviving masonry from these phases represents reuse of the earlier wall or a replacement of it.

Some evidence was also revealed for the robbed lines of two possible north–south internal walls flanking the gate hall. The east wall was identified as a linear feature [1940] *c.* 0.83m wide; the west wall was represented by another linear feature *c.* 3.5m long × *c.* 0.7m wide [1956]. The continuation of this feature to the south is by no means certain and neither robber trench was subjected to detailed investigation. It remains possible that the western arch abutment [attached to context 1119], currently ascribed to Phase 2, belongs to this earlier phase indicating that the western gate hall wall in fact steps westwards before continuing southwards to join the south wall.

To the south of the suggested early gatehouse, a large, possibly circular pit was found in the centre of Trench 12 [1230], cutting through a possible make-up deposit of light brown sandy clay [1272] which lay above the natural. The pit fills were predominantly light-coloured sands, containing abundant quantities of decayed and crushed sandstone pieces. It is possible that this pit was dug to extract gravel for the production of mortar and that it was used subsequently for mortar mixing, perhaps for the construction of the early gatehouse just to the north.

The evidence for an early gatehouse structure is extremely limited, and its existence hinges on the presence of the rather tenuous and disturbed remains of the south wall – a structural element that, unlike the other walls, cannot be associated with any of the later phases in a coherent way. The reconstruction suggests a single pile building measuring externally *c.* 12.87m (42.2 feet) east to west, by 7.5m (24.6 feet) north to south. Although the north–south span is large, the unequal dimensions of the gate hall and flanking rooms could indicate an east–west axial roof rather than a separate transverse roof over each bay. This theory is supported by the substantial nature of the north wall of the building compared with the comparatively slight north–south walls on either side of the gate hall.

No secure dating evidence was recovered for this early gatehouse, although it is likely to be of the twelfth or thirteenth century, since the major remodelling of the building in Phase 2 has been ascribed to the fourteenth to fifteenth century. If correct, this date raises an interesting problem regarding the relationship of the Phase 1 gatehouse with the precinct walls and a number of possible interpretations emerge:

a) The line of the north precinct wall originally ran much further south to link with this early gatehouse, just 15m north of the church. No evidence for this has emerged so far from earlier excavations or from the results of geophysical survey, although if the wall had been completely robbed this is unsurprising. Another possible objection might be that the precinct wall would be too close to the church. However, if this gatehouse and early boundary are twelfth century, it is likely that the church was aisleless at this stage, making it over 20m away.

b) As (a), but with parallel walls running north, projecting beyond the line of the precinct wall, terminating with an outer gate, to form a type of bastion arrangement as noted at Thornton Abbey.[102]

c) The same arrangement as in the later medieval period – the precinct wall in the same position as now and the bastion arrangement as above, but contained wholly within the precinct, forming a 'halt-way' as described in the Crown Commissioners' Survey.

Only further excavation or remote sensing may resolve these questions. However, if the arrangement was originally as (a), it is tempting to see the construction of the later gatehouse and boundary wall as part of a major programme of works, perhaps including the enlargement of the church with the addition of a north aisle, a factor which may have forced the extension of the precinct to the north.

Phase 2: c. 1350–1500 (figs. 17 and 18)

The 1538/9 Crown Commissioners' Survey describes, 'a square lodging on either side of the gatehouse in which are five chambers with chimneys and large glazed windows, the walls being of stone and covered with lead, and with four stone turrets at the corners of the same'. This description tallies with the image of the eastern half of the south facade shown on the Buck brothers' engraving of the 'South View of Leicester Abby' (below p. 102, fig. 2). Here, there are at least three polygonal turrets and windows of sixteenth-century form indicative of pre-Dissolution fabric and suggesting that the original gatehouse was extended south, east and westwards to create lodgings of a high standard with heated rooms. Some walls of the early gatehouse must have been retained; certainly the north and probably the flanking walls of the gate hall were reused, but the south wall must have been demolished. Evidence for this was found in the form of a robber trench [1961] filled with orangey-brown clay and mortar [1960, 1979, and 1986] which produced ten sherds of pottery in Potters Marston and the Chilvers Coton fabrics (CC1 and CC2) dating from the twelfth or thirteenth to the fourteenth or fifteenth centuries.[103] Single fragments of thirteenth-century and later medieval ridge tile (in CC1 and MP2 fabric respectively), a piece of worn floor tile (possibly fourteenth century in date), a flat roof tile and four fragments of coarse building material, including a moulded brick, were also found. The building materials as a group could date from as early as the fourteenth century providing a possible 'terminus post quem' for the construction of the gatehouse. However, it should be borne in mind that it would be unusual to find brick as early as this in Leicester and also that the finds derived from robber-trench contexts which were contained entirely within the gate hall area and therefore not, in stratigraphic terms, demonstrably earlier than any of the Phase 2 walls, and were in an area with many modern intrusions. Thus the dating evidence should be regarded with caution.

The corners of the Phase 2 medieval gatehouse were probably formed by the western and eastern turrets, as shown on the Buck engraving. Excavation has added evidence for the plan and

102. Although at Thornton these walls are considered to be post-Dissolution; A. W. Clapham, *Thornton Abbey* (London 1956), 4, 9, with a description of the monastic buildings by P. K. Ballie Reynolds.

103. D. Sawday, 'The pottery and medieval floor and ridge tile from excavations at Leicester Abbey (season 4)' in Jones and Buckley, ed. (2004b), 16–24.

Fig. 18. View west of the 2001 excavation, showing the south wall of the Phase 2 gatehouse. The west gate hall turret is just above the ranging rod

phasing of the southern façade, including the foundations of the polygonal towers flanking the gate hall, parts of the wall linking the westernmost of these to the south-western corner turret, and the south-western corner turret itself. Only limited evidence for internal walls or for the arrangement of the northern façade has emerged .

South-western turret
Trench 15 excavated within the garden of Abbey House revealed a wall [1503], 0.9m wide, forming the western and south-western sides of a polygonal structure interpreted as the south-western corner turret of the gatehouse (fig. 19). Unlike the western gate hall turret [1207], which was solid

Fig. 19. View west of the west turret of the south wall of the Phase 2 gatehouse

Fig. 20. View east of the western gate hall turret excavated in 2001. Note the insubstantial stone foundation on the right of the photograph, possibly 18th century, which relates to the structure shown on the Buck brothers' engraving of 1730 (fig. 2, p. 102)

(see below), this turret was hollow internally, suggesting it contained a newel staircase serving the upper floors of the building and a cellar or undercroft (the interior space was well below the anticipated ground floor level of the building).

An east–west wall [1504], 1.1m long × 0.9m wide, abuts the western side of this turret and is interpreted as a later addition to the gatehouse to link it to a structure which may have been a detached kitchen as indicated by a double chimney stack wall to the west (and which also appears on the Buck brothers' engraving).

Western gate hall wall and turret

Trench 12 confirmed the existence of the western gate hall turret [1207] with a substantial foundation measuring 2.80m east to west, 2.55m north to south and at least 0.90m deep, constructed of rough sandstone blocks bonded with lime mortar (fig. 20). A kerb of large sandstone blocks was found around the south-eastern and southern edges of the tower, although it had been removed on the south-westerm side perhaps as a result of earlier excavations. The turret had a small (*c.* 1.0m) projection [1206] to the east, constructed of large sandstone and granite blocks with lime mortar on the upper parts and clay bonding for the lower foundations. A large sandstone block on the top of the wall marked the boundary between the tower and this butt-ended projection, although the phasing could not be determined clearly. This large block included a right-angled notch cut into the eastern edge. Based on the evidence from the Buck brothers' engraving, this feature almost certainly represents the respond of an archway spanning the gate hall, with the western timber gate closing against the notch (see below, 38). Running westwards from the turret was a wall [1405], 1.4m thick and built of rough-hewn granite block foundations at least 0.85m deep. One course of the superstructure survived, comprising a chamfered sandstone plinth course bonded with lime mortar on its southern edge. The western end of the wall was truncated by a modern brick-built structure. Without excavation, the stratigraphic relationship between this wall and adjacent turret remains uncertain.

A wall [1255] projects north of the tower base with granite and sandstone rubble footings, bonded by lime mortar and clay and with traces of superstructure surviving in the form of three, faced sandstone blocks, bonded with orangey lime mortar. This wall was partially covered by a spread of lime mortar from the tower base [1207] and used granite in its foundations. This would seem to suggest two distinct phases of construction, with the tower base as a later addition.

This wall [1255] joined another [1119] constructed mostly of sandstone blocks with a little granite, that angled north-east before joining a north–south robber trench [1956], assumed to represent a wall retained from the Phase 1 structure. A projection from wall 1119 was constructed from large irregular granite blocks and probably represents the footings of the respond of another archway spanning the gate hall.

Eastern gate hall wall and turret

Later disturbance has damaged the eastern gate hall turret [1267], leaving only the south-western and southern facets, but again its form was polygonal. As far as could be ascertained, the footings for this tower were no deeper than 0.36m and were constructed of rough-hewn sandstone blocks and mortar, with a kerb of larger, faced sandstone blocks around the surviving faces. As with the western turret, there was evidence of a short stretch of wall [1223], *c.* 1.5m long × 1.5m wide × 0.6m deep, forming an abutment facing the gate hall and constructed of sandstone and large granite blocks. Any evidence for the remainder of the south façade east of the turret appears to have been destroyed by a large pit feature.

South-eastern corner turret

A small trench excavated in the predicted position of the south-eastern corner turret, max. *c.* 1.3m deep, revealed that this area had been subject to extensive modern disturbance, perhaps quarrying, removing any evidence of earlier features.

Northern façade

Evidence for the appearance and position of the north wall of the Phase 2 gatehouse is entirely lacking from either the pictorial or archaeological record, and the present reconstructed line is based effectively on a process of elimination from a series of targeted trenches that produced negative results. Initially, it was thought possible that the Phase 1 gatehouse had been demolished entirely and that the north wall of the Phase 2 structure lay further to the north, under the present ruined north façade wall of the south wing of Cavendish House. A stone projection in the cellar of the west range of Cavendish House provided possible support for this theory, as it coincided with the junction of the surviving ruined façade wall of the south range, taken to be a fragment of the north-western corner turret.

In order to test this theory, Trenches 18/24 and 23 were excavated at the presumed locations of the north-east and north-west turrets respectively. Trench 18 was located on the north side of the ruined north façade of Cavendish House, at its eastern end where it joins the eastern halt-way wall. Beneath the stone footings of the present line of the latter [1809] and the footings for the Phase 3 east cellar wing of Cavendish House [1808] (see below, p. 105), some evidence emerged for an earlier feature consisting of an area of very rough limestone fragments, perhaps relating to a robbed feature, the alignment of which coincided with a scar of rough unfaced rubble on the lower part of the Phase 3 east cellar wing of Cavendish House. It lay also on the same line as the east halt-way wall some 20m to the north, where it steps in about 1m to the west. This all seems to suggest that the halt-way wall to the south of this point was rebuilt, perhaps when the Phase 4 stair tower was added to Cavendish House after the Dissolution, and that the structural feature identified represents the robbed remains of the original halt-way wall.

No evidence that could be interpreted as a polygonal turret base was identified. An additional trench, no. 24, to the east of the Phase 3 cellar wing was dug to determine whether the turret lies further to the east, but no earlier structures were identified.

Trench 23 was excavated on the north side of the surviving ruined north façade of Cavendish House, at its junction with the east wall of the west range. Excavation to a depth of *c.* 1m revealed a north–south orientated linear feature containing mortar and sandstone fragments. As on the eastern side, this feature lined up with a step in the west halt-way wall to the north, suggesting that the southern portion of this wall was demolished when the west range was constructed in the post-Dissolution period. Parts of the footings of this wall may have been retained for the foundations of the north façade wall [2304] and east wall of the west range [2305] of Cavendish House. Again no evidence for a polygonal foundation was revealed.

These negative results suggest that the Phase 2 gatehouse reused the north wall of the Phase 1 gatehouse. The north-eastern corner turret was therefore destroyed by the construction of the Phase 3 projecting cellar wing, perhaps in the late sixteenth century (see below, p. 105). To test the revised projected position of the north-western turret, a trench was excavated in this area. However, this revealed an area of well-preserved flagstone paving associated with the post-Dissolution phases of Cavendish House which it was considered desirable to preserve in situ, so the area was not investigated further.

A possible detached kitchen

A substantial double chimney breast now incorporated into an outbuilding west of the gatehouse is shown on eighteenth- and nineteenth-century engravings of the south façade. The survival of chimneys and towers on many ruined buildings reflects, in part, the structural integrity of compact building cells rather than the elongated cells used for constructing living accommodation.[104] In the Buck engraving, it is shown topped with the remnants of four stone chimney flues of classical pedimented form, probably of the last quarter of the sixteenth century (see below, p. 116). This, together with a small blocked window perhaps of similar date, has led to an assumption that the chimney breast relates to the post-Dissolution mansion. However, the stone fabric in the chimney has the appearance of an original build and is stylistically of medieval form. Hence, it most likely relates to a late medieval detached, or semi-detached, kitchen block, serving the adjacent gatehouse.

Unfortunately, the extensive coverage of ivy on the walls of Cavendish House in this area has prevented examination of the fabric and its relationship with other upstanding remains. Although the internal fabric is largely obscured by later brick additions, the springing of two substantial stone archways is evident in the eastern portion of the building, suggesting, on the basis of the length of the surviving east–west wall, that there were perhaps originally two arched fireplaces, each over 3m across. The overall internal dimensions of the building could have been as much as 11.3m (37 feet) east–west by 7.01m (23 feet) north–south (the latter measurement is entirely speculative). The small blocked window at the base of the westernmost chimney is not visible inside the building, but may relate to a now-vanished dry chamber or perhaps a 'squint' in the rear of the fireplace.

The stub walling and gable end (which now forms an outbuilding incorporated into the chimney at the eastern end) appears to be part of the original fabric; there is evidence from the Buck engraving and from excavation of the south-western corner turret of the gatehouse, to suggest that the two buildings were linked, perhaps by a passage. The wall found in excavation clearly post-dated the turret, indicating that the passageway, at least, was a later addition to the gatehouse.

Discussion

On the basis of this evidence, Leicester Abbey's Phase 2 gatehouse appears to have been a rectangular building measuring internally 20.88m (68.5 feet) × 8.31m (27.26 feet, along the east gate hall wall), with a gate hall measuring 3.47m (11.38 feet) wide reducing to 2.31m (7.58 feet) (minimum) at the archway positions. Its closest parallel is the well-preserved gatehouse of Thornton Abbey in north Lincolnshire (figs. 21 and 22).[105] This is a three-storey building with a central gate hall, corner turrets and inner gate hall turrets, built partly of stone, but more substantially of brick with stone dressings. It was constructed in the 1360s and enlarged and defended in 1382, when the abbey received a licence to crenellate.[106] It is approached via an outer barbican, added perhaps in the sixteenth century, com-

104. D. Smith, 'Assessment of Cavendish House and outbuildings' in 'Abbey Park, Leicester' ed. Buckley (1997), 44.

105. Thanks to Dr G. Coppack for a guided tour of Thornton and plans of that gatehouse.

Fig. 21. The west, principal, elevation of the gatehouse at Thornton Abbey

Fig. 22. The gatehouse plans of Leicester abbey (above) and Thornton Abbey (below, based on a 19th-century survey in the possession of English Heritage)

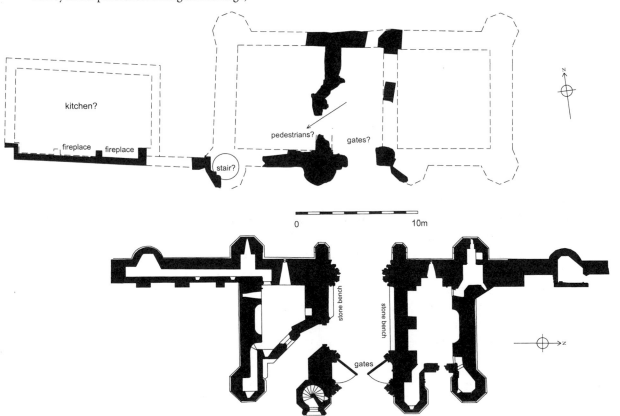

prising a pair of crenellated parallel walls with wall walks terminating in circular towers, rather like the Leicester halt-way, but projecting beyond the precinct wall and originally equipped with an outer drawbridge to span a wet moat. Archways divide the gate hall into two unequal bays, the large outer bay furnished with stone benches to accommodate waiting visitors. Pedestrians could then enter the precinct via a side passageway past the porters' rooms, while vehicular traffic proceeded through a pair of (surviving) oak gates that swung back against the gate hall walls of the inner bay. Access to the upper floors was via a single newel staircase in one of the gate hall turrets or from the wall walk. A great hall at first floor level had further rooms on the floor above.

The gatehouse at Thornton was used for administrative purposes and housed the abbey's exchequer; it has no kitchen or other domestic offices and so is not considered to have been the abbot's lodging.[107] Figure 23 shows the plan of the Leicester gatehouse at the same scale as that at Thornton. The dimensions of Thornton are similar to those at Leicester, at 15.75m (51.67 feet) × 7.6m (24.93 feet) (measured along the north gate hall wall) and a gate hall 3.38–5.31m wide (17.42–11.08 feet). The rather odd arrangement of the west gate hall wall at Leicester may suggest that, like Thornton, it too had a separate pedestrian passageway. An objection to this is the stretch of wall to the west of the west gate hall turret, where one would expect the pedestrian exit to be. Here, the surviving chamfered plinth course might indicate no exit at this point, although it is entirely possible that this is a later blocking, perhaps of the post-Dissolution phase. Alternatively, a pedestrian access may have been on the east side of the gate hall.

The Buck brothers' engraving (below p. 102, fig. 2) of the south façade of Cavendish House indicates that the medieval turrets were crenellated and that the central pair, flanking the gate hall, were taller than the corner turrets, as at Thornton (fig. 21). Another feature at Leicester resembling the arrangement at Thornton is in the position of the gates themselves, which may have opened southwards, against the walls of an inner bay of the gate hall, as suggested by a fragment of rebated stone on the arch abutment of the western gate hall turret.

As discussed above, dating of the construction of the Phase 2 gatehouse using archaeological evidence is not entirely certain, relying on a short stretch of the robbed south wall of the postulated Phase 1 structure which has no stratigraphic relationship with the building which succeeded it and which was heavily disturbed by later intrusions. Finds from this robber trench, including Midland Purple Ware ridge tile and nibbed roofing tile, suggest a fourteenth-century date for the robbing, although the presence of a fragment of brick would, on the face of it, be anomalous.[108] The use of brick at Thornton and elsewhere was becoming increasingly common by the fourteenth century. However, it is usually thought that brick was not used in Leicestershire until the late fifteenth century at Ashby de la Zouch Castle (c. 1470s), Kirby Muxloe Castle (1480–4) or Groby Manor House (c. 1450–1500).[109] Similarly, nibbed flat roofing tile is comparatively unusual in the county, due to the presence of good sources of slate, and the evidence from documentary sources suggests that it was only used on high-status buildings in Leicester, such as the Castle and the Guildhall, from the fourteenth century onwards.[110]

Interestingly, Nichols tell us that, 'to the account of abbot Clowne who died 1377, the Rental of Charyte enables us to add that in his time, the gates of the abbey were new built with brick'.[111] The

106. Clapham, *Thornton Abbey*, 4, 9.

107. Ibid, 9.

108. Nibbed ceramic roofing tile appears at the Austin Friars site in Phase 3c, dated to the fourteenth century; C. E. Allin, 'The ridge tiles' in *The Austin friars, Leicester*, ed. J. Mellor and T.

Pearce, Council for British Archaeology research report 35 (Leicester 1981), 52–70 at 65.

109. McWhirr, 'Brickmaking in Leicestershire', 39.

110. Allin, 'The ridge tiles', 65.

111. Nichols, *Leicester*, i pt. 2, 262.

close agreement between the dates of Thornton Gatehouse and Nichols' reference, tempts us to set the rather tenuous archaeological dating evidence aside and to assign the construction of the gatehouse instead to the late fourteenth century, with the use of brick perhaps a hundred years earlier than elsewhere in the county. The Buck brothers' engraving does not seem to suggest brick for the south façade, although it is possible that this fashionable and indeed prestigious new material was used only for the principal external elevation.[112] Unfortunately, evidence from the wall foundations uncovered in the excavations sheds little light on the materials of the superstructure, as both stone and early brick walls are likely to have had stone foundations.

The description of the gatehouse in the Crown Commissioners' Survey indicates that it had comfortable, well-appointed accommodation by the 1530s, with heated rooms and glazed windows, whilst the postulated kitchen to the west suggests that the complex could have functioned as an independent residential unit by the end of the medieval period. All of this adds weight to the theory that the gatehouse had become the abbot's lodgings, perhaps by the fifteenth century. Such lodgings, at the very least, normally included a chapel, dining room, bedchamber and parlour, and, in later periods, the entertainment of important visitors increasingly became a requirement for the abbot. For this reason, it was not uncommon for abbots to have separate dining halls constructed, together with guest accommodation and, in the greater houses, a separate kitchen.[113] The most notable example of the latter is the Abbot's Kitchen at Glastonbury Abbey (Somerset), which at about 10.15m (33 feet 4in) square internally, was slightly larger than the monastic kitchen itself (see below, 61).

If the gatehouse at Leicester was indeed the abbot's lodging, it is likely that the first floor was occupied by a great hall with a solar or great chamber at the eastern end, opposite the postulated service range. This is of course highly speculative and raises the question whether the first floor of the gatehouse would be large enough for both hall and solar. If the first floor were divided along the line of the east wall of the gate hall, this would create a hall 13.17m (43 feet) long, east–west, by 8.56m (28 feet) north–south, with the solar bay 7.63m (25 feet) east–west and 8.56m (28 feet) north–south. Although this does not seem to be a particularly large space for the abbot's private apartments, additional rooms at second floor remain a possibility. Lodgings for guests within the gatehouse do not seem particularly likely, in view of its size, and references in the Crown Commissioners' Survey to 'the great dining chamber' and the 'King's lodging' to the south of the claustral range suggests that it was here that visitors were accommodated and took their meals (see below, 67).

2. Courtyard with farm buildings

Although a number of stone or part-stone buildings survive within a courtyard on the western side of the northern enclosure, and could relate to agricultural buildings of the monastic period, they have been subject to significant later alterations to the extent that no features may be identified which are unequivocally medieval in character.

3. The inner court

The eastern side of the inner court described by the Crown Commissioners is clearly shown in the plan of the 1929–31 excavations, bounded by the church and claustral buildings. The location of

112. T. P. Smith, *The medieval brickmaking industry in England 1400–1450* British Archaeological Reports, British series 138 (Oxford 1985), 6.

113. L. Butler and C. Given-Wilson, *Medieval monasteries of Great Britain* (London 1979), 71.

the brew-house, bake-house and stables is uncertain, although the fragmentary buildings excavated in the early 1920s south-west of the cloister may include some of these.

4. The church and claustral buildings

The church

The abbey church is cruciform in plan, orientated east to west with a western tower and is constructed on what is thought to be an artificial terrace about 0.5m higher than the claustral buildings to the south. It was largely completed by the end of the twelfth century, as the nave was constructed under the patronage of Petronilla (d. 1212), wife of Robert Blanchmains, third earl of
Leicester (c. 1130–1190).[114]

Transepts that extend beyond the north and south aisles mark the crossing, with large side
chapels at their eastern ends. The chapel in the northern transept is thought to have been the Lady
Chapel, dedicated to the Virgin, and burials from it are recorded by Bedingfield. According to
Nichols, this chapel was enriched with pictures and fittings presented by William Geryn, a fourteenth-century canon, who also designed and painted the ceiling of the choir and church in about
1340.[115] The chapel in the south transept is thought to have been dedicated to St Augustine, with an
altar to John the Baptist. Of the remaining seven chapels the church is said to have had, no evidence survives.[116]

The excavation plan clearly shows the outline of the church with nave, aisles, transepts and
chapels, although there are ambiguities. The west tower is shown on the traced plan but without
explanation and it is likely that its west wall, as now laid out on the ground, is based on supposi-
tion rather than physical remains. The lines of the nave arcades are shown as continuous strip
foundations on the traced plan, but as pillars on the published plan (and are laid out as such).
Similarly, at the crossing, substantial piers are depicted on the published plan and laid out on the
ground, on the assumption that there was a central crossing tower, although there is no evidence
for this on the excavation plan. Two parallel walls shown at the east end of the nave are presumably part of the choir stalls, and there is possible evidence of the night stair from the dormitory in
the south transept. Three small areas of tile paving are marked on the plan, indicating the survival
of floor levels. The arrangements at the east end are unclear, particularly the internal walls defin-
ing the chapels, presumably because of extensive robbing. At the time of writing, the 1930s reconstruction walls are in the process of being restored and evidence for some genuine masonry, particularly the south wall of the south aisle, together with reused architectural fragments, is being
revealed. It is to be hoped that evidence can be found to clarify the ambiguous parts of the plan.

The cloister

The cloister lies south of the church, following conventional monastic practice. The excavation
plan shows that the foundations of the wall of the north cloister walk were well preserved with
nine small buttresses projecting into the cloister garth. About half of the west wall and a small section of the northern part of the east wall were also revealed. The rest was robbed but their lines are
indicated by buttresses that the stone robbers missed. The south wall had been completely robbed,
except for one possible buttress at the south-west corner. The cloister walk was tiled and four

---

114. *ODNB s.n.* 'Grandmesnil, Petronilla de, Countess of
Leicester (d. 1212)' and 'Breteuil, Robert de, third earl of Leicester
(c. 1130–1190)'; Fox, *Leicester Abbey*, 6.

115. Nichols, *Leicester*, i pt. 2, 276.
116. Bedingfield, 'Presidential address', 22.

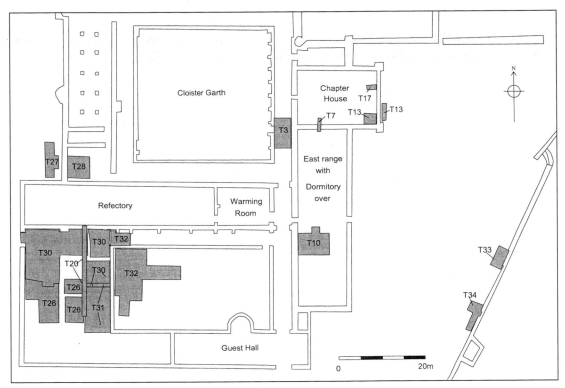

Fig. 23. Plan of trenches within the claustral ranges (2000–5)

Fig. 24. Plan of Trenches 3 and 7, east cloister walk and Chapter House

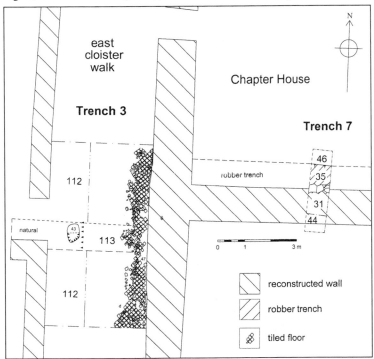

Fig. 25. View south of the medieval tiled floor in the east cloister walk revealed in 2001

patches of surviving tiles were found, most extensively in the east cloister walk (apparently that which was found by Nevinson in the nineteenth century).[117] No photograph has yet been traced of the pavement in situ but Thompson published drawings of the designs.[118]

A trial trench dug in 2000 revealed the same pavement (figs. 23–5).[119] A layer of grey brown, silty sand lay beneath the turf and contained modern debris and fragments of medieval ridge and floor tile. Directly beneath this layer the medieval tiled paving lay in situ. The square tiles were bedded in lime mortar and laid on the diagonal; many were cracked and loose. Although some tiles, particularly those immediately adjacent to the reconstructed east wall of the cloister walk, retained a green glazed finish, most were worn, revealing fabrics ranging in colour from oxidised dark red varieties to reduced grey types. Analysis of the tile suggests a fourteenth-century date, the likely source being the Chilvers Coton kilns at Nuneaton.[120] Fragments of decorated tile, recovered from the backfill of the trench, suggest that the floor was not entirely plain. Many examples of decorated floor tiles have previously been recovered from the site, and include the arms of Leicester Abbey, an alphabet tile, a fleur-de-lys and a 'Wessex' tile.[121] These tiles, together with others recovered from earlier excavations, indicate an elaborately ornamented series of floors in the complex.

Beneath the tiled floor lay a sand deposit [113], presumably fourteenth century or earlier in date, although no artefacts substantiated this. An area directly to the west of the tiled pavement had been stripped down to the natural Mercia Mudstone probably in the 1930s and backfilled with a deposit [112] which contained modern brick, slate, stone and lime mortar. Below this layer was a small pit cut into the natural sub-stratum [42] which contained Cistercian ware dating to the fifteenth or sixteenth century, a sixteenth-century sherd of earthenware and a sherd of 'imitation' Mottled Ware dating from the seventeenth century.

Two burials were discovered in the 1920s excavations under the east cloister walk and probably mark the Chapter House door. The other feature of the cloister is a stone tank in the west cloister

117. Bedingfield observed that 'the Brothers Nevinson by an irony of fate found the tiles in the Cloyster, but failing to appreciate their significance, desisted'; Bedingfield, 'Presidential Address', 19.

118. Thompson, *Leicester Abbey: a historical paper*, 19.

119. Buckley and Derrick, ed. 'An archaeological evaluation', 9 (Trench 3).

120. Sawday, 'The pottery and other finds'; E. S. Eames, 'Appendix 1: the decorated floor tiles' in *Pottery kilns at Chilvers Coton, Nuneaton* ed. P. Mayes and K. Scott, Society of Medieval Archaeology Monograph 10 (London 1984) 173–87 at 184.

121. N. R. Whitcomb, *The medieval floor tiles of Leicestershire* (Leicester 1956).

walk, a remnant of the 'laver' (or 'lavatorium') where the canons washed before eating. It had a piped water supply (traced on the west side of the west range as a lead pipe) and a drain that is almost certainly the curved stonework recovered under the west range. This suggests that waste water, including rainwater from the cloister roofs, was carried beneath the west range in a drain which ran along the west side of the west range to join the complex of drains adjacent to the kitchen (below, 57).

The west range

The west range has substantial stretches of east wall (to which the 'laver' is attached) and south wall, plus three internal pillar bases and a series of wall fragments. Bedingfield thought that three fragments of walling made up the west wall, and reconstructed the pillar bases as the easternmost of two rows of pillars supporting a complex vaulted roof. A better solution has the three fragments as two buttresses and a semi-circular base (perhaps for a chimney or a stair), attached to the west wall; these may have been missed by the stone robbers in the same way that they missed some of the cloister buttresses. This would make the range narrower and the surviving pillar bases would then be in the correct position for a simpler vaulted roof based on a single row of pillar bases. The passageway through the range in the present reconstruction is also doubtful. The north side as shown is probably the laver drain rather than a wall, and the south side is on a slightly different alignment and may well be from a different phase of building (along with other fragments of walls in this area). The thickening at the north-west corner could be a stair turret, to give access to the church from a first floor suite of rooms in the west range.

It is likely that the west range consisted of a vaulted undercroft, in which food, drink and other materials were stored under control of the cellarer, above which perhaps was high-status accommodation.[122] On many sites, at least in the early period, this is often the location of the abbot's lodging; in the later medieval period, abbots frequently built separate mansion houses rivalling those of wealthy courtiers. It seems possible, as discussed above, that the gatehouse complex was re-modelled in this way and was furnished with its own kitchen, which may explain why it was chosen as the nucleus of the post-medieval mansion.

Trenches 27 and 28 were excavated in 2003 to investigate the southern portion of the west range, in an area shown on the 1930s excavation plan to have a complex series of drains and wall foundations of uncertain date and form. The work revealed a wall, probably modern in date, together with a possible drain, destruction deposits and an undated pit. The trenches were not examined further as this would have required complete removal of archaeological strata in order to characterise any underlying structural details.

The south range: refectory and warming house

The plan of the south range is very clear from the excavated data. The north wall is represented by five wall fragments and four buttresses missed by the stone robbers. The south wall is a continuous foundation with buttresses for most of its length; it was robbed at its east end, but can be traced by extant buttresses. The east wall survives for about a third of its length (and has an internal buttress), but the west wall was not found. Thinner walls on a slightly different alignment are

---

122. J. P. Greene, *Medieval monasteries* (Leicester, London and New York 1992), 9.

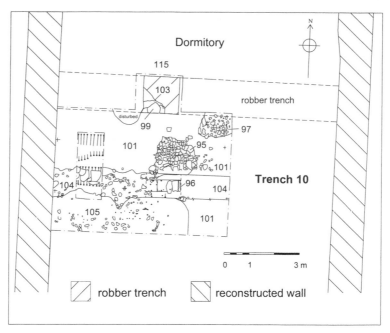

Fig. 26. Plan of Trench 10, to the south of the dormitory

probably from a different phase. The south range is likely to have been the refectory, perhaps at first floor level with storage in undercrofts below and a warming house in the partitioned-off east end.[123] The identification of this range as the refectory, which is its common position in claustral buildings, is supported by the 1538/9 Crown Commissioners' Survey and the location of a kitchen to the south. Evidence for the south wall of the refectory revealed in the 2004 excavations is considered below, 59, in relationship to the kitchen.

The east range: dormitory, undercrofts, chapter house and slype
The east range is the most difficult to interpret as it is the most heavily robbed. The west wall can be traced from two fragments of masonry (one with two buttresses attached), and the edge of the paving in the east cloister walk. The rest is a confusion of small, detached pieces of walling. Bedingfield had the advantage of actually seeing these and assessing their direction in drawing up his reconstruction, but the results do not ring true. The length of the building, projecting a considerable distance past the south range, seems excessive (fig. 6). A drain was traced running immediately south of the south range. This kinks southwards as it approaches the east range, most probably to run around the south end of the building. In this position, one might expect a latrine block or reredorter projecting over the drain. North of the drain-course is an isolated block of masonry and another block may represent the south-east corner of the range. In an attempt to resolve some of the difficulties with the interpretation of the southern end of the dormitory range, a small evaluative trench (no. 10) was excavated in 2000 (fig. 26) on the projected line of the drain referred to above.[124] This sought to determine accurately the plan of the dormitory and to examine the drain

123. Ibid. 148.

124. Buckley and Derrick, 'An archaeological evaluation', 10–11 (Trench 10).

itself that was likely to contain waterlogged deposits with high potential for environmental analysis. Initial stripping of the area revealed deposits [101 and 105] probably relating to the back-fill of Bedingfield's excavations.

Evidence for the south wall of the dormitory was discovered to the north of Trench 10, where a robber cut [103] was aligned east–west. This contained part of a mortared granite wall [99] in situ, on the same alignment as a fragment of masonry recorded on Bedingfield's excavation plan. It appears, therefore, that the southern extent of the dormitory is as shown on Liddle's interpretative plan (fig. 15) and not as laid out on the ground. The difference in character between the archaeological deposits on either side of the robber trench [103] is significant. A substantial and homogeneous rubble deposit to the north of the robber trench, present for the full depth of its cut, suggests a partially subterranean floor level in the rooms beneath the dormitory. The Crown Commissioners' Survey of 1538/9 mentions that the dormitory was positioned above 'large cellars' and it is possible that the rubble deposit [115] is post-Dissolution back-fill. In contrast, the character of the deposits on the south the side of the robber trench seems indicative of ground-level features outside the dormitory and its possible undercrofts. This area was hand cleaned and recorded, but subject to only limited investigation.

A linear deposit of light grey sandy rubble [104] ran west–east across the trench. A trial section across this deposit showed that it formed the upper fill of a cut (0.65m deep) that contained a stone-capped, slate-lined drain [96] which cut deposits of dark greyish-brown clay silt; these deposits were not examined, but appeared similar in character to pit fills. The drain was aligned west–east, on the projected line of the drain shown on the plan of the 1920s excavations. Although the main drain of the abbey was anticipated in this area, the dimensions here were clearly too small to suggest anything other than a minor drain flowing beneath the alley to the south of the refectory and dormitory. It must then (as shown on Bedingfield's published plan) have joined the main drain that discharged into the Soar through the large arch visible in the precinct wall. This minor drain appears to be the eastern end of a stone-lined drain examined in 2004, between the kitchen and refectory, and was almost certainly for rainwater rather than effluent.

At the time of writing, the 2005 season of excavation has just been completed. It included excavation of a trench adjacent to the inner face of the east precinct wall, at the position of the exit point of the main drain. This revealed the sandstone side walls of the main drain and its inner arch, while an arch in its north wall indicates that it was fed by another substantial drain, perhaps serving buildings to the north. Of considerable interest was the fact that the partially-filled main drain had been cut by a small stone-lined and capped drain, of similar character to the rainwater drains already discovered, running along the south side of the refectory and dormitory. Although not recognised in the trench excavated to the south of the dormitory, it is possible that drain [96] also cut the backfill of the main drain. This raises the question of whether the 'reredorter' (latrine block) was perhaps originally at the southern end of the dormitory (as represented by robber trench 103) and served by the main drain, but was later relocated. It is possible that the dormitory was extended to the south, the original main drain backfilled and a new reredorter erected further south yet.

Trench 10 also contained two possible structural features of uncertain date and function. One lay just to the north of the drain and consisted of a neat pile of un-mortared granite and sandstone rubble [95] measuring approximately 1.75m square × 0.7m tall. Although this was not excavated, it was clear from the adjacent section through the drain that the feature rested on a substantial stone foundation below ground level. That foundation appears on the tracing of Bedingfield's excavation plan; the superstructure of this feature is more likely to be a fabrication of the late 1920s when the excavations were backfilled. A similar pile of un-mortared stones [97] was located just to the south of the wall line marked by robber trench [103]. Again, this may be work of the 1920s but could mark the position of a buttress to the south wall of the dormitory. Another possibility is that these features relate to the foundations of the reredorter that may have been located here originally.

(i) *Chapter house*

It was normal in medieval religious houses for the dormitory to be at first floor level, running over the western end of a major east–west building (the chapter house or a vestibule leading to it) with access to the church at the north end by way of a night stair to allow easy access for the midnight service. There are few walls shown in the vicinity of the chapter house on the 1930s excavation plan, suggesting that they are likely to have been heavily robbed. The burials in the cloister walk have already been noted and these probably mark the chapter-house door (above, 42). Abbots' graves are commonly found inside chapter houses, and three burials are recorded in this area. The abbot generally sat at the east end of the chapter house (which was frequently, but not invariably, apsidal or polygonal), and often sat with his feet on his predecessors to symbolise continuity in the governance of the abbey. Two burials lying together may mark the abbot's chair and the east end of the chapter house. Bedingfield places these beyond the east end. One of the burials in the cloister walk (both in stone coffins) contained cloth fragments with gold thread presumably from the vestments of an abbot; a fragmentary inscription suggests one of the two burials may have been that of Abbot Paul (1186–1204/5).[125]

A small trench [7] was excavated (fig. 24) to clarify the line of the south wall of the chapter house.[126] This located the line of a robber trench on an east–west orientation running slightly north of the 'south wall' of the chapter house as reconstructed in the 1930s. The foundations of the wall were constructed with rough squared sandstone blocks with fragments of granite, bonded with dark orange-brown sandy clay. A cut for the wall was observed on the south side, though comparable evidence was absent on the north due to partial robbing. The robber trench [35] cut through a deep deposit of orange clay sand [46] to its north, indicating perhaps a sunken floor within the chapter house. Another trench [13] was excavated (fig. 27), which confirmed that this wall continued to the east with an east–west robber trench cut [1314] on the northern side of the reconstructed chapter house wall.[127] This feature again cut through non-natural make-up material on its northern side, adding weight to the suggestion that the chapter house floor was lower than those of the adjacent rooms. Bedingfield's reconstruction of this wall lies slightly to the south of the correct line and it is clear that the robbed portion was not recognised by him.

Trench 13 also examined the accuracy of the reconstructed east wall of the building and revealed the sandstone foundations of a north–south wall [1307] beneath what appeared to be demolition spreads of crushed sandstone and mortar fragments. These spreads measured *c.* 2.3m across the length of the trench by 1.4 × 0.50m deep. Natural ground was exposed on both sides of the wall, but was evidently higher on the eastern side compared to the west, suggesting that the wall had deep foundations and that it surrounded a sunken-floored area, indicating that it probably represents the east wall of the chapter house, lying slightly to the west of the reconstructed line

125. See above, 10, note 63.
126. Buckley and Derrick, 'An archaeological evaluation', 10 (Trench 7).
127. Meek and Buckley, 'An archaeological evaluation', 17–18 (Trench 13).

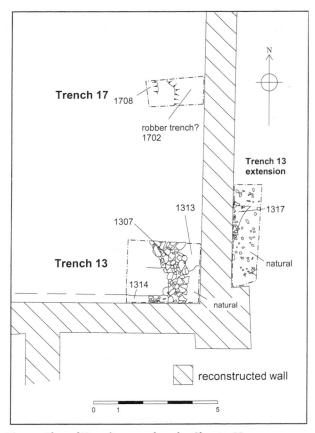

Fig. 27. Plan of Trenches 13 and 17, the Chapter House

(which lacks underlying evidence for masonry or robbing). Another trench was excavated to the north [17] (fig. 27), but the area was extensively disturbed and no definite evidence for the continuation of this wall was detected.[128]

An extension to Trench 13 was excavated on the eastern side of the reconstructed chapter house wall. This trench revealed undisturbed natural ground less than 0.30m beneath ground level, with disturbed soils and rubble above. Apart from a thin spread of sandy material [1317], no other feature was found.

(ii) Slype
Between the chapter house and the south transept at many sites is a passageway known as a slype, leading from the cloister alley beneath the dormitory out to the monastic cemetery. However, at Leicester, the excavated remains suggest a small room at this point.

5. Yard, guest facilities and kitchen
South of the claustral buildings, Bedingfield's excavation plan shows fragmentary stone buildings that probably represent some of the guest facilities. Immediately south of the warming room, at

---

128. Context 1702 may be a robber trench; ibid, 19.

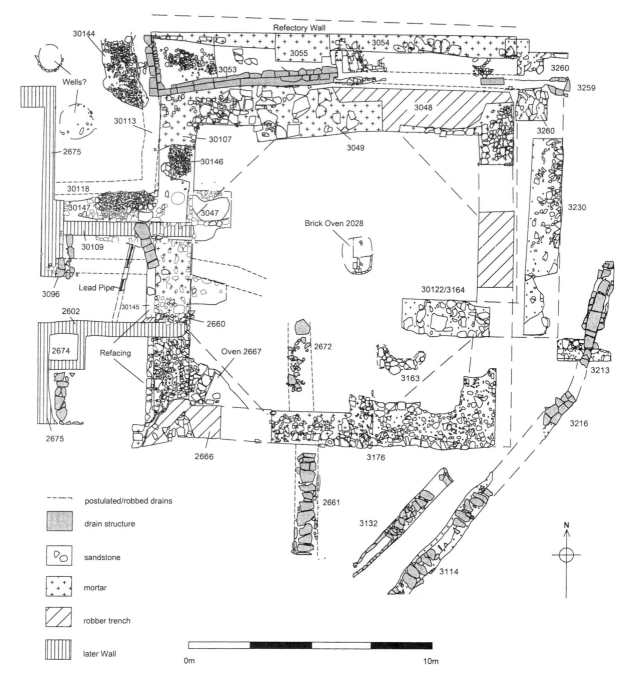

Fig. 28. Plan of the results of the excavations on the site of the kitchen (2002–5)

the east end of the south range, is a walled yard with possible buildings or covered walkways on its west side (again added to the plan in pencil), and on its south side a large rectangular building with an apsidal foundation projecting from its north wall. This seems to indicate the position of an oriel window, supporting the identification of this building as the guest hall referred to in the 1538/9 Survey. To the south are further drains and fragments of buildings, including an irregular

structure with walls that are not at right angles to one another; this could be another yard or perhaps a stable block.

Excavation of the kitchen 2002–2004 (figs. 23 and 28)

South of the refectory was a thick-walled building, aligned with the west range. The south and east
walls are marked on Bedingfield's traced plan (fig. 3), somewhat disturbed by a post-medieval
brick wall built across them; a north wall is added in pencil. This is almost certainly the kitchen,
served by a system of drains running southwards (rather than the drain that ran between this
building and the south range). The kitchen was not marked out with low walls after Bedingfield's
excavation as the rest of the complex had been.

A narrow exploratory trial trench (20) in 2002 located the north and south walls of the building, so the kitchen was investigated more thoroughly in 2003–4.[129] Further trenches (31 and 32)
were opened in 2005, although detailed analysis of the results of the work have yet to be undertaken and only the major conclusions are summarised here.

Trench 26 revealed the south-west corner of the kitchen with an oven constructed within the
internal angle of the walls and the remains of a stone-lined and capped drain running southwards,
matching that on the 1920s excavation plan. Evidence for structures apparently post-dating the
kitchen to the west was also located. Robbed lines of the northern and western walls of the kitchen
were revealed in 2004 (Trench 30, fig. 29). These indicated the presence of more corner fireplaces,
represented by substantial sequences of superimposed burnt deposits and stone arch abutments. A
complex water-management system was found outside the kitchen, comprising several stone-lined
and capped drains of different phases to take rainwater from the refectory and kitchen roofs, some
of which may then have been used to flush the foul drain within the kitchen.

Trench 30 also revealed cobble yard surfaces, some contemporary with the kitchen, others
post-dating its demolition and associated with a later medieval structure or with reoccupation of
the site in the late sixteenth to early seventeenth century (fig. 30). Two circular, stone-lined features, probably wells, were also found here. Evidence for a pair of parallel walls at right angles to
the west wall of the kitchen was also uncovered. These suggest that a wide passageway led to the
kitchen from another range of buildings to the west, as yet undiscovered. Pre-dating these features
was a lead water pipe, which ties in with a course of lead piping illustrated on the 1920s excavation
plan, indicating the provision of a piped supply of fresh water into the kitchen. Evidence for the
south wall of the refectory range was also revealed, confirming the position of its south-western
corner and the possible point of access from the kitchen block.

The 2005 trench examined evidence for the east wall of the kitchen and the south-eastern
corner fireplace. This revealed the corner of the building and evidence for a substantial wall post-
dating it, perhaps relating to a later kitchen structure.

Kitchen walls

The south wall of the kitchen [2032/2625] was located in Trenches 20 and 26. The wall was overlain
by the disturbed dark grey-brown, silty-clay backfill of Bedingfield's 1920s excavation trench and it
was apparent that he had removed the fill of a post-Dissolution robber trench to reveal the footings of the wall. Although a 4m stretch of wall footings, 1.37m wide, survived beneath these later

129. Jones and Buckley, ed. 'An archaeological evaluation'
(2004a) 6–13.

deposits, the western end of the wall was entirely robbed, as shown by robber trench [2666]. This lay beneath a compact orange-brown sandy-silt demolition layer, c. 0.2m deep [2637/2652]. Below this layer, the west wall of the kitchen [2660] was exposed on a north–south axis for a length of about 5m. The 1920s excavation trench [2663] truncated its junction with the south wall. The west wall was constructed with a mortared rubble core faced with sandstone, two courses of which survived. It had an overall width of 1.72m, but had been refaced with sandstone ashlar on its western (external) face; the original west wall was same width (1.37m) as the south wall. At the external south-west corner, three large sandstone blocks, c. 0.4m × 0.4m, suggest the truncated remains of a buttress that had also been exposed in Bedingfield's trench.

The width of the south and west walls of the kitchen at 1.37m (before re-facing) is at variance with the evidence gained from Trench 20, where part of the south wall was revealed to be over 2m wide. Unfortunately it was not possible to excavate further to resolve this discrepancy, but the most likely explanation is that the south wall of the kitchen was thickened at its mid point to accommodate the footing for a fireplace arch abutment.

The northward continuation of the west wall was identified in Trench 30 [30107]; it was c. 1.8m wide and continued for c. 7m northwards before turning east, and adjoined the footings of the north wall of the kitchen [3049]. The west wall here consisted predominantly of light grey fine-grained sandstone blocks (c. 0.25 × 0.35 × 0.45m) bonded with an orange-brown soft sand mortar. The depth of the footings was unclear, and unexcavated, but likely to be at least two or three courses deep. A well-faced offset [30145] was visible on the western side of this part of the wall, presumably part of the same refacing visible further south. Excluding the later re-facing, the wall measured approximately 1.4m in width. The offset formed by the re-facing overlay of a deposit of mortar, rubble and silt [30108], presumably relating to a demolition or construction phase, suggesting that the re-facing was associated with a later remodelling of the kitchen. Although buttresses had been postulated for the south-west corner of the kitchen, there was no further evidence for a similar arrangement at the north-western corner. However, it is possible that any such remains are hidden by later (unexcavated) deposits.

The north wall of the kitchen [3049] was revealed for a total length of c. 12.7m (fig. 31). Just as in Trench 20, Bedingfield had clearly followed and removed the rubble deposits of the post-Dissolution robber trenches down onto the intact kitchen wall remains. Towards the eastern end of the footings of the north wall [3049] some of these original robber trench deposits [3048], remained in situ, undisturbed by Bedingfield. The wall measured c. 1.4m wide and consisted of predominantly light-grey, soft, fine-grain sandstone with occasional blocks of granite and pale-grey sandstone, bonded with a similar mortar to the west wall [30107].

Trench 30 was extended south-east to locate the kitchen's east wall. The remains of the north east corner [30110] were more fragmentary than the other exposed wall footings, suggesting that the eastern side of the building was more extensively robbed. The northern end of the east wall was visible as poorly-bonded sandstone rubble, and appeared to be completely robbed beyond the baulk in the south-east extension trench. It was unclear whether the latter had resulted from the 1930s excavation or from post-Dissolution robbing.

The south-eastern corner of the kitchen was revealed in Trench 31 which was excavated in 2005 and the results have yet to be evaluated in detail (fig. 32). However the walls were similar in width and composition to those examined elsewhere. The south wall increased in thickness slightly two metres or so from the corner, perhaps indicating the position of the abutment for a corner fireplace arch.

Fig. 29. View north of the excavation of the western side of the kitchen (2004)

Fig. 30. View north of the excavation of the western side of the kitchen, showing the west wall, later passageway, cobbled surfaces and drains (2004)

Fig. 31. View east of the excavation of the western side of the kitchen showing the
north-west corner of the building, cobbled surfaces and drains (2004). The
standing wall on the left of the photograph is a 1930s reconstruction of the south
wall of the refectory

Internal features

It was clear from the initial trial trench in 2002 that the interior of the kitchen contained deep
stratified deposits, perhaps in excess of 1m in thickness. In line with the stated objectives of the
project, these were not excavated, the record of them deriving only from sections revealed by the
removal of later intrusions. Other internal features identified were structural in nature, comprising drains, ovens and a fireplace, providing indications of the form of the building at least in its
final phase.

(i) Fireplaces and ovens

In Trench 26, a possible demolition deposit [2637] within the internal angle formed by the west
and south kitchen walls, exposed an orange sandy rubble spread [2662], *c.* 0.2m deep, containing a
fragment of Potters Marston Ware dating to the twelfth or thirteenth century. Beneath, the

remains of an oven base [2667] were revealed, possibly set within a corner fireplace constructed across the south-western internal angle of the kitchen. To the north, Trench 30 revealed an area of compact rubble [30121], *c.* 1.8 × 1.2m across, which butted up against the west kitchen wall [30107]. This could be associated with the footing of the abutment of the fireplace arch.

The oven was roughly circular, approximately 1.2m in diameter internally and constructed of sandstone blocks measuring *c.* 0.3m². Lying over the floor of the oven, a shallow charcoal spread [2668], *c.* 0.05m deep, was half-sectioned and sampled for environmental evidence. The sieved samples showed that burnt remains in the oven included wheat and barley grains with a little bread-wheat chaff and arable weed seeds.[130] These remains may have been waste from cleaning cereals to prepare food such as potage. The oven fill also contained other domestic rubbish including fish scales, including those of the carp family, bones of eel and herrings, and hazelnut shells. Animal bones were recovered, and included those of domestic fowl (cf. *gallus* sp.), mouse bones (cf. *mus domesticus*) and bones from the thrush family (including cf. *turdus merula* and an unrecognised passeriform). The bones do not seem to represent food preparation or table waste. The domestic fowl bones were from the wing tips, which would have been removed soon after slaughter. There is no direct evidence whether the thrushes were used for food, however, their small size and the fact that the bones are not clearly associated with other food debris makes it less likely. The mouse bones are indicative of scavenging animals living in and around the kitchen.

In the north west corner of the kitchen, Trench 30 revealed the remains of another probable fireplace or oven structure beneath a demolition deposit of orange sandy rubble [3047]. The remains were also visible in the north-face of the east–west section (as revealed by the excavation

Fig. 32. General view north of the excavation of the east side of the kitchen, showing the south-west corner of the building (beneath the ranging rods) and the complex of drains first discovered in 1923 (2005)

130. A. Monckton, 'Charred plant remains from evaluative excavations at Leicester Abbey in 2002 and 2003 (A8.2000)' in Jones and Buckley, ed. (2004b), 28–30.

of the 1920s trench) covering an area *c.* 0.6 × 2m; this area was unexcavated. Other layers associated with the structure (or more likely its robbing), comprised deposits of mortar, re-used slate and burnt layers of red sand and charcoal. The charcoal layer [30106] at the base of the structure (possibly associated with an in situ deposit) was also sampled for environmental evidence. The sample contained abundant charcoal and a few charred plant remains, mainly weed seeds with a few burnt straw fragments, perhaps cleanings from cereals or straw used as kindling.

Beneath a series of deposits probably associated with robbing of the building, were the remains of a masonry structure, *c.* 2.3m south of the north west corner [30111]. This was constructed from sandstone blocks (*c.* 0.22m wide) set within yellowish-white mortar that could represent the southern abutment for the north-western corner fireplace arch.

Evidence for the fireplace structures in the north-east and south-east corners of the kitchen was less clear, although burnt deposits in these areas did at least point to their presence there. In Trench 30, a substantial section of wall [30122] was revealed, thought at the time to represent the abutment of a fireplace in the south-east corner. It consisted of sandstone blocks *c.* 0.2–0.4m across and covered an area *c.* 1.95 × 1.6m. In this area, the 1930s excavation plan shows thickening of the east wall just north of the south-east corner. This was re-examined in 2005; Trench 31 indicated that the sequence here is rather more complicated than anticipated, revealing evidence for the corner of a substantial stone building apparently post-dating the kitchen but on the same orientation, the south wall of which is represented by the wall [30122] discussed above. The east wall of this later building [3230] abutted the kitchen's east wall, and continued north to join with the south wall of the refectory. Trench 31 also revealed the floor of the south-eastern corner fireplace, composed of a scorched surface of fine pebbles, together with at least one later circular stone oven or hearth constructed about one metre away from the corner. The hearths were truncated by the south wall of the later building.

The internal angles of the walls of the kitchen have yet to be examined in detail and it is not possible at present to know if they contained circular ovens as found in the south-west corner. Tantalising evidence of another oven, located in the central part of the kitchen, was revealed in Trench 20. This consisted of a circular brick structure [2027 and 2028], *c.* 1.23m wide × 0.2m deep, one course wide and two to three courses deep, truncated on its north side by a robber pit [2030]. The base of the feature [2034] was also made of brick, and was sealed by a compact pale yellow mortar layer [2033]. Above this was a dark greyish-brown silty-clay fill [2009], *c.* 0.16m deep, containing brick, charcoal, Midland Yellow pottery and a fragment of glass goblet dating to the mid-sixteenth or early seventeenth century.[131] Environmental samples from this deposit revealed charred legumes (including peas and beans) and barley and oat grains consistent with domestic waste from a kitchen, perhaps representing spillage during cooking together with cleanings from the crops burnt in the oven or hearth. Similar material could have been raked from hearths and accumulated or been dumped in this area. The deposit also contained a small number of carp fish scales together

131. Wide mouthed bowl – Woodfield form 'Obj'; P. Woodfield, 'Midland yellows', *West Midlands Pottery Research Group Newsletter* 2 (1984). This ware is dated generally from *c.* 1500 at Leicester, R. Woodland 'The pottery' in Mellor and Pearce, ed. (1981), 81–129 at 128; D. Sawday, 'The post-Roman pottery' in 'An excavation in the north-east quarter of Leicester: Elbow Lane 1977' ed. J. Lucas, *TLAHS* 63 (1989), 28–51 at 35, with a terminal date in the eighteenth century. For the fragment of a goblet (a knobbed stem in the form of an inverted baluster of the mid-sixteenth to early seventeenth century) see, H. Willmott, 'The majority of high quality sixteenth-century drinking vessels found on monastic sites can be attributed to occupation on the site after the Dissolution', *Early post-medieval vessel glass in England c. 1500–1650*, Council for British Archaeology Research Report 132 (York 2002), 21, pl. 7, fig. 156.10.2.

with small fragments of eggshell and a rib fragment probably from a sheep, representing waste from kitchen activities. This feature could relate to an oven, partially robbed after disuse some time after the mid sixteenth to early seventeenth century. Whether it was constructed before or after the Dissolution, or indeed inside or outside a building, however, remains uncertain.

(ii) Drains

Further 1920s activity was visible in Trench 26, adjacent to the south-east stretch of the south wall of the kitchen. An earlier investigative trench [2631 and 2641], *c.* 1.94 × 0.7m, containing residual medieval and post medieval pottery had evidently been excavated in 1923 (fig. 3) exposing a substantial slate-capped drain [2661]. This drain crossed the line of the south wall of the kitchen and was uncovered for a length of some *c.* 4m; another 3m stretch was also exposed further north following the removal of more of the 1920s trench back-fill. Due to the level of truncation from earlier excavations, the true relationship between the drain and the south wall of the kitchen cannot be fully determined. However, the most likely interpretation is that it continued through the wall, probably built into the structure when the kitchen was constructed in the medieval period. A less attractive theory, although one which should not be discounted, is that the drain could be a later feature, truncating the robbed walls of the kitchen but serving another structure altogether.

The drain structure consisted of a pair of narrow sandstone walls capped with substantial Swithland slates, *c.* 0.6 × 0.3m. The drain was about 0.26m deep and contained a dark greyish-brown silt fill [2671] with fragments of shell and a single sherd of Cistercian or Midland Blackware dating to the fifteenth or sixteenth century.[132] The fill was sampled for environmental evidence, revealing numerous fish scales including those of the carp family and perch, numerous fish vertebrae including eels and herrings. Charcoal and ash was also found suggesting that the drain had become filled with domestic rubbish. The charred material included occasional charred cereal grains and a few charred seeds of docks, knotgrass, vetch and fat-hen which grow as weeds of disturbed ground and gardens. Numerous small bones were present, including those of frogs or toads that had lived in the drain, and pygmy shrews, and small rabbits, perhaps from later burrowing.

Evidence from the 1920s–30s excavation plan suggests that the drain flowed south out of the kitchen, joining up with other branches to feed a single outlet to the river, although this has yet to be located. Levels taken over the length of the base of the drain showed very little difference, implying that the fall was slight.

External features
(i) Later passageway to the east of the kitchen

In the north-western corner of Trench 26 a series of walls associated with structures west of the kitchen were identified. Cutting across the west wall of the kitchen [2660] was a stretch of wall [2602] *c.* 4.2 × 0.6m, constructed of sandstone blocks, *c.* 0.28 × 0.25m, faced on both sides and bonded with pale-white lime mortar. This was set on a single course of rough foundations, offset *c.* 0.15m north and south. An area of mortar just visible north of wall [2602] may represent a floor surface associated with this structure. This lay beneath rubble layer [2656], which contained late medieval pottery and a fragment of medieval floor tile.[133]

---

132. Sawday, 'The pottery and medieval floor and ridge tiles', 19.   133. Ibid.; Midland Purple Ware 2.

The western end of the wall [2602] abutted a north–south wall [2675] (exposed for a length of 4.1m) with a straight joint, indicating that they were probably of different phases albeit similar in appearance and make-up. Both walls were probably similar in width, although the western edge of wall [2675] was concealed by the modern reconstruction wall. A continuation of wall [2675] was located further north turning to the west. A drain or soakaway was built into the angle of the two walls, represented by an L-shaped wall [2674]. The walls of this feature (*c.* 1.4 × 0.3–0.4m and at least 1.1m deep) were similar in construction to the east–west wall [2602]. An open drain [2676] oriented north–south led into the soakaway through a small opening in its southern wall. The open drain was lined with sandstone blocks, *c.* 1 × *c.* 0.2m, with a slate base. The drain lay beneath an orange, sandy clay [2678] similar in appearance to layer [2637] which was interpreted as a post-Dissolution demolition deposit) suggesting that the drain may be medieval. The soakaway, however, contained a modern backfill and this whole area appears to have been exposed and truncated comparatively recently as it appears on the surviving excavation plan, dated 14 June 1923. On 19 June 1923, a short stretch of granite wall oriented north–south was also exposed. At the time of this work, a large shed appears to have been standing to the east of the soakaway, perhaps explaining why the east–west wall [2602] was not located at the same time.

Another wall running parallel and *c.* 3.4m to the north of wall 2602 was revealed for a length of about 3.8m [30109]. The walls ran at right angles away from the approximate mid-point of the west wall of the kitchen and clearly post-dated it. Neither wall extended eastwards beyond the inner face of the kitchen wall suggesting that they represent a later passageway structure added to the pre-existing building. Unfortunately, the area between these two walls had already been excavated, perhaps in the late 1920s after the removal of the large shed mentioned above. The upper layers [3018] exposed in this area were *c.* 0.25m deep, and those below it [3036], *c.* 0.45m deep; these consisted of disturbed deposits containing frequent fragments of rubble, brick and tile and much residual medieval and post-medieval pottery. The lower fill [3036] did initially appear to be an early deposit, but is evidently redeposited backfill since it contained Earthenware 3 pottery of mid-seventeenth- to eighteenth-century date and a sherd of modern flowerpot. Removal of this backfill revealed a section just north of the south wall of the passageway in which a number of floor layers were evident, generally consisting of mortar, red clay and occasional charcoal. These were not excavated.

Removal of the redeposited backfill between the passageway walls, revealed a number of other earlier deposits that pre-dated the passageway and its floors, including a possible north–south wall line and a 1.1m length of lead pipe, running approximately north–south. At its northern end was a square join, *c.* 0.06m wide, while at the other end there were a number of small holes where the pipe had been worn or damaged. It was set within a construction trench [3097], *c.* 0.2m wide, which contained a sherd of Potters Marston Ware of the twelfth or thirteenth century. Around 20m further north, additional lead pipes are shown on Bedingfield's 1930 excavation plan that apparently served the west range. Since some of those pipes are north–south aligned, it is possible that the pipe located beneath the later passageway could represent its southerly extent, presumably serving the kitchen.

(ii) Cobbled yard

A cobbled yard surface [30144 and 30147] was uncovered to the north-west and west of the kitchen. This consisted of rounded medium to large sized pebbles (*c.* 0.06 > *c.* 0.11m in diameter) set within dark-grey, silt-sand clay, *c.* 0.1m deep. Some resurfacing was identifiable, with some areas of larger, slightly less compacted cobbles overlying the surface. The majority of the cobbled surface is interpreted as a yard external to the kitchen, but a small patch of cobbling different in character [3072/30146] clearly overlay the northern end of its west wall [30107] suggesting it related to a later medieval structure or perhaps to post-Dissolution activity. Two circular stone-lined features, possibly wells, together with fragments of possible robbed walls relating to buildings of unknown date to the west of the kitchen were also identified, but were not examined in detail. Trench 31 to the east of the kitchen, also revealed extensive cobbled surfaces apparently associated with a substantial structure post-dating the kitchen.

Rainwater drains

(i) East–west drain, north of kitchen (fig. 31)

Between the north wall of the kitchen and the south wall of the refectory was a stone-lined and capped drain [3053], running along the north face of the kitchen wall [3049]. It was constructed from pale grey sandstone or fine grained oolitic grey limestone blocks, typically 0.25 × 0.23m, most of which appeared to be re-used architectural fragments. At its western point, the southern wall of the drain had been robbed, possibly at the same time as the kitchen wall [3049], although it is possible that the kitchen wall may have served as the north face of the drain. Just south-east of the refectory wall buttress [3055], a later re-build [3050] of the southern wall of the drain was evident, consisting of sandstone, granite and slate bonded within red clay. This section appeared to post-date the robber trench fill [3048] below it, suggesting that it was in use after the demolition of the kitchen. A similar re-build [3051] of the northern part of the drain was also visible, again suggesting a later re-use. Just south-east of the refectory wall buttress [3055], a drain inlet or chute [3052], *c.* 0.24m wide and constructed out of white mortar, slate and red clay was found, which presumably channelled water from the refectory roof into the drain.

Although the eastern end of the drain was not excavated, its line could be traced beneath a mortar-rich rubble layer [30112]. East of this point, the drain was found to cut across the line of the east wall of a substantial building thought to post-date the kitchen. The drain, therefore, is either contemporary with or later than the wall. The 1920s excavation plan indicates that the drain continued eastwards, along the south side of the south range, to the south of the dormitory, eventually joining a larger drain close to the infirmary before discharging into the river Soar via an arch in the precinct wall. However, as discussed (above, 45), excavations adjacent to the drain outlet in the eastern precinct wall now indicate that the main drain was probably backfilled before the end of the medieval period as a smaller rainwater drain cuts its fill.

(ii) A north–south drain, west of the kitchen

At the western end of the north wall of the kitchen, drain [3053] fed into a north–south drain represented by a linear feature [30113] (probably a robber trench, *c.* 7m × *c.* 0.6–8 × 0.35m). This feature truncated the cobbled surface [30144] and was filled with loose, dark-brown sandy-silt [3037], containing fragments of brick, slate, small stones, clay pipe, shell, bone and post-medieval and modern pottery. Part of the base and the eastern wall of the northern end of the drain remained intact and consisted of sandstone blocks, *c.* 0.4 × 0.3m, linking up with the western point of drain 3053. The date of the drain relative to the cobbled surface is unclear because of the robbing. The southern end of the drain appears to have fed into the kitchen (see below, 58). An east–west linear feature [30118], measuring *c.* 0.5 × 3.4m, was found and may represent a robbed drain feeding into the robbed out drain [30113]. Its fill [3027] was very similar to the fill of the north–south drain [3037] and contained late medieval Cistercian Ware pottery and clay pipe.

The robbed out north–south drain [30113] seems at one time have fed into the kitchen via a channel through the west wall, *c.* 0.8m deep. Slate capping for this was visible in situ at its southern end, some of which also overlay this stretch of the kitchen wall. Two blocks of sandstone, *c.* 0.6 × 0.3m, appeared to form part of the end of the structure. The fill of the drain [30105] was a very dark-brown silt 0.4m deep and contained frequent fragments of animal bone; a soft, pale grey-brown silt deposit [30103], *c.* 0.4 × 0.2m, containing many charcoal flecks and fragments of animal bone was associated with it. These two deposits [3013 and 3015] contained fragments of cattle, sheep/goat, domestic fowl and a butchered goose humerus, suggestive of food refuse. Environmental samples from these two deposits contained large animal bones, abundant charcoal, a few charred plant remains, numerous fish remains (including scales of the carp family and bones of herring and some larger fish, as yet unidentified). These samples represent domestic waste, although it is possible that the fish remains were washed into the drains from food preparation in the kitchen. The sample from the drain end [30104] in the kitchen lacked the animal bones and fish remains (although a frog/toad humerus and fish scales were collected) and consisted entirely of charcoal with more charred plant remains, and appeared similar to the deposits associated with the ovens (see discussion below, 63).

It was impossible to determine whether the drain [30113] was contemporary with the west wall or whether it had been introduced later when the wall was breached and the passageway built to serve another range of buildings. However, it did seem clear that the later re-facing of the wall [30145] respected the drain and was therefore later than it. After the drain was robbed, rainwater still flowed freely through it southwards, now via a surface-channel *c.* 0.4m wide constructed from a single course of flat laid flagstones (*c.* 0.2 × 0.6m) set within the cobbled surface.

The entrance of a drain running into the kitchen was also exposed on the eastern side of the north–south kitchen wall [30107], consisting of a channel set into the face of the wall, constructed from slate and sandstone, *c.* 0.4 × 0.2m which contained a loose, mixed deposit [3014] of red and grey-brown silt, mortar and charcoal which contained a fragment of modern drainpipe. The drain channel leading from this entrance, taking water into the kitchen had been robbed.

(iii) An east–west drain, west of the kitchen

Some evidence for an east–west rainwater drain heading towards the opening in the western kitchen wall was also recovered. It survived as a small opening in the masonry of the north–south wall [3096] west of the kitchen, but the remainder of it had been destroyed presumably by later excavation of the area between the passageway walls.

It was considered at the time of the excavation that the area between the parallel walls of the passageway was in fact a sump or cistern for the storage of rainwater, later backfilled with rubble and floored over. The evidence for this was thought to comprise a stretch of north–south wall to the west, forming the western end of the feature, a number of silt deposits, together with the fact that a number of drains appeared to converge at this point. This theory is now considered rather less likely and is discussed in more detail below (62).

(iv) Drains to the south and east of the kitchen

Two additional branches feeding drain [2661] were noticed during the 1923 excavations and re-examined in Trench 31. The westernmost branch of the drain [3132] had stone walls and a stone capping, and its projected alignment cut across the corner of the kitchen, implying that it post-dates it and perhaps relates to the later building identified by recent excavation [30122, 3164, 3230]. The eastern drain [3213] was slate-capped, and seems to have taken water from the kitchen roof (suggested by a fragment of slate run-off located close to the corner of the kitchen). It was also fed from the north by other drains.

South wall of the refectory

The south-western corner of the refectory was found just north of the north wall of the kitchen [3049]. The evidence consisted of a stretch of wall, 14.48 × 0.8m [3054], (slightly to the south of the wall reconstructed in the 1930s) and what is likely to be the south-west corner buttress [3055], measuring *c.* 2m wide. Both buttress and wall were made of materials similar to the north wall of the kitchen [3049]. The buttress was located slightly east of its reconstructed counterpart and, on the assumption that it is a corner buttress, indicates that the reconstructed wall continues rather too far to the west than it should.

It is assumed that there was a door in the mid point of the north wall of the kitchen [3049] providing access into the refectory undercroft, although no secure evidence for this exists. Trench 32 showed that the wall of the substantial building post-dating the kitchen [3260] abutted the south wall of the refectory, indicating that the refectory wall remained standing at the time of its construction.

Discussion

The 1923 excavation plan indicates that the south wall and south-eastern corner of what we now know to be the abbey kitchen was uncovered at that time, together with three substantial drains, one emerging from within the building and two others possibly relating to an adjacent structure to the east; these drains converged just to the south of the kitchen into a single, larger drain which continued for some distance to the south. A short stretch of north–south wall and a small square structure to the west of the kitchen (the soakaway revealed in 2003 [2674]) also appears on the 1923 plan. The investigations of 1929–31 located part of the east wall of the kitchen, the south wall of the refectory, as shown on the survey plan of 'Aug. & Sept. 1930', together with some of the north wall and an east–west drain running between the kitchen and refectory that were added to the tracing of the plan of 'foundations disclosed up to Sept 1930' now in the Jewry Wall Museum.[134]

This area is labelled on the published plan as the probable site of the kitchen and the 'Kynges lodging', based on the nature of the remains discovered and the description of this part of the site in the Crown Commissioners' Survey of 1538/9.[135] The Survey also describes a yard to the south of the claustral ranges, surrounded by a hall and chambers, guest facilities including a tower called the King's Lodging and a great dining chamber (with bay window). These are linked by 'galleries' – perhaps covered walkways – to the kitchen and officials' quarters.

The earliest high-status medieval kitchens were generally detached buildings, presumably to reduce the risk to adjacent structures in the event of fire, and were commonly square or octagonal in plan. The hearth may initially have been located centrally, the smoke being carried out through a great timber or stone-vaulted louvered roof.[136] Commonly, the fireplaces were later moved to the sides. Some kitchens were square externally, but octagonal internally, such as the Abbot's Kitchen

134. ROLLR DE6218/1.
135. Fox, *Leicester Abbey*, 14–15.

136. G. Coppack, *Abbeys and priories* (London 1990), 75.

at Glastonbury.[137] Other square kitchens had fireplaces in the side walls, or in both the walls and corners; pairs of fireplaces adjoining at right angles are not uncommon, as at South Wingfield.[138]

From the evidence encountered so far, the kitchen at Leicester Abbey was a substantial building measuring approximately 39 feet square (11.88m square) internally with walls c. 4 feet 6 inches (1.4m) thick, except for the west wall that was refaced thereby increasing its thickness to c. 5.7 feet (1.74m). The trenches excavated in 2003–5 suggest it had corner fireplaces, at least one of which (in the south-west) contained a circular oven; the south-east corner contained a later complex of ovens or hearths set out from the corner. Evidence for possible fireplace arch abutments was also located, adding weight to the suggestion that the kitchen was octagonal internally, and similar in plan to the kitchen at Fontevrault (Maine et Loire) and the Abbot's Kitchen at Glastonbury (fig. 33). The latter measures c. 10.15m² internally (c. 33 feet 4ins) and has corner fireplaces, each containing a circular oven.[139] The flues run along the plane of the roof, exiting via a central octagonal lantern, supported by diagonal vaulting ribs that spring from either side of each fireplace. Externally the building is buttressed.

In the north-western corner of the kitchen at Leicester, the remains of an oven or hearth were also partially exposed, flanked by projecting foundations, echoing the design of that at Glastonbury which has archways over fireplaces in each corner and ribs running diagonally across the building forming a vaulted roof. The 1930 excavation plan at Leicester also seems to show a thickening of the east wall towards its southern end, perhaps indicating an abutment for a fireplace arch in the south-east corner. The thickening of the south wall noticed in Trenches 20 and 31 is more difficult to explain, but could indicate an additional fireplace in the centre of the wall or, alternatively, the position of an arch abutment.

Interestingly, the lengths of the internal walls of the building, at 39 feet, are neatly divisible by three to locate the position of the fireplace arch abutments, thereby creating the internal octagon plan. It is tempting to suggest that the numbers themselves are symbolic: the number three equates to the Trinity and thirteen represents Jesus and the twelve apostles. However, it has been suggested elsewhere that the unit of measurement used on many sites was a 'medieval foot' of 0.295m, which would make the dimensions of the kitchens at Leicester and Glastonbury approximately 40 and 35 medieval feet square respectively.[140]

A substantial kitchen like this must surely have served not only the refectory, but also the adjacent guest hall, the corrodian's lodgings (as yet unlocated) and, in the early period at least, the abbot's lodging perhaps on the first floor of the west range. Clearly there must have been many modifications over a long period of time not only to the building itself, but also by constructing passageways and pentices linking the kitchen with neighbouring buildings and alterations to the associated water management systems. Investigations in 2003–4 provided some archaeological evidence of such activities and a complex sequence was identified. A number of modifications and built-up floor levels inside the kitchen were evident, creating the accumulation of stratified layers c. 0.50m deep.

Outside, a wide passageway was added to western side of the kitchen, probably serving another range of buildings yet to be revealed by excavation, but perhaps the 'Kings Tower' complex known from the Commissioners' Survey. The date of this passageway is uncertain, but the substantial

137. M. Wood, *The English medieval house* (London 1965, repr. 1971), 250–1.

138. Ibid. 251.

139. V. Dawson (pers. comm.) for measurements and plans of the abbots' and monks' kitchens at Glastonbury.

140. Greene, *Medieval monasteries*, 67.

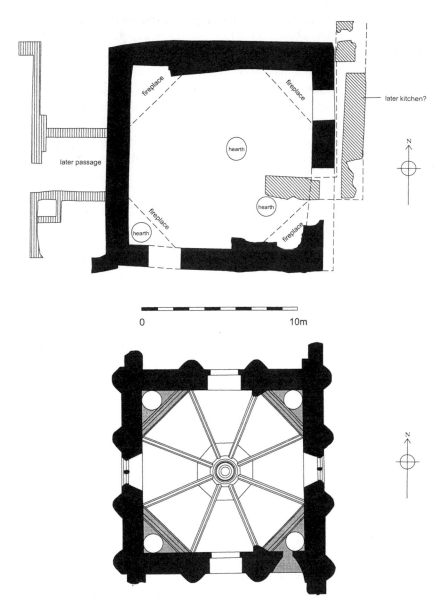

Fig. 33. The kitchen plans of Leicester Abbey (above) and the Abbot's Kitchen, Glastonbury (below)

depth of surviving floor levels and layers within it suggests that it was built some considerable time before the Dissolution. Two circular stone-lined features, probably wells, were identified which may have supplemented the piped supply of water to the kitchen. Other activity identified in Trench 30 included cobbled yard surfaces, some contemporary with the kitchen though others seem to post-date its demolition and are presumably associated with later occupation of the site in the pre or post-Dissolution periods. The 2005 excavations, revealed unexpected evidence that the kitchen was probably demolished before the end of the medieval period and replaced with another substantial structure, perhaps another kitchen, this time attached to the south wall of the refectory. The plan of this building remains uncertain as no evidence for the westerly extension of its south wall, or indeed its return northwards, has been identified in previous seasons, and clearly there is more to be learned from this area of the site.

Investigation of the area to the west and north of the kitchen revealed the comparatively well-preserved remains of a number of drains, providing an insight into the complexity of the water-management systems that existed on the site. One stone-lined drain, presumably to carry rainwater from the refectory roof, was located in the alley between the kitchen and refectory and ran eastwards along the full length of the latter (traced on the 1930s excavation plan), ultimately to join the outlet of the main drain which discharged into the river Soar via an archway in the eastern precinct wall. A small stretch of this rainwater drain was also examined just to the south of the dormitory (above, 44). At that time, it was assumed that the line of the drain marked on the 1930s excavation plan represented that of the abbey main drain, taking effluent from the reredorter (expected to be at the southern end of the dormitory). Instead, a narrow-stone-capped drain was revealed almost certainly for rainwater rather than sewage. Excavations in 2005 indicated that the eastern end of this drain cut the backfill of the abbey's main drain at its outlet in the precinct wall; the same situation may also have occurred south of the dormitory. If correct, this evidence for the disuse of the main drain may suggest that the reredorter was relocated further to the south in the later medieval period, perhaps when the dormitory was extended.

Other rainwater drains ran southwards along the western side of the kitchen, including one which turns east to go through the kitchen wall, suggesting that a supply of rainwater into the kitchen was carefully controlled to flush away food-preparation debris down the wider stone-capped drain inside the building. The evidence from the western side of the kitchen has led to the suggestion that a head of water was created for this purpose by channelling the rainwater into a stone-lined sump or cistern c. 3.5 × 5m and 1.45m deep constructed adjacent to the west wall of the building. Interpretation of this feature, however, remains problematic. It was identified initially as a rubble-filled area between the parallel walls forming a later passageway connecting the kitchen to another range of buildings. Removal of the rubble – which appeared to represent backfill from the 1930s excavations – revealed (or perhaps created) a rectangular flat-bottomed feature bounded by a number of walls and apparently fed by at least two rainwater drains.

More likely, however, in the 1930s an area of stratified deposits was excavated between the passage walls, effectively destroying all relationships between structural features and creating the illusion of a rectangular feature. This interpretation may be supported by the presence of a narrow block of stratified layers running along the north face of the south wall of the passageway that may incorporate the fragmentary remains of floor surfaces, presumably relating to the passage itself. The environmental sample from deposit [3098] at the base of the feature argues against the presence of standing water in this area, since it produced only a small number of snails normally associated with damp places, unlike samples from other drains examined on the site. The presence of a cistern or sump in this position is, therefore, unlikely although there is no doubt at all that rainwater entered the kitchen through its west wall via stone-lined drains.

Of particular interest was the discovery of a length of lead piping in situ beneath the later passageway, pointing to a supply of fresh water to the kitchen at an earlier date. The line of the pipe, approximately north–south along the side of the west wall of the kitchen, ties in with a course of lead piping illustrated on the 1930s excavation plan. Although the source of the abbey's fresh water supply remains unclear, the 1613 Senior map shows a small circular building surmounted by a cross west of the 'ruynes' which may represent a conduit or well house. A plentiful supply of fresh water to the kitchen for the preparation and cooking of food was essential, and evidence from other sites indicates that a piped supply, usually under pressure, was provided to other buildings, such as the scullery, refectory and guest hall, and to the laver where the canons washed before meals.[141]

During the 2002–4 excavations, a number of environmental samples were taken from key deposits associated with the kitchen with the aim of identifying evidence for food preparation and cooking. Samples from the fireplace in the north-west corner and the south-west corner contained abundant charcoal and ash together with charred cereal grains, weed seeds and occasional chaff fragments, probably representing waste sorted from the cereals before use and accidentally spilled cereal grains. Some of the burnt material in the oven may represent the remains of fuel which would normally be raked out when the oven was at the correct temperature before food was put in; other grains found in the oven may have resulted from the cooking process itself, having been scattered on the oven floor to stop cooking bread from sticking. Some un-charred fish remains were found in this hearth suggesting that the deposit also includes general kitchen waste.

In the centre of the kitchen, a brick hearth was excavated, dating probably to the sixteenth or early seventeenth century and therefore may belong to the post-Dissolution use of the site. It is impossible to determine whether the hearth represents an internal feature, indicating that the building that post-dated the kitchen survived into the mansion phase of the site, or whether it is an external feature. Environmental evidence from the hearth included charred peas, a small variety of bean and hazelnut shell, probably waste or spillage from preparing meals.

Environmental samples from the drains contained numerous fragments of fish scales and bones probably from preparing fish for consumption, or from clearing away after meals, together with domestic rubbish from the kitchen area. The fish remains include eels, perch and carp, and sea fish such as plaice, cod and herrings. Similar fish remains have been found on other medieval to post-medieval sites in Leicester such as at Causeway Lane.[142] The Augustinians had a rather more relaxed attitude to meat eating than the Cistercians (whose rule initially prohibited meat eating).[143] Meat was, however, still banned on many days throughout the year, so fish was particularly important in the Augustinians' diet. The evidence from animal bones suggests that beef, mutton, pork and chicken were consumed; domestic birds may also have contributed to the diet, together with venison (as indicated by the recovery of a single deer bone). The presence of mice bones in one of the oven fills confirms, unsurprisingly, that vermin were present in the kitchen. The drains and ovens included abundant charcoal with small numbers of charred cereal grains and weed seeds, peas, beans, fruit-stones of sloe or cherry and bramble, indicating that the deposits probably represent an accumulation of waste from the kitchen area.

6. The infirmary houses

East of the guest hall area and constructed against the precinct wall is another complex of buildings, excavated in 1931–2, which can probably be identified as the infirmary. This would have been used for infirm or aged monks and may have included a hall, chapel, latrines and other small

141. Ibid. 119.

142. R. Nicholson, 'Fish remains' in *Roman and medieval occupation in Causeway Lane, Leicester*, ed. A. Connor and R. Buckley,

Leicester Archaeology Monographs 5 (Leicester 1999), 333–7.

143. Greene, *Medieval monasteries*, 147.

Fig. 34. View east of the outlet of the abbey main drain through
the eastern precinct wall, together with a later drain constructed
within its backfill in the centre of the photograph

rooms. It is difficult to interpret the excavated plan in detail, but it appears to include two large
structures.

One, a long and narrow building, adjoins the precinct wall and is sub-divided, creating two
rooms, the southernmost of which contains a small chamber. A wall runs westwards from the
mid-point of the building towards the dormitory range, effectively demarcating the infirmary
complex from the area to the north that formed the monastic graveyard. Running beneath the
southern room of the building, and exiting via an arch in the precinct wall to the Soar, is what has
been interpreted as the main drain, carrying rainwater from the refectory range and effluent from
the (as yet undiscovered) reredorter adjacent to the dormitory. Excavation here in 2005 (fig. 34)
revealed the side walls of the main drain, the northernmost one of which contained evidence of an
archway, indicating the junction with another large drain. The main drain was found to have been
backfilled in the medieval period (above, 45). The building is linked by a pair of curved walls (perhaps drains or a passageway) to another large rectangular building to the south which has an eastern annexe, and a structure which projects beyond the precinct wall over the course of the Soar,
interpreted as a garderobe (above, 19). Two thinner walls run west from the building and may
have formed part of a covered walkway or, possibly, the heavily robbed remains of a more substantial structure (in view of the presence of a drain leading from them to the north-east, presumably to join the main drain). Between this structure and the building interpreted as the guest hall is
a patch of tile that may relate to another building or external walkway.

7. Outer court

Finally, south-west of the guest hall are walls found in the 1923–5 campaign. The site plans and
photographs and full press accounts (partly written at the time by Marcus Dare who was involved
in the excavations), give us a good basis for assessing this phase of the excavations. Despite this,
they are difficult to understand. There is a mixture of brick and stone walls (and some stone footings carrying brick at one edge). This suggests several phases and rebuilds, as do discontinuities in

the plan. The 1923–5 work was essentially a trenching exercise between standing trees in an orchard rather than an open area excavation, and it is not surprising that the results are slightly incoherent. There are, however, unambiguous fragments of major buildings, several of which had chimneys attached. This is suggestive of guest accommodation. A brick 'tank' with concrete floor suggests an industrial process. The excavators (on the advice of the eminent Romanist, Major Bushe-Fox) considered it a Roman dyeing tank. It certainly seems to have been designed to hold water. It was possibly part of the brew-house but dating is difficult. To the south of this group are a pair of two-storey structures, perhaps residential accommodation, shown on an eighteenth-century engraving, constructed against the south wall of the northern precinct (discussed above, 20).

Conclusion

The aim of archaeological excavation at the site of Leicester Abbey in the nineteenth and earlier twentieth centuries was little different to that adopted elsewhere at the time, namely to uncover as much of the plan of the church and claustral buildings as possible. Little attempt was made to gain a detailed understanding of the stratigraphic sequence of layers, to prepare an adequate record of deposits excavated or to catalogue and correctly provenance finds recovered. Although today it is easy to be critical of such an approach and to bemoan the lack of records, it is also important to remember the constraints that the excavators were working under. In the nineteenth century, the site was still a thriving market garden and only available for minimally-intrusive trenches, whilst the excavators – as elsewhere – had little experience of the techniques of archaeological excavation and limited resources. The campaigns of 1923–25 had similar constraints. Following the acquisition of the site by the City in 1925, and its subsequent conversion to a public park in 1929–32 (which placed a considerable financial burden on the council at a time of economic depression), the archaeology of the site remained uncharacterised and was under considerable threat from landscaping proposals. It was only through the foresight of Bedingfield that a major programme of archaeological fieldwork was mounted at all and that plans which would have involved considerable damage to the church and claustral ranges were shelved as a result of his investigations. Bedingfield also had the vision to interpret the archaeological remains discovered for the public benefit and used his architectural knowledge to prepare reconstructed plans of the buildings and to arrange for them to be laid out on the site with low walls. No doubt the work at Leicester Abbey raised public consciousness of the importance of archaeology and must surely have influenced subsequent pre-war investigations of the Roman baths at the Jewry Wall site.[144]

In the late twentieth century, the assumption was that the majority of the archaeology on the site of Leicester Abbey had been destroyed as a result of earlier excavations and that there was therefore little to gain from undertaking any further fieldwork. In the event, a programme of geophysical survey and trial trenching as student training exercises from 1997–2005 has indicated that in fact much remains to be discovered, and that earlier investigations have caused comparatively little damage to buried archaeological remains, leaving areas of deep and complex stratification in situ. Today, the approach to investigation is influenced by similar constraints to those faced by earlier excavators, in that the site is not all accessible due to current recreational uses and limited resources. Hence, a programme of minimally-intrusive trial trenching was undertaken, with the aim of causing as little damage as possible to buried remains. Although work such as this places

---

144. K. M. Kenyon, *Excavations at the Jewry Wall site, Leicester* (Oxford 1948).

considerable limitations on the interpretation of the evidence, especially when few stratified deposits are sampled and dated by finds, the investigations have still added considerably to our knowledge of the plan and development of two buildings in particular: the gatehouse and the kitchen. For each, the archaeology has proved unexpectedly complex due not only to the longevity of the structure, with many phases of alteration, but also as a result of later robbing and post-Dissolution activity. The evidence from both has indicated the presence of monumental buildings on a similar scale to those seen at high status sites elsewhere, in particular the Abbot's Kitchen at Glastonbury and the gatehouse at Thornton. These comparisons amply demonstrate the architectural grandeur and temporal power of Leicester Abbey in the medieval period.

The survival of the 1930 excavation plan has made it possible to undertake a number of other small, targeted trenches to answer specific questions relating to the layout of particular buildings. Priorities for the future are clearly to characterise buildings to the south and east of the main claustral ranges, such as the guest accommodation, infirmary and possible ancillary buildings, whose plans are by no means clear due to extensive robbing. It is also to be hoped that the environmental sampling programme can continue, with the objective of characterising more fully the diet, health and living conditions of the inhabitants of this important site, work which was beyond the scope and skills of the earlier investigators of Leicester Abbey.

Appendix: Crown Commissioners' Survey of Leicester Abbey (1538 or 1539)
The text below is reprinted from Fox, *Leicester Abbey*, 14–15 (TNA SC12/10/11), previously printed in *The Archaeological Journal* 27 (1870), 204–6, and *TLAAS* 4 (1878), 33–4.

The viewe of the scytuacion of the late monasterye of Leycester
The scyet conteynyth xv akers and inclosyd all about with a wall of stone parte bryke standyng halfe a myell from Leycester towardys the Northe, all invieorned on the South parte with a freyshe water ryver curraunt by the same . . .

    The Churche the mansyon houses and other buyldynges standyth in the myddyst of the scyet. And a halt way cast out of the Northe parte thereof inclosyd with hyghe walles of stone and inbattelyd leydyng into the seyd scyet, and to a basse court of barnys stabbeys and other housses of husbondrye and to a small gate house withe one turret opeynyng into an other bascourt, and with a square lodgyng of ayther syed the gatehouse wherin be v chaumbers with chymneys and large wyndowes glasyd, the walles of stone and coveryd with leyd, and foure turrettes of stone at the foure cornerres of the same. In the South Est parte of the seyd court standyth the backhouse brewhouse and ij stables all of stone coveryd with tyell. On the West parte standyth the Churche conteynyng in leyngth cxl fote and in bredyth xxx fote with a large crose yell in the mydyst of the same conteyning in leyngth c fote and xxx fote in bredyth and nygh to the hyght of Westminster churche with a hyghe squayr Tower stepyll standyng at the West end of the same wherin ys a great dorre and a large wyndowe glasyd openyng at the entre in to the seyd scyet. And a great square house leydyng from the West end of the seyd churche to the West end of the frater wherin be iij great chaumbers with chymneys and large wyndowes parte glasyd with stayres of tymber leydyng uppe to the same, the walles parte stone and coveryd with leyde which wolde be muche more comodyouse yf yt werr performed after an uniforme all with stone to the prospecte and view of the same. The Frater is a great large house and well proporcyoned withe a large wyndowe glasyd openyng into the Courte the dorter standyng at the Est end thereof of lyke proporcyon with stayres leydyng on hygh to the same and valtyd under and belowe wherin be great large sellers. The churche withe they foreseyd housses chapter house and librarye be all of stone and coveryd with leyd, and buyldyd squayr about the cloyester yerde and a entree leydyng furth of the cloyester in to the hall and chaumberes, and other houses of offyce buylded square about a yarde adjoynyng to the seyd cloyester parte stone and parte tymber part coveryd with leyd and parte with tyell with gallerees leydyng above and belawe to the same hall and chaumberes kychyn and other housses of offyce. And att the entree out of the bascourt to the same standyth a tower the forefrunte all bryke with a turret well proporcyoned callyd the Kynges lodgyng, wherin ys two fayr chaumberes with wyndowes glasyd, with chymneys and two inner chaumbers with chymneys and belawe a parler with two inner chaumberes of lyke proporcyon, and a gallere leydyng from the seyd tower belawe to iij chaumberes with chymneys and to the hall all of stone and covered with tyell, and to serten chaumberes above and belawe for offycers, and a hygh galere above leydying from the foreseyde tower at the gate to iiij chaumberes above with chymneys. And to the gret dynyng chaumber standyth on hyghe at the upper end of the hall well sealyd above with the out caste of large bey wyndowes and within the same one fayr lodgyng chaumber with an iner chaumber with chymneys and wyndowes glaysed the wallys stone and coveryd with leyd, and an lawe galere leydyng frome the hall to the keychyn and housses of offyce and to vj chaumberes for offycers. And an entree ledyng owt of the same to the fermore housses wherof parte ys newly and lately buyldyd wherin be vj chaumbers with chymneys. And there be in the utter court dyvers chaumbers for servantes in severall placys and all the foresayd houses with the churche be in good repayr . . .

An incense-boat cover from Leicester Abbey

David Dawson

One of the most interesting finds recovered during excavations of Leicester Abbey in the 1920s and 1930s is the hinged lid of a Limoges enamel incense-boat, found in the sacristy and dating to the thirteenth century (colour plate D and fig. 1).[1] The complete vessel would have been boat-shaped, with a hinged D-shaped lid, standing on a flattened ovoid foot.

Form (fig. 1)

The cover from Leicester Abbey is formed by a copper D-shaped plate with the rounded end drawn out into a hook handle with an animal-head terminal, measuring 86mm long, by 80mm wide and 3mm thick. At the centre of the plate is riveted an openwork roundel, depicting a contorted dragon-like animal with speckled body and ribbon limbs. Surrounding the roundel is a circle containing a flower-like design with eleven pointed petals. Each petal has a base of black enamel, the rest of the flower is infilled with turquoise enamel, and between each petal is a teardrop shaped gilded dot. In each of the three corners is a motif of a small flower with shallow petals and a central dot, accompanied by two elongated diamond-shaped teardrops. On the two curved edges of the plate is a double line, the outer of these two lines being nicked. On the straight edge by the hinge, the outer of the two lines is an engraved zig-zag pattern. The plate is pierced by eleven rivet holes, two are used to fasten the roundel, and the remaining nine are arranged around the edges. These suggest that the plate was fastened onto the bowl of the incense-boat, and that this was not the lifting lid.

Fig. 1. The incense-boat lid found at Leicester Abbey, vertical view (reduced)

Acknowledgments: This article is a revised version of a paper written in 1984, as an artefact study for the Museum Studies at University of Leicester. I would like to thank the staff of the Jewry Wall Museum, Ms V. Pirie and Mr R. Rutland for their assistance when writing the original article, and to Richard Buckley for contacting me twenty years later to encourage me to edit the article for publication.

1. R. Buckley, 'The archaeology of Leicester Abbey', above pp. 1–67.

Manufacture

Manufacture of the item would have started with a sheet of copper, since it is on this base that enamels fuse, rather than with a copper alloy.[2] The copper is likely to have been mined and smelted in the Massif Central, the closest source of copper to the place of manufacture. The copper sheet was cut to shape and the handle drawn out. The plate was then filed to give a smooth edge, and the animal-head terminal formed with a graving tool. Next, it is likely that the design for the enamel work was drawn onto the plate, and the areas to be filled with enamel chiselled away to a depth of approximately 1mm. The base of the cells were left rough but clean to ensure good cohesion with the enamel and to reflect light back into the enamel, enhancing the colour. The cells were then filled with enamel.

Enamel is a ground glass, made from flint or sand, red lead and soda or potash. By varying the proportions, the enamel can be made either more brilliant or more durable. The clear enamel is then coloured by the addition of various metallic oxides and minerals. The ingredients of the enamel were mixed and then heated until fused into a lump of glass or 'frit', which was then ground into a pestle and mortar into a powder. This was then washed to remove the finer particles of enamel, and the dust from the mortar. These fine particles make the raw enamel appear white, despite the colouring agents. The enamel, suspended in water, was then painted into the prepared hollows. This method of enamelling is known as champlevé, where hollows are cut into the metal; an alternative technique, known as cloisonée, requires thin strips of metal soldered to the metal base to create a raised border for the enamel. Once the enamel had been painted into the cells, the object was placed in an oven and heated until the enamel fused. The fusing temperature for each colour of enamel is different, so the enamel with the highest fusing temperature was laid down first, with the others being added in descending order of fusing temperature. This incense-boat would have needed three different firings, probably in the following order, black, turquoise and lastly, blue.

After the final firing, the enamel was smoothed and polished with abrasives, firstly with a fine stone such as 'Water of Ayr stone' and water, finally with rouge and leather. The areas of exposed metal were then gilded (as a preliminary the metal was painted with mercury to amalgamate the surface) and then painted with an equal mixture of mercury and powdered gold. The object was then gently heated for a number of days before being brought to a dull red heat to drive off the mercury vapour. The cover required need final burnishing and polishing before assembly.

The roundel, made of bronze or copper, was probably cast in a cire perdue mould, where a wax model is encased in a fire-clay mould heated to evaporate the wax. Molten metal is poured into the mould, filling the hollow left by the wax. When cool, the mould is broken open to allow the removal of the cast roundel. As the two halves of the cover of the incense-boat are likely to have had identical roundels, the wax model of the roundel was probably itself moulded, and the areas of openwork cut away by hand. The roundel was filed and burnished before being riveted to the incense-boat cover and gilded.

Limoges enamels

The origin of enamelling in the Limoges area is uncertain, but is first recorded in a letter of 1167–9, when a member of Archbishop Thomas Becket's entourage related the marvels of the enamelled

2. H. Maryon, *Metalwork and enamelling* (Dover 1971), 174.

reliquaries of the Infirmary of St Victor in Paris. Before this time, the main centres of enamel working during the earlier medieval period had been further east, in the region around the River Meuse.[3] In the eleventh century, new workshops were established in Limoges by the Abbey, partly because of local ecclesiastical demand and partly because of the access to local mineral deposits.[4] The high level of craftsmanship of the early products of the workshop make it clear that the skills, if not the artistic style, of Germany were imported at this time.

The area of the Massif Central provided many of the raw materials for the production of metal and enamel work. The exceptions were the exotic colouring agents such as cobalt blue, lapis lazuli and sapphire, which came from the East. The trade routes that brought these materials to Venice, and thus further into Europe, broke down in the early thirteenth century after the onset of Mongol invasions. This led to a search for new colouring agents available locally, resulting in cruder colours and, coupled with increased output, led to a general decline in quality.[5] The output of the later thirteenth century was prodigious, with one particular type of candlestick still surviving in many hundreds of examples.[6] This volume of production must have necessitated a factory-like production, indeed the process outlined above falls into a number of clearly defined specialisations: metal-working; layout; enamel preparation; enamel painting; gilding and finishing. No doubt the workshops were organised in this way. Some confirmation of this comes from the assembly marks and the marks probably indicating the work of individual craftsmen found on some pieces.[7] These individuals (who are sometimes historically-recorded as heading workshops) imply that the trade was highly organised. The incense-boat cover from Leicester Abbey appears to carry no marks, and the simple design of large cells to hold the enamel, the limited colour range and the quality of workmanship all indicate that the item was one produced in quantity.

Parallels (fig. 2)

The incense-boat from Leicester can be compared with an example now in the Victoria and Albert Museum, London (fig. 2), and with another unprovenanced example in the Kofler Collection, which is dated to the third decade of the thirteenth century.[8] Its thirteenth-century date is confirmed by the openwork roundel, which may be compared to a medallion now at Biella, Piedmont, by two roundels in the Keir Collection and by a censer now in Limoges.[9] A similar incense-boat to the one from Leicester Abbey is currently on display at the Museu Nacional d'Art de Catalunya, in Barcelona; this item is unprovenanced, but is also from Limoges and has a similar openwork mount, and is dated to the early thirteenth century.

The incense-boat at Leicester Abbey

There are no records of the purchase of this item by Leicester Abbey, or of its donation to the Abbey. However, its acquisition can be understood in the context of increasingly complex

3. For evidence of earlier enamelling workshops around the French city of Conques (c. 1100) see, E. Taburet-Delahaye, 'La naissance de l'emallerie méridionale' in F. Douar, B. Petit and C. Ehm, ed. *La France romane au temps de premiers Capétiens (987–1152)*, exh. cat. (The Louvre: Paris 2005), 370–7.

4. M-M. Gauthier, *Émaux du Moyen Âge occidental* (Fribourg 1972), 106.

5. Ibid. 187.

6. M-M. Gauthier and G. François, *Medieval enamels: master-*

pieces from the Keir collection (London 1981), no. 27.

7. W. F. Stohlman, 'Assembling marks on Limoges champlevé enamels as a basis for Classification', *Art bulletin* 16 (1934), 14–18 at 14.

8. 'La collection de E. et M. Truniger', *Bulletin de la Société archéologique et historique du Limousin* 93 (Limoges 1966–8), 17–34, E113.

9. Catalogued respectively in Gauthier *Émaux du Moyen Âge*, no. 139; Gauthier and François, *Medieval enamels*, nos. 29–30; Gauthier, *Collection de E. et M. Truniger*, no. 135.

Fig. 2. A complete, thirteenth-century incense-boat with pierced roundels on both parts of the lid (one now lost), now in the Victoria and Albert Museum, London (M. 320–1926) (reduced)

liturgical practices during the medieval period, as shown in the practice of Sarum.[10] Additionally, the products of enamellers workshops were recommended by Pope Innocent III and subsequently adopted at Winchester in 1229, as suitable receptacles for relics of saints.[11] However, even a wealthy foundation such as Leicester Abbey may not have owned many such items; a visit in 1518 by Bishop Attwater found that there was no proper receptacle for the consecrated host.[12] A suitable container, or pyx, was essential for the elevation of the Host, a practice introduced from France in the thirteenth century.[13] The fact that such an important item was not available in the abbey in the early sixteenth century may imply that liturgical vessels were not acquired as sets, including items such as paten, chalice, pyx, censers, incense-boats and altar cruets, but that they were obtained individually, perhaps presented by benefactors. A suite of vessels would be needed for each altar; at Leicester there were two chapels in addition to the high altar, and there would have been several more in the main body of the nave. However, there may have been just one incense-boat at the abbey, kept either in the aumbrey, or cupboard, next to the high altar, which may also have held the store of incense, or in the sacristy. The incense-boat is likely to have been among the stores and ornaments of the abbey valued at its Dissolution in October 1538 at £228.

   The incense-boat cover was found in the sacristy, between the south transept and the chapter house, during the excavations by W. K. Bedingfield in 1930.[14] This may have been where the incense-boat was kept, or the liturgical vessels and furnishings may have been gathered here before being removed from the abbey at the Dissolution. It is, so far, the only extant liturgical vessel from the Abbey, and it must be assumed that either the incense-boat was already damaged, or that the

10. T. Bailey, *The processions of Sarum and the western Church* (Toronto 1971)

11. Gauthier, *Émaux du Moyen Âge*, 187.

12. A. Hamilton Thompson, *The abbey of St Mary of the Meadows, Leicester* (Leicester 1949), 65.

13. J. G. Davies, *Dictionary of liturgy and worship* (London 1972), 197.

14. Buckley, 'The archaeology of Leicester Abbey', above p. 10.

cover was removed in order for it to be sold for secular use. The discovery of the incense-boat cover was recorded in an article in the Leicester Mercury, and was identified at the time by the Victoria and Albert Museum.[15] The cover was donated to Leicester Museum on the death of Bedingfield.[16] Unfortunately, few records of the excavation remain, but these are amplified by a number of newspaper reports and a note by the excavator.[17]

Incense-boats in England

It is difficult to identify how common incense-boats were in medieval England. All Limoges enamels have primarily been treated as art-historical items, and have been collected as such since the eighteenth century. This history means that provenances are rarely known, especially when items passed into private hands following the Dissolution. Archaeologically, Limoges enamels have been found in a variety of contexts, from the priory at Rusper in Sussex to a plaque for decorating a book cover by the master craftsman G. Alpius found at the small parish church of Rottingdean, also in Sussex.[18] In Leicestershire Museums, there are two Limoges enamel items in addition to the incense-boat: namely, an unprovenanced crucifix, and a plaque from a processional cross from St Martin's, Leicester.

In a wider context, the Portable Antiquities Scheme currently records 43 artefacts identified as Limoges enamels; one of these, a figurine, is from Frolesworth in Leicestershire.[19] Approximately 50% of these artefacts are figures, mounts from reliquaries or from crucifixes, and there appears to be a reasonably even distribution across Britain. In addition, part of an incense burner, dated mid-twelfth to mid-thirteenth century and possibly of German origin, was found at Medbourne.[20]

Incense in the medieval church

The incense-boat was used as a container for burning a mixture of the solidified resins of frankincense and myrrh. These resins are found in the Horn of Africa and the Arabian Peninsula, and were traded through the Eastern Mediterranean to Venice, and from there to the rest of Europe. The burning of incense burnt in worship is recorded in the Old Testament, as well as being the gift of two of the Magi to the infant Jesus. Despite these associations, the use of incense was regarded by the early church as a pagan ritual, as a result of the sacrificial use of incense in the worship of the Roman Emperor. In the fourth century, incense began to have an honorific use, being carried before the priest at his entrance into church. From this use developed the censing of the altar, the Gospels, ministers and the choir.[21] By the sixth century, incense began to have a sacrificial use in Christian worship, in the sense that it was used in an act for which blessings were sought in return. In England, incense was used in processions in the late Saxon period, shown by the censer covers from Canterbury and Pershore.[22] The introduction of the elevation of the Host from France in the thirteenth century, led to incense being used in the new focal point of the Mass. By the time of the

15. 'Discoveries at Leicester Abbey', Leicester Mercury (18.2.1930).

16. LCMS acc. no. A241.1951

17. W. K. Bedingfield, 'Presidential address 1930–31', Transactions of the Leicester Literary and Philosophical Society 32 (1931), 5–24.

18. G. Zarnecki, J. Holt and T. Holland, ed. English Romanesque art, 1066–1200, exh. cat. (The Hayward Gallery: London 1984), 278; A. Hussey, 'Notice on an ancient engraved copper', Sussex archaeological collections 5 (1852), 105–10. See also the ciborium of c. 1200 signed by 'Magister G. Alpais', which is now in The Louvre, acc. no. MRR0098; J. Evans, Art in medieval France,

987–1498 (London 1948), pl. 59.

19. Portable antiquities scheme, Finds database (2005), LEIC-CF6E30 (www.finds.org.uk).

20. Portable antiquities scheme, Finds database (2005), NARC915 (www.finds.org.uk).

21. Davies, Dictionary of liturgy, 197.

22. J. Backhouse, D. H. Turner and L. Webster, ed. The golden age of Anglo-Saxon art 966–1066, exh. cat. (British Museum: London 1984), nos. 73–4.

Sarum Breviary, the use of incense was ubiquitous; simple processions had two thurifers (incense burners) and incense was burnt during the lesson at Matins. The Sarum Breviary also includes the blessing of the incense itself.[23] Thus, incense in the later medieval church had a whole range of ritual uses and meanings; in addition to its use during daily services, it was also used during the consecration of new altars and at funerals when its use was probably demonifugal, driving away evil spirits. The importance of incense declined with the rise of Protestantism, but was still used in the Protestant Church into the seventeenth century, before being revived by the Oxford Movement in the 1870s.

The use of an imported item of metalwork to contain a material laden with symbolic and liturgical meaning serves to illustrate the widespread contacts of the medieval church in general and of Leicester Abbey in particular. The quantity of Limoges enamel metalwork in England and the popularity of English enamels at home and abroad show the close contacts with the continent in artistic style, liturgy and trade.[24] The importation of incense demonstrates the length of trade routes, and their predictability despite the political changes that were taking place in the Mediterranean. The removal of the incense-boat from its place near the high altar, and the removal and loss of the cover, speak of the upheaval of the Dissolution. The stripping of the consecrated altars of the gifts of benefactors must have been a severe blow to the ex-monks of Leicester Abbey. One may speculate that the incense-boat cover was removed to allow the bowl to be sold into private hands for use at table. But it is one of the few remnants that, along with the extant manuscripts and documentary evidence, tell of the furnishings of Leicester Abbey at its height.

23. Bailey, *Processions of Sarum*, 111.
24. C. Onan, 'English medieval base-metal church plate', *The Archaeological Journal* 119 (1962), 195-207.

The landscape of Leicester Abbey's home demesne lands to the Dissolution

Anthony Squires

From its foundation by Earl Robert II le Bossu, earl of Leicester (1118–68), the abbey of St Mary de Pratis – St Mary of the Meadows – prospered to become the wealthiest religious house in Leicestershire.[1] Its income at the Dissolution was a little over £1000, which was approximately twice that of the second wealthiest, Garendon Abbey near Loughborough. From the monastic complex on the north bank of the River Soar, St Mary's Abbey managed a multitude of properties, large and small, which were acquired over four centuries. The monastic site, together with its immediate surroundings, is now widely known as Abbey Park and is owned and administered by Leicester City Council. The present landscape was laid out in the late nineteenth century as a typical urban amenity park for the benefit of the expanding population of Leicester. Virtually all the land of the surrounding area is built over with factories, commercial units and housing estates that form the city's busy northern suburb.

The history of Leicester Abbey as a religious house and an outline of the administration of its estates have been described by Hamilton Thompson and Hilton.[2] A number of writers, including Hoskins, have touched on the landscape of the abbey's holdings in different parts of the county, including those that fourteenth- and fifteenth-century abbots enclosed and depopulated in favour of sheep farming.[3] Most recently, excavations of the monastic precincts are producing new insights into the layout and nature of the former buildings and closes.[4] However, as yet no attempt has been made to describe the landscape of the surrounding and extensive home estate of the abbey, and it is the purpose of this paper to make some account of this.

The recent discovery in the archives at Chatsworth in Derbyshire of a detailed map of the former demesne estate presents an opportunity for drawing together many scattered data and references and for reassessing some of the findings of earlier writers who used the better-worked sources. The map was made in 1613 by William Senior for William Cavendish, the first earl of Devonshire and new owner of the abbey site, and is hereafter referred to as the 'William Senior Leicester Abbey Map' (colour plate B).[5] The present work uses, at all times, the lands shown on the

1. *ODNB*, s.n. 'Robert [Robert de Beaumont], second earl of Leicester (1104–1168)'; D. Crouch, 'The foundation of Leicester Abbey, and other problems', *Midland History* 12 (1974), 1–12 suggests a possible foundation date of 1138 against the traditional date of 1143.

2. A. Hamilton Thompson, *The Abbey of St Mary of the Meadows, Leicester* (Leicester 1949); R. Hilton, *The economic development of some Leicestershire estates in the fourteenth and fifteenth centuries* (Oxford 1949).

3. W. G. Hoskins, 'Seven deserted village sites in Leicestershire', *TLAHS* 33 (1956), 36–51 at 46–7.

4. R. Buckley et al., 'The archaeology of Leicester Abbey', above pp. 1–67.

5. D. V. Fowkes and G. R. Potter, ed. *William Senior's survey of estates of the 1st and 2nd Earls of Devonshire c. 1600–1628*, Derbyshire Record Society 13 (Chesterfield 1988). See further, Buckley et al., 'Leicester Abbey after the Dissolution', below p. 98.

William Senior Map as its definition of the boundaries of the home demesne estate at the time of the surrender of the abbey in 1538 (that is, the lands that were held and worked directly by the abbey). Other surveys of the monastic estate adjacent to the abbey and the anomalies they present are referred to below. Considerations of geology and topography have been included, and extensive ground survey, carried out on foot, has produced some results. An assessment of the abbey's estate as seen against the early woodland of the Chace (later the Royal Forest) of Leicester has also been taken into account. Moreover, all the major documentary sources have been consulted, particularly the abbey's surviving fifteenth-century 'novum Rentale', now in the Bodleian Library.[6] Omitted from this study is the landscape within the walls of the monastic precinct and the abbey's lands – held in demesne or otherwise – lying near the town and elsewhere on the northern bank of the River Soar. This paper attempts to outline the growth of the home demesne lands, to account for the landscape to the Dissolution and to indicate the influence of the layout of the estate on the northern part of the modern city.

The physical background

The uncertain effects of a number of major, relatively recent landscape changes limit any study of the landscape of the abbey and its estate. These include changes to the pattern of drainage which is, or was, predominantly from north-west to south-east, brought about by the canalisation of the River Soar and the effects of major flood alleviation schemes carried out in the nineteenth century. In addition, earth moving on a huge scale over the last century-and-a-half has caused major modifications in the contours and surface geology. Fortunately, the first edition of the Ordnance Survey Geological Map (1892) appeared before much of the area was built over, and from this source it is clear that the layout and land use of the abbey's estate closely mirrored the earlier topography.[7]

The monastic site and the River Soar

Until the end of the eighteenth century, the River Soar, in the area of the abbey, was divided into two channels (see figs. 1 and 2). The Tudor traveller John Leland described the river thus:

> Downstream the whole river flows around half the town and through the north bridge, which has seven or eight stone arches. Then it divides into two . . . the larger stream flowing past St Mary's Abbey on its far bank. The other stream is called the Bishop's Water, because tenants of the Bishop of Lincoln enjoy rights over it; before long its rejoins the main river, and by so doing forms an island out of a large pleasant meadow.[8] (fig. 3)

Alluvial material was deposited and re-deposited over the river's floodplain both in the neighbourhood of the abbey and to the west of the town, as indicated by the many wetland place-names. This pattern of flooding together with the very poor drainage effectively prevented urbanisation of the land of the West Field of Leicester until the third decade of the nineteenth century. The river also formed an effective barrier between the abbey and the town, communication with which was chiefly via the North Bridge (fig. 1). This separation, throughout the middle ages and beyond, gave the abbey a sense of isolation which was emphasised and maintained by the fact that the suburban develop-

---

6. Bodl. Laud misc 625; M. Gullick and T. Webber, 'Summary catalogue of surviving manuscripts from Leicester Abbey', below pp. 173–92, no. 17.

7. Ordnance Survey, *Geological map of England at scale one inch*

to the mile (1892).

8. J. Chandler, *John Leland's itinerary: travels in Tudor England* (Stroud 1993), 279.

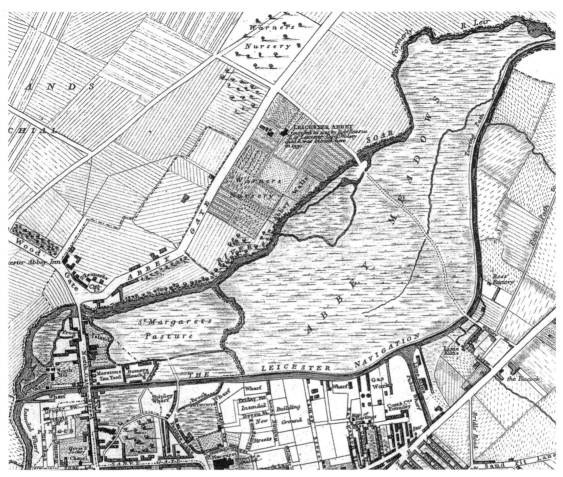

Fig. 1. Detail from Fowler's 'Plan of Leicester Showing the Limits of the Borough' (1828) (from Fielding Johnson, *Glimpses of ancient Leicester*)

ment of Leicester during the abbey's existence took place mostly outside the South and East Gates.

The abbey buildings situated in the northern part of the monastic precinct occupied a terrace of well-drained river gravel, which stood a little above the floodplain. The southern part of the site, the areas shown on the William Senior Map as containing 'Meryvale' and 'Abbat Garden', was more low-lying and may well have been subject to occasional flooding.

Geology and topography

Away from the river gravel terraces and the site of the abbey buildings, the land rises steadily and gently westwards across small patches of glacial soils and gravels. It reaches the 200ft contour in the neighbourhood of what eventually became the abbey's north-western boundary. Northwards and eastwards of this line the land becomes more strongly rolling and reaches the 250ft contour in the area of the modern Stocking Farm Estate. The present community centre there commands fine views southwards over Leicester and beyond. Much of this upland, including the area of the abbot's later medieval park and the 'Stocking' closes, is overlain by boulder clay (colour plate B).

Fig. 2. The site of the former abbey and the modern Abbey Park looking south. The partly altered course of the northern branch of the River Soar can be seen above the site of the abbey buildings, a little to the left of the 'oval'. Above these, the southern canalised course of the Soar can be seen sweeping from right to left along the southern edge of Abbey Park. The two waterways unite on the centre left edge of the view

Fig. 3. A view of Cavendish House on the site of the former Abbey in 1796. The stream here is the former southern channel of the River Soar which was canalised in 1791 as part of the Leicester Navigation. The land beyond is the meadows, now the site of the modern Abbey Park (from Nichols, *Leicester*, i. 294)

This deposit extends in a huge sweep from Thurcaston in the north to Huncote, far to the south-west of Leicester, although it is interrupted in places by lighter soils and gravels. The nature of the boulder clay is variable but for the most part it is heavy and difficult to cultivate. Drainage, now much changed, was predominately from the clay belt to the river. These three features, topography, soils and drainage, were the major physical determinants of the immediate pre-Conquest landscape which, during the middle ages, was to form much of the royal forest.

The early woodland

The single most important biotic factor accounting for the development of the abbey's demesne lands north of the River Soar was woodland. Its presence also greatly influenced the determination of the parish boundaries of local communities, especially those on the edge of the upland clay belt. Involved here are the settlements of Birstall, Belgrave and Thurcaston together with the small settlement – of whatever nature – at Bromkinsthorpe (fig. 4).

Domesday Book (1086) attributes a number of woods to Birstall, Belgrave and Thurcaston; at Birstall, the wood occupied approximately 50 acres, at Belgrave 126 acres and at Thurcaston 1200 acres. These figures are the result of using the middle form factor of the method devised by Rackham to calculate woodland areas, but of course they are only approximations.[9] Also present, and in much the same general area north and west of Leicester, was the county's largest wood called 'Hereswode', which occupied almost 5000 acres. The meaning of this name has been much discussed and its origin appears to lie in the probability that the inhabitants of Leicester, and possibly of some surrounding communities, had common rights of wood and pasture there.[10] Hereswode's northern boundary may well have been marked by the Anstey Lane out of Leicester (fig. 4), from which line it swept southwards and eastwards to its southern-most point near Tooley Park by Earl Shilton. After the Conquest, its northern section, perhaps half its total area, became know as 'the Frith'; Cox considers this term to be derived from the Old English 'fyrho', meaning 'wooded countryside' and also from Middle English meaning 'park'.[11] Both derivations agree with our knowledge of the area from the evidence of later centuries. Its southern part appears to have had no general name, and it is to this area that the Royal Forest had contracted by the late sixteenth century.

The woodland recorded from the three manors of Birstall, Belgrave and Thurcaston was not part of 'the Frith'. It is now becoming apparent, from topographical assessment together with later documentary evidence, that the large wood of Thurcaston swept southwards from the settlement of that name, closely followed the upland clay belt and terminated somewhere in the region of the present Fosse Road and its northern extension, Blackbird Road (figs. 4 and 5). Much of this area of woodland later attracted the name Beaumont Leys, which today is a community mostly occupied by industrial areas and residential estates.

Size apart, a view of the nature of the woodland is also important. This may be gained by comparison with other large Domesday woodlands, not only in Leicestershire but elsewhere in England.[12] To this may be added the topographical background and later documentary evidence. To be brief, it seems most likely that the eleventh-century 'Wood of Thurcaston' was not a landscape of continuous or unbroken woodland but rather one of trees, wood-pasture and open

9. O. Rackham, *Ancient woodland* (Colvend 2003), 114.

10. J. Bourne, *Understanding Leicestershire and Rutland place-names* (Loughborough 2003), 59; L. Fox and P. Russell, *Leicester Forest* (Leicester 1948).

11. B. Cox, *The place-names of Leicestershire. Pt. I: the Borough of Leicester*, English Place-Names Society 75 (Nottingham 1998), 224.

12. A. Squires and M. Jeeves, *Leicestershire and Rutland woodlands past and present* (Newtown Linford 1994), 26–30.

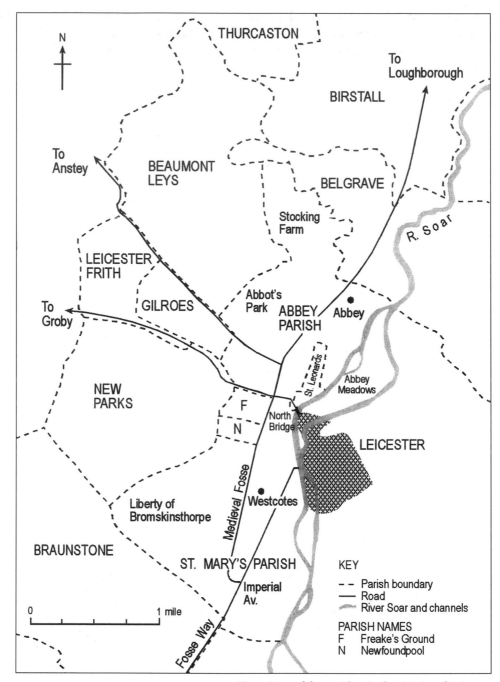

Fig. 4. Map of the parishes in the vicinity of Leicester

grassland. The woodland products and substantial grazing it offered were exploited by the inhabitants of local communities; the deer and other species of wild animals were considered as sources of sport and meat by the manorial lords who regarded their preservation as part of their manorial economies.

The decline of the Domesday woodland

By the thirteenth century, the assarting (or conversion of woodland to arable) around the periphery of the Wood of Thurcaston was well underway and the wooded element of the landscape was

Fig. 5. Current roads and the boundaries of the Leicester Abbey estate

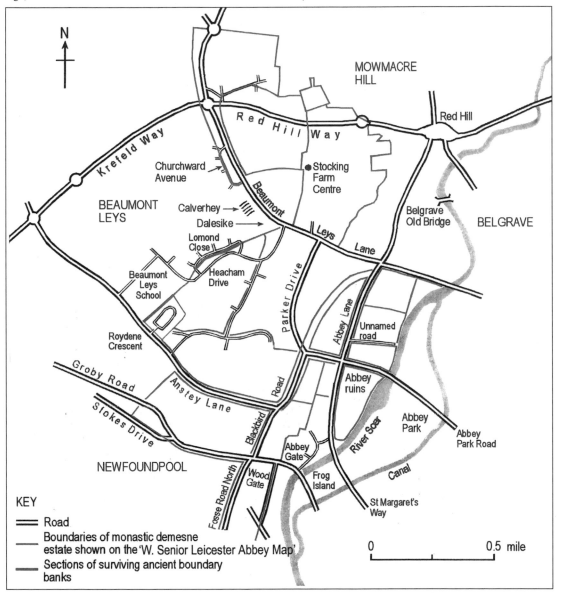

in decline. Here, as in other parts of Leicestershire, measures were being taken to protect the best of the remaining woodlands, with varying degrees of success. Enclosures such as 'Dovelands', 'Beaumont Wood' and 'The Stocking' persisted for many centuries, simply because they were regarded as valuable assets and as such were carefully protected and maintained. By the early thirteenth century, the Domesday Wood of Thurcaston was mostly open pasture scattered with trees, but with some large wooded areas. The south-eastern portion extended to the western boundary of Belgrave manor and the south-western boundary of the manor of Birstall, that is, to the area of the modern Stocking Farm and Mowmacre Estates (fig. 4). Here the land is very strongly rolling and the tops are covered with boulder clay and exposed to the wind. It seems likely that the Domesday woodlands of both Belgrave and Birstall lay very close to one another and may have even adjoined. In topographical terms they may have formed one wood, but were divided between the inhabitants of both manors. The remaining part of the modern parish of Birstall slopes gently eastwards to the River Soar and is much more suited to grazing and tillage. Moreover, there were extensive meadows along the course of the river. The same broad topographical considerations apply to the parish of Belgrave. However, where the remarks on the history of the woodland at Birstall are largely based on inherent topographical probability, those for the woodland of Belgrave are augmented by details on a map of the parish made in 1657.[13]

There is, then, a view that in the late eleventh century at the time Domesday Book was compiled, a landscape of woodland and pasture completely surrounded the north and west of the town of Leicester. It began at Thurcaston and swept southwards, following the clay uplands of the later Beaumont Leys, and terminated possibly along the line of the modern Fosse and Blackbird Roads. Moving again, and this time in a south-westerly direction, it crossed the Anstey Lane and the Groby Road out of Leicester to come to an end in the region of Tooley Park.

The origins of the demesne estate

The immediate post-Dissolution history

A study of the William Senior Map allows a fresh appraisal of not only the origins of the abbey's demesne estate but also of its immediate post-Dissolution history. The particular value of this document is that for the first time it maps accurately the boundaries of the various closes and supplies precise acreages. An accompanying text also provides firm indications of how the land was being used. Moreover, the map fixes place-names that had been previously unknown.

Many earlier descriptions of what were usually referred to as, 'the lands of the late dissolved monastery of Leicester' are of limited value and even misleading to modern topographical research. Before the Cavendish family, earls and later dukes of Devonshire, acquired the property, it had been granted on four occasions. The following sequence of events between 1539 and 1613 records these exchanges. The acreages given represent the best estimate in each case.

1. In 1539, the year following the surrender to the king, the abbey site and its estate totalling 496 acres were granted to Sir Francis Cave.[14] Not included were Stocking Wood and the Stocking Closes. Also excluded was the abbey's valuable woodland of Doveland that lay in Bromkinsthorpe manor.

---

13. John Coffyn, map of 'The manor and parish of Belgrave' (1657); Leicester University Library SCT 00869 and ROLLR 28 DE 64/317.

14. *Calendar of Patent Rolls, 1553–54*, 282.

2. In 1550 what appears to have been the identical properties were granted to the Marquess of Northampton who was attainted three years later.[15]

3. In 1563 Sir Edward Hastings received the Marquess' abbey lands of 495 acres.[16] Five years later the two woods of Stocking and Doveland were added.[17] The 'Stocking' was presumably that area shown on the William Senior Map as 'The Abbats' Woode at Stockinges', in which case the acreage would have risen to 559, but not including Doveland which is of unknown area. If the Stocking Closes were included, as is probable, the total area of the grant would have risen to 720 acres. On the imprisonment of Sir Edward, the property passed to his brother, the earl of Huntingdon. Sir Edward later re-acquired the estate, again presumably unchanged at 553 or 720 acres, plus Doveland.[18]

4. The Hastings family surrendered the property to Queen Elizabeth who granted it to Sir Christopher Hatton in 1572.[19] There were, in addition, a 'Leicester Meadow' and a 'Barne Close' the location of which was unspecified.

5. Finally, in 1613, the estate passed to the Cavendish family whose surveyor, William Senior, drew the map. The demesne land at that time is stated as totalling 867 acres minus the 40 acres of 'Burstal More', which formed a detached holding of meadow by the River Soar in Birstall. Doveland Wood was not included in the grant to the Cavendishes and is not included in the final total – for present purposes – of 827 acres (colour plate B).

Early grants

The abbey's founder, Earl Robert le Bossu (d. 1168), was followed by many distinguished and wealthy patrons. These included Amice his wife, his son Robert (the third earl, d. 1190) and Robert's wife Petronilla (or Pernell, d. 1212), his grandson Robert (the fourth earl, d. 1204), his granddaughter Margaret, her husband Saer de Quincy, earl of Winchester (d. 1219) and their second son Roger de Quincy (d. 1264), Simon de Montfort (d. 1265), and others.[20] Grants by these patrons were subsequently confirmed by four kings: Stephen, Henry II, John and Henry III.[21]

Le Bossu's foundation grant included most if not all the lands of the college of St Mary de Castro, which lay within the walls of town near the castle and which had been founded c. 1107, by his father.[22] Precisely where these lands lay is not known, but some were presumably immediately adjacent to the site of the new building and most likely included the meadowland between the two courses of the River Soar. Also, it appears, some lay in the manor of Bromkinsthorpe.[23] Throsby identified former de Castro lands called 'biggin'.[24] Cox considered the name, first recorded in 1323, as meaning 'building' or 'outbuilding' but failed to find any other 'biggin' place-name in the area north-west of the Soar.[25] However, the William Senior Map identifies two closes called 'Bigins' to the west of the abbey (colour plate B). If these are indeed the former de Castro lands, it is of particular interest that on their west sides the two biggin closes border the very ancient line of the post-Roman Fosseway (figs. 4 and 5). This is popularly known as the 'medieval Fosse' on account

15. *Calendar of Patent Rolls, 1549–51*, 370.
16. *Calendar of Patent Rolls, 1553–54*, 283.
17. VCH *Leics.* iv, 452.
18. Ibid.
19. *Calendar of Patent Rolls, 1571–72*, 482.
20. *ODNB, s.n.* 'Breteuil, Robert de, third earl of Leicester (*c.* 1130–1190)', 'Grandmesnil, Petronilla de, countess of Leicester (d. 1212), 'Breteuil, Robert de, fourth earl of Leicester (d. 1204)', 'Quincy, Saer de, earl of Winchester (d. 1219)', and 'Quincy, Roger de, earl of Winchester (*c.* 1195–1264)'.
21. See further, D. Crouch, 'Early charters and patrons of Leicester Abbey', below pp. 225–87 especially nos. 3, 8, 9, 20, 25–6, 34.
22. Ibid. pp. 228–9 and n. 21; VCH *Leics.* ii, 45.
23. VCH *Leics.* iv, 369.
24. J. Throsby, *The history and antiquities of the ancient town of Leicester* (Leicester 1791), 83.
25. Cox, *Place Names of Leicestershire*, 181.

of its being an early bypass for Leicester, and is discussed below. The line is also important in relation to the mid thirteenth-century grant of land by Simon de Montfort (discussed below) since from this a northern boundary of the demesne estate in the mid thirteenth century can be proposed.

Other early grants of land to the abbey, whether former de Castro lands or otherwise, are few and unhelpful for present purposes. Le Bossu's foundation charter granted 'five carrucates of land outside the north gate of the town' and 'one carrucate at the north bridge by the site of the mint'. There were also eight houses in Leicester and the mill that had been the bishop's.[26] The foundation charter also recalls the grant of lands by Seward Pitefrid 'in Brunchenestorp' (Bromkinsthorpe).[27] A charter of Henry II confirmed to the abbey the earl of Leicester's grant of 'seven virgates and one bovate of land outside the West Gate' with all appurtenances and liberties in 1155 x 58.[28] Ranulph Ianitoris / Portarius gave land in Bromkinsthorpe, 'in our manor of West Gate' which may have been the origin of the grange established by St Mary de Pratis and which came to be known as Westcotes (fig. 4).[29] The mid twelfth-century royal confirmation of the foundation charter also records the gift by Joscelin Marshal of six assarts of his woodland 'de North', that is, near the North Bridge.[30] The inference here is that the Wood of Hereswode, in whatever form, extended as far south as the river gravel terraces on the north bank of the Soar. Through it the road from Leicester to Groby wound its way (fig. 4).

The William Senior Map presents at least two anomalies which must be taken into account. The first is the extension of the estate southwards, indicated by the position of the 'North Meadow' and two areas called 'Reedes Close' (colour plate B). The meadow is on the alluvium but the two closes occupy a distinct patch of gravel terrace above the flood plain. Cox suggests the name Reede may derive from two seventeenth-century local men, John and Lawrence Reide.[31] However, there is no evidence to link any of these properties with the former de Castro lands. Also, it is interesting that they alone of all the closes shown on the William Senior Map remained in the parish of St Mary rather than being included in Leicester Abbey Parish (fig. 4).

The second point of interest is the existence of the tiny parish of St Leonard's (fig. 4). This occupied land not only on the west bank of the Soar but also that area within the town walls which was subsequently known as Frog Island. The parish's origin is believed to have been related to the facility, whatever it was, for persons crossing the river beyond the north gate. St Leonard's was already established by 1220 but became dominated by St Mary's Abbey that, in the twelfth century and later, obtained grants of land there.[32] However, virtually nothing is known of these grants, but since St Leonard's parish lay almost wholly on the alluvium of the flood plain, the land was predominantly pasture and meadow. At the Dissolution, the monastic lands in this parish were granted separately and, not appearing on the William Senior Map, are not investigated further here.[33]

26. Crouch, 'Early charters and patrons', below pp. 234–5 no. 1; J. Nichols, *The history and antiquities of the county of Leicester*, 4 vols in 8 (London 1795–1815) i, 258. A 'carrucate' was a unit of land that could be ploughed by a single team of oxen in a year; the area of land was variable depending on its nature.

27. Crouch, 'Early charters and patrons', pp. 234–5 and 249–52 nos. 1 and 24; Nichols, *Leicester*, iv, 565–6.

28. Crouch, 'Early charters and patrons', pp. 238–41 no. 8; VCH *Leics.* iv, 382. A 'virgate' was an early term of land measure that could amount to as much as 30 acres, and a 'bovate' was a variable unit of land that could be ploughed by a single ox annually.

29. The reference is from Charyte's 'novum Rentale'; Nichols, *Leicester*, iv, 565–6 and ibid. i, appendix, p. 71. For another grant from Ranulph, here called Ianitoris (ie: 'the doorkeeper'), see Crouch, 'Early charters and patrons', pp. 269–70 no. 58. On Bromkinsthorpe and Westcotes see, Cox, *Placenames*, i, 218–19.

30. Crouch, 'Early charters and patrons', pp. 238–41 and 249–52 nos. 8 and 24; Nichols, *Leicester*, ii, 259.

31. Cox, *Place-names of Leicestershire*, 191.

32. VCH *Leics.* iv, 348.

33. Ibid.

An almost rectangular block of land lies to the west of 'Reedes Close', the northern portion of which in modern times became known as Freake's Ground and the southern part as Newfoundpool (fig. 4). Its northern border is Pinders Close and its southern one is the manor of Bromkinsthorpe. Earlier writers have pointed out that almost nothing is known of the early history of both areas; but these areas can hardly be ignored since they appear to form a clear buffer, devoid of any abbey holdings as far as one can tell, between the Cavendish lands and Bromkinsthorpe.[34] The regular rectangular outline strongly suggests that they are lands carefully and deliberately excised from the Frith for an unrecorded purpose and at an unknown date.

In time, the lands of St Mary de Castro that lay west of the River Soar became part of the parish of St Mary. Within this was the liberty or manor of Bromkinsthorpe. Westcotes Grange apart, the abbey is known to have held other lands in parts of the same parish west of the Soar and at least some of these appear to have been tenanted. The wood of Doveland, in the north-western tip of Bromkinsthorpe, was certainly one property held in demesne. It was originally granted to the abbey by Simon de Montfort in 1255 in exchange for the abbey relinquishing its rights to collect wood and to pasture animals in parts of the Frith reserved for deer.[35] Hilton concluded that the main bulk of the abbey's possessions, held in demesne or otherwise, as existed at the time of the Dissolution, had been acquired by the end of the thirteenth century.[36] Thereafter there was to be little or no change in the boundaries of abbey lands.

The abbey's western and northern boundary

Incomplete though it is, this discussion of the abbey's holdings to the south of the monastic precinct leads to a consideration of the abbey's western and northern boundary. This, as shown on the William Senior Map, forms a broad sweep from the Groby Road in the south, along the northern edge of the close shown as 'High parke' and as far as the present Beaumont Leys Lane (fig. 5). From here is swings north-westwards along Barn Close and, if we ignore Batts Close for the present, along the edge of Abbot's Stocking. The origin of much of this line can be interpreted by reference to a grant by Simon de Montfort (dated by Crouch 1239 x 1240) which is worth quoting at length:

> [Simon de Montfort] gave three hundred and twenty acres of land and wood in his forest called 'Defensa' by Leicester with all things there growing; which land lies from the road to Anesty to Dalesike crossways, and from Dalesike beyond Sterkeshull to Oldefield crossways upon the path from Cropston as shown by the metes and bounds, and from Oldefield round by the field of Belgrave and by the field of the said canons to the road to Anstey; and all cloyhegges with all things there growing; to be held by the said canons in frank almoign [free alms], so that they enclose the same with a dike and cultivate it or make such profit thereof as they will, as free of all service, demand, suits or customs . . . saving to the grantor his venison . . .[37]

First, an interpretation of this important material is called for. The actual course on the ground

34. VCH *Leics.* iv, 449, 455.

35. Crouch, 'Early charters and patrons', pp. 269–70 no. 58; Nichols, *Leicester*, iii, 1080.

36. Hilton, *Some Leicestershire estates*, 17.

37. *Calendar of Charter Rolls*, 1226–57, 408, from where this translation is obtained and where the charter is dated 1252. See, however, Crouch, 'Early charters and patrons', pp. 267–8 no. 55.

has now been accurately determined by field survey. It begins at the point where the line of the gardens in the northerly section of the present Roydene Crescent leaves Anstey Lane and extends to form the boundary of the playing fields of Beaumont Leys School (fig. 5). From there it continues to Heacham Drive where it crosses the road and continues along the ends of the gardens of the houses on the northern side. The original bank and ditch is clearly visible behind the wooden fence in Lomond Close (fig. 6). 'Dalesike' is the very deep and now tree-covered ditch which once drained eastwards from Beaumont Leys and which separates the former close known as Calverhay from the south-east corner of what is now Beaumont Walk (figs. 5–9). Near this corner 'the path from Cropston' is that line clearly marked on the first edition of the Six Inch Ordnance Survey Map of 1886.

In the area of the Stocking Closes, the de Montfort boundary has left only an echo in the modern street pattern and becomes difficult to trace in the housing estate to the northeast. 'Sterkeshull' is clearly Stocking Hill and 'the Oldfeld' refers to the western-most of the open fields of Birstall (figs. 4 and 5). Thereafter, the de Montfort line moves southwards along the edge of the western-most field of Belgrave (the parish was not enclosed until 1654), the position of which is discussed below.

The total area mentioned in the grant is 320 acres and this may well be an approximation. However, one sees the area as forming a huge sweep of land granted to accommodate the abbey's need to expand but at the same time to disrupt, as little as possible, the expanse of woodland identified above as the later Beaumont Leys. We may also infer that 'Sterkeshull' was already an established Stocking, although actual details are lacking.

A reading of the entry of de Montfort's grant suggests that 'Cloyhegges' [Clay Hedges] lay within the area of the grant or at least adjacent to it. However, the abbey's late fifteenth-century 'novum Rentale', 'compiled and written' by William Charyte, mentions 'Clay Hedges under Anstey' and describes it thus:

> We have in that place [Anstey] an assart called Clay Egges, Litel Stocking, otherwise Otylsyke which was bought of Simon de Montfort with woods growing on it . . . lying outside the western part of the manor of Bealmont [Beaumont] and is attached to the chief fishpond of Bealmont . . .[38]

It seems that Clay Hedges and 'Litel Stocking' may be one and the same. If, however, they were two separate areas, they lay near to each other and near to 'Otylsyke', which again may even have been an alternative name for 'Litel Stocking'. At least Clay Hedges lay to the south of Anstey and well over a mile from the abbey's northern border.

The mention of 'Litel Stocking' at Anstey is important because it establishes that the abbey had a second holding called 'Stocking'. Hilton confuses the two when referring to the breaking down of the abbey's gallows by rioters in 1337. There is only one 'Stocking Farm' on the Ordnance Survey Six Inch map to which he refers and that is at Belgrave.[39] In addition, the names 'Stockingford' and 'Stockingforth' also mentioned in the 'novum Rentale' do not refer to places in Leicestershire, but to Leicester abbey's holdings near Nuneaton in Warwickshire.[40]

De Monfort's 'grant' had in reality been a sale and the transfer from earl to abbey was meant to be permanent. The land concerned was to be fenced and managed by the monks to their best

38. Bodl. Laud misc. 625, f. 199v.
39. Hilton, *Some Leicestershire estates*, 60.

40. S. J. Wager, *Woods, wolds and groves: the woodland of medieval Warwickshire*, British Archaeological Reports, British series 269 (Oxford 1998), 230.

Fig. 6. A view along Lomond Crescent looking north. Behind the wooden fence (left) which screens the ends of the gardens of Heacham Drive lie the remains of the bank and ditch sanctioned in 1352 by the duke of Lancaster. It was constructed along the line of the de Montfort grant of 1239 x 1240

Fig. 7. Beaumont Leys Road and the eastern end of Beaumont Walk looking north. In the foreground, the modern path leads around part of a former small enclosure called Calverhey which is first recorded in 1477. On the left of the path in the distance is the land and ditch (hidden by trees) referred to as 'Dalesike' in the de Montfort grant of land to the abbey in 1239 x 1240

Fig. 8. Churchward Avenue looking south. Beneath the tangled vegetation marking the ends of the gardens (left) of houses in a section of Beaumont Leys Lane lies a very substantial bank and ditch (see fig. 9). This marked a section of the western boundary of the abbot's holding known as Batts Close which adjoined his Stocking Wood

Fig. 9. Section of the bank (left) and ditch in Churchward Avenue

interest and profit. This arrangement, where land was sought for more or less unrestricted development, was typical of the activities of Augustinian monasteries elsewhere in Britain.[41] The only reservation was that de Montfort reserved the right to enter the property to chase deer. A century was to pass before a bank and ditch could be established along the boundary.

The boundary at Stocking Hill

It is necessary to account for the origins of the abbey's lands in the area of Stocking Hill, in the approximate centre of which is now a modern Community centre. The area has already been noted as one of steep, clay-covered slopes that are partly north-facing and exposed to the winds. At the time of Domesday Book, it was the location of the woodlands of Belgrave and Birstall and part of that of Thurcaston, and its resources of wood and grazing were shared by the local communities. The grant by de Montfort of at least part of the area may well have cut across these activities although there is no direct evidence for this. The abbey received other gifts of land in the area, notably from members of the prolific Belgrave family. Among these was one from Richard Belgrave who gave, 'all his waste land lying between the wood called Brokkytt [a brockett: a two year old male red deer] and his own grounds near that wood'.[42] The purpose was to allow free passage for the abbey's servants whenever the hedges or ditches around their closes might need repair. Again, the abbey received a similar grant enabling them to make a ditch and a hedge between Belgrave's land (not specified) and the abbey's wood (not named) in order to provide freedom of passage for both parties.[43] It is difficult to date the various gifts in the 'novum Rentale' but they probably belong to the period 1250–1350. Thus it would appear that the abbot was formalising and consolidating his boundaries at a time when the demand for land for grazing and tillage was growing and when 'waste' land was being encroached upon.

This view of the landscape under pressure from an expanding agricultural economy is supported by an extraordinary event in 1337 as reported by Henry Knighton. One night the brothers John and Steven Lawrence of Belgrave, together with a group of villagers, riotously threw down the gallows of the abbot in a corner of the field called Stocking, and pulled up stakes and fences which the abbot had erected there. To hammer home their message of grievance, they dug trenches over the Fosseway and blocked the bridge over the River Soar (fig. 5). This proved to be, 'to the great grievance of the convent' because it prevented servants of the abbey from bringing supplies from the demesne lands and elsewhere from the south of Leicester.[44] One suspects that the men of Belgrave had been quietly making encroachments on to the waste land of the Abbey and the abbot had decided to call a halt to their activities. It is probable that the precise boundary of the open field of Belgrave, shown on the William Senior Map, was finally determined as a result of this incident.

The William Senior Map produces three other indications regarding access to the Stocking Wood and Closes. The smallest of these is called 'Barley hill', from which extends a tongue of land, indicating provision for ingress and egress for stock to and from the field of Birstall. The long, narrow nature of Batts Close west of 'the Abbates' Woode at Stockinges' suggests it was laid out as an access, particularly because it was adjoined by the former tiny close called Calverhey, the position of which is indicated on figs. 5, 7 and 8. Finally, the road known as Stoney Lane, separating 'Great

41. M. Aston, *Monasteries in the landscape* (Stroud 2000), 133.
42. Nichols, *Leicester*, iii, 173 and appendix, p. 11.
43. Ibid.

44. G. H. Martin, ed. *Knighton's Chronicle 1337–96* (Oxford 1995), 155–7.

Stockins' and 'Lowe Parke' and gated at both ends, linked Beaumont Leys with the field of Belgrave.[45] All three closes: Batts Close, Calverhay and Stoney Lane now form just one length of the modern and very busy Beaumont Leys Lane.

Communications

Long before the abbey's foundation, the dominant influence on communications north of Leicester was the River Soar and its flood plain. On the eastern bank was the town, defined by the outline of its Roman walls and once a major centre along the Roman Fosseway from Exeter to Lincoln. Long-distance travellers along this road often wished to avoid the town with its narrow streets, the restricted access of the town's gate and the tolls for crossing the bridges. The alternative route left the Roman Fosseway at its junction with the modern Imperial Avenue and followed a line that became known as the 'medieval Fosse' or 'post-Roman Fosse' (figs. 4 and 5).[46] This is now the line of the present Fosse Road South, Central and North and Blackbird Road. Having bypassed the town, travellers drew close to the abbey precincts. At the place where the present Parker Drive strikes off in a north-westerly direction, the original line of the medieval Fosse continued in a north-easterly direction to join the modern Abbey Lane in the general area of Welbeck Avenue. This extension of Blackbird Road is now lost. It is marked on Prior's map of 1777 but does not appear on Fowler's map of 1828 (fig. 1).[47] The present sharp turn eastwards in Blackbird Road seems to have originated as a direct route for travellers wishing to reach the abbey's gates.

Communication between town and abbey was chiefly by means of the North Gate and North Bridge. Before the abbey's foundation, the road known today as Abbey Gate, partly along the line of the present St Margaret's Way, was no more than a track. It wound its way along the edge of the flood plain where it gave access to the meadows. With the rise of the abbey and the development of its home demesne, this track grew to become an important routeway.

Travellers leaving the town via the North Bridge were able to avoid the abbey precinct by following Woodgate, crossing the medieval Fosse and continuing along the Groby Road. This was one of only two pre-Conquest routes from the town which enabled travellers heading to the north-west to avoid areas of marshy or rising ground. This road followed very closely the western edge of Pinders Close. The rising land here produced the two abrupt changes in direction. One also suspects that this alignment was connected with the same action that produced the block of land containing Freake's Ground and Newfoundpool, mentioned above.

The other route northwards from Leicester was the Anstey Lane which led directly to that village and beyond to Charnwood Forest. Its course followed a shallow valley between the wooded uplands of Beaumont Leys to the north-east and Gilroes and Leicester Frith to the south-west. Along one section of its course it was, as now, noticeably wide and it can be seen as a drove road for stock being moved in and out of Leicester. At its eastern end it met the medieval Fosse, whence the route to the town was via Woodgate.

The abbot's park

It was by no means unusual for a religious house in Leicestershire to manage part of its estate as a

45. ROLLR 28D64/12 (Beaumont Leys Papers, Bargain and Sale 1568, Edward Lord Hastings to Roger Wigston).
46. VCH Leics. iii, 72.
47. J. D. Welding, ed. Leicestershire in 1777: an edition of John

Prior's Map of Leicestershire, Leicestershire Libraries and Information Service (Leicester 1984), 38; Fowler's 'Plan of Leicester showing the limits of the borough (1828)' in T. Fielding Johnson, Glimpses of ancient Leicester (Leicester 1906).

deer park. The abbey's park marked on the William Senior Map was the antithesis of the late Victorian creation known today as Abbey Park. The early park was an enclosure where deer were raised and hunted by a select group of the abbot's social equals and where controlled grazing by domestic stock and other carefully regulated profit-making activities took place.

The early abbots held a park in the Frith in 1297 but little is known about it.[48] Its relationship with the New Park created by Henry VIII, now the site of the New Parks housing estate, will be examined elsewhere. However, it is the abbot's other park – the 'Lowe Parke' and 'High Parke' shown on the William Senior Map (colour plate B and fig. 4) – which concerns us here. It was established in 1352 when Henry, duke of Lancaster, gave the abbot permission to empark the land and wood which Simon de Montfort had sold the abbey a century earlier. In return, the abbot gave up his claim to receive wood from the duke's forest (or chace) of Leicester.[49] The creation of the park was unusual in that it took place only four years or so after the arrival of the Black Death in the county and at a time when large numbers of parks were falling into decay and being abandoned. With labour in short supply, the ditching and fencing of the 180 acres concerned represented a considerable effort and outlay. In 1516 the abbot enlarged his park by withdrawing 20 acres from tillage.[50] This land was presumably the area known as Barley Close. The move did not involve any of the depopulation seen when the abbey had enclosed their lordship of Ingarsby in 1469 and where the village had been abandoned.[51]

Initially the park was stocked with deer from the duke of Lancaster's woodlands, probably that part from which the abbot had given up his right to take wood. Knighton relates that the first move was to pull down the fences separating the two properties. Deer were then enticed across the road from forest to park by the laying down of hay and oats. Additional deer were caught in nets by the foresters and forcibly moved.[52] The transfer appears to have taken place at a point along the Anstey Lane in the region of the southern part of the close called Warldsend (now Roydene Crescent) and the western edge of Brick Close (fig. 5). One sees the landscape of the abbot's park as one of predominantly open grassland, with some woodpasture and a few smaller fenced and carefully managed woodlands. Deer were still present at the Dissolution and were last recorded in Hatton's grant of 1572.

The land use of the demesne estate

Religious considerations apart, a monastery was at heart a commercial enterprise, the success of which at any one time depended upon the motivation, business skills and control of the chief executive, the abbot. The commercial life of a wealthy abbey such as St Mary de Pratis generated a considerable volume of records and it is unfortunate that so little of the early year-to-year accounts have survived. Also, there are no details for the use of specific closes before the Dissolution. At that time, and of the 496½ acres covering the Cave grant, only 56 were arable and these occupied two closes. A further ten closes accounted for 157½ acres of pasture and there were 103 acres of meadow. In addition there were the 180 acres of pasture (and probably woodland) within the park.[53] Northampton's grant of 1550 repeats these details and mentions 'a lodge' within

48. Nichols, *Leicester* iv, 763.

49. Ibid. 462.

50. W. G. D. Fletcher, 'On the efforts made to convert arable land into pasture in Leicestershire in the fifteenth and sixteenth centuries', *TLAAS* 8 (1899), 308–13 at 312.

51. Hoskins, 'Seven deserted villages', 46.

52. Martin, *Knighton's Chronicle*, 121.

53. Hilton, *Some Leicestershire estates*, 55.

Fig. 10. Leicester Abbey from the north (Throsby, *History and Antiquities*, opposite p. 281, detail). This view of haymaking in 1790 was drawn from a point in either Brick Close or Low Park. It looks towards the then still substantial remains of Cavendish House with the spires of Leicester beyond

the park. Since the Stocking closes were not included in either grant there is no positive mention of woodland.

The William Senior Leicester Abbey Map

It is fortunate that, accompanying the list of closes and their acreages on the William Senior map, are some valuable annotations by the surveyor. Fowkes and Potter have quite reasonably interpreted these as meaning the following: excellent meadows; good meadow; excellent pasture; best pasture; good pasture; good arable.[54] It is debatable whether these descriptions apply to the land's potential rather than its actual use at the time of the survey, but the latter appears to be much more likely. If we discount the abbey precinct of 29 acres and the 40 acres of detached meadow called 'Burstal More', but include all the Stocking Closes, we arrive at a figure of 789 acres. Of these $40\frac{1}{2}$ (5%) were arable; 617 acres (to include the whole of the park) (77%) were pasture; 82 acres (10%) were meadow and $63\frac{1}{2}$ acres (8%) were wood. This last figure takes no account of trees that grew in Ash Close and those which were present in the park.

The picture emerges of a home demesne rich in meadow along the River Soar, with large areas of pasture occupying the adjacent flat and slightly raised river gravel terraces (fig. 10), then rising to the clay uplands as far as the abbey's border with Beaumont Leys. The 'arable' of the four small closes: Shield Close (11 acres); the Copie (5 acres); Barley Hill (5 acres) and Barley Close ($13\frac{1}{2}$ acres) cannot be explained in terms of gross geology. They must have occupied areas of more easily worked soils. The whole situation accords well with the description of an anonymous writer who, in the reign of Henry VIII, remarks on:

54. Fowkes and Potter, ed. *William Senior's survey*, 163.

good battyll [rich and productive] and fruitful pastures, and wood there with
the park wherein is deer parcel of the demesne within xl perches of the site [of
the abbey precinct] part high and champion [open] ground very comodyouse
and parkly, nigh adjoining to the great woods and pasture called the Frith and
Beaumont Leys . . .[55]

Ogilvy on his road map of 1698 records 'pasture' in the area of the park which, by that time, had
been disparked.[56] An engraving entitled, 'The South Prospect of Leicester' drawn by the Buck
Brothers and dated 1743, presents a convincing panorama of the scene. In particular it shows the
ruins of Cavendish House with the great closes of pasture rising to the high land of Beaumont Leys
in the north-west and Stocking Wood to the north.[57]

Other aspects of the landscape

Although the abbey was endowed with 'fruitful pastures' there is no direct indication, apart from
the mention of deer, as to how these were grazed. Sheep seem to have been the most likely domestic stock, but Leicester Abbey did not possess anything like the numbers spread across the great
sheep ranches of the abbeys in the north of England. Hilton suggests St Mary de Pratis had flocks
totalling about 6000 in 1477 but adds that perhaps half of these were not on the abbey's demesne
lands.[58] The number on the abbey's home demesne is not known but, in view of the extensive

Fig. 11. An aerial view of the site of the former abbey and the modern Abbey Park looking north, taken in 1991. The
boundaries of the William Senior map have been superimposed to show their approximate positions

55. J. Burtt, 'Contributions to the history of Leicester Abbey',
TLAHS 4 (1878), 32–6 at 33.

56. J. Ogilvy, *Britannia, or an illustration of the kingdom of
England and dominium of Wales* (London 1675), sheet 40.

57. S. and N. Buck, 'The south prospect of Leicester', published
according to Act of Parliament, March 1745.

58. Hilton, *Some Leicestershire estates*, 67–8.

pastures, one suspects it was considerable. Cattle and horses too, would have been present but there is no mention of rabbits and none of a rabbit warren.

Windmills appear to have been absent from the estate. There is no record of one in the 'novum Rentale' or on the William Senior Map. The Buck brothers' engraving shows one which may have stood in Brick Close. Since most grain came from the Abbey's other lands either the community used their water mill adjacent to the precinct, or the grain was delivered as bags of flour. There are no records of mineral resources except perhaps of clay in Brick Close. There were no deposits of iron or any other metals and no mention of forges. It is even not certain where the stone for the monastic buildings was quarried. Any coal used originated in the coal mines at Oakthorpe which the abbey owned and leased out.[59] Fishponds in the southern enclosure of the abbey, as suggested on the William Senior Map, have been confirmed by recent geophysical survey; presumably the community's needs were supplemented by the River Soar which contained 'fish of all kinds'.[60] Finally, the sources of water for the abbey remain obscure as there seems to have been few streams or wells.[61] The discovery from recent excavations of what appear to have been drains may well provide pointers to further investigation.

Until well into the nineteenth century the landscape of the former abbey demesne retained much of the rural and timeless character of its earlier days. An account of the area's transformation under a sea of houses and industrial areas belongs elsewhere (fig. 11). The development of the demesne estate has also something to tell us about the much earlier and wider landscape on to which it was imposed and raises questions, the answers to which offer most interesting lines of research.

59. *Calendar of Patent Rolls, 1572–75*, 451.
60. Burtt, 'Contributions to the history', 33; Buckley et al., 'Archaeology of Leicester Abbey', above p. 21.
61. Ordnance Survey 25 Inch Map (1887), sheets 31/6 and 31/10.

Leicester Abbey after the Dissolution

Richard Buckley
with Steve Jones, Paul Courtney and David Smith

Leicester Abbey was surrendered to the king by its last abbot, John Bourchier, on 28 August 1538; Dr Francis Cave, the commissioner who negotiated its surrender, became interim custodian of the site. His role, although not specifically recorded, was presumably to wind up the financial affairs of the abbey and make arrangements to ensure that the principal monastic buildings were rendered uninhabitable to remove any possibility of the return of the community and the resumption of religious life.[1] When Cave wrote to Thomas Cromwell to report on progress he noted that, in addition to the debt owed to the king, the abbey was left with a debt of £411 10s 0d.[2] He advised that this would be settled by the sale of the church bells and various items from the church and monastic buildings, and provided details of amounts obtained from the sale of these goods and added:

> The church and house remeyneth as yet undefacede, and in the church be many things to be made sale of; for the wych yt may plese your lorshippe to let me knawe yowre pleysure, as well for the further sale to be made, as for the defacinge of the chirche and other superfluous byldinges wiche be abowt the monastery. A hundrithe marks yerly will not susteyne the charges in reparying this house yt all byldinges be lette stande, as yowr lorshippe shall knowe more herafter.[3]

Commissioners were normally instructed to 'pull down to the ground all the walls of the churches, steeples, cloisters, fraters, dorters, chapter houses, with all other houses, saving them that may be necessary for the farmer' (the interim custodian).[4] In fact, destruction was not always thorough because demolition costs were prohibitive; other factors, such as the demand for building stone, must have influenced the pace of the work.[5] At the very least, prior to the sale of a site, the lead was normally removed from the roofs of the principal buildings and melted down for dispatch to the

Acknowledgments: This article is based on survey and excavation by University of Leicester Archaeological Services between 1997 and 2005, directed by the author and supervised by Neil Finn, Michael Derrick, James Meek and Steve Jones. The results of the survey and each excavation season are presented in a series of unpublished reports deposited with the Leicester City Sites and Monuments Record: Buckley (1997), Buckley and Derrick (2001), Meek and Buckley (2002) and Jones and Buckley (2004). I am especially grateful to all students, staff and volunteers who were involved with the fieldwork and to Marilyn Palmer, Neil Christie, James Meek, Steve Jones, Peter Liddle and Neil Finn for their helpful suggestions for improvements to the text, and to Matt Beamish for assistance with illustrations.

1. J. P. Greene, *Medieval monasteries* (Leicester, London and New York 1992), 183.

2. J. Nichols, *The history and antiquities of the county of Leicester*, 4 vols. in 8 (London 1795–1815), i pt. 2, 274; L. Fox, *Leicester Abbey: history and description* (Leicester 1938, 2nd edn. 1949), 12.

3. Nichols, *Leicester*, i pt. 2, 274; Fox, *Leicester Abbey*, 12.

4. C. Platt, *The abbeys and priories of medieval England* (London 1984), 229.

5. Greene, *Medieval monasteries*, 183.

Crown, along with the bell metal. On 24 March 1539, almost seven months after the surrender, Cave obtained a 21-year lease of the site for the annual sum of £41 15s 4d.[6] It has been noted elsewhere that most monastic sites were sold at the market rate or leased, usually for 21 years, bringing much needed funds into the Exchequer and satisfying the considerable demand from the Tudor gentry for land acquisition.[7] Although it is difficult to be sure of Cave's motives in leasing the site, he probably saw the sale of the building materials as a potentially lucrative source of income. Certainly there is no evidence that he converted any of the buildings into a gentleman's residence at the heart of an agricultural estate, or that he ever lived here, as his seat is known to have been at Baggrave, an abbey estate granted to him by Henry VIII in 1543.[8]

James Thompson, the nineteenth-century historian, suggested that the abbey buildings fell into decay some 30 years after the Dissolution, but it is much more likely that the demolition of some of the conventual buildings proceeded very quickly under Cave's stewardship.[9] Unlike other monastic sites, such as the abbeys of Thorney and Ramsey, where stone was reused for construction works at specific buildings such as Cambridge colleges, there is no evidence in the documentary sources of the final destination of the materials from Leicester. They may have been re-used on site for new building projects during Cave's time or some may have found their way to Baggrave; W. K. Bedingfield (the 1920s excavator of Leicester Abbey), argued that parts of the hall there, 'have the appearance of being constructed out of the materials derived from the abbey'.[10]

In 1551 the abbey was granted to William Parr, Marquess of Northampton, brother of Catherine Parr, Henry VIII's queen, and a prominent member of court, having been made Baron Parr in 1539 and Earl of Essex in 1543.[11] He retained influence during the reign of Edward VI and was a supporter of Lady Jane Grey and later of Elizabeth I.[12] The particulars of the sale survive and are of considerable importance in providing details both of Cave's progress with the destruction of the monastic buildings and of the character and extent of lands within and surrounding the precinct.[13] The lands are listed in the grant by name with approximate areas; some fields, such as Meryvale Close, Asheclose Meadow and Harpe Orchard, can be identified on the William Senior map prepared for William Cavendish in 1613 when he acquired the estate (colour plate B). The lands included meadows, pasture, orchards and arable land; specifically excluded from the grant were all great trees and woods and, 'does and deer being and herafter happening to be in the park aforesaid'. Within the precinct, much of value remained:

> The farm of the house and scite of the same late Monastery of Leicester, together with all houses, edifices, barns, stables, dovecotes, yards, orchards, gardens, lands and soil within the scite and precincts of the said monastery. And one water-mill with the appurtenances to the said late Monastery adjacent . . . and also all such and such kind of houses and edifces within the scite of the said late Monastery which the Lord the King has there ordered to be pulled down and taken away.

6. W. K. Bedingfield, 'Presidential address 1930–31', *Transactions of the Leicester Literary and Philosophical Society* 32 (1931), 5–24 at 14.

7. Greene, *Medieval monasteries*, 187.

8. *TLAAS* 6 (1888) 90–98 at 97–8; Nichols, *Leicester*, iii pt. 1, 288.

9. J. Thompson, *Leicester Abbey: an historical paper* (1855), 16 (ROLLR L726).

10. Bedingfield, 'Presidential address 1930–31', 14.

11. Nichols, *Leicester*, i pt. 2, 287.

12. *ODNB* s.n. 'Parr, William, marquess of Northampton (1513–1571)'.

13. Augmentation Office, Particulars for Grants. William Marquess of Northampton 4 Edw VI, Section 3; W. D. G. Fletcher, 'Some unpublished documents relating to Leicestershire, preserved in the Public Record Office', *Associated Architectural Societies Reports and Papers* 23.1 (1895), 213–52 at 240–2.

This suggests that, apart from those purely practical and non-religious buildings suitable for retention as part of the post-Dissolution estate, a number of other structures, perhaps relating to the claustral ranges, still survived. The lack of a specific mention of the church would seem to indicate that it had already gone by this time, while a reference to lead-pigs on the site shows that Cave had made considerable progress with stripping the roofs of the monastic buildings, although much remained to be done:

> There is remaining w[th]in the p'cincte of the said late Monasterie in the Custode
> of the said Fr[a]unc' Cave ferm' there in Leade Molten in Sowes (besid iiij[xx]vij
> foders of lead remaininge opon Howses w[th]in the said Scite as yet not taken
> down and moulten)[14]

The reference to the lead 'sowes' (pigs) remaining within the precinct is of considerable interest as these should have been stamped with the King's mark and delivered to the Crown in advance of the sale or lease of the site. Lead from monastic sites did not always reach its required destination, as shown by the discovery of four lead ingots marked with the Tudor rose at Rievaulx (Yorks.) and another from the Augustinian abbey at Kenilworth (Warwicks.).[15] The particulars of sale conjure up a picture of a site in turmoil, with buildings partially demolished and valuable materials lying around, indicating that there was not a smooth and rapid transition to a secular estate with landscaped gardens and a mansion house. As discussed above, Cave probably lived at Baggrave and perhaps expended his energies in improving and extending the house there, rather than adapting the remains of buildings at the abbey for residential accommodation. He probably fulfilled the minimum requirements of the Crown, to demolish or render uninhabitable, the principal monastic buildings (church, chapter house, dormitory and refectory) thereby preventing the return of the community. The process of demolition must have been a considerable financial burden so, perhaps for financial reasons, most of the other buildings remained largely intact and there was still much clearance to be undertaken. It has been noted elsewhere that few monastic sites saw any significant building activity in the twenty years following their dissolution; perhaps in a climate of religious turmoil, it was unwise to expend significant capital sums on property which, theoretically at least, could have been reinstated to its former purpose at the whim of the monarch.[16] Former monastic buildings instead provided a convenient source of materials for supply to building projects elsewhere, although this process perhaps did not begin in earnest at Leicester Abbey until the site was in the possession of Henry Hastings later in the sixteenth century.

It is unlikely that William Parr had much impact on the site; in 1553 he was attainted by Mary I, with the loss of all of his titles and the estate was confiscated by the Crown and granted to the catholic Sir Edward Hastings, later Lord Loughborough.[17] In 1561, after Elizabeth's accession, Hastings was imprisoned for hearing mass and the abbey was granted to his nephew Henry Hastings, third earl of Huntingdon, who sold it back to his uncle later the same year.[18] In 1572, Hastings of Loughborough returned the abbey lands to the queen, who granted them to Sir Christopher Hatton the same year.[19] The grant to Hatton appears to have been preparatory to a

---

14. 1 Foder = 1912 cwt, almost 1 tonne; Greene, *Medieval monasteries*, 185.

15. Ibid.

16. M. Airs, *The Tudor and Jacobean country house: a building history* (Stroud 1995), 29.

17. *ODNB s.n.* 'Hastings, Edward, Baron Hastings of Lough-borough (1512 x 15?–1572)'; P. Courtney, 'Leicester Abbey: historical background' in 'Abbey Park, Leicester: an archaeological desk-based assessment and survey', ed. R. Buckley, unpubl. ULAS report 97/12 (1997), 13–25.

18. VCH *Leics.* iv, 451.

19. Ibid.

new grant to Henry Earl of Huntingdon, who repurchased the property in 1572 for £1,149 13s. 2d.[20] He is said by Nichols to have built a 'fair house' on the site out of the old materials, and stayed at the abbey in 1579–80.[21] Henry sold Leicester Abbey in 1580 to his younger brother, Sir Edward Hastings who appears to have lived there during the later part of his life, probably in the modified and enlarged monastic gatehouse (see below, 104), where he could supervise the affairs of the town on behalf of his brother, frequently acting for him in the 1580s and 90s.[22] In 1590, Lord's Place, another property owned by Henry earl of Huntingdon, also passed to Sir Edward.[23]

Sir Edward Hastings died in 1603 and his son, Henry, appears to have lived at Leicester Abbey from at least 1605, probably until its sale in 1613 to William Cavendish, first Earl of Devonshire, son of Sir William Cavendish and his third wife, Elizabeth Hardwick (afterwards the Countess of Shrewsbury).[24] At this time, the earl was actively expanding his Derbyshire-centred estates, and probably arranged for Leicester Abbey to be surveyed by William Senior shortly after purchase (colour plate B). In 1619 his wife Elizabeth founded a charity to feed the poor at the abbey gates.[25] In 1626, William was succeeded by his son, the second earl William, a leading figure at court and intimate friend of James I, who had knighted him in 1609.[26] The second earl had married Christian (or Christiana) Bruce in 1612, daughter of the first Lord Kinloss; their lavish lifestyle led to financial problems in his last years and he died in 1628 leaving his wife as ward of his children and manager of the family estates on behalf of their son William, the underage third earl. The occasional visits of the first three earls of Devonshire to Leicester is recorded in various sources especially those relating to expenditure on the ringing of bells at St Martin's church.[27]

Household books for the dowager countess Christian for 1635–7 demonstrate that she visited Cavendish House en route from Derbyshire to London and Surrey in April and October 1635.[28] She stayed longer from 18 February to 20 July 1637 when she entertained several relatives. The borough spent £3 13s 11d on a present of sack and claret for the third earl who came to the abbey on 13 May 1637 during this residence. It also paid 5s to the countess' surveyor for surveying the mayor's parlour at the town hall (now the Guildhall).[29] This suggests that building work was being undertaken at the abbey in 1636–7. A case before the justices in 1632 implies that the countess made use of St Martin's church during her sojourns, a suggestion confirmed by the purchase of a mat for her seat there in 1641.[30] The church of St Martin's was closely linked to the borough's ruling elite. Christian may have made more use of Cavendish House when her son came of age; in 1645 Richard Symonds described it as having been her chief residence.[31]

20. C. Cross, *The puritan earl: the life of Henry Hastings, third earl of Huntingdon 1536–1595* (London 1966) 312, 340.

21. Nichols, *Leicester*, i pt. 2, 287; although this is more likely to be a misreading of the inscription on the 1730 Buck brothers engraving of the 'South view of Leicester Abby', which uses a similar phrase in relation to William Cavendish who purchased the property in 1613; M. Bateson, ed. *Records of the Borough of Leicester*, 4 vols (London 1899–1923), iii, 184 (hereafter *RBL*).

22. Nichols, *Leicester*, i pt. 2, 287; Cross, *The puritan earl*, 117; eadem, 'Dynastic politics: the local and national importance of the Hastings family in the sixteenth century' in *The aristocratic estate: the Hastings in Leicestershire and south Derbyshire*, ed. M. Palmer (Loughborough 1982), 16–34 at 30. See also *ODNB*, *s.n.* 'Hastings, Henry, third earl of Huntingdon (1536?–1595)'.

23. TNA C54/1361; Cross, *The puritan earl*, 68.

24. *ODNB s.n.* 'Cavendish, William, first earl of Devonshire (1551–1626)'; *s.n.* 'Cavendish, Sir William (1508–1557); *s.n.* 'Hard-

wick, Elizabeth, countess of Shrewsbury (1527?–1608)' ; P. Courtney, 'Lord's Place, Leicester: an urban aristocratic house of the sixteenth century', *TLAHS* 74 (2000), 37–58 at 42; *RBL* iv, 5, 37 and 103, and VCH *Leics.* iv, 452.

25. *RBL* iv, 187.

26. *ODNB s.n.* 'Cavendish, William, second earl of Devonshire (1590–1628)'.

27. T. North, ed. *Accounts of the churchwardens of St Martin's 1489–1844* (Leicester 1884) 159, 166, 170, 173; *RBL* iv, 292–3; Derby Record Office D258/20/2/7. On Christian see *ODNB s.n.* 'Cavendish, Christian, countess of Devonshire (1595–1675)'.

28. Nichols, *Leicester*, i pt. 2, 290–2.

29. *RBL* iv, 292–3.

30. *RBL* iv, 267; Nichols, *Leicester*, i pt. 2, 578.

31. E. Long, ed. *Diary of the marches of the royal army during the Great Civil War kept by Richard Symonds*, Camden Society 74 (London 1859), 184.

From monastic site to secular estate

There is a presumption, based entirely on Senior's survey of 1613 (colour plate B; above p. 14, fig. 8), that a mansion house was established at the abbey during the last quarter of the sixteenth century and that the grounds were laid out as gardens. His survey shows a thriving minor estate with a mansion (now known to incorporate the medieval monastic gatehouse), a 'dovecote garden', an 'apricocks garden', monastic barns and a 'hog yard'. On the site of the claustral ranges are a number of other buildings, some with pitched roofs, perhaps intact, and others are labelled as 'Ruynes'. A domed structure surmounted by a cross is also depicted which could be a spring or conduit house, again surviving from the medieval period. In the southern part of the precinct are a series of fishponds – almost certainly medieval – whilst outside the precinct wall, on the east bank of the river, is a 'hopyard'. All this suggests that Cavendish had purchased from the Hastings family an established estate with extensive gardens, agriculturally productive land, fishponds and a mansion house, admittedly of comparatively modest proportions.

In the period following the Dissolution, buildings were selected for re-use as part of the new estate primarily for their suitability for new secular purposes. At the majority of monastic sites we might expect that the choice was narrowed down to those buildings which were essentially secular or at least utilitarian in character, such as ancillary buildings (bake-house, brew-house stables, etc.) or buildings such as the abbot's lodgings or guest accommodation which had a degree of refinement making them suitable for conversion into residential accommodation at the centre of a new estate. This is, however, an oversimplification as on many sites significant claustral buildings survived and in some cases these formed the nucleus of a post-suppression mansion.[32] This was certainly so at some local sites, such as Grace Dieu (Leics.) which became the Beaumonts' mansion after the Dissolution and where the monastic buildings remained substantially complete in the early seventeenth century.[33] Similarly, at Laude Abbey (Leics.), parts of the church, dormitory, and refectory ranges were re-used in the later mansion.[34] At Leicester, the 1538/9 Crown Commissioners' Survey makes it clear that the medieval gatehouse was not simply a utilitarian structure controlling access into the abbey; it implies that the building had comparatively comfortable accommodation, with heated rooms, glazed windows and, perhaps, its own kitchen. It is entirely possible that these apartments had been created not long before the Dissolution, perhaps as the residence of the abbot or other senior obedientiary, rendering them eminently suitable for conversion to secular accommodation.

At Leicester, architectural aesthetics may have played a part in decisions about what to preserve, with some buildings perhaps not being held in particular regard. This is suggested by a comment in the Commissioners' Survey that the refectory would 'be muche more comodyouse yf yt werr performed after an uniforme all with stone to the prospecte and view of the same'.[35] An additional overriding concern undoubtedly was the need to render certain of the monastic buildings unusable, to guard against the return of the former community at a later date.

Hence, the precinct walls of the abbey remained, together with the outer gateway in the north wall and a number of buildings on the western side of the site, such as the monastic barns. Archaeological, documentary and pictorial evidence also indicates that other buildings were

32. G. Coppack, *Abbeys and priories* (London 1990), 136–42.

33. P. Liddle, 'The abbeys and priories of Leicestershire and Rutland', *TLAHS* 69 (1995), 1–21 at 14.

34. R. T. Schadla-Hall, A. Green and P. Liddle, 'Launde Abbey'

in *Leicestershire and Rutland, report and proceedings of the 149th summer meeting of the Royal Archaeological Institute*, ed. B. Dix (2003), 234–71 at 268.

35. Fox, *Leicester Abbey*, 14: also above p. 67.

Fig. 1. North façade of Cavendish house from the south .

retained, including the inner gatehouse, the water mill and some structures within and adjacent to the claustral ranges. Some at least of these may be those mentioned in the 1551 grant to Parr. In addition, engravings by Pridden from the late eighteenth century, published by Nichols, indicate the survival of possible medieval two-storey structures abutting the south wall of the north precinct (see above fig. 12, p. 20).

Archaeology, so far, has been unable to add much to our knowledge of the processes of demolition since the excavators of 1929–32 largely ignored evidence of destruction being more concerned with tracing the plans of the principal buildings. Hence most of the destruction deposits were simply removed, few finds retained, and many wall lines were 'chased', destroying robber trenches and any associated dating evidence. Recent excavations have suggested that important evidence for post-Dissolution activity does still survive on the site. In 2002 the remains of a circular brick oven, possibly later sixteenth century in date, were identified within the monastic kitchen, indicating that the building probably survived the Dissolution (above, p. 54). Elsewhere, unexcavated robber trenches and demolition deposits have been identified, unfortunately without clear dating evidence.[36]

It is therefore possible to argue that by the later part of the sixteenth century most of the claustral buildings had been demolished and their materials dispersed. Some buildings with an economic function were retained, and the medieval gatehouse (later known as Cavendish House) was enlarged to create a mansion at the heart of the estate. Although it is possible to identify people linked to Leicester Abbey after the Dissolution, the pattern of occupation and reuse of the site is far

36. R. Buckley et al., 'The archaeology of Leicester Abbey', above pp. 1–67.

from certain. It was only one of a series of properties used by both the Hastings and Cavendish families and it is unclear if Sir Edward Hastings of Loughborough or William Parr, the Marquess of Northampton, ever used it as a residence. The earl of Huntingdon is unlikely to have used it as he owned a more convenient dwelling at Lord's Place in Leicester. It is possible that his brother, Sir Edward Hastings, dwelt there from 1580, perhaps prior to his acquisition of Lord's Place in 1590. The only certain occupant before the Cavendishes was Henry Hastings in the early seventeenth century, but he appears to have sold both the abbey and Lord's Place within a few years. Quite probably Leicester Abbey served as William Cavendish's main residence from 1613–26 but after that date it was a subsidiary residence to the family's main seat at Chatsworth. It was certainly visited by the countess as indicated by her household books for 1635–6, and she seems to have chosen Leicester Abbey as her chief residence after her eldest son came of age, probably in 1638.[37] It is possible also that Elizabeth, the dowager countess of Devonshire (d. 1642), may also have dwelt there at some point, as the hospital and associated charity outside the abbey entrance was named after her.[38]

Cavendish House (fig. 1) was destroyed in the Civil War, probably during one of the two sieges of Leicester in 1645. An itinerary of the king, said to have been compiled by an attendant, states that it was burnt by the Royalists at the time of the first siege.[39] Richard Symonds who was part of the Royalist army at Leicester states that Charles stayed there on the night of the siege until the army marched south on the 4 June.[40] Nichols reconciles these sources by suggesting the house was burnt after Charles left and notes that it was 'said by some' to be the work of an envious Lord Loughborough, Henry Hastings.[41] Nichols may have had in mind the early eighteenth-century 'manuscript history of Leicester' by Rev. Samuel Carte who laid the blame on Hastings, 'afterwards made Lord Loughborough', raiding from Loughborough.[42] Certainly Ralph Josselin noted on 17 September 1645 that of the house, 'nothing standing but ye stone works'.[43]

The meagre sources are not explicit about the date or responsibility for the destruction of Cavendish House. Had its destruction indeed been the work of the Royalists, it was an unusual response to the hospitality of the Countess of Devonshire who was, after all, a supporter of the king. Alternatively, it is possible that the fire had been started accidentally or that it was a deliberate act of arson by the Royalist army fleeing after their defeat at the battle of Naseby.

The Cavendish family remained owners of the abbey until 1733 when it was sold to Sir John Manners, brother of the Duke of Rutland.[44] In the eighteenth century, a number of engravings of the site were prepared: the Buck brothers' 'South View' of Cavendish House in 1730 (fig. 2); the same elevation in 1775 (fig. 3); engravings by Newton in 1787 of the large chimney at Cavendish House; a view south from the outer gateway on what is now Abbey Park road.[45] It is not clear when the name 'Cavendish House' entered general usage since all these engravings are labelled 'Leicester Abbey'. Nichols also published a number of drawings, some probably produced on demand by his son-in-law, the Rev. J. Pridden. By the nineteenth century, the site had passed into the ownership of the earls of Dysart, who sold Abbey Meadows to the Leicester Town Council in 1876 in order

37. See above, note 31; Nichols, *Leicester*, i pt. 2, 288–90.

38. VCH *Leics.* iv, 410.

39. 'Iter Carolinum' in *A collection of scarce and valuable tracts*, ed. J. Somers, 2nd edn. revised and enlarged by W. Scott, 13 vols (London 1809–15), x, 296.

40. Long, ed. *Diary of the marches of the royal army*, 185.

41. Nichols, *Leicester*, i pt. 2, 293.

42. Samuel Carte's 'manuscript history' is unprinted (a version, copied by Thomas Cave, is ROLLR DE5463/38) but was used

by Nichols and Throsby; R. Sweet, 'John Nichols and his circle', *TLAHS* 74 (2000), 1–20.

43. E. Hockliffe, ed. *The diary of the Rev. Ralph Josselin 1616–1683*, Camden Soc. 3rd ser. 15 (London 1908), 28–9.

44. VCH *Leics.* iv, 452.

45. J. Throsby, *The history and antiquities of the ancient town of Leicester* (Leicester 1791), following p. 282, 'Leicester Abbey' and 'West view of Leicester Abbey' by Newton.

Fig. 2. 'The South View of Leicester Abby' by Samuel and Nathaniel Buck (1730)

Fig. 3. J. Throsby, *The history and antiquities of the ancient town of Leicester* (1791), plate following p. 288

that they might proceed with the Leicester Flood Relief scheme which involved widening the river Soar, deepening its bed by 3ft 6ins and raising the land either side by seven feet.[46] The land east of the river was subsequently developed as a public open space, Abbey Park, opened by the Prince

46. T. Williamson, 'The history of Abbey Park' in 'Abbey Park restoration management plan' III, Leicester City Council unpubl. report (Leicester 1997), 1–33 at 5.

Fig. 4. John Flower, 'Leicester Abbey in 1826'

and Princess of Wales in 1882. The site of the abbey itself had remained in the ownership of the earls of Dysart and was used as a market garden from the 1830s, firstly by Thomas Warner and later by James Wright. The site of Cavendish House was illustrated on a number of occasions in the nineteenth century, most notably by John Flower in 1826 (fig. 4), an unnamed artist in about 1830[47] and by Frances Flora Palmer in 1842–3. These show a three-storey farmhouse, perhaps of late eighteenth-century date, constructed within a corner of the ruined south range of the mansion. Photographs of the late nineteenth century show further structures added to the north side of this range and at about the same time, the west range was re-roofed and provided with projecting square bay windows to its western elevation. These habitable parts of the building became known as Abbey House. The Abbey Grounds were given by the earl of Dysart to the City Council in 1925 to be developed as an extension to the existing park. As part of this process, the ruins of Cavendish House were restored by Bedingfield, who may also have been responsible for demolishing the later additions on either side of the ruined façade of the south range.

Identifying the post-Dissolution estate

Having outlined the historical framework for the abbey's demise, subsequent patterns of owner-ship, and the possible extent of the destruction of its principal buildings, we turn next to the supporting archaeological data for the nature of the post-Dissolution estate in the sixteenth and

47. W. Dugdale, *Monasticon Anglicanum. A history of the abbies and other monasteries, hospitals, frieries and cathedral and collegiate churches*, ed. J. Caley, H. Ellis and B. Bandinel, 6 vols in 8 (London 1830), vi.ii, plate following p. 462, 'Leicester Abbey' drawn and engraved by John Coney.

seventeenth centuries. The evidence for the nature and constructional phases of the mansion (now generally known as Cavendish House), which incorporated the earlier monastic gatehouse, derives from a survey of the buildings undertaken in 1997 using eighteenth- and nineteenth-century engravings and from archaeological excavation in 2000–5.[48] The engravings in particular indicate that the fire of 1645 probably gutted the entire mansion and that the shell survived substantially intact until *c.* 1730 (fig. 2 and colour plate c). By 1775, most of the south range, including all surviving remnants of the medieval gatehouse that formed the core of the building, had disappeared. Later in the eighteenth century, parts of the ruined mansion were re-roofed and inhabited again and a small farmhouse (now demolished) was constructed within the ruined south range.

The account that follows represents an initial interpretation of the phasing and dating of the building although it should be noted that at the time of the survey, much of the fabric was obscured by ivy (since partly cleared), precluding detailed investigation of the upstanding fabric. This has caused difficulties in establishing certain key structural relationships, in particular the junction between the out-building adjoining the large double chimney breast in the south west of the building (discussed above, p. 36). Although the combination of limited building survey and trial excavation has enabled the identification of a relative chronology for the development of the post-Dissolution mansion, ascribing definite date ranges to the identified phases remains difficult since there are few closely dateable stylistic features. For this reason it is impossible to link in any definitive way identifiable building campaigns with specific people known to have been associated with the site.

Today, the complex of buildings, now known as Abbey House, consists of the following main elements:

1. A south range, of which only the north wall survives. This range, which incorporated the footprint of the monastic gatehouse, is at the southern end of the halt-way leading from the outer gateway, referred to in the Crown Commissioners' Survey of 1538/9.
2. A west range with cellars, and a possible stair turret, restored in the 1930s.
3. A building at the junction of the west and south ranges, characterised by the large double chimney, thought to be the remnant of a kitchen perhaps medieval and re-used in the post-medieval period.

The main post-Dissolution structural phases of Cavendish House identified by excavation and from the survey of surviving fabric are as follows:

Phases 1 and 2: The medieval gatehouse structure, discussed above, pp. 28–39.

Phase 3: *c.* late sixteenth-century additions to the north façade of the pre-existing medieval gatehouse (hereafter referred to as 'the south range').

Phase 4: *c.* late sixteenth to seventeenth-century modifications to the south range and the addition of a west range.

Phase 3: the late sixteenth-century mansion

The monastic gatehouse, described at the time of the Dissolution in the Crown Commissioners' survey of 1538/9, and partly identified through excavation and evidence from engravings, seems to have consisted of a large rectangular structure of three storeys in height, with corner turrets, a central gate-hall flanked with turrets, glazed windows, heated chambers and possibly a detached

48. D. Smith, 'Assessment of Cavendish House and outbuild-ings' in 'Abbey Park, Leicester', ed. Buckley, 41–65.

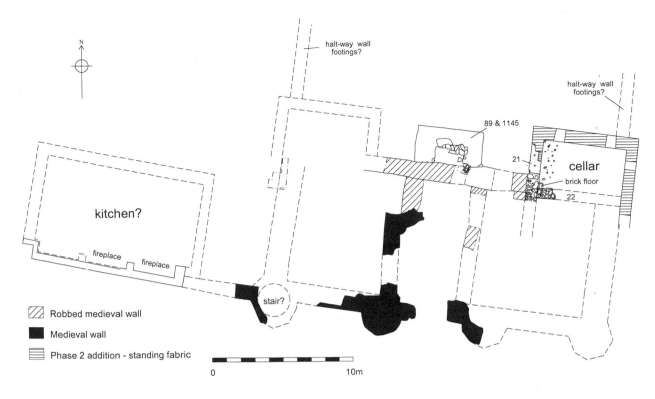

halt-way wall
footings?

halt-way wall
footings?

89 & 1145

21

cellar

brick floor

22

kitchen?

fireplace   fireplace

stair?

Robbed medieval wall

Medieval wall

Phase 2 addition - standing fabric

0   10m

Fig. 5. Plan of Phase 3 mansion, showing additions and modifications to the existing Phase 2 gatehouse

kitchen to the west. At ground floor were perhaps rooms for the porter, while on upper floors there was probably a hall and heated apartments. Although documentary evidence is lacking, it is suspected that in the later medieval period the gatehouse formed the abbot's lodging. The local Dane Hills sandstone formed a major component of the fabric of the building, but it is thought possible that early brick was also used extensively (above, pp. 38–9).

From the archaeological evidence, the first identifiable post-Dissolution change to the monastic gatehouse appears to have been the remodelling of the northern, principal elevation. This may have occurred during the ownership of the Hastings family in the second half of the sixteenth century, perhaps even during the period of Henry Hastings, 1562–80, said by Nichols to have built a 'fair house' on the site out of the old materials.[49] Excavations in 2000 against the interior face of the surviving north façade wall of the later mansion, at its eastern end (Trenches 1 and 2, fig. 5, and above, p. 29, fig. 17), revealed a cellar with a brick floor pre-dating a later stair tower. The cellar, stratigraphically later than the robbed north wall of the medieval gatehouse, was represented by the lower portion of the surviving northern facade wall, and excavated evidence for its west and south walls [21 and 22]. The internal faces of the latter walls were rendered with mortar but, where missing, the wall fabric of well-coursed sandstone bonded with lime mortar was visible.

Both the west and north walls of the cellar showed evidence for single-light windows with sloping sills at present ground level. The windows on the external face of the north wall are the best

49. Nichols, *Leicester*, i pt. 2, 287.

preserved – rectangular, square-headed, with plain chamfered jambs and of an earlier design than those higher up. In addition, the north wall here is off-set slightly to the north of the higher level masonry, the junction marked by a course of chamfered stone (fig. 6), reinforcing the suggestion that it is from an earlier phase. The north wall also bears the scar at its eastern end of rough un-dressed stonework, which marks the original junction of the north cellar wall with the halt-way wall. The southern portion of the halt-way was demolished at a later date and rebuilt slightly further to the east to accommodate the Phase 4 stair tower.

The window in the west wall of the cellar almost certainly opened out to exterior space, providing natural light to the interior, indicating that this wing projected beyond the line of the north wall of the pre-existing medieval gatehouse. A small area of flagstones [65] to the west of the cellar wall, originally thought to represent courtyard paving, is now thought more likely to relate to later interior flooring. Excavation of a small sample section through the rubble backfill of the cellar showed that the floor was paved in brick, 1.6m below the level of the flagstones. The bricks, which cannot be dated accurately, were hand-made, with some coarse inclusions, and measured $9\frac{1}{2}$ inches × $4\frac{1}{8}$ × 2 inches (241mm × 125mm × 50mm). Loose stone laid on top of the west and south walls [21 and 22] may represent reconstruction at the time of Bedingfield's excavation.

The foundations of the north wall of the medieval gatehouse survive at its junction with the cellar wing suggesting that the wall was largely retained during this phase and not taken down and robbed out until later, perhaps when the northern façade was remodelled in Phase 4. No finds were recovered from the robber trench fills in Trenches 2, 5 and 11 (above, pp. 29 and 32, figs. 17 and 18) to confirm this.

It is conceivable – if not probable – that the cellar wing was balanced by a similar wing on the west side of the northern elevation, and a wide offset of the lower part of the wall is indeed visible on the exterior face, again with a course of chamfered stone perhaps indicating a later rebuild of

Fig. 6. Phase 3: north face exterior showing the Phase 4 east stair tower of the south range with the cellar walls and windows retained from Phase 3

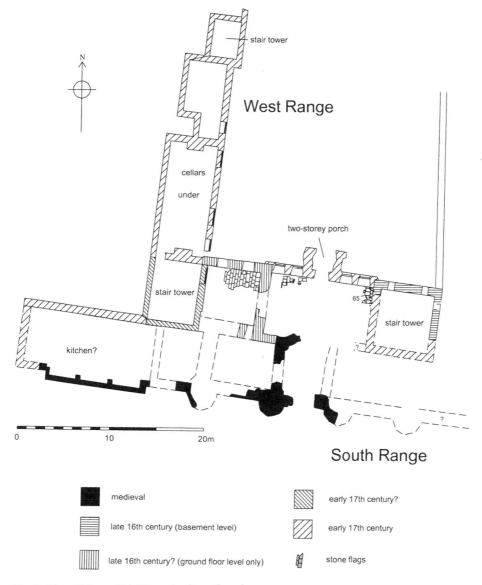

Fig. 8. Plan of Cavendish House in the early 17th century

the medieval gatehouse, although it lacked dating evidence. The large dimensions of the chimney breast suggest it serviced either a kitchen or a suite of heated chambers. If the former, it may indicate a detached or semi-detached kitchen servicing the late medieval gatehouse which, perhaps by the late fifteenth century, may have served as high-status residential accommodation. Alternatively, it could have been added after the Dissolution, perhaps at the same time as the initial remodelling of the northern façade described above. A final possibility is that the chimneys serviced a suite of heated rooms to the west of the core medieval fabric, probably added in the late sixteenth or early seventeenth century (Phase 4) to judge by the classical window forms and balustraded parapet (below, p. 112). However, it is unlikely, on stylistic grounds, that such a chimney was contemporary with the late, 'classical' form of this range, suggesting that it was probably an earlier feature incorporated into the new building work. The favoured interpretation is that the chimney breast represents a kitchen either of the late medieval period (perhaps associated with abbatial accommodation in the gatehouse) or is an addition to the first post-Dissolution mansion phase (Phase 3) made in the later sixteenth century.

Phase 4: the mansion in the late sixteenth and seventeenth century (fig. 8)

The south range was extended to the west to add a suite of rooms; a stair tower was constructed at its east end and the northern façade was remodelled. At the same time, or perhaps shortly afterwards, a west range of at least two storeys (orientated north–south) was constructed above a high basement, together with another stair tower, at right angles to the south range to create an L-shaped plan. Subsequently, a small structure (perhaps another tower) appears to have been built to link the west and south ranges. The west range still survives as Abbey House, but the westerly extension to the south range is known only from a few fragments of masonry and from eighteenth-century engravings, principally that by the Buck brothers (fig. 2). On stylistic grounds, these additions and modifications can only be dated between the late sixteenth century and 1645 when the building was destroyed by fire. In the sections that follow, the detailed examination of structural features undertaken during the surveys of 1997–2004 is considered in more depth.

Modifications to the south range

1. North façade wall and east stair tower

The north façade of the south range, with its projecting central porch and flanking wings was flattened by the construction of a wall linking the two wings together, creating a continuous frontage. As part of this remodelling both the porch and the north wall of the medieval gatehouse seem to have been demolished, and the wall was robbed of its stone. The eastern cellar wing was replaced with a square stair tower (fig. 9) and the upper portion of the projecting west wing was rebuilt. At the centre of the façade, the remains of parallel foundations projecting c. 2m north of the elevation suggests that either a porch (perhaps with balustraded balcony) or a staircase giving access to the first floor hall was built here. Inside the building, excavation revealed evidence for stone flagged floors (fig. 10).

The quality of fenestration in the surviving north facade implies that this part of the building was the original hall block. This raises the question of whether or not there were any other related buildings eastwards of the surviving fabric. Existing survey evidence has not revealed any structures and, since the fragment of return wall forming the east gable of the stair tower contains evidence of windows, it seems that the building ran no further east. The stair tower at the east end of the range is identified by surviving structural details in the form of a series of stepped windows, together with evidence from topographical drawings, where scars in the masonry probably deriving from the staircase strings are shown. Examination of the eastern end of the north wall shows it to be an external facade wall pierced by windows with no doorways. If this interpretation is correct it precludes a courtyard enclosing a wing running northwards from this point.

2. Western extension to the south range

A suite of rooms appears to have been added at the western end of the south range, incorporating what has been interpreted as the medieval detached kitchen block. The Bucks' engraving shows a

Fig. 9. Phase 4: interior of the east stair tower of the south range, showing staggered windows and fabric at basement level retained from Phase 3

Fig. 10. Phase 4: view south-east of 2004 excavation of part of stone flagged floor and wall foundations at the west end of the south range

range projecting westwards from the south-western corner tower of the medieval gatehouse and running slightly to the north of the large double chimney breast feature, but presumably utilising it as part of its south wall (fig. 2). Architecturally, the range is classical in style, with a balustraded parapet, tall mullioned and transomed windows and square pedimented chimneys, while the south-eastern corner of the block has pronounced quoins. The parapet requires the building to have had a shallow-pitched roof, as a steep pitch would negate the silhouetted form of the balustrade that was a vital part of its visual impact feature.[52]

Apart from the double chimney, only fragments of the walling of this range have survived, and in many places the stone has been replaced with brick. Where stonework does survive, it appears to be coursed more regularly and finished more evenly than that on the chimney breast. Areas of erosion on both internal wall-faces contrast with the quality of stonework surviving externally, perhaps reflecting heat damage from the fire in 1645. A surviving ground floor window opening has substantial proportions, confirming the dimensions shown by the Bucks' engraving. Today, a north–south wall closes off the remnant of the west end wall, linking it to a small outbuilding constructed against the double chimney. This wall contains a number of joist housings at first floor level, although they do not relate to any known feature, and may instead be an 'antique' rebuild of the nineteenth century. A late nineteenth-century photograph of this feature, reproduced on a number of postcards, is titled 'Leicester Abbey, The Entrance (with modern arch)'.[53]

Comparing their engravings of other sites and locations, the Buck brothers' illustration of Cavendish House shows that they thought the 'South View' was the original principal elevation of the house. From the extant physical evidence, with its emphasis on the larger dimensions of the windows, and the balustraded parapet, this extension seems intended to introduce a new series of socially-superior rooms to the elevation of the house facing the present line of Abbey Lane. A view from this approach diminishes the impact of the large chimney breast that offers little aesthetic quality to any elevation.

West range

The west range – now known as Abbey House – is a single pile stone structure of two storeys and a high basement, orientated at right angles to the ruined north wall of the earlier south range. At the northern end of this range is a probable stair turret. The east wall of the west range overlaps the chamfered plinth course of the north wall of the south range, with a butt joint above, indicating that it is a later addition (fig. 11). Apart from the arrangement of windows, there is little evidence for the original internal plan of this range: it is now divided transversely in the centre by a staircase and it is possible that the range originally contained two large heated chambers at first floor level. The basement appears to be contemporary with the superstructure of the west range, but is covered by a nineteenth-century brick vault, has three modern brick transverse walls and has been extended to the south with the addition of a brick cellar to which the present staircase provides access. On the inside face of the south wall of the original basement, a short series of descending stones, apparently contemporary with the wall, may represent the remains of the original staircase leading into the cellar.

A series of twelve stone windows, three with splayed jambs and mullions, eight with splayed

52. At Aylestone Hall parapets were added to pre-existing steeply-pitched roofs indicating an attempt to modernise the building whilst avoiding the expense of reproofing. N. Finn pers. comm.

53. C. H. Compton, 'The Abbey of St Mary de Pratis, Leicester', *TLAAS* 9 (1904–5), 197–204 plate following p. 202.

Fig. 11. Phase 4: junction of the north façade of the south range and the west range

jambs, mullions and transoms and one with splayed jambs, are recorded on the east-facing wall of the west range, at basement, ground and first floor levels. A two-light mullion window is in the north wall of the basement and fragments of others are on its western side; at first floor level there is a north-facing four-light window with splayed jambs, mullions and transoms in what is thought to be the stair turret at the northern end of the range. There are several similarities and some dissimilarities between the splayed mullions of the surviving cellar level windows and those elsewhere in the ruined north wall of the south range. What appears to be a mason's mark of an interlocking Λ form [Μ] can be identified on several of the window jambs in the ruined north wall and is also present on the jambs of the small window in the large chimney breast. The same mark appears on several window jambs in the west range suggesting they are broadly coeval, although more detailed examination is required to confirm this point. The dressing work on a few of the stone windows seems more pronounced and of Victorian form rather than the sixteenth- or early seventeenth-century date of most of the windows. These may be replacement pieces from an earlier restoration; significantly, none of them appears to be associated with the mason's mark.

A series of relieving arches running over the stone mullioned and transomed windows at ground floor and cellar level in the west range are similar in form to those surviving in the ruined north wall of the south range. Similar arches are also described over the two two-light cellar windows on the east side of the west range, which are the most original of all those surviving in the cellar area.

On the western elevation of the west range, the original stone mullioned windows have been removed at first floor level and were probably replaced with sashes in the nineteenth century (now

Fig. 12. Phase 4: view east of the structural break in the masonry marking the
junction of the west range (left) with possible stair tower (right)

replaced by modern windows) as evidenced by the survival of fragments of stone jambs. At ground
floor level, two large square bay windows were added in the late Victorian period (fig. 12). Also on
this side, evidence of a straight joint in the stonework – coinciding with the line of the original
south wall of the basement – indicates the addition of a square unit of build, which is interpreted
as a possible tower at the southern end of this range. This is confirmed by evidence that, at each
level of the house from cellar to roof space, the south wall of the original west range had been broken through to provide access into an adjacent structure. Allowing for discrepancies in perspec-
tive, Pridden's west-north-west prospect of 1786 shows a small recessed section coinciding with
the position of this postulated tower between the west range and the westerly extension of the
south range that, with the exception of the large chimney breast, had disappeared by this time.[54]
This, apparently later linking-unit of build, raises questions concerning the relationship of the
newly constructed west range to the pre-existing south range. Without the linking tower, the two
ranges effectively touch corner to corner and are completely separate, each served by its own stair
tower. This may indicate that the suggested stair tower merely replaced another linking structure
for which no evidence survives, perhaps set back slightly from the west façade, otherwise the evidence implies a curious arrangement of two entirely self-contained and independent wings.

On the western side of the roof of the west range are six purlins that appear to be re-used timber joists and may represent salvaged fabric from the abbey complex. All are short (no more than
2.5m long) and are joined by splayed scarf joints with two face-pegs and carry a series of joist mor-
tices at approximately 375mm intervals. The sequence of carpenters' marks relating to the joist
joints run uninterrupted from I to XXVII along the six timbers confirming that what survives in the

54. Nichols, *Leicester*, i pt. 2, plate xviii following p. 282.

roof are the original cut lengths. The joist joints (fig. 13) are probably of a sixteenth- to seventeenth-century type, coeval with the building, and their close positioning suggests they originally supported a substantial first floor. In their re-used position, the purlins sit on top of brick piers with a packing piece of square section timber to support them. This combination of brick piers supporting roof members is similar to a roof support for barns described by Marshall in his 1790 *Rural economy of the Midland counties*, as an innovative form and so may help date when this building was refurbished.[55]

The present rafters are set on a substantial wall-plate most of which is hidden by later plasterwork. However, an area where the wall-plate located onto the tie-beam was exposed during the survey, revealing a lapped dovetail with housed shoulders and secret notch (fig. 13), a joint hitherto unrecorded in Leicestershire and for which no comparitor form has been identified. The illustration also shows the notched housing for the feet of the common rafters on the top of the wall-plate. A distinctive feature of

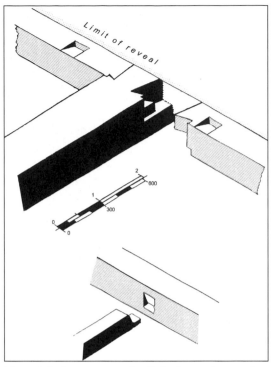

Fig. 13. Jointing carpentry details in the roofspace of the west range: wallplate and tie bottom (above) and joist details on the present side purloins (below)

this jointing arrangement is that the wall-plates form a series of bridging pieces running between the trusses. The wall-plates are jointed onto the topside of the tie beam, not clasped by the tie beams as they pass under them.

At the northern end of the west range is a small square structure interpreted as a stair turret and capped with a later mono-pitched roof at first floor level. On its western elevation, at ground floor, are the remnants of a blocked window which is the first of a rising, staggered sequence of mullioned windows, of which two survive, one each on the north and east facing walls. At wall-plate level, the wall continues to rise and, from the east side, is higher than the remainder of the side wall. Evidence in the roof space also indicates that the side walls of the turret originally rose to a greater height than at present and that the current roof was constructed when the side walls were graded at their present level.

Discussion of Phase 4

Perhaps the most noticeable difference on the Buck brothers' engraving between the core of the medieval gatehouse and the apparent later additions and modifications of Phase 4, principally on the western side, is that the latter are characterised by overtly classical architectural forms, such as

---

55. W. Marshall, *The rural economy of the Midland counties including the management of livestock in Leicestershire and its environs*, 2 vols (London 1790), i, 26–36.

a balustraded parapet, pedimented chimneys and tall windows. Balustraded parapets similar to those shown on the west range and western extension to the south range survive in other sixteenth-century East Midlands great houses, such as Hardwick Hall (Derbys.) (1590–7), Wootton Lodge (Staffs.) (*c.* 1607/8–11)[56] and Wollaton Hall (Notts.) (1582–8). The architect at all of these houses was Robert Smythson, who undertook several commissions for the Cavendish family and lived at Wollaton while building the hall; the village became his permanent home until his death in 1614.[57]

Another feature of Smythson houses which may be relevant to the Phase 4 additions is that they tend to be high and compact, with no courtyards or only small ones, owing their height partly to high basements.[58] Buildings constructed on high basements are known at Barlborough Hall (Derbys.) 1583–4 and its twin, Heath Old Hall (Yorks.) *c.* 1585.[59] The latter also has a balustraded parapet, whilst both have principal elevations enlivened by long flights of steps and two-storey projecting porches. Barlborough has other features of Smythsonian origin, such as the location of chimneys within internal walls, leaving the outer façades free for an imposing display of windows.[60] Unfortunately, the identification of similar features at Cavendish House does not really help to refine the dating of Phases 3 and 4 as they may be seen in both – for example the two storey projecting porch of Phase 3 and the high basement and balustraded parapet of the west range in Phase 4. Another stylistically datable element appears on the 1775 engraving of Cavendish House (fig. 3), where two cranked volute forms are shown alongside the pedimented chimneys of the large chimney breast. They do not appear on the Buck brothers' view, but are too pronounced to be a misinterpretation of fragments of balustrading. These are details associated with late sixteenth- or early seventeenth-century balustrade work, referred to by contemporaries as 'cresting', first introduced by Smythson at Longleat (*c.* 1575) and Wollaton (*c.* 1582–8).

Hence, Phase 4 of Cavendish House seems to incorporate a number of elements of apparent Smythsonian inspiration (though the same may also be partly true of Phase 3). Although many of the Phase 4 architectural features could, on stylistic grounds, be as early as the late sixteenth century, it is considered more likely that they are associated with the ownership of the Cavendish family from 1613 until the building was destroyed by fire in 1645. Despite the fact that the Cavendish family who built the house at Leicester Abbey were the cadet branch of the family, and no direct link with Robert Smythson can be demonstrated, it is likely that they were aware of his work and influences. His son, John Smythson, worked on a fairly continuous basis for the Cavendishes from the early years of the seventeenth century and by 1615 had become a permanent Cavendish employee.[61] He died in 1634. A single reference in the Cavendish accounts survives to suggest that he was probably involved in alterations at Leicester Abbey, although the size of the sum does not suggest major building work: in August 1621, £13 6s. 8d was 'given Mr Smithson' at Leicester.[62]

The substantial double chimney breast is shown on the Buck brothers' engraving topped with the remnants of what was originally a series of four stone chimney flues set on a moulded pediment. These bear a close resemblance to the classical pedimented chimney form first recorded in the East Midlands at Kirby Hall (Northants.). Although the designer of Kirby Hall is unknown, Thomas Thorpe, mason-builder from Kingscliffe (Northants.) is believed to have been the super-

---

56. Girouard, *Robert Smythson*, 204.
57. Ibid. 37.
58. Ibid. 187.
59. Ibid. 120.

60. Ibid. 123.
61. Ibid. 245.
62. Ibid. 270.

visor of that great house, commenced by Sir Humphrey Stafford in 1570, and completed by Sir Christopher Hatton, c. 1583.[63] Evidence from eighteenth-century engravings indicates that this classical pedimented chimney form proliferated across the roofscape of Cavendish House. The fact that they are present on what appear to be amongst the latest phases of build – the west range and the stair tower on the east side of the south range – may suggest that they could be as late as the early seventeenth century, perhaps introduced during the Cavendish's ownership.

Although the proportions of the majority of the splayed window forms identified in the present Abbey House almost certainly originate in the final quarter of the sixteenth century, this form of window never entirely lost its medieval characteristics. Similar dates for flat splay mullions and jambs have been recorded in areas close by. Marsden, studying Rutland examples, gave them a dating spread of c. 1575 to 1720.[64] Like Summerson, Marsden suggested the flat splay mullion was seldom used in buildings in the Northamptonshire uplands; there the ovolo mullion form was more popular. By way of contrast, Wood-Jones' study of the Banbury region found the flat splay 'ubiquitous' in that area and provided evidence of dated examples running from c. 1574 to 1719.[65] In the Cotswolds, Wood-Jones noted that the form persisted until 1750. Discussing the universality of the flat-splay form, Wood-Jones observed that, 'the poorer properties of the marlstone in working and weathering are probably responsible for this general acceptance of the simpler profile within the region'.[66] This may also be true of the sandstone used for the window details at Cavendish House.

The plan of Cavendish House in its final form was L-shaped, a form created by the west and south ranges; this placed considerable emphasis on the fashionable principal break-fronted north elevation with its central porch and imposing display of tall mullion and transomed windows at first floor level. The windows presumably marked the location of the hall that, despite many alterations to the building following the Dissolution, retained its medieval position. Hence, at the time of the modifications, a visitor approaching from the north, via the outer gate towers and halt-way would have been presented with the impressive vista of an apparently fashionable – if modest – new house, which concealed, at the rear, a rag bag of mixed architectural styles dating back to the medieval period. By the time that the Buck brothers produced their drawing of the South View, nearly a hundred years after Cavendish House was destroyed by fire, they regarded this as the principal elevation of the house or, rather, the elevation most worth illustrating.

By the mid-sixteenth century, the hitherto fashionable quadrangular enclosed courtyard plan was beginning to be replaced by an arrangement which placed greater emphasis on an open front and considerably less on attendant details such as gatehouses. An early example of this new plan type can be seen in the surviving fragments of nearby Bradgate House. Also by this time, halls were increasingly becoming centres of social contact and private quarters for the family were becoming essential. At Cavendish House the surviving built fragments cause a certain amount of confusion when trying to interpret the domestic organisation of the house along conventional lines. The eastern staircase that, by its scale, appears to have been the main staircase, can only have served a limited number of rooms such as the Great Hall and chambers at second floor level. The west range, perhaps containing domestic apartments, was served by a staircase at its northern end, whilst the service facilities, probably located in the postulated medieval kitchen, and additional

63. Hatton was briefly associated with Cavendish House in 1572.
64. E. Marsden, 'Minor domestic architecture of the Rutland district', unpubl. PhD thesis, University of Manchester (1953).
65. R. B. Wood-Jones, *Traditional domestic architecture in the Banbury region* (Manchester 1963), 257.
66. Ibid. 257.

domestic quarters at the west end of the south range, were serviced by a less substantial staircase, perhaps located in the small tower thought to link the west and south ranges. This may represent one of the final improvements to the building.

Through a combination of standing building survey, documentary research and limited excavation, it has been possible to gain an initial understanding of the nature and development of the post-Dissolution mansion which formed the heart of the Leicester Abbey estate in the late sixteenth and early seventeenth centuries. The study of this period in the history of the site has been neglected in the past and there is clearly considerable scope for clarifying the complex transitions from a major monastic site to a comparatively short-lived post-Dissolution estate. Cavendish House retains future research potential, both through excavation and standing building survey, to clarify the structural sequence. Elsewhere within the precinct, there is still much to be learned not only about the about the processes of Dissolution – the dating and sequence of the demolition of monastic buildings – but also about the character of the wider landscape of the later sixteenth-century estate.

Henry Knighton's *Chronicle* and Leicester Abbey

Geoffrey Martin

The Augustinian abbey of St Mary of the Meadows, Leicester, was a well-endowed house, established in Stephen's reign on the high tide of the Augustinians' fortunes, and brought by the currents of politics into royal patronage. The earldom of Leicester had a tumultuous journey to the point at which, in the late thirteenth century, it became part of a royal appanage, first in the hands of Edmund Crouchback, younger son of Henry III, and subsequently in those of Henry of Grosmont, first duke of Lancaster, and at last John of Gaunt, whose son Henry Bolingbroke became King Henry IV in 1399. As it happened, Leicester castle was the favourite residence of both Duke Henry and of his son-in-law Duke John, so the canons of St Mary's were in constant touch with a distinguished and busy household, always close to the royal court.

The canons who professed the rule of St Augustine were members of a distinctive order. Though bound to a monastic regime they were not monks: they were ordained priests, and they were expected to undertake pastoral duties outside their houses, among the laity, and in particular in the parish churches committed to their care. The order was so popular in the early years of its presence in England that St Mary's was from the beginning overwhelmed with such churches, some fifty in thirteen counties, a number plainly beyond the capacity of a single convent, however well found. Like other professed religious, however, the Augustinians had also to maintain the daily round of services and requite the benefactions of their patrons, great and lesser, by intercessory prayer and counsel, besides preaching and pursuing learning.

All religious houses kept records of their communal life and works, and in Augustinian abbeys and priories the precentor was charged with the care of the library and the production and maintenance of books. The late-fifteenth-century catalogue of the library at Leicester has survived, and is a work of outstanding value. It reveals an assembly of more than a thousand books, only a handful of which are to be found today, scattered among a small number of libraries (Webber, below pp. 127–46; Gullick and Webber, below pp. 173–92, no. 16). We can therefore, with a few exceptions, only infer the use that the canons made of them. By the same token no administrative records have survived from the abbey before the last half-century of its existence, denying us the chance of studying the recruitment of its community and the day-to-day management of its affairs.

Henry Knighton, the author of the Chronicle which bears his name, is one of the few canons whom we can identify, and even so our knowledge of him is scanty.[1] His name suggests that he

---

1. For Henry Knighton and his chronicle, see *Knighton's Chronicle, 1337–1396*, ed. G. H. Martin, Oxford Medieval Texts (Oxford 1995), referred to here as *Knighton's Chronicle*.

came from Knighton on the outskirts of Leicester. He was in Leicester, and most probably already a member of the convent, in 1363, when he saw and heard Edward III there. He was certainly a canon by 1370, when he had a brush with the law, and he paid the clerical poll tax in 1377, and was writing his Chronicle soon afterwards. He struggled with failing sight in his later years, and seems to have abandoned the Chronicle in 1396, when he probably died. The principal text of his Chronicle, which is now in the British Library's Cottonian collection (BL Cotton Tiberius C vii) (fig. 1; Gullick and Webber, below, no. 14), is in a number of hands, one of which may be Knighton's own, and contains several strictures on its writing and presentation which appear to be his. Only one other copy of the work survives, made perhaps two decades later and apparently in Leicester. It contains no additional material, but some changes in spelling suggest that it was made c. 1420 or a little later (BL Cotton Claudius E iii). It is a large folio volume in a plain hand, and was probably made to be read aloud. The earlier volume, Tiberius, though not a draft, is evidently rather closer to the author.[2]

The content of the Chronicle is richly informative, and makes it a major source for its period, which covers the greater part of the fourteenth century. It seems that Knighton's first intention was to commemorate both Edward III and Abbot Cloune of Leicester, a celebrated figure, who died in 1378, a year after the old king. He accordingly began with a threnody of King Edward and of his eldest son, Edward the Black Prince (1330–76), and a lengthy obituary of the great abbot. It seems then to have occurred to him to write a history of England from the Conquest to his own day, and for the rest of his life he worked on parallel texts, which he did not quite succeed in joining together, as the first part of the Chronicle ends in 1372 and Prince Edward died in 1376. In both parts, however, he maintained a vigorous and well-informed narrative.

Like other historians of his time, Knighton's first care in the extended Chronicle was to obtain a reliable history which he could copy and then continue. The medieval mind had a strong respect for established authority, and no sense whatever of a proprietorial interest in the written word – no notion of an authorial copyright as we understand it.[3] In the event Knighton found two respectable supports: the first was Ranulph Higden's 'Polychronicon', the work of a Benedictine monk of Chester, and the second the 'Chronicon de gestis regum Anglie' of Walter of Guisborough, an Augustinian canon of Guisborough priory in the North Riding of Yorkshire. Higden was a comprehensive work of reference such as any well-equipped library would include.[4] The importance of Guisborough's chronicle here is that someone before Knighton had added some material to it relating to Leicester, and especially a unique and highly interesting account of Earl Thomas of Lancaster's negotiations with representatives of King Edward II's party during the political crisis of 1318. It is a document that most probably came – must have come – from Leicester castle, and its preservation suggests that someone before Knighton, who carefully attributes it to the copy of Guisborough which he was using, was aware of its historical significance. With that secure foundation taking his story to the outbreak of the war between England and France in 1337, Knighton took up the narrative, observing wryly that from that point he would be on his own, a state of affairs with which we, as his successors in the exposition of history, can all sympathise.[5]

2. On the manuscripts, see further *Knighton's Chronicle*, xx–xxiii. Claudius E iii must have been copied directly or at one or more stages removed from a Leicester manuscript; see also, T. Webber, 'The books of Leicester Abbey', below pp. 127–46 at 145.

3. On that important matter, see E. P. Goldschmidt, *Medieval texts and their first appearance in print*, Bibliographical Society (London 1943), 89–114.

4. Webber, 'The books of Leicester Abbey', below p. 42, note 99.

5. See *Knighton's Chronicle*, xxx–xxxi.

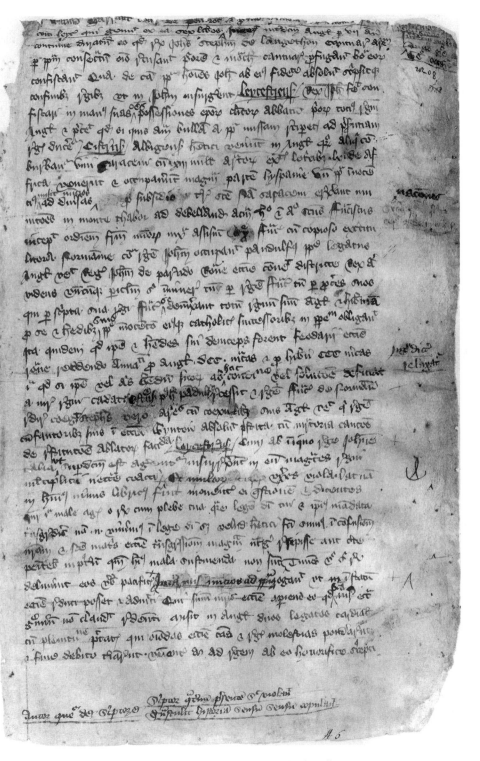

Fig. 1. London, British Library, Cotton Tiberius c. vii, f. 62r (reduced)

The vigour of Knighton's account of the English operations against the French, including their recovery of control in Gascony, a principal theatre of contention, and Edward III's efforts to construct an alliance amongst the German princes of the Rhineland, shows that half a century after those events he did not lack resources. The narrative immediately reveals that he had collected a remarkable archive of material, ranging from official decrees and communiqués to market prices, which he worked carefully into his narrative, There are also a number of items which seem to be personal reminiscences, such as reports of merchants familiar with the markets of the Low Countries, and gossip at various levels from Leicester castle. The perceptible documents in the text number more than a hundred, and represent a considerable outlay of time and energy.[6] Any member of a religious house who wished to write a history, or anything else, needed the permission of his abbot or prior, the means to collect writing materials and, as the task might require, information. Knighton evidently wrote with the approval and perhaps even the encouragement of his superiors. If he had correspondents he does not name them, but occasionally an individual does emerge, as when the keeper of Gaunt's palace of the Savoy described with horror the destruction of that great house and its sumptuous contents by the mob in London in 1381. We are not often so close, not only to events, but to the ways in which news travelled from place to place, and from witness to auditor seven hundred years ago.[7]

From the 1330s to the short-lived treaty of Bretigny in 1361 there is an immediacy about the narrative that seems almost personal. Its hero is Henry of Grosmont, the first duke of Lancaster, who was Edward III's most valued captain in France, and who died of the plague in 1361. Knighton can hardly have witnessed the events of the 1330s and 1340s himself; though he may have seen and known Duke Henry. The first event in his own life which is dated, in 1363, is only two years later than Henry's death, and at the least he must have known members of Henry's household who could have provided him with details of the campaigns in Gascony and northern France, which are explicit and vivid, He most probably also had access to newsletters from the same source. Edward III was careful to publish accounts of his own campaigns in the first years of the war, and his captains will have informed their households of their successes. The lists of casualties in battle and of prisoners taken – important for the money that could be raised by ransoms – are another written source which circulated widely but eventually were lost or buried in family papers. The mangling of titles and place-names in the examples preserved by Knighton is a reminder of the exigencies of writing anything in the aftermath of battle, especially on such a field as Poitiers in 1356, with armies drawn from all parts of France and its neighbouring territories. The descriptions of Duke Henry's prowess, stratagems, and booty, however, have a more personal ring.

The second part of the Chronicle clearly falls in Knighton's adult lifetime. It is as carefully documented as the first, and not less arresting in its detail, but it is dominated by two particular themes, one the developing political crisis of Richard II's reign (1377–99), and the other the concurrent rise of the heresy known as Lollardy of which Knighton had an uncomfortable personal knowledge. The hero of the second strophe is John of Gaunt (1340–99), Duke Henry's son-in-law. The two make for interesting contrasts. Henry was a distinguished soldier, a fighting man and a strategist of courtly accomplishments. He remarked once that he had found more pleasure in the embraces of common wenches than of ladies of quality because they did not trouble his conscience with the reflection that he had led them into sin in the first place. That is not one of Knighton's

6. Ibid. xxxii–xlvi.   7. Ibid. 214–16.

stories, but Henry is a living presence in the Chronicle, whether Knighton knew him, glimpsed him once or twice, or fed on the reminiscences of those about him, who kept his story alive.[8]

Gaunt was Edward III's third son, born at Ghent in 1340 when Edward was seeking allies in the Rhineland, and opportunely married to Blanche, the heiress of the Lancastrian estates as Henry of Grosmont had no son to succeed him. He campaigned because it was expected of him, but without distinction. His gifts were those not of a soldier but of a diplomat, politician, and courtier. He was the titular king of Castile, a title which he acquired by a second marriage and maintained by diplomacy. In England he had extensive estates mainly in the North and the Midlands, and he exercised a royal authority over his palatinate duchy, from Clitheroe in the Pennines to the Mersey. There he had his own chancery and exchequer, and his writ ran as did the king's commands in the rest of the kingdom.[9]

There is no doubt that Knighton knew Gaunt and the senior members of his household. He also commented freely upon Gaunt's *crise de conscience* in 1381 when the duke attributed his misfortunes to the irregularity of his private life. On the one hand it is difficult at first sight to imagine Gaunt listening meekly in company to such a narrative. On the other it seems unlikely that Knighton would have written a passage ringing with moral purpose if it were not intended for the duke's ears. On balance it seems likely that the attitude of public figures to publicity, when allowance is made for individual temperament and circumstances, was not greatly different in the fourteenth century from that of their successors in more recent times.[10]

If Knighton felt any diffidence in recording Gaunt's soul-searching he evidently resolved his problems. It was otherwise with another issue which would have exercised his audience and was manifestly embarrassing to him as a privileged observer. In the last quarter of the fourteenth century the English church was shaken by a movement known as Lollardy. The Lollards wanted access to the Scriptures in the vernacular, with individuals free to exercise their own judgement in spiritual matters. They disowned the papal monarchy and the expedients by which the international church was funded. The debate was sharpened by the scandal of the Great Schism (1378–1416) which saw first two and at last three rival popes and colleges of cardinals, and which Knighton witnessed from its inception. What made Lollardy most dangerous, however, was that it was simultaneously a popular movement, prefiguring much of sixteenth-century Protestantism, and an academic creed, begotten and sustained by John Wyclif (*c.* 1340–84), the most formidable metaphysician in the schools at Oxford. Wyclif attracted able young men to his classes, precisely those who would fill the commanding posts in the church over the following decades – from archdeaconries to bishoprics.

The crisis in Oxford was short-lived, and effectively over by 1382. The authorities moved to suppress academic Lollardy, and its champions either conformed or disappeared into obscurity. One of their leaders, however, was Philip Repingdon, a canon of Leicester, doctor of divinity, subsequently abbot of Leicester from 1393 to 1404, and then bishop of Lincoln and a cardinal. Repingdon made his peace with the church readily enough, but he was apparently not ashamed of his former heresy, and he provided Knighton with documents which the chronicler would really have preferred not to see. To make matters worse, Leicester itself was an early focus of popular Lollardy, which Repingdon had also helped to promote. Knighton found himself torn between his

---

8. On Duke Henry, see K. Fowler, *The King's Lieutenant: Henry of Grosmont, duke of Lancaster, 1310–1361* (London 1969).

9. On Gaunt, see A. Goodman, *John of Gaunt: the exercise of princely power in fourteenth-century Europe* (Harlow 1992).

10. See *Knighton's Chronicle*, 234–8.

own orthodoxy and conservatism, and an unrivalled view of the discontents of those who rejected the established practices of the church, and what they denounced as the abuses of clerical power and privilege. He was plainly embarrassed by what many of his successors, especially in the present day, would have regarded as a heaven-sent opportunity to run with the hare and the hounds together. As things were, he did his best, seeking especially to shield his indiscreet abbot from opprobrium.[11]

The Chronicle therefore gives us a detailed but carefully edited account of the academic movement and its sudden end, and a wider ranging but still circumspect account of the popular discontents. Lollardy flared in the 1370s, and despite proscription and persecution survived underground until its beliefs were subsumed in the Protestantism of the sixteenth-century Reformation. Knighton witnessed only the beginning of that process. He deplored it but presented a thoughtful and well-balanced account of the sect, of its beliefs, and especially of such attributes as dress, vocabulary, and the disputes and enthusiasms which divided families and congregations.

After describing Lollardy, Knighton turned, perhaps with some sense of relief, to national and political matters, describing Gaunt's expedition to Spain in 1386–9 and the crisis which erupted in his absence, when Richard II and his ministers effectively lost control of the kingdom in 1387–8. Knighton followed the process in detail, apparently drawing material from Henry Bolingbroke, Gaunt's son and heir, who eventually usurped the crown in 1399 as Henry IV. Once again he found himself with divided loyalties, weighing his reverence for the king against his respect for and the abbey's long commitment to the house of Lancaster. In the event, he kept his nerve and balance very well.[12]

In both halves of his narrative, before and after the death of Edward III in 1376 and, incidentally, from the descent of the duchy of Lancaster from Henry of Grosmont to John of Gaunt, Knighton achieves an uncommonly consistent note of personal involvement. As it would have been physically difficult for him to have witnessed in his maturity public events both in the 1330s and the 1390s, the freshness of his descriptions, of battles, expeditions, pageantry, visions in the sky, must reflect the range and quality of the information that he collected and his own skill in assembling it. That in turn suggests something about his intended audience as well as his own tastes and interests. If Knighton envisaged those who might 'read and hear' his history as a larger company than his fellow canons alone, and he undoubtedly did, we might assume that they would include members of the nobility and their knights and captains, who were greatly given to tales of blood and thunder, whether they had a part in them or not, of the official classes at various levels, and of merchants and civic dignitaries. When Knighton recited the spoils of Duke Henry's campaign in Gascony, or the names of prisoners taken in battle, he excited both pride and the spirit of emulation in those who had been to France, or had ever thought of seeking their fortunes there. When the mayor of Leicester wrung his hands over the reported approach of the rebels in 1381 he probably agonized in private, but he saw to it that, as soon as the crisis was past, Knighton both knew of his misgivings and of his resolute action in the face of danger. Merchants who brought home news from the markets of the Low Countries were probably also gratified to find an attentive audience and to have their experiences noted.

It is notable that Knighton says relatively little about the life of the abbey itself, or its buildings. He refers to an attempted robbery in 1364, when the thieves entered the church through a window

---

11. Ibid. xlii–xlvi.   12. Ibid. xlvi–viii.

above the altar of St John, and to a chamber in the church occupied for a time by William Swinderby, who was subsequently busy among the Lollards. Beyond that he has nothing to say of his fellow canons, or their day-to-day affairs.[13] There is, however, one particular feature of the Chronicle that seems to reflect a particular interest of Knighton's, and may relate to his own experience at Leicester. He shows a concern for what would now be called economic affairs – prices, commodities, and supply. He knew that when the king, or a general like Gaunt or his father-in-law organized an expedition there was shipping to be collected, and stores to be assembled and carried. When he reported on the incidence of the plague, the Black Death, he noted its effects upon wages and on the attitudes and expectations of those who earned them. Those concerns, together with a lively interest in the progress and incidents of military campaigns, run through the Chronicle. It may be that Knighton's own experience extended only to the management of the abbey and its estates. He may, on the other hand, have been closer in his time to the ducal household than any of his fellows. Whatsoever the origins of his insight, his Chronicle is an exceptionally wide-ranging account of his time, and a striking record of national and local affairs as they impinged upon the canons of St Mary of the Meadows. There were many others who experienced such events: posterity has been grateful to Knighton who recorded them.

13. Ibid. 193, 309 and note 2.

The books of Leicester Abbey

Teresa Webber

By the late fifteenth century Leicester Abbey possessed around 1100 books. Only sixteen are known to survive, bearing powerful witness to the scale of loss in the aftermath of the Dissolution of the monasteries.[1] The late medieval holdings are recorded in an unusually comprehensive catalogue (now Bodl. Laud Misc. 623), which lists not only around 940 books for study and personal devotion but also some 170 liturgical books in the abbey church, the infirmary, and the chapel in the abbey's grange at Ingarsby, as well as a number of rentals and other administrative records.[2] The catalogue is of particular interest as probably the most complete listing of the accumulation of books by any single religious house in Britain during the Middle Ages.[3] Nevertheless, although it shows what was available at the abbey towards the end of the fifteenth century, it is by no means a straightforward guide to the use of the books at that time or earlier.[4] Furthermore, there are too few surviving volumes to permit a detailed study of the history of the books, as has been possible, for example, for the Benedictine abbeys of St Albans and Reading.[5] Nevertheless, information in the catalogue, combined with evidence from the surviving books, can be used in conjunction with what is known from richer materials from other religious houses to provide brief glimpses of the acquisition, use and dispersal of the books of Leicester Abbey.

Acknowledgements: I am very grateful to Michael Gullick for reading and commenting upon a draft of this paper, and for much helpful discussion about the Leicester catalogue. I am also grateful to the following for providing information about manuscripts or facilitating my use of them: James Willoughby, Karen Begg, Kenneth Dunn, and the librarians and staff of the Wren Library, Trinity College, Cambridge University Library, the National Library of Scotland, the British Library and the Bodleian Library.

References to entries in M. Gullick and T. Webber, 'Summary catalogue of surviving manuscripts from Leicester Abbey', below, 173–92 are given in the form 'Gullick and Webber, no. 000'. Entries in the medieval library catalogue of Leicester Abbey are referred to by the entry number in T. Webber and A. G. Watson, *The libraries of the Augustinian canons*, Corpus of British Medieval Library Catalogues 6 (London 1998), 104–399 (e.g. 'A20.000'). With the exception of fig. 1, all the figs. in this paper are reproduced at same size; references to figs. elsewhere in this volume are by page and figure number, and the colour plates are between pp. 8 and 9 above.

1. For summary descriptions of these books, and of five administrative volumes, three further books which may have been owned by the abbey or its members before the Dissolution, and the sole surviving original charter, see Gullick and Webber, 'Summary catalogue', below.

2. The catalogue is edited in Webber and Watson, *Libraries of the Augustinian canons* (catalogue A20). Inconsistencies in the catalogue make it impossible to calculate precise numbers.

3. An inventory from Exeter Cathedral of 1506 also provides detailed lists of liturgical and non-liturgical books, which may represent the full communal holdings: G. Oliver, *Lives of the bishops of Exeter and a history of the cathedral* (Exeter 1861), 323–76.

4. The contents are surveyed in A. Hamilton Thompson, *The abbey of St Mary of the Meadows, Leicester* (Leicester 1949), 204–30.

5. R. M. Thomson, *Manuscripts from St Albans Abbey 1066–1235*, 2 vols (Woodbridge 1982); R. Vaughan, *Matthew Paris* (Cambridge 1958); V. H. Galbraith, *The St Albans Chronicle 1406–20* (Oxford 1937), xxxvi–lxxvi; D. R. Howlett, 'Fifteenth-century Manuscripts of St Albans Abbey and Gloucester College, Oxford' in *manuscripts at Oxford: an exhibition in memory of R. W. Hunt*, ed. A. C. de la Mare and B. C. Barker-Benfield (Oxford 1980), 84–7; A. Coates, *English medieval books: The Reading Abbey collections from foundation to dispersal* (Oxford 1999).

The Leicester Abbey holdings in the late fifteenth century

> The monastic library, even the greatest, had something of the appearance of a
> heap even though the nucleus was an ordered whole; at the best, it was the sum
> of many collections, great and small, rather than a planned articulate unit.[6]

In order to discern how the 'heap' recorded so comprehensively in the Leicester catalogue was accumulated, and the use made of the books, it is necessary to understand the nature of the catalogue itself. It is a handsome fair-copy of one or more lists of uncertain date, scope and character, produced between 1477 and 1494, with a small number of additions made shortly after (p. 184, fig. 12).[7] A few other British medieval library catalogues are larger, but none is as comprehensive.[8] The function of the catalogue, however, is unclear. It is in several sections, beginning with a preface that briefly outlines the contents. But beneath the superficial coherence suggested by the uniformity of its script, layout and arrangement of the entries it is possible to detect a patchwork of different records, not fully adapted to form an integrated whole. Only the first two sections – a *tabula* of authors and a subject catalogue of the books for study and devotion – are obviously linked, the order of the former following the arrangement of the latter. A heading describes the *tabula* as having been made by a Leicester canon, William Charyte, who is also named in a subsequent heading as responsible for revising ('renovatum') the subject catalogue during his time as precentor.[9] It is unclear whether this revision involved substantial changes to the form and arrangement of the entries or simply the addition of more recently acquired books. The next two sections describe again (in a shortened form of entry) between a quarter and a third of the volumes recorded in the subject catalogue, arranged by their location on lecterns in the *libraria* and the *scriptoria*. But no location references are provided in the subject catalogue to facilitate its use in conjunction with these two lists, merely references to two books located in the abbey church (one in the choir and one on the pulpitum), and a two-volume bible in the refectory.[10] The *libraria* and *scriptoria* lists may well derive from a different source from the subject catalogue revised by Charyte. This is more demonstrably the case with the next section, a list of the books and their locations within the abbey church, which is datable to between 1477 and 1494, some time after Charyte had ceased to be precentor.[11] The same may also be true of the brief lists of books in the infirmary and at Ingarsby, and the list of rentals, but their relationship to each other and to the earlier parts of the catalogue is as yet unclear. Although the list of rentals is the last item mentioned in the description of the contents given in the preface, it is followed in the catalogue by lists of the books for which William Charyte was in one way or another responsible for producing or acquiring. These lists evidently became incorporated only after all the other elements had been brought together, and perhaps only in the final fair-copy itself.

The catalogue as a whole was evidently not intended as a finding-list, since the location of almost all of the non-liturgical books housed outside the *libraria* is nowhere specified. In common with a number of other religious houses, the *libraria* accommodated only a portion of such books;

6. D. Knowles, *The religious orders in England*, II. *The end of the middle ages* (Cambridge 1955), 332.

7. Gullick and Webber, no. 16, superseding Webber and Watson, *Libraries of the Augustinian canons*, 107–8.

8. The extensive catalogues from St Augustine's, Canterbury, and Syon Abbey, for example, do not include service books: M. R. James, *The ancient libraries of Canterbury and Dover* (Cambridge 1903), 173–406 (a new edition, including a revised opinion of the date of the catalogue, is

forthcoming, ed. B. C. Barker-Benfield, in the Corpus of British Medieval Library Catalogues); V. Gillespie, *Syon Abbey with the libraries of the Carthusians, edited by A. I. Doyle*, CBMLC 9 (London 2001).

9. Some time before 1463, by which date he held the higher office of prior.

10. A20.600 and 654; A20.1.

11. Gullick and Webber, no. 16, superseding Webber and Watson, *Libraries of the Augustinian canons*, 107–8.

the remainder, if not on temporary loan, were probably shelved in cupboards or recesses in or near the cloister and in other convenient places within the abbey.[12] The arrangement of the entries in the subject catalogue is unlikely to reflect a shelf-order, since scattered among them are volumes located variously in the *libraria*, as well as the few stated as being elsewhere (in the refectory and the abbey church). Instead, the entries are organized by the main author and subject of each volume, following a more-or-less classified order that reflects a long-recognized hierarchy of authority of Christian texts and writers: biblical manuscripts and glossed books on the Bible, followed by the works of the Church Fathers, more recent interpreters of Scripture and the teachings of the Church, then other (primarily) Christian writings: histories and chronicles, letters, and various kinds of pastoral, penitential and devotional literature. The remainder of the subject catalogue is arranged by the subjects of the medieval curriculum: grammar, rhetoric and logic, philosophy, arithmetic, music, geometry and astronomy, followed by the higher studies of medicine, civil law, and canon law. It ends with a short series of entries describing volumes containing statutes of the realm, a small collection of romances and other texts in Anglo-Norman, and fourteen missals and psalters (presumably surplus to those required in the abbey church).

The conspectus of authors in Charyte's *tabula* follows this order, acting as a table of contents rather than an alphabetical index. It is, however, a far from complete listing of the authors represented in the catalogue. Furthermore, many books described in the subject catalogue contained works by more than one author, yet the arrangement of entries follows the author or subject of the first or main item in the book. This issue was partially addressed by the inclusion of cross-references for the other contents and their authors, but these were not provided systematically for every text. The *tabula* and subject catalogue thus lack the sophistication and scope of the remarkable late medieval catalogues from Dover Priory and Syon Abbey, which provide a comprehensive author/title index, and use each volume's pressmark as a reference to link the index to the main catalogue.[13]

Despite its limitations, the Leicester catalogue may yet have been of practical assistance to the precentor as an *aide-memoire* when carrying out his duties, such as checking the holdings, and providing canons and others with the books they requested.[14] The lack of references to location need not have been a source of difficulty. None of the surviving Leicester manuscripts bears a location mark (including those with their medieval bindings still intact),[15] which indicates that precentors at Leicester, as at some other houses, were able to manage their holdings without such aids.[16] The entries do, however, contain other information, perhaps included to enable the precentor to distinguish between copies of the same text. Most useful for this purpose were *secundo folio* references supplied in almost every entry. These consist of the first word or two of the second leaf of a book, which, in most instances, would differ from copy to copy of the same text. The inclusion (albeit less systematically) of information about the binding and donors may also have served the same purpose, although these details may simply have been transferred mechanically from earlier lists.

12. See, for example, A. J. Piper, 'The libraries of the monks of Durham' in *Medieval scribes, manuscripts and libraries: essays presented to N. R. Ker*, ed. M. B. Parkes and A. G. Watson (London 1978), 213–49.

13. Gillespie, *Syon Abbey*; W. P. Stoneman, *Dover Priory*, CBMLC 5 (London 1999).

14. The custumal used by the canons of Leicester is unknown, but the arrangements for the care of books may have been broadly similar to those of the *Liber ordinis* of the highly influential abbey of Saint-Victor in Paris, which were drawn upon, for example, by the Augustinian priory of Barnwell: *Liber ordinis Sancti Victoris Parisiensis*, ed. L. Jocqué and L. Milis, CCCM 61 (Turnhout 1984), 78–83; *The observances in use at the Augustinian priory of S. Giles and S. Andrew at Barnwell, Cambridgeshire*, ed. J. W. Clark (Cambridge 1897), 62–9.

15. See M. Gullick, 'The binding descriptions in the library catalogue from Leicester Abbey' in this volume, pp. 142–72 below.

16. R. Sharpe, 'Accession, classification, location: shelfmarks in medieval libraries', *Scriptorium* 50 (1996), 279–87, esp. 286.

It is possible that the catalogue may have not been solely practical in function. The use of the highest grade of script, *Littera textualis quadrata* (occasionally incorporating elements from Anglicana), for headings, and a formal grade of Anglicana for the entries, together with the large format and spacious layout, are indicative of a formal record rather than a working document (p. 184, fig. 12).[17] This level of formality was perhaps intended to convey the significance that the community attached to their books collectively, whatever their various functions as individual volumes and collections, and whether they were in current use or not. A commemorative function is also suggested by the references to William Charyte in the first two headings in the catalogue, and the inclusion of lists recording his industry in providing books for the liturgy, for study, and for administering the abbey's estates. The precision with which the nature of his involvement is recorded in the headings to each of the lists is striking; they distinguish between the books he caused to be made, the books for which he supplied the musical notation, the books he either copied or compiled himself, and the books he purchased.[18]

The very inclusiveness of the catalogue, however, creates problems in using it as evidence of the religious and intellectual climate of the abbey towards the end of the fifteenth century. While it provides a remarkably full picture of the resources available for study and devotion, it only partially reveals the role played by the books in the life of the community. The accumulated 'heap' doubtless included unplanned and unwelcome additions as well as books no longer consulted. An unusually rich survival of books and booklists from Durham Cathedral Priory demonstrates that over time books went in and out of use, and were moved to and from more or less accessible places of storage in response to changing patterns of use.[19] Since no earlier records survive from Leicester, and locations are not given for around three-quarters of the books listed, such patterns are not detectable from the catalogue alone. Nevertheless, some indication of the perceived utility, if not the actual use, of some of the books may be inferred from the books that had been placed in the *libraria*, the *scriptoria*, the abbey church and the infirmary.

By the later fifteenth century, a library room had been created at Leicester as at many other religious houses – a development that took place at English religious houses and cathedrals from the end of the fourteenth century onwards, no doubt in imitation of similar rooms at Oxford and Cambridge colleges.[20] By contrast with the book rooms already existing in some houses, which had little natural light and appear to have been used essentially as store-rooms (although this did not preclude a more or less systematic shelf-arrangement by subject), the new library rooms were places where books were arranged on lecterns for consultation *in situ*. For communities with larger accumulations of books, such an arrangement would not have permitted all of the books to be shelved in this way.[21] A process of selection was probably involved, or an existing 'core' collection may have been transferred to the lecterns in the new room.[22] At Leicester, the books were disposed

---

17. For further reproductions, see Hamilton Thompson, *Leicester Abbey*, pls between 208–9 and Webber and Watson, *Libraries of the Augustinian canons*, pls 6–7.

18. A20.1878–1958.

19. Piper, 'Libraries of the monks of Durham'.

20. J. W. Clark, *The care of books* (Cambridge 1901), 101–70.

21. Few catalogues of monastic and cathedral library rooms survive. The list of books compiled by William Ingram in 1508 (James, *Ancient libraries*, 152–63) is now generally thought to include all or almost all of the books in the fifteenth-century library room at Christ Church, Canterbury; the 293 books recorded were only a small proportion of the holdings which, in the early fourteenth century, numbered at least 1830 volumes

(*Ancient libraries*, 13–145); see also C. F. R. de Hamel, 'The dispersal of the library of Christ Church, Canterbury, from the fourteenth to the sixteenth century' in *Books and collectors 1200–1700: essays presented to Andrew Watson*, ed. J. P. Carley and C. G. C. Tite (London 1997), 263–79. For the inventories of the library rooms at the secular cathedrals of Exeter and Lincoln, see Oliver, *Lives of the bishops of Exeter*, 366–75 and R. M. Wooley, *Catalogue of the manuscripts of Lincoln Cathedral chapter library* (Oxford 1927), ix–xiv. New editions of all these lists are forthcoming in the Corpus of British Medieval Library Catalogues.

22. On the process of selection at Durham, see Piper, 'Libraries of the monks of Durham', 223–5.

among the eight lecterns according to a fairly systematic subject-arrangement.[23] Five of the lecterns held books that were typical constituents of library rooms elsewhere, to judge from surviving lists and what may be inferred from pressmarks. These included the standard tools for biblical study, comprising both the technical and academic literature of the thirteenth and fourteenth centuries (such as a biblical concordance, Nicholas of Lyra's Postills on the Old and New Testaments, Aquinas on the Gospels, and Robert Holcot on Wisdom) as well as the inherited wisdom of the Fathers incorporated within the *Glossa ordinaria* and the *Magna glosatura* of Peter Lombard on the Pauline epistles and the Psalms; a selection of patristic and later exegesis and theology; the university textbooks and commentaries of the higher studies of theology and canon law, and (to a lesser extent) civil law and philosophy.[24] The *libraria* at Leicester, like that at Christ Church, Canterbury, also contained a number of volumes of history. But it is also unusual in a number of respects, most notably the heavy preponderance of works of Augustine (occupying the whole of the second lectern) by comparison with other patristic authors; the large number of medical books, and, perhaps most striking, the quantity of sermons, penitentials and other pastoral handbooks which took up the entire fourth lectern. These included not only well-known works but also the penitential of the Augustinian canon, Robert fitz Gille, archdeacon of Totnes (died 1186).[25] Such emphasis upon the practical application of biblical study, theology and canon law may explain the presence among the tools for exegesis of Richard Barre's *Compendium ueteris et noui testamenti* – a late-twelfth-century collection of biblical extracts, chosen and organized as a handy source for preaching and teaching the faithful.[26]

The bulk of the *libraria*, therefore, was devoted to the higher studies and to preaching and pastoral activity, for the most part reflecting the character of the abbey's holdings over-all. The final lectern, however, contained texts studied as part of the preliminaries to higher study, and these are generally less-well represented: just six volumes of logic (out of some forty volumes possessed by the abbey); three astronomical compendia, two arithmetical and geometrical volumes, Martianus Capella on the seven liberal arts, and a mere five volumes for the teaching and study of grammar.

A ninth lectern is described as being in the *scriptoria*, which may have been an annexe to the *libraria*. It is unclear whether this was a 'scriptorium' in the more generally understood meaning of the term, in other words a space for writing and correcting books. Since most of the books located there were the standard grammatical textbooks, as well as a 'ludus puerorum' (perhaps a liturgical drama), the *scriptoria* may have been used for teaching.[27] The canons were required to provide instruction in grammar to the junior canons as well as to boys in the almonry school, but where that teaching took place is not known.[28]

The books listed in the abbey church and in the chapel of the abbey's grange at Yngwardby

23. For the physical arrangement of the room, see below, Gullick, 'The binding descriptions', Appendix 2.

24. The latest authors represented are (for theology) the fourteenth-century Oxford theologians, Thomas Bradwardine (died 1349) and Richard FitzRalph (died 1360), (for philosophy) Walter Burley (died after 1344) and Peter of Auvergne (fl. 1300).

25. See note on A20.765.

26. R. Sharpe, 'Richard Barre's *Compendium Veteris et Noui Testamenti*', *Journal of Medieval Latin* 14 (2004), 128–46. Barre gave five books to the abbey: see below, n. 64.

27. A. I. Doyle, 'Book production by the monastic orders in England (c. 1375–1530): assessing the evidence' in *Medieval book production: assessing the evidence*, ed. L. L. Brownrigg (Los Altos

Hills, CA, 1990), 1–19. The cathedral chapter at Salisbury, when discussing the construction of a new library room in 1445, agreed that the works should include 'certain schools suitable for lectures . . . such schools and library to be built . . . over one side of the cloister of the church': Clark, *Care of books*, 121 and n. 2. I am grateful to Professor M. B. Parkes for this reference and for discussion about the meaning of the term 'scriptoria'.

28. Complaints about the lack of a grammar teacher to perform this requirement were made at Bishop William Alnwick's visitation in 1440: *Records of visitations held by William Alnwick bishop of Lincoln, Part 1*, ed. A. Hamilton Thompson, *Visitations of religious houses in the diocese of Lincoln* ii, Canterbury and York Society 24 (London 1919), 208–9 and 214.

were overwhelmingly liturgical volumes, although those on the pulpitum included a legendary, a copy of Nicholas Trevet's commentary on the Augustinian rule, five 'libri collacionum' and John de Burgo's pastoral manual, the *Pupilla oculi* (these were perhaps a small collection of books used for public reading within the abbey).[29] This section of the catalogue is of special interest as a rare conspectus of the number and precise location of the books involved in the liturgical life of a community at the end of the fifteenth century.[30] It reveals the number of volumes at each canon's stall, from the antiphoner, gradual, psalter, processional, breviary ('portiferium') and diurnal (containing the day hours of the Office) for the senior members of the community, to the antiphoner, gradual, psalter and processional for the more junior, with four canons (including the cellerer and sub-cellerer) having just a breviary and/or a diurnal. Earlier owners of these volumes can be glimpsed here and there.[31]

The books in the infirmary were wholly liturgical, which corresponds with the contents of other known infirmary collections, the various volumes of practical medicine recorded in the subject catalogue being kept elsewhere.[32] The books used for public reading in the refectory and at collation are not listed separately in the catalogue, unless the group of books kept on the pulpitum had this purpose. A two-volume bible is described in the subject catalogue as lying in the refectory (A20.1), and a volume containing the sermons of Bernard, Innocent III and Peter Lombard (A20.300) as being used for reading at collation. Other books recorded in the subject part of the catalogue may perhaps have been temporarily assigned for this purpose.

Unlike the slightly later catalogue from Syon Abbey, which was used for some years as a working document, and in which numerous deletions and additions cast light upon the use of books at the Abbey during the early decades of the sixteenth century (in particular, the impact of the introduction of printed material),[33] the Leicester catalogue contains too few alterations for changes in reading to be traced. The few surviving volumes acquired after the catalogue was made are also insufficient to indicate developments in the years before the Dissolution.[34]

The history of the collections

The earlier history of the books is only partially recoverable from information provided in the catalogue and from the surviving volumes. The most plentiful source of evidence is the names mentioned in just over a fifth of the entries in the subject catalogue (and occasionally in other sections, including the remarkably full record of the books made or acquired by Charyte himself). It is unclear how complete a record of donations this is, or how systematically such information had been recorded in earlier lists and then transmitted in the subsequent copies and compilations that lie behind the catalogue.[35] Close study of the binding descriptions has indicated that information in earlier lists was not always fully transmitted, or that categories of information had been

29. A20.1833–5, A20.1843.

30. A similarly detailed listing of the disposition of the liturgical books is found in the 1506 inventory from Exeter Cathedral: Oliver, *Lives of the bishops of Exeter*, 323–76.

31. A20.1721 and A20.1901–2 (listed with their current users at A20.1783 and 1770). Cross-references in the subject catalogue refer to psalters of Iohannes Blaby and W. de Thornton 'in the choir' (A20. 626 and 927), but, unless they were among the unnamed senior officers, these men were no longer canons when the list of books in the church was drawn up.

32. D. Nebbiai Dalla Guarda, 'Les livres de l'infirmerie dans les monastères médiévaux', *Revue Mabillon* n.s. 5 (1994), 57–81.

33. Gillespie, *Syon Abbey*, xlix–lxiii.

34. Cambridge, King's College 2 (a single-volume bible), Bodl. Rawlinson A 445 (sermons), and perhaps BL Harley 7333 and Bodl. Bodley 636: see below, Gullick and Webber, nos 1, 18, 22 and 24.

35. All but one of the entries that describe books also entered in the lists of books that Charyte was involved in producing or acquiring for the abbey, mention Charyte's name, but given his special status in relation to the document, such comprehensive treatment may have been exceptional. The only omission is A20.975, which does not mention the *tabula* purchased by Chartye (A20.1938) and which came to be bound with the copy of Hugutio's *Liber deriuationum* described in that entry.

included in lists of some parts of the holdings and not others.[36] The same may be true of information concerning former owners and donors. Individuals' names are found disproportionately in entries for certain types of book: single volume bibles, glossed books of the Bible, canon law and grammar; to a lesser extent in entries involving the academic texts of theology, natural philosophy, and logic, and even more occasionally, sermons, pastoral literature and devotional books. By contrast, surprisingly few names (just two) are found among the entries on civil law.[37] Many more of the books that, from their contents, must date from the fourteenth and fifteenth centuries may have been donated. All but 200 of the 1400-plus volumes recorded in the final recension of the catalogue of the brethren's library at Syon Abbey (founded in 1415) had been acquired in this way.[38]

Unfortunately, only eighteen of the eighty-odd names recorded in the Leicester catalogue as donors or procurers of books can be identified, all but four of them canons. Others may well have been members of the community or local clergy, to judge from the number of surnames formed from Leicestershire place-names, such as Aylestone, Barkby, Hathern, Ibstock, Kegworth and Shepshed.[39] Since names are not always given in full, it is not possible to calculate the precise number of individuals represented, or to match with confidence a Christian or surname with a name recorded fully elsewhere in the catalogue.

The role played by those named is not always clear. Two forms of wording are used: the author and/or title of the text plus a name in the genitive case (for example, 'Biblia parua Iohannis Barkby': A20.10), or the author and/or title of the work followed by 'per' and the name in the accusative ('Decreta glosata per R. Kegworth': A20.1276). The former probably records the previous owner, and was also commonly used as a form of donation inscription.[40] The meaning of the latter, however, is ambiguous, since it could refer not to an owner or donor but to some other kind of involvement in the procurement of the book. Such entries cannot therefore be used unreservedly as evidence for the personal book collection of the person named, or of his religious and intellectual interests. Nevertheless, since the alternative wording was almost exclusively used in the catalogue only for a very restricted range of texts (single volume bibles, and volumes of sermons, meditations and practical medicine), it is likely that 'per' was used in some instances to refer to a former owner.

Surviving manuscripts constitute a much smaller body of evidence from Leicester. All but two of the non-administrative volumes, including the two most recent identifications, can be matched with entries in the catalogue on the basis of their *secundo folio* references.[41] More may yet be identified among collections for which modern catalogues do not yet exist, or in which such information is not recorded.[42] Two survivors have been identified only from donation inscriptions

---

36. See below, Gullick, 'The binding descriptions', pp. 161–5.

37. A20.1262–3.

38. Gillespie, *Syon Abbey*, xliv.

39. Webber and Watson, *Libraries of the Augustinian canons*, 567–70 (Leicester Abbey donors or former holders of books).

40. N. R. Ker, *Medieval libraries of Great Britain*, 2nd edn (London 1964), xvii–xviii and xxvi.

41. Bodl. Rawlinson C 153 lacks its first leaf, so the *secundo folio* reference is now found on f. 1.

42. The use of *secundo folio* references as the sole means of identifying survivors is not without its hazards. Some texts are more likely to exist in copies with identical references, either because the constraints of their layout reduced the degree of variation likely to occur (as in the short-line layout of verse texts, or the arrangement of blocks of text and music in liturgical books), or where the second leaf marked the beginning of the text proper, the first containing prefatory matter: see Ker, *Medieval libraries*, xx, n. 6. The latter is the case in some copies of the *Institutes* of Priscian (M. T. Gibson, 'Priscian, *Institutiones grammaticae*: A handlist of manuscripts', *Scriptorium* 26 (1972), 105–24), and for this reason, in the absence of any other evidence to confirm a Leicester provenance, the identification of Edinburgh, University Library 137 with the copy recorded at A20.996, is unreliable (D. Williman and K. Corsano, 'Medieval Latin manuscripts in Scotland: some provenances', *Edinburgh Bibliographical Society Transactions* 6/5 (2002), 178–90, at 184).

Fig. 1. Cambridge, King's College 2, f. 494v

Fig. 2. Edinburgh, National Library of Scotland Advocates 18.5.13, f. 1r

(Cambridge, King's College 2 and Bodl. Rawlinson A 445) (fig. 1). These demonstrate that the books were given to the abbey after the catalogue had been compiled.[43] One more manuscript that may once have been owned by the abbey or one of the canons is a fourteenth-century copy of the *Decretals*, discarded by the late fifteenth century when a few leaves were reused as end-leaves by Charyte for his rental (now Bodl. Laud Misc. 625). Only York Minster XVI.M.6 bears an *ex libris* inscription in the strict sense of the term (colour pl. F).[44] The absence of such inscriptions from two manuscripts still in their medieval bindings (Cambridge, Queens' College 2 and 8) suggests that such inscriptions were never entered systematically in the books at Leicester. This may not have been unusual, although Augustinian houses are among those who more commonly adopted such inscriptions from the late twelfth and early thirteenth centuries.[45]

The surviving manuscripts range in date from the mid twelfth until the late fifteenth century. Their date of production on its own is an unsafe guide to when they entered the abbey's holdings. At least two of the earlier manuscripts were acquired late on. Edinburgh, National Library of Scotland, Advocates 18.5.13, ff. 1–47 (a late-twelfth-century copy of Ovid's *Fasti* of perhaps French origin) was acquired for the abbey by William Charyte in the later fifteenth century (fig. 2), whilst Cambridge, King's College 2, a thirteenth-century bible, was donated *c.* 1500.[46] Unfortunately the lack of early marks of ownership or donation (none of the surviving inscriptions predates the fifteenth century) or early annotating hands makes it difficult to establish by what date books produced elsewhere may have been acquired.

43. See below, Gullick and Webber, nos 1 and 18.

44. '[. . .] Mon' beate M[arie] Leycestr' in p[ra]tis', now partly trimmed away.

45. Ker, *Medieval libraries*, xvi.

46. Gullick and Webber, nos 10 and 1.

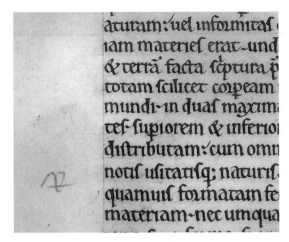

Fig. 3. Cambridge, Queens' College 8, f. 3v   Fig. 4. Cambridge, Trinity College B.14.7, f. 144r

The earliest evidence of a common (and perhaps Leicester) ownership are scruffy pencil annotations, including a characteristic **R** added in the margins in four manuscripts (fig. 3).[47] Dating
such notes is not easy, but the character of the script employed and the use of arabic numerals suggest a date in the thirteenth or earlier fourteenth century. A Leicester provenance for the remainder of the books can be firmly established only from the fifteenth century. For some, the catalogue
entries are the earliest evidence, but eight contain marginal annotations in the same or very similar
hand datable to the late fourteenth or first half of the fifteenth century (fig. 4 and see also fig. 7).[48]

The twelfth and thirteenth centuries

Religious houses founded during the twelfth century drew to varying degrees upon their own
scribal resources or upon commissions, donations and other forms of acquisition to build up their
fundamental collections of books for the liturgy, public reading at mealtimes and collation, and
for private study and devotion.[49] Substantial numbers of twelfth-century books survive from only
two English Augustinian foundations, Cirencester and Lanthony Secunda.[50] The Lanthony books
have yet to receive sufficient detailed study to bring to light the extent of in-house production, but
contemporary inscriptions in several of the Cirencester books show that the canons themselves
were involved in producing books in the middle quarters of the twelfth century.[51] These books display the hands of a number of good scribes, well-executed minor initials and a homogeneity in
their bindings – evidence of a well-established tradition of book production at the abbey.[52]

No comparable tradition was established at Leicester, to judge from the few remaining books
that may have formed Leicester's earliest holdings. Five contain fundamental patristic and exeget-
ical texts that typically formed the core of the book collections of religious houses in the late
eleventh century and twelfth centuries: Cambridge, Queens' College 2 (Ambrose, *De officiis, De*

47. Gullick and Webber, nos 2, 3 and 5–6.

48. Gullick and Webber, nos 2–8 and 19.

49. N. R. Ker, *English manuscripts in the century after the Norman
Conquest* (Oxford 1960).

50. Ker, *Medieval libraries*, 51–2 and 112; A. G. Watson, ed.
Medieval libraries of Great Britain, supplement (London 1987), 14
and 41–3.

51. See, for example, A. G. Watson, *Catalogue of dated and
datable manuscripts c. 435–1600 in Oxford Libraries* 2 vols. (Oxford
1984), i, nos 798–803; ii, pls 56–8 and 60.

52. M. Gullick 'The bindings' in R. A. B. Mynors and R. M.
Thomson, *Catalogue of the manuscripts of Hereford Cathedral library*
(Cambridge 1993), xxvi–xxxii, at xxvii, xxix and n. 114. A study of the
Cirencester books is being prepared by Michael Gullick.

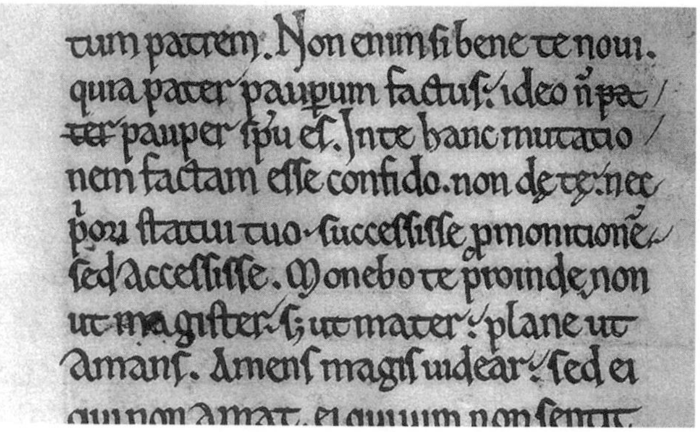

Fig. 5. Cambridge, Queens' College 8, f. iiir

Ioseph patriarcha and *De patriarchis*, and Augustine on the epistle of St John; p. 175, figs. 1 and 2) and 8 (Odo of Canterbury on the Pentateuch, attributed here to Haymo; figs. 3 and 5); Cambridge, Trinity College B.2.22 (Gregory on Ezekiel; p. 177, figs. 3 and 4) and B.3.27 (Ambrose on Luke; p. 178, figs. 5 and 6); Bodl. Rawlinson C 153 (*ps.* Augustine, *De mirabilibus sacrae scripturae*) (p. 187, figs. 14 and 15).[53] Although no hands common to two or more of these books have been identified with certainty, the quality of the parchment, handwriting and decoration is generally so modest as to suggest local manufacture.[54] The scribes in the two Queens' manuscripts, and the three scribes of the original end-leaves of the twelfth-century binding of Queens' 8 (from an abandoned copy of Bernard's *De consideratione*) also share the same distinctive scribal habit: a wavy-line mark of medial punctuation (figs. 3 and 5).[55] BL Additional 57533, a copy of Geoffrey of Burton's Life of St Modwenna, is a similarly modest book made at the turn of the twelfth/thirteenth centuries, which may perhaps have been produced locally.[56] The rather conservative character of the hand is a feature shared with that of the sole surviving original charter from the abbey, the confirmation charter of Robert IV, earl of Leicester, 1190–1204. This was almost certainly produced by a scribe from the abbey rather than by one of Robert's own clerks, since the scribe wrote a competent medium-size bookhand rather than the informal business hands more typical of the clerks of royal and baronial households (p. 250, fig. 1, and p. 192, fig. 22).[57]

The quality of parchment, handwriting and decoration of two of the remaining twelfth-century volumes, Cambridge, Trinity College, B.16.5 (Peter Lombard's *Sentences*) (pp. 180–1, figs 8–11 and colour pl. E) and York Minster XVI.M.6 (Cicero, *De inuentione*, etc.) (p. 188, figs 16–18 and colour pl. F), reflect markedly more refined traditions of book production.[58] At present it seems likely that the Lombard was an import, though at how early a date cannot be established, but the Cicero may have been produced locally: its arabesque initials share decorative motifs with the major arabesque initial in Queens' 2 (compare p. 175, fig. 1 with p. 188, figs. 16 and 17).[59] York XVI.M.7, a modest but well-written copy of commentaries on Cicero, may be an import (p. 189, fig. 19).[60]

53. Gullick and Webber, nos 2–3, 5–6 and 19.

54. Trinity B.2.22 may be an exception. Although similar to the others in its general characteristics, it contains rather more elaborate arabesque initials which are similar to those from St Albans: see Gullick and Webber, no. 5, n. 10.

55. On the use of this symbol, see Ker, *English manuscripts*, 47–9.

56. Gullick and Webber, no. 11.

57. For a more detailed description of the hand, see Gullick and Webber, no. 25.

58. Gullick and Webber, nos 9 and 20.

59. I am grateful to Michael Gullick for this observation.

60. Gullick and Webber, no. 21.

How many more of the volumes of *patristica*, pre-thirteenth-century exegesis and other texts recorded in the catalogue were produced or acquired during the first fifty-hundred years after the abbey's foundation cannot be determined. Only seven entries record names identifiable as donors during this period. Two psalters were associated with the abbey's founder, Robert II, earl of Leicester (died 1168), and his wife Amice: both are named in one entry, Amice alone in the other.[61] Abbey tradition, as transmitted by the chronicler Henry Knighton, a canon of Leicester from *c.* 1370–*c.* 1396, claimed that Robert entered the community in his retirement and was buried in the abbey church, but other evidence suggests that he took the habit only on his death-bed.[62] After his death, Amice entered one of his other foundations, the nunnery at Nuneaton.

Five volumes of the fundamental texts of the higher studies of theology, civil and canon law from the later twelfth century had been owned (and presumably donated) by Richard Barre. The precise nature of his association with the abbey is unknown, although he may have been a younger brother of Hugh Barre, a *familiaris* in the household of the earls of Leicester and, for a time, archdeacon of Leicester, who by the early 1160s was a canon of Leicester.[63] Richard was archdeacon of Lisieux in the 1180s, archdeacon of Ely in the 1190s, and in 1202 was a judge-delegate for Pope Innocent III.[64] Hugh, for a few years, combined the office of archdeacon with his being a canon. Unless Richard had done the same, what is known of his career leaves little scope for him also to have become a member of the community. Nevertheless, his association with Leicester would appear to have been close. The abbey also possessed a copy of his commentary on the Old and New Testaments, and two copies of his verses 'De molestiis curie' (for which no witnesses are known to survive).[65] A locally-made thirteenth-century miscellany (but perhaps not from the abbey) contains two copies of an otherwise unattested short set of verses attributed to him.[66]

The catalogue also records fifteen glossed books of the bible and a volume of sermons formerly owned and perhaps donated by an as yet unidentified Henry Whatton.[67] Similar sets of glossed books were acquired by individual masters and prelates and donated by them to religious houses during the second half of the twelfth and first half of the thirteenth century.[68] These books may have been acquired by the abbey early on, but a later date is not impossible.

Surviving manuscripts and information in the catalogue otherwise provide very little certain evidence for the production and acquisition of books during the thirteenth century. Cambridge, Trinity College B.1.8 comprises two originally independent volumes, written by the same scribe and brought together shortly afterwards, when a contents list was added in the late thirteenth or early fourteenth century (fig. 6).[69] The character of the handwriting (rather irregular and incorporating features of cursive script), the very modest initials, and the somewhat roughly and incompletely supplied rubrics, give the manuscript a home-made appearance. The first part contains a copy of William of Tournai's, *Flores Bernardi*, the second (now incomplete) contained several texts of Augustine, a Life of St Bernard and William of Conches' *Moralium dogma philosophorum*. It may have been made at Leicester, since phi-shaped marginal *notae*, probably in the hand of the

61. A20.66 'Psalterium fundatorum'; A20.67 'Psalterium fundatricis'.

62. J. R. Lumby, *Chronicon Henrici Knighton vel Cnitthon, monachi Leycestrensis* i, RS 92 (London 1895), 63; D. Crouch, *The Beaumont twins: the roots and branches of power in the twelfth century* (Cambridge 1986), 95–6.

63. Sharpe, 'Richard Barre', and Crouch, *Beaumont twins*, 150–1, revising *Fasti Ecclesiae Anglicanae, 1066–1300*, iii. Lincoln, ed. D. E. Greenway (London 1977), 33.

64. The volumes comprised glossed books of the Psalms and Pauline epistles (A20.57 and 179), Peter Lombard's *Sentences*

(A20.508), Justinian's *Codex* (A20.1263) and Gratian's *Decretum* (A20.1285).

65. A20.146, 469h and 618b.

66. Bodl. Bodley 57. Its contents suggest a local origin: see Gullick and Webber, no. 23.

67. A20.23, 30, 35, 39, 40, 43–4, 48, 54, 58, 80b, 81, 109, 119, 126, 133 and 840.

68. C. F. R. de Hamel, *Glossed books of the bible and the origins of the Paris booktrade* (Woodbridge 1984), 5–13.

69. Gullick and Webber, no. 4.

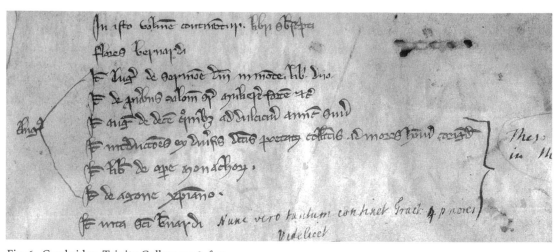

Fig. 6. Cambridge, Trinity College B.1.8, f. 1r

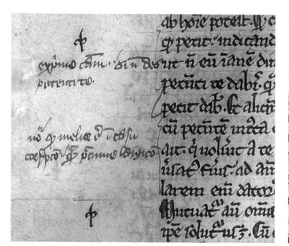

Fig. 7. Cambridge, Trinity College B.1.8, f. 15v

Fig. 8. Cambridge, Trinity College B.14.30, f. 33r

text scribe, resemble a similar annotation found in Cambridge, Trinity College B.14.30, a late-eleventh-century collection of contemporary booklets, probably produced at Exeter Cathedral but, like Trinity B.1.8, certainly at Leicester by the fifteenth century (compare figs. 7 and 8). In the fourteenth-century it was collated with another copy of the *Flores Bernardi* and, at the same time, carefully annotated with marginalia identifying the sources of the extracts comprising the *Flores*, but this hand is not found in any other surviving Leicester book.

None of the names of former owners or donors is securely identifiable as a member of the community during the thirteenth century. The donations of glossed books of the bible by the otherwise unknown Richard Hastyng, Richard Pepyn and Richard Scott may, like the more substantial donation of Henry Whatton, date from the late twelfth or thirteenth centuries.[70] The surname Pepyn, named in connection with a bible (A20.15) may be that of Richard Pepyn, but could refer to William Pepyn, fifth abbot of Leicester (1204/5–1222/4).[71]

70. A20.106, 127, 178; A20.61, 107, and A20.46–7.   71. Hamilton Thompson, *Leicester Abbey*, 14 and 184.

The fourteenth and fifteenth centuries

More certain evidence of the role played by canons in the provision of books exists only from the fourteenth century onwards. Six members of the community are identifiable from the names recorded in the catalogue: Henry Stretford, a canon in 1318;[72] William Cloune, canon, then abbot 1345–78;[73] Ralph Thurlestone, canon in 1345, and prior of Mottesfont from 1352–*c.* 1356;[74] Geoffrey Salow, treasurer in 1357;[75] John Thorpe, abbot of Wellow from 1374–1410,[76] and the chronicler, Henry Knighton, canon from at least 1370 until *c.* 1396.[77] In his Chronicle, Knighton depicts the abbacy of William Cloune as a period during which the abbey flourished.[78] The books associated with Cloune and two of his contemporaries, Ralph Thurlestone and Geoffrey Salow, and other evidence in the catalogue, give further substance to Knighton's account.

William Cloune and Ralph Thurlestone are known to have been in Oxford in 1339, the same year that Pope Benedict XII, in his *Constitutiones ad canonicos nigros*, laid down formal requirements for larger Augustinian houses to send canons as students to university.[79] The books they procured for the abbey may well have been acquired during the course of their studies at Oxford, and strongly suggest that both studied canon law.[80] If Ralph is the 'Thurleston' named in A20.1184 and 1223 as procuring copies of medical works by Constantinus Africanus, Isaac Iudaeus and Galen, then he may also have studied medicine. Their contemporary, Geoffrey Salow, may have

72. Hamilton Thompson, *Leicester Abbey*, 22. He owned or procured A20.7 (Bible), 826 (a volume known as *Omne bonum*, containing sermons and *ps.* William of Conches, *Moralium dogma philosophorum*), and 1294 (Gregory IX, *Decretales*).

73. A. B. Emden, *A biographical register of the University of Oxford to A.D. 1500* 3 vols. (Oxford 1957), i, 446–7, hereafter *BRUO*; Hamilton Thompson, *Leicester Abbey*, 28–39. He is named in A20.176 (glossed Pauline epistles), 1300–1 (two copies of Gregory IX, *Decretales*, the first of which was glossed), 1310 (*Liber Sextus Decretalium*, with the commentaries of Cardinal Jean le Moine, Jesselin de Cassagnes and Iohannes Andreae), and 1357 (Guido de Baysio on the *Decretum*).

74. Emden, *BRUO* iii, 1872; Hamilton Thompson, *Leicester Abbey*, 27 and 35–6. He owned or procured A20.1290–1 (two copies of Gregory IX, *Decretales*, glossed) and 1356 (Guido de Baysio on the *Decretum*). A20.436 also passed through his hands (now Cambridge, Trinity B.14.7, containing *ps.* Bonaventure, *Meditationes de passione Christi*; James of Milan, *Stimulus amoris*; *ps.* Augustine, *De diligendo Deo*, *Liber soliloquiorum animae ad Deum*, and *Meditationes de Spiritu Sancto*; Anselm and *ps.* Anselm, Prayers and meditations: see below no. 7). Either Thurlestone or a fifteenth-century canon, Ralph Seyton may be the Ralph named in A20.1102 (Duns Scotus's commentary on Porphyry's *Isagoge*), 1112 (Walter Burley on Aristotle's *Posterior analytics* and a commentary on the same text by 'Alkok'), and 1140 (Antonius Andreae on Aristotle's *Metaphysics*). He may be the Thurleston named in entries recording two medical manuscripts: A20.1184 (Constantinus Africanus, *Pantegni*; Isaac Iudaeus, *Liber febrium* and four standard medical texts of Galen), and 1223 (Constantinus Africanus, *Liber graduum*).

75. Bodl. Laud Misc. 625, f. 185r. He is named in the catalogue (A20. 244e) as the author of a pentitenial *summa* entitled *Lucerna conscientiae*, of which two complete copies and an excerpt are known to survive (R. Sharpe, *A handlist of the Latin writers of Great Britain and Ireland before 1540* (Turnhout 1997), 128); three more copies are recorded anonymously in the catalogue (A20. 868a, 869a and 870). Salow was the donor or procurer of A20.8 (Bible and *Interpretationes nominum hebraicorum*), 333 (a primarily devotional miscellany), 435 (*ps.* Bonaventure, *Meditationes de passione Christi*; James of Milan, *Stimulus amoris*; *ps.* Augustine, *De diligen-*

do Deo, *Liber soliloquiorum animae ad Deum*, and *Meditationes de Spiritu Sancto*; Anselm and *ps.* Anselm, Prayers and meditations), 477 (Ambrosius Autpertus, *De conflictu uitiorum et uirtutum*; glossed gospels of Matthew and Luke, and sermons), 510 (Peter Lombard, *Sentences*), 534 (Sermons of Peter Comestor), 570 (Thomas Bradwardine, *De causa Dei contra Pelagium*), 572–3 (two volumes of 'Quaestiones theologice'), 960 (devotional poems of John of Howden, and the *Sigillum sanctae Mariae* attributed to Honorius Augustodunensis), 980 (a 'Liber de rhetorica', perhaps Cicero, *De inventione* and/or *ps.* Cicero, *De ratione dicendi*), 981 (a 'liber de grammatica'), 1067 (an 'Opus de rhetorica super Tullio': perhaps a duplicate entry for 980, or a commentary on Cicero or *ps.* Cicero), 1094 ('Logicalia'), 1095 ('Tractatus plurimum insolubilium'), 1132 (Averroes on Aristotle's *Metaphysics*), and 1284 (Gratian, *Decretum*).

76. Hamilton Thompson, *Leicester Abbey*, 36. His name is recorded only in A20.986 (Hugutio of Pisa, *Liber deriuationum*).

77. G. H. Martin, 'Henry Knighton' in *ODNB*. He owned or procured A20.742 (Bartholomaeus Anglicus, *De proprietatibus rerum*), 903 (John Beleth, *Summa de ecclesiasticis officiis*), 928 (a cross-reference to a lapidary not recorded as a main entry, which contained a copy of Honorius Augustodunensis, *Elucidarium*); 959 (John Howden's devotional poems), and 963 (a commentary on the Lord's prayer and a penitential). For his Chronicle (A20.636), see G. H. Martin, ed. *Knighton's Chronicle 1337–1396* (Oxford 1995); the earlier and less original part of the chronicle is edited in Lumby, *Chronicon*.

78. Martin, *Knighton's Chronicle*, esp. 199–203.

79. H. E. Salter, *Chapters of the Augustinian canons*, Canterbury and York Society 29 (London 1922), 229–30; S. Forde, 'The educational organization of the Augustinian canons in England and Wales and their university life at Oxford, 1325–1448', *History of Universities* 13 (1994), 21–60, at 25–7 and 34. The catalogue records two copies of Benedict's *Constitutions*: A20. 1327 and 1834b; the latter was kept in the abbey church on the pulpitum as part of a volume that also contained Nicholas Trevet's commentary on the Augustinian rule and the *Constitutions* of Cardinal Otto and others.

80. Forde, 'Educational Organization', 42, and above, nn. 73–4.

studied theology at university: the books he acquired included Thomas Bradwardine's *De causa Dei contra Pelagium* (a text completed in 1344), as well as two glossed books of the bible, Peter Lombard's *Sentences* and two volumes of 'Quaestiones theologice').[81]

The Benedictine Constitutions of 1339 recommended that, where possible, copies of the required texts should be provided from the resources of the mother-house and distributed among the student canons for their use at university.[82] No records survive of the books sent to Oxford or Cambridge by any English Augustinian house. Nevertheless, the Leicester catalogue describes significant numbers of set texts, commentaries and other compilations associated with the teaching of philosophy, theology and canon law at the universities, a proportion of which is likely to have come to the abbey during the fourteenth century, and may have been used by its students.

One striking absence from the names recorded in the catalogue is that of Leicester's most outstanding student canon, Philip Repyngdon (*c.* 1345–1424), canon by 1369 and abbot from 1394–1405, who incepted at Oxford in 1382, was chancellor of the university from 1400 until at least 1403, and bishop of Lincoln from 1405 until 1419. Repyngdon studied theology, and was an early disciple of John Wyclif, although he subsequently recanted.[83] It was perhaps through him that the abbey came to acquire copies of Wyclif's sermons, logic and *Trialogus*.[84] Repyngdon put his learning to practical use in a set of *Sermones super euangelia dominicalia*, probably composed between 1382 and 1393.[85] Some of his sources, such as the gospel commentaries of William of Nottingham and Nicolas de Gorran are not represented in the Leicester catalogue, but others are: for example, the *Sermones dominicales* of Jacopo da Voragine;[86] the Postills of Nicholas of Lyra,[87] and various works of Augustine, Robert Grosseteste and Bernard of Clairvaux. In the absence of any documentary record of his books, it is not possible to know how far he drew upon a personal book collection or upon the holdings of the abbey. Only one of his books is known to survive: an illuminated copy of Petrus de Aureolis' *Compendium super bibliam*, which he donated to Lincoln.[88]

More is known about Repyngdon's career than that of any other canon. His activities may allow some speculation about the practical applications of some of the other canons' studies and reading during the fourteenth century. Repyngdon was a close friend and, by 1404, confessor to Henry IV. He was perhaps responsible for the compilation of Cambridge, Trinity College B.2.16, a devotional and theological compendium produced for Henry before he became king, part of which is textually so closely related to the devotional compendium associated with Ralph Thurlestone (Cambridge, Trinity College B.14.7), as to indicate that it was copied from it.[89] Other canons may also have acted as confessors or religious advisers to members of the aristocracy. A connection of this kind perhaps lay behind the donation of a book of meditations by Sir Roger Aungerville, lord of the manor of Ingarsby, Leicestershire, who made a covenant with the abbey in

81. See above, n. 75.

82. Salter, *Chapters*, 236; Forde, 'Educational organization', 40.

83. Emden, *BRUO* iii, 1565–7; S. Forde, 'Philip Repyngdon' in *ODNB*.

84. A20.858, 1107 (his *Logica*, and/or his *Logica continuatio*) and 611. Noting the presence of these works in the late-fifteenth-century catalogue and the possible role played by Repyngdon, Professor Hudson observes that 'while there is no direct proof that they were there a century earlier, there is less reason for their acquisition at a later date': A. Hudson, *The premature reformation: Wycliffite texts and Lollard history* (Oxford 1988), 77, n. 106.

85. S. Forde, 'Social outlook and preaching in a Wycliffite *Sermones dominicales* collection' in *Church and chronicle in the*

middle ages: essays presented to John Taylor, ed. I. Wood and G. A. Loud (London 1991), 179–91.

86. A20.478. Copies recorded at A20.479–80 were procured after Repyngdon's death.

87. A20.144–5 and 610.

88. BL Royal 8 G.iii, perhaps specially commissioned as a gift: R. M. Thomson, *Catalogue of the manuscripts of Lincoln Cathedral Chapter library* (Woodbridge 1989), xviii.

89. A20.436. The quality of the script and decoration indicate that it was the work of professional craftsmen. For a preliminary account of the manuscript, see *The Cambridge illuminations: ten centuries of book production in the medieval west*, ed. P. Binski and S. Panayotova (London/Turnhout 2005), 258–9, no. 118.

1350 for the provision of a chaplain for the chapel of St Nicholas at Ingarsby.[90] Abbot William Cloune was licensed to hear confessions in the archdeaconry of Leicester in 1358.[91] How far this or other pastoral activity carried out by the canons extended beyond the abbey's precincts, or what form it took, cannot be known, but the quantity of sermon material and pastoral handbooks among the holdings of the community is very striking.

Entries in the catalogue also suggest a significant interest in devotional literature.[92] Geoffrey Salow, for example, possessed or procured a second copy of the devotional compendium that had passed through the hands of Ralph Thurlestone, as well as a volume containing devotional poems of John of Howden, and the *Sigillum sanctae Mariae* attributed to Honorius Augustodunensis, and a miscellany containing primarily devotional items.[93] Knighton also acquired a copy of John of Howden's devotional poems.[94]

Enthusiasm for learning and standards of religious observance could fluctuate, and were affected by the energy or otherwise of the abbot and the senior canons. In 1440, at Bishop William Alnwick's visitation, several canons complained that numbers of pupils in the almonry school had fallen to six from the sixteen or twenty-four they remembered had once been there, and that there was no one to teach either them or the novices and younger canons in grammar and the other elementary parts of knowledge.[95] Their view of happier times some decades before, presumably during the abbacies of Repyngdon and his successor, Richard Rothley (1405–17), is perhaps supported by the five volumes of grammatical texts procured by Thomas Bathe, a canon in 1408.[96] A large proportion of the books purchased or procured for the abbey by William Charyte during the second half of the century contained texts used for the teaching and study of grammar, which may reflect efforts to improve the resources for elementary instruction in the abbey.[97]

Nevertheless, visitations were prone to elicit criticism against unpopular abbots, and the canons' depositions may present a misleading picture. The Benedictine Constitutions' requirement to send canons to university was being fulfilled in 1440, in the person of Ralph Seyton,

90. A20.958; Hamilton Thompson, *Leicester Abbey*, 151. The manor of Ingarsby came into the abbey's possession during Cloune's abbacy (Martin, *Knighton's Chronicle*, 201).

91. Emden, *BRUO* i, 447.

92. T. Webber, 'Latin devotional texts and the books of the Augustinian canons of Thurgarton Priory and Leicester Abbey in the late middle ages' in *Books and collectors 1200–1700: essays presented to Andrew Watson*, ed. J. P. Carley and C. G. C. Tite (London 1997), 27–41 at 30–5.

93. A20.435, 960 and 333.

94. A20.959.

95. Hamilton Thompson, *Visitations*, 208–9.

96. A rental attributed to him is dated 1408 in Bodl. Laud Misc. 625, f. 12r; it is recorded in the catalogue (A20.1871, attributed to 'Bathe'), and may also be the rental mentioned in A20.1875, which is attributed, perhaps incorrectly, to 'Iohannis Bathe'. In addition to the grammar books (A20.982–3, 1000–1001 and 1006), he also gave a Bible (A20.14), a volume containing Hrabanus Maurus on Matthew, Augustine, *De opere monachorum*, and other unspecified contents (A20.493), and a medical compilation, including a 'tractatus in anglico' (A20.1204).

97. A20.1023 (a grammatical compendium), 1052–61 (ten volumes of grammatical reading-texts: Lucan, *De bello ciuili*; Ovid, *Heroides*, *Epistulae ex Ponto*, *Fasti* and *Ars amatoria*; *Claudianus maior*; a commentary (perhaps that of Remigius) on Martianus Capella; a commentary on ps. Boethius, *De disciplina scholarium*; Alan of Lille, *Anticlaudianus*, and Macrobius's commentary on

Cicero's *De somno Scipionis*), 1933 (Alexander de Villa Dei, *Doctrinale* and Eberhard of Béthune, *Graecismus*), 1938 (*tabula* on Hugutio of Pisa, *Liber deriuationum*), 1953 (Guido Faba, *Epistolae*), 1954 (a 'Dialogus creaturarum moralizatus, etc.'), 1955 (*Vita Æsopi*), and 1956 (perhaps William Brito, *Expositiones uocabulorum Bibliae*). In addition to the liturgical and administrative books and rolls that Charyte acquired or copied (A20.1892–1925), he was also involved in the production or acquisition of A20.80 (glossed Proverbs, Song of Songs and Ecclesiastes), 325 (Hugh of Saint-Cher, *Sermones de tempore et de sanctis*), 433 (Boethius, *Philosophiae consolatio*), 755 (Iohannes de Burgo, *Pupilla oculi*), 824 (John of Bromyard, *Distinctiones*), 861 (Richard de Bury, *Philobiblon* and a miscellany of other texts), 862 (Ranulf Higden, *Ars componendi sermones* and a miscellany of other texts, including a number of mathematical items and Nicholas Bollard's *De cultura arborum et plantarum*), 971 (a devotional miscellany), 972 (Henry Suso, *Horologium sapientiae*), 1150 (a book of logic), 1151–2 (Aristotle, *De anima* and *Metaphysica*), 1309 (Gregory IX, *Decretales*), 1930 (a book called 'Vnus omnium', presumably some kind of miscellany), 1952 (the *Speculum Christiani*), 1957 (the commentary on the rule of Augustine attributed to Hugh of Saint-Victor), and 1958 (a *tabula* on unspecified works of Aquinas). Charyte also acquired two astronomical instruments: a 'navis' (also known as a 'navicula': a kind of portable sundial) and a 'triangulus' (listed after A20.1167), one of which was designated for the use of a student canon, Thomas Halom (in 1506 the *prior studentium* at the Augustinian college of St Mary at Oxford: Emden, *BRUO* ii, 849 s.v. Thomas Hallam).

canon-scholar at Oxford.[98] The books he procured unfortunately do not indicate whether he attended lectures in the higher faculties of theology or canon law.[99] John Pomerey, sub-prior and master of the novices in 1440 (and abbot 1442–74), was competent to deliver the visitation sermon, and his acquisitions included university texts on natural philosophy and logic, including the commentary on Aristotle's *Categories* by the late-fourteenth-century Oxford master, Robert Alyngton (died after 1395).[100]

Four other canons are also named as donating or procuring books for the abbey during the fifteenth century: William Sadyngton, abbot 1420–42;[101] John Sadyngton, cellerer in 1440;[102] John Schepeschede, sub-cellerer in 1440 and abbot 1474–85,[103] and Thomas Asty, canon in 1440.[104] As far as the higher studies are concerned, their acquisitions were more restricted than those of canons during the fourteenth century. The most notable donation was William Sadyngton's purchase of nine books of academic medicine from a 'medicus', John Bokedene. These substantially supplemented the abbey's holdings of twelfth-century and earlier medical texts, with works from the thirteenth and fourteenth centuries, such as the *Lilium medicinae* and *De prognosticiis* of Bernard de Gordon (died *c.* 1320) and the *Rosa medicina* of John of Gaddeston (died before 1349). Natural philosophy and logic are the only other university subjects well-represented among their acquisitions.

Marginal annotations in several of the surviving books provide further evidence of learned activity at the abbey some time between the late fourteenth and mid-fifteenth century.[105] There are slight variations in the size and appearance of the handwriting, but most, if not all, are probably the work of a single individual (figs. 4 and 7). They are found almost exclusively in copies of patristic texts, and draw attention (usually in the form 'Nota quod . . .') to noteworthy words, phrases or statements, perhaps for future use in sermons. Both the handwriting and contents of these marginalia deserve more thorough treatment than has been possible for this article, as does the precise nature of the relationship between the set of annotations supplied in the copy of Augustine's *De diligendo Deo* in Cambridge, Trinity College B.14.7 (the early fourteenth-century book which

98. Emden, *BRUO* iii, 1676; Hamilton Thompson, *Visitations*, 206–217; Hamilton Thompson, *Leicester Abbey*, 63 and 68–71.

99. A20.466 (Alexander Nequam on the Song of Songs), 467 (Alexander Nequam, *De naturis rerum*, his commentary on Ecclesiastes and *De laudibus diuinae sapientiae*), 480 (perhaps Iacobus de Voragine, *Sermones de tempore*) and 646 (Ranulf Higden, *Polychronicon*); four volumes of grammatical treatises or reading-texts: 1009 (Alexander de Villa Dei, *Doctrinale* and Eberhard de Béthune, *Graecismus*), 1042 (Geoffrey of Vinsauf, *Poetria noua*), 1043 (Alan of Lille, *Anticlaudianus*), 1045 (Alan of Lille, *De planctu naturae*), and 1330–1 (two copies of Raymond of Pennafort, *Summa de casibus poenitentiae*). He was perhaps the Ralph who acquired copies of Duns Scotus on Porphyry's *Isagoge* (A20.1102), Walter Burley on Aristotle's *Posterior analytics* and a commentary on the same text by 'Alkok' (A20.1112), and Antonius Andreae on Aristotle's *Metaphysics* (A20.1140), although Ralph Thurlestone is another possibility.

100. A20.366 (*tabula* to Richard of Saint-Victor, *Beniamin minor*), 501 (letters of Peter of Blois), 785 (sermons of Peter Comestor), 1046 (Alan of Lille, *De planctu naturae*), 1099 (Thomas Sutton, commentary on Aristotle's *Categoriae*), 1100 (Duns Scotus, *Quaestiones* on Aristotle's *Categoriae*), 1101 (Robert Alyngton, Commentary on Aristotle's *Categoriae*), and 1138 (Averroes on Aristotle's *Physica* and *De anima*). He was probably the 'Iohannes abbas' who acquired a copy of Hrabanus Maurus on Matthew (A20.495).

101. Hamilton Thompson, *Leicester Abbey*, 61–9. A20.498 (letters of Peter of Blois) and 1169–77 (nine medical volumes containing the standard texts of the Articella and academic treatises and commentaries from the eleventh to the fourteenth century, purchased from a *medicus*, John Bokedene). On Abbot Sadyngton, see also A. Roe, 'Abbot Sadyngton of Leicester Abbey and onychomancy' below, 217–24.

102. Hamilton Thompson, *Visitations*, 207. A20.499 (letters of Peter of Blois), 1122 (Aristotle, *Libri naturales*), and 1123 (Aristotle, *Metaphysica* and *Ethica*).

103. Hamilton Thompson, *Visitations*, 206–17. A20.366 (*tabula* to Richard of Saint-Victor, *Beniamin minor*), 386 ('Odo super evangelia': perhaps Odo of Cheriton, *Sermones dominicales*), 479 Iacobus de Voragine, *Sermones de tempore*), and 492 (Hrabanus Maurus on Matthew).

104. Hamilton Thompson, *Visitations*, 209 and 211–12. A20.17 (Bible).

105. I have not yet been able to date the hand closely. The notes are written in a tiny Anglicana, largely free from any features of the continental cursive that began to influence handwriting in England from the late fourteenth and early fifteenth century onwards, apart from the use of single-compartment a, yet displaying little if any of the stylistic features (such as hook-shaped ascenders) that characterize the writing of Anglicana during the fourteenth century.

passed through the hands of Ralph Thurlestone) and an identical set in Trinity B.2.16, the theological and devotional miscellany made for the future Henry IV, written in the hand of the text scribe (which must therefore predate 1399). Only closer dating of the handwriting of the annotator will be able to prove whether the scribe of B.2.16 could have transcribed the annotations from B.14.7, or whether the annotator was active after the late fourteenth century, and drew upon existing marginalia in other copies of the texts.

Book-production in the later Middle Ages

The far greater number of identifiable names of donors and procurers of books from the fourteenth and fifteenth centuries compared with the first 150 or so years of the abbey's history suggests that, at Leicester as elsewhere, donation or acquisition of new and second-hand books were the main sources of book provision in the later Middle Ages. The catalogue, however, is an important witness to in-house monastic book production during this period. The detailed statements that form the headings to the lists of the books with which William Charyte was associated are the best evidence of such activity at Leicester. Inferences about local production may also be drawn from identical combinations of texts in two or more entries in the catalogue, which point to the abbey's holdings being used as exemplars for further copies for members of the community.

Charyte's lists distinguish between the thirty-three books he purchased and those in whose production he was involved, either causing others to make them (twenty-one volumes, plus another sixteen which he himself notated with music), or writing them himself (another twelve volumes and twenty-three rolls). With the exception of a copy of the sermon collection of Hugh of Saint-Cher, all of the books he was instrumental in producing at the abbey were either liturgical or business volumes, whereas the books he purchased were all for study or private devotion. Charyte's own scribal activity involved supplying the musical notation in service books and producing rentals and other administrative records. In only one instance did he act as the text scribe of a book for study, when he compiled a 'liber de certis vocabilis biblie', written on paper (A20.1912), but he nevertheless got another scribe to make a fair copy of this compilation on parchment (A20.1887). Charyte, therefore, does not appear to have produced formal copies of either books or documentary records himself. The catalogue does not tell us whether the scribes involved were members of the community, salaried living-in laymen, or other local scribes.

The lists of Charyte's achievements are a valuable reminder that the scribal resources of a community were directed towards the production of administrative records as well as books, and that those individuals who demonstrated particular care for the management of their community's books were often also engaged in producing other forms of written record.[106] Charyte's own preoccupations may lie behind the inclusion of lists of administrative books and rolls in the catalogue, and the comments on the importance of such records incorporated in two of the entries.[107] Administrative records and books are usually treated separately in modern scholarship, but the handwriting of the former is important evidence of scribal skills and resources. Of the five

---

106. The range of Charyte's activities is comparable with that of Henry of Kirkstead, librarian at Bury St Edmunds (died c. 1378), William Curteys, successively cellerer, prior and abbot there between 1417 and 1446, and John Whytefelde, precentor at Dover Priory towards the end of the fourteenth century: Doyle, 'Book production', 5–7; R. H. Rouse and M. A. Rouse, *Henry of Kirkstede, Catalogue de libris autenticis et apocrifis*, CBMLC 11 (London 2004); Stoneman, *Dover Priory*, 3.

107. A20.1873 and 1875. In A20.1875, for example (an omnium gatherum entry for rentals compiled since the fourth year of the reign of Henry IV, 1403–4), the rentals are described as 'valde bona'. The entry ends by emphasizing the utility of these rentals: 'Ista bene notentur et custodiantur quia valde necessaria sunt in multis casibus, et in tempore necessitatis prudenter et diserte demonstrentur'.

surviving business manuscripts surviving from Leicester, only Bodl. Laud Misc. 625 is written in informal hands, and is obviously a working document, with numerous additions (p. 185, fig. 13). The others, like the catalogue, are all well-made, large-format books, carefully articulated with headings in a large ornate script which blends the forms and stylistic features of the highest grade of script, *Littera textualis formata* with the occasional element derived from cursive bookhands; the capital letters are touched in yellow.[108] Most of the handwriting (the work of a small number of scribes) is a generally fluent and sometimes formal grade of Anglicana, which by this date was often used as a bookhand.

The books that Charyte caused to be made, or had a hand in producing himself were the types of book most commonly produced in-house in the later Middle Ages, namely liturgical and administrative volumes.[109] Copies of works by house-authors are also likely to have been produced at the abbey, either by members of the community, by salaried laymen or scribes employed on a more *ad hoc* basis. The abbey's copy of Knighton's Chronicle, the work of several scribes and modestly decorated with plain or pen-flourished initials, was almost certainly a local product (p. 121, fig. 1).[110] So, too, were probably the several copies of Geoffrey Salow's *Lucerna conscientiae.*[111]

Personal copies of sermons and devotional texts, and other compendia, may also have been produced locally. This is perhaps the best explanation for recurrence of the same combinations of contents in different entries in the catalogue. The devotional compendium that was associated with Ralph Thurlestone (Cambridge, Trinity College B.14.7: A20.436), a well-made if modestly decorated book, written in *Littera textualis*, was perhaps produced elsewhere. It is, however, likely to have been the exemplar for a now-lost duplicate copy procured by Thurlestone's contemporary, Geoffrey Salow (A20.435). One or other of these copies may then have lain behind elements of three large miscellany volumes – A20.225ae–ag, A20.244k–m, s–aj and A20.971e, h–j, u – this last being a volume listed among the books that Chartye is said to have purchased (A20.1949). Since a Leicester book was almost certainly one of the exemplars used, it is likely that this book was produced locally, but that Charyte used his own allowance to pay for the materials and the labour involved. A20.244 contained a further three items that correspond with three adjacent texts recorded in another book acquired by Geoffrey Salow (A20.333a–c), and also a copy of his *Lucerna conscientiae* (A20.244e). A20.469, a large compendium of pastoral and pentiential texts may also have been compiled from Leicester books. It contained one of only two attested copies of Richard Barre's 'De molestiis curie', a copy of the *ps.* Anselmian meditation known in this and other Leicester copies as 'Anselmus contra vanas cogitationes' (the last in the series of meditations in Trinity B.14.7, and also presumably its derivatives),[112] a pair of unidentified penitentials, one attributed to William de Montibus, the other anonymous, which correspond with two adjacent items in another compendium, (A20.303l–m), and an unidentified text, 'Hugo de quatuor potenciis anime racionalis', also found with this title in A20.155b.

Leicester books were also used as exemplars for books for individuals outside the abbey. The best evidence of this is a statement of William Wymondham, a canon of the Augustinian priory of Kirby Bellars, Leicestershire, who produced a scientific compilation that survives as Cambridge, Trinity College O.2.40. On f. 52v, he noted 'Incipiunt clausule diuerse sparsim abstracte de libro noue compilacionis magistri iohannis de sacro bosco quas ego willelmus womyndham canonicus

108. See Gullick and Webber, nos 12, 13 and 15.
109. Doyle, 'Book production'.
110. Cotton Tiberius C vii (A20.636); see Gullick and Webber, no. 14.

111. A20.244e, 868a, 869a and 870.
112. On this text, see Webber, 'Latin devotional texts', 31–2 and 33–5.

de Kyrkeby Beller abstraxi de quodam libro monasterii beate marie de pratis leycestrie Anno christi m cccc lxxxxij'. These extracts (the various 'clausule' taken from John of Sacro Bosco) and several other texts found on ff. 9v–58 have been shown to derive from the volume of scientific and other texts described in A20.862 (a book purchased by Charyte: A20.1935).[113] Textual evidence indicates that a least one Leicester book acted as an exemplar for the theological and devotional compendium made for the future Henry IV (Cambridge, Trinity College B.2.16, see above), and a fifteenth-century copy of Knighton's Chronicle (of unknown medieval origin or provenance), now BL Cotton Claudius E iii, must also derive directly or indirectly from a Leicester manuscript.[114]

Loss and dispersal

The history of the abbey's books in the aftermath of the Dissolution, like that of all other religious houses in the East Midlands, is largely unknown. The scale of loss throughout this region was uniformly high. In the years immediately following the dissolution, if monastic books were not either left *in situ*, at the mercy of the elements, or put to other uses, their continued survival was dependent upon the personal initiative of members of the community, local families or clergy, and antiquaries. The sooner books re-entered institutional ownership, the more likely their survival, since books in private ownership became vulnerable at the death of their owners.[115] Two surviving Leicester books bear inscriptions or scribbles that indicate they passed into local private ownership. Cambridge, King's College 2 bears a number of mid-sixteenth-century pentrials, including references to denizens of Shepshed (Leicestershire), and to one Ralfe Cossby, probably the Ralph Cosseby presented by the abbey as vicar of Shepshed in 1538.[116] Bodl. Rawlinson A 445 had been owned by Thomas Peeke, rector of Burton Overy (seven or eight miles south-east of Leicester), and then passed through the hands of three members of the Weston family, who succeeded each other as rectors of the next-door parish of Carlton Curlieu.[117] A third volume perhaps owned by the abbey by *c.* 1500 (BL Harley 7333), also passed into the hands of Leicestershire families.[118]

The abbey's archives fared no better than the books.[119] It is not known how Sir Robert Cotton came by three administrative compilations from the abbey (as well as the abbey's copy of Knighton's Chronicle), nor how two others were acquired by Archbishop Laud in 1635.[120] These exceptions apart, Leicester manuscripts are barely found among the collections of the major antiquaries and collectors of the late sixteenth and early seventeenth centuries. BL Add. 57533, which by an unknown route came into the hands of William Marshall, formerly a Fellow of Merton and Principal of St Alban Hall (died 1583), was subsequently acquired by Thomas Allen (died 1632).[121] Also in Oxford by 1600 was a book with Leicester connections, Bodl. Bodley 57, when it was owned by Henry Jackson of Corpus Christi College.[122] Most of the remaining volumes had probably become part of the London booktrade by at least the early decades of the seventeenth century, which is presumably how they came to be acquired by their first known post-medieval owners.

113. D. Britton, 'Manuscripts associated with Kirby Bellars Priory', *Transactions of the Cambridge Bibliographical Society* 6 (1972–76), 267–84 at 269–70. For the speculation that William Wymondham may have been educated at the abbey's almonry school, see ibid. 274.

114. Martin, *Knighton's Chronicle*, xxiii, n. 32.

115. For the various factors shaping patterns of loss and survival, see N. R. Ker, 'The migration of manuscripts from the English medieval libraries', *The Library*, 4th ser. 23 (1942–3), 1–11, repr. in his *Books, collectors and libraries: studies in the medieval heritage*,

ed. A. G. Watson (London [1985]), 459–70, and Coates, *English medieval books*, 122–42.

116. See Gullick and Webber, no. 1.

117. See Gullick and Webber, no. 18.

118. See Gullick and Webber, no. 22.

119. See D. Crouch, 'Early charters and patrons of Leicester Abbey' in this volume, pp. 225–87 below.

120. Gullick and Webber, nos. 12–17.

121. See Gullick and Webber, no. 11.

122. See Gullick and Webber, no. 23.

A group of six was among a donation of thirty-nine books given to Trinity College by George Willmer (died 1626), a former fellow-commoner, who was admitted to the Inner Temple 1601–2, and remained active as a lawyer in the London area.[123] Sir James Balfour (died 1657) bought Edinburgh, National Library of Scotland, Adv. 18.5.13 between 1628 and 1630/1631, whilst at the College of Arms in London.[124] It was also probably while studying law in London c. 1633–4 that Francis Tyndall (died 1634) acquired the two Leicester books that were among the collection of at least six books donated to his former college, Queens' Cambridge.[125] The history of the three remaining survivors is unknown before the later seventeenth century. BL Harley 7333 was acquired by Lord John Somers (died 1716), who also owned Bodl. Rawlinson c 153,[126] while York Minster XVI.M.6 and 7 were recorded as part of the York Minster library in Edward Bernard's compendium of catalogues published in 1697.[127]

123. See Gullick and Webber, nos 4–9.

124. See Gullick and Webber, no. 10.

125. Cambridge, Queens' College 2 and 5–9; Queens' 10 was also perhaps given by him. See Gullick and Webber, nos 2–3.

126. See Gullick and Webber, nos 22 and 19.

127. See Gullick and Webber, nos 20–21; E. Bernard, *Catalogi manuscriptorum Angliae et Hiberniae* (Oxford 1697) nos 31–2.

The binding descriptions in the library catalogue from Leicester Abbey

Michael Gullick

The catalogue of the books at Leicester Abbey drawn up by William Charyte in the fifteenth century is remarkable for several reasons. It appears to be a comprehensive account of all the books at the abbey, whereas most British medieval catalogues or booklists from institutions are not. Secondly, it includes descriptions of many of the bindings of the books, whereas binding descriptions are usually either infrequent or completely absent elsewhere. As the catalogue reveals that the abbey had quite a respectable number of books for its size and importance (about 1100), there are a significant number of binding descriptions and these are of national rather than of merely local importance. The nature of these descriptions, including the terms employed, is the principal subject of this paper. For clarification and comparison extensive use has been made of comparable descriptions elsewhere, and details regarding all the source material is set out in fig. 1.[1] Unfortunately, not many manuscripts have been identified from Leicester, and only three of these have medieval bindings. Two of them are twelfth century, and both were described in the abbey catalogue and both may have been made there, but the third is fifteenth century, and this was neither described in the catalogue nor made at the abbey.[2]

The catalogue is arranged in several sections. The first and largest lists works by subject and author (1–1449), and therefore books containing more than one work are usually described more than once. It may be termed a 'subject catalogue'. There is usually one full description of all the content of a volume (with *secundo folio* reference and often, but not always, a description of the binding), with single works listed under their respective authors and a cross-reference of some kind to the

Acknowledgements: I am grateful to Karen Begg, librarian at Queens' College, Cambridge, for kindly allowing me to study two manuscripts in her care by depositing them for a short period in the Cambridge University Library, and to Godfrey Waller, superintendent of the manuscript reading room at the CUL, for his help in this matter. I am also grateful to Teresa Webber for several helpful discussions about medieval library catalogues in general and the Leicester catalogue in particular, and for kindly reading and commenting upon a draft of the present paper.

1. Only a few works have been concerned with collecting terms relating to bindings in medieval catalogues and inventories. One of the earliest is W. Wattenbach, *Das Schriftwesen im Mittelalter* (3rd ed., Leipzig 1896), with terms collected on 386–408, and some

more recent studies will be cited below. All the English material is post-Conquest as the only bindings mentioned in the few (and generally fairly short) pre-Conquest booklists are of treasure bindings (bindings whose exterior was decorated with metalwork) over gospelbooks (M. Lapidge, 'Surviving booklists from Anglo-Saxon England' in *Learning and literature in Anglo-Saxon England. Studies presented to Peter Clemoes on the occasion of his sixty-fifth birthday*, ed. M. Lapidge and H. Gneuss (Cambridge 1985), 33–89, nos. II.3 and VIII.1).

2. For the surviving manuscripts see M. Gullick and T. Webber, 'Summary catalogue of surviving manuscripts from Leicester Abbey', below pp. 173-92. Brief technical descriptions of the twelfth-century bindings (Cambridge, Queens' College 2 and 8) are in Appendix 1 below. The fifteenth-century binding is on Bodl. Rawlinson A 445.

The British and continental medieval library catalogues referred to in this paper are listed below. First are the British ones edited in the Corpus of British Medieval Library Catalogues series (London 1990–   ) (= CBMLC), in which each catalogue is referred to by a letter and number, and individual items in each catalogue by the same letter and number followed by a period and the item number. (Therefore A20 is the fifteenth-century Leicester catalogue, and A20.105 is item 105 in that catalogue.) Second are the British catalogues not in the CBMLC series and one continental one, referred to by their place of origin, with individual items referred to by either page number (if the items are not numbered) or by item number (if they are).

A16 = Lanthony secunda (*c.* 1355–60): CBMLC 5, 38–94
A20 = Leicester (s. xv²): CBMLC 5, 109–399
A36 = Thurgarton (s. xv): CBMLC 5, 415–26
B10 = Bermondsey (1310 x 1328): CBMLC 4, 22–32
B30 = Evesham (s. xiv ex): CBMLC 4, 138–50
B39 = Glastonbury (1247/8): CBMLC 4, 169–215
B71 = Reading (s. xii ex.): CBMLC 4, 421–47
B79 = Rochester (1202): CBMLC 4, 499–526
B81 = Rochester (s. xiii in.): CBMLC 4, 529–31
B105 = Westminster (*c.* 1376): CBMLC 4, 615–25
B124 = Rumburgh (1482): CBMLC 4, 794–7
C3b = Hulne (1366): CBMLC 1, 167–77
P2 = Bradsole (s. xiii ex.): CBMLC 3, 161–78
P6 = Titchfield (1400): CBMLC 3, 183–254
UC18 = Corpus Christi College, Cambridge (*c.* 1376): CBMLC 10, 170–84
Z7 = Flaxley (s. xiii in.): CBMLC 3, 17–26

Candia = San Francesco, Candia (northern Crete) (1417): G. Hofmann, 'La biblioteca scientifica del monastero di San Francesco a Candia nel medio evo', *Orientalia Christiana Periodica* 8 (1942), 317–60
Christ Church = Christ Church, Canterbury (*c.* 1170): M. R. James, *Ancient Libraries of Canterbury and Dover* (Cambridge 1903), 7–12
Exeter = Exeter Cathedral (1327): G. Oliver, *Lives of the Bishops of Exeter and a History of the Cathedral* (Exeter 1861), 301–10

The important late medieval catalogues from Christ Church and St Augustine's, both in Canterbury, and Durham do occasionally mention bindings, but the terms that occur are all to be found in the British catalogues listed above. The Canterbury and Durham catalogues exist in elderly and unsatisfactory editions, and, as new editions of all of them will soon appear in the CBMLC series, none have been cited below.

Fig. 1. Primary source material

full description.[3] The cross-references sometimes use a binding description as a means to distinguish the volume with the full description, and therefore the binding of a volume may be described more than once, although, as will be seen, these 'duplicate' descriptions are not always identical

3. Other means provided to distinguish one volume from another was the duplication of other features of the full description such as the *secundo folio* reference (the opening words of the second leaf that is an almost infallible means of distinguishing one volume from another) or the donor's name. Leicester books do not have pressmarks or any notes concerning their location, and, although a reader could identify from the catalogue how many copies of a particular work was owned by the abbey and in which volumes they were contained, there is no means of identifying where individual volumes were housed. This shortcoming can be contrasted to the similar catalogue from St Mary's, York, in which references are always provided to the pressmarks of the relevant volumes containing individual works (CBMLC 4, 684–748 (= B120)). See further R. Sharpe, 'Accession, classification, location: shelfmarks in medieval libraries', *Scriptorium* 50 (1996), 279–87 (mostly concerned with English material).

and sometimes they contain conflicting information.[4] However, descriptions of bindings are fewer at the end of the first section, mostly describing law books (1251–1449), than earlier. The second section lists 227 books *in libraria* (1450–1677) and 21 *in scriptoria* [sic] (1678–98), nearly all of which are also in the first section.[5] The arrangement of the books in the library shows that this part of the catalogue is a 'shelf-list' and the nature of the books in the *scriptoria* suggests that it is a small collection of schoolbooks. Although none of the entries in either section have binding descriptions, the bindings of many of the volumes are described in the first section. The third section describes liturgical books in the church and a few books elsewhere (1699–1862), and this is followed by several short sections listing cartularies and registers (1863–77), books written or notated by or for William Charyte (1878–1925), and books acquired by William (1926–58). Almost none of the liturgical books or the volumes in the last sections have their bindings described, although as a few of these are in the first section some volumes do have their bindings described.

While there are 1958 numbered items in the catalogue, the total number of volumes described is about 1100, and of these about 570 (51%) have their bindings described.[6] (A precise figure is impossible to calculate as there is a small number of internal inconsistencies in the catalogue.) However, of the 227 volumes in the main library, 141 (62%) have their bindings described. Although the descriptions are the principal source material for this study, the material is limited in that virtually all of them are of either library books or books for study, with very few of either liturgical or archival books.

The descriptions show that the bindings nearly all fall into one of three groups. The first and largest consists of bindings with wooden boards ('stiff-board' bindings), and the second group consists of books with semi-stiff or limp covers ('limp' bindings). The third group (miscellaneous) has mostly either ambiguous or unclear binding descriptions that cannot be put into either of the first two groups.

In addition to the binding descriptions, the catalogue also occasionally provides other information about the books. The sizes of some of the volumes are given, usually either 'magno' ('large') (32), 'larga' (1) or 'paruo' ('small') (35), with only one as 'medio' ('medium').[7] One each of the 'magno' and 'paruo' volumes have survived, the larger 350 × 250 mm, and the smaller 195 × 140 mm, although both have been retrimmed in modern times.[8] Twenty-three books, including two archival books, were said to be on paper ('papiro' or similar).[9] Six books were described as 'spisso' ('thick'),[10]

---

4. There are about 320 of these 'cross-reference' descriptions of which twenty four have binding descriptions (A20.75–7, 82, 172, 173, 187, 229, 232, 252, 408, 413, 417, 422, 456, 484, 555, 672, 675, 754, 898, 914, 916 and 925). There are a small number of manuscripts with single works entered in more than one place, and some of these have their bindings described more than once (see, for example, A20.623 and 678).

5. There are 228 entries for the library but, as there are two numbered 1553 in error and two books have each been entered twice (1479 = 1563 and 1480 = 1564), the total number of volumes is 227. There are no cross-references in the subject/author section to books in the library section or vice-versa. For a note concerning the abbey library room see Appendix 2 below.

6. The binding terms used in the catalogue are collected in Appendix 3 below.

7. The 'larga' volume is A20.1845 and the 'medio' one is

A20.828. The size of 245 of the 514 volumes in the Lanthony catalogue (A16) are described as either large, medium or small, and the size of books was occasionally recorded in other catalogues and booklists.

8. A20.504 (= Cambridge, Trinity College B.16.5), and 222 (= Cambridge, Trinity College B.14.30) respectively.

9. A20.71, 175, 196, 478, 577, 610, 786, 819, 834, 835, 836, 839, 852, 887, 1084, 1109, 1162, 1163, 1215, 1403 and 1912. The two archival books are 1871 and 1906.

10. A20.5 ('spissa'), 156, 178, 303, 1216 and 1863. I cannot recall the use of 'spisso' in any other British catalogue. It occurs twice ('spissus') in the fourteenth-century catalogue of the papal library (2059 items, most of which have their bindings described), see P. Gasnault, 'Observations paléographiques et codicologiques tirées de l'inventaire de la librairie pontificale de 1369', *Scriptorium* 34 (1980), 269–75, on 270.

and two as 'lato' ('broad' or 'thick').[11] Six books, three of them in the church, were described as 'cathenacum' or similar ('chained').[12] Twelve books were described as 'pulchro' ('handsome' or 'beautiful'),[13] and the decoration of two bestiaries was mentioned, one as being well decorated ('bene illuminatus', also described as a 'pulchro' volume) and the second without illustrations ('non illuminatum nec figuratum' and later as 'non figuratum').[14] There are two service books described as well decorated ('bene illuminatum'), and a copy of the *Elementa* of Euclid (a work on geometry) with diagrams ('figuris').[15] What appears to be a description of the general condition, appearance or both, of three books is given as 'vtilis et bona' or 'bone et vtiles' ('useful' and 'sound' or 'good').[16] One binding had its cover described as 'lacerato' ('torn').[17] Finally, one manuscript had its former and present binding described ('quondam . . . modo . . .').[18] Otherwise there is nothing much else that the cataloguer considered necessary to mention about the physical features of either the books or their bindings.

William Charyte appears to have drawn up a substantial part of the catalogue before 1463. It survives in a fair copy well written by one good scribe that is datable to between 1477 and 1494, although there are some additions and corrections by at least two scribes, one of whom was William.[19] (The additional volumes have been included in the totals of the books given above, and will be included in subsequent ones.) There is, however, one very important matter concerning the interpretation and understanding of the binding descriptions in this and all other medieval library catalogues. A significant number of stiff-board bindings from about the middle of the eleventh century to the end of the middle ages had a primary cover pasted to their boards, as well as another cover, now usually called either an 'overcover' or 'chemise'. These covers were usually made with 'flaps' (rather like a modern dust-jacket) that were each sewn at their three outer edges to make what are termed 'sleeves'. The boards of a binding, already with its primary covering, were slipped into the sleeves of its overcover, and the result was a snugly fitting cover offering addition protection.[20] The skin of overcovers was usually extended at one or more edges (these extensions are known as 'skirts'), and these could be wrapped around the book to give further protection. (Overcovers would have been inconvenient as soon as books began to be stored vertically rather than horizontally, and many have

11. A20.1178 and 1386. A one-quire grammar book (A20.1004, Boethius of Dacia on Priscian) with no covering at all is also described as 'lato' ('in uno quaterno lato'). A breviary at Hulne in 1366 was described as 'magnum et grossum' (C3b.97), and a missal at Exeter in 1506 was described as 'magnum longum et latum' (G. Oliver, *Lives of the bishops of Exeter and a history of the cathedral* (Exeter 1861), 330), both likely to be large and thick books.

12. A20.441, 534, 1342, 1706, 1842 and 1843.

13. A20.44, 433, 738, 872, 1122, 1275, 1276, 1296, 1298, 1310, 1316 and 1336. Seven of these were law books.

14. A20.872 (= 922) and 873 (= 923).

15. A20.1723, 1724 and 1159.

16. A20.38, 820 and 1325. Two manuscripts are described as 'vtilis' in the Lanthony catalogue (A16.72 and 229), but the most numerous comments about the general condition and appearance of books occur in the thirteenth-century Glastonbury catalogue, where 'bona' or similar is quite common, and where about sixteen books are described as 'inutilia' or similar ('useless'), B39.17, 32, 38, 44, 45, 59, 80, 179, 180, 122, 182, 257, 273, 288, 290, 295 and 303.

17. A20.326. The same term is used once in another British catalogue (UC18.48), and it also occurs several times in *Candia* (nos. 16, 22, 53–5 and 181).

18. A20.8. In the customary from the small house at Barnwell (the only known customary from an English Augustinian house), surviving in a manuscript written in the late thirteenth century, it is stated that it was the duty of the precentor to care for the books, and it appears to state that he ought to bind them himself if necessary (J. W. Clark, *The observances in use at the Augustinian priory of S. Giles and S. Andrew at Barnwell, Cambridgeshire* (Cambridge 1897), 64). Whether William Charyte or any other Leicester precentor bound or repaired books is unknown.

19. See Gullick and Webber, no. 16 superseding the account by Teresa Webber in CBMLC 6, 107 and 109.

20. For overcovers see J. A. Szirmai, *The archaeology of medieval bookbinding* (Aldershot 1999), 164–6, 234 and figs. 8.21 and 8.22, and for two English examples see *Book bindings at the Public Record Office* (Kew 1999), [no. 3] (s. xiv), and G. Barber, *Textile and embroidered bindings* (Bodleian Library: Oxford 1971), pl. 1 (s. xv Italian velvet overcover on a s. xiv English manuscript). For further discussion and reproductions see F. Bearman, 'The origins and significance of two late medieval textile chemise bookbindings in the Walters Art Gallery', *Journal of the Walters Art Gallery* 54 (1996), 163–87. (Bearman's description of bindings with overcovers as 'chemise bindings', a term used by earlier writers, seems to me one that should be abandoned.)

had their skirts cut off or have been entirely removed.) A well-made overcover usually 'hides' nearly all of the primary cover, and as primary and overcovers on books in institutions were usually made of animal skin, it is uncertain whether a medieval cataloguer ever looked at the primary covering of books with overcovers.[21]

The cataloguer who described the library books at Saint-Claude (Jura) in 1492 certainly did not look closely at least one book with an overcover. One binding is described as 'couvert de peaul blanche', and, as the manuscript has survived in its contemporary reddish-brown covering that was blindstamped, this must be a description of an overcover, now lost.[22] One of the two twelfth-century bindings from Leicester still has its overcover, and the manuscript is described in the catalogue as 'in asseribus coopertoriis cum albo'.[23] As will be seen, this is a common form of description in the catalogue, and there is nothing in them to indicate whether the cataloguer was describing a primary cover or an overcover. It is probably to be presumed that this form of description was used to describe both, and, so far as I know, there is no British catalogue or booklist that distinguishes one from the other.

Stiff-board bindings

The most numerous binding description in the catalogue in its fullest form is as follows:

. . . in asseribus cum albo coopertorio ('wooden boards with white covering')

The extensive recording of boards in the catalogue is a little unusual. It occurs regularly in the catalogue from Hulne, sometimes in a twelfth-century Christ Church catalogue, but only occasionally elsewhere.[24] The term used is almost always 'asseribus' (or similar), and this is common in continental sources.[25] A few of the descriptions have their covering described as 'subalbo', and one as 'quasi albo', that I take to indicate an off-white of some kind.[26] Although the details of construction varied from time to time and place to place, a significant number of surviving medieval bindings correspond to this description: wooden boards (in England nearly always made of oak) covered with tawed skin, just as all three of the surviving bindings from the abbey.[27] However, none of the descriptions are as full as

21. Privately owned books, especially books of devotion, liturgical books, and some other, special kinds of books, could (and did) have overcovers made from textile, although coverings of textile are rarely mentioned in British catalogues. An inventory from Christ Church of 1315 has a 'novum Missale magnum cum coopertorio de serico consuto' (J. W. Legg and W. H. St John Hope, *Inventories of Christchurch, Canterbury* (London 1902), 75), and a breviary described as 'bonum cum auro illuminatum' that was given to Exeter was 'cum velvet cooperto' (*Exeter*, 318), and these may be early descriptions of either a cover or overcover of textile. The earliest covering of textile ('pannum aureum et siricum') found in a survey of continental sources occurs in a list of 1339, see M.-P. Laffitte, 'Le vocabulaire médiéval de la reliure d'après les anciens inventaires' in *Vocabulaire du livre et de l'écriture au Moyen Age*, ed. O. Weijers (Turnhout 1989), 61–78, on 65. (This survey was based upon catalogues, lists and inventories mostly from France, see ibid. 61–2 and the list on 72–8.) See also Barber, *Textile and embroidered bindings*, 3–4, M.-P. Laffitte, O. Valansot, D. de Reyer and W. Novik, 'Trois reliures médiévales à elements de tissu', *Bulletin du Centre International d'Etude des Textiles Anciennes* 74 (1997), 50–63, esp. 51–4 (with references to the earlier literature), and, for further references, C. de Mérindol, 'Couleurs des couvertures et continus des livres à la fin du Moyen Age', *Bulletin de la Société Nationale des Antiquaires de France* (1991), 212–26, on 216–17.

22. C. F. R. de Hamel, *Glossed books of the Bible and the origins of the Paris booktrade* (Woodbridge 1984), 77, with references.

23. A20.41 (= Cambridge, Queens' College 8).

24. C3B, and *Christ Church*, nos. 1–4, 6, 39, 40, 46, 47, 117–20, 125–7, 130, 131, 163 and 164. There are eight bindings described as with or without boards ('asseribus') in *Exeter*, pp. 304, 306, 308 and 309, and see also (for example) two books described as without boards ('sine asseribus') in B105.11 and 25, and two books described as with boards ('asseribus') in z7.67 and 68.

25. J. Vezin, 'Le vocabulaire Latin de la reliure au moyen age' in *Vocabulaire du livre et de l'écriture au Moyen Age*, ed. O. Weijers (Turnhout 1989), 56–60, on 58, and Laffitte, 'Le vocabulaire médiéval de la reliure', 64. One English catalogue uses 'tabulis' for boards (UC18.4, 6, 10, 15, 47–9 and 53), a term that also appears in continental sources, and another once uses 'asseribus ligneis' (*Exeter*, 306).

26. A20.1 (two volumes), 509, 814 and 876, and 49 respectively.

27. For twelfth-century bindings see C. Clarkson, 'English monastic bookbinding in the twelfth century' in *Ancient and medieval book materials and techniques*, ed. M. Maniaci and P. F. Munafò, Studi e Testi 357–8 (1993), ii, 181–200. No authoritative account of later English medieval bindings has yet been made. Here and below I use the neutral term 'tawed skin' to avoid being specific about the precise nature of covering material, as far too little is known about the manufacture and preparation of medieval skins used for binding books.

those of some that occur in an earlier catalogue from Cambridge (*c.* 1376) in which mention is made of clasps, never mentioned in the Leicester catalogue although common on late medieval English bindings, and the nature of the covering skin (deerskin).[28]

There are nine duplicate descriptions. Two of these are identical, and there are two which have minor textual variants.[29] Two appear in an abbreviated form as 'sub albo coopertorio' and 'cum alb [sic] coopertorio',[30] and there are nearly seventy comparable descriptions elsewhere in the catalogue.[31] Whether the other descriptions are for books in boards, books with limp covers, or a mixture of the two is unknowable. (The abbreviated descriptions will be discussed below.) Two other shortened descriptions are as 'in asseribus',[32] and there are fifty identical descriptions in the catalogue.[33] It is unknowable whether these were books with covered or uncovered boards, or a mixture of both. Finally, there is one duplicate description that records the covering as black ('nigro'), not white, and therefore the two descriptions of the same book provide contradictory information.[34]

There are also bindings described in an identical fashion but with a coloured covering (43 = 7.5% of the binding descriptions), the commonest being red ('rubeo') (24). Four of the red covers are described as 'subrubeo' that I take to indicate a pale red, although a duplicate description of one of these has 'subalbo', and a duplicate description of another does not include 'asseribus'.[35] The next commonest colour is black ('nigro') (16). However, one of these is described as 'denigrato' and another as 'quasi nigro', and a duplicate description of a third has 'albo coopertorio'.[36] Two covers are described as 'viridi' ('green'), and there is one described as 'glauco' ('grey'),[37] both colours rarely found elsewhere.[38] Other than red, surviving British bindings with coloured covers are unusual, and most of them are probably later than 1200 as twelfth-century bindings are usually 'white'. The paucity of coloured bindings other than red might be due to a combination of the fugitive nature of the pigments used to stain the covering skin, and abrasion from handling and storage.[39]

28. UC18.10, 15 and 53. A characteristic description is 'continentur in tabulis cum claspis et corio ceruino' (15).

29. A20.518c (= 617) and 864 (= 1911), and A20.459 (= 802 as 'in asseribus albo coopertoriis') and 392 (= 41 as 'in asseribus coopertoriis cum albo') respectively.

30. A20.920 (= 876) and 736 (= 1335).

31. A20.2, 4–6, 8–10, 12, 14, 15, 20, 31, 44, 57–61, 65, 92, 97, 107, 109, 110, 119, 126, 135, 177–82, 202, 203, 208, 211, 214, 222, 278, 294, 304, 328, 329, 332, 365, 389, 440, 510, 531, 544, 545, 569, 593, 615, 738, 753, 822, 860, 909, 918, 974, 1257 and 1263.

32. A20.924 (= 339) and 952 (= 572).

33. A20.67, 71, 146,189, 336, 366, 415, 417, 479, 492, 493, 673, 716, 742, 785, 806, 818, 824, 829, 847, 868, 884, 885, 941, 954, 965, 991, 995, 1000, 1011, 1076, 1096, 1099, 1103, 1107, 1115, 1125, 1126, 1136, 1184, 1204, 1255 and 1270–4.

34. A20.975 (= 987).

35. A20.69, 164 (also as 'impresso'), 228, 284, 303, 424 ('subrubeo'), 458, 507 (also as 'impresso'), 508 ('subrubeo' also as 'impresso'), 551, 635, 737 ('subrubeo' = 1334 as 'subalbo'), 739, 740 ('subrubeo' = 754 but wanting 'asseribus'), 816, 863, 955, 956, 1172, 1174 ('subrubeo'), 1175, 1193, 1196 and 1251. Blindstamped bindings will be discussed below.

36. A20.27, 68 (wants 'coopertorio'), 129, 143, 210, 244, 284, 299, 369 ('denigrato'), 506, 518b, 549, 815, 987 (= 975 as 'albo'), 1086 ('quasi nigro') and 1212.

37. A20.548 and 553, and 1087 respectively.

38. For six lost bindings with a green covering see A16.239 ('viride pelle'), A36.32 ('viridi'), C3b.17 and 55 ('viridi coreo' and 'viridibus'), and UC18.11 and 12 ('corii uiridis' and 'corio uiridi'). TNA E164/9 (s. xiv, England) has an overcover of tawed skin stained green (*Book bindings at the Public Record Office*, [no. 3]). I cannot recall that I have ever seen any bindings with what could be identified with certainty as a grey covering, unless the cataloguer was describing a grubby white tawed skin.

39. At Hulne (C3b) the commonest colour was 'white' (40%), followed by red (20%), black (4%) and green (2%), with the others not specified. The commonest colour in the fourteenth-century catalogue of the papal library was green, followed by red, 'white', and black. There were also a few bindings with either a yellow ('croeceum') or violet ('violaceum') covering (Gasnault, 'La libraire pontificale', 274). However, the commonest colour in the *Candia* catalogue was red (23%), followed by 'white' (19%), black (7%), yellow ('croceo') (2.5%), green (1.5%) and 'zallo' (probably for 'gallo', modern *giallo*, meaning yellow) (1%), with the others not specified. It should be noted that tawed skins can be stained with colour, but not dyed, and for some instructions (s. xv/xvi) for colouring tawed skins see *Report on the manuscripts of the late Reginald Rawdon Hastings, Esq., of the Manor House, Ashby de la Zouche*, Historical Manuscripts Commission, 4 vols. (London 1928–47), i, 431. Other recipes may be recovered from M. Clark, *The art of all colours: medieval recipe books for painters and illuminators* (London 2001).

Three bindings have boards covered with tanned skin:

... in asseribus cum coopertorio bercato ('wooden boards with tanned covering')[40]

Medieval bindings with undecorated tanned skin covers are very rare, and tanned skin covers are usually decorated with blindstamped tools. There are some blindstamped bindings in the Leicester catalogue (to be discussed below), but none of these have covers described as 'bercato'. There is certainly nothing unusual about the three manuscripts with bindings with tanned skin, although two of them cannot be earlier than the mid thirteenth century because of their content.[41] No covering of tanned skin appears to be specified in any other British catalogue, and I have not noticed the term 'bercato' elsewhere.[42]

Five bindings have boards with a covering whose surface is described:

... in asseribus cum hispido coopertorio[43]

The term 'hispido' could either be a description of a roughly textured surface or a skin still with hair, and a few overcovers with hairs have survived.[44] One of the Leicester bindings is probably twelfth century as the manuscript (a Psalter) is associated in the catalogue with the founders of the abbey, Robert, earl of Leicester (d. 1167), and his wife.[45] I have not noticed 'hispido' in any other British library catalogue.

One binding is unusual for having its boards described:

... in asseribus tenuibus ('thin boards')

The binding was over a copy of Priscian, *Institutiones grammaticae* (a common text), and it might well have been a small book only requiring thin boards.[46]

One covering cannot be identified with certainty:

... in asseribus cum coopertorio vltimo

It has been suggested that 'vltimo' might be an error for 'vitulino' ('calfskin').[47] This is quite possible, although 'vitulino' otherwise occurs only once in the Leicester catalogue to describe a limp covering, and it has not been noticed in any other British catalogue.[48] However, 'vltimo' seems as

---

40. A20.455, 741 and 808.

41. I can only recall seeing four stiff-board bindings with an undecorated tanned skin covering: Hereford Cathedral P.iv.3 (s. xii med., Hereford-made) and P.iv.12 (s. xii med., probably Hereford-made), Uppsala, Universitetsbibliotek C 222 (s. xiii, probably German-made), and Worcester Cathedral Q.7 (s. xii med., probably French-made). Worcester Cathedral F.40 (s. xii², Worcester-made), and Q.75 (s. xii², probably Bordesley-made), both have a primary covering of tawed skin, but both are unusual for having an overcover of tanned skin with tawed skin sleeves. For the Hereford and Worcester manuscripts noticed here and below, see the relevant descriptions in R. A. B. Mynors and R. M. Thomson, *Catalogue of the manuscripts of Hereford Cathedral Library* (Cambridge 1993), and R. M. Thomson, *A descriptive catalogue of the medieval manuscripts in Worcester Cathedral library* (Cambridge 2001), neither of which will subsequently be cited.

42. Compare 'coriis...barkandis' used in 1335 and 'pellibus...barcatis' in 1478, both recorded s.v. *bercare* in the *Dictionary of medieval Latin from British sources*. In the fourteenth-century catalogue of the papal library there were forty-four manuscripts with a tanned skin ('tannatum') covering (Gasnault, 'La libraire pontificale', 274).

43. A20.18, 66 (as 'hispide' and wanting 'coopertorio'), 128, 282 and 297.

44. Cambridge, Queens' College 5 (s. xii², England), Cambridge, Queens' College 6 (s. xii², England), Lincoln Cathedral 31 (s. xii med., probably Lincoln-made) (R. M. Thomson, *Catalogue of the manuscripts of Lincoln Cathedral Chapter library* (Cambridge 1989),

pl. 3), Oxford, Corpus Christi College 206 (s. xii med., Fountains-made) and Wormsley, J. P. Getty s.n. (s. xii med., Byland-made) (*The Wormsley Library*, exh. cat. (Pierpont Morgan Library: New York 1999), no. 3 with plate) have sealskin overcovers. BL Add. 63077 (s. xii med.) and Worcester Cathedral F.12 (s. xiii) each have an overcover with hair (source uncertain). The binding of a service book (Gradual + Troper) is described in a document of 1361 as 'cum corio piloso coopertum' (Hereford Cathedral, Dean and Chapter Archives 1448A), and a few books with a Clairmarais provenance are said still to have hair on their covers, identified as deerskin (B. van Regemorter, 'La reliure des manuscrits à Clairmarais aux xiie au xiiie siècles', *Scriptorium* 5 (1951), 99–100, on 99). A covering with hair is occasionally mentioned in some continental sources (Laffitte, 'Le vocabulaire medieval de la reliure', 67).

45. A20.18, 66 (associated with the founders), 128, 282 and 297.

46. A20.995.

47. In the commentary to the relevant entry, A20.547.

48. A20.138. There are a few references to 'ceruino' ('deerskin'), but identifying the animal species from which a covering skin was made is rare in British catalogues, see (for example) UC18.10 ('corio cerui') and 15 ('corio ceruino'), and B79.152 ('ceruino'). The specification of the nature of covering skin was also rarely noted in the sources used by Laffitte ('Le vocabulaire médiéval de la reliure', 66–7). The catalogue from *Candia* sometimes specifies 'asinino' ('ass'), see nos. 9, 10, 19, 40, 56, 58, 152, 156, 178, 180, 184 and 185, and 144 as with hair ('asinino piloso'). For the variety of skins used for covering books it is necessary to turn to accounts. For example,

likely to be from *ultimus*, and refer back to the 'previous' binding.[49] This was in boards with a white covering, and it and the 'vltimo' binding both covered copies of the first part of the *Summa theologica* of Thomas Aquinas.

The bindings described so far had full covers, but in addition to these there are twelve partly covered bindings that can only be descriptions of a primary covering:

... in asseribus seminudis cum albo coopertorio ('wooden boards with a partial white covering') These bindings would have had a covering skin that was on the spine, but which only extended over part of each of the two boards.[50] Only two of the twelve Leicester bindings have their covering specified, the other ten described only as either 'asseribus seminudis' or 'seminudis asseribus'.[51]

Thirty-three books are said to have no covering at all, and these are described as either 'in asseribus nudis' or 'in nudis asseribus'.[52] Such a description is otherwise only found in the catalogue from Hulne, where there are four books 'in asseribus nudis'.[53]

Blindstamped bindings

There were six blindstamped bindings, described as 'impresso' (one has 'inpresso'), and these can only be descriptions of a primary covering. The colour of the covering of three was described as 'rubeo', one as 'subrubeo', one as 'nigro', and one was not specified.[54] The covering of surviving blindstamped bindings is usually tanned skin, as this is easier to stamp than tawed, and therefore the 'red' covering in the Leicester catalogue might be reddish-brown, and the 'black' a very dark brown. Four of the six binding descriptions do include 'asseribus', but the two bindings not to be said in boards probably were.[55] I have not noticed the term 'impresso' in any other British catalogue or booklist.[56]

---

calfskins and sheepskins occur in 1371/2, '8 Coreis vitulin: et 4 coreis ovin: de albat' (M. Gullick, *Extracts from the precentors' accounts concerning books and bookmaking of Ely Cathedral Priory* (Hitchin 1985), 11, from an eighteenth-century transcript), and 1399, 'corio magni cervi' and 'pellibus vitulinis' (J. Raine, *The fabric rolls of York Minster*, Surtees Society 35 (1859), 132). In 1412/13 a binder working for Exeter Cathedral bought calfskins ('coreis vitulinis' and 'pellibus vitulinis'), sheepskins ('pellibus ouium'), as well as red skins ('pellibus rubeis') and one horseskin ('coreo equino') (J. W. Clark, 'On the work done to the Library of Exeter Cathedral in 1412 and 1413', *Proceedings of the Cambridge Antiquarian Society* 10 (1904), 294–306, on 300–1), and in 1508 a binder working for Christ Church, Canterbury, was provided with 'rams skyns, calvys skyns, and hors ledyr' (M. Beazeley, 'History of the Chapter Library of Canterbury Cathedral', *Transactions of the Bibliographical Society* 8 (1904–6), 113–85, on 141). Between 1421 and 1425 calfskins, sheepskins and red skins were bought for covering books at King's Hall, Cambridge (CBMLC 10, 317).

49. A20.546. The entry before this one has a book described as 'in consimili volumine', and this must be a reference back to the preceding entry. However, while 'consimili' occurs elsewhere in the catalogue (A20.1b, 203, 388, 467, 658, 835 and 1123 ('simili')), 'vltimo' does not.

50. I have seen very few such bindings in British collections, and none much earlier (I think) than s. xiii med. One is Hereford Cathedral o.i.4 (s. xiii ex.), and three others were Worcester Cathedral F.70 (s. xiii med.), F.111 (s. xiv¹), and F.144 (s. xiv in.), but the covering of all three Worcester books has been replaced in modern times. An Italian example is New Haven, Yale University, Beinecke Library, Marston 262 (s. xv²) (B. A. Shailor, *The medieval book* (New Haven 1988), no. 67). For some in French collections see J.-L. Alexandre and C. Maître, *Catalogue des reliures médiévales con-*

servés à la Bibliothèque municipale d'Autun (Paris 1997), figs. 26 (s. xv), 47 (s. xv), 51 (s. xv), 56 (s. xv), 119 (s. xv), 130 (s. xv) and 138 (s. xv), and J.-L. Alexandre, G. Grand and G. Lanöe, *Bibliothèque municipale de Vendôme*, Reliures médiévales des bibliothèques de France (Paris 2000), figs. 8 (s. xv) and 68 (s. xv). (Note that the binding descriptions in these two works are very inadequate, see the reviews of the last volume by M. Gullick in *Manuscripta* 43/4 (1999–2000), 189–93, and N. Pickwoad in *The Library* 7th ser. 5 (2004), 80–2).

51. A20.62 and 63 (both with white covering), and 85, 183, 185, 262, 330, 390, 448, 760, 990 and 1207. Two descriptions, one as 'in asseribus albis abreviatus' (c3b.39) and another as 'cum nigro corio in dorso' (B124.30), are probably other ways of describing a part-covering. For partially covered boards (often referred to as 'quarter-' or 'half-bindings') see Szirmai, *Medieval bookbinding*, 233–4.

52. A.20.28, 75, 83, 120, 136, 141, 158, 173 (= 189, where as 'in asseribus'), 186, 286, 301, 378, 397, 634, 842, 902, 930, 988, 989, 996, 1089–92, 1098, 1253, 1256, 1261, 1262, 1265, 1268, 1319 and 1362.

53. c3b.18–20 and 48.

54. A20.64 ('nigro'), 121 ('rubeo' and as 'inpresso'), 164 ('rubeo'), 507 ('rubeo'), 508 ('subrubeo') and 1208 (not specified).

55. 20.64 and 121 are not said to be in boards. However, for some blindstamped bindings with 'boards' of tanned skin see Appendix 4 below, and, for a French-made limp binding with a blindstamped cover of tannned skin, see J. Vezin, 'Une reliure souple en cuir souple estampé du xiiie siècle (Paris, Bibliothèque Nationale, lat. 6637A)', *Revue française d'histoire du livre* 36 (1982), 243–9.

56. The term *impressio* (or similar) was also used in association with several processes that involved stamping, such as making coins and using seals, and, at the end of the middle ages, with printed books, see *Dictionary of medieval Latin from British sources* s.v. *impressio*.

Five bindings enclosed manuscripts of either glossed books of the Bible (three) or the *Sentences* of Peter Lombard (two).[57] The manufacture and dissemination from France of these kinds of books, some with blindstamped covers, all over Europe, where they were soon copied locally and their bindings imitated, is well known.[58] Although it is impossible to be certain that all five of the Leicester books were twelfth-century, it is very likely as the fashion for blindstamped books had declined by the middle of the thirteenth, not to be revived until the second half of the fifteenth. However, one of the five was certainly earlier than 1200 as the name of its donor is known, Richard Barre (active s. xii²).[59] Whether the Leicester books (and their bindings) were English or continental is, of course, quite unknown.[60]

The sixth binding was over a manuscript containing a medical text (Gariopontus, *Passionarius Galeni*),[61] not a kind of work usually associated with twelfth-century blindstamped bindings, and the date and nature of the binding is unknown.[62] Only one other British catalogue, the late twelfth-century Reading catalogue, described blindstamped bindings ('corio presso'), three of which are over glossed books and the fourth an epistolar.[63]

Chained books

Six books are described as chained ('cathenacum', 'catenata', 'catenatus', 'cathenato', 'catenatum', and 'cathenatur'), three of which were in the church and three elsewhere. One of those not in the church was a copy of Peter Comestor, *Sermones*, that appears twice in the subject/author section but not elsewhere, so that its location is unknown, although it was described as chained only once.[64] The two others were in the main library (not housed in the same lectern), one a copy of Isidore, *Etymologiae*, the other a copy of the *Summa confessorum*, either that by John of Freiburg or that by Thomas of Chobham. The first of these was listed twice in the subject/author section (once as 'magno volumine'), but only once mentioned as chained, and the second was also mentioned twice in the subject/author section (twice as 'pulchro'), but only once described as chained.[65]

---

57. A20.64 (Glossed Psalter), 121 (Glossed Mark) and 164 (Glossed Acts), and 507 and 508.

58. de Hamel, *Glossed books of the Bible*, ch. 6, to be supplemented by P. D. Stirnemann, 'Où ont été fabriqués les livres de la glose ordinaire dans la première moitié du xiie siècle' in F. Gasparri, ed. *Le xiie siècle: tournant et renouveau 1120–1150* (Paris 1994), 257–301.

59. For Richard see the commentary to A20.57, and R. Sharpe, 'Richard Barre's *Compendium Veteris et Noui Testamenti*', *Journal of Medieval Latin* 14 (2004), 128–46. Richard gave five books to the abbey, two of them glossed books and two law books, all of which had a white covering (A20.57, 179, 1263 and 1285), and the fifth the *Sentences* with a blindstamped binding (A20.508). He had the opportunity to acquire his books in France, Italy and England, for he either studied or worked in all these countries.

60. For Romanesque blindstamped bindings see F. A. Schmidt-Künsemüller, *Die abendländischen romanischen Blindstempel-einbände* (Stuttgart 1985), and, for a recently discovered English binding, M. Gullick, 'A Romanesque blind-stamped binding' in *'For the love of binding'. Studies in bookbinding history presented to Mirjam Foot*, ed. D. Pearson (London and Newcastle 2000), 1–8.

61. A20.1208. The author probably lived in the eleventh century, and the date of this copy of his work (which circulated fairly widely) is impossible to estimate.

62. A medical manuscript at Cambridge, St John's College E 29 (132) (s. xiii, ?Mersea) has a blindstamped binding, and there are

two medical manuscripts at Worcester Cathedral, Q.39 (s. xiii, France or Italy) and Q.52 (s. xiii, France), that were said to have blindstamped bindings (the former with a red covering, the latter brown), but now unfortunately rebound. The significance of this, to which can now be added the evidence of the Leicester catalogue, cannot be assessed at present.

63. B71.140–2 and 200. The term *presso* (or similar) appears to have been used more in association with processes concerned with applying pressure than stamping, for example with cider, cheese, clothes and printing presses, see R. E. Latham, *Revised medieval Latin word-list from British and Irish sources* (Oxford 1965), s.v. *presso*. In the fourteenth-century catalogue of the papal library there were twenty-six blindstamped bindings ('impressatum' or 'impressum') (Gasnault, 'La libraire pontificale', 274).

64. A20.534 (= 782).

65. A20.441 (= 984 and 1530) and 1342 (= 738 and 1618). Donors of books to medieval institutions sometimes specified that their gifts were to be chained. The donor of one of the chained books (A20.534) was a canon at Leicester in the mid fourteenth century (Geoffrey Salow), and he gave sixteen other books (see the commentary to A20.8). None of the other chained books were associated with a donor. It is an odd coincidence that a catalogue that does not often mention whether a book is 'magno' and rarely if 'pulchro', should record that two such books were also chained, although perhaps it was because they were 'magno' or 'pulchro' that they were chained.

The chained books in the church comprised one whose content was described as 'deuo-cionum', a breviary, and the third was a copy of Johannes de Burgo, *Pupilla oculi*. The last of these books was purchased by William Charyte, and it may have been chained at about the time that it entered the abbey.[66]

M. R. James noticed these descriptions of chained books, and he wondered whether all the books in the main library might have been chained.[67] However, there is no evidence from the sur-viving Leicester manuscripts to confirm this suggestion, and, writing a little later, N. R. Ker has pointed out 'that chaining was uncommon in monastic libraries'.[68] The few references in British catalogues and booklists to chained books are usually descriptions of 'liturgical' (rather than 'ref-erence') books kept in a church.[69] The presence of the three chained library books at Leicester is, at present, puzzling.

Limp covers

The fullest form of description of bindings with limp covers is as follows:

 . . . in quaternis cum albo coopertorio ('quires with a white covering')

and there are twenty-six bindings described in this manner, although only one of them was in the main library.[70] In addition to these, there are nine others, one in the main library, with different coloured or textured covers. Five are 'nigro' (one of these as 'quasi nigro') and two as 'rubeo', and there were two described as 'hispido'.[71]

Black, red and roughly textured or hairy covers are to be found on limp and stiff-board bind-ings, but there were also a few limp bindings with a covering not found on stiff-board bindings. One is described as 'panno lineo' ('cloth/textile of linen'), another as 'vitulino' ('calfskin'), and a third as 'scakcariato' ('checkered' [textile]).[72] A slightly mysterious description records one bind-ing as 'in quaternis nigro coopertorio panno blodio duplicato', perhaps a black skin lined with blue textile.[73]

There is an abbreviated form of description used for forty books in which the colour or nature of the covering was not specified ('in quaternis cum coopertorio').[74] However, eight of these have duplicate descriptions as 'in quaternis'.[75] Including these eight, there are 100 books with limp covers described as 'in quaternis', three of which were in the main

---

66. A20.1706, 1842 and 1843 (= 755 and 1950).

67. 'Catalogue of the library of Leicester Abbey', *TLAHS* 19 (1935–7), 118–61, at 127–8.

68. N. R. Ker, 'Sir John Prise', *The Library* 5th ser. 10 (1955), 1–24, on 18 (note on J.17), repr. in his *Books, collectors and libraries. Studies in the medieval heritage*, ed. A. G. Watson (London 1985), 471–95, at 489.

69. B71.167 (four Psalters, two in the church and two in the infirmary), B79.15 (Psalter in church), and *Exeter*, p. 309 (Breviary + Psalter in two volumes in church 'ad deserviendeum populo'). A number of the many books in the church at Exeter described in an inventory of 1506 were said to be chained (Oliver, *Lives of the bish-ops of Exeter*, 357, 359, 359–60 and 361).

70. A20.35, 54, 74, 133 (wanting 'coopertorio'), 162, 166, 220, 370, 401 (= 1591 in the main library), 470, 517, 666, 830, 831, 836–9, 899, 919, 953, 957, 1189, 1192, 1211 and 1223.

71. A20.163, 171, 761, 1206 and 1164 (= 1668 in the main library), 148 and 1210, and 391 and 638 respectively. BL Add. 32050 (1310/11) is a royal archival book with a limp cover of skin still with hair, almost certainly manufactured for use as a covering. Two other royal archival books with similar covers are TNA E101/14/22 (1311/12) and E101/368/27 (1305/6) (*List of documents relating to the household and wardrobe John to Edward I* (London 1964), repro-duction on the front cover).

72. A20.160, 538 and 1217 respectively. For a limp parchment cover on an English manuscript (s. xv) see P. R. Robinson, 'The "Booklet", a self-contained unit in composite manuscripts', *Codicologica* 3 (1980), 46–69, on 52–3 and pls. 1–3.

73. A20.50. For 'blodio' see *Dictionary of medieval Latin from British sources* s.v. *blodius* and *bludus*. The word was used for blue in descriptions of illuminations and decoration in a cata-logue of c. 1376 (UC18.1, 21, 26, 28, 34, 36, 37 and 39). Worcester Cathedral Q.44 (s. xii/xiii, England) has an outer cover of skin and an inner one of textile, and Worcester Cathedral Q.78 (s. xii ex. England) had a outer cover of parchment and an inner one of tex-tile but it has been disbound and the cover is now preserved sepa-rately as Q.78A.

74. A20.223.

75. A20.25 (= 370), 76 (= 899), 77 and 81 (= 171), 187 (= 166), 229 (= 223), 252 (= 220), 573 (= 953) and 875 (= 919).

library.[76] Five of the 100 have duplicate descriptions, but in these the description of the covering is the same in both.[77]

One other book 'in quaternis' is also described twice, but the second description, one of the additions to the manuscript, records the binding as 'in asseribus'. The manuscript is also listed among the books purchased by William Charyte, and therefore it appears that he bought it in a limp cover, and that it was subsequently rebound in boards.[78]

The total number of books at Leicester in limp covers was at least 132 (= 23% of the binding descriptions). Manuscripts described as 'in quaternis' or 'in quaterno' are quite common in British library catalogues and booklists, the earliest a single example in a twelfth-century Christ Church catalogue, but there are substantial numbers in the catalogues from Bradsole, Lanthony, and Titchfield, as well as in catalogues and lists from elsewhere.[79] The fuller descriptions in the Leicester catalogue clearly show that a variety of material was used for limp covers, but it is usually not very easy to match a catalogue description with a surviving book. However, there is at least one in the English sources. A mid twelfth-century copy of Cicero, *De officiis*, with a St Augustine's, Canterbury, provenance still has its former limp cover of parchment bound with its modern binding, and the fifteenth-century St Augustine's catalogue describes the book as 'in quaterno'.[80]

I suspect that such descriptions are rarely of a series of quires without a covering of any kind.[81] Why this term was applied to quires enclosed limp covers is unclear, but it has a long history as 'in quaternionibus' occurs in a ninth-century catalogue from St Gall, as well as in an eleventh-century catalogue from Lobbes ('in quaternionibus').[82] The crucial feature of books 'in quaterno' (or similar) is the absence of wooden boards.[83] However, there are three basic structural types of books enclosed in limp covers. First, books whose quires were *sewn* directly to a cover (in effect using the cover as a support), secondly books whose quires were *stitched* to a cover directly by tackets,[84] and, thirdly, books whose quires were *sewn* to supports that were integrated, by a variety of means, with a cover.[85] Unfortunately, the descriptions of books with limp covers in British catalogues and booklists, including the Leicester catalogue,

76. A.20.22, 25 (= 370), 26, 42, 43, 73, 76 (= 899), 77 (= 171), 156, 157, 159, 187 (= 166), 196–8, 229 (= 223), 249, 252 (= 220), 295, 372, 408, 430–3, 465, 526, 552, 573 (= 953), 576, 643, 649, 745, 813, 840, 845, 854, 856, 875 (= 919), 886, 887, 911, 986, 992–4, 999, 1001–3, 1027, 1028, 1030–2, 1034–7, 1038 (= 1673 in the main library), 1071, 1072, 1078, 1081, 1088, 1100, 1108, 1109, 1114, 1120, 1134, 1161 (= 1667 in the main library), 1165 (= 1660 in the main library), 1166, 1190, 1213, 1214, 1218–20, 1222, 1224–8, 1229 (as 'in quaterno'), 1230–4, 1236, 1243, 1245, 1247, 1264, 1327, 1348 and 1380.

77. A.20.22 (?= 195), 249 (= 854), 430 (= 1074), 431 (?= 1075) and 432 (= 1077).

78. A20.433 = 1076 = 1927.

79. *Christ Church*, no. 53, and P2, A16 and P6 respectively.

80. BL Royal 15 A.vi f. 1 + one unfoliated (= M. R. James, *Ancient libraries of Canterbury and Dover* (Cambridge 1903), 304 no. 1011). The size of the manuscript is 180 × 120 mm.

81. For a review of the written evidence see J. Vezin, '"Quaderni simul ligati": Recherches sur les manuscrits en cahiers' in *Of the making of books. Medieval manuscripts, their scribes and readers. Essays presented to M. B. Parkes*, ed. P. R. Robinson and R. Zim (Aldershot 1997), 64–70, at 64–9, and see also Szirmai, *Medieval bookbinding*, 285.

82. P. Lehmann, *Mittelalterliche Bibliothekskataloge Deutschlands und der Schweiz. I Band. Die Bistümer Konstanz und Chur* (Munich 1918), 71, and F. Dolbeau, 'Un nouveau catalogue

des manuscrits de Lobbes aux XIe et XIIe siècles', *Recherches Augustiniennes* 13 (1978), 3–36, nos. 29–31.

83. This is a feature isolated and emphasised by A. Scholla, 'Early western limp bindings. Report on a study' in *Care and conservation of manuscripts 7*, Proceedings of the seventh international seminar held at the Royal Library, Copenhagen 18–19 April 2002, ed. G. Fellows-Jensen and P. Springborg, (Copenhagen 2003), 132–58, at 132. This fundamental structural feature is explicit in the descriptions of forty books in the fourteenth-century papal library. These include 'coopertus de pergameno sine postibus', 'coopertus corio rubeo sine postibus' and 'coopertus sidone rubea sine postibus' (Gasnault, 'La libraire pontificale', 273). *Candia* has 'sine tabulis cum corio . . .' (or similar) (nos. 7, 34, 157–9, 170 and 171).

84. For tacketing see Szirmai, *Medieval Bookbinding*, pp. 287–90.

85. For a typology of limp covers see Scholla, 'Limp bindings', 135–6. The structural features of books in limp covers are discussed and illustrated by Scholla, and also by Szirmai, *Medieval Bookbinding*, 285–319. There is also much valuable information concerning post-medieval bindings (mostly sixteenth-century), in many respects continuing medieval traditions and techniques, in N. Pickwoad, 'Tacketed bindings – a hundred years of European bookbinding' in *'For the love of the binding'. Studies in bookbinding history presented to Mirjam Foot*, ed. D. Pearson, (London and Newcastle 2000), 119–68.

are never detailed enough to be certain which of these three types of limp covers was being described.

One manuscript was described as 'in quaternis non ligatis', and this may be a description of a collection of loose quires, perhaps enclosed in a loose wrapper. It is the last of a run of ten copies of Priscian, *Institutiones grammaticae*, and it might well have been either a small, worn or damaged volume.[86] There are similar descriptions elsewhere that seem to point to the use of 'non ligatis' to mean loose quires that were not attached to each other (in contrast to quires sewn to supports), although the sheets of individual quires might be attached to each other with tackets:

. . . cum septem quaternis non ligatis ('in seven quires unbound')

. . . gradale nouum non ligatum ('new Gradual unbound')

and

. . . partes librorum non ligatorum ('part [ie incomplete] book unbound')[87]

The evidence suggests that books described as 'in quaterno' could either be sewn to supports or have their quires tacketed, but that such books were usually enclosed in limp covers of some kind.[88] Books described as 'ligatus' were probably usually sewn to supports, but such books were not always enclosed in boards.[89] However, while books can sometimes be found described in British catalogues and booklists as *non ligatorum* (or similar), books described as *ligatorum* are much less frequent, and 'non ligatus' can either mean a book not sewn or one sewn but without boards. The fluidity of medieval vocabulary and the context in which a particular word may appear always need to be taken into account. This can be illustrated in the headings to two Cambridge booklists. The first is a list of thirty-five books, mostly printed, drawn up at Corpus Christi College, Cambridge, *c.* 1525 that is headed 'libri in quaternis et pergameno clausi'.[90] These books were clearly bound in limp covers of parchment. However, an inventory of ninety books drawn up at Clare College, Cambridge, in 1496 is headed 'omnium librorum in biblioteca non ligatorum'.[91] It has been plausibly suggested that this is a list of *electio* books (books available for loan), and that these were bound in limp covers for practical convenience. They were very unlikely to have been unbound, and the use of 'non ligatorum' here must be for books that were either sewn to supports or tacketed but that none were enclosed in boards.

Manuscripts with limp covers are not poor cousins of stiff-board bindings, but often bindings of sound and even sophisticated construction. There are a few ninth-century continental examples,[92] and there are others from subsequent centuries but, unfortunately, there are not many of them, especially in British libraries as most have been rebound in modern times in boards by tidy-minded collectors and librarians. One example (probably English), over a copy of Alan of Lille,

86. A20.997.

87. B105.19, and B10.65 and 102. For other similar descriptions see A16.252 ('non ligatus') and 254 ('quaternus non ligatus'), B10.64, 86 and 87 ('non ligatum'), 71 ('non ligatus'), and 103 ('non ligatis'), B30.46 ('non ligatus'), P2.60 and 72 ('non ligato'), and *Exeter*, p. 308 ('non ligatus').

88. The earliest manuscript I have seen sewn to supports not laced through its limp cover is Italian (s. xii in., with a cover of tawed skin), New Haven, Yale University, Beinecke Library, Marston 24. (For a summary description of the binding see M. Gullick, 'From scribe to binder: quire tackets in twelfth-century European manuscripts' in *Roger Powell: The Compleat Binder. Liber Amicorum*, ed. J. L. Sharpe, Bibliologia 14 (Turnhout 1996),

240–59, at 256 n. 26, and for an illustration showing something of its structural details see Shailor, *The Medieval Book*, no. 55). The earliest English such binding that I have seen is a royal archival book, TNA E101/368/27 (1305/6).

89. There are exceptions to this generalisation, see, for example, 'i quaterno ligato' (A36.21) and 'quaternus ligatus' (A16.29), both of which appear to be single-quires with their sheets attached together in some manner.

90. CBMLC 10, 235.

91. CBMLC 10, 143.

92. See, for example, J. Vezin, 'Une reliure carolingienne de cuir souple (Oxford, Bodleian Library, Marshall 19)', *Revue française d'histoire du livre* 36 (1982), 235–41.

Fig. 2. Cambridge, Pembroke College 119, lower (back) cover. The cover
is a much abraded tawed skin stained red

Anticlaudianus, of *c.* 1200 is reproduced in fig. 2.[93] This has a fore-edge flap (these are a near-universal feature of limp bindings until about 1300),[94] but its tie, which would have passed around the book, has broken off.[95] The origin of the manuscript and its medieval provenance is unknown, but it is likely that at least some of the Leicester volumes looked something like this.[96]

Miscellaneous

There are a number of ambiguous or unclear descriptions of bindings. Nearly seventy are recorded as 'albo coopertorio' (or similar) that merely indicate a 'white covering'. In addition to the 'albo coopertorio' descriptions, there are thirty-six others such as 'coopertorio quasi nigro',

93. Cambridge, Pembroke College 119 (145 × 115 mm). (In this binding the quires were sewn directly to the cover.) Three other examples of such a binding in English collections are Worcester Cathedral Q.44 (s. xii ex., France or England) (Thomson, *Catalogue of the medieval manuscripts in Worcester Cathedral*, pl. 5a), Worcester Cathedral Q.76 (s. xiv in., England), and TNA DL42/7 (s. xiv, England) (*Book bindings at the Public Record Office*, [no. 1]). Three English-made examples, now unfortunately disbound with their covers preserved separately, are BL Add. 40165 (s. xii med.), and Oxford, Jesus College 6 (s. xii med.) and 18 (s. xiii²), and an Icelandic book with a cover made from sealskin, also now disbound, is Stockholm, Kungliga Biblioteket Isl. perg. 4° 15 (s. xii/xiii).

94. Scholla, 'Limp bindings', 145–6.

95. One British catalogue mentions 'ligulas', and these must be either straps or ties (UC18.6, 8, 9 and 11–14), see *Dictionary of medieval Latin from British sources* s.v. *ligula*.

96. There were three copies of Alan's work at Leicester, but, unfortunately, none had their bindings described (A20.1043, 1044 and 1060, the last of which was purchased for the abbey by William Charyte).

'hispido coopertorio', 'rubeo coopertorio', 'nigro coopertorio' or similar that also record only the colour or nature of the covering.[97]

Several of these bindings have duplicate descriptions, and there are two in which one clarifies the other. One binding is recorded as 'asseribus cum sub rubeo coopertorio' in one place but 'sub-rubeo coopertorio' in another, and a second is recorded as 'in asseribus cum subalbo coopertorio' in one place but as 'subalbo coopertorio' in another, thereby removing the uncertainty about the second description in each case.[98] On the other hand, one binding is recorded as 'albo' in one place but as 'albo coopertorio' in another, a second as 'nigro coopertorio' in one place but 'albo cooper-torio' in another, and a third as 'subrubeo coopertorio' in one place but 'subalbo coopertorio' in another, in each case one description not clarifying the other.[99]

What may be another description of the binding of a manuscript with one of these ambiguous or unclear descriptions occurs in one of the surviving abbey archival books. The catalogue descrip-tion is of another archival book and reads 'liber vetus vocatus Chartwary . . . cum nigro coopero-rio', and there is a description of an abbey archival book as 'uetere libro euidentiarum cum nigro copertorio in quaternis'.[100] There is real possibility that the two descriptions are of the same book. If this is so, the catalogue description appears to be an abbreviated one, but what gives this pair of descriptions a special interest is that they are both of archival rather than library books, for few of the archival books in the catalogue had their bindings described.

Another binding is described as 'in nudis asseribus cum albo coopertorio', and this is either an error or a description of uncovered boards with some kind of loose cover of skin.[104]

One ambiguous description is 'coopertorio duplicato cum panno blodio', and this is perhaps a cover formed from two layers, one of them blue textile.[105] This might be for a limp covering with a lining of blue textile, but it is also possible that it is an abbreviated description of a stiff-board binding with a covering of skin and a textile overcover. The book is a one-volume Bible, not only likely to have been a fairly small book, but also a kind of book that might have had an overcover.[106] 'Duplicatio' occurs only once elsewhere in the catalogue for a binding described as 'in quaternis cum nigro coopertorio panno blodio duplicato'.[107] This covered an unidentified commentary of some kind on Job, and therefore its size cannot even be guessed at. The book must have had a limp covering comprising an unspecified black material combined with a blue textile, perhaps (as sug-gested above) a black skin at the exterior lined with blue textile.

There are three descriptions that include either 'ligantur' or 'ligatur', and, in each case, these appear to mean 'bound up' (that is 'sewn') with other matter. The first has 'ligantur cum aliis', the

---

97. A20.13, 16, 55, 122, 134, 176, 204, 379, 396, 398, 413, 422, 435, 456, 495, 540, 555, 583, 675, 724, 751, 823, 898, 914a, 914c, 998, 1073, 1097, 1124, 1209, 1215, 1259, 1329, 1340, 1346 and 1864.

98. A20.740 (= 754) and 920 (= 876).

99. A20.92 (= 258), 531 (= 615) and 737 (= 1334).

100. A20.1864, and Bodl. Laud misc. 625 f. 143r. The catalogue description occurs in a section headed *Libri et Rotule euidenciarum nostrarum* . . . (I owe my knowledge of the binding description in the Laud manuscript to the paper by David Crouch in this volume, where it is quoted on 225, n. 2.) The description in the Laud manu-script may have been made to distinguish the volume from another book described as 'liber qui vocatur The Chartwary in magno et spisso volumine . . .' (A20.1863) that contained similar material.

101. A20.67, 71, 189, 336, 339, 415, 417, 492, 493, 572, 673, 716, 742, 785, 806, 818, 829, 847, 868, 884, 885, 941, 954, 965, 991, 995, 1000, 1011, 1076, 1103, 1115, 1125, 1126, 1136, 1204, 1255 and 1270–4.

102. A20.189 (= 173) and 572 (= 952).

103. A20.1076 (= 433).

104. A20.1267. It might be that the description is for uncovered boards and an overcover, although I cannot recall ever seeing a medieval binding in a British collection with such an arrange-ment.

105. A20.7.

106. A20.7. A20.1–17 are bibles belonging to the abbey, five of which were described as 'parua' and two as either 'magna' or 'magno'. (A20.1, a two-volume bible in the refectory, almost cer-tainly comprised two large books, but their size was not noted.) However, the bible of concern here did not have its size noted, and it is the only one said to have a textile covering. (All but A20.11, whose binding was not described, had a white covering, although not all are said to be 'in asseribus'.)

107. A20.50.

second 'ligatur in libro qui vocatur . . .' and the last 'ligatur cum . . .'.[108] The term *ligatus* appears to have been used in the sense of 'unsewn' (as noticed above), but also to the operation of binding in general as in these three occurences.[109] A twelfth-century dialogue concerned with the Rule of St Augustine mentions the tasks that canons could undertake, and these included 'libros scribere illuminare regulare notare emendare atque ligare' ('writing, illuminating, ruling, notating, correcting and also binding books').[110] A note in a Rochester catalogue concerning a manuscript sent to be bound has 'in quaternis fecit ligare' ('quires to be bound'), and a continental description of 1334 has 'ligatam inter duas asseres, coopertam de corio' ('bound between two boards and covered with leather').[111] In the first two of these texts *ligatus* appears always to be used in the sense of 'binding', and the third appears to distinguish the operations of sewing and board attachment ('ligatum') and covering ('coopertam'). A similar distinction also appears to be made in a later description of a book as 'xvii quaternis ligatus et sine asseribus' ('seventeen quires and without boards') in which 'ligatus' was used to describe quires that were only sewn.[112]

Abbreviated descriptions

Abbreviated forms of descriptions have been mentioned several times above, and there is a real possibility that at least some of these are shortened versions of long ones rather than complete short ones. The fullest form of the description of a stiff-board binding has five words (no. 1 below), and the variant forms (nos. 2, 3 and 4) appear to have one word 'missing' in each case:

    1: in asseribus cum albo coopertorio

    2: in asseribus cum albo [   ]

    3: in asseribus cum [   ] coopertorio

    4: in asseribus [   ] albo coopertorio

However, the following description could either have been heavily abbreviated or be complete:

    5: in asseribus [   ]

'Missing' words also appears to explain the variant forms of the description of limp bindings:

    6: in quaternis cum albo coopertorio

    7: in quaternis cum albo [   ]

    8: in quaternis cum [   ]

    9: in quaternis cum [   ] coopertorio

although the following could either have been heavily abbreviated or be complete:

    10: in quaternis [   ]

It is also clear that one short form of description could refer to a binding with either boards or limp covers.

108. A20.871, 892 and 1066.

109. See the texts collected in Wattenbach, *Das Schriftwesen im Mittelalter*, 390–5, and, for an assessment of the written sources, see Vezin, 'Le vocabulaire Latin de la reliure', 56–7. *Ligatur* (or similar) was also used to describe other activities concerned with 'enclosing', see *Dictionary of medieval Latin from British sources* s.v. *ligare* and *ligatio. Ligator* was a common description of a bookbinder.

110. M. L. Colker, 'Richard of St Victor and the Anonymous of Bridlington', *Traditio* 18 (1962), 181–227, at 217. See also a grant of 1206 made to an Evesham precentor for supplying 'incaustum omnibus scriptoribus monasterii, et pergamenum ad breuia, et colores ad illuminandum, et necessaria ad ligandum libros' (*Thomas of Marlborough. History of the Abbey of Evesham*, ed.

J. E. Sayers and L. Watkiss, Oxford Medieval Texts (Oxford 2003), 523).

111. B81.14, and Vezin, 'Le vocabulaire Latin de la reliure', 57.

112. F. M. Powick, *The medieval books of Merton College* (Oxford 1931), 50. Two copies of the same text, a work on canon law by Bernard of Parma and therefore unlikely to be small books, in the Lanthony catalogue are described as 'libri duo quorum vnus ligatus et aliter quaternus' (A16.274). The first of these is likely to have been bound in boards, and the second to have had a limp cover. A Cîteaux library catalogue dated 1480 includes in its heading the statement that the books were 'aptari, ligari et cooperiri' (*Catalogue général des manuscrits des Bibliothèques Publiques de France*, 8° ser. 5 (Paris 1889), 339).

11: in [   ] albo coopertorio

What the full descriptions (nos. **1** and **6**) and those that were almost certainly abbreviated (nos. **2**, **3**, **4**, **7**, **8** and **9**) show, together with those elsewhere in the catalogue, is that they are formulaic to a degree that suggests they may have been the work of one person. However, the short descriptions (nos. **5** and **10**, and, perhaps, **11**) could either have been abbreviated or be complete.

The binding descriptions and earlier catalogues

Because the only manuscript of the Leicester catalogue is a fair copy of an earlier one, the date of the fullest forms of the binding descriptions and the terms they employed, is uncertain. Based upon the textual evidence just discussed, an obvious suggestion is that the scribe of the fair copy abbreviated many of the binding descriptions in the subject/author section where nearly all of the descriptions occur. (In what follows, reference to 'the catalogue' should be understood to refer almost always to the author/subject section, and it will clear from the context when reference is being made to the whole catalogue.) This raises the possibility that at least some of the entries in the catalogue without binding descriptions may once have had one. It is notable that, although the fair copy has a number of corrections and a few additions, there does not appear to be any correction made to any of the binding descriptions, and it is also notable that the scribe of the fair copy otherwise appears to have been careful in his work. However, there are errors and omissions in the catalogue not concerned with the binding descriptions, and it is uncertain whether these were in the exemplar or made by the scribe. Some single works listed give a cross-reference to a full description of a volume for which no description is present.[113] Furthermore, other single works give a cross-reference to a full description of a volume that is present but which has no mention of the work.[114] As William Charyte was one of the two scribes who made corrections to the fair copy, it appears that he may not have been concerned about the integrity of the descriptions in the fair copy either, for little of this appears to have been concerned with errors and omissions. That William may not have been much concerned with describing bindings is shown in the sections with books that he had either acquired or had made (1878–1958), sections that William might well have composed himself. Only two of these had their bindings described, one as 'in quaternis' that is described elsewhere as 'in asseribus', probably because William had bought it in a limp cover and had it rebound in boards, and the other as 'in asseribus'.[115] However, the two descriptions that he did make might well be complete and not have been abbreviated, and this raises the possibility that at least some of the comparable descriptions in the catalogue may also have been his work.

Confirmation that William did probably describe bindings in the catalogue is to be found in the entries for books given to the abbey by John Pomerey, abbot 1442–74, and his successor, John Shepeshede, abbot 1474–85. John Pomerey gave eight, and probably a ninth, and he is named as abbot in the catalogue. Four of his books are described as 'in asseribus', and a fifth, the book that is probably his gift, as 'nigro volumine'.[116] John Shepeshede gave four books (one jointly with John Pomerey), but he is never named as abbot, and three of them were described as 'in asseribus'.[117] As William Charyte was born about 1421 and entered Leicester about 1439 he is unlikely to have been precentor much before about 1450, becoming prior in 1463.[118] The chronology suggests that the

113. See, for example, A20.324 and 377. This may be termed a 'ghost' volume.

114. See, for example, A20.425 and 472.

115. A20.1927 (= 433 and 1076) and 1926 (= 824).

116. A20.366, 785, 1099 and 1100 were his certain gifts with their bindings described, and 495 his probable gift (see the commentary to the entry). A20.501, 1046, 1101 and 1138 were his other gifts.

117. A20.366 (given with John Pomerey), 479 and 492 have their bindings described, and A20.386 does not.

118. For all this see CBMLC 6, 107.

books given by the two Johns might have been described by William, and it is significant that all the binding descriptions are short ones.

M. R. James wondered whether the entries with binding descriptions were taken over by William from an older list.[119] It now appears that this question should probably be directed mainly at the full descriptions and their abbreviated forms (nos. 1, 2, 3, 4, 6, 7, 8 and 9 above), to allow for the possibility that at least some of the short descriptions (nos. 5 and 10) should be associated with William Charyte. This would mean that the long descriptions, as well perhaps as other errors and omissions, might all belong to an earlier stage in the transmission of the catalogue than the exemplar of the present one that was drawn up by William. There were at least three catalogues or lists of books at the abbey described in the surviving catalogue, although one of these may be a reference to the present catalogue.[120] The dependence of William Charyte on earlier material is implied in a heading to the catalogue describing it as 'renouatum'.[121] Elsewhere William appears to have claimed authorship of the list of authors ('tabula') at the beginning of the catalogue ('facta'), but not the catalogue itself.[122] Might one or more of the earlier lists used by William have had binding descriptions (and one or more of them not) as James suggested? One entry in the catalogue does describe the former and present binding of a manuscript ('quondam in nigro modo in albo cooperta'), and this does suggest that an earlier description was used in making the later one.[123] The implication is that the author of the later list, whether William or another, must have had an earlier list with binding descriptions and the relevant volume in front of him when making the later description.

Another entry refers to the binding together of two volumes, one a copy of works by Cicero and the other commentaries on Cicero that have separate entries in the catalogue. The entry concerning the commentaries has a note written by the principal scribe stating that the volume was 'ligatur cum textu' ('bound with [a copy of] the text') with 'modo' ('now') added before by William Charyte, presumably to clarify and give additional emphasis to the original note.[124] This pair of entries is especially informative for the light it casts on the making of the catalogue. The note concerning the binding together of the two volumes appears to have been an addition to an earlier catalogue because it follows the *secundo folio* reference, whereas binding descriptions are usually before, and uses a term ('ligatur') that only occurs in two other entries in the catalogue. It is significant that in both of these the term also comes after the *secundo folio* reference, so it is likely that these notes were also added to an earlier catalogue, to be dutifully copied by the scribe of the present catalogue.[125] One of these notes also appears to refer to the binding together of two volumes that had separate entries. The entry is for an unidentified work concerned with instructing novices said to be in one quire ('quaternus'), with the added note stating that it was bound up in another volume ('ligatur in libro qui vocatur philomena'). Unfortunately, this volume does not appear to be described anywhere else in the catalogue.[126] The note added to the other entry ('ligantur cum aliis'), a volume containing eleven works, is a little ambiguous. It appears to be a

---

119. 'Catalogue of the Library', 128.

120. A20.844 item g ('Registrum librorum'), 1297 item b ('Registro librorum nostrorum') and 1867 ('Registrum omnium librorum nostrorum'). The last of these might be the surviving catalogue, see the commentary to the entry.

121. CBMLC 5, 120 ('Registrum librorum . . . renouatum').

122. CBMLC 5, 109 ('tabula facta per fratrem Willelmum Charyte').

123. A20.8. As this book was given to the abbey by one of its canons (Geoffrey Salow) sometime in the middle of the fourteenth century, the earlier description cannot have been more than about one hundred years old when William Charyte began his work on the catalogue.

124. A20.1064 and 1066. The two volumes have survived as York Minster XVI.M.6 and XVI.M.7.

125. A20.871 and 892.

126. A20.892. The lost volume is therefore another ghost volume.

comment on the content of the volume ('bound up with other works not specified'), but these other works may once have been in another volume.[127]

Who added these three notes copied unchanged into the present catalogue from an earlier one is unknown, and there is certainly nothing to show that they were the work of William Charyte as he could merely have taken them over from an earlier catalogue. One putative earlier catalogue with binding descriptions can be roughly dated. A surviving Leicester manuscript has an inscription that suggests it was acquired by 'frater Iohannes Neuton' from 'Radulfus Thurkeston' when it was enclosed a limp cover ('in quaternis non illuminatum nec ligatum et continet in se xvij quaternis').[128] Ralph Thurlestone was a Leicester canon in 1339, later to be the prior of Mottesfont (Hants.), and presumably John was also a Leicester canon, although he is otherwise unknown. The manuscript was said in the catalogue to have been the gift of John Neubolt (not described as a canon), also otherwise unknown, and it was then described as 'in asseribus cum albo cooperto-rio'.[129] This shows that in about the middle of the fourteenth century the manuscript was in a limp cover, and that by the second half of the fifteenth it was in a stiff-board binding. Therefore at least one putative list with binding descriptions used by William cannot have been earlier than about the middle of the fourteenth century.

It is very difficult to separate a significant number of the entries with binding descriptions from a significant number of those without, and therefore it is very difficult to understand the nature and scope of the lists that may lay behind the present catalogue. Both groups of entries contain books with similar contents that might well be of similar date, and whose contents are described in a similar fashion. So far it has proved impossible to observe any notable distinction or characteristic that points to a significance difference or differences between the two groups, in particular that the entries with binding descriptions contain manuscripts likely to be of an earlier or later date than those entries without.[130] The only peculiar feature is that the bindings of a large number of law books at the end of the first section of the catalogue (1251–1435) usually do not have their bindings described. The reason for this may simply be fatigue on the part of a scribe somewhere in the transmission (including the scribe of the fair copy) who abbreviated or dropped more descriptions towards the end of this section.[131]

It appears from all this that the work of William Charyte was probably based upon one or more earlier lists, and that one or more of them contained full binding descriptions. Whether these were faithfully taken over by William or not when he drew up his catalogue is also uncertain, for they could either have been abbreviated by him or by the scribe of the fair copy of his catalogue. It does appear that William did supply some binding descriptions, but that these were only

127. A20.871. The volume appears again at A20.1323, but there its content is identical to the first description.

128. Cambridge, Trinity College B.14.7, f. 197r. 'ligatum' appears to be used here in the sense of 'sewing'. Compare the description of a manuscript bought in Oxford in the 1450s as 'in quaternis non illuminatis nec ligatis' (*Duke Humfrey's Library and the Divinity School 1488–1988*, exh. cat. (Bodleian Library: Oxford 1988), no. 105).

129. A20.436. For Ralph Thurleston, who was the owner or donor of at least three volumes in the catalogue and who may have given another five, see the commentary to A20.1290.

130. As the groups cannot apparently be distinguished by date, one other obvious distinction could be by location. However, it may be difficult to show that a list of books in one location had their bindings described and that a list of books in another did not.

If these putative lists were somewhat earlier than the mid fifteenth century, it is possible that they were drawn up before the library room at the abbey existed.

131. Of the 184 entries only thirty-five include descriptions of bindings (19%), twenty-four of which are at the beginning of the run (A20.1251–74). On the other hand, of the first 201 entries in the catalogue (including a number of descriptions of the same volume where the binding is usually only described once) 134 (67%) have binding descriptions (A20.1–201). The majority of the law books contained only one work, and therefore there are few cross-referenced descriptions. As noted above, one means of identifying a volume in a cross-referenced description was its binding, so perhaps the need to record bindings in the law book section of the catalogue was considered to be less pressing than earlier.

ever short ones. Therefore, the date of the form of the long descriptions, and the terms that were employed, appear to belong to a period before the mid fifteenth century when William Charyte began work.[132]

Stiff-board bindings and limp covers

The catalogue describes the bindings of about 570 books (51%) from a total of about 1100. Of these about 65% were in boards, about 30% in limp covers, and about 5% have ambiguous or unclear descriptions. However, these relative figures for different kinds of binding are not the same when the percentages for books in the main library and the books elsewhere are calculated separately. About 141 (62%) of 227 books in the library have their bindings described, and of these about 73% were in boards, about 3.5% in limp covers, and about 23.5% have ambiguous or unclear descriptions. Of the books elsewhere, about 54% were in boards, 36% in limp covers and about 10% have ambiguous or uncertain descriptions. Nevertheless, there is enough evidence to suggest that about 70% of the collection was bound in boards and about 30% in limp covers.

The Leicester figures can be compared to those in the few other British catalogues with many binding descriptions, a mid fourteenth-century one from Lanthony, one dated 1400 from Titchfield and a late thirteenth-century one from Bradsole. The Lanthony catalogue lists 514 volumes housed in five cupboards, representing the main collection of the priory, and of these volumes about 157 (30%) have their bindings described.[133] About 85% of these are of books in limp covers ('in quaternis') and about 15% of the descriptions are ambiguous or unclear. No stiff-board bindings are described at all. However, it appears that the cataloguer only described bindings with limp covers, and it can be safely presumed that a significant number of the manuscripts whose bindings were not described had stiff-board bindings.[134] In addition, the books whose bindings were not described usually had their sizes noted, and it appears that the cataloguer usually only recorded one physical feature of a book, either its size or whether it had a limp covering.

The books in the Lanthony catalogue with limp covers comprised a little less than 30% of the collection, and this figure is virtually identical to the proportion of the Leicester books with limp covers. The majority of the Lanthony books with limp covers were on the last shelves of the fourth cupboard and throughout the fifth cupboard. They were probably mostly medium or small sized books, and most were either schoolbooks, scientific and medical texts, or modern theology, together with small handfuls of glossed books of the Bible, law books, and sermons.[135]

The Titchfield catalogue lists 224 volumes in four cupboards that, like the Lanthony catalogue, described the main collection of the priory. Seventy-six (33%) of the books were said to have limp covers ('in quaterno'), and it seems virtually certain that most, if not all, of the others had stiff-board bindings. Not only were the relevant volumes described as 'in quaterno', but also at the end

---

132. The matter might be understood better when the nature of the list or lists with long binding descriptions can be contrasted with the nature of the list or lists without them. It is always possible (I suppose) that earlier descriptions of manuscripts used by William all had binding descriptions, and that nearly half of them were subsequently 'lost' entirely.

133. A16. The books were arranged by subject, and the nature of the collection, as well as its arrangement, shows that it was the main library of the priory.

134. London, Lambeth Palace 343 (s. xii med.) is a Lanthony manuscript still with its contemporary stiff-board binding, and this is not mentioned in the catalogue description (A16.25).

135. Most of the books from A16.364 (about one third of the way into the fourth shelf of the fourth cupboard) to A16.463 (the last entry for the sixth shelf of the fifth cupboard) had limp covers. The usual form of the descriptions is a title followed by 'quaternus', occasionally qualified as (for example) 'quaternus rubeus', 'quaternus simplex', and 'quaternus ligatus'. It should not be presumed that books in limp covers were never large. The former upper cover of parchment over BL Royal 2 C.viii (England, s. xiii/xiv) has survived as an endleaf in the manuscript (171) that is 325 × 230 mm. The manuscript may not have been bound in boards until s. xv as may be seen from the stains of the former upper paste-down (1r).

of each of the ten sections of the catalogue the number of books in limp covers is noted, thereby distinguishing these bindings twice.[136] However, while only eight (12%) of the sixty-eight volumes containing theology (Bibles, glossed books of the Bible, patristics, and some other material) had limp covers, six (68%) of the nineteen volumes with medical works and six (50%) of the dozen volumes with grammatical works had limp covers.[137]

The Bradsole catalogue lists 143 volumes but gives no information concerning where or how they were stored. The books are usually described as either 'in volumine' (72%) or 'in quaternis' (12.5%), and it appears that these are descriptions of books in stiff-board bindings or limp covers.[138] A small number of books (12%) have no descriptions, and there are two said to be 'non ligato' and three whose number of quires are specified, presumably because these were loose.[139]

The majority of the books without a binding description are in the last third of the list, and most of them are schoolbooks containing poetry. Therefore these are certainly the kind of book that was as likely to be in a limp cover as a stiff-board binding, but this must remain a matter of uncertainty. Bradsole was a very small Premonstratensian house with a small collection of books, and it is probably safest to treat the figures at face value and conclude that the proportion of books in limp covers at Bradsole was smaller than at Lanthony and Titchfield.

The Leicester collection of books with about 70% in boards and 30% in limp covers is a feature also found in the Lanthony and Titchfield collections. This might well have been the case in collections elsewhere, possible from as early as the end of the twelfth century, although the evidence of the Bradsole collection cautions against making this a universal generalisation. I suspect that the number of books in large and medium collections bound in limp covers could have been as many as about one third, but perhaps rarely much more, and may have been as little as about one fifth.[140]

It is virtually certain that fundamental texts and basic reference works concerned with theology in the broadest sense were usually bound in boards, and, in larger houses, by the end of the fifteenth century often housed together as a reference collection in a library room (such as the one at Leicester). Supplementary and subsidiary collections of works concerned with subjects such as science and medicine, as well as schoolbooks and practical theology, were as likely to have been bound in limp covers as boards. However, the range of these collections appears to have been more variable in their numbers and subjects from place to place than basic reference collections, almost certainly due to variable and changing local conditions over centuries. At present, the evaluation of the evidence cannot support more than these broad generalisations, not least because the variety of bindings in medieval collections, and the manner in which this reflects different attitudes to different types of books and their storage and use, in both institutional and

136. P6. The books were arranged by subject into ten divisions, and the nature of the collection and its arrangement show that it was the main library of the priory. At the end of the catalogue is a list of service books, almost certainly housed elsewhere (perhaps in the vestry or sacristy), none of whose bindings were described.

137. The Theological section with 68 volumes (12% with limp covers) comes first in the catalogue. The other figures, following the subject divisions of the catalogue, are as follows: 31 Canon Law (20%), 7 Civil Law (two), 29 Medical (68%), 24 Grammar (50%), 20 Miscellaneous (30%), 8 Logic (75%), 5 Philosophy (20%), 13 Statutes (23%) and 18 books in French (70%).

138. P2.1–121, but, as this lists several multi-volume works and multiple copies of one work each as one item, the total number of volumes is 143. The cataloguer divided the books into sections by subject, with books concerned with the bible listed first. The head-

ings in the catalogue are 'De Theologia' (1–78 = 83 volumes), 'De Iure' (79–88 = 12 volumes), 'De Phisica' (89–102 = 14 volumes) and 'De Grammatica' (103–21 = 24 volumes). P2.123–6 lists a large collection of psalters and service books, and 127–47 is a list of the books 'in ecclesia'. The Bradsole catalogue may be a list of all the books owned by the house.

139. P2.60 ('non ligato') and 72 ('vno volumine non ligato'), and 73 ('sex quaterni'), 78 ('tres quaterni') 118 and ('duobis quaternis'). The suggestion that the books 'in quaternis' were loose collections of quires (CBMLC 3, 160) should, in the light of evidence presented here, be disregarded.

140. It may be recorded here that of the nearly 100 books on a wide range of subjects acquired by Prior Nicholas of Evesham (d. 1392) for his house, about one third appear to have had limp covers (B30.1–97).

individual collections, has not received much attention from those interested in books and libraries.[141]

The Leicester catalogue in its present form poses several problems concerning its making, including the origin, development and form of the list or lists that almost certainly lay behind it, that have only been briefly touched upon here. That just over half of the books in the catalogue had their bindings described is remarkable, although the number and range of the terms used to describe them is fairly limited. Many of the descriptions are unambiguous, although there is a significant number whose meaning is not entirely clear, but both the descriptions here and elsewhere can sometimes be clarified by understanding the context in which they appear. Medieval terms used for describing bindings cannot always be fully understood if they are taken in isolation, for medieval library catalogues and booklists have considerable variety in their form, ambition and expression. Nevertheless, the terms in the Leicester catalogue, as well as those that have survived in catalogues and booklists from elsewhere, together with those too few medieval bindings that have survived to the present day, are the principal source material for studying the variety of medieval bindings to be found in late medieval British libraries.

141. See further on the matters raised in this paragraph Szirmai, *Medieval bookbinding*, 285, and Scholla, 'Limp bindings', 149–51.

Fig. 3. Cambridge, Queens' College 8, upper (front) board inner face

Appendix 1: Two twelfth-century bindings from the abbey
Cambridge, Queens' College 2 and 8 are the only two surviving twelfth-century manuscripts from Leicester with their contemporary bindings, and it is possible that both manuscripts were written and bound at the abbey. Both the bindings are typical of twelfth-century English work with nothing especially unusual in their materials or structure.

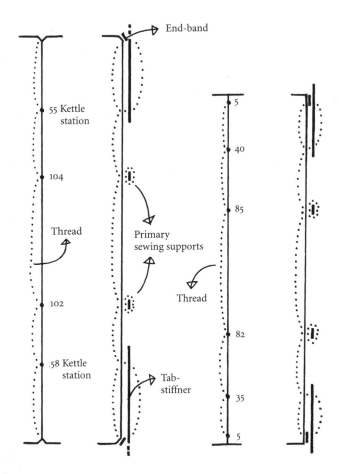

Fig. 4. Diagramatic representation of the spine-folds of Cambridge, Queens' College 2 (left) and 8 (right), from the interior (left) and in section (right). Measurements are in millimeters, taken from either the head- or tail-edge, whichever is the closer

The quires of both books were sewn to two primary sewing supports made of tawed skin straps slit across the spine, employing kettle stations, and both have end-bands with similar straps. The position of the primary stations divides the height of the leaves into roughly three equal parts with the kettle stations placed halfway between the primary supports and the outer edges of the leaves (fig. 4).[142] The ends of the spines were treated differently. Queens' 2 has the back corners cut (deeply cut) with the end-band thread passing to the

142. See Szirmai, *Medieval Bookbinding*, fig. 8.7 for sewing patterns.

end-band support in the lowest part of the V made by the cuts (fig. 4). In Queens' 8 on the other hand the end-band thread passes to the end-band support through pierced holes in the spine-folds of the quires, but with the spine-folds cut from the leaf edges to the stations (fig. 4).[143] (This was done to relieve the tension created in the spine-folds at the ends of the spine by a thick thread passing through a station close to the leaf edges.) Neither of the bindings have end-bands with a secondary sewing.

Both bindings had tab-stiffners extending inwards from the leaf edges to just past the kettle stations (fig. 4).[144] The tabs that project away from the leaf edges that are one of the most marked features of nearly all stiff-board pre-1200 bindings are still present in Queens' 8, but have been cut off in Queens' 2 (fig. 4). The tabs in Queens' 8 have a shallow curved profile and were not attached to the covering skin with a perimeter sewing.

The boards in both bindings were made of oak with the grain running vertically, and are a little thicker at the spine-edges than the fore-edges. Both sets of boards had their three exterior edges slightly shaped to ease the passing of the covering skin around them and to present a slightly rounded look to the finished binding. Both sets of boards have a short lacing path pattern for the primary supports (fig. 3),[145] and both sets of boards had their back corners cut. In Queens' 2 the cut is more or less straight and matches the cut of the leaves, but in Queens' 8 the cut is quite shallow and appears to have made with a rounded chisel. The boards were covered with tawed skin, and Queens' 8 has the remains of a tawed skin overcover, its skirt that once extended on all four sides having been neatly cut off close to the board edges (fig. 3). The overcover appears to have had an early, if not contemporary, title in handsome pen-drawn capitals running down the spine, but now only one letter (an **M**) is clearly visible. The covering at the spine of Queens' 2 must have become damaged for it has been renewed with modern skin.

Fig. 5. Cambridge, Queens' College 2, lower (back) board outer face

The fastening system in both bindings was a single strap fixed in a recess cut at the centre fore-edge of the upper board passing to a side pin at the centre of the lower board. Queens' 2 had a tawed skin strap and Queens' 8 one of tanned skin, but both have been cut off at the board edges and neither binding has retained its pin.

The most unusual feature of the bindings occurs on Queens' 2. At the centre foot of the lower board is a hole passing through its thickness, but one that does not completely penetrate the lower paste-down, surrounded by four nails forming a square shape (fig. 5). There is no evidence that anything of metal passed through the hole, and there is no depression in the covering skin that might show what the four nails might have fixed down. This all makes it rather unlikely that the hole and the nails are evidence of some kind of staple used to attach a chain, and at present this physical evidence is puzzling.[146]

Appendix 2: A note on the library room at the abbey
During the course of the fourteenth- and fifteenth-century specially built library rooms were commonplace

143. See ibid. fig. 8.16 for end-band constructions.
144. See ibid. fig. 8.14 for tab-stiffners.
145. See ibid. fig. 8.12 a–c for lacing paths.
146. During the preparation of this paper the Old Library at Queens' College was undergoing renovation, and I have been unable to examine any of the other Queens' manuscripts to see whether there is anything to suggest that this feature occurs on other of its books, and therefore that the evidence has nothing to do with Leicester. I have pointed out above that there is little to suggest that a significant number of books at Leicester was ever chained.

in Oxford and Cambridge colleges. From at least the early fifteenth century onwards, a significant number of ecclesiastical institutions also had them, but whereas colleges could plan and build a library room during their earliest building programmes, ecclesiastical institutions usually fitted such a room somewhere into their extant claustral buildings.[147] The presence of one at Leicester is known from its catalogue where there is a list of books headed *Registrum librorum qui sunt in libraria*.[148] The books were disposed on eight lecterns ('stallo'), although when the room was built (presuming that it was newly built and not an adaptation of an extant room) is unknown.[149]

There are 228 entries for the library, but among these are five added by a corrector at the end of the section listing books on the first lectern (1478–82). However, two of these entries (1479 and 1480) are for books that were entered by the original scribe (1563 and 1564), and presumably these two were moved from their original location on the fourth lectern to the first. As two entries were given the same number (1553) in the CBMLC edition, this means that the catalogue originally listed 224 volumes. In what follows the movement of two books from one lectern to another and the three that were added are ignored.

As was common elsewhere, the books were arranged by subject. The first lectern was biblical (29 volumes), the second contained Augustine (21 volumes), and the third mostly church fathers (Gregory, Bede, Ambrose and Jerome, as well as Bernard of Clairvaux and a few others) (27 volumes). The fourth and fifth contained mostly relatively modern theology followed by philosophy (35 and 20 volumes respectively). The sixth contained law books (30 volumes), the seventh mostly history followed by medicine (34 volumes), and the eighth a miscellany (including logic, astronomy and poetry) (17 volumes). The average number of volumes on each lectern was twenty-eight, although the eighth appears to have had noticeably fewer volumes than the others.

Each lectern would almost certainly have had two sides, each with a surface (probably sloped) on which books could have been laid when not in use that doubled as a surface on which to consult books. There may have been one or two shelves to store books, one above the sloped surface and, if there was a second, one below. This would mean an average of fourteen volumes on each side of a lectern. The classic arrangement would have been with lecterns projecting into the library room, at 90° to the walls, either side of a rectangular room on the longer sides, with windows in the walls between each lectern. However, it is also possible that the lecterns ranged along one wall of a long and narrow room.

There is confirmation concerning the disposition of the books in three of the lecterns in the manuscript of the catalogue itself where, in the middle of the sections listing the books in the fifth, sixth and seventh, the scribe left spaces of either two, three or four lines. In the fifth lectern the division comes after a run of twenty volumes of mostly modern theology, and before a run of twelve volumes of mostly philosophy. In the sixth, containing only law books, the division divides the volumes into two runs of fifteen volumes each. In the seventh the division comes between a run of seventeen history books and seventeen miscellaneous volumes.[150] These divisions seem hardly likely to be mere coincidences, and the obvious conclusion is that the exemplar used by the scribe of the catalogue had some kind of visual device marking off the volumes on one side of a lectern from those on the other.[151]

Although there is no such division of the volumes in the other lecterns, those in the first can be also be divided into two. This comes after a run of thirteen volumes of mostly commentaries on all or parts of the Bible, and before a run of fourteen volumes of mostly glossed books of the Bible.[152] The only other feature of the catalogue likely to reflect the arrangement of the volumes concerns the eighth lectern with only seventeen

147. For early library rooms and the lectern system see J. W. Clark, *The care of books* (Cambridge 1901), 101–70, and B. H. Streeter, *The chained library* (London 1931), 9–41, with a summary of these in Szirmai, *Medieval bookbinding*, 268–70.

148. A20.1450–1677.

149. The term used for the furniture that housed books was varied considerably. For example, Cambridge colleges used *distinctio* (King's), *gradus* (Queens'), *lectrinum* (Peterhouse), *stallum* (St Catherine's), and *staulum* and *descus* (University Library) (CBMLC 10, lxiii).

150. In lectern five (A20.1565–96) the division comes after 1584, in six (1597–1626) after 1611, and in seven (1627–60) after 1643. These divisions were noticed in the CBMLC edition, where it was

also noticed that the scribe of the catalogue also left line spaces following the last volume on each lectern, before the heading to the next, unless a new lectern was begun at the top of a page.

151. In the third lectern there is a two-line space after nine volumes (eight by Gregory and one by Bede), followed by two volumes of Ambrose, then another two-line space followed by sixteen volumes by various authors. It is uncertain whether either of these divisions might reflect any physical arrangement of the volumes or not. The line-spaces occur after A20.512 (not noticed in the edition, although an abortive entry 'Am' on the first line is noticed), and 1514 (correcting the edition that notes only a one-line space).

152. In the first lectern (A20.1450–77) the division comes after 1463.

miscellaneous books. From their content, it is likely that several of them were small, and there is a real possibility that this lectern had only one side.[153] If this was so, the average number of books on each lectern rises to about thirty, with fifteen on either side.

The library room at Leicester is the only one from an English Augustinian house about which anything much is known. Few of the houses have much of their fabric remaining, and the only surviving catalogue of such a library in an Augustinian house is the one from Leicester. However, a post-Dissolution survey of Leicester, drawn up in 1538 or 1539, mentions a 'librarye' and from the context it appears that it was in the east claustral range.[154] One is also mentioned in a similar survey of the abbey at Cirencester and it appears that it too was somewhere in or off the cloister.[155]

Appendix 3: The terms used to describe books and bindings in the catalogue
Terms that occur ten times or less are marked with an asterisk.

albus: white	**illuminatio**: illumination*	**pannus**: textile*
antiquus: ancient*	**impressio**: blindstamped*	**pulchrum**: beautiful*
asseribus: wooden board	**lacer**: torn*	**quaternis**: limp cover
bercare: tanned*	**largus**: large*	**rubeus**: red
blodius: blue*	**latus**: thick or broad*	**scacario**: checkered*
bonus: good*	**ligatio**: sew	**spissus**: thick*
catenatus: chained*	**lineus**: linen*	**tenuis**: thin*
cooperio: cover	**magnus**: large	**utilis**: useful*
duplicatio: double*	**medius**: medium*	**vetus**: old*
figura: illustration*	**niger**: black	**viridus**: green*
glaucus: grey*	**nouus**: new*	**vitulinus**: calfskin*
hispidus: hairy	**nudus**: uncovered	

Appendix 4: Semi-limp and flexible boards
A fourteenth-century Cambridge catalogue is unusual as it specifies 'boards' of cuir-bouilli, as either 'guerbulie' or 'quebulie' ('. . . guerbulie/quebulie cum coopertorio corii . . .').[156] The manuscripts that I have seen with boards of leather are constructed in the manner of stiff-board bindings, and therefore they ought to be regarded as a sub-group of stiff-board bindings rather than one of bindings with limp or semi-limp covers.[157] The same catalogue has a binding described as '. . . cum bredis flexibilibus albi corei . . .',[158] but it is unclear whether this is a book with 'boards' of white leather or with flexible boards covered with white skin, as the crucial word 'coopertorio' is not present.

---

153. For example, the volumes of Boethius (A20.1669), Euclid, (1670), Virgil (1673) and Cicero (1674), were all likely to have been small books, and one of them was described as 'paruo' earlier in the catalogue (1669 = 1154). M. R. James suggested that this lectern might have had only one side ('Catalogue of the library', 121), and he also suggested that the second (with twenty-one volumes) might also have had only one side, leading to the further suggestion that if this was so, the lectern was described out of sequence. However, the second lectern contained only works by Augustine and its natural place would be following the biblical material in the first. Most, if not all, of the Augustine volumes were probably large books, and one of them was described as 'magno' earlier in the catalogue (1500 = 211).

154. The full text of the survey is printed as an Appendix by R. Buckley et al., 'The archaeology of Leicester Abbey' in this volume, above, p. 67.

155. A. K. B. Evans, 'Historical evidence for the Anglo-Saxon church and medieval abbey' in *Cirencester Anglo-Saxon church and medieval abbey*, ed. D. Wilkinson and A. McWhirr (Cotswold Archaeological Trust: Cirencester 1998), 14–18, at 17.

156. UC18.8, 9, 11 and 14 ('guerbulie'), and UC.18.6, 12 and 13 ('quebulie'), all of which are thirteenth- or fourteenth-century law books. The earliest use of cuir-bouilli (tanned leather boiled to

harden it) in the *Oxford English Dictionary* dates from *c.* 1375.

157. Cambridge, St John's College E 29 (132) (s. xiii, ?Mersea provenance) (with blindstamped covers), Worcester Cathedral F.69 (s. xiv in., perhaps Oxford-made) and F.87 (s. xiii ex., England). Three continental examples are BL Egerton 2900 (s. xii²) (with blindstamped covers), London, Lambeth Palace 232 (s. xii med.), and Washington, Library of Congress Rosenwald 1 (s. xii²) (with blindstamped covers). London, Society of Antiquaries 154 (s. xii med., Winchester-made) (with blindstamped covers) has boards made from laminated leaves of parchment (discarded from a tenth-century manuscript) that is also structurally related to stiff-board bindings (H. Nixon, 'The binding of the Winton Domesday' in *Winchester in the early middle ages*, ed. M. Biddle, Winchester Studies 1 (Oxford 1976), 526–40). New Haven, Yale University, Beinecke Library 494 (s. xv¼, England) appears to have boards of leather reinforced with leaves of parchment at the interior faces (Shailor, *The medieval book*, no. 54). A few other examples of bindings with leather boards (none of which I have seen) are noticed in de Hamel, *Glossed books of the Bible*, 68.

158. UC18.5, a copy of Peter Comestor, *Historia scholastica*, a work usually in a large or largeish format. 'Bredis' must derive from an obsolete word for board, see *Oxford English Dictionary* s.v. *bred*.

Summary catalogue of surviving manuscripts from Leicester Abbey

Michael Gullick and Teresa Webber

The arrangement of the following descriptions is self-evident, although note that in the physical descriptions the leaf count includes medieval paste-downs but no post-medieval leaves. The bibliography is minimal, mostly limited to some basic works of reference in which the manuscripts are noticed. No references are given to printed library catalogues, but the catalogue numbers from M. R. James' catalogue of the manuscripts of Trinity College, Cambridge, and from the Bodleian Library's *Summary Catalogue* (= *SC*) have been provided. References in the form 'A20.000' are to the main entry and, where relevant, the entry in the list of books in the *libraria*, taken from the edition of the late-fifteenth-century Leicester library catalogue in the Corpus of British Medieval Library Catalogues (CBMLC) 6, 104–399.

The catalogue below is divided into three parts. The first (nos. **1–21**) lists books certainly owned by the abbey, the second (nos. **22–4**) books that may have been owned by the abbey, and the third part the only known original charter from the abbey archives (no. **25**). N. R. Ker, in his *Medieval libraries of Great Britain* (2nd edn., London 1964), 113, a work that does not include archival books, listed nos. **1–10, 14, 18** (with a query), **20–1** and **23** (with a query), but not nos. **11, 13, 19, 22** and **24** as their certain or possible Leicester provenance is due to subsequent discoveries. Unless stated otherwise, the illustrations in the catalogue are reproduced at same size. This is also often the case with the illustrations of the manuscripts elsewhere in this book, references to which are given below by page and fig. number. The colour plates are between pp. 8 and 9.

Manuscripts owned by Leicester Abbey

1. Cambridge, King's College 2

303 × 205 mm (retrimmed). i + 491 + i leaves, foliated 1–190, 192–222, 224–451 and 453–494. Three leaves (191, 223 and 452) are now lost.

Bible; Stephen Langton, *Interpretationes nominum hebraicorum*

s. xiii²

Moderate parchment. Two columns. One good scribe, writing below top line. Good historiated and decorated initials at major divisions; pen-flourished initials. The manuscript is French. Given to Leicester s. xv ex. by John Willscheyr, vicar of All Saints, Leicester, 1481–96' (494v) (p. 143, fig. 1):

> Orate pro anima domini Iohannis Wylchur vicarii omnium sanctorum leycestrie qui dedit istum librum ad usum allatis leycestrie

Several s. xvi med. pen trials show that the book was owned locally after the Dissolution: for example,

---

1. A. Hamilton Thompson, *The Abbey of St Mary of the Meadows, Leicester* (Leicester 1949), 160.

'Rychardus Barton of Shepished' (307v); 'ralfe cos(s)by' (177r and 205v; perhaps Ralph Cosseby, presented by the abbey as vicar of Shepshed, Leicestershire, in 1538).[2] Other pen trials are partial drafts of documents dated to the second year of Edward VI (218r and 283v).

2. Cambridge, Queens' College 2 A20.251 and 1513

302 × 212 mm. i + 126 leaves. Leaves have been cut out following ff. 70 and 83. Contemporary binding.

Ambrose, *De officiis, De Ioseph patriarcha, De patriarchis*; Augustine, *In epistulam Iohannis ad Parthos tractatus x*

s. xii[2] (probably s. xii[3]₄)

Poor parchment. Two columns. Written by one moderate scribe and rubricated by a better one. The text scribe used a form of medial punctuation described by N. R. Ker as 'wavy-line' (pp. 135–6, figs. 3 and 5).[3] Two moderate arabesque initials, a large one at the beginning and a much more modest one later on (1r and 75v) (fig. 1). The text scribe twice extended the lower bowl of the **g** on the last line of a page and added an arrow to make the bowl appear like a bow (10r and 31v) (fig. 2), a scribal trick found in some west-country manuscripts.[4] A contents list of s. xiii/xiv with the last three words added later, partially over erasure, on the upper pastedown: 'Ambrosius mediolanensis de officiis / augustinus super epistolis johannis'. Contains pencil annotations (s. xiii or xiv), including a majuscule **R** found also in nos. **3** (p. 135, fig. 3), **5** and **6**, and annotations in a hand of s. xv[1], the same or similar to that of annotations in nos. **3–8** and **19**.

   Given *c.* 1631–4 to Queens' by Francis Tyndall (see inscription on upper paste-down), as was no. **3**.[5]

3. Cambridge, Queens' College 8 A20.41

258 × 182 mm. iii + 162 + iv leaves. Contemporary binding with the remains of an overcover.

Odo of Canterbury, Commentary on Genesis-Numbers

s. xii ex.

Poor parchment. Two columns. Several (five or six) mostly mediocre scribes, the best scribe being the first (p. 135, fig. 3).[6] On the overcover is the remains of what is probably a contemporary title in handsome pen-drawn ink capital letters running down the spine. (The only letter that can be read with certainty is an **M**.) A later written title of probably s. xiv running up the spine, partly obscured by a modern paper label, reads *haymo super pe*[*ntatechum*].[7] (The reading of most of the last word is taken from the catalogue of the Queens' manuscripts by M. R. James.) Plummet-written additions of s. xii–xiii on ff. 110v (Prayer), 150v (Poem on John the Baptist) and 162v (Verses on John the Baptist) noted by James are very difficult to read and cannot be identified. Contains pencil annotations (s. xiii or xiv), including a majuscule **R**, found also in nos. **2, 5** and **6**, and annotations in a hand of s. xv[1], the same or similar to that of annotations in nos. **2, 4–8** and **19**. A late medieval or early modern erased three-line inscription at the top of the sleeve of the chemise at the inner face of the upper board appears to open *Iste liber*, followed by one long or two short words, followed by *ad*, followed in turn by a word that appears to begin with **l** and the third letter of which appears to be **y** (p. 168, fig. 3).

   The end-leaves (ii–iii and 163–165) contain the preface, book 1 and the beginning of book 2 of Bernard of Clairvaux, *De consideratione*, written s. xii[2] (after 1153, the date of the composition of the work, and probably before about 1180), and were rejected because of scribal incompetence. (The leaves cannot be arranged so that the text is consecutive.) Three scribes, the first the best although only mediocre (p. 136, fig. 5), but the second and third very poor.[8] No rubrication and blank spaces for initials but for two, probably added a little

---

2. Ibid. 190.

3. N. R. Ker, *English manuscripts in the century after the Norman Conquest* (Oxford 1960), 47–9.

4. Ibid. 7.

5. Francis Tyndall matriculated fellow-commoner at Queens' in 1631, and died *c.* 1634: J. Venn and J. A. Venn, *Alumni Cantabrigiensis. A biographical list of all known students, graduates and holders of office at the University of Cambridge, from the earliest times to 1751,* 4 vols. (Cambridge 1922–5), iv, 284,

6. Scribe A wrote ff. 1r–14va, Scribe B ff. 14vb–40v and 111r–118v, Scribe C ff. 41r–43v, 46r–50v and 111r–118v, Scribe D ff. 44r–45v, Scribe E ff. 50r–110v and 119r–150r, and Scribe F ff. 151r–162v. Scribe D may be Scribe E, but writing quite large. Scribes A, B, C and E used the wavy-line form of medial punctuation (see no. 2).

7. The hand of the scribe looks rather like the hand of the scribe who wrote the contents list in no. 2.

8. Scribe A wrote ff. ii–iii and 163, Scribe B f. 164ra lines 1–27, and Scribe C ff. 164ra line 28–165v. Scribe A used the wavy-line form of medial punctuation (see no. 2).

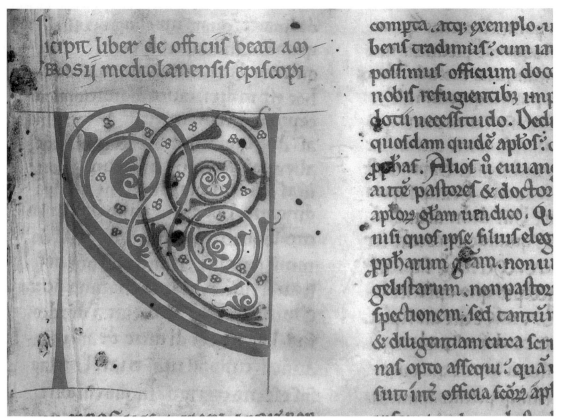

Fig. 1. Cambridge, Queens' College 2, f. 1v

Fig. 2. Cambridge, Queens' College 2, f. 10r

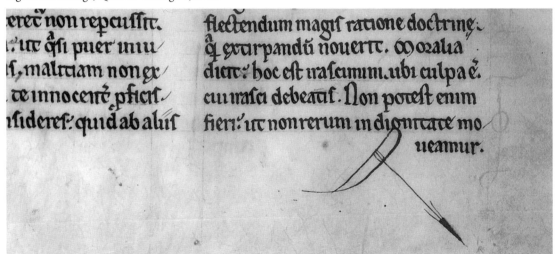

later. If, as is possible, the manuscript itself was written and bound at Leicester, these reject leaves are also likely to have been written at the abbey

Given *c.* 1631–4 to Queens' by Francis Tyndall (see inscription on ii recto), as was no. 2.

4. Cambridge, Trinity College B.1.8 (7)   A20.298 and 1517

126 × 195 mm (retrimmed). A composite manuscript of two contemporary parts, written by the same scribe but with different quire and ruling patterns, bound together by s. xiii/xiv: ii + 97 + 55 leaves, foliated 1–2 + 3–99 + 1–55; an additional leaf, supplying a lacuna, is stitched to the base of f. 95. A medieval contents list and the library catalogue entry indicate the subsequent loss of a substantial number of leaves following part 2 (see below).

1. (3–99) William of Tournai, *Flores Bernardi*

2. (1–55) Augustine, *De sermone Domini in monte, Sermo de muliere forti, De octo quaestionibus Dulcitii* (here entitled 'De decem questionibus . . .')

A contents list of s. xiii/xiv (1r) (p. 138, fig. 6) and the catalogue (A20.298 and cross-references at A20.940 and A20.942) record four further items, now lost: William of Conches, *Moralium dogma philosophorum*; Augustine, *De opere monachorum*, *De agone christiano*, and a *Vita S. Bernardi*

s. xiii med.

Poor parchment. Two columns. Both parts written by one mediocre scribe, writing below top line; partially rubricated in the same or very similar hand. Very modest flourished initials in red or blue. Part 1 is quired in 12s and part 2 in 8s, and both parts have parchment arranged with the flesh-side outside of the outermost bifolium. Marginal annotations of s. xiv in the same hand as that which supplied a large lacuna on f. 95v and a shorter one on f. 97r. Later marginal annotations of s. xv[1] are in perhaps the same hand as those found in nos. 2–3, 5–8 and 19.

Given to Trinity by George Willmer (d. 1626), as were nos. 5–9.[9]

5. Cambridge, Trinity College B.2.22 (65)   A20.283

285 × 198 mm (retrimmed). 189 leaves.

Gregory, *Homiliae in Ezechielem* (Books 1–2)

s. xii med.

Mediocre parchment. Two columns. One moderate scribe. Modestly decorated arabesque initials (1r, 99r and 160v) (figs. 3 and 4).[10] Contains pencil annotations (s. xiii or xiv), including a majuscule **R**, found also in nos. 2, 3 and 6, and annotations in a hand of s. xv[1], the same or similar to that of annotations in nos. 2–4, 6–8 and 19.

Given to Trinity by George Willmer (d. 1626), as were nos. 4 and 6–9.

R. Gameson, *The manuscripts of early Norman England (c. 1066–1130)* (Oxford 1999), no. 134 [dated too early]; T. N. Hall, 'The early English manuscripts of Gregory the Great's *Homiliae in Evangelia* and *Homiliae in Hiezechihelem*: A preliminary survey' in *Rome and the North: The early reception of Gregory the Great in Germanic Europe*, ed. R. H. Bremmer, K. Dekker and D. F. Johnson (Paris 2001), 115–136, on 130 n. 61

6. Cambridge, Trinity College B.3.27 (106)   A20.250 and 1514

310 × 230 mm (retrimmed). 123 leaves.

Ambrose, Commentary on Luke

s. xiii in.

Moderate parchment. Two columns. Two scribes, both writing above top-line, the hand of the first (fig. 5) rather conservative. Rubrics in red and green. Modest, arabesque initials, also rather conservative; mediocre flourished initials added s. xv (e.g. 6r) (fig. 6). Contains pencil annotations (s. xiii or xiv), including a majuscule **R**, found also in nos. 2, 3 and 5, and annotations in a hand of s. xv[1], the same or similar to that of annotations in nos. 2–5, 7–8 and 19.

Given to Trinity by George Willmer (d. 1626), as were nos. 4–5 and 7–9.

---

9. Matriculated fellow-commoner of Trinity College in 1598: Venn and Venn, *Alumni Cantabrigiensis* iv, 424.

10. The arabesque initials are very close to comparable initials in some s. xii med. manuscripts made at St Albans (R. M. Thomson, *Manuscripts from St Albans Abbey 1066–1235*, 2 vols.

(Woodbridge 1982), ii, pls. 79, 96–9, 153, 155, 160–2 and 170). Such initials do occur in manuscripts from elsewhere, but their number and the influence of St Albans in their making, with the possibility that they represent a regional style, has yet to be determined.

Fig. 3. Cambridge, Trinity College, B.2.22, f. 1r

Fig. 4. Cambridge, Trinity College, B.2.22, f. 99r

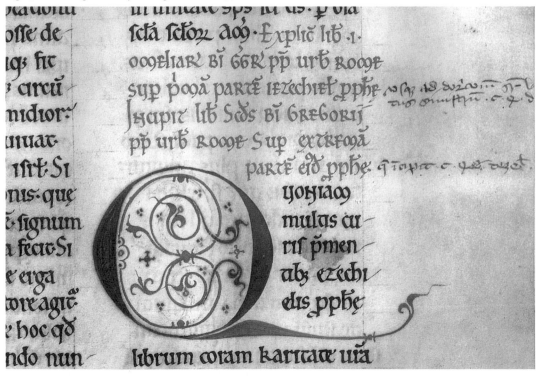

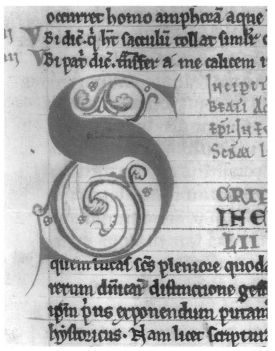

Fig. 5. Cambridge, Trinity College, B.3.27, f. 2r   Fig. 6. Cambridge, Trinity College, B.3.27, f. 6r

7. Cambridge, Trinity College B.14.7 (293)   A20.436

230 × 160 mm (retrimmed). 198 leaves.

Ps. Bonaventure, *Meditationes de passione Christi*; James of Milan, *Stimulus amoris* (in the expanded three-part version); *ps.* Augustine, *De diligendo Deo, Liber soliloquiorum animae ad Deum, Meditationes de spiritu sancto*; seventeen prayers and meditations by or attributed to Anselm; three prayers to BVM[11]

s. xiv in.

Moderate parchment. One good scribe, writing *Textualis*. Plain blue or red initials. According to the catalogue (A20.436), acquired for Leicester by John Neubolt (unidentified); a note on f. 197r refers to Ralph Thurlestone, canon of Leicester in 1345 and prior of Mottesfont from 1352. Marginal annotations of s. xv[1] are in perhaps the same hand as those found in nos. **2–6**, **8** and **19**.

   Given to Trinity by George Willmer (d. 1626), as were nos. **4–6** and **8–9**.

8. Cambridge, Trinity College B.14.30 (315)   A20.222

195 × 140 mm (retrimmed). A composite manuscript of four contemporary parts with a common ruling pattern bound together by s. xv ex.: 32 + 17 + 10 + 72 leaves, foliated 1–32 + 33–39, 39a, 40–44, 44a, 45–47 + 48–57 + 58–129

1. (1–32) Ten Marian sermons

2. (33–47) Odilo of Cluny, *De moribus et uita beatae Mariae*; Paschasius Radbertus, *De assumptione beatae Mariae uirginis*

11. The content is identical to that of another book recorded in the catalogue (A20.435). Three items (*ps.* Augustine, *De diligendo Deo, Liber soliloquiorum animae ad Deum*, and the set of Anselmian prayers and meditations) are textually very closely related to Cambridge, Trinity College B.2.16, part 1, made for Henry IV prior to his accession in 1399; the first of these items in Trinity B.2.16 is accompanied (in the hand of the text scribe) by an almost identical set of marginal annotations as that added to B.14.7. (T. Webber, 'Latin devotional texts and the books of the Augustinian canons of Thurgarton Priory and Leicester Abbey in the late middle ages' in *Books and collectors 1200–1700: essays presented to Andrew Watson*, ed. J. P. Carley and C. G. C. Tite (London 1997), 27–41, on 33–34, 39 and 40.)

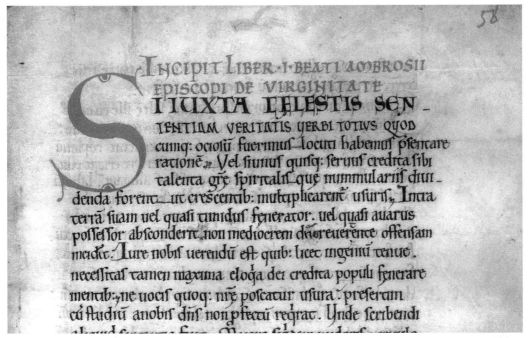

Fig. 7. Cambridge, Trinity College, B.14.30, f. 58r

3. (48–57) *Lectiones* on the life of BVM[12]

At the end of the penultimate lection is a scribal prayer in the hand of the text scribe (55r): 'Virgo beata manum salua scriptoris in euum'.

4. (58–129) Ambrose, *De uirginibus, De uiduis, De uirginitate, De institutione uirginis* and *Exhortatio uirginitatis*; ps. Ambrose, *De lapsu uirginis consecratae*; prayers: 'Incipit ad uiolatorem. De te autem quid dicam . . .'; 'Lamentatio super se. Quis consoletur . . .'.

s. xi ex.

Mediocre parchment. Six scribes, one of whom (scribe 3), who contributed to parts 1 and 2, has been identified in two manuscripts connected with Exeter Cathedral (Cambridge, Trinity College O.10.3 and BL Royal 6 B.viii). For the hand of another scribe, see fig. 7. Contains annotations in a hand of s. xv[1], the same or similar to that of annotations in nos. 2–7 and 19, and distinctive nota marks (p. 138, fig. 8).

Given to Trinity by George Willmer (d. 1626), as were nos. 4–7 and 9.

T. A. M. Bishop, 'Notes on Cambridge manuscripts, Part III', *Transactions of the Cambridge Bibliographical Society* 2 (1954–8), 192–9, at 198–9; Gameson, *Manuscripts of early Norman England*, nos. 160 [parts 1–3] + 161 [part 4]; R. Gameson, *The scribe speaks? Colophons in early English manuscripts*, H. M. Chadwick Memorial Lectures 12 (Cambridge 2001), 48 no. 37, and pl. 8

9. Cambridge, Trinity College B.16.5 (381)   A20.504 and 1565

350 × 250 mm (slightly retrimmed). 229 leaves.

Peter Lombard, *Sententiae*

s. xii² (after 1158)[13]

12. A similar set of Marian texts as those comprising parts 1–3, occurred in a slightly different sequence in a now lost manuscript from Salisbury: N. R. Ker, 'Salisbury Cathedral manuscripts and Patrick Young's catalogue', *Wiltshire Archaeological and Natural History Magazine* 53 (1949–50), 153–83, on 170 no. 109, items 2, 4–5, 6–8, plus 9–11 not noted by Ker but corresponding with the contents of part 3 (ibid. 177); repr. in his *Books, collectors and libraries: studies in the medieval heritage*, ed. A. G. Watson (London 1985), 175–208, on 193 and 200.

13. The year 1158 is about when the work is usually thought to have become available for copying.

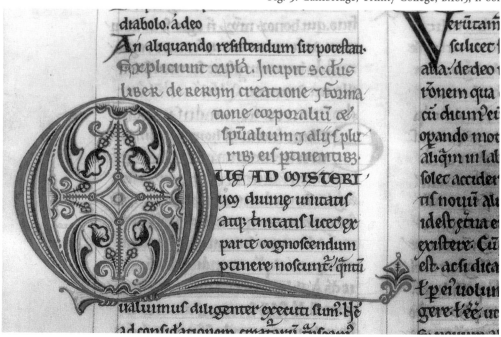

Fig. 8. Cambridge, Trinity College, B.16.5, f. 3v

Fig. 9. Cambridge, Trinity College, B.16.5, f. 68r

Fig. 10. Cambridge, Trinity College, B.16.5, f. 122r   Fig. 11. Cambridge, Trinity College, B.16.5, f. 165v

Good parchment. Two columns. Written and rubricated by one expert scribe. The opening initial (1r) is historiated, depicting a seated untonsured figure holding a scroll, with a scribe (also untonsured) working at his feet (colour pl. E).[14] Good arabesque initials in the same style, perhaps a little conservative for their date (3v, 68r, 122r, 165v) (figs. 8–11). Marginal apparatus in red.[15]

Given to Trinity by George Willmer (d. 1626), as were nos. **4–8**.

10. Edinburgh, National Library of Scotland Advocates 18.5.13 ff. 1–47   A20.1055 and 1941
214 × 110 mm (retrimmed). 47 leaves. Two leaves missing between ff. 43 and 44 (Book 4, vv. 305–472), and more than one gathering after f. 47 (Book 4, vv. 726 to the end).

Ovid, *Fasti*

s. xii ex.

Poor parchment. Prickings in outer margin only. Text written by one scribe; marginal and interlinear glosses probably in the same hand as the text. Very modest initials in red or blue. The hand of the scribe does not look English, and the manuscript may be French. Acquired for Leicester by William Charyte, s. xv² (1r) (p. 134, fig. 2): 'per adquisicionem fratris Willelmi Charyte'.

The manuscript was bound up with ff. 48–106 from the sixteenth century. Owned by Sir James Balfour (d. 1657).

I. C. Cunningham, 'Latin classical manuscripts in the National Library of Scotland', *Scriptorium* 27 (1973), 64–90, at 81–2; I. C. Cunningham, 'Sir James Balfour's manuscript collection: the 1698 catalogue and other sources', *Edinburgh Bibliographical Society Transactions* 6/6 (2004), 191–255, at 222; B. Munk Olsen, *L'Etude des auteurs classiques latins aux xie et xiie siècles*, 4 vols. in 3 (Paris 1982–9), ii, 131, and iii/1, 133

14. The iconography appears to be unusual. If the principal figure was intended to show the author, the figure has none of the common attributes used to identify Lombard, and we are not aware of any pre-1200 manuscript of the *Sentences* showing Lombard with a scribe at his feet. (For portraits of Lombard see P. D. Stirnemann, 'Historia tripartite: un inventaire des livres de Pierre Lombard, un exemplaire de ses *Sentences* et le destinataire du Psautier de Copenhagen' in *Du copiste au collectionneur. Mélanges d'histoire des textes et des bibliothèques en l'honneur d'André Vernet*, ed. D. Nebbiai Dalla Guarda and J.-F. Genest, Bibliologia 18 (Turnhout 1998), 301–18, on 312 and pl. 8, and J. P. Turcheck, 'A neglected manuscript of Peter Lombard's *Sententiarum* and Parisian illumination of the late twelfth century', *Journal of the Walters Art Gallery* 44 (1986), 48–69, on 56–60 and figs. 1 and 14–16, mostly discussing French manuscripts.)

15. For this (common in s. xii manuscripts) see Stirnemann, 'Historia tripartite', 312–13, citing I. Brady, 'The rubrics of Peter Lombard's Sentences', *Pier Lombardo* 6.1–4 (1962), 5–25.

11. London, British Library, Add. 57533[16]   A20.660
282 × 192 mm (not retrimmed). A composite manuscript of two contemporary parts: i + 80 + 33 leaves, foliated iv + 1–80 + 81–113

1. (1–80) Aelred of Rievaulx, *Vita S Edwardi regis et confessoris* and *Vita Dauidis Scotorum regis*; *Miracula beatae uirginis Mariae*; Fulbert of Chartres, *Sermones in natiuitate beatae uirginis Mariae* (two); Innocent III, *De miseria humanae conditionis*

2. (81–113) Geoffrey of Burton, *Vita S Modwennae*[17]

s. xii/xiii (after 1198)[18]

Poor parchment. Probably two scribes, one in each part, and one very mediocre old fashioned arabesque initial (1r) in part 1, and in part 2 pen-flourished initials as far as f. 88 and thereafter plain initials. Shortly after the catalogue was produced, the manuscript came into the hands of Hector Rydyng,[19] as is shown by an inscription on f. iv recto:

Iste liber constat Ectori Rydyng vicario de Radclyff super sorarii . . .

Following the inscription is a note on a legal transaction by another, slightly later scribe.

The manuscript was later owned by William Marshall (d. 1583),[20] Thomas Allen (d. 1632), and Sir Thomas Mostyn (d. 1692), and it remained in the Mostyn collection until sold in 1920 (Sotheby's 13.vii.1920 lot 1). It was later owned by Professor Francis Wormald and given to the British Library after his death in 1972.

> A. G. Watson, 'Thomas Allen of Oxford and his manuscripts' in *Medieval scribes, manuscripts and libraries: Essays presented to N. R. Ker*, ed. M. B. Parkes and A. G. Watson (London 1978), 279–314, at 290 and 309; D. Huws, 'Sir Thomas Mostyn and the Mostyn manuscripts' in *Books and collectors, 1200–1700: Essays presented to Andrew Watson*, 451–72, at 461 no. 9; *Geoffrey of Burton. Life and miracles of St Modwenna*, ed. R. Bartlett, Oxford Medieval Texts (Oxford 2002), xxxvii–xli

12. London, British Library, Cotton Galba E iii ff. 83–173
352 × 258 mm (retrimmed). 91 leaves.
Liber de terris dominicalibus[21]

s. xv/xvi

Moderate parchment. Mostly the work of one good but variable scribe, and the initials touched with yellow throughout. Physically the manuscript is like no. **13**. There was at least one copy of this work at the abbey. One was bound up with a catalogue of books (A20.1867), and this might be Bodl. Laud misc. 623 (no. **16** below) although the Cotton manuscript is now noticeably smaller than the Laud one. (However, the Cotton manuscript has been retrimmed, perhaps drastically). Whether the Laud manuscript is the manuscript referred to in the catalogue, and whether the Cotton manuscript is the copy bound up with it is, at present, uncertain.[22] The script of the Cotton manuscript suggests that it may have been written after the present catalogue was drawn up.[23]

> R. H. Hilton, *The economic development of some Leicestershire estates in the fourteenth and fifteenth centuries* (Oxford 1947), esp. 19–20

13. London, British Library, Cotton Nero D x ff. 140–197
368 × 274 mm. 58 leaves.
Matriculus

s. xv/xvi

16. This was identified as a Leicester manuscript several years ago by Professor Richard Sharpe, and his discovery was first published by one of us (TW) in CBMLC 6, 239–40 (commentary to A20.660).

17. One of only two surviving copies of the full text (Bartlett, ed. *Geoffrey of Burton*, xxxvii–xli).

18. Lotario dei Segni is referred to as Innocent III (65v).

19. Vicar of Holy Trinity, Ratcliffe-on-Soar (Notts.) 1497–1509 (Bartlett, ed. *Geoffrey of Burton*, xxxviii).

20. Formerly a fellow of Merton College, Oxford, and Principal of St Alban Hall; A. B. Emden, *A biographical register of the University of Oxford, A.D. 1501 to 1540* (Oxford 1974), 382 and 727.

21. The arrangement is alphabetical, running from 'Barkeby' to 'Wover'.

22. It may be noted that another copy was on paper, and this was used as an exemplar by William Charyte to produce another copy on parchment (A20.1906). This new copy appears to have been bound up with other matter (A20.1885, 'cum multis aliis'). Both paper and parchment copies had the *secundo folio* 'in qua et Rod', which is probably a corruption of 'iij qᵃ (for 'quarentene' = furlongs) et \i/ rod', the start of the entry found under the heading 'Barkeby' on f. 2r of Galba E iii.

23. This is not the only manuscript associated with William at Leicester of which there was more than one copy. Among the manuscripts in the catalogue described as compiled and written by William are several (A20.1887, 1888, 1890 and 1891) that appear elsewhere among those described as written for William, presumably in fair copies using William's manuscripts as exemplars (A20.1912, 1914, 1916 and 1918).

Moderate parchment. Mostly the work of one good but variable scribe, and the initials and many of the capital letters touched with yellow throughout. There are two added notes of Leicester abbey interest in the margins of ff. 142r and 145r, and physically the manuscript is like no. **12**. There were two copies of the *Matriculus* of Hugh of Wells, bishop of Lincoln (1209–32), at Leicester, but both were in roll form (A20.652). It is likely that the Cotton manuscript is a Leicester Abbey book, so it must be another copy, and its script does suggest that it may have been written after the library catalogue was drawn up.

14. London, British Library, Cotton Tiberius C vii   A20.636 and 1637

237 leaves, foliated 3–239. The manuscript suffered damage in the 1731 Cotton fire, and the leaves are now singletons with loss at all the outer edges and some shrinkage at the head edge. The size of the leaves is now about 270 × 180 mm.

Henry Knighton, *Chronicon*[24]

s. xiv ex.

Moderate parchment. One column. Several moderate scribes, and blue initials modestly pen-flourished in red as far as f. 75v and thereafter mostly plain red initials (p. 121, fig. 1).

> V. H. Galbraith, 'The Chronicle of Henry Knighton' in *Fritz Saxl, 1890–1984: A volume of memorial essays from his friends in England*, ed. D. Gordon (London 1957), 136–48; *Knighton's Chronicle 1337–1396*, ed. G. H. Martin, Oxford Medieval Texts (Oxford 1995), lxxxviii–ix and plates

15. London, British Library, Cotton Vitellius F xvii

iv + 42 + v leaves, foliated 1–4 + 5–46 + 47–51. The manuscript suffered badly in the 1731 Cotton fire with losses to the leaves, especially at the head, and much shrinkage, and the leaves are all now singletons.

Rental[25]

s. xv/xvi

Moderate parchment. Perhaps mostly the work of one scribe. The capital letters are touched throughout with yellow. There are some contemporary additions in some of the foot margins. The end-leaves are discards from an unidentified s. xiv English manuscript. Damage from the Cottonian fire makes it impossible to verify whether this was the copy that William Charyte 'caused to be made' (A20.1873).

> G. R. C. Davis, *Medieval cartularies of Great Britain* (London 1958), no. 549

16. Oxford, Bodleian Library, Laud misc. 623

390 × 275 mm. i + 51 + i, foliated ii + 1–51 + 52. Formerly part of a composite manuscript, perhaps of two parts, for an early modern foliation of the text-leaves runs 90–140.

Catalogus librorum[26]

s. xv² (1477 x 1494)

Fine parchment. One column. One expert scribe with additions and amendments by at least two near-contemporary scribes, one of them William Charyte (fig. 12). The initials are touched with yellow throughout. The end-leaves (ii and 52) are opened out bifolia from a copy of *Novae Narrationes* (s. xiv/xv), but, at present, these appear more likely to have been supplied by Laud's binder than to be the remains of an abbey book.

The manuscript is a fair copy of an earlier one. The opening rubric (4r) states that the catalogue was 'renouatum' by William Charyte when he was precentor and, as he was prior by 1463 (Bodl. Laud misc. 625 f. 170r), this suggests the earlier catalogue was completed by that year.[27] The fair copy is datable 1477 x 1494 as it includes reference to a rental, known as the 'novum Rentale', compiled and written by William Charyte (A20.1872), now Bodl. Laud misc. 625 (no. **17** below), which includes a copy of a rental that had been

---

24. This is the earlier of the two known copies (the other is BL Cotton Claudius E iii (s. xv)) (Martin, ed. *Knighton's Chronicle*, xv–xvi and xxii–xxiii).

25. A longer version of this is no. **17**.

26. The edition of M. R. James ('Catalogue of the library of Leicester Abbey', *TLAHS* 19 (1935–7), 118–61 and 378–440, and ibid.

21 (1939–41), 2–88) has now been superseded by that in T. Webber and A. G. Watson, *Libraries of the Augustinian canons*, CBMLC 6 (London 1998), 109–399. However, the introduction by James to his edition is still worth consulting.

27. Webber and Watson, *Libraries of the Augustinian canons*, 107 and 120.

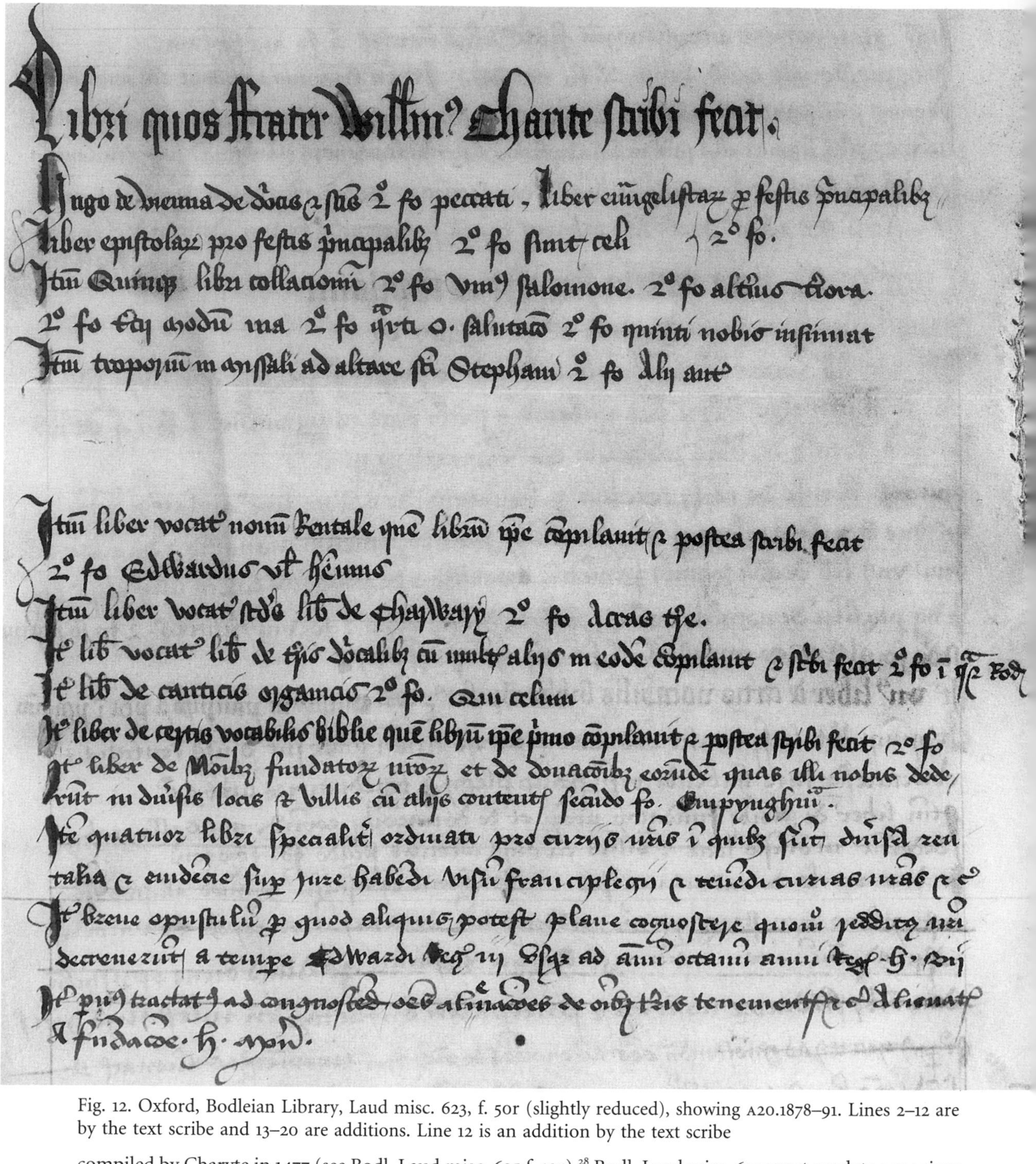

Fig. 12. Oxford, Bodleian Library, Laud misc. 623, f. 50r (slightly reduced), showing A20.1878–91. Lines 2–12 are by the text scribe and 13–20 are additions. Line 12 is an addition by the text scribe

compiled by Charyte in 1477 (see Bodl. Laud misc. 625 f. 12r).[28] Bodl. Laud misc. 623 must predate 1494 since it refers to John Penny who became abbot in 1494 as 'capellanus' (A20.1794).

The manuscript may be listed in the catalogue itself, bound up with a work titled *liber de terris dominical-*

28. The identification of Bodl. Laud misc. 625 with A20.1872 supersedes the identification of that entry with Charyte's lost rental of 1477 as given in Webber and Watson, *Libraries of the Augustinian canons*, 107.

ibus (A20.1867) that might be BL Cotton Galba E iii ff. 83–173 (no. **12** above), although the Laud manuscript is now noticeably larger than the Cotton one. (However, the Cotton manuscript has been retrimmed, perhaps drastically.) Whether the Laud manuscript is the manuscript referred to in the catalogue, and whether the Cotton manuscript is the copy bound up with it is, at present, uncertain.[29]

At the foot of the first text-leaf (1r) is an inscription (s. xvi): '+ Sub De Re Le Te +'. The meaning of this is unclear, but M. R. James noted that he had found the same inscription in six other manuscripts, none from Leicester, sometimes associated with the initials 'J H'.[30]

Hamilton Thompson, *Leicester Abbey*, pls. betw. pp. 208–9; CBMLC 6, 107–9, 120 and pls. 6–7.

17. Oxford, Bodleian Library, Laud misc. 625   A20.1872

350 × 230 mm (retrimmed). ii + 210 + v leaves, foliated 1a, 2 + 3–212 + 213–17.

Rental[31]

s. xv²

Moderate parchment (sheepskin). One column. Mostly the work of one scribe (fig. 13), although most of ff. 186r–211r are clearly by another scribe. There are numerous corrections, amendments and additions by the main scribe and other contemporary or near-contemporary scribes on virtually every page. Initials and capital letters are touched with colour throughout in either red or yellow.

There is one early addition: ff. 10 and 12–19 appear to have been an early insertion (together with f. 11 that is a slip), of either s. xv/xvi or s. xvi in. On f. 10r–v is a contents list with folio references, and the hand that wrote these appears to have foliated the whole manuscript at the same time. This hand foliated the leaf with the original contents list and a genealogy of abbey founders (4r–v) as '1' and the next leaf that begins with charters of the founders (5r) as '2'. The opening words of this leaf are 'habemus ex dono', and these are given as the *secundo folio* reference in the abbey library catalogue for a book described as *Rentale vocatum nouum Rentale compilatum et scriptum per manu fratris Willelmi Charite...*[32] It therefore appears that the Laud manuscript was compiled and written by William Charyte, and that William is to be identified as the main scribe. The manuscript is clearly his working copy.

The recto of the third leaf of the inserted matter (12r) opens:

Fig. 13. Oxford, Bodleian Library, Laud misc. 625, f. 170r (reduced)

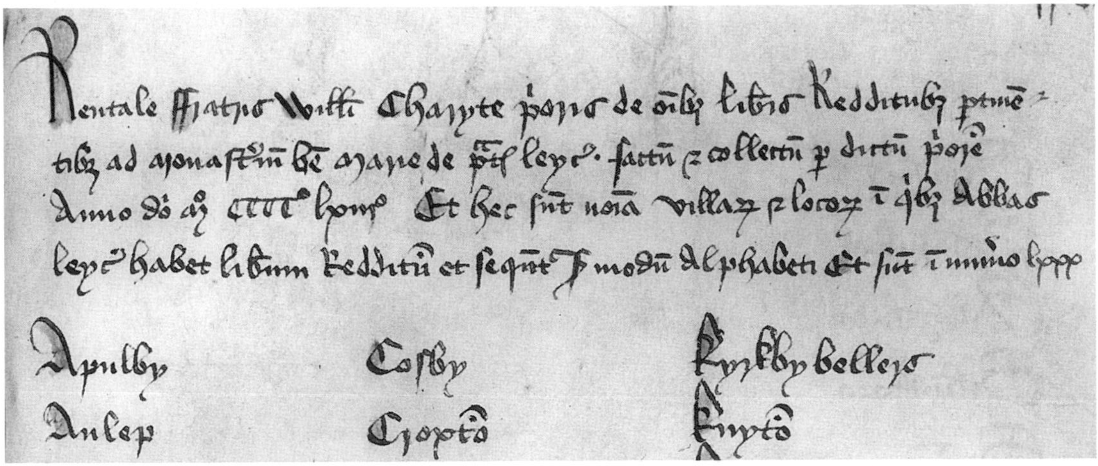

29. The suggestion that the Laud manuscript may once have been bound with the Cotton one was first made by R. W. Hunt in the 1973 reprint of the nineteenth-century catalogue of the Laud manuscripts.

30. James, 'Catalogue of the Library', 128.

31. Excerpts were printed by J. Nichols, *The history and antiquities of the county of Leicester*, 4 vols. in 8 (London 1795–1815), i.2, Appendix 17 (53–100). A shorter version is no. **15**.

32. This book also appears in the catalogue among those described as compiled and written by William Charyte (A20.1905). The structure of the opening leaves of the Laud manuscript has been seriously disrupted at an unknown date, and the original collation of ff. 3–9 is uncertain.

Rentale monasterii beate mar[i]e pratio leycestre generale

followed by:

de *aduocacionibus ecclesiarum. de pencionibus et porcionibus* deciarum. *de molendinis et* de *decimus mol-endinorum de decima feni pasture et bosci et de firmis et Redditubus uoluntaris* ac *liberis . . .*

and the words in *italic* occur in the description of William's *nouum Rentale* in the abbey catalogue.

Probably to be associated with the insertion of ff. 10–19 is the formal inscription 'Memoriale fratris Willelmi Charite' in the foot margin of f. 5r. And at the foot of page whose opening has just been quoted is another inscription:

Memoriale fratris Willelmi Charyte quondam prioris . . . istum librum compilauit et propria manu scripsit

All this appears to show that within a few years of William's death (the use of 'quondam' suggests that William was no longer prior and had presumably died), the present manuscript was intimately associated with him, and there appears no reason to doubt the veracity of the information concerning William's role in its production.

The six end-leaves (2 and 213–17) are from a copy of the *Decretals* (s. xiv), some partially erased and written over by William. The leaves are likely to have come from an abbey book that, for one reason or another, was discarded, broken up and leaves reused.

Davis, *Medieval Cartularies*, no. 548; Hilton, *Economic development of some Leicestershire estates*, esp. 18–19 and 150–1

18. Oxford, Bodleian Library, Rawlinson A 445

195 × 145 mm. i + 307 leaves, foliated i + 1–137. Contemporary binding with overcover.

Sermones dominicales

s. XV

Moderate parchment. One scribe. The opening initial is red, but all the others were never supplied. The manuscript came very late to the abbey (1536/7) as is shown by a inscription, partially lost, at the end (307v):

liber [ ] ecclesie beate mar[ ] leycestrie Anno regni regis henrici octau[ ] vicesimo octauo

The post-Dissolution history of the manuscript is recorded in a series of sixteenth-century inscriptions, printed below in the order in which they appear in the manuscript:

1572 Liber Hugonis Weston Ecclesia Carleton Rectoris (i recto)

Liber Willimus Weston rectoris ecclesia parochialis Carleton Curle (1r)

Liber domini Robertti Weston de dono domini Thome thorpe et Johannis Moore executorum domini thome peeke quondam rector ecclesie de Burton Ouerey, anime cuius propitietur deus, ad quem quidem presens liber pertinebat pro anima orate precor (307r)

Liber Hugonis Weston Rectoris Ecclesiae de Carleton Curlewe Anno domini 1579 Anno R. reginae Elizabethae 20 (307v)

On the turn-in of the cover at the beginning is written 'Wyllimus Weston' and 'Wyllimi', and on the upper end-leaf (i recto) two names written by the same hand (perhaps s. xv/xvi) 'William' and 'Richard'. All of the places named are in Leicestershire. William Weston, Robert Weston and Hugh Weston became rectors of Carleton Curlieu in 1534, 1560 and 1576 respectively.[33]

19. Oxford, Bodleian Library Rawlinson C 153   A20.214 and 1490

268 × 195 mm (retrimmed). 106 leaves, foliated 1–106. The former first leaf has been cut out.

Ps. Augustine, *De mirabilibus sacrae scripturae*; Origen, *Homiliae*; Baldric of Dol, *De visitatione infirmorum*; Bernard of Clairvaux, *Sermo de diuersis*

s. xii med.

Moderate to poor parchment. One column. Written, corrected and rubricated by one expert scribe (figs. 14 and 15), with at least one correction (70r) by a second scribe. Modest arabesque initials (1r and 97r) (figs. 14 and 15) and a few modestly decorated initials (20r, 35v, 42v and 73v). The manuscript is a little unusual for being quired in 12s.

33. Nichols, *Leicester*, ii, 546; *Lincoln episcopal records in the time of Thomas Cooper, S.T.P., Bishop of Lincoln* A.D. *1571 to* A.D.   *1584*, ed. C. W. Foster, Canterbury and York Society 11 (London 1948), 38 and 266.

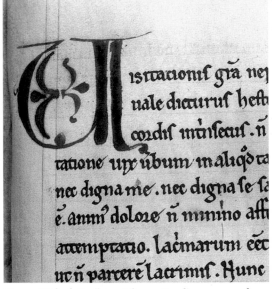

Fig. 14. Oxford, Bodleian Library, Rawlinson c 153, f. 97r   Fig. 15. Oxford, Bodleian Library, Rawlinson c 153, f. 1r

F. Dolbeau suggested that this manuscript might be a Leicester book from the identity of its content with an entry in the abbey library catalogue.[34] This suggestion has been confirmed by the identity of the *secundo folio* given in the catalogue to that of manuscript,[35] as well as the presence in the manuscript of annotations in a hand of s. xv[1], the same or similar to that of annotations in nos. 2–8. The manuscript was owned by Lord John Somers (d. 1716) and passed, with the rest of his library, to his son-in-law, Sir Joseph Jekyll (d. 1738). (Another Leicester manuscript that was in these two collections is no. 22 below.) The Somers–Jekyll collection was sold in 1740, and the manuscript, together with many others, was acquired by Richard Rawlinson (d. 1755).

20. York Minster XVI.M.6   A20.1064 and 1674

255 × 175 mm (retrimmed). iii + 120 + ii leaves, foliated 1–120.[36] The quires have been misbound with viii, vi and vii following xiv. The contents are described in their original order.

Cicero, *De inuentione rhetorica*; ps. Cicero, *Rhetorica ad Herennium*; Boethius, *De differencis topicis* (Book 4)[37]

s. xii med.

Fine parchment. One column. One expert scribe and good arabesque initials (1r, 2v, 27r, 53v, 64r and 89r) (figs. 16–18 and colour plate F). There is an *ex libris* of s. xv (partly lost through retrimming) at the head of f. 1r: '[. . .] Mon' beate M[arie] Leycestr' in p[ra]tis' (colour plate F).

The manuscript was at York by 1691.

Munk Olsen, *L'Etude des auteurs classiques latins* iii/1, 133, and iii/2, 47; N. R. Ker and A. J. Piper, *Medieval manuscripts in British libraries*, 5 vols (Oxford 1969–2002), iv, 744–5

34. Review of Webber and Watson, *Libraries of the Augustinian canons* in *Revue Mabillon* n.s. 10 (1999), 347–8, on 348. Dolbeau noted that this manuscript and two others (London, Lambeth Palace 363 (s. xii/xiii) and Shrewsbury School xxxi (s. xii ex.)), both of English origin, are the only ones to attribute the third item in the present manuscript to Baldric.

35. The *secundo folio* in the manuscript is for a chapter title ('de duobus signis'), where it is preceded by the number 'xv' in red. The library catalogue does not have the number, and the decision whether to include or exclude such numbers in the catalogue and elsewhere must have been a common one.

36. It is over twenty years since one of us (MG) saw this and the following manuscript, and we are uncertain how many of the endleaves are medieval; their number has been taken from the description of Ker and Piper cited below.

37. Book 4 of the last work by itself appears commoner in manuscripts later than 1200. Other pre-1200 copies include Cambridge University Library Ii.6.6, BL Harley 3509 and Sotheby's 19.vi.2001 lot 3, all of which are probably French. The York manuscript was missed by M. T. Gibson and L. Smith in their *Codices Boethiani: a conspectus of manuscripts of the works of Boethius*, Warburg Institute surveys and texts 25 (London 1995).

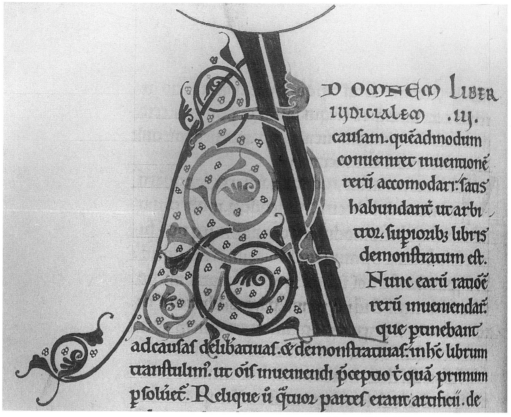

Fig. 16. York Minster, XVI.M.6, f. 53v

Fig. 17. York Minster, XVI.M.6, f. 2v   Fig. 18. York Minster, XVI.M.6, f. 38v

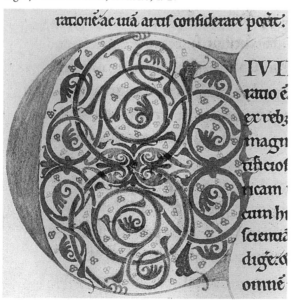

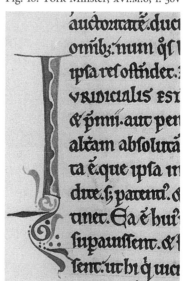

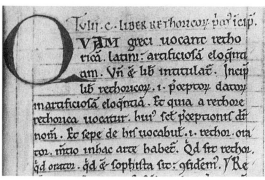

Fig. 19. York Minster, XVI.M.7, f. 1r

21. York Minster XVI.M.7   A20.1066
255 × 160 mm. ii + 71 leaves, foliated 1–41, 41*, 42–57, 57* 58–69.

Manegold of Lauterbach, *In Ciceronem de Inuentione* (preface); Commentaries on Cicero, *De Inuentione* and ps. Cicero, *De ratione dicendi ad Herennium*;[38] notes on 'demonstratiuum' and 'translatiuum'

s. xii med.

Moderate parchment. Prickings in the outer and inner margins. Two columns. Two moderate scribes (fig. 19). The manuscript was at York by 1691.

> Munk Olsen, *L'Etude des auteurs classiques latins* iii/1, 133; Ker and Piper, *Medieval manuscripts in British libraries* iv, 745–6

Manuscripts perhaps owned by the abbey or made locally

22. London, British Library, Harley 7333
450 × 325 mm. 211 leaves, foliated 1–211. Leaves have been lost at the beginning and end. There is a medieval foliation in the head margins, the first surviving leaf foliated 'xxv' and the last 'xxᶜ lv'.

Miscellany of English verse[39]

s. xv/xvi

Moderate parchment. One column. Perhaps eight good scribes, but mostly the work of three (fig. 20).[40] The initials are all blue decorated with pen-made flourishes in red.

The manuscript has several names and sketches in the margins. The name 'Stoughton' (s. xv) and a rebus (a stock in a tun) (32v, 41r and 45v) have been associated with William Stoughton, canon and cellarer of Leicester abbey in the late fifteenth century. The note (s. xv) 'Doctor peni writ this booke' (150r) (fig. 20) has been associated with the Leicester canon John Penny who was elected prior in 1493 and abbot in 1496, later becoming the bishop of Bangor (1504) and of Carlisle (1508), and who perhaps owned no. **24**.[41] Although the note appears to suggest that John wrote some part of the manuscript, this is very unlikely.[42] It is also very unlikely that the manuscript was made at the abbey, but the names do appear to show that it was there by *c.* 1500.

---

38. The commentaries also occur in Durham Cathedral c.iv.29 (s. xii med.) and Vatican City, Biblioteca Apostolica Vaticana, Borghese lat. 57 (s. xii) (M. Dickey, 'Some commentaries on the *De inventione* and *Ad Herennium* of the eleventh and early twelfth centuries', *Medieval and Renaissance Studies* 6 (1968), 1–41).

39. The contents (including works by Lydgate, Hoccleve and Chaucer) are listed in H. L. D. Ward and J. A. Herbert, *Catalogue of romances in the Department of Manuscripts in the British Museum*, 3 vols. (London 1883–1910), iii, 252–3, and J. M. Manly and E. Rickert, *The text of the Canterbury Tales*, 8 vols. (Chicago 1940), i, 207, and they are included in C. Brown and R. H.

Robbins, *Index of Middle English verse* (New York 1943) but need to be retrieved from R. Hamer, *A manuscript index to the 'Index of Middle English verse'* (London 1995).

40. See the scribal analysis by Linne Mooney in her paper (on 198) cited below. We are very grateful to Dr Mooney for drawing our attention to her work.

41. For John see Emden, *A biographical register, A.D. 1501 to 1540*, 1458.

42. The suggestion that John was a scribe was made by Manly and Rickert, *Canterbury Tales* i, 214–5.

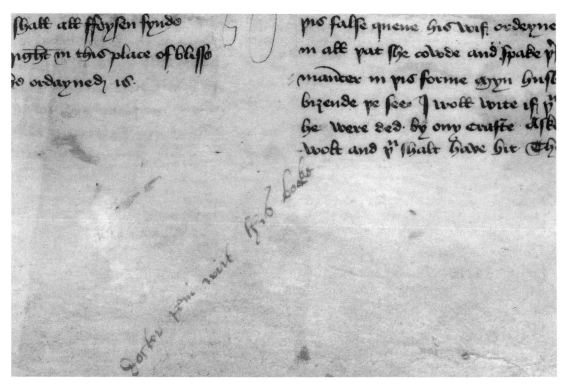

Fig. 20. London, British Library, Harley 733, f. 150r

Later names suggest that after the Dissolution the manuscript was owned by families linked by marriage, first in Leicestershire and later in Surrey, the earliest owner being Geoffrey Ithell (d. 1599).[43] The manuscript was later owned by Lord John Somers (d. 1716) and passed, with the rest of his library, to his son-in-law, Sir Joseph Jekyll (d. 1738). (Another Leicester manuscript that was in these two collections is no. **19** above.) The Somers–Jekyll collection was sold in 1740, and the manuscript soon passed into the Harley collection.

> C. E. Wright, *Fontes Harleiani* (London 1972), 204 and 308–9; L. R. Mooney, 'John Shirley's Heirs' in *Medieval and early modern literary miscellanies*, ed. P. Hardman, *Yearbook of English Studies*, special number 33 (2003), 182–98, at 190–4 and 198

23. Oxford, Bodleian Library, Bodley 57 (*SC* 2004)

170 × 125 mm. ii + 214 + ii leaves, foliated ii–iii + 1–214 + 215–17. A collection of booklets (at least twelve) bound together early.

Miscellaneous theological and moral pieces (mostly Latin, but some in French)

s. xiii/xiv

Moderate parchment. A large number of scribes all of whom were competent and some of whom were quite good. Red or blue initials throughout, some of them decorated with modest pen flourishes.

On ff. 68v and 89v are copies of a short set of verses attributed to 'magister Barre de porco uacuo dato', and the author may be Richard Barre (active in the 1160s and known to be alive in 1202) who gave several volumes to the library at Leicester.[44] On f. 191v is a metrical poem ridiculing the complaints of the people of Stoughton against the abbey at Leicester in or soon after 1296.[45]

43. The evidence of the names, from Stoughton to Ithell, and the later provenance of the manuscript is set out by Manly and Rickert, *Canterbury Tales* i, 214–17.

44. For Richard (who was not a Leicester canon) see the commentary to A20.57, and R. Sharpe, 'Richard Barre's *Compendium Veteris et Noui Testamenti*', *Journal of Medieval Latin* 14 (2004), 1–16.

45. R. H. Hilton, 'A thirteenth-century poem on disputed villein services', *English Historical Review* 56 (1941), 90–7, reprinted in his *Class conflict and the crisis of feudalism: essays in medieval social history* (London 1985), 108–13.

The manuscript was owned by Henry Jackson of Corpus Christi College, Oxford, in 1600, and was purchased by the Bodleian Library in 1619/20.

24. Oxford, Bodleian Library, Bodley 636 (*SC* 2002)[46]

192 × 138 mm (retrimmed). A composite manuscript of three parts probably bound together soon after writing, as indicated by the stains of the boards of s. xv type on the end-leaves and an ownership inscription on f. 224r that refers to the *secundo folio* reference on f. 2r: ii + 24 + 119 + 79 + ii leaves, foliated i–ii + 1–24 + 25–143 + 144–222 + 223–224.

1. (1–24) 'De raptu anime tundali et eius uisione' (excerpt from Vincent of Beauvais, *Speculum Historiale*)

2. (25–143) Miscellaneous theological and devotional texts

3. (144–222) Miscellaneous theological and devotional texts[47]

s. xv^2

Part 1 is on paper, and parts 2 and 3 on paper and parchment. Part 1 was written by one scribe (A), part 2 by three (B, C and D) and part 3 by six (E, F, G, H, I and J), with the scribal changes always occurring at the beginning of a new item.[48] Scribe A is mediocre, but the others are mostly competent, a few quite good. Part 1 has blue initials pen flourished in red. In Part 2 the stint of Scribe B has plain blue or red initials, the stint of Scribe C blue initials, some decorated in red and yellow, and the stint of Scribe D red initials. In part 3 the stint of Scribe E has some well-drawn lettered scrolls and blue initials decorated in an orangey-yellow. The stints of scribes F and I have blue initials, some decorated in red and yellow. The stints of scribes G and H have no initials, and in the stint of Scribe J the initials are all red. The initials in the stints of scribes C (in part 2), and F and I (in part 3) are very similar, and, if not by the same hand, point to a common origin. The initials are generally mediocre.[49]

There is a near-contemporary inscription (now partially cropped) at the top of f. 224r (fig. 21):

Iste liber constat domino J. peny secundo folio bibisset Data

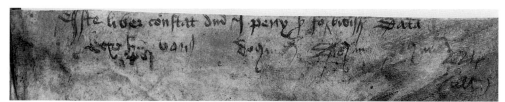

Fig. 21. Oxford, Bodleian Library, Bodley 636, f. 224r

with some illegible scribbles under. The last four words appear to have been written with a finer pen and paler ink than the first six, but all appear to be the work of the same scribe. 'J. peny' may be John Penny, canon and subsequently prior (1493) and abbot of Leicester (1496), then bishop of Bangor (1504) and later of Carlisle (1508), and who may also be the 'Doctor Peny' named in no. **22** above.

The manuscript was owned by Walter Cope (d. 1614) and was given, with many others, to the Bodleian Library in 1602.

A. G. Watson, 'The manuscript collection of Sir Walter Cope', *Bodleian Library Record* 12 (1985–8), 262–97, at 288 no. 153

46. We are very grateful to James Willoughby for drawing this manuscript to our attention, and for providing preliminary notes on it.

47. The content of all three parts is itemised in the *Summary Catalogue*.

48. Scribe A wrote part 1 (item 1). In part 2 Scribe B wrote item 2, C items 3–4, and D items 5–7. In part 3 Scribe E wrote item 8, F items 9–10, G an unnumbered item following item 10 (f. 187r line 16–187v), H item 11, I items 12–13, and J item 14.

49. The general aspect of the manuscript suggests that it might have been produced at an ecclesiastical centre. However, this is perhaps unlikely to be Leicester, as at least several of the works in the manuscript do not occur in the abbey catalogue and therefore the scribes of the manuscript probably could not have used local exemplars.

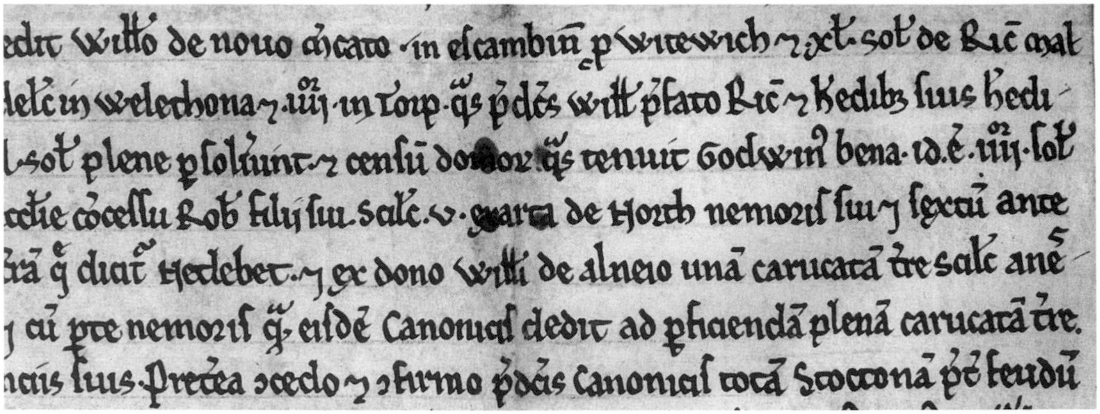

Fig. 22. London, British Library, Sloane ch. xxxii.22

Single-sheet charter

25. London, British Library, Sloane ch. xxxii.22
410 × 242 mm. 53 lines of text, ruled in pencil. Two endorsements, one s. xiv, the other s. xv.
Confirmation charter of Robert iv, earl of Leicester

1190 X 1204

One scribe, writing a medium-size bookhand (fig. 22, and p. 250, fig. 1). Ascenders in line 1 and occasionally elsewhere are elongated and embellished with a small serif located not at the top of the stroke (as was usual in bookhands), but part-way down the left-hand of the shaft – a stylistic feature typical of the handwriting of charters and more formal classes of document by the late twelfth and early thirteenth centuries. The hand displays none of the proportions or stylistic features of *Littera Textualis*, which had become common in larger bookhands by this date. Instead, it retains the rounded proportions and appearance of twelfth-century minuscule. The scribe employed variant forms of **d** (with a straight or with a curved shaft) and round **s** (one resembling the capital form, and an elongated variety found especially at the end of words). The treatment of the tops and bottoms of minims, and of the headstroke of **a** and the shaft and headstroke of the tironian *nota* for 'et' also vary; from line 34, the shaft of the *nota* is longer and noticeably more upright. **i** is sometimes marked with a diacritical stroke, but usually only the first of a pair of adjacent **i**s is thus marked. Tie-marks indicating word division at line-ends are supplied at both the end of the line and at the beginning of the next.

    D. Crouch, 'Early charters and patrons of Leicester Abbey', below pp. 249–52 (no. 24)

On the outside looking in: Leicester Abbey's urban property in Leicester

David Postles

Like the other major houses of Austin Canons, Leicester Abbey accumulated significant urban property. In part, the ease with which these houses acquired urban property derived from the purpose of their Order: to proselytize and preach in the rapidly expanding urban centres of the eleventh and more particularly the twelfth century. The impulsion to maintain the 'purity' of the Church combined with the new challenge of urban development necessitated new religious orders that were not irrevocably cloistered, but could venture into the world; and so evolved the status of the Black Canons, the first order of secular canons, living under a strict rule but one that was not simply coenobitical.[1]

Accordingly, the largest houses of the order had a special association with urban centres. Some, like Cirencester and Dunstable, acquired the lordship of urbanizing centres producing inevitable tension between townspeople and religious overlord. Other of these major houses of the order, through their location in or near boroughs, acquired extensive urban property, often in what (later) developed into boroughs, formally constituted. Without investigating this phenomenon in great detail, Leicester Abbey, Osney Abbey, Darley Abbey and Barnwell Priory were all located on the periphery of boroughs, outside the walls, but received substantial urban property inside the borough. Although some, like Darley, had originally been established inside the walls of the borough, migration outside to a more contemplative site quickly ensued. Their position was therefore on the outside of the borough looking in, certainly in terms of possessions. To what extent their proximity assisted the welfare of the souls of the townspeople remains a moot point. Through gift and purchase, nevertheless, their material, if not spiritual, presence in boroughs was profound.[2]

The abbey's urban acquisitions in the borough of Leicester did not attain the levels of, for example, Osney Abbey in Oxford, but its acquisitions made a considerable impact on the town. Urban property was valuable to the house for a number of reasons: its proximity; its association

1. J. C. Dickinson, *The origins of the Austin Canons and their introduction into England* (London 1950); D. M. Robinson, *The geography of Augustinian settlements in medieval England and Wales*, 2 vols. British Archaeological Reports, British series 80 (London 1980); idem, 'Site changes of Augustinian communities in medieval England and Wales', *Mediaeval Studies* 43 (1981), 425–44; for nuances of the earlier position, G. Rosser, 'The cure of souls in English towns before 1000' in *Pastoral care before the parish*, ed. J. Blair and R. Sharpe (Leicester 1992), 267–84.

2. *The cartulary of the monastery of St Frideswide at Oxford*, ed. S. R. Wigram, Oxford Historical Society 27 (Oxford 1894); *Cartularium prioratus de Gyseburne*, ed. W. Brown, Surtees Society 2 vols. (Durham 1889–94), i, 18–90; *The cartulary of Darley Abbey*, ed. R. R. Darlington, 2 vols. (Kendal 1945); *Liber memorandum ecclesie de Bernewell*, ed. J. W. Clark (Cambridge 1907); *The cartulary of Cirencester Abbey*, ed. C. D. Ross and M. Devine, 3 vols. (Oxford 1964–7); for the disputes between Dunstable and its townspeople, N. Trenholme, *The English monastic boroughs: a study in medieval history* (Columbia, MO, 1927), 12–18, 48–50.

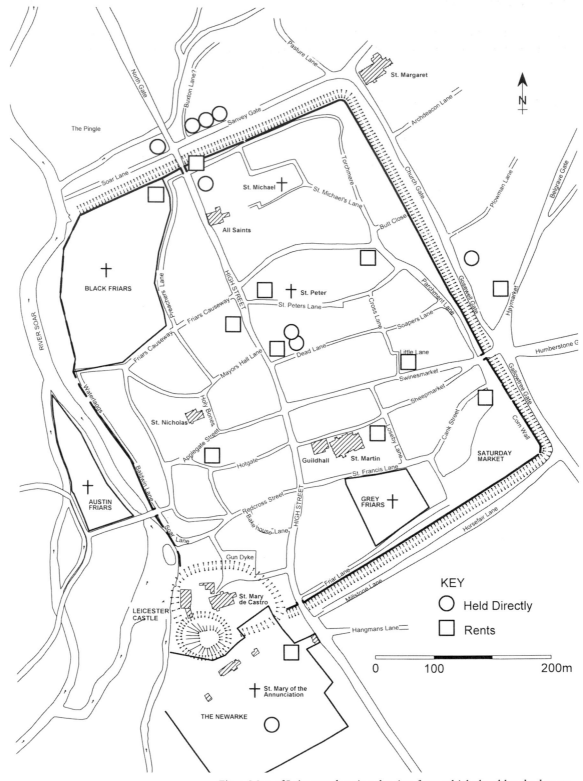

Fig. 1. Map of Leicester showing the sites from which the abbey had rents

with the burgesses; and the fluidity and liquidity of the urban land market. To elaborate the last point, the freedom of alienation of burgage tenements allowed the easier accumulation of rents.[3]

The abbey's position of as an outsider looking into the borough was complicated by the circumstances of its foundation within the Bishop's Fee, that is, the liberty of the Bishop of Lincoln just outside the walls of the borough. Continuous tension existed between the burgesses and the inhabitants of the Bishop's Fee over inclusion within and exclusion from the privileges of the borough and the infraction of those rights. In the case of Leicester Abbey, the precise location of the foundation might have owed much to local territorial politics, a jurisdictional conflict in the early twelfth century between the earl of Leicester and the bishop, the earl invading the Bishop's Fee for the foundation of the abbey.[4]

The consequences of the foundation and location of the abbey were the influence of an external force in the property market, topography, demography and development of the borough and also, perhaps more importantly, of its suburbs outside the walls. It was outside the Northgate that that exercise of seigniorial rights had the greatest impact.

First, however, it is advisable to consider the distribution of all of the abbey's urban and suburban holdings, which can most easily be accomplished through the rental traditionally assigned to 1341 and known as 'Geryn's Rental'.[5] Geryn's Rental describes the rents received from properties topographically by parish. Excluding the grange outside the Southgate, the rents received derived predominantly from properties designated as tenements, the characteristic urban property; the abbey received rents from 199 tenements. Over half the tenemental rents – 105 – were located in the parish of St Leonard, whilst a further forty-two were contained within the parish of All Saints. Almost three-quarters of the abbey's principal rents thus emanated from the northern sector of the borough or outside the Northgate. (See table 1 and fig. 1).

Parish	Rents from types of property	Number of properties		Parish	Rents from types of property	Number of properties
St Mary	grange	1		All Saints	plots of land	several
	plots of land	2			houses	3
	capital messuage	1			croft	1
	tenements	10			tenements	42
St Nicholas	cottages	2		St Margaret	capital messuage	1
	tenements	7			cottages	7
St Martin	tenements	21			plots of land	several
					tenements	3
St Peter	plot of land	1		St Leonard	capital messuage	1
	cottages	6			cottages	7
	tenements	10			crofts	10
St Michael	plots of land	3			houses	6
	tenement	1			tenements	105

Table 1. Distribution of the abbey's rental income in Leicester in 1341

3. M. de W. Hemmeon, *Burgage tenure in medieval England* (Cambridge, MA, 1914).

4. D. Crouch, 'The foundation of Leicester Abbey, and other problems', *Midland History* 12 (1987), 1–13.

5. Bodl. Laud misc 625 is the extant volume of rentals of the house; the relevant section of Geryn's Rental for the urban property of the abbey is on ff. 185r–189r. Several rentals are described in the Abbey's library catalogue, including a 'rentale vocatum Geryn'; T. Webber and A. G. Watson, *The Libraries of the Augustinian Canons*, CBMLC 6 (London 1998), A20.1870. See also, M. Gullick and T. Webber, 'Summary catalogue of surviving manuscripts from Leicester Abbey', above pp. 173–92, no. 17.

In total, the house had, according to the rental, accumulated 221 rents from urban and suburban properties of all types. The freedom of devise of burgage property allowed the fragmentation of rents, so that there might be a multitude of interests in any urban property – each interest collecting a proportion of the rent. For that reason, the levels of rents received by the abbey from the various urban properties ranged from 4½d. to 20s. 6d. Although the rental does not conclude with a sum total of expected receipts from rents, the total amount to be collected appears to have been about £33 13s. 5d.

Compared with the anticipated income of Osney Abbey from its urban rents in Oxford, that amount diminishes in importance, for the sum total of the Osney rental of urban property in 1317 was calculated by the abbey as £174 8s. 10d. before outgoings ('resoluciones').[6] About 1280, the manciple – the obedientiary of Osney receiving most of the urban rents – accounted for an income from rents in Oxford and its suburbs of £151 9s. 11d. with arrears of the previous two years amounting to £12 8s. 9d.[7] Osney, however, was exceptional and Leicester Abbey's rental interest in Leicester was otherwise substantial and certainly of vast importance to the house itself.[8]

Despite the disparities between the two houses, it is also instructive to compare the composition of their urban interests. Leicester Abbey's rents derived preponderantly from properties described as tenements, whilst those of Osney in Oxford were received from a wider range of urban properties: sixty-nine commercial properties ('selde'), ten market stalls and one smith ('fabrica'); 115 'houses' ('domus'); sixty-five cottages; numerous buildings employed for educational purposes (twenty 'aule' and ten 'scole'); eleven parcels of land and two gardens; and only eleven properties described as tenements. Thus, although Osney had around forty percent more rents in number than Leicester Abbey (just over 300 rents to Leicester's 221), its expected rental income was more than five times as much. It may be, however, that the preponderant description of tenements in Leicester Abbey's rental concealed the precise usage of urban buildings.

In addition to the money rents, Leicester Abbey received symbolic rents in kind – in fowl. However, since the rental uses suspensions for 'galli' and 'galline' erratically, it is not possible to calculate these fowl rents precisely by type. Suffice to record, however, that the abbey expected to receive 178 fowl, mainly cocks or hens, but with a small complement of capons, from its urban income. Since most of the fowl rents emanated from outside the North Gate, this form of rent was largely associated with suburban status. Whilst burgage tenements within the borough were subject only to money rents or 'gafol', suburban rents contained a bucolic element, although only of small livestock consistent with and symbolic of their non-burghal status.

Of course, accounting for the reception of rents does little to assess the abbey's influence in the borough through lordship of urban property. Despite the ambiguities of the rental, we can estimate the extent of the abbey's direct interest as the chief lord of some urban properties. The language of the rental allows us in places to identify the tenurial arrangement of these properties, especially where the fully descriptive phrase, 'tenet de nobis ... ad placitum' ('holds from us ... at will/pleasure') recurs as the formula. There is less certainty, however, where the more abbreviated formula 'ad placitum' is deployed. In these cases, the shortened phrase acts as a potential guide but

6. *The cartulary of Oseney Abbey*, ed. H. E. Salter, 6 vols. Oxford Historical Society 89–91, 97–8, 101 (Oxford 1929–36), iii, 134–48; for the rental income in 1359–60, Bodl. Oseney Roll 27.

7. Salter, ed. *Cartulary of Oseney Abbey*, vi, 195.

8. A. Butcher, 'Rent and the urban economy: Oxford and Canterbury in the later middle ages', *Southern History*, 1 (1979), 11–43 at 18–19, estimated that 75 percent of assessed income from rents in Oxford in 1312 belonged to ecclesiastical interests and that Osney's alone amounted to some 20 percent of the assessment of rents.

requires confirmatory evidence (through the size of the rent, for example). Nevertheless, some estimation of the abbey's influence through direct lordship can be established.

In the parish of St Nicholas, five tenements were described as being held 'de nobis . . . ad placitum', three at rental income of 2s. each, but two at the accordingly higher amounts of 12s. and 15s. since the whole rent was directed to the abbey without other interests. Another rent in St Martin's parish was inscribed in the rental as 'de tenemento nostro' ('from our tenement'), also held 'ad placitum', with the rental income to the house at the higher level of 4s. An even higher amount, a half mark (6s. 8d.), was collected by the abbey from another tenement in St Martin's, next to the churchyard stile; this too was held 'ad placitum'. When the rental evaluated St Peter's parish, it recorded five tenements held 'ad placitum' producing rental income to the abbey of 2s., 3s. 6d., 4s., 7s. and 8s., so we might suppose that the abbey had the principal interest in those tenements as well. Merely two tenements were held 'ad placitum' in St Michael's parish, from which the house expected rental receipts of 2s. and 8s. To the east, in St Margaret's parish, the only properties held 'de nobis . . . ad placitum' consisted of seven contiguous cottages, six of which contributed 3s. each to the abbey, whilst one only 1s. 3d.

Moving north in the borough, we now encounter the location of the abbey's major interest as a lord of urban property. In the parish of All Saints, ten tenements were described as held 'de nobis . . . ad placitum', the abbey receiving 3s., 3s. 6d., 4s., 4s. 6d., 6s. (from two), 11s., 14s. (from two) and 20s. In the same parish, seven other tenements were held 'ad placitum', from which the abbey expected rental income of 6d., 9d., 5s. (for two combined tenements), 6s., 10s. 6d. and 11s. Additionally, three houses ('domus') were held 'de nobis . . . ad placitum' at a total rental income to the abbey of 6s. 3d.

It was further north, mostly outside the walls of the borough in St Leonard's parish, that the abbey's seigniorial interest was paramount. Whilst the tenements here were described only as 'ad placitum' rather than 'de nobis . . . ad placitum', the income accruing to the house implies a major interest as lord in the properties. Eighty-four tenements in St Leonard's were described as being held 'ad placitum' in the rental. Table 2 shows the anticipated income to the abbey from these tenements. So dominant was the abbot's interest in this location that in Charyte's late-fifteenth-century rental of the abbey's possessions, it was designated 'vicus abbathie'.[9]

Correlating the interests in rents described in Table 1 with the local built environment presents inordinate difficulties and any attempt is likely to be highly speculative. It is fortunate that contemporaneously with Geryn's rental, several instalments of the 'nonae' ('ninths') tax of Edward III

Rental income to the abbey	Number of tenements				
1s. 3d.	1	2s. 6d.	12	5s	9
1s. 8d.	1	3s.	24	5s. 6d.	1
1s. 9d.	1	3s. 3d.	1	6s. 8d.	1
1s. 10d.	1	3s. 6d.	4	7s.	4
2s.	13	4s.	7	9s.	1
2s. 3d	2	4s. 6d.	1		

Table 2. Expected rental income from tenements in St Leonard's in 1341

9. Charyte's rental is contained within Bodl. Laud misc. 625, at ff. 82v–102v; Webber and Watson, *Libraries of the Augustinian* *Canons*, A20.1872 and Gullick and Webber, 'Summary catalogue', above pp. 185–6, no. 17.

(1340–2) were collected. The assessments for the 'nonae' are significant because they comprehended a much larger number of taxpayers than the borough's internal subsidies, since the 'nonae' captured all those – including singleton women – who had any amount of wool. The first instalment thus embraced 400 townspeople, the second 508, and the final almost 550.[10]

During the late eleventh, twelfth, and more particularly, the thirteenth centuries, the development of suburbs outside the gates of the borough altered the topography of urban settlement.[11] Although expansion happened outside the East Gate, it was the suburb outside the North Gate where, it seems, suburban development was strongest. Among the remarkably small corpus of extant charters concerning transactions in Leicester's urban property, those relating to this suburb outside the North Gate are most numerous before 1350. These surviving charters pertain to just fewer than twenty transactions 'in vico fullonum' and a couple of dozen to other locations within this suburban development, in the parishes of All Saints, St Leonard and St Margaret, all of which coalesced in the suburb. Yet it is unclear to what extent the taxation rolls represent the full population of the suburbs. Nevertheless, the assessments do provide some sort of idea of the housing stock of the built environment of the borough.

The assignments of rents in the unrestricted urban land market and the composition of rents in the northern sector of the borough and its northern suburb are illustrated by these charters. For example, a charter of 1292 concerning a tenement in the suburb outside the North Gate reserved the rent to the abbot of Leicester, chief lord of the fee, comprising 2s. 6d., two hens and a cock.[12] Rent from another tenement in the northern suburb was assigned and re-assigned, the payment consisting of 2s., three hens and a cock.[13] From these transactions, the nature of the rents counted in the rental of 1341 can be perceived.

Material interest was not the only source of influence of the abbey in the borough since, from the earliest time, it had acquired the advowson of all the parish churches in the borough except for St Margaret's which remained a prebendal church of the bishop of Lincoln in his fee in the suburb.[14] The abbot thus influenced the spiritual provision for the townspeople by presenting to the livings at All Saints, St Clement, St Leonard, St Martin, St Peter and St Mary de Castro; indeed, the abbot's appropriation over the last of these constituted a peculiar jurisdiction contained within the liberty of the castle. An integral part of the original endowment had comprised the property of the college of secular canons in St Mary, including urban possessions.[15]

Unlike the controversy between some other houses of Austin Canons and their urban neighbours, however, the relationship between Leicester Abbey and the burgesses appeared at most times to be quite harmonious. As the abbot was appointed one of the collectors of the 'nonae' of 1340–2, he received a 'douceur' ('sweetener') from the mayor of four gallons of wine costing 2s. 8d.[16] A generation later, the labourers of the abbey assisted in quarrying for the repair of the West Bridge and the house's masons were engaged in the borough's affairs.[17] In between those arrange-

10. M. Bateson, ed. *Records of the borough of Leicester 1103–1327* (London 1899), 51, 55; these rolls have not been subjected to the examination they deserve.

11. The importance of suburban growth has been examined by C. Dyer, 'Towns and cottages in 11th-century England' in *Studies in medieval history presented to R. H. C. Davis*, ed. H. Mayr-Harting and R. I. Moore (London 1985), 91–106, and D. Keene, 'Suburban growth' in *The English medieval town: a reader in English urban history*, ed. R. Holt and G. Rosser (London 1990), 97–119.

12. Bateson, *Records of the borough 1103–1327*, 393 (xxxvi); see also 389 (xxvi) for fowl rents in this suburb.

13. Bateson, *Records of the borough 1103–1327*, 394 (xxxviii–xl).

14. A. Hamilton Thompson, *The Abbey of St Mary of the Meadows, Leicester* (Leicester 1949), 157.

15. Hamilton Thompson, *Leicester Abbey*, 157; Crouch, 'The foundation', 2–3.

16. M. Bateson, ed. *Records of the borough of Leicester 1327–1509* (London 1901), 47.

17. Bateson, *Records of the borough 1103–1327*, 140–1.

ments, in 1351–2, two of the abbot's carters were seconded to carry stone from Ibstock for main-tenance of the borough's gates, by the abbot's permission.[18] Such neighbourly acts might have sustained cordiality between the two corporations, secular and spiritual.

On the other hand, the acquisition of interests in the borough and its perimeter by the abbey did introduce some serious changes. Firstly, there can be little doubt that the abbey was a pro-moter of the suburb outside the North Gate. The genesis of that extra-burghal area might well have been organic, but it was also stimulated by the proximity of the abbey, and the house almost certainly encouraged its development and progress. How can that active involvement be per-ceived? One of the traits is the imposition of tenure 'ad placitum', a non-urban, non-burghal form of tenure. That tenurial constraint was associated with tenements for which the abbey was the chief lord. One further aspect is that it appears that the abbey's tenements were to some extent populated by immigrants from its own manors.[19] Whether that movement was encouraged by the abbey or simply a consequence of an 'information field' (as geographers call the area within which knowledge about opportunities is exchanged) within the abbey's lordship and estates, those immi-grants were attracted to these tenements, particularly in St Leonard's parish, by the association of the abbey and the properties.

Analysing the toponymic bynames of the tenants in the parish of St Leonard's in the abbey's rental reveals this connection between the abbey's estates and its urban and suburban tenants. The toponymic bynames indicate a migration at some stage, although we cannot infer from them the migration of their current bearer since bynames were becoming hereditary in the borough from the early thirteenth century. To take an extreme example illustrating the connection between rural estates and urban property, in the rental Adam de Cokerham/Kokerham held two tenements and two crofts in St Leonard's parish; his migration to Leicester had been influenced by the abbey's possessions in Cockerham in Lonsdale Hundred in Lancashire, where the abbey also sustained a priory with cure or cell.[20] In 'le Byggyng', William de Cokerham held another tenement. On the same principle (that toponymic bynames indicate a migration at some time from placename of origin to suburb), significance can be attached to the bynames of tenants designated 'de Ansty', 'de Stoucton', 'de Hatherne' and 'de Schepeshed'. Perhaps too the byname 'de Pecco' was associated with the abbey's holding in Youlgreave and elsewhere in the Peak District.

Even more interesting is the number of independent women, ostensibly spinsters rather than widows, holding abbey tenements. Amongst the tenants of the abbey in the parish of St Leonard's, over twenty holding property 'ad placitum' – and thus probably directly from the abbey – were women whose bynames suggest an independent status: Margery Russell; Helen de Rothele; Helen de Lauda; Emma Borer; Agnes de Bernewell; Helen Haluemar'; Christine de Ansty; Helen de Dyngelee; Alice de Pecco; Felicia Grodye; Diana Squirt; Agnes la Roper; Helen la Ropere; Amice de Wodegate; Matilda de Donemowe; Petronilla de Wetherby; Alice Ladde; Agnes de Hatherne; Magg' de Rotheley; Amice Seynt; and Letice de Stafford. These tenants do not necessarily betray any particular abbatial policy, but what can be observed here is that these expanding suburbs pro-vided a harbour for spinsters to hold tenements and that the abbot was not averse to female ten-ants. The abbot therefore was benign to female tenants of independent means, but it was the sub-urban environment which attracted them and furnished shelter for them. It was medieval

18. Bateson, *Records of the borough 1103–1327*, 78.

19. For the abbey's rural estates, R. H. Hilton, *The economic development of some Leicestershire estates in the fif-* *teenth centuries* (Oxford 1947).

20. Hamilton Thompson, *Leicester Abbey*, 121.

Leicester's equivalent of 'spinster clustering' and, indeed, four of the female tenants were seemingly in contiguous tenements and all in the same neighbourhood.

Advertently or not, then, the abbey's intrusion into urban property and rents had consequences or catalysed processes already under way. The abbey fostered the expansion of the northern suburb or existed at least as a stimulant. Its property in that suburb allowed immigration of tenants from its rural estates, sometimes – although rarely – over enormous distance, so that lordship influenced urban immigration. Those suburbs and the abbot's benign attitude to female tenants also provided shelter for spinsters who could engage in some way in the urban economy without burghal privilege. Although its engagement in or domination of urban place was not as intense as that of some other houses of Austin Canons, the experience of some in the urban society and economy of Leicester and its suburbs was certainly affected by the abbey.

Appendix: Oxford, Bodleian Library, Laud misc. 625 ff. 185r–189r
In the translation, I do not normalise bynames of any kind into a modern equivalent; all are left as in the original. Blanks in the manuscript are indicated by '. . .', the manuscript's orthography is retained throughout except where indicated in a footnote, and obvious omissions are supplied in square brackets.

[f. 185r head]
Edwardi tercii sextodecimo
Geryn

The sixteenth year of Edward III
Geryn

[f. 185r foot]
Ecclesia sancte Marie
Habemus ibi unam placeam ubi grangia nostra deccimalis Scituatur in le Bernegate extra portam australem ex concessione et quieta clamacione Roberti Amphelys de Torpe Ernalde quam ipse emit de Willelmo Daubeney de Leyc'

St Mary's church
We have there a plot where our tithe grange is located in le Bernegate outside the south gate by grant and quitclaim of Robert Amphelys of Thorpe Arnold which he bought from William Daubeney of Leicester

Item habemus ibi de Domino Comite Leyc' Redditum de duabus Placeis terre sibi per nos traditis super le Barbekan ex

Item we have there from the lord Earl of Leicester a rent from two plots of land leased by us to him on the Barbican on

[f. 185v]
Australi parte fossati turris castri inter terram quondam Ade Emelot & terram quondam Johannis de Asheby quam Idem Johannes habuit ex feoffamento Ricardi de le Gardiner' & inde usque ad terram quondam Roberti le Gardiner Et est illa terra inclusa inter murum terreum & fossatum turris ubi nuper habuimus grangiam nostram deccimalem & inde reddit nobis dictus Comes allocando nobis annuatim de redditu unius marce quam sibi debemus pro terra Janitoris & piscarie supra Ponte de North'

the south side of the castle turret ditch between the land once of Adam Emelot and the land once of John de Asheby which that John had by feoffment of Richard de le Gardiner' and from there up to the land once of Robert le Gardiner. And that land is enclosed between the earth wall and the turret ditch where we lately had our tithe grange and the earl pays rent to us for it through an allowance to us yearly from a rent of one mark (13s. 4d.) which we owe to him for the gatekeeper's land and the land of the fishery on the north gate

De Roberto Palmer pro capitali mesuagio suo quod Thomas de Melbourne & Willelmus de Ayleston' quondam tenuerunt in ij mesuagiis iijs. ij gallos ij gallinas j Whitur

From Robert Palmer for his chief messuage which Thomas de Melbourne and William de Ayleston' once held in 2 messuages 4s., 2 cocks, 2 hens, and 1 whitur

De Thoma de Thurmaston' pro tenemento quod Johannes Faber quondam tenuit xviijd. ij Gall'

From Thomas de Thurmaston' for a tenement which John Faber once held 18d., 2 fowl

De Johanne de Petelyng' pro medietate illius tenementi quod Petrus Stake quondam tenuit ijs. j Caponem Releuium

From John de Petelyng' for half of that tenement which Peter Stake once held 2s., 1 capon, relief

De Cecilia Blancharde pro altera medietate dicti tenementi quondam dicti Petri Stake ijs. j Caponem

From Cecily Blancharde for the other half of this tenement once of Peter Stake 2s., 1 capon

De Domino Roberto de Holand pro tenemento quod Johannes Passelewe quondam tenuit xijd.

From Sir Robert de Holand for the tenement which John Passelewe once held 12d.

De Ricardo le Huscher pro tenemento quod Rogerus de Cramford' quondam tenuit xijd.

From Richard le Huscher for the tenement which Roger de Cramford' once held 12d.

De . . .

De . . . Northfolke pro tenemento quod . . . quondam tenuit xviijd.[21]

De Johanne leueriche pro tenemento quondam J. de Threngston' & quod . . . quondam tenuit ijs. iijd.[21]

De Waltero Baker' pro tenemento Kent' & quod . . . quondam tenuit xijd.[21]

De Johanne Attemaydnes pro tenemento quondam Gilofr' & . . . quod . . . quondam tenuit vjd.[21]

De Magistro Willelmo de Barkeby pro tenemento quondam Walteri Wantoun ixd.[21]

De Thoma Martyn pro tenemento quondam Willelmi Lord vjd.[21]

Parochia Sancti Nicholai
De Johanne Kynttecote pro tenemento quod Hugo loueman quondam tenuit ijs. vjd. ij Capones Releuium

De Roberto Aumblere pro tenemento jacente ibidem proximus & quod W. Bawdewyn quondam tenuit vjd.

De Rogero Pestel pro tenemento quod tenet de nobis ad Placitum xvs.

De Johanne de Brantiston' pro tenemento quod tenet de nobis iuxta[22] ad Placitum xijs.

De Jordane[23] de Neuton' pro tenemento quod tenet de nobis ad Placitum ijs.

De Leticia de Newton' pro tenemento iuxta quod tenet de nobis ad Placitum ijs.

De Willelmo Carter pro tenemento quod tenet de nobis ad Placitum ijs.

De ij Cotagiis que Walterus Barker & Willelmus Wareyn' tenent ex parte boriali dicti tenementi que quedem tenementa Willelmus Baldewyne quondam tenuit vjd.

Parochia Sancti Martini
De Nicholao Blancherd pro tenemento quod tenet iuxta Scalam Ecclesie & quod Henricus Houchel Willelmus Blound Ricardus de Cosyngton' & Galfridus Spick quondam tenuerunt in iiij tenementis vjs.

From . . .

From . . . Northfolke for the tenement which . . . once held 18d.[21]

From John Leveriche for the tenement once J. de Threngston's and which . . . once held 2s. 3d.[21]

From Walter Baker for Kent's tenement and which . . . once held 12d.[21]

From John Attemaydnes for the tenement once of Gilofr' and . . . which . . . once held 6d.[21]

From Mr William de Barkeby for the tenement once Walter Wantoun's 9d.[21]

From Thomas Martyn for the tenement once William Lord's 6d.[21]

St Nicholas's parish
From John Knyttecotte for the tenement which Hugh Loveman once held 2s. 6d., 2 capons, relief

From Robert Aumblere for the tenement lying there nearest and which W. Bawdewyn once held 6d.

From Roger Pestel for the tenement which he holds from us 'ad placitum' 15s.

From John de Brantiston' for the tenement which he holds from us next along[22] 'ad placitum' 12s.

From Jordan[23] de Neuton' for the tenement which he holds from us 'ad placitum' 2s.

From Letice de Newton' for the tenement next along which she holds from us 'ad placitum' 2s.

From William Carter for the tenement which he holds from us 'ad placitum' 2s.

From 2 cottages which Walter Barker and William Wareyn' hold on the said tenement's north side which tenements William Baldewyne once held 6d.

St Martin's Parish
From Nicholas Blanchard for the tenement which he holds next to the church stile and which Henry Houchel, William Blound, Richard de Cosyngton' and Geoffrey Spick once held in 4 tenements 6s.

---

21. These items are bracketed together by the word 'Releuium'.
22. This wording is used often, signifying the next tenement in a sequence.

23. MS sic.

De Symone de Camera pro tenemento quod Hugo de Camera quondam tenuit ex alia parte vie in eodem vico vjd.

From Simon de Camera for the tenement which Hugh de Camera once held on the other side of the street in that place 6d.

De Alicia de Barnesby pro tenemento quod Johannes Pistor quondam tenuit ex orientali parte forni[24] vjd.

From Alice de Barnesby for the tenement which John Pistor once held on the east side of the oven[24] 6d.

[f. 186r]

De Johanne Turueye pro tenemento quod Symon de Okam quondam tenuit ibidem in Calido vico[25] xijd.

From John Turveye for the tenement which Simon de Okam once held there in Hot Place[25] 12d.

De Willelmo de Asheby pro tenemento quod Amicia filia Johannis Waryne quondam tenuit xiiijd.

From William de Asheby for the tenement which Amice, John Waryn's daughter, once held 14d.

De uxore[26] Johannis Marwe quod[27] tercia pars tenementi quod Alicia de Oadeby quondam tenuit vjd. j gallinam Releuium

From John Marwe's wife[26] [who holds][27] the third part of a tenement which Alice de Oadeby once held 6d., 1 hen, relief

De Radulpho Mac3on' pro tenemento quod fuit due partes dicti tenementi quod dicta Alicia de Oudeby tenuit ibidem usque ad Cornerium venelle modo Freman xijd. ij gallinas

From Ralph Mac3on' for the tenement which was two parts of this tenement which Alice de Oudeby held there up to the lane's corner, now Freman's, 12d., 2 hens

De Willelmo de Foxton' capellano pro tenemento quod Rogerus de Wykyngston' quondam tenuit vjd.

From William de Foxton' chaplain for the tenement which Roger de Wykyngston once held 6d.

De Christoforo de Enderby pro tenemento quod Radulphus Fode quondam tenuit vjd.

From Christopher de Enderby for the tenement which Ralph Fode once held 6d.

De Dicto Christoforo pro tenemento quod Galfridus Curleuache quondam tenuit super Cornerium ijs. Releuium

From the said Christopher for the tenement which Geoffrey Culevache once held on the corner 2s., relief

De Thoma Marwe Capellano pro tenemento quod Willelmus Doucepeper' quondam tenuit ixd.

From Thomas Marwe chaplain for the tenement which William Doucepeper' once held 9d.

De uxore[26] Johannis Marwe pro tenemento iuxta & quod Walterus de Okam quondam tenuit ixd. Releuium

From John Marwe's wife[26] for the tenement next along and which Walter de Okam once held 9d., relief

De Anselmo Baldewyne pro tenemento quod Willelmus de Sileby quondam tenuit xijd. j Caponem Releuium

From Anselm Baldewyne for the tenement which William de Sileby once held 12d., 1 capon, relief

De Johanne Schirforde pro tenemento iuxta & quod Reginaldus le Parmonter' quondam tenuit xijd. ij Capones Releuium

From John Schirforde for the tenement next along and which Reginald le Parmentor' once held, 12d., 2 capons, relief

De Thoma de Wilughby pro tenemento uxoris sue in vico parcamenti[28] quod Ricardus de Schelton' quondam tenuit & post[29] Editha de Burton' tenuit xijd. ij Gallinas Releuium

From Thomas de Wilughby for his wife's tenement in the parchment place[28] which Richard de Schelton' once held and afterwards[29] Edith de Burton' held, 12d., 2 hens, relief

---

24. MS sic; *furni* is meant.
25. i.e. Hot Gate.
26. i.e. probably widow (here and below).

27. MS sic.
28. i.e. Parchment Lane.
29. MS sic (*recte* postea).

De Gilberto lauener' pro tenemento quod tenet in Cimitorio Sancti Martini & quod Radulphus le mercer' quondam tenuit xijd.

De Dicto Gilberto pro tenemento quod Willelmus le Blound' quondam tenuit iuxta Scalam Cimiterii contra fratres Minores ad placitum dimidia marca

De . . .

De Willemo de Okam pro tenemento quod tenet iuxta furnum ex parte boriali scale Cimiterii ijs.

De Johanne Kelyng' pro tenemento Johannis de Folleuile & quod Robertus Sturdy quondam tenuit in Swynsmarket iijs. ixd. Releuium

De Tenemento quondam Johannis de Melton' in foro Sabbati iuxta tenementum R. Pikeryng' quod habuit de J. Galeys . . .

De Hered'[30] Walteri de Busseby pro Schopa quod ut patet iijd.

De tenemento nostro iuxta tenementum relicte Ade de Syleby quondam[31] Radulphus le Baylli tenet ad placitum iiijs.

Parochia Sancti Petri
De Nicholao Hendeman pro tenemento quod tenet ad antiquam Gildhall' ad Placitum ijs. ij Gallinas

De Willelmo Stiworman pro tenemento quod tenet ibidem ad placitum iiijs.

De eodem Willelmo pro alio tenemento iuxta dictum tenementum quod tenet ad placitum iijs. vjd.

De ij aliis tenementis ibidem quod Willelmus Aldith' tenet ad Placitum vijs.

De Willelmo Aldith' pro quadam Placea terre ibidem retro antiquam Gildhall' ex parte boriali quam Willelmus de Grescote quondam tenuit libere vjd.

De Reginaldo Pestel pro tenemento quod tenet in mortuo vico[32] usque aliam stratam ad placitum viijs.

De Rogero de Wylughby pro vj Cotagiis edificatis in quoddam tenemento quod Laurencius Seman quondam tenuit prope Ecclesiam Sancti Petri libere ijs. ij Capones Releuium

From Gilbert Lavener' for the tenement which he holds in St Martin's churchyard and which Ralph le Mercer' once held 12d.

From the said Gilbert for the tenement which William le Blound' once held next to the churchyard stile up against the Friars Minor 'ad placitum' half a mark [6s. 8d.]

From . . .

From William de Okam for the tenement which he holds next to the oven on the north side of the churchyard stile 2s.

From John Kelyng' for the tenement of John de Follevile and which Robert Sturdy once held in Swinesmarket 4s. 9d., relief

From the tenement once John de Melton's in the Saturday Market next to R. Pikeryng's tenement which he had from J. Galeys . . .

From Walter de Busseby's heir(s)[30] for the shop as is evident 3d.

From our tenement next to Adam de Syleby's widow's tenement which[31] Ralph le Baylli holds 'ad placitum' 4s.

St Peter's Parish
From Nicholas Hendeman for the tenement which he holds at the old Gildhall 'ad placitum' 2s., 2 hens

From William Stiworman for the tenement which he holds there 'ad placitum' 4s.

From the same William for the other tenement next to the said tenement which he holds 'ad placitum' 4s. 6d.

From 2 other tenements there which William Aldith' holds 'ad placitum' 7s.

From William Aldith' for a certain plot of land there behind the old Gildhall on the north side which William de Grescote once held freely 6d.

From Reginald Pestel for the tenement which he holds in the Dead Place[32] up to another street 'ad placitum' 8s.

From Roger de Wylughby for 6 cottages built on a certain tenement which Laurence Seman once held freely near St Peter's church 2s., 2 capons, relief

---

30. Either *Herede* or *Heredibus*.
31. MS sic (*recte* quod).

32. i.e. Dead Lane.

De Henrico de Barkeby pro tenemento quod dominus Willelmus Musseburt[33] quondam tenuit iuxta borialem scalam vjd.

[f. 186v]
De Domino W. Herle pro tenemento ex australi parte Cimiterii quod Willelmus de Burscena quondam tenuit xijd.

De Willelmo Aurifabro pro tenemento quod Johannes Cagge quondam tenuit in alta strata[34] iiijs. ij Capones Releuium

De Waltero Tannatore pro tenemento quod Willelmus de Broghton' quondam tenuit vjd.

Parochia Sancti Michaelis
De Galfrido de Osberton' pro quadam placea terre nostre iacent'[35] ex orientali parte Ecclesie continent' in longitudine vj^{xx} et iij pedes & in latitudine viij^{xx} pedes ad placitum xijd.

De quoddam tenemento iacente iuxta scalam orientalem Cimiterii omnium sanctorum quod W. fischer' tenet ad placitum ijs.

De Ricardo Coco pro quadam placea iuxta Cimiterium Sancti Michaelis quod quondam fuit Walteri Choloun vjd. j Caponem

De quadam placea terre quam Robertus Sturdy tenet que pertinet ad ecclesiam Sancti Michaelis iuxta terram ad placitum viijs.

Parochia Omnium Sanctorum
De Willelmo le Spicere pro tenemento quondam Nicholai Burgeys & quod Robertus Castel Patris[36] tenuit in vico fullonum[37] xijd. Releuium

De Johanne de le Waynhous pro ij tenementis quod Robertus filius Henrici Houchl' quondam tenuit iuxta dictum tenementum xxjd. ij g' j g[38]

De Symone Coureyour' pro tenemento quod leticia Houchl' & Willelmus de nouo Castello quondam tenuerunt quondam erat Situm & quod idem Symon Tenet ad Placitum vjs. ij Gallinas

De Henrico de Thorneton' pro tenemento quod tenet iuxta Cornerium vici fullonum quod Willelmus Sampson' Solebat tenere iuxta fabricam Et pro tenemento super Cogueir ubi fabrica est

From Henry de Barkeby for the tenement which Sir William Musseburt[33] once held next to the north stile 6d.

From Sir W. Herle for the tenement on the south side of the churchyard which William de Burscena once held 12d.

From William Aurifaber for the tenement which John Cagge once held in High Street[34] 4s., 2 capons, relief

From Walter Tannator for the tenement which William de Broghton' once held 6d.

St Michael's parish
From Geoffrey de Osberton' for a certain plot of our land lying[35] on the east side of he church containing 123 feet in length and 160 feet in width, 'ad placitum' 12d.

From a certain tenement lying next to the east stile of All Saints' churchyard which W. Fischer holds 'ad placitum' 2s.

From Richard Cocus for a certain plot next to St Michael's churchyard which was once Walter Choloun's 6d., 1 capon

From a certain plot of land which Robert Sturdy holds which belongs to St Michael's church next to the land 'ad placitum' 8s.

All Saints' parish
From William le Spicere for the tenement once Nicholas Burgeys's and which his father[36] Robert Castel held in the fuller's place[37] 12d., relief

From John de le Waynhous for 2 tenements which Robert son of Henry Houchl' once held next to the said tenement 21d, 2 cocks, 1 hen[38]

From Simon Coureyour' for the tenement which Letice Houchl' and William de Novo Castello once held and which the same Simon holds 'ad placitum' 6s., 2 hens

From Henry de Thorneton' for the tenement which he holds next to the corner of the fullers' place which William Sampson used to hold next to the smithy. And for the tenement on Cogweir where the

---

33. The name is unclear in the MS.
34. i.e. Highcross Street.
35. Above and below, this word is extended by the *scriptor* as *iacente* but it, as *continent'* below, should be *iacenti*.
36. MS sic.

37. i.e. Fullers Lane.
38. Here (and elsewhere), the abbreviation makes it impossible to know which are cocks and which hens, although the usual order was male animals before female.

quod Robertus filius H. tenuit xijd. ob. iij gallinas j Caponem

De uxore Roberti Sire pro tenemento quondam Radulphi olm' Willelmus Sampson' quondam tenuit xixd. ob. iij Capones

De Emma de Houby pro tenemento quod Ricardus de Howby tenet & quod filia Henrici Alby quondam tenuit jd. ob. ij Capones Releuium

De Roberto Bryde pro tenemento quod r'[39] retro fabricam & quod Robertus filius Henrici tenet iuxta tenementum predictum ixd. Releuium

De Willelmo Fouk' pro tenemento quod uxor J. de Evyngton' tenet & quod J. Makcpays quondam tenuit xviijd. Releuium

De Johanne le[40] Waynhous pro tenemento quod Willelmus Proudfote quondam tenuit vjd. Releuium

De uxore Willelmi de Clounham pro tenemento quod Willelmus Balle quondam tenuit xijd. iiij gallinas Releuium

De uxore Ricardi de Cramforth' pro tenemento quod Johannes de Dauentr' quondam tenuit xijd. ij gallinas Releuium

De Willelmo Turnour pro tenemento quod dictus Johannes de Dauentr' quondam tenuit xijd. ij gallinas Releuium

De Willelmo de Donyngton' pro tenemento quod Ricardus Trunchoun quondam tenuit xviijd. Releuium

De Alicia Inglod[41] pro tenemento quod tenuit Robertus de Enderby & quod Matildis de Roley quondam tenuit xijd. ij gallinas Releuium

De Roberto Kelyng' pro tenemento quod Henricus Kelyng' quondam tenuit vjd.

De uxore Johannis Becke pro tenemento quod tenet de nobis cum una placea terre eidem coniuncta ad placitum vjs. ij gallinas

De Johanne de Enderby pro tenemento quod tenet de nobis Ad Placitum xjs. ij g'

De Rogero Blysse pro tenemento quod tenet de Nobis Ad Placitum iijs. vjd.

smithy is which Robert son of Henry held 12½d., 3 hens, 1 capon

From Robert Sire's wife for the tenement once of Ralph Olm [which] William Sampson' once held, 19½d., 3 capons

From Emma de Houby for the tenement which Richard de Howby holds and which Henry Alby's daughter once held 1½d., 2 capons, relief

From Robert Bryde for the tenement behind[39] the smithy and which Robert son of Henry holds next to the aforesaid tenement 9d., relief

From William Fouk' for the tenement which J. de Evyngton's wife holds and which J. Makepays once held 18d., relief

From John [de][40] le Waynhous for the tenement which William Proudfote once held 6d., relief

From William de Clounham's wife for the tenement which William Balle once held 12d., 4 hens, relief

From Richard de Cramforth's wife for the tenement which John de Daventr' once held 12d., 2 hens, relief

From William Turnour for the tenement which the said John de Daventr' once held 12d., 2 hens, relief

From William de Donyngton' for the tenement which Richard Trunchon once held 18d., relief

From Alice Inglod[41] for the tenement which Robert de Enderby held and which Matilda de Roley once held 12d., 2 hens, relief

From Robert Kelyng' for the tenement which Henry Kelyng' once held 6d.

From John Becke's wife for the tenement which she holds of us with a plot of land joined to it 'ad placitum' 6s., 2 hens

From John de Enderby for the tenement which he holds of us 'ad placitum' 11s., 2 fowl

From Roger Blysse for the tenement which he holds of us 'ad placitum' 3s. 6d.

---

39. MS sic.
40. MS sic, but it should be *de le*.

41. MS sic, but *Ingold'* would be expected (i.e. metathesis).

De Roberto de Groby pro tenemento quod tenet de Nobis Ad Placitum iiijs.

From Robert de Groby for the tenement which he holds from us 'ad placitum' 4s.

[f. 187r]

De Isabella de Schepeshed pro tenemento quod tenet de nobis Ad Placitum vjs. ij [d.]

From Isabel de Schepeshed for the tenement which she holds from us 'ad placitum' 6s. 2d.

De Johanne Burgeys pro tenemento suo & terra quam W. de nouo castillo tenet & medietate tofti Willelmus[42] peronell' iijs.[43] ij g'

From John Burgeys for his tenement and land which W. de Novo Castillo holds and half William[42] Peronell's toft 3s.,[43] 2 fowl

De Eodem Johanne pro terra ubi[44] sepes gardini sui plantantur si de quadam particula terre sue nobis concesse eiciamur vjd.

From the same John for land where[44] his garden's border is planted if we are evicted from a parcel of land leased to us 6d.

De Ricardo de Swepston' pro tenemento quod Robertus filius Alani Rotarii quondam tenuit ijs. vjd. ij g' Releuium

From Richard de Swepston' for the tenement which Robert son of Alan Rotarius once held 2s. 6d., 2 fowl, relief

De Helia le Tayllour pro tenemento quod tenet de Nobis ad Placitum iiijs. vjd. j g' Releuium

From Elias le Tayllour for the tenement which he holds from us 'ad placitum' 4s. 6d., 1 fowl, relief

De Johanne filio Hugonis le Barkere pro terra xijd.

From John son of Hugh le Barkere for land 12d.

De Margareta Geryn' pro quadam placea cum gardino suo quod N. Burgeys quondam tenuit ixd. j g'

From Margaret Geryn' for a certain plot with its garden which N. Burgeys once held 9d., 1 fowl

De Willelmo le Diker' pro tenemento quod tenet de nobis ex altera parte vici ad Placitum iijs.

From William le Diker' for the tenement which he holds from us on the other side of the place 'ad placitum' 3s.

De Johanne filio Hugonis le Barker' pro tenemento quod tenet retro predictum tenementum quod fuit Roberti Dole Dufhous vjd. j g' Releuium

From John son of Hugh le Barker' for the tenement which he holds behind the aforesaid tenement which was Robert Dole's Dufhous 6d., 1 hen, relief

De magistro Hospitalis Sancti Leonardi pro quodam tenemento quod tenet super stagnum Molendini xijd.

From the master of St Leonard's Hospital for a certain tenement which he holds on the millpond 12d.

De Johanne de Thurmaston' pro tenemento quod ad boriale cornerium vici molendini[45] ad Placitum ixd.

From John de Thurmaston' for the tenement which [lies][45] at the north corner of the mill site 'ad placitum' 9d.

De Rogero de Sibbisdon' pro quadam placea terre ex occidentali parte dicti tenementi ad placitum vjd.

From Roger de Sibbisdon' for a certain plot of land on the west side of the said tenement 'ad placitum' 6d.

De Tenemento quondam Simonis Priour quod fuit Galfridi de Stanton' iiijd.

From the tenement once Simon Priour's which was Geoffrey de Stanton's 4d.

De Ricardo le Sawer & Willelmo Scriptore pro ij tenementis quod tenent ad Placitum vs.

From Richard le Sawer and William Scriptor for 2 tenements which they hold 'ad placitum' 5s.

De Symone le Quarreour pro tenemento quod Willelmus de Belgraue tenuit as Placitum vjs.

From Simon le Quarreour for the tenement which William de Belgrave held 'ad placitum' 6s.

---

42. MS sic.
43. Altered from ij.

44. *Ubi* superscript.
45. MS omits verb.

De Henrico de Boresworth' pro tenemento quod tenet de Nobis Ad Placitum xjs.

De Magistro Willelmo Coco pro tenemento quod tenet iuxta ecclesiam omnium sanctorum & quod Gryffyn quondam tenuit libere ixd.

De Eodem Willelmo pro tenemento quod tenet iuxta tenementum predictum ad Placitum xs. vjd.

De Ricardo Plummer' pro tenemento quod tenet de nobis ad Placitum xiiijs.

De Margeria Russell' pro tenemento quod tenet ibi de nobis ad Placitum xiiijs.

De Stephano Campanar' pro tenemento quod tenet ad cornerium de nobis ad Placitum xxs.

De Thoma Vescy pro tenemento quod tenet infra portam borialem & quod Hawisa uxor Johannis Fabri quondam tenuit iuxta portam in principio venelle qua itur versus fratres predicatores vjd. Releuium

De Magistro J. Coco pro tenemento Rodyngton' & quod . . . quondam tenuit . . .

De Johanne filio Hugonis Tannatoris pro tenemento suo quod . . . quondam tenuit iijd.

De Tribus domibus iuxta vicum molendini que tenentur de nobis ad Placitum vjs. iijd.

De Crofto ad capita eorum quod Willelmus le freman tenet ad Placitum xijd. j g'

Parochia Sancte Margarete
De Roberto le Porter in Belgrauegate pro capitali mesuagio suo quod fuit Dauid' de Kent ijs. ij g' Releuium

De Magistro Johanne Coco pro tenemento quod Ricardus Cokenbred quondam tenuit vjd. ij g' Releuium

De Ricardo de Staunford pro tenemento quod Alicia de haldenby quondam tenuit xijd. Releuium

[f. 187v]
De Waltero le Barker pro tenemento quondam J. northern' quod fuit Symonis[46] flandr' xijd. Releuium

De Septem Cotagiis quondam Amphelisie de Thorp que diuersi tenent de nobis ad Placitum

46. MS *Symon*.

From Henry de Boresworth' for the tenement which he holds from us 'ad placitum' 11s.

From Mr William Cocus for the tenement which he holds next to All Saints' church and which Griffin once held freely 9d.

From the same William for the tenement which he holds next to the aforesaid tenement 'ad placitum' 10s. 6d.

From Richard Plummer' for the tenement which he holds from us 'ad placitum' 14s.

From Margery Russell' for the tenement which she holds from us 'ad placitum' 14s.

From Stephen Campanar' for the tenement which he holds from us at the corner 'ad placitum' 20s.

From Thomas Vescy for the tenement which he holds inside Northgate and which Hawise, John Faber's wife, once held next to the gate at the head of the lane which leads towards the Friars Preachers 6d., relief

From Mr John Cocus for Rodyngton's tenement and which . . . once held . . .

From John Hugh Tannator's son for his tenement which . . . once held 3d.

From 3 houses next to the mill site which are held from us 'ad placitum' 6s. 3d.

From the croft at their heads which William le Freman holds 'ad placitum' 12d., 1 fowl

St Margaret's parish
From Robert le Porter in Belgravegate for his chief messuage which was David de Kent's 2s., 2 fowl, relief

From Mr John Cocus for the tenement which Richard Cokenbred once held 6d., 2 fowl, relief

From Richard de Staunford for the tenement which Alice de Haldenby once held 12d., relief

From Walter le Barker for the tenement once J. Northern's which was Simon[46] Flandr's 12d., relief

From 7 cottages once Amphelis de Thorp's which several hold from us 'ad placitum'

De Primo Cotagio incipienti ab oriente usque occidentem quod tenetur de nobis ad placitum iijs. ij g'

From the first cottage beginning from east to west which is held from us 'ad placitum' 3s., 2 fowl

De Secundo Cotagio quod Matilda de Thurmeston' tenet Ad Placitum xvd.

From the second cottage which Matilda de Thurmeston holds 'ad placitum' 15d.

De Tercio Cotagio quod tenetur . . . Ad Placitum iijs. ij g'

From the third cottage which is held . . . 'ad placitum' 3s., 2 fowl

De Quarto Cotagio quod tenetur . . . Ad Placitum iijs. ij g'

From the fourth cottage which is held . . . 'ad placitum' 3s., 2 fowl

De Quinto Cotagio quod tenetur . . . Ad Placitum iijs. ij g'

From the fifth cottage which is held . . . 'ad placitum' 3s., 2 fowl

De Sexto Cotagio quod tenetur . . . Ad Placitum iijs. ij g'

From the sixth cottage which is held . . . 'ad placitum' 3s., 2 fowl

De Septimo Cotagio quod tenetur . . . Ad Placitum iijs. ij g'

From the seventh cottage which is held . . . 'ad placitum' 3s., 2 fowl

De una Placea terre inter dictum Cotagium & tenementum quondam Willelmi Baldewyn quod . . .

From a plot of land between the said cottage and the tenement once William Baldewyn's which . . .

De Terra quam Johannes le Tannour quondam tenuit iiijd. ob.

From the land which John le Tannour once held 4½d.

Parochia Sancti Leonardi
De Galfrido le Barkere pro tenemento quod Ricardus de Barkeby quondam tenuit ante pontem ligneum vjd. j g' Releuium

St Leonard's parish
From Geoffrey le Barkere for the tenement which Richard de Barkeby once held before the wooden bridge 6d., 1 fowl, relief

De Willelmo Geryn pro tenemento quod Johannes de Sibbesdon' quondam tenuit vjd. j g' Releuium

From William Geryn for the tenement which John de Sibbesdon' once held 6d., 1 fowl, relief

De Waltero Barker' pro capitali mesuagio suo quod Robertus Petit quondam tenuit ijs. ij g' Releuium

From Walter Barker' for his chief messuage which Robert Petit once held 2s., 2 fowl, relief

De Elena Geryn pro tenemento quod Willelmus Cockowh' quondam tenuit iuxta Pontem iiijd. j g' Releuium

From Helen Geryn for the tenement which William Cockowh' once held next to the bridge 4d., 1 fowl, relief

De Waltero Tannatore pro tenemento quod tenet inter capitale mesuagium suum[47] & ad vicum ad terram vijs.

From Walter Tannator for the tenement which he holds between his[47] chief messuage and at the place at land 7s.

De Tenemento ubi vicarius manet & quod tenet Ad Placitum dimidia marca

From the tenement where the vicar resides and which he holds 'ad placitum' half a mark [6s. 8d.]

De Tenemento quod Johannes Scot tenet Ad Placitum iiijs. ij g'

From the tenement which John Scot holds 'ad placitum' 4s., 2 fowl

De Tenemento quod Johannes Sutor tenet Ad Placitum iiijs. ij g'

From the tenement which John Sutor holds 'ad placitum' 4s., 2 fowl

De Tenemento quod Henricus de Boresworth' tenet & quod Amori de Sadyngt' quondam tenuit xviijd.

From the tenement which Henry de Boresworth' holds and which Amory de Sadyngt' once held 18d.

47. MS *suo*.

De Waltero Tannatore pro tenemento quod . . . quondam tenuit xijd. iiij g' Releuium

From Walter Tannator for the tenement which . . . once held 12d., 4 fowl, relief

De Magistro Sancti Leonardi pro ij Croftis iuxta Hospitale xs.

From the master of St Leonard's for 2 crofts next to the hospital 10s.

De Septem Cotagiis cum uno crofto & Stagno in Wodgate quod tenentur ad Placitum xxs. vjd. vij g'

From 7 cottages with a croft and pond in Woodgate which are held 'ad placitum' 20s. 6d., 7 fowl

De tenemento de nouo edificato quod tenetur . . . Ad Placitum . . .

From a newly-built tenement which is held . . . 'ad placitum' . . .

De Willelmo le Macʒon' pro tenemento nouo in vico Abbatie quod tenetur Ad Placitum vijs. ij g'

From William le Macʒon' for the new tenement in the abbey's precinct which is held 'ad placitum' 7s., 2 fowl

De Domo iuxta quod tenetur . . . Ad Placitum vijs. ij g'

From the house next along which is held . . . 'ad placitum' 7s., 2 fowl

De Adam[48] de Kokerham pro tenemento quod fuit Willelmi Gregori xviijd. j g' Releuium

From Adam[48] de Kokerham for the tenement which was William Gregori's 18d., 1 fowl, relief

De Elena de Rothele pro tenemento quod tenet in Wodgate iuxta campum Ad Placitum vs. ij g'

From Helen de Rothele for the tenement which she holds in Woodgate next to the [North] field 'ad placitum' 5s., 2 fowl

De Radulpho de Barton' pro tenemento iuxta campum ex altera parte Ad Placitum iijs.

From Ralph de Barton' from the tenement next to the field on the other side 'ad placitum' 4s.

De Willelmo de Doueland pro tenemento iuxta predictum Radulphum ijs. vjd. ij g'

From William de Doueland for the tenement next to the aforesaid Ralph 2s. 6d., 2 fowl

De Johanne de Pecco pro tenemento iuxta usque Ecclesiam Ad Placitum iijs. j g'

From John de Pecco for the tenement next along up to the church 'ad placitum' 3s., 1 fowl

De eodem pro tenemento iuxta predictum tenementum versus ecclesiam Ad Placitum iijs. vjd. j g'

From the same for the tenement next to the aforesaid tenement towards the church 'ad placitum' 3s. 6d., 1 fowl

[f. 188r]
De Thoma de Pecco pro tenemento iuxta predictum versus ecclesiam Ad Placitum iijs. j gallum

From Thomas de Pecco for the tenement next to the aforesaid towards the church 'ad placitum' 3s., 1 cock

De Ricardo Carpentar' pro tenemento iuxta predictum versus ecclesiam Ad Placitum iijs. vjd.

From Richard Carpentar' for the tenement next to the aforesaid towards the church 'ad placitum' 3s. 6d.

De Willelmo de[49] Cropston' pro tenemento iuxta predictum versus Ecclesiam Ad Placitum iijs.

From William de[49] Cropston' for the tenement next to the aforesaid towards the church 'ad placitum' 3s.

De Willelmo de Doueland pro tenemento iuxta terram Hospitalis Sancti Leonardi ijs. j gallum ij gallinas

From William de Doueland for the tenement next to St Leonard's Hospital's land 2s., 1 cock, 2 hens

De Johanne de Pakyngton' pro Deuoncroft' Ad Placitum vs.

From John de Pakyngton' for Devoncroft' 'ad placitum' 5s.

---

48. ᴍꜱ sic.

49. *de* superscript.

De Ricardo Chede pro tenemento iuxta tenementum Amicia[50] de Pakyngton' Ad Placitum ixs. j gallum j gallinam

From Richard Chede for the tenement next to Amice[50] de Pakyngton's tenement 'ad placitum' 9s., 1 cock, 1 hen

De Ricardo de Pollesworth' pro Bondcroft Ad Placitum vs.

From Richard de Pollesworth' for Bondcroft 'ad placitum' 5s.

De Johanne Fatte pro tenemento ad Cornerium iuxta predictum tenementum Ad Placitum ijs. vjd.

From John Fatte for the tenement at the corner next to the aforesaid tenement 'ad placitum' 2s. 6d.

De Willelmo de Pyrye pro tenemento quod tenet iuxta Ad Placitum ijs. vjd.

From William de Pyrye for the tenement which he holds next along 'ad placitum' 2s. 6d.

De Rogero de Codyngton' pro tenemento iuxta Ad Placitum ijs. vjd. ij g'

From Roger de Codyngton' for the tenement next along 'ad placitum' 2s. 6d., 2 fowl

De Elena de Lauda pro tenemento iuxta Ad Placitum ijs. vjd. ij g'

From Helen de Lauda for the tenement next along 'ad placitum' 2s. 6d., 2 fowl

De Johanne Gold pro tenemento iuxta Ad Placitum iijs.

From John Gold for the tenement next along 'ad placitum' 3s.

De Emma Borer pro tenemento iuxta Ad Placitum iijs.

From Emma Borer for the tenement next along 'ad placitum' 3s.

De Willelmo Blisse pro tenemento iuxta Ad Placitum iijs.

From William Blisse for the tenement next along 'ad placitum' 3s.

De Agnete de bernewell' pro tenemento iuxta Ad Placitum ijs. j g'

From Agnes de Bernewell' for the tenement next along 'ad placitum' 2s., 1 fowl

De Elena Haluemar' pro tenemento iuxta Ad Placitum ijs. j g'

From Helen Halvemar' for the tenement next along 'ad placitum' 2s., 1 fowl

De Christiana de Ansty pro tenemento iuxta Ad Placitum ijs. j g'

From Christine de Ansty for the tenement next along 'ad placitum' 2s., 1 fowl

De Elena de Dyngelee pro tenemento iuxta Ad Placitum ijs. vjd. j g'

From Helen de Dyngelee for the tenement next along 'ad placitum' 2s. 6d., 1 fowl

De Johanne de Tacker pro tenemento iuxta Ad placitum ijs. j g'

From John de Tacker for the tenement next along 'ad placitum' 2s., 1 fowl

De Henrico de Burstalle pro tenemento quod ad terminum vite[51] nichil quia Redditus ibi condonatur

From Henry de Burstalle for the tenement which [he holds][51] for a life term nothing because the rent there is remitted

De Roberto le Armerer pro tenemento iuxta Ad Placitum ijs. vjd.

From Robert le Armerer for the tenement next along 'ad placitum' 2s. 6d.

De . . . pro tenemento iuxta Ad Placitum xxijd.

From . . . for the tenement next along 'ad placitum' 22d.

De Rogero glide pro tenemento quondam Thome de Bramdoon' Ad Placitum iiijs.

From Roger Glide for the tenement once Thomas de Bramdoon's 'ad placitum' 4s.

De Johanne De Pakyngton' pro crofto retro dicto[52] duo tenementa Ad Placitum xvjd.

From John de Packyngton' for the croft behind the said[52] 2 tenements 'ad placitum' 16d.

---

50. MS sic.

51. MS omits verb.
52. MS sic.

De Waltero Hexham pro tenemento iuxta Crofto[53] Ad Placitum vs.

From Walter Hexham for the tenement next to the croft[53] 'ad placitum' 5s.

De Johanne de Stoucton' pro tenemento iuxta cum crofto Ad Placitum vs.

From John de Stoucton' for the tenement next along with a croft 'ad placitum' 5s.

De Roberto de Burstale pro tenemento iuxta cum Crofto Ad Placitum vs.

From Robert de Burstale for the tenement next along with a croft 'ad placitum' 5s.

De predictis ij Tenementis Scilicet Braundoun & Whiteby solebamus percipere xijd. redditus ad officium Fabrice ferrar'.[54]

From the aforesaid 2 tenements, that is Braundon and Whiteby, we used to collect 12d. rent for the office of the farriery.[54]

De Ricardo Fox pro tenemento quod tenet ad Cornerium ex opposito le Thewh'[55] Ad Placitum iijs. j gallum j gallinam

From Richard Fox for the tenement which he holds at the corner opposite le Thewh'[55] 'ad placitum' 3s., 1 cock, 1 hen

De Adam[56] de Cokerham pro crofto retro dictum tenementum Ad Placitum ijs.

From Adam[56] de Cokerham for the croft behind the said tenement 'ad placitum' 2s.

De Roberto de Stocton' pro tenemento iuxta Ricardum Fox Ad Placitum iijs.

From Robert de Stocton' for the tenement next to Richard Fox 'ad placitum' 3s.

De Galfrido Strippelyng' pro tenemento iuxta Ad Placitum iijs. vjd. j gallum

From Geoffrey Strippelyng' for the tenement next along 'ad placitum' 3s. 6d., 1 cock

De Nicholao de haywode pro tenemento iuxta Ad placitum iijs. j gallum j gallinam

From Nicholas de Haywode for the tenement next along 'ad placitum' 3s., 1 cock, 1 hen

De Alicia de Pecco pro tenemento iuxta Ad Placitum iijs. j g'

From Alice de Pecco for the tenement next along 'ad placitum' 3s., 1 fowl

Sunt iuxta due domus de Sacristaria de quibus prius fit mencio

There are next along 2 houses of the Sacristy of which mention might be made before

De Roberto de gardener' pro tenemento iuxta Ad Placitum iijs. j g'

From Robert de Gardener' for the tenement next along 'ad placitum' 3s., 1 fowl

De Willelmo Comyn pro tenemento iuxta Robertum Gardener' Ad Placitum iijs. j g'

From William Comyn for the tenement next to Robert Gardener' 'ad placitum' 3s., 1 fowl

De Felicia Grodye pro tenemento iuxta Ad placitum iijs. j g'

From Felice Grodye for the tenement next along 'ad placitum' 3s., 1 fowl

De Henrico Trompur pro tenemento iuxta Ad Placitum iijs. j g'

From Henry Trompur for the tenement next along 'ad placitum' 3s., 1 fowl

De Adam[57] de Kokerham pro Crofto retro tenementum suum Ad Placitum vd.

From Adam[57] de Kokerham for the croft behind his tenement 'ad placitum' 5d.

[f. 188v]
Idem Adam tenet tenementum ibidem de Sacristaria libere quod fuit Willelmi gregori de quo ante[58] fit mencio

The same Adam holds a tenement there freely from the Sacristy which was William Gregori's, mention of which might be made above[58]

---

53. MS sic.
54. MS sic but later (correctly) *ferrarie*.
55. The former name for Sanvey Gate.

56. MS sic, here and below (*recte* Ada).
57. MS sic.
58. MS sic (*recte* antea).

De Willelmo Mac3on pro tenemento iuxta tenementum Ade de Cokerham Ad Placitum ijs. vjd. ij g'

From William Mac3on for the tenement next to Adam de Cokerham's tenement 'ad placitum' 2s. 6d., 2 fowl

De Thoma de Wetherby pro tenemento iuxta Ad Placitum ijs. vjd. ij g'

From Thomas de Wetherby for the tenement next along 'ad placitum' 2s. 6d., 2 fowl

De Adam[59] Taylour pro tenemento super Cornerium le Byggynge Ad Placitum iijs. ij g'

From Adam[59] Taylour for the tenement on the corner of le Byggyng 'ad placitum' 3s., 2 fowl

De Willelmo de Cokerham pro tenemento intrando in le Byggynge Ad Placitum . . .

From William de Cokerham for the tenement entering into le Byggyng 'ad placitum' . . .

De Willelmo de[60] Palycere pro tenemento iuxta Ad Placitum xxjd.

From William le[60] Palycere for the tenement next along 'ad placitum' 21d.

De Diana Squirt pro tenemento iuxta Ad Placitum ijs. j g' j gallum

From Diana Squirt for the tenement next along 'ad placitum' 2s., 1 fowl, 1 cock

De Rogero de Sybbesdon' pro tenemento iuxta Ad Placitum xviijd.

From Roger de Sybbesdon' for the tenement next along 'ad placitum' 18d.

De Willelmo de bramleye pro tenemento iuxta Ad Placitum ijs.

From William de Bramleye for the tenement next along 'ad placitum' 2s.

De Agnete de[61] Roper' pro tenemento iuxta Ad Placitum iijs.

From Agnes la[61] Roper' for the tenement next along 'ad placitum' 3s.

De Radulpho godehewer pro tenemento iuxta Ad Placitum iijs.

From Ralph Godehewer for the tenement next along 'ad placitum' 3s.

De . . . pro tenemento quod W. Fole[62] Ad Placitum vijs. j g' j g'

From . . . for the tenement which W. Fole [holds][62] 'ad placitum' 7s., 1 cock 1 hen

De Clemente de Burstalle pro tenemento iuxta Ad Placitum vijs. j g' j gallum

From Clement de Burstalle for the tenement next along 'ad placitum' 7s., 1 hen, 1 cock

De Stephano le Roper pro tenemento iuxta Ad Placitum vs. j g' j gallum

From Stephen le Roper for the tenement next along 'ad placitum' 5s., 1 hen, 1 cock

De Roberto de Eton' pro tenemento iuxta Ad Placitum iijs. iijd. ij g'

From Robert de Eton' for the tenement next along 'ad placitum' 3s. 3d., 2 fowl

De Adam[63] Cromber pro tenemento iuxta Ad Placitum iijs. vjd. j g' j gallum

From Adam[63] Cromber for the tenement next along 'ad placitum' 4s. 6d., 1 hen, 1 cock

De Willelmo le Bene pro tenemento iuxta Ad placitum iijs. vjd. ij g'

From William le Bene for the tenement next along 'ad placitum' 3s. 6d., 2 fowl

De Elena le[64] Ropere pro domo in fronte le Byggyng' Ad Placitum ijs. ij g'

From Helen le[64] Ropere for the house in front of le Byggyng 'ad placitum' 2s., 2 fowl

De Reginaldo Scot pro tenemento iuxta Ad Placitum ijs. j g'

From Reginald Scot for the tenement next along 'ad placitum' 2s., 1 fowl

De Willelmo le Ropere pro tenemento iuxta Ad Placitum ijs. j g'

From William le Ropere for the tenement next along 'ad placitum' 2s., 1 fowl

59. MS sic.
60. MS sic (*recte* le).
61. MS sic (*recte* la).

62. MS omits verb.
63. MS sic.
64. MS sic.

De Henrico le Scheperd pro tenemento iuxta
quondam Roberti de Malthous Ad Placitum iiijs. j g'
j g'

From Henry le Scheperd for the tenement next
along once Robert de Malthous's 'ad placitum' 4s., 1
cock, 1 hen

De uno Crofto ad Capud dicti tenementi quod
Rogerus de Stocton' tenet Ad Placitum xvjd.

From a croft at the head of the said tenement which
Roger de Stocton' holds 'ad placitum' 16d.

De Stephano Borhog pro tenemento suo iuxta quod
tenet libere iijs. j g' j g'

From Stephen Borhog for his tenement next along
which he holds from us freely 3s., 1 cock, 1 hen

De . . . pro tenemento quod tenet de Elemosinaria
Ad Placitum . . .

From . . . for the tenement which s/he holds from
the Almonry 'ad placitum' . . .

De Roberto Atthall' pro tenemento iuxta Ad
Placitum iijs.

From Robert Atthall' for the tenement next along
'ad placitum' 3s.

De Amicia Wodegate pro uno crofto quod tenet ad
capud dicti tenementi Ad Placitum viijd.

From Amice Wodegate for a croft which she holds
at the head of the said tenement 'ad placitum' 8d.

De Rogero de Stocton' pro tenemento iuxta
predictum tenementum Ad Placitum iijs.

From Roger de Stocton' for the tenement next to
the aforesaid tenement 'ad placitum' 3s.

De Ricardo le latoner' pro tenemento iuxta Ad
Placitum iijs.

From Richard le Latoner' for the tenement next
along 'ad placitum' 3s.

De . . . pro tenemento quod tenet de Elemosinaria
iuxta dictum tenementum ad placitum . . .

From . . . for the tenement which s/he holds from
the Almonry next to the aforesaid tenement 'ad
placitum' . . .

De . . . pro tenemento quod tenet de Elemosinaria
iuxta[65] Ad Placitum . . .

From . . . for the tenement which s/he holds from
the Almonry next along[65] 'ad placitum' . . .

De una domo ubi commune furnum est . . .

From a house where the common oven is . . .

De Roberto Mareshall' pro tenemento iuxta furnum
cum alia domo contigua Ad Placitum vs. j g'

From Robert Mareshall' for the tenement next to
the oven with another adjacent house 'ad placitum'
5s., 1 fowl

De Ricardo Glouere pro tenemento iuxta Ad
Placitum ijs.

From Richard Glovere for the tenement next along
'ad placitum' 2s.

De Matilda Donemowe pro tenemento iuxta Ad
Placitum ijs.

From Matilda Donemowe for the tenement next
along 'ad placitum' 2s.

De Petronella de Wetherby pro tenemento iuxta Ad
Placitum ijs.

From Petronilla de Wetherby for the tenement next
along 'ad placitum' 2s.

De Johanne Blynde pro tenemento iuxta quod tenet
de Cantaria Ad Placitum . . .

From John Blynde for the tenement next along
which he holds from the Cantarist 'ad placitum' . . .

De Eodem pro tenemento iuxta Ad Placitum iijs.

From the same for the tenement next along 'ad
placitum' 3s.

De Rogero Nottyng pro tenemento iuxta Ad
Placitum xvd.

From Roger Nottyng for the tenement next along
'ad placitum' 15d.

[f. 189r]
De Reginaldo Moyses pro tenemento iuxta Ad
Placitum iiijs. vjd.

From Reginald Moyses for the tenement next along
'ad placitum' 4s. 6d.

65. MS sic.

De Alicia ladde pro tenemento iuxta Ad Placitum iiijs.

From Alice Ladde for the tenement next along 'ad placitum' 4s.

De Alicia uxore Rogeri Staleworth' pro tenemento iuxta quondam Joh'[66] de Anecote Ad Placitum vs. j gallum j gallinam[67]

From Alice, Roger Staleworth's wife, for the tenement next along once Joan/John[66] de Anecote's 'ad placitum' 5s., 1 cock, 1 hen[67]

De Henrico Steyne pro tenemento iuxta Ad Placitum ijs. vjd. j gallinam

From Henry Steyne for the tenement next along 'ad placitum' 2s. 6d., 1 hen

De Agnete de Hatherne pro tenemento iuxta Ad Placitum ijs. vjd. j gallinam

From Agnes de Hatherne for the tenement next along 'ad placitum' 2s. 6d., 1 hen

De Johanne de Wheston' pro tenemento iuxta Ad Placitum vs.

From John de Wheston' for the tenement next along 'ad placitum' 5s.

De Magg' de Rotheley pro tenemento iuxta Ad Placitum ijs. vjd. j gallinam

From Magg' de Rotheley for the tenement next along 'ad placitum' 2s. 6d., 1 hen

De Amicia Seynt pro tenemento iuxta Ad Placitum ijs. iijd. j gallum

From Amice Seynt for the tenement next along 'ad placitum' 2s. 3d., 1 cock

De Willelmo de Schepeshed pro tenemento iuxta Ad Placitum ijs. iijd. ij gallinas

From William de Schepeshed for the tenement next along 'ad placitum' 2s. 3d., 2 hens

De Ricardo de lauda pro tenemento iuxta Ad Placitum vs. vjd. j gallinam

From Richard de Lauda for the tenement next along 'ad placitum' 5s. 6d., 1 hen

De Crofto Retro tenementum suum Ad Placitum xviijd.

From the croft behind his tenement 'ad placitum' 18d.

De Ricardo de Pollesworth' pro tenemento iuxta Ad Placitum iiijs. ixd. j gallum

From Richard de Pollesworth' for the tenement next along 'ad placitum' 3s., 1 cock

De Henrico Mareshall pro tenemento iuxta Ad Placitum vs.

From Henry Mareshall for the tenement next along 'ad placitum' 5s.

De Leticia de Stafford' pro tenemento iuxta Ad Placitum iiijs. j gallum

From Letice de Stafford' for the tenement next along 'ad placitum' 4s., 1 cock

De uxore Th' Elmete pro tenemento iuxta Ad Placitum iiijs. j gallinam

From Thomas Elmete's wife for the tenement next along 'ad placitum' 4s., 1 hen

De Roberto Atthalle pro tenemento quod tenet libere vjd.

From Robert Atthalle for the tenement which he holds freely 6d.

De Johanne Russell' pro tenemento iuxta ubi sedet & cum salario quod tenet de Sacristaria unde percipiebamus ad officium Fabrice ferrarie xijd. Et ad officium Elemosinarie . . . Et ad officium Sacristarie . . .

From John Russell' for the tenement next along where he lives and with the wage which he holds from the Sacristy from which we take 12d. for the Farriery and . . . for the Almonry and . . . for the Sacristy

Liber Thome Catere militis[68]

The book of Thomas Catere, knight[68]

---

66. MS sic, and so gender cannot be determined.
67. From here the nouns are extended sufficiently in the MS.

68. In a later hand: at f. 189v ensues Bromkinthorpe, and at f. 191r Knighton.

Abbot Sadyngton of Leicester Abbey and Onychomancy: an Episode of Clerical Divination in the Fifteenth Century

Anthony Roe

On 25 July 1910 the Leicestershire Architectural and Archaeological Society organised a half-day excursion to Houghton on the Hill, Ingarsby and Quenby. An account of this outing, by the Reverend S. T. Winckley, contains some notes upon the building at Ingarsby.[1] The Old Hall there is of stone and, as the manor of Ingarsby formerly belonged to Leicester Abbey, the building is known by local tradition as 'the chapel' although no signs of any such structure remain. In his nineteenth-century directory, White notes that a building adjoining the Old Hall, used as a stable, was supposed to have been a chapel before the Reformation and that there were still a few fragments of stained glass in its windows.[2] In the fifteenth century the manor was the venue for a strange episode involving William Sadyngton, abbot of Leicester Abbey.

St Mary of the Meadows, the Abbey of the Assumption of the Blessed Virgin, was founded in Leicester in 1139 or 1140 and became one of the largest houses of the Augustinian order.[3] There had been forty canons there and twenty-six boys in the almonry for education but by 1440 there were only fifteen canons, with just six boys in the almonry.[4] William Sadyngton had been installed as abbot some twenty years earlier, in 1420.

In his historical introduction to the abbey, Fox noted that the first intimate glimpse of the internal working of the abbey is afforded by the record relating to the visitation of Bishop Alnwick conducted in 1440.[5] On the whole the state of things was not very satisfactory. Fifteen canons gave evidence before the bishop; a sixteenth was away. This number was far fewer than that which the house, if managed along proper lines, could support. Sadyngton was the cause of much dissatisfaction and the object of complaint. Apparently domineering and avaricious, he had engrossed the whole temporal business of the abbey. He ruled his brethren by terror and was suspected and accused of practising sorcery.[6] Moreover, he proved refractory at the visitation, refusing to submit the usual documents and with the canons showing no willingness to support him. The annual

Acknowledgements: Thanks are accorded to Dr Nicholas Bennett of Lincoln Cathedral Library, to Adrian Wilkinson, Archivist with Lincolnshire County Council, and to the Diocesan Registrar of Lincoln for granting access to the Visitation Book in Lincolnshire Archives. Grateful thanks are also recorded to Ms Joan Elliott of Leominster for her calculation of the 1439 horoscope. The interest and support of Professor Kieckhefer of Northwestern University in Evanston, Illinois, was very much appreciated, and his comments were obligingly received. Last but not least indebtedness is due to Mrs Linda Brookes for word-processing the article.

1. S. T. Winckley, 'Excursion to Houghton on the Hill, Ingarsby and Quenby', *TLAAS* 10 (1911–12), 254–6.

2. W. White, *History, gazetteer and directory of Leicestershire and the small county of Rutland* (Sheffield 1846), 440.

3. D. Crouch, 'The foundation of Leicester Abbey and other problems', *Midland History* 12 (1987), 1–13 at 3–4, and *idem*, 'Early charters and patrons of Leicester Abbey', below, pp. 225–87.

4. D. Knowles and R. N. Hadcock, *Medieval religious houses in England and Wales* (London 1971), 163.

5. L. Fox, *Leicester Abbey: history and description* (3rd edn. Leicester 1971), 7.

6. VCH *Leics.* ii, 15.

income of the house was estimated at £1,180 (over a quarter of a million pounds in today's money) and it was reckoned that the abbot must have had at least a thousand pounds in hand, of which he gave no account. Perhaps in response to his hard rule, an accusation of sorcery was made against Abbot Sadyngton; he narrowly escaped from this charge, evading deprivation of his office by the bishop.

Further details of the exercise by the abbot of what the Bible calls 'curious arts' (Acts 19:19) are given by Kittredge in his survey of witchcraft.[7] He tells us that some of the abbot's money apparently had been stolen and that he called the brethren together and declared that one of their number must be the thief. Nobody would confess and so he had recourse to sorcery to find the culprit. Sadyngton took himself away from the abbey to the grange at Ingarsby to perform his rituals. After certain incantations he anointed the thumbnail of a boy and bade him tell what he saw. As a result of the boy's vision, the abbot accused Canon Thomas Asty of the theft. Bishop Alnwick subsequently allowed the abbot to purge himself of the consequent charge of sorcery.

Scrying in its several species – employing variously a mirror, a crystal stone, a basin of water, a sword-blade, or a polished fingernail (this latter practice properly called onychomancy) – has a long history in England. The object of the exercise was ordinarily to detect a thief, or to discover the whereabouts of lost or stolen items, although it could be applied to any kind of secret. The scryer (one who descries, reveals, or discovers with the eye) was regularly a young boy, for the doctrine was that spiritual visions were only vouchsafed to the pure in heart in accordance with the sixth beatitude, 'Blessed are the pure in heart, for they shall see God' (Matthew 5:8).

'Specularii' was the technical, Latin term applied to users of scrying. Such persons, according to John of Salisbury, the twelfth-century scholastic philosopher and bishop of Chartres, defended their art on the ground that they make no offerings, harm nobody, often do good service by revealing thefts, seeking only truth that is useful or necessary.[8] However, these pretexts, John contended, were groundless, since the invocations that preceded the scryer's vision were by no means orthodox. Chaucer's parson had no doubt on this point: 'Lat us go now thilke horrible swering of adiuracioun and coniuracioun, as doon this enchantours or nigromanciens'.[9]

Indeed, when John of Salisbury was a boy he had been entrusted to a priest to learn the Psalter. This priest was a practitioner of magic, and he attempted to use John and another boy as scryers. After invoking certain demons, he had the boys look at their fingernails, which he had smeared with holy oil, and at a polished bowl. The other boy saw some indistinct and cloudy images, but John could discern nothing of the sort, and was therefore shut out whenever his tutor undertook these experiments in the speculary art.[10]

In 1311 Ralph Baldock, Bishop of London, sent a letter to his archdeacon directing him to investigate the matter of sorcery and magic in the city and the diocese, since he had learned that these arts had many practitioners there. Among other abuses it appeared that, for the recovery of lost articles or for the revelation of the future, certain persons 'professed that they invoked spirits in fingernails, mirrors, stones, and rings, or similar materials, which spirits, as they pretend, give vain responses and make signs'.[11]

7. G. L. Kittredge, *Witchcraft in Old and New England* (Cambridge, MA 1929), 187.

8. John of Salisbury, *Policraticus* ii.28; C. C. J. Webb, ed. *Iohannis Saresberiensis episcopi Carnotensis Policratici*, 2 vols (Oxford 1909), i, 161

9. Chaucer, 'The Parson's Tale'; W. W. Skeat, ed. *The complete works of Geoffrey Chaucer*, 7 vols (Oxford 1899), iv, 607.

10. John of Salisbury, as n. 8.

11. R. C. Fowler, ed. *Registrum Radulphi Baldock*, Canterbury and York Society 7 (Woodbridge 1911), 144–5.

Such thief-catching magic had been condemned previously by Robert Brunne in 1303: 'If you ever had to do with nigromancy, or made sacrifices to the devil through witchcraft, or paid any man to raise the devil in order to disclose anything stolen, you have sinned. If you have made any child look in sword or basin, or thumbnail or in crystal – all that, men call witchcraft'.[12]

In 1467 William Byg was accused of heresy and sorcery in the court of the Archbishop of York. He confessed that for the past two or three years he had practised scrying for the recovery of stolen goods but claimed that he never saw anything himself. His scryer was a boy of less than twelve years. He put in the boy's hand a crystal stone ('unum lapidem cristallum') and made him repeat a pater noster, an ave, and a credo, as well as the prayer that follows: 'Lord Jesus Christ send us three angels from the right-hand direction who shall tell or show us the truth about these things which we shall ask'. Sometimes the boy saw the stolen goods in the crystal, sometimes the thieves, sometimes one or two angels. When the boy saw an angel or angels, Byg adjured them in Latin to reveal the truth, and then the boy saw the thieves and the stolen goods. A score of times the boy had seen nothing. Byg gave examples of items and money recovered, with names. Interestingly, he had learned the art from one Arthur Mitton of Leicester, some three years earlier.[13]

Abbot Sadyngton's experiments in magical divination are recorded in the account of the bishop of Lincoln's visitation to Leicester Abbey, written down by Thomas Colstone, a public notary, and contained in the official account of the bishop's visitations for the years 1436–49. The surviving manuscript record of 135 leaves, originally comprised of seventeen unbound quires, found in a decayed state in the Alnwick Tower of the Old Palace in Lincoln early in the last century, now forms a bound volume in the Diocesan Registry held by Lincolnshire Archives. Folios 104–6 cover the visitation of the bishop of Lincoln to the abbey on 3 December 1440. Folio 105 bears the telling relation of Abbot Sadyngton's misdemeanour. The last paragraph on the recto of that leaf (fig. 1) details the accusation against him regarding onychomancy, in the following words:

> Frater Willelmus Sadyngtone, abbas . . . vt vel in fide dubius vel a fide et determinacione ecclesie catholica deuians, contra huismodi fidem et determinacionem pro certa sui pecunia a cista sua ablatis, circiter v marcis vel eo amplius, exercuit in persona sua sortilegium siue incantaciones hoc modo, videlicet in vigilia vel in die festi sancti Mathei apostoli, anno Domini mccccxxxix, apud Ingwardeby sumpsit sibi unum puerum nomine Mauricium, et obseruata quadam supersticione dampnata vnxit vnguem pollicis illius pueri, mandans

Fig. 1. Lincolnshire Archives, Visitation Book vj 1, f. 105r

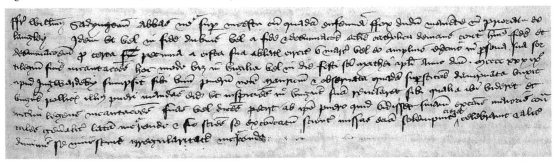

12. F. J. Furnivall, ed. *Robert of Brunne's Handlyng Synne*, Roxburghe Club (London 1862), 12–13, vv. 339–54.

13. G. Nevill, 'William Byg alias Lech, a fifteenth-century wizard', *The Archaeological Journal* 13 (1856), 372–4.

eidem vt inspiciens in vnguem suam reuelaret sibi qualia ibi videret, et interim legens incantaciones suas vel dicens peciit ab ipso puero quid vidisset, sentenciam excommunicaciones maioris contra tales generaliter latam incurrendo; et sic sciens se excommunicatum, missas eciam solempniter citra celebrauit et aliter diuinis se inmisciut, irregularitatem incurrendo.[14]

Such was the testimony, possibly of Robert Grene, sub-sacrist, in his deposition to the bishop against the abbot. It indicates that the abbot followed the time-honoured practice of taking a boy ('sumpsit sibi unum puerum'), then anointed the boy's thumbnail, and asked him to relate what he saw therein whilst the abbot himself recited incantations. Hamilton Thompson translates the tell-tale paragraph, thus:

> Brother William Sadyngton, the abbot . . . whether as one wavering in faith or straying from the faith and the fixed judgement of the catholic church, did practice in his own person, contrary to such faith and fixed judgement, divination or incantations after this manner, to wit, on the eve or on the day of the feast of St Matthew the apostle, in the year of our Lord 1439, at Ingarsby, he took to himself a boy, Maurice by name, and observing a damnable superstition, smeared the boy's thumbnail, bidding him look upon his nail and discover to him what sort of things he saw there, and, reading or saying his charms the while, asked of the same boy what he had seen, incurring the sentence of the greater excommunication passed against such persons in general; and knowing himself to be thus excommunicate, has since then celebrated masses, even in solemn wise, and otherwise has taken part in divine service, incurring irregularity.[15]

In his study of Leicester Abbey where the episode involving Sadyngton and Maurice is related, Hamilton Thompson notes that by the end of the fifteenth century the abbey library contained numerous astrological books.[16] Abbot Sadyngton would have been aware of the injunction, 'To every thing there is a season, and a time for every purpose under the heaven' (Ecclesiastes 3:1). He might well have chosen an astrologically suitable time to pursue his exercise of the scryer's art, applying rules perhaps taken from astrological manuals in the library. Presumably he chose Ingarsby as being away from prying eyes and the bustle of the abbey.

A catalogue of the abbey library, datable to between 1477 and 1494, copied in part by Prior William Charyte (Bodl. Library, Laud Misc. 623) was published by M. R. James in the *Transactions* of the Society, edited by Hamilton Thompson.[17] They were of the view that the tastes of Abbot Sadyngton, who had enriched the library signally in its medical side – he had brought nine medical books from John Bokedene, a 'medicus' – may have increased its resources in kindred sciences, such as alchemy and astrology.[18] Late medieval medicine operated along astrological lines: for example, in *The Canterbury Tales*, Chaucer's doctor was guided by natural magic, and had a copy of a handbook by Haly Imbrani to help him treat his patients according to the precepts of astrology.[19]

14. Lincolnshire Archives, Visitation Book, vj i, f. 105.

15. *Records of visitations held by William Alnwick, bishop of Lincoln, Part 1*, ed. A. Hamilton Thompson, *Visitations of religious houses in the diocese of Lincoln* ii, Canterbury and York Society 24 (London 1919), 212.

16. A. Hamilton Thompson, *The Abbey of St Mary of the Meadows, Leicester* (Leicester 1949), 217.

17. M. R. James, 'Catalogue of the library of Leicester Abbey', *TLAS* 19 (1936–7), 111–61, 377–440, and ibid. 21 (1940–1), 1–88. See now T. Webber and A. G. Watson, *The Libraries of the Augustinian canons*, CBMLC 6 (London 1998), 104–399, catalogue A20 where the astronomical books are listed as A20.1160–7; also T. Webber, 'The books of Leicester Abbey', above pp. 127–46 and M. Gullick and T. Webber, 'Summary catalogue of surviving manuscripts from Leicester Abbey', above no. 16.

18. Hamilton Thompson, *Leicester Abbey*, 215. On the books acquired by Sadyngton for the abbey, see Webber, 'The books of Leicester Abbey', above p. 142, n. 101.

19. Skeat, ed. *Geoffrey Chaucer*, iv, 416.

In one item described in the abbey library catalogue, among a collection headed 'Astronomia',[20] we find this very handbook on the choice of hours (*De electione horarum*) by Haly Imbrani and the book of nine judges (*Liber novem judicum*), a compilation of various authorities, together with necessary rules to observe in 'Canones austrologie', and various 'computi' or calculation books for the reckoning of times and seasons, calendars and tables on the Alphosine model from Toledo, as 'Tabule solis de anno bisextili et iij annis sequentibus'. The catalogue also notes a small collection of astronomical instruments.[21] At this period astronomy and astrology were a united discipline. The inclusion of an opuscule titled 'Liber de arte notaria' ('Book on the art of notation') might be considered out of place within the same catalogue item, unless perchance it was misdescribed as a manual of 'ars notoria', the 'angelic art', which used invocations comprised of many mystical names, well-known later from a seventeenth-century English version by Robert Turner.[22] Other, singular works of astrological symbolism are found listed, including one by Thebit ben Corat, the sage from Harran, the last repository of ancient star lore inherited from Babylon, and even a book by the Egyptian mystagogue Hermes. All these works point to a treasury of ancient knowledge held in the abbey library to which Abbot Sadyngton had ready access. The library was thus well provided with guidance on occult practice.

Primed with these and cognate sources it is possible to appraise the circumstances of the actual rite carried out by Sadyngton and performed for him by the boy Maurice. Onychomancy is a mode of divination under the auspices of the sun, according to the old authority, John Gaule in 'Mysmantia' (1652).[23] This prompts an astrological analysis as being most apposite. Astrology relates planets to their position in the zodiac. The circle of the celestial regions is divided into twelve thirty-degree sections, called Houses of Heaven; the positions of the planets (and the sun and moon) represent powers active within the Houses, and their relationship to each other (angular distances called aspects) significantly influence the meanings attached to them at any given moment for which a diagram of their positions – known as a horoscope – is drawn up.

The sun is most potent at noon and so, given this time for the enactment of the rite of nail divination, such being under solar auspices, a horoscope cast for 20 September 1439 (St Matthew's Eve), gives the zodiac sign Sagittarius as the sign ascending on the eastern horizon, the key position of the whole chart. With deference to the jargon of astrologics, the sun is in the fifth degree of Libra which was the sign designated since Graeco-Roman times for works of necromancy – an effective demon of that sign being 'a spirit of justice and truth'.[24] In horary astrology, which provides answers to specific queries, the second house of heaven is given over to personal possessions and lost items. Abbot Sadyngton most likely would have been familiar with the Campanus system of house division (originated by Johannus Campanus towards the end of the thirteenth century), which gives the cusp or first point of the second house in our chart as nineteen degrees of Capricorn. Jupiter, which governs priests, is conjunct this point within two degrees. Moreover, Jupiter is Lord of the Ascendant, and in close favourable sextile aspect with Venus, herself ruler of the sun in this chart. The sun is also in conjunction with Mercury in Libra, and Mercury, the Prince of Thieves, is posited in the eleventh house yet lord of the seventh, betokening some friend

20. Webber and Watson, *Libraries of the Augustinian canons*, A20.1160; James, 'Catalogue', 20–1, no. 682.

21. Webber and Watson, *Libraries of the Augustinian canons*, 324–5, and Webber, 'The books of Leicester Abbey', above p. 141, n. 97.

22. R. Turner, *Ars Notoria: The notory art of Solomon* (London 1657).

23. R. H. Robbins, *The encyclopaedia of witchcraft and demonology* (London 1970), 139.

24. P. Christian, *The history and practice of magic*, 2 vols (London 1952), ii, 477.

or person in trust, or that has done the querent (i.e. the Abbot) some service. This would certainly include Canon Asty whom Abbot Sadyngton accused.

Thus the astrological scenario is well 'elected' – to use the astrological term – for performance of the nail divination. The meridional prayers used, recited between the canonical hours of sext and none, would have included the customary Psalm 119 (Psalm 118 in the Vulgate, beginning, 'Beati immaculati in via, qui ambulant in lege Domini': 'Blessed are the undefiled in the way, who walk in the law of the LORD') for that time of the day. This psalm is unique in having the names of the letters of the Hebrew alphabet as the initial words of each verse in turn, the perfect text to facilitate the required concatenation of sounds to enunciate the divine names as dictated by the notory art. To enhance the ritual performance, the abbot could have used a seal of the sun as described in the manual by Thebit ben Corat, or frankincense as an appropriate matutinal incense prior to a noon rite. Sadyngton might also have enjoined Maurice to recite prayers, perhaps like those William Byg was accused of using in 1467 which he claimed to have learned from a Leicester source. If the abbot himself had invoked a particular spirit it could have been Adnachiel, the angel of the ascendant at the time of the operation, being the ruler of Sagittarius, as we learn from a listing given by Benjamin Camfield, a seventeenth-century rector of Aylestone, in his discourse on celestial beings.[25]

As to the actual ritual and incantations used by Abbot Sadyngton, there is an intimation from a rare manuscript from the period, now Munich, Bayerische Staatsbibliothek Clm 849, which contains a work entitled 'Liber de nigromancia' that some suggest was used by a cleric.[26] Kieckhefer, in a preliminary chapter to his edition of the work, suggests that in all likelihood necromancy was studied and practised within a kind of clerical underworld through much if not most of Western Europe in the later Middle Ages.[27] For example, Johannes Hartlieb, who served the Duke of Bavaria in Munich, wrote a 'Book of All Forbidden Arts', between 1456 and 1464, in which he describes many of the practices detailed in the manuscript, including the anointing of a boy's fingernail for scrying. It is not possible, however, to establish a clear connection between Hartlieb and the Munich manuscript.

This necromancer's manual of the early fifteenth century has five divinatory experiments requiring a child medium to gaze at his own fingernail or thumbnail. The rituals are elaborate, with an initial regimen followed by repeated conjurations and questioning of spirits who appear in the polished nail, the focus of attention for the juvenile scryer. The thumbnail, of the left hand, is first scraped clean. A slip with magical names is then bound to the thumb on its underside. The master of the operation, who has chosen the pure boy ('accipe puerum virginem'), recites his conjurations meanwhile, some into the ear of the boy, perhaps three times. The child may become aware of various degrees of brightness and is commanded to describe truthfully what he sees. Signings of the cross are used at various points and sundry spirits are summoned by name. Some of the rituals take place within a triple circle drawn with the boy's and other, holy names, in which the child sits on a three-legged stool. In one version the master brandishes a sword. In another instance the master places one of the boy's thumbs over the other and anoints with olive oil the uppermost thumbnail. Prayers are directed towards the East; the Trinity is invoked; Christ is addressed and his miracles recited; conjurations are uttered in the names of the nine orders of blessed angels; apparitions are constrained by the tears of the Virgin Mary.[28]

25. B. Camfield, *A theological discourse of angels and their ministries* (London 1678), 67.

26. R. Kieckhefer, *Forbidden rites* (Stroud 1997).

27. Ibid. 34.

28. Ibid. 108–12 for details of the ceremonies.

The boy Maurice, used by Abbot Sadyngton, was probably a lad from the abbey rather than a local boy from Ingarsby Grange. To be useful as a medium the child would have needed to be sensitive, intelligent and articulate, and perhaps beholden to the abbot in some way. Hamilton Thompson noted that in 1440 according to Canon Belgrave there were only six boys left in the almonry: they were under-nourished, received no elementary instruction, and were paid by the canons for running their errands, while the abbot had brought lads who were entirely unsuitable into the almonry for a fee.[29] It is certain that Abbot Sadyngton was disposed to worldly interests and pleasures. At the visitation of Bishop Alnwick that year he also stood also accused of an affair with Euphemia Fox who lived at Langley priory. He traded in horseflesh and had seemingly accumulated unaccounted funds. An alleged loss of money had previously led him to send his manservant William Banastre to Market Harborough to consult a wise woman regarding its recovery.[30] A penchant for mystical practices for the accumulation of wealth is evidenced from his employment of an alchemist, Robert, who lodged in the gatehouse of the abbey. The abbot's attitude to such things may have disposed him to engage in the experiment with Maurice.[31]

When Sadyngton and the boy returned to Leicester after their magical retirement in Ingarsby, the abbot summoned the convent to chapter and, based upon Maurice's vision of the thief, accused Thomas Asty of the latest theft of his monies. When Asty endeavoured to exculpate himself in confession, the abbot refused to absolve him and went away 'in a passion'. Afterwards, because Asty threatened to complain to the bishop, the abbot retaliated by repeating Asty's confession.[32] It should be remembered that the object of an episcopal visitation was not just the collection of examples of virtue but also the reformation of abuses; hence the records show evidence of what Hamilton Thompson has called 'petty frivolity' and 'mutual jealousy'.[33] He argued that if such abuses were prominent it need not follow that virtues were wholly excluded by them. In examining the documentary evidence such circumstances should be kept in mind, with due allowance for the strength of human nature, even in lives which had taken shelter from it behind the barrier of monastic vows.

Abbot Sadyngton undoubtedly felt the lure of the outer world and yielded to financial temptations that he sought to indulge by means both secular and sacerdotal. His behaviour certainly did not foster orthodox spirituality. Yet on the whole the abbey survived the searching test of the bishop's visitation fairly well and no serious immorality was disclosed. The charge of incontinence against the abbot appears not to have been sustained and he was allowed to purge himself of the charge of having practised divination.[34]

Kieckhefer has suggested that the case of William Sadyngton is related to the divinatory procedures found in the Munich handbook of necromancy, although he is not sure that he would assume that the incantations Abbot Sadyngton was alleged to have used were necessarily demonic.[35] Perhaps Sadyngton accepted licence for his art from the authority of Augustine of Hippo, founding father of his order. In his 'De incantationibus et divinationibus' the renowned scholar Ivo of Chartres (c. 1100) claimed the authority of Augustine to adjudge: 'Divination is not anything to do with evil, but a human concern with the doubtful, and a means of indicating the divine will'.[36]

29. Hamilton Thompson, *Leicester Abbey*, 64; idem. *Visitations*, 208–9.

30. Ibid. 209.

31. Ibid. 210.

32. Ibid. 211.

33. A. Hamilton Thompson, 'The monasteries of Leicestershire in the fifteenth century', *TLAAS* 11 (1913–14), 89–108 at 108.

34. VCH *Leics.* ii, 15.

35. Kieckhefer, pers. comm.

36. 'Sors non aliquid mali est, scilicet res in dubitatione humana, divinam indicans voluntatem'; Ivo of Chartres, *Panormia*, PL 161, col. 77.

Considering the serious nature of the evidence brought against him, Abbot Sadyngton was treated leniently in the carefully composed injunctions issued by a compassionate bishop in the course of the month following the visitation. Bishop Alnwick 'came with his hoe' to root out weeds that grew in the Lord's garden. Testimony at the visitation indicates that the behaviour of Sadyngton was generally reprehensible. Attempts at divination are consonant with this conclusion. Later ages would condemn such practices as superstitious but in the milieu of the fifteenth century such activities were at least a veracious, albeit not a valid, procedure for a cleric to indulge in. Abbot Sadyngton was recalcitrant in front of the bishop but the occult antics attributed to him were in no way flagitious, as the judgement of the bishop confirms. John Pomery, sub-prior (who had preached the visitation sermon from Matthew 21:5, likening the bishop's arrival to the Lord's entry into Jerusalem) succeeded Sadyngton as abbot, and ruled for thirty-two years. We know nothing more of the boy Maurice or what happened to Thomas Asty. The Old Hall at Ingarsby stands in the place where the abbot of Leicester Abbey was said to have performed his unorthodox rites. Of Sadyngton, however, we know little more, except that he died within a year of the bishop's visitation to Leicester.

Early charters and patrons of Leicester Abbey

David Crouch

The charters of Leicester abbey did not, for the most part, survive the Reformation. The abbey's muniments, comprising many hundreds of deeds, fines, rentals, terriers and inquisitions, were not among those which found a home in some gentry archive or in Henry VIII's Court of Augmentations. In the case of some abbeys and priories whose original charters were also lost, this sort of documentary tragedy is softened by the survival of a pre-Reformation cartulary, a register of transcripts of the charter texts. Cartularies were created for the sake of ease of reference and insurance against the perishing of the originals. What makes things a little worse in the case of Leicester abbey is the fact that the abbey had produced several cartularies by the end of the fifteenth century. We hear about an 'old cartulary' ('vetus Chartwary'; A20.1864) or the 'old book of evidences', probably written in the later thirteenth century; a more comprehensive later cartulary ('The Chartwary'; A20.1863) probably of the fourteenth century,[1] which included records of concords and pleas as well as charters; and a further fifteenth-century single volume work, compiled by William Charyte ('secundus liber de Chartwary'; A20.1865) specially to include charters the earlier volumes had omitted.[2] But the cartularies did not survive the Reformation any more than did the abbey's charters. With them went a lot of Leicestershire's history, as well as the history of the abbey. The charters and cartularies had been lost long before they could come to the notice of any sixteenth- or seventeenth-century antiquary with a mind to transcribe medieval Leicestershire deeds.

The one consolation in this catalogue of archival disasters is that in the 1470s William Charyte, prior of Leicester, who had himself compiled and 'caused to be written' the last of the cartularies, compiled along with it a number of breviates or registers, summarising the content of the cartularies, complete with material from now-lost abbey rentals of 1254 (called 'de Pyn'; A20.1868),

Acknowledgments: I would like to thanks all those who assisted in the compilation and editing of this collection, some are thanked particularly in the appropriate place, but special mentions are due to Dr Margaret Bonney of the Leicestershire Archives Service, and to Judy Burg of the Brynmor Jones Library, University of Hull. For help with dating, I must thank Professor Richard Sharpe and Leofranc Holford-Strevens.

1. The fourteenth-century date of the second cartulary (A20.1863) is implied by the date of the handwriting of the endorsement on the one surviving original charter of the abbey, which may be associated with the compilation of the cartulary (on this charter see M. Gullick and T. Webber, 'Summary catalogue of surviving manuscripts from Leicester Abbey', above p. 192, no. 25

and below, 249–52 no. 24).

2. For the cartularies see the 'libri et rotule evidenciarium nostrarum' in the surviving catalogue of the abbey library; M. R. James, 'Catalogue of the library of Leicester Abbey', TLAHS 19 (1935–37), 118–61, 378–440; 21 (1939–41), 2–88, especially, 21, p. 53, and T. Webber and A. G. Watson, ed. The libraries of the Augustinian canons, CBMLC 6 (London 1988), 389–90 (reference numbers A20.1863–7 also used here). See also the reference in Bodl. Laud misc. 625, f. 143r, 'Ista carta est in uetere libro euidentiarum cum nigro copertorio in quaternis' which may be a reference to A20.1864 (see M. Gullick, 'The binding descriptions in the library catalogue from Leicester Abbey', above p. 160 and n. 100). The digest of the catalogue in J. Nichols, The history and antiquities of the county of Leicester, 4 vols in 8 (London 1795–1815), i. pt 2, Appendix p. 167, is misleading.

1341 (called 'Geryn'; A20.1870) and 1408 (called 'Bathe' in the catalogue; A20.1871). He also abstracted material from the Lincoln diocesan archives, notably the 'matriculus' of Bishop Hugh de Wells, and some secular records, including the lost account rolls of the twelfth-century earldom.[3] The intention was to provide a consolidated digest of matter relating to the title of all the abbey properties for easy reference. Unlike Charyte's cartulary (A20.1865), this work does survive as a working copy written largely in William Charyte's own hand, labelled at the front of the book (on f. iir) by a post-medieval scribe as the 'rentale novum generale monasterii beate Marie de Pratis Leycestr[ie]'. It is now amongst the Laudian manuscripts in the Bodleian Library in Oxford, and is in very good condition.[4] A fire-damaged and shorter copy of the breviate by Charyte is amongst the Cotton manuscripts in the British Library.[5] The significance of Charyte's work for anyone studying the fragments of the archive of Leicester abbey is that he gives us at least a guide to the contents of the lost cartularies and some idea of the way they had been compiled.

Prior Charyte's register did not summarise the full contents of the lost cartularies, but it does tell us something of their structure. It indicates that the 'old cartulary' (A20.1864) containing charters of founders and benefactors was compiled at the end of the thirteenth century, for no donor whom Charyte noted as featuring in it lived later than the 1260s. Like many cartularies it commenced with sequences of charters of founders, kings, popes, and bishops, and it also seems to have had a brief foundation chronicle as an introduction.[6] Most of the rest of the volume seems to have been devoted to charters relating to properties in the town of Leicester itself, of which there were at least 183, as appears from a reference to a charter concerning land outside the east gate as 'carta clxxxiijᵒ'.[7] The second and later cartulary (A20.1863) concerned rural properties and was organised under topographical headings in alphabetical order.[8] We can glimpse some of the contents of those chapters. For instance, the section on the estate of *Berwode* (in Curdworth, Warwicks.) contained at least fourteen charters. It began with two charters of the original donor, Hugh of Arden, then copied two successive confirmation charters of Hugh's overlords, William (1153–84) and Waleran (1184–1203), earls of Warwick. The succeeding ten charters included confirmations and further grants from Hugh's heirs, Thomas I and Thomas II of Arden, and other earlier charters relating to the property which were not directed to the abbey but which reflected on its title.[9]

This all gives us some indication of the volume of material that has been lost since 1539. But not all has been lost. For a variety of reasons a large number of twelfth- and thirteenth-century

3. A copy of the 'matriculus' made at Leicester after the compilation of the catalogue (s. xv/xvi) is BL Cotton Nero D x ff. 140–197 on which see Gullick and Webber, 'Summary catalogue', above pp. 182–3, no. 13.

4. Bodl. Laud misc. 625, on which see Gullick and Webber, 'Summary catalogue', above pp. 185–6, no. 17. It can be identified as the 'nouum Rentale' in the catalogue, A20.1872. On the identification of Charyte's hand, see Webber and Watson, *Libraries of the Augustinian canons*, 170.

5. In his catalogue of the library, Charyte mentions two 'new rentals' that he had 'caused to be made', one of which he had copied himself; James, 'Catalogue', xxi, 59 and Webber and Watson, *Libraries of the Augustinian canons*, 390–1 (A20.1872–3). Bodl. Laud misc. 625 would seem to be the first of the two he described 'compilatum et scriptum per manu fratris Willemi Charite'; the second of them, which had lists of advowsons and

rents, mills and titles, may be the fire-damaged Leicester register, now BL Cotton Vitellius F xvii (see Gullick and Webber, 'Summary catalogue', above p. 183, no. 15).

6. See the 'cronica brevis de fundatore nostro', A20.648, with fuller details at A20.1332.

7. The charters of the earls of Leicester were apparently provided in a book called 'le primo libro de Chartwary' (that is, either A20.1863 or A20.1864 in the library catalogue) see Bodl. Laud misc, 625, on f. 88v. For the 183rd Leicester charter, ibid. f. 84v.

8. There is a reference in Bodl. Laud misc. 625, f. 8r to the 'ijᵒ libro de Chartwary' (ie: A20.1865) containing the first, second and seventh charters in a section of charters relating to the abbey's properties in King's Norton. The charters of Gotham, Stoughton and Knighton were also in 'iᵒ libro de Chartwary', ibid. ff. 65v, 81r, 128v.

9. Ibid. f. 22r–v.

Leicester abbey charter texts survive. These amount to ninety-four texts. All but one of them are copies of the originals. There remains to us the original of one early charter, preserved now amongst the Sloane charters in the British Library (see below, Appendix no. 24).[10] This is a confirmation to the abbey by Earl Robert IV of Leicester of his predecessors' grants. It is clear that it was once a part of the abbey's archive, because it was endorsed with archival press marks, notably a fourteenth-century hand that marked it: 'ij^a in [cartis] fund[atorum] pro pastura in Desforde'. This would indicate that it once lay in a box of founders' charters in a bundle collected together as evidences concerning the abbey's pasture at Desford, west of Leicester. It is the same charter that was copied into the abbey's second cartulary, according to Charyte, as 'the confirmation of Robert son of Petronilla by his charter of all the grants namely which his grandfather, father and men gave us, as in his first charter'.[11]

The bulk of the surviving early Leicester abbey texts exist only in the form of later copies. These are drawn from a variety of sources and most have only recently come to light. A few charters were transcribed rather than summarised by Prior Charyte in the fifteenth century, but most come from enrolments by medieval Exchequer and Chancery clerks. The great prize, the text of the abbey's lost foundation charter resurfaced only in 1985, discovered by myself while working on London sources in the fourteenth-century plea rolls of the Exchequer (class E13 in the National Archives). A second and later version of it was discovered in 1991 by Nicholas Vincent in a volume of early sixteenth-century transcripts of monastic deeds deposited in Winchester Cathedral library.[12] The plea roll E13/76, dating to 1351, in fact contained a total of seventy-one enrolled texts of deeds, by far the biggest collection of early material relating to Leicester abbey.[13] The roll includes copies of almost all of the abbey's charters relating to its lands in Barkby, Hungarton and Thurmaston in Leicestershire and Bramcote and Curdworth in Warwickshire, a substantial fraction of its lost muniments. A further five otherwise unknown copies of texts relating to the abbey turned up in 1988 entered in the Chancery Confirmation Rolls (C56) of the reign of Henry VII: including two charters of Earl Simon de Montfort and three of Earl Roger de Quincy to the abbey.

The foundation of Leicester Abbey

We are therefore now in a far better position than was A. Hamilton Thompson in 1949 to assess the politics and patronage behind the foundation of Leicester abbey. In another place I have pointed out how the issue of the foundation charter can be dated to the end of 1139 or the beginning of 1140 at the latest.[14] The date of 1143 adopted by modern reference books for the foundation was therefore untenable. The date of 1143 had been taken by Prior Charyte from the work of his fourteenth-century predecessor, Henry Knighton.[15] Knighton's Chronicle reproduced the abbey's

---

10. There was a series of five original acts granting and confirming land at Kirby Bellars, Leics. to Leicester abbey amongst the Hastings deeds at the time they were catalogued in the 1920s. They are not now amongst the Hastings deeds at the Huntington Library in San Marino, and are yet to be located, see *Report on the manuscripts of the late Reginald Rawdon Hastings, Esq. of the Manor House, Ashby de la Zouche*, 4 vols. Historical Manuscripts Commission (London 1928–47), i, 87–8. These charters are also not listed in the digest of abbey charters in the Bodleian register.

11. Ibid. f. 5v. Also noted in the *Desforth* section, ibid. 59r.

12. For this remarkable source, N. Vincent, 'The early years of Keynsham Abbey', *Transactions of the Bristol and Gloucestershire Archaeological Society* 111 (1993), 95–113 at 95–7.

13. Two of these enrolled charters are omitted here, as the church of Barkby was the beneficiary in them, not the abbey.

14. D. Crouch, 'The foundation of Leicester Abbey and other problems', *Midland History* 12 (1987), 1–13 at 3–4.

15. *Chronicon Henrici Knighton*, ed. J. R. Lumby, Rolls Series 92, 2 vols. (London 1889–95), i, 62. See also G. H. Martin, *Knighton's Chronicle 1337–1396* (Oxford 1995); the earlier and less original part of the chronicle is edited in Lumby, *Chronicon*.

own list of its abbots, and is the 'Cronica Leycestr[ie]' listed in Prior Charyte's catalogue (A20.636).[16] Charyte abstracted this information and gave the date of the institution of the first abbot, Richard, as the eighth year of King Stephen (that is December 1143 to December 1144).[17] Knighton and Charyte both made the understandable assumption that the abbot had been elected and consecrated as soon as the community had been established. But in fact Leicester Abbey seems to have preserved an alternative tradition that its origins were earlier. When Charyte made his abstract of the foundation charter he added to it the observation: 'The date of this charter [is] around the year of Our Lord 1137'.[18] Since Charyte did not have the apparatus that we have to calculate the date from the charter's internal evidence, he must have found this nugget in a Leicester Abbey chronicle or document he had seen in his library that was unknown to Knighton.

The foundation charter most likely belongs to the autumn of 1139 but it is axiomatic now amongst historians of monasticism that the foundation process of any regular house could be a long and involved process. This would be particularly the case where, as in the case of Leicester Abbey, it was created out of an earlier and very different religious institution. The earlier institution in this case was the secular collegiate church of St Mary de Castro which stands to this day in the bailey of Leicester castle. Its origins are obscure. It is not known whether the church was a pre-Conquest foundation and whether it stood on its present site before the castle was built c. 1069. Several writers have played with the idea that St Mary de Castro might have been the pre-Conquest cathedral church of the defunct Anglo-Saxon see of Leicester.[19] This is unlikely, but the comparable case of the minster church of All Saints in Warwick, which was enclosed within the castle there when it was also built c. 1069, indicates that there is nothing unlikely about the idea of an intramural church being older than the castle which enclosed it. It is certainly possible that St Mary de Castro was one of the two churches in Leicester listed as held by Earl Robert's predecessor, Hugh de Grandmesnil, in the Domesday Survey.[20]

Some information about the early St Mary de Castro was preserved in the records of the abbey which succeeded it. Charyte copied out a historical memorandum concerning the minster which he found in the Geryn rental of 1341. It is in part a dubious source as it begins by saying that Count Robert of Meulan, father of Earl Robert the founder, received Leicester and its earldom from William the Conqueror. In fact he obtained it in 1107 from the Conqueror's son, Henry I. But the narration then takes on more detail, and it can be reasonably assumed that the rest of it was based on more than just legend, and most likely on an early text still then possessed by the abbey:

> Robert count of Meulan . . . rebuilt the same church of St Mary within the Castle, instituting there twelve secular canons and a dean, conferring on them and appropriating to them all the churches of Leicester (except the church of St Margaret, which was not in his power because it was and is a prebend of Lincoln cathedral) with five carrucates of land outside the north gate of the town and other possessions within it, and with all the churches of the soke of Shepshed and Halse and many other rents and possessions.[21]

16. Knighton's Chronicle survives in a late fourteenth century manuscript, BL Cotton Tiberius C vii; see Gullick and Webber, 'Summary catalogue', above p. 183, no. 14 and Webber and Watson, *Libraries of the Augustinian canons*, 236 (A20.636) where Webber identifies the Cotton manuscript on the basis of the second folio reference given in Charyte's catalogue.

17. Hence 'Monasterium istud fundatum fuit A° do[min]i M°.C°.XLIII°', Bodl. Laud misc. 625, f. 4v.

18. Ibid. f. 5r: 'Datum huius carte circa ann[um] domini M°.C°.xxxvij°'.

19. A. Hamilton Thompson, *The Abbey of St Mary of the Meadows, Leicester* (Leicester 1949), 1.

20. *Domesday Book seu liber censualis Willelmi primi regis Angliae*, ed. A. Farley and H. Ellis, 4 vols. (London 1783–1816), i, f. 230r.

21. Bodl. Laud misc. 625, f. 89r, and compare ibid. f. 185r.

Confirmatory evidence that the Geryn rental was citing Count Robert of Meulan's original diploma for St Mary de Castro can be found in the reference to the church of Clifton in Warwickshire, with its chapels of Over and Rugby, having formed one of the prebends 'of the castle of Leicester' in a digest of a charter of Arnold III du Bois, the seneschal of Earl Robert II.[22] This is confirmation that there had indeed been a reform and endowment of the collegiate church before 1118, which had involved the allocation of specific prebends. The other evidence is the abbey's foundation charter itself, which refers to the prebends of the secular canons of Leicester and the liberties and quittances they had enjoyed from Count Robert of Meulan. It even names the former dean, Gubert (see below).

The pre-1139 collegiate church of St Mary de Castro had been from this evidence very large and very wealthy, one of the greater secular colleges in the Anglo-Norman realm. It compared in size with other large contemporary collegiate churches, such as Christchurch in Twynham, which also had twelve canons and a dean.[23] Count Robert was in his day much involved with secular colleges. With his town of Meulan he had inherited in 1080 an ancient college of canons dedicated to St Nicaise, and he possessed an eleventh-century college dedicated to Holy Trinity within his castle of Beaumont in Normandy. In his castle at Meulan he himself built a small collegiate church dedicated to St Nicholas, the counterpart of St Mary de Castro at Leicester. King Henry also gave Count Robert the patronage of another large collegiate minster at Wareham in Dorset. We know that the count had been perfectly capable of taking a hand in the affairs of the collegiate churches under his patronage, because at some time between 1093 and 1115 he had converted his college of St Nicaise of Meulan into a Benedictine priory under the Norman abbey of Bec.[24]

In 1139 the count's younger twin son, Earl Robert II, did much the same with St Mary de Castro as his father had done with St Nicaise of Meulan a generation before. He also converted around the same time the collegiate church of St Mary at Wareham, which he had also inherited from his father, into a Benedictine priory dependent on his southern Norman abbey of Lyre. It cannot be a coincidence that in March 1139 in France, the other twin, Count Waleran of Meulan and Worcester, had granted his collegiate church of St Nicholas in the castle of Meulan to the abbey of Bec. We can probably put this sudden flurry of reform down to a movement in favour of the monastic orders within Earl Robert's immediate family. In the autumn of 1139 Count Waleran had founded a large abbey at Bordesley in Worcestershire, drawing the monks from his brother's Cistercian abbey of Garendon in Leicestershire. From the evidence of this and the Leicester foundation charter, it would seem that Leicester and Bordesley abbeys were literally twin foundations, even though Leicester was Augustinian and Bordesley was Cistercian. This in turn was related to the ascendancy of the twins at the court of King Stephen, which had been growing since the end of 1137, when the king had fallen under Waleran's spell on his Norman tour. Waleran had acquired an English earldom, and both twins amassed huge influence, which could partly be expressed through the foundation of large and prestigious abbeys.[25]

Another influence in the foundation of Leicester Abbey was undoubtedly the recent history of

22. Ibid. f. 43v.

23. For Twynham in 1114 see, Hermann of Laon, *De miraculis sancte Marie Laudunensis*, PL 156, col. 979. The choice of twelve canons and a dean is significantly the same as the basic complement necessary for founding an abbey, the apostolic number reflecting Christ and his disciples. It is possible that this comple-

ment might have been the result of a post-Conquest reform imposed on St Mary de Castro to improve its common life.

24. For this, Versailles, Archives départementales des Yvelines, 24 h 9, no. 13.

25. Crouch, 'Foundation of Leicester Abbey', 3–4; idem, *The reign of King Stephen, 1135–54* (London 2000), 68–70.

the relations between the earl and Bishop Alexander of Lincoln. In June 1139 Earl Robert had been one of a cabal of aristocrats who overthrew the bishop's uncle, Bishop Roger of Salisbury, the king's chief justiciar. Earl Robert had also taken an active part in persecuting Bishop Alexander. He had seized the bishop's castle of Sleaford and his estates in Leicestershire during the period when the king held Bishop Roger and his relatives in custody. Before the end of the summer, Earl Robert had been placed under an interdict until he returned the bishop's possessions. Earl Robert had since the 1120s been in dispute with the bishop over his estates within the town of Leicester and in the fields outside, based on the episcopal estate of Knighton. The earl went so far as to seize them in or soon after 1123, but by 1129 had returned them to Bishop Alexander under pressure from the king. The summer of 1139 was a crisis point in the relationship between the two great men. The foundation of Leicester Abbey may well have been part of the peace process to bring them together. It can be deduced that the earl returned to Alexander his castle of Sleaford and the bishop's urban properties in Leicester, but held on to Knighton outside the walls. Bishop Alexander's presence and consent at the formal foundation of the new Augustinian abbey in Leicester must have been part of the process of reconciliation and formalisation of the new order in Leicester.[26]

The scale of the earl's commitment to his Augustinian foundation seems not to have been profligate. The new abbey was financed on the back of the generosity of previous generations. The bulk of its endowment was formed from the prebends of the old minster. This is most clear in the case of the supposed grant by Arnold du Bois III to the new abbey of the church of Clifton-upon-Dunsmoor in Warwickshire. From the notice of Arnold's own charter to the abbey it appears that it was not a grant at all, but a confirmation: Clifton and its chapels (which included the church of Rugby) had previously been a prebend of the old minster, presumably granted to it in the time of the Grandmesnils or the count of Meulan. The same must be true of the lands and churches formerly of Dean Gubert and Osbert the canon, both former chaplains of the count of Meulan, and the same might reasonably be true of many of the other churches mentioned in the foundation charter. The extent of the earl's own generosity with land was no more than the grant of the manor of Asfordby, an acquisition from the king in the previous reign. His other major concession was the extension of the old minster's area of judicial exemption outside the North Gate. Even the abbey site itself had once been a possession of the minster. This is not to imply that the earl was ungenerous. There were undoubtedly invisible costs to the foundation, most notably the funds to construct a fitting new abbey church and buildings, and the costs of coming to a settlement with those of the former secular canons who had no intention of entering the cloister, even if the opportunity had been offered them. The involvement of the Augustinian prior and a canon of Kenilworth in the foundation charter and the absence of any Leicester Augustinians at that time, indicates that the charter was issued at an early stage of the foundation. Maybe the Kenilworth canons had been called in by the earl as consultants about the needs of instituting regular monastic life for the new foundation. Perhaps there were not in 1139 sufficient priests willing to enter the new abbey to commence its liturgical life. Complications and expenses such as these might very

---

26. For the fall of Bishop Roger and his relatives, K. Yoshitake, 'The arrest of the bishops in 1139 and its consequences', *Journal of Medieval History* 14 (1988), 97–114. For the rest see D. Crouch, 'Earls and bishops in twelfth-century Leicestershire', *Nottingham Medieval Studies* 37 (1993), 9–15. For the place of ecclesiastical assemblies and monastic foundations in the process of peace-making in England in the mid twelfth century, P. Dalton, 'Civil war and ecclesiastical peace in the reign of King Stephen' in *War and society in medieval and early modern Britain*, ed. D. Dunn (Liverpool 2000), 53–75 at 61–6.

well explain how it was that the first abbot was not installed until 1144, between four and five years after the formal act of foundation.

Earl Robert undoubtedly benefitted from the impressive new abbey eventually built on the northern meadows of his town. It would have offered a different scale of liturgy for Leicester, suitable for the court of such a princely figure as he was in mid twelfth-century England, a prime mover in the succession of Henry II to the throne in 1153–54 and, from 1155 onwards, chief justiciar of England. On his deathbed he was dressed in the habit of a canon of Leicester. He died on 5 April 1168. His body was buried in front of, and to the north of the abbey's high altar. The abbey had benefitted from his death and conversion with a grant of the manor of Stoughton and the mill at Belgrave, Leics. Since the earl's heart and internal organs were buried at the hospital he founded at Brackley in Northamptonshire, it is probable that he died and was embalmed at his castle there, and that he never actually lived as a canon within the precinct of Leicester, as later abbey legend said he did.[27]

Long before the earl died, his abbey had become a focus for his local political activity. His immediate family had offered their support. His elder twin brother offered the abbey twenty measures of salt per annum from his salt works at Droitwich in Worcestershire. His wife offered a rent of four pounds a year from her own revenues in Eversley in Wiltshire for the support of the fathers confined in the infirmary.[28] The earl's first cousin, Earl Roger of Warwick, had made a grant to the abbey of his church of Narborough, Leics. before he died in 1153. More intriguingly, Earl Ranulf II of Chester, Earl Robert's great rival for power in the Midlands, felt obliged at some time after they came to terms in 1149 to offer the abbey the church of his manor of Barrow-on-Soar, Leics. and a carrucate of land there, as well as a gift of two carrucates of land and some meadow near Rothley in Leicestershire.[29]

It was not until 1153 that the abbey received its first royal confirmation (Appendix no. 3). It was issued as one of many royal writs recognising in retrospect acts which had been carried out during the period of civil war. Such a confirmation was needed for two reasons. The first was that the king had by custom the right to appoint abbots to any house called an abbey, unless he had conceded it to another patron.[30] Earl Robert wanted it made clear that his new abbey was in his own patronage. The second reason was that the grants it concerned were made to the abbey at Droitwich and Rothley out of land which had once been part of the royal estates. Droitwich had come to Count Waleran in 1136 and Rothley (officially) to Earl Ranulf in April 1153. But over the summer of 1153 the shape of the settlement of the civil war had become clear, and it was to involve the reclamation by the king of the estates he had possessed in 1135. Both grants were therefore at risk, and Earl Robert was making efforts to secure them to the abbey by an act of royal recognition.[31] His plan was frustrated, if not by Stephen, then by Henry II when he came to the throne in 1154. Droitwich and Rothley are significantly absent from the later deeds and records of the abbey, although the earl of Chester's gift of the church of Barrow-on-Soar remained among its possessions, as it was granted out of the earl's own estates.

---

27. For his death, D. Crouch, *The Beaumont twins: the roots and branches of power in the twelfth century* (Cambridge 1986), 95 and note.

28. Bodl. Laud misc. 625, ff. 5v, 6v, 63v.

29. Ibid. f. 6v. For the long-term rivalry and eventual settlement between the two earls, *c.* 1129 x 49, see E. J. King, 'Mount-sorrel and its region in King Stephen's reign', *Huntingdon Library Quarterly* 44 (1980), 1–10; Crouch, *Reign of King Stephen*, 253–4.

30. D. Crouch, *The image of aristocracy in Britain, 1000–1300* (London 1992), 329 and note.

31. For other such manoeuvres, Crouch, *Reign of King Stephen*, 274–6.

The full and impressive extent of grants made to the abbey by people other than Earl Robert is revealed by the confirmation it received from King Henry II most probably in 1156 (Appendix no. 8). There were two considerable grants made at quite a distance from Leicester. The first was the grant by William of Lancaster, lord of Kendal, of the whole manor of Cockerham in Lancashire. William had in fact married a daughter of Earl Robert II's cousin, Earl Roger of Warwick, himself a benefactor, and this family link may have been the main reason for the grant. It is probably the case that William planned to set up his own Augustinian house at Cockerham, although the project was slow to come to fruition. A similar reason may lie behind the substantial grants to the abbey by William Avenel in Derbyshire and Buckinghamshire, centred on the manor of Conkersbury, Derbys. Avenel had earlier made grants to the Nottinghamshire Cluniac house at Lenton, including land at Meadowplace (*Medopleke*) near Youlgrave, Derbys. It would seem that the monks of Lenton had disappointed his expectation of founding a cell there, for we find the grant at Meadowplace had been transferred to Leicester by 1156. Two canons of Leicester in the end constituted a cell in *Medweplek* until at least the middle of the thirteenth century.[32] The fact that the abbey failed to make good all of Avenel's grants, is some indication that there was an even greater scheme under discussion which was dropped after 1158, and a compromise reached. But great gifts or small, successful or unsuccessful, Henry II confirmed over a score of grants to Leicester Abbey which were made by people outside the earl's honor. From this it can be reasonably deduced that the new abbey was able to attract a good degree of enthusiasm amongst the twelfth-century landowners of the Midlands.

The enthusiasm faded in the decades after the death of Robert II. His son, Robert III, made no major grants to the abbey, although he offered the canons from his forests and fishponds the means to make suitable feasts on the four principal Marian feasts of the year. Robert III's checkered career between 1168 and 1190 led to a decline in the wealth and the power of his family, and the bulk of his own patronage was directed to his Benedictine Norman abbey of Lyre. Nonetheless the next generation saw a revival of family interest in the abbey. Earl Robert IV (1190–1204), a famous crusader and one of the great military heroes of the reign of Richard the Lionheart, was a formidable patron, as the diocese of Lincoln discovered to its cost when he intervened in its attempts to regain the manor of Knighton, which had come into the abbey's possession. A major defeat in the *curia regis* led to the bishop losing not just Knighton, but his urban estate in Leicester and other lands formerly offered and exchanged during Robert II's painstaking diplomacy to negotiate a final settlement of his claims on the bishop's estate in his county.[33]

The extinction of the first line of the earls of Leicester with the death of Earl Robert IV in 1204 was a serious reverse to the abbey. Although Robert's collateral descendants (the children of his sisters) made a decent show of keeping up a connection with the abbey, none of them was a patron of particular generosity. The most generous in terms of charters was Earl Roger de Quincy of Winchester, who issued twelve known acts to the benefit of the abbey. Most are to do with forest privileges, for his forests were one of the earl's known enthusiasms, and although doubtless benefitting the abbey, none of his charters make any great grants.[34] There is evidence of the abbey's continuing popularity amongst the local gentry of Leicestershire. Although he made no grants of

32. For the grant to Lenton see, W. Dugdale, *Monasticon Anglicanum*, ed. J. Caley and others, 6 vols in 8 (London 1817–30), v, 111. The abbey negotiated the status of its two canons in Youlgrave with Sir Richard (1) de Vernon, the husband of William Avenel's grand-daughter and heir, at some time in the later years of Henry III, Bodl. Laud misc. 625, f. 112v. For Richard see G. le Blanc Smith, *Haddon* (London 1906), 4–5.

33. Crouch, 'Earls and bishops in twelfth-century Leicestershire', 16–17.

34. Bodl. Laud misc. 625, f. 6r.

land, the leading Leicestershire *curialis*, Stephen de Segrave (d. 1241), cultivated strong links with the abbey. He had begun his career as a clerk in minor orders before taking knighthood, and he may have been educated under the abbey's auspices, as it was a major landowner in Seagrave itself. Certainly he took refuge in its cloister during a crisis in his career in 1234 and he ended his days as a canon there.[35] Before the mid thirteenth century the abbey had begun to expand its estates by purchase from local landowners in the vicinity of its core estates. We can see this particularly in Thurmaston and Barkby, Leics. and in Bramcote, Warwicks. In all three cases the abbey had acquired a patrimonial estate there in the twelfth century, and it used its purchasing power to buy up parcels of land in the 1240s and 1250s. It seems likely that this was a policy developed and pursued by Abbot Henry of Rothley (1247–70). The recovery of the texts of many of the thirteenth-century charters which recorded the expansion of Leicester abbey's lands in the 1240s and 1250s opens up the possibility of analysing how it was accomplished, and at whose expense. But this would be a task for another place and time.

---

35. Matthew Paris, *Chronica Majora*, ed. H. R. Luard, 7 vols.
Rolls Series 57 (London 1872–84), iii, 293; iv, 107.

Appendix: The charters of Leicester Abbey, 1139–1265

The conventions adopted for editing generally follow those of the English Episcopal Acta series (q.v.). Punctuation is that of the original or copy, with the *punctus elevatus* replaced by commas. Capitalisation has been standardised.

The thirteenth-century cartulary of Leicester Abbey '(*vetus Chartwary*)' (A20.1864), now lost, is referred to in the notes as the 'Leicester Cartulary', while the fourteenth-century cartulary of Leicester Abbey '(*The Chartwary*)', also now lost, is referred to as the 'Second Leicester Cartulary' (A20.1863). A third, fifteenth-century cartulary compiled by Charyte ('*secundus liber de Chartwary*', A20.1865) is also lost and is not drawn upon in this edition. The Rental of Leicester Abbey of Prior William Charyte (dated 1477 in Bodl. Laud misc. 625 f. 12r) is now lost but a copy survives in Bodl. Laud misc. 625 (s. xv²–xvi in.) and is the 'novum Rentale' that was 'compiled and written by William Charyte' (A20.1872). This (lost) 1477 rental is referred to in this edition as the 'Leicester Rental'. The other extant Leicester rental, now BL Cotton Vitellius F xvii (s. xv/xvi), is referred to in this edition as the 'Second Leicester Rental' (and may be that described in the medieval catalogue at A20.1873).

1. Robert II, earl of Leicester   February x June 1139, or September 1139 x May 1140

For the souls of himself, his wife, his children, his brother Waleran, King Henry, his father and mother, the earl has founded a church of St Mary outside the North Gate of Leicester for the use of regular canons. He has transferred the prebends and possessions that were of the secular canons of the church of St Mary within the castle by the agency of Bishop Alexander of Lincoln. He concedes to the canons the said church of St Mary, with all the liberties conceded to it by his father, Count Robert of Meulan, and extends the liberty outside the North Gate. He concedes five carrucates, eight houses in another part of the town, three virgates and three bovates; six pounds annually from the rents of Leicester; the churches of Leicester inside and outside the walls, which are in his gift; the church of Lilbourne, Northants. and sixty shillings rent there; three carrucates and a virgate in Thurmaston, Leics.; a virgate in Burton Overy, Leics. granted by his mother Countess Isabel (to St Mary de Castro); six carrucates and three bovates in Seagrave, Leics.; the manor of Asfordby, Leics. which King Henry gave the earl in exchange for the land of the bishop of Lincoln outside the walls of Leicester and the manor of Knighton, Leics.; a carrucate of land at the North Bridge which once lay at the mint; the rents and houses which Dean Gubert held of the earl at the South Gate; the tithe of colts from the earl's studs; the mill once the bishop's; what Osbert the chaplain held of the earl in the sokes of Shepshed, Leics. and Halse, Northants. namely all the churches of both sokes with the church of Syresham, Northants. which is known to be subject to that of Brackley; the church of West Isley, Berks.; the church of Thurnby, Leics. from the grant of Ralph the butler; the church of Theddingworth, Leics. from the grant of Robert his son, in exchange for the thirty shillings which his father had previously conceded to the canons of St Mary de Castro from Blynfield, Dorset; the churches of Clifton-upon-Dunsmoor, Warwicks. and Thorp Arnold, Leics. and a rent of a mark in Leicester of the grant of Arnold du Bois; the church of Bulkington, Warwicks.; a half a hide in Bramcote, Warwicks. and a meadow in Weston-on-Avon, Gloucs. of the grant of Roger de Vatteville; land in Bromkinsthorpe, Leics. of the grant of Siward Pitefrid; and rights of wood and freedom from pannage in the earl's forests.

> A = Original, now lost. B = Leicester Cartulary (from A). C = TNA E13/76 (Plea Rolls of the Exchequer), m. 69d. (dated 1351) (from A). D = Leicester Rental incomplete abridgement probably from B, now lost. E = Second Leicester Rental, f. 10r (partial abridgement probably from B). F = Bodl. Laud misc. 625, f. 5r (from D). G = Winchester Cathedral Library xxB, copy by William Say (dated *c.* 1536) (from A).
>
> Pd. Nichols, *Leicester*, i pt. 2, Appendix p. 54 (from E); Dugdale, *Monasticon Anglicanum*, vi pt. 1, 464 (from E); Crouch, 'The foundation of Leicester Abbey', 8–9 (from C).

[CG]

Vniversis sancte dei ecclesie fidelibus, Robertus comes Legrec[estrie], salutem. Nouerint cuncti fideles tam posteri quam presentes quod ego Robertus comes pro salute anime mee et vxoris mee et filiorum meorum et Wal[eranni] fratris mei et pro anima Henr[ici] r[egis][a] et pro animabus patris et matris mee fundaui ecclesiam in honore sancte Marie extra portam aquilonalem Legrec[estrie] ad opus canonicorum regularium. et omnes prebendas et possessiones que fuerunt canonicorum secularium ecclesie sancte Marie infra castellum concessi. et per manum Alex[andri] Lincoln[ensis][b] episcopi transtuli et iure perpetuo confirmaui in vsus canonicorum regularium. In primis videlicet concedo eisdem canonicis regularibus prefatam ecclesiam sancte Marie cum tota possessione et parrochia sua cum terris et decimis et pratis et omnibus aliis pertinentiis suis. cum omnibus libertatibus et quietudinibus quas Rob[ert]us comes Mellenti pater meus predicte ecclesie ante concesserat. Item concedo eis extra portam de Norht eadem libertate .v. carrucatas terre et .viij. mansiones hominum. Et in alia parte ciuitatis .iij. virgatas et .iij. bouatas terre et de redditibus Legrec[estrie] .vj. libras per annum. Ecclesias quoque omnes Legrec[estrie] tam infra muros quam extra que mee dicionis sunt cum domibus et mansuris cum terris et decimis et omnibus pertinentiis suis. Ecclesiam quoque de Lilleburna cum terris et decimis et omnibus pertinentiis suis et .lx. solidos per annum de redditibus eiusdem ville. In Turmodestona .iij. carucatas et vnam virgatam terre. ex dono Isabel comitisse matris mee .j. virgatam terre in Burtona. In Setgraua .vj. carrucatas et .iij. bouatas terre. et manerium Asfordeby[c] totum et integrum cum molendinis et omnibus pertinentiis suis liberum et quietum cum omnibus libertatibus et consuetudinibus suis ab omni seruitio seculari quod Henricus rex Angl[ie] de suo dominio dedit mihi[d] in escambium pro terra episcopi Linc[olnie] extra muros Legrec[estrie] et pro manerio Cnichtetona.[e] ad pontem de Norht[f] carrucatam terre que iacebat olim ad cuneos monete et censum et domos quas Gubertus decanus de me tenebat ad portam de Suth et decimam pullorum de mea equaria. et molendinum quod fuit episcopi. et quicquid ad ipsum molendinum pertinet et quicquid Osbertus capellanus de me tenebat in soca de Sepeheua et in soca de Halsou. Omnes videlicet ecclesias de vtraque soca cum ecclesia de Sigresham que de parrochia de Brachaleya esse congnoscitur. cum terris et decimis et omnibus pertinentiis suis. et decimam denariorum meorum de vtraque soca et de pannagio. Item ecclesiam de Indeslai que est in Berchesira cum terris et decimis et omnibus pertinentiis suis. Ecclesiam quoque de Turneby[g] ex dono Rad[ulfi] pinc[erne] cum terris et decimis et omnibus pertinentiis suis. et ex dono Roberti filii eius ecclesiam de Tamgenuurd[h] in escambium pro .xxx. solidos quos pater suus canonicis sancte Marie antea in Blingesfeld concesserat. Ex dono Ernaldi de Bosco ecclesiam de Cliftona et ecclesiam de Torp iuxta Meltonam cum terris et decimis et omnibus pertinentiis suis et vnam marcatam redditus in Legrec[estria]. Ex dono Rogeri de Wateuilla ecclesiam de Bulchintona cum terris et decimis et omnibus pertinentiis suis. et dimidiam hidam terre in Brancota et pratum quod fuit de dominio de Westona.[i] Et ex dono Siwardi Pitefrid terram quam de me tenebat in Brunchenestorp. Item concedo supramemoratis canonicis omnes donationes quas homines totius terre mee eis fecerint iuste in ecclesiis et decimis et aliis elemosinis. Has igitur terras et ecclesias possessiones redditus volo et firmiter constituo vt predicti canonici libere et quiete et honorifice teneant ab omni seruitio et exactione seculari erga me et heredes meos. vbicumque vero in forestis meis ad proprios vsus ligna sumpsero, ibi et canonici cum tribus carecis cotidie ad ignem suum libere ligna sumant. Et vbicumque tempore pascionis mei dominici porci fuerint, ibi et canonici suos dominicos porcos libere et sine pannagio habeant. AMEN. Huius mee concessionis sunt testes. Bernardus prior Kiniguurd[e]. A[micia] comitissa. Robertus filius meus. Ernaldus de Bosco. Ernaldus junior. Rad[ulfu]s pincerna. Robertus et Gaufr[idus] abb[as] filii eius. Gaufr[idus] de Craft. et Robertus filius eius. Adam de Cirre. Reginaldus de Borden[eio]. Ioh[ann]es de Iohi. Ric[ard]us Fremnel. Rad[ulfus] fil[ius] Gilleb[erti]. Robertus capellanus. Simon canonicus de[k] Kiningeuurd[a]. Ric[ardus] camerarius. Rog[erus] de Cranford. Rog[erus] Walensis.

[a] Henrici reg[is] G. [b] Alexandri Lincol[nensis] G. [c] Asfordebi G. [d] et G. [e] Cnichetona G. [f] North' G. [g] Turnebi G. [h] Tamgeuurd' G. [i] de Westona de dominio G. [k] de omitted in G.

The date of this charter is established by the evidence in it that Countess Isabel, the earl's mother was dead. Since we can calculate that she was alive till at least February 1139, the charter must date after that. The fact that Ralph the earl's butler is active in the foundation provides the other limit. Ralph had retired to Alcester Abbey in Warwickshire by May 1140 (Crouch, 'The foundation of Leicester Abbey', 5). This can be narrowed further by the amicable presence in it of Bishop Alexander of Lincoln. The bishop had placed Earl Robert under an interdict, with the pope's support, probably in the late summer of 1139 after his complicity in the fall of the bishop's family in June. The likelihood is that this act was issued in the autumn of 1139, after a reconciliation and settlement between earl and bishop.

2. Eugenius III, pope   1 January 1148 x 24 March 1149

Protection for the abbey and its possessions (list omitted) with exemption from tithes on the produce of their lands; admonition to the abbots not to alienate its estates; injunction to the abbot to appoint priests to its churches from among the canons and to present them to the bishop, or if not others suitable, who are to be obedient to the abbot; the abbey in its parishes to have the burial of those who die within them or who express a wish to be buried within them, unless they be excommunicate, saving the rights of mother churches. Threat of excommunication against anyone, lay or secular, wilfully troubling the abbey over its possessions if they fail to make suitable amends on summons.

A = Original, now lost. B = Leicester Cartulary (from A). C = Leicester Rental (partial transcript from B, now lost). D = Bodl. Laud misc. 625, ff. 180v–181r (from C).

[D]

Eugenius papa etc. Ea propter etc. dilecti in domino filii ecclesiam beate Marie de Leyc[estria] in qua diuino mancipati est obsequio sub beati Petri et nostra protectione suscipimus etc. Statuentes vt quascumque possessiones quecumque bona. eadem ecclesia in presentiarum iuste et canonice possidet aut in futurum concessione pontificum largitione regum uel principum oblatione fidelium seu aliis iustis modis deo propitio poterit adipisci. Firma vobis vestrisque successoribus et illibata permaneant in quibus hec propriis duximus exprimenda vocabulis ecclesiam sancte Marie iuxta castellum cum parochia possessionibus libertatibus et omnibus pertinentiis suis etc vsque huc. Sane laborum vestrorum quos propriis manibus aut sumptibus colitis siue de nutrimentis vestrorum animalium. nullus omnino a vobis decimas exigere presumat. Libertates quoque et immunitates a regibus siue principibus vobis pia deuotione concessas presentis scripti pagina confirmamus. Obediente vero te nunc eiusdem loci abbate vel tuorum quolibet successorum. nullus ibi qualibet surreptionis austicia seu violencia proponatur nisi quem fratres communi consilio etc prouiderint eligendo. Statuimus eciam vt in parochialibus ecclesiis quas tenetur de fratribus vestris sacerdotes eligatur et episcopis presentetis. quibus si idonei fuerint episcopi curam animarum commitant vel huiusmodi sacerdotes de plebis quid cura episcopis rationem reddant. vobis de professione sua et ordine et rebus temporalibus debitam subiectionem exhibeant. Sepulturam quoque ipsius loci liberam esse decernimus vel eorum qui se illic sepeliri deliberauerint deuotioni et extreme voluntati nisi forte excommunicati vel interdicti sint nullus obsistat. salua tamen iusticia matricis ecclesie. Decernimus vt nulli omnino hominum liceat prefatam ecclesiam temere perturbare aut eius possessiones auferre vel ablatas retinere arripere aut aliquibus vexationibus fatigare etc. Si qua igitur in futurum ecclesiastica secularis ne persona hanc nostre confirmationis paginam sciens contra eam temere venire temptauerit secundo tercio ne commonita si non satisfactione congrua emendauerit potestatis honorisque sui dignitate careat reamque se diuino iudicio existere de perpetrata iniquitate connoscat et a sacratissime corpore ac sanguine dei et domini nostri Iehsu Christi aliena fiat atque in extremo examine districte vltioni subiaceat. Cuntis autem eidem loco iusta seruantibus sit pax domini nostri Iehsu Christi quatinus et hic fructum bone actionis percipient et apud districtum iudicem premia eterne pacis inueniant. Amen. Dat[um] etc.

The date of this bull is indicated in the rubric of the register as 'made subsequent to the foundation of the abbey of Leicester, in the year of grace 1148', Bodl. Laud misc. 625, f. 180v. The dates of the incarnational year 1148 are therefore adopted above.

3. Stephen, king of England   August x December 1153
Confirmation of the foundation of the church of St Mary by Earl Robert II and the appointment by the earl of an abbot. Confirmation of the grants recorded in his foundation charter, with confirmations also of the subsequent grants by Count Waleran of Meulan of twenty measures of salt annually at Droitwich, Worcs, and by Earl Ranulf II of Chester of two carrucates of land called Hanechestoft *at Rothley, Leics.*

A = Original, now lost. B = Leicester Cartulary (from A). C = Leicester Rental (partial transcript from B, now lost). D = Bodl. Laud misc. 625, f. 6v (from C).
Pd. Nichols, *Leicester*, i pt. 2, Appendix p. 54 (from D); Dugdale, *Monasticon Anglicanum*, vi pt. 1, p. 466 (from D); *Regesta Regum Anglo-Normannorum, 1066–1154*, ed. R. H. C. Davis and H. A. Cronne, 3 vols. (Oxford 1913–69), iii, no. 436 (from D).

[D]

Stephanus rex Anglie etc. Sciatis me concessisse Roberto comiti Leyc[estrie] fundare ecclesiam sancte Marie etc. et ibi constituere abbatem etc. Et concedo deo et beate Marie et Ricardo abbati et canonicis regularibus etc. omnes donationes quas Robertus comes Leyc[estrie] dedit concessit uel adquisiuit siue adquisierit seu que deinceps eis dabuntur in elemosinam. In primis concedo etc. ut in carta originali fundatoris nostri usque huc. Item ex dono Walerani comitis de Mell[ento] xx mitas salis in Wich' de Wiricestresira. Ex dono Ranulfi comitis Cestr[ie] duas carucatas terre in Roleia que vocatur Hanechestoft cum prato adiacente etc. Has donationes terras etc. que eisdem canonicis pertinent liberas et quietas concedo ab omni expedicione infra Angliam etc. et omni seruicio seculari etc. Et volo et firmiter precipio ut prefata ecclesia et canonici bene et pacifice libere et quiete teneant et libertatem curie sue habeant cum saca et soca et toll et team et infangnenethof et omnibus aliis consuetudinibus etc. in nemore et plano etc. sicut aliqua ecclesia tocius terre mee de elemosina mea melius et quietius et honorificencius tenet etc. ut in carta.

> The date of this charter is established by the later grants included within it. Both Count Waleran and Earl Ranulf were at odds with the king until the settlement which began to be negotiated between the king and the Angevin party in August 1153. The other limit to the date is the death of Earl Ranulf in December 1153, after which the grants made him at Rothley were taken back into the royal estates (Crouch, *The reign of King Stephen*, 277–8), Waleran's earldom of Worcester was almost certainly confiscated on Duke Henry's departure from England in March 1154, if not before. Significantly, the grants at Droitwich and Rothley do not feature in the abbey's later records. The charter must then date between August and December 1153.

4. William of Lancaster   1139 x 1156

Grant, with the agreement of his wife Gundreda and William his son and heir, of the manor of Cockerham, Lancs.

> A = Original, now lost. B = Leicester Rental (partial transcript from A, now lost). C = Bodl. Laud misc. 625, f. 45r (from B).
> Pd. *The Lancashire Pipe Rolls and Early Lancashire Charters*, ed. W. Farrer (Liverpool 1902), 391.

[C]

Vniuersis sancte dei ecclesie fidelibus Will[elmu]s de Lancastr' salutem. Notum sit vniuersitati uestre me assensu etc. vxoris mee Gundrede et Will[elm]i filii mei et heredis etc. dedisse et concessisse etc. deo et ecclesie sancte Marie de Pratis Leirc[estrie] et canonicis regularibus ibidem deo seruientibus totum manerium meum de Cokerheim cum omnibus pertinentiis suis in bosco et plano in aquis pratis pascuis piscariis et mariscis cum salinis et molendinis et cum omnibus libertatibus et liberis consuetudinibus ad eandem terram pertinentibus.

> The date of this charter must precede the confirmation by Henry II, which mentions its grants (see no. 8). It is impossible to say how long before 1156 it was made. It quite likely preceded 1153, if it was made under the influence of Earl Roger of Warwick, William's father-in-law, for the earl died that year. It could conceivably have been issued as early as 1139.

5. William of Lancaster   1139 x 1156

Grant, with the agreement of his wife Gundreda and William his son and heir, of the manor of Cockerham, Lancs. along with its church, the chapel of Ellel and the settlement of Crimbles.

> A = Original, now lost. B = Leicester Rental (partial transcript from A, now lost). C = Bodl. Laud misc. 625, f. 45r (from B).
> Pd. *Lancashire Pipe Rolls and Early Lancashire Charters*, ed. Farrer, 391–2.

[C]

Vniuersis sancte dei ecclesie fidelibus Will[elmu]s de Lancastr' salutem. Notum sit vniuersitati uestre me consilio et assensu Will[elm]i filii mei et heredis et Gundrede vxoris mee etc. dedisse et concessisse et hac presenti carta confirmasse in puram et perpetuam elemosinam deo et ecclesie sancte Marie de Prato Leirc[estrie] et canonicis regularibus ibidem deo seruientibus totum manerium meum de Cokerheim cum ecclesia eiusdem ville cum capella de Elhale et cum omnibus pertinentiis suis et cum Crimblis tam ultra Cokir quam citra cum omnibus pertinentiis suis etc.

> The date would be the same as the preceding charter.

6. Robert de Vatteville   1139 x 1156

Grant of the mill of Bramcote, Warwicks. to the abbey with the consent of Earl Robert of Leicester, with confirmation of the things previously granted by his brother Roger de Vatteville.

> A = Original, now lost. B = Second Leicester Cartulary (from A). C = TNA E13/76 m. 71, copy dated 1351, from A. D = Leicester Rental (digest from B, now lost). E = Bodl. Laud misc. 625, f. 34r (from D).

[C]

Vniuersis sancte dei ecclesie fidelibus, Rob[er]tus de Wateuilla, salutem. Nouerint cuncti fideles tam posteri quam presentes quod ego Rob[er]tus pro salute anime mee et animabus patris et matris mee et fratrum meorum in perpetuam elemosinam concedo ecclesie sancte Marie Legrecestr' de Prato et canonicis regularibus ibidem deo seruientibus molendinum de Brancota cum terra et prato et omnibus ad ipsum molendinum pertinentibus et hoc concessu domini mei Rob[er]ti comitis Legrec[estrie]. de cuius feodo est. Quare volo et firmiter constituo vt predicta ecclesia et prefati canonici hanc[a] meam elemosinam cum omnibus que eis ante frater meus Rog[er]us concesserat libere et quiete et honorifice teneant sine omni exactione et seruitio seculari. Test[ibus] Amic[ia] comitissa Legrec[estrie] Ernaldo de Bosco Gaufr[ido] abbate Malerba Will[elm]o dispensatore abbatis Rad[ulf]o janitore Rann[ulfo] pistore Hug[one] aucupe.

[a] hac C.

This grant is mentioned in Henry II's confirmation charter to the abbey, so must date to before 1156. It could have been made at any time after 1139.

7. Robert son of Ralph   1148 x 1156

Grant of the churches of Knipton and Harston, Leics. to the abbey with the consent of his sons, and in particular his youngest son, Gervase, who will retain a life interest in the churches.

A = Original, now lost. B = Copy in W. Dugdale, *Monasticon Anglicanum* (3 vols, London, 1653–73), i, 315 'ex autographo in Officio Armorum' (from A).
Pd. Nichols, *Leicester*, i pt. 2, Appendix p. 55 (from B).

[B]

Uniuersis sancti dei ecclesie fidelibus Robertus filius Radulfi salutem. Notum sit universitati vestre quod ego Robertus pro anima patris mei et matris mee et pro anima Aveline coniugis mee et Willelmi fratris mei et pro animabus parentum et amicorum meorum in perpetuum, concessi et dedi ecclesie sancte Marie de Legrecestria et canonicis regulariter ibidem deo seruientibus ecclesiam de Cnipeton et ecclesiam de Arestona cum terris et decimis et mansuris et omnibus pertinentiis et hoc concessu Willielmi filii et heredis mei et Roberti filii mei et Gervasii filii mei, ita tamen quod idem Gervasius teneat de predicta ecclesia sancte Marie de Legrecestria prenominatas ecclesias libere et quiete quamdiu vixerit. Volo autem et firmiter constituo ut predicta ecclesia sancte Marie et canonici has prenominatas ecclesias bene et in pace libere et quiete et honorifice teneant, cum omnibus libertatibus et liberis consuetudinibus que ad easdem ecclesias pertinent et cum omni libertate et communitate pasture utriusque ville. Hiis testibus: Roberto Lincolnie episcopo, Roberto comite Legrecestrie, Roberto de Croft, Ivone de Harcurt, Willielmo Basset, magistro Edmundo, magistro Bernardo, Willielmo capellano, Hugone de Blabi, Gumfredo presbitero, Gervasio filio Turgis, Roberto filio Suani, Walcellino, Johanne et Willielmo scriptoribus, Hugone de Bedeford, Abei filio eius, Willielmo dispensatore, Rogero, Johanne, Petro famulis abbatis.

The date of this grant must be after the consecration of Robert de Chesney as bishop of Lincoln, and before the confirmation of Henry II (below no. 8) in which the grants feature.

8. Henry II, king of England   Dover, 1155 x 58, probably January 1156

Confirmation of the foundation of the abbey and the grants recorded in its foundation charter, with confirmations of further grants. These include the place of Stockingford, Warwicks. with woodland and neighbouring land the earl exchanged with William de Neufmarché; forty shillings rent in Welton and Thorpe, Northants.; four shillings rent in Leicester from the houses of Godwin Bena; six assarts from the grant of Joscelin Marshal; a carrucate called Anastalesleia from the grant of William de Launay; land called Nettlebed, Oxfords. from the grant of Geoffrey de Tourville; four pounds rent in Eversley, Wilts, from the grant of Countess Amice of Leicester; the church of Langton and the chapels of Thorp and Tirlington, Leics. from the grant of William de Neufmarché and Reginald de Bordigny; the church of Barrow-on-Soar with the chapel of Quorndon, Leics. with tithes and a carrucate of land in his demesne from the grant of Ranulf II, earl of Chester; the church of Narborough with the chapel of Huncote, Leics. from the grant of Earl Roger of Warwick; a meadow in Six Hills (Segeswold), Leics. from the grant of Geoffrey of Dalby; the church of Bulkington and six carrucates in Bramcote, Warwicks. from the grant of Roger de Vatteville, and a mill in Bramcote from the grant of Roger's brother, Robert; the village of Conkersbury, its mills, the banks on both sides of the river [Wye] and twenty acres in the field of Haddon, Derbys. and the church and a carrucate at Adstock, Bucks. from the grant of William Avenel; a virgate in Eastwell, Leics. from the grant of Henry Tuschet; two thirds of the tithes of garbs from his lordship of Gotham, Notts. from the grant of Hugh de Launay and Heloise his wife; the mill of Belgrave and the village of Stoughton (except the land of Ralph Friday), Leics. from the grant of Earl Robert of Leicester; half the church of Chesham Bois, Bucks. from the grant of Robert de Chiffrewast; the church of Sharnbrook, Beds. from the grant of William Triket; the church of Eydon, Northants. from the grant of Richard son of Walo; the church of Billing Magna, Northants. from the grant of William Barre; the church of Billesdon with the chapels of Rolleston and Goadby, Leics. from the grant of William de Chiffrewast; the churches of Thornton, Leics. and Syresham, Northants. from the grant of Thomas Sorel; the church of Aldeby and the chapel of Whetstone, Leics. from the grant of Earl Robert of Leicester; the church of Blaby and the chapel of Countesthorpe, Leics. from the grant of William of Ladbroke; the church of North Kilworth, Leics. from the grant of Robert Rabbaz; the church of Husbands Bosworth, Leics. and a carrucate from the grant of Robert of Bosworth and Roger Cute his son; a virgate in Husbands Bosworth from the grant of Roger Sampson; two virgates in Mowsley, Leics. from the grant of Reginald of Mowsley; a virgate in Humberstone, Leics. from the grant of Ralph son of Richard de Martinwast; a virgate in Norton-by-Twycross, Leics. from the grant of Robert of Burton; the churches of Barkby and Hungarton, Leics. with their chapels, from the grant of Walter le Poer; the church of Eaton, Leics. from the grant of William de Envermeu; the church of Eastwell from the grant of Robert Arraby; the churches of Harston and Knipton from the grant of Robert son of Ralph; the churches of Youlgrave, Derbys. and Bitteswell, Leics. with chapels and tithes from the grant of Robert son of Robert son of Col; the church of Curdworth, and the hermitage and wood of Barwood, Warwicks. with the mills, from the grant of Hugh of Arden; a carrucate in Sutton Cheney, Leics. from the grant of Geoffrey of Croft; a carrucate of land in Stoke Golding, Leics. from the grant of Robert of Croft; the church of Croft, Leics. from the grant of Ralph de Tourville; a bovate in Shuckburgh, Warwicks. from the grant of Osbert of Leamington; the church and six virgates at Wanlip, Leics. from the grant of Richard Labbé; a carrucate of land in Empingham, Rutland, from the grant of the same Richard and of Richard son of Philip; the place of Pinslade (in Husbands Bosworth), Leics. from the grant of Earl Robert of Leicester; three virgates in Kilby, Leics. from the grant of William of Kilby; five virgates in Bitteswell, Leics. from the grant of Godfrey Patroc; a carrucate in Theddingworth, Leics. from the grant of William of Kirby; the entire manor of Cockerham, Lancs. with its church and the chapel of Ellel and its liberties according to the charter of William of Lancaster; the church of Queniborough, Leics. from the grant of Ralph of Queniborough; a virgate in Lilbourne, Northants. from the grant of Richard Labbé; three virgates in Old Dalby, Leics. from Geoffrey of Dalby; a virgate in Foxton, Leics. from the grant of Robert of Cotes.

A = Original, now lost. B = Leicester Cartulary (from A). C = TNA C53/104 (Charter Roll 11 Edward II) m. 4 (dated 1318) (from A). D = TNA C53/123 (Charter Roll 10 Edward III) m. 2 (dated 1336) from C. E = TNA E13/76, m. 77d. (dated 1351) (from A). F = Leicester Rental (partial transcript from B, now lost). G = TNA C56/16 (Confirmation Roll 3 Henry VII, pt. 3), m. 17 (from D). H = Bodl. Laud misc. 625, f. 6v (from F). I = TNA C56/27 (Confirmation Roll of 1 Henry VIII, pt. 3) m. 23 (from G).

[CE]

H[enricus] rex Angl[orum] dux Norm[annorum] et Aquit[annorum] et comes Andeg[avorum] archiepiscopis episcopis comitibus baronibus iustic[iis] vic[ecomitibus] et omnibus fidelibus suis Angl[ie] salutem. Sciatis me concessisse et in perpetuam elemosinam confirmasse deo et ecclesie sancte Marie de Prato Leyc[estrie] et canonicis regularibus ibidem deo seruientibus quicquid Rob[er]tus comes Leicestr[ie] eis dedit vel daturus est in terris et ecclesiis et decimis et omnibus aliis rebus et quicquid alii eis rationabiliter dederunt vel daturi sunt, ex dono videlicet predicti com[itis] Rob[er]ti Leicestr[ie] ipsum locum in quo abbatia fundata est. Et ecclesiam sancte Marie de castello Leic' cum omnibus prebendis et possessionibus eiusdem ecclesie et cum omnibus pertinentiis suis sicut Rob[er]tus comes Mellend' predicte ecclesie olim concesserat, et ceteras omnes ecclesias Leic[estrie] et ecclesiam de Cossibi que pertinet ad ecclesiam sancti Augustini de Leic[estria] cum omnibus rebus predictis ecclesiis pertinentibus. Et extra portam de Nort de Leic[estria] sex carucatas terre et dimidiam cum illa que olim iacebat ad cuneos monete et octo mansiones extra portam de West septem virgatas terre et vnam bouatam. De redditibus Leic[estrie] sex libras per annum et omnes domos quas Gilbertus decanus tenebat ad portam de Suth' et decimam pullorum de equaria comitis et totum molendinum iuxta abbatiam cum soca et prato adiacente. Et ecclesiam de Lilleburna et quadraginta solidos de redditibus eiusdem ville. Et ecclesiam de Sepeheua et omnes ecclesias de eadem soca et decimam denariorum de redditibus et decimam de pasnagio in eadem soca. Et ecclesiam de Brackel[eia] cum capellis de Alsou et de Sigresham cum omnibus pertinentiis suis et cum decimis denariorum de redditibus de Brackel[eia] et de sooca de Alsou et ecclesiam de Farningehou cum pertinentiis suis. Et in Turmodeston' tres carucatas terre et tres virgatas terre. in Burton' vnam virgatam terre et totum manerium de Aisfordeby cum ecclesia et cum molendinis et cum omnibus pertinentiis suis. in Sedgraue sex carucatas et tres bouatas terre. et ecclesias de Cnapetoft' et Erdesby et de Turnebi et de Tamgwrtth et de Stantona et de Ilmesdon' et de Hildeslai in Berkesira cum omnibus pertinentiis suis et locum de Stockiford' cum nemore et terra adiacente sicut comes Leic' eam escambiauit Willelmo de Nouo Mercato pro Witewich'. et de Ric[ard]o Mallori et de heredibus suis quadraginta solidos pro terra de Welton' et de Trop. et quatuor solidos in Leircestr[ia] de domibus Godwini Bena. et sex exsarta de dono Iocelini marscaldi. Ex dono Willelmi de Auneia vnam carucatam terre que vocatur Anestalesleia. Ex dono Gaufridi de Turuuilla terram que dicitur Netlebehd. Ex dono Amicie comitisse quatuor libratas terre in Euerlais. scilicet nonam partem eiusdem villa cum pertinentiis suis. Ex dono Ernaldi de Bosco ecclesiam de Clifton' cum capellis de Rokebi et de Wauere et ecclesiam de Thorp cum capella de Brantingeby. et ecclesias de Euintona et de Humberstan. Ex dono Willelmi de Nouo Mercato et Rogeri de Bordeni ecclesiam de Langeton' cum capellis de Torp et de Turlinton'. Ex dono Ranulphi comitis Cestr[ie] ecclesiam de Barwa cum capella de Querendona cum terris decimis et omnibus pertinentiis suis. et cum illa carucata terre quam idem comes de suo dominio in Barewa et in Querendona accreuit eidem ecclesie. Ex dono Rog[er]i comitis de Warrewych' ecclesiam de Norburgh' cum capella de Honecote et cum omnibus pertinentiis suis. Ex dono Gaufridi de Dalby vnum pratum in Segeswold. Ex dono Rogeri de Wateuilla ecclesiam de Bulkinton' cum capellis et omnibus pertinentiis suis et sex virgatas terre in Bramcote. Ex dono Roberti fratris eiusdem Rogeri molendinum eiusdem ville cum terra et prato adiacente. Ex dono Will[elm]i Auenel villam de Cankersburiam totam cum molendinis et cliuam ex altera parte aque et viginti acras terre in campo de Haddona et ecclesiam de Adestok' cum vna carucata terre in eadem villa. Ex dono Henrici Tuschet vnam virgatam terre in Asseuella. Ex dono Hugonis de Alnaia et Helewise vxoris eius duas partes decime garbarum de dominio de Gaham. Item ex dono Roberti comitis Leyc[estrie] molendinum de Belegraua et villam de Stoctona totam preter terram Rad[ulf]i Fridai. Ex dono Rob[er]ti de Sifrewast medietatem ecclesie de Cestresham. Ex dono Will[elm]i Triket ecclesiam de Sharnebrok'. Ex dono Ric[ard]i filii Walonis ecclesiam de Eindona. Ex dono Will[elm]i Barre ecclesiam de Billynges. Ex dono Will[elm]i de Sifrewast ecclesiam de Billesdon' cum capellis de Rolueston' et de Gouteby et omnibus aliis pertinentiis suis. Ex dono Thome Sorel ecclesias de Thorentona et de Sigresham. Ex dono Rob[er]ti com[itis] Leyc[estrie] ecclesiam de Aldebi cum capella de Whetstan et omnibus aliis pertinentiis suis. Ex dono Will[elm]i de Lodbrok' ecclesiam de Blabi cum capella de Torp et omnibus aliis pertinentiis suis. Ex dono Rob[er]ti Rabbaz ecclesiam de Keuelingworth. Ex dono Rob[er]ti de Bareswrth' et Rogeri Cute filii eius ecclesiam de Barewswrth' cum pertinentiis suis et vnam carucatam terre in eadem villa. Ex dono Rog[er]i Sampson vnam virgatam terre in Bareswrth'. Ex dono Reginaldi de Muslai duas virgatas terre in Muslai. Ex dono Rad[ulf]i de Martiuall' filii Ricardi de Martiuall' vnam virgatam terre in Humberstan. Ex dono Rob[er]ti de Burton' vnam virgatam terre in Nortona. Ex dono Walteri le Poher ecclesias de Barkeby et de Hungertona cum capellis et omnibus aliis pertinentiis suis. Ex dono Willelmi de Euermou ecclesiam de Ettona. Ex dono Rob[er]ti Arabi ecclesiam de Estwella. Ex dono Rob[er]ti filii Rad[ulf]i ecclesias de Harestan et Kniptona. Ex dono Rob[er]ti filii Rob[er]ti filii Col ecclesiam de Ialgraue cum capellis terris decimis et omnibus aliis pertinentiis suis. Item ex dono ipsius Rob[er]ti ecclesiam de Bitmeswella. Ex dono Hugonis de Hardena ecclesiam de Croddeworth' et ermitagium et nemus de Berewode cum molendinis et omnibus aliis pertinentiis suis. Ex dono Gaufr[idi] de Creft vnam carucatam terre in Sutton'. Ex dono Rob[er]ti de Creft vnam carucatam terre in Stok'. Ex dono Rad[ulf]i de Turuilla ecclesiam de Creft. Ex dono Osberti de Lementona vnam bouatam in Sugkebergia. Ex dono Ric[ard]i Labbe ecclesiam de Anlep' et sex virgatas terre in eadem villa. Item ex dono eiusdem Ric[ard]i et Ric[ard]i fil[ii] Ph[ilipp]i vnam carucatam terre in Empingham. Ex dono Rob[er]ti comitis locum de Pineslade. Ex dono Will[elm]i de Kelebi tres virgatas terre in Kelebi. Ex dono Godefridi Patroc quinque virgatas terre in

Bitmeswella. Ex dono Will[elm]i de Kereby vnam carucatam terre in Themgworth'. Ex dono Rad[ulf]i pincerne ecclesiam de Themgworth' cum pertinentiis suis. Ex dono Will[elm]i de Lancastro totum manerium de Cokerham cum ecclesia eiusdem ville cum capella de Elhale et cum omnibus aliis pertinentiis et libertatibus suis sicut carte predicti Will[elm]i testantur. Ex dono Rad[ulf]i de Queneburcht ecclesiam eiusdem ville cum terris decimis et omnibus aliis pertinentiis suis. Ex dono Ric[ard]i Labbe vnam virgatam terre in Lilleburna. Ex dono Gaufridi de Dalby tres virgatas terre in eadem villa. Ex dono Roberti de Cocis vnam virgatam terre in Foxtona. Quare volo et firmiter precipio quod prefati canonici has predictas terras teneant et habeant bene et in pace libere et quiete et honorifice cum omnibus libertatibus et liberis consuetudinibus prefatis terris pertinentibus sicut carte donatorum testantur. Hiis testibus Rog[er]o archiepiscopo Ebor[acensi]. Rob[er]to Lincoln[ensi] episcopo. Nigello Heliensi episcopo. Thoma cancellario. Rob[er]to comite Leic[estrie]. Reg[inaldo] comite Cornub[ie]. Ric[ardo] de Humez constabul[ario]. Henr[ico] de Essex constab[ulario]. Ric[ardo] de Lucy. Warino filio Geroldi. apud Doueram.

Dates between Henry II's accession and the death of Warin fitz Gerald in August 1158. It may date to the known visit of Henry II to Dover in January 1156, and be one of a series of acts in favour of the abbey. Many thanks to Professor Nicholas Vincent for his advice on this text and its date, discussion of which will feature in the forthcoming Acta of the Angevin Kings. For the identification of places, Hamilton Thompson, *Leicester Abbey*, 92–201, *passim*.

9. Henry II, king of England   Rouen, February 1156

Takes the abbey under his personal protection, as if it were one of his own houses, with exemption from all secular exactions and free passage on land and through his ports.

A = Original, now lost. B = TNA c52/22 (Cartae Antiquae Rolls), m. 23 (s. xiii in.) (from A). C = Leicester Cartulary (from A). D = Leicester Rental (partial transcript from C, now lost). E = Bodl. Laud misc. 625, f. 7r (from D). F = BL Harley 84, ff. 271v–272r (s. xvii) from B. G = BL Harley 6748, f. 13v (s. xvii) (abbreviated copy from B).

Pd. Nichols, *Leicester*, i pt. 2, Appendix p. 58 (from B).

[B]

H[enricus] rex Angl[orum]. dux Norm[annorum]. Aquit[annorum]. com[es] And[egauorum]. archiepiscopis. episcopis. abbatibus. comitibus. baronibus. baill[iuis]. ministris. et omnibus fidelibus suis. Franc[is] et Angl[is] salutem. Sciatis me recepisse in mea propria manu et custodia et protectione sicut unam de meis elemosinis ecclesiam sancte Marie Leirc[est]r[ie] de Prato cum omnibus pertinentiis suis. Quare volo et firmiter precipio. quod canonici in predicta ecclesia deo seruientes, omnia tenementa sua teneant bene et in pace. et libere et quiete. et integre. et plenarie et honorifice. in bosco et plano. in pratis et pascuis. et aquis. et mariscis. in piscariis. in toftis et croftis. in viis. in semitis. et in omnibus locis tam in burgo quam extra burgum. liberam et quietam de geldis et danegeldis. et auxiliis et wapentacis. et hundredis et schiris et tennemanetale. et murdro. et scuagio. et assisis. et summonitionibus et de omnibus placitis et querelis et occasionibus. et consuetudinibus. et de omni terreno seruitio. et seculari exactione. cum saca et socha et toll et theam. et infangenetheof. et aliis omnibus consuetudinibus et libertatibus. Et volo ut predicti canonici et homines sui habeant saluum conductum meum et sint liberi et quieti a passagio et pontagio et teloneo et stallagio per omnes ciuitates meas et burgos. et uendant et emant libere et quiete. et volo ut sint quieti a trauerso, per omnes portus meos. et si quis uersus domum illam aliquid de possessionibus eius clamauerit, prohibeo ne pro aliquo respondeant. nec in placitum ponantur nisi per me et in presentia mea. T[estibus]. Tom[a] cancell[ario]. Philippo episcopo Baioc[ensi]. Ric[ardo] de Hum[et]. Manes[sero] Biset. Apud Rothom[agum].

For date see R.W. Eyton, *Court, household and itinerary of King Henry II* (London 1878), 17. This charter might well be linked with the preceding act of the king, as part of a series of benefactions to the principal abbey of his new chief justiciar, Earl Robert II.

10. Alexander III, pope   1 January 1161 x 24 March 1162

Protection for the abbey and its possessions (list omitted) as no. 2, with admonition against any unjust imposition on the abbey on pain of excommunication. At times of interdict, the abbey may celebrate the holy office behind closed doors with minimal ceremony. The abbey may receive clerks and lay persons into its cloister and community. No canon to leave the abbey after making profession there without the abbot's licence, and no one should receive a refugee from the abbey without its licence. The abbey to receive oil of chrism, consecration of altars and ordinations from the bishop of the diocese, providing he is in communion with Rome.

> A = Original, now lost. B = Leicester Cartulary (from A). C = Leicester Rental (partial transcript from B, now lost). D = Bodl. Laud misc. 625, f. 181r (from C).

[D]

Alexander episcopus etc. Ea propter etc. vt in priori bulla vsque. statuentes. et inde per totum sic prius vsque illum locum. sane laborum vestrorum. Quibus adiecit Alexander papa predictus. Ex dono comitis Rob[er]ti Leyc[estrie] etc. manerium de Knyton' cum terris etc. Statuimus preterea vt nulli ecclesiastice seculari ne persone liceat indebitas et iniustas exactiones in prefata ecclesia exercere. Preterea quando commune interdictum terre fuerit liceat vobis clausis ianuis exclusis excommunicatis et interdictis non pulsatis tintinabulis suppressa voce in ecclesia vestra diuina officia celebrare. Liceat quoque vobis clericos siue laicos liberos et absolutos de seculo fugientes ad conuersionem suscipere et in vestro collegio retinere. Prohibemus autem vt nulli fratrum vestrorum post factam in eodem loco professionem absque abbatis sui licencia de claustro discedere. Discedentem vero absque communi litterarum cautione nullus audeat retinere. Crisma oleum sanctum consecrationes altarium ordinationes clericorum qui ad sacros ordines fuerint promouendi a diocesano suscipietis episcopo si quid catholicus fuerit et gratiam atque communionem sedes apostolice habuerit et ea . . . et absque prauitate vobis voluerit exhibere. Alioquin liceat vobis quem malueritis adire antistetem qui . . . nostram subtus auctoritate quod postulatur indulgeat.

> The date of this bull is indicated in the rubric of the register as 'privileges of Pope Alexander in the year of our Lord 1161', Bodl. Laud misc. 625, f. 181r. The dates of the incarnational year 1161 are therefore adopted above.

11. Robert of Croft   1156 x 1163

Grant to the abbey of the church of (West) Kilworth, Leics. and notification that he has presented Abbot Richard to Hugh Barre, archdeacon of Leicester, as the incumbent of the church, saving only the interest of Nicholas of Knaptoft. Also a confirmation of the land in Sutton Cheney, Leics. granted to the abbey by Robert's father, Geoffrey, when he became a canon there.

> A = Original, now lost. B = TNA E13/76, m. 68, copy of 1351 (from A).

[B]

Vniuersis sancte matris ecclesie fidelibus, Robertus de Crest, salutem. Nouerint cuncti fideles tam posteri quam presentes quod ego Rob[er]tus pro salute mea et pro animabus patris et matris mee et pro animabus omnium antecessorum et successorum meorum dedi et presenti carta mea confirmaui deo et ecclesie sancte Marie de Prato Leircestr' et canonicis regularibus ibidem deo seruientibus ecclesiam de Westkyuelyngwrd' que est de feudo meo cum terris et omnibus aliis pertinentiis et libertatibus suis in perpetuam elemosinam. et presentaui Ric[ardu]m abbatem Hugoni Barre archidiacono Leircestr' qui eum ad presentationem meam recepit et personam in prefata ecclesia eundem abbatem instituit saluo tenemento Nich[ola]i de Cnapetoft. Preterea concessi et presenti carta mea confirmaui prenominatis canonicis in perpetuam elemosinam totam terram illam quam Gaufridus pater meus habuit in Sutton' cum omnibus libertatibus suis in pratis pascuis et in omnibus locis liberam et quietam ab omni seruitio et exactione seculari quam scilicet terram idem pater meus prenominatis canonicis dedit quando ibidem se in canonicum reddidit. Quare volo et firmiter constituo vt prefati canonici omnia que predicta sunt habeant et teneant bene et in pace libere et honorifice quieta ab omni seruitio et exactione seculari erga omnes homines quia ego et heredes mei illos adquietabimus erga omnes homines. Hiis testibus. Rob[er]to comite Leircestr' Ern[aldo] de Bosco Iuone de Allespatha Ansch[etillo] de Creft. magistro Ric[ard]o de Sallau Rob[er]to et Math[e]o capell[anis] Will[elm]o Genus. Rog[er]o Stori. Richerio de la Bara Rogero de Cranford Gilleb[erto] Pesceremne Hugone de Dunham Barth[olome]o de Sifrewast Christiano Ern[aldo] de Cam[er]a Henr[ico] Clement.

> The dates of this charter are dictated by the tenure of Hugh Barre of the archdeaconry of Leicester, a post he had resigned by 1163 at the very latest (see, *Fasti Ecclesiae Anglicanae 1066–1300 3, Lincoln*, ed. D. E. Greenway (London 1977), 33). This charter was issued after the confirmation charter of Henry II to the abbey, which does not mention Kilworth or Robert's confirmation of his father's grant.

12. Geoffrey L'Abbé   1155 x 1168

Grant, with the consent of his wife, Emma, and his son, Richard, of six virgates in Bramcote, Warwicks. which Roger de Vatteville had given him. Grant also of a half carrucate of land in Rothley, Leics. and the land in Leicester which Ralph of Blaby held of him.

> A = Original, now lost. B = Second Leicester Cartulary (from A). C = TNA E13/76 mm. 70d–71, copy dated 1351, from A. D = Leicester Rental (digest from B, now lost). E = Bodl. Laud misc. 625, f. 34r (from D).

[C]

Vniuersis sancte dei ecclesie fidelibus, Galfr[id]us Labbe salutem. Sciatis me dedisse deo et ecclesie sancte Marie Legrecestr' de Prato et canonicis regularibus deo ibidem seruientibus concessu vxoris mee et Ric[ard]i fil[ii] mei sex virgatas terre in Brancothe quas Rogerus de Wateuilla michi dedit et carta sua confirmauit cum hominibus et omnibus pertinentiis suis in perpetuam elemosinam liberam et quietam ab omni seruitio seculari erga me et heredes meos et eadem libertate dimidiam carucatam terre de Ruelawa cum omnibus pertinentiis suis et illam terram in Leic[estria] quam Rad[ulfu]s de Blaby de me tenebat. Hanc donationem feci predictis canonicis pro salute anime mee et vxoris et filiorum meorum et pro animabus patris et matris mee. Quare volo et firmiter concedo vt prefati canonici hanc meam elemosinam libere et quiete et honorifice teneant. Test[ibus] Emma vxore mea Ric[ard]o fil[io] meo magistro Waltero medico et Rob[er]to et Math[e]o capellanis Rad[ulf]o de Cratfh Will[elm]o de Chereby Ioh[ann]e et Rogero hominibus abbatis Legrecest[rie].

> The grants recorded here are not mentioned in Henry ii's confirmation, and so must have been made after 1155. The chaplains mentioned as witnesses are those of the households of Earl Robert ii and Countess Amice (see Crouch, *The Beaumont twins*, 149–50), and so the charter must date before the earl's death in 1168.

13. Robert ii, earl of Leicester   September 1164 x April 1168

Refoundation of the collegiate church of St Mary de Castro for a dean, chaplain and six other canons, to be nominated by the abbey of St Mary of Leicester. The college is to receive all the offerings and tithes of the church of St Mary, except offerings of fruits. The sacrist of the abbey to provide for two prebends and devote twenty shillings from the earl's exchequer for upkeep of the services of the church. The eighth prebend is to provide for a chaplain in the church of St Mary, who is to continue to receive the upkeep paid by the abbey to the previous chaplains. The dean and canons are to take an oath of good faith and canonical subjection to the abbot. Any vicar choral appointed is to be instituted by the bishop of Lincoln.

> A = Original, now lost. B = Leicester Rental (from A, now lost). C = Bodl. Laud misc. 625, f. 95r (from B).

[C]

Vniuersis sancte matris ecclesie filiis Robertus comes Leyc[estrie] salutem. Notum sit universitati vestre quod Ricardus abbas et conuentus ecclesie sancte Marie de Prato prouiderunt ex concensu et consilio meo etc. octo clericos honestos etc. ad seruiendum in ecclesia sancte Marie de Castello ab eis eligendos. ad quorum sustentacionem concesserunt omnes oblaciones et omnes decimas exceptis manipulis frugum et omnia beneficia parochie illius ecclesie que antea commune uocabatur. Ita quod due porciones cedent sacriste qui ecclesie seruicio prouidebit cum .xx. s[olidis] de scaccario etc. Relique sex porciones dabuntur sex clericis cum eo etc. Octauus erit capellanus qui ad sustentacionem suam habebit quod priores capellani ante eum habere solebant. Sacramento singuli fidelitate et canonicam subiectionem ecclesie sancte Marie de Prato promittent etc. + Decanus et ceteri canonici instituendi sunt per abbatem. Vicarius instituendus est per episcopum etc.

> The date of this charter is fixed by the existing constitution for the refounded chapter issued by Abbot Richard (*Ancient charters prior to 1200*, ed. J. H. Round, Pipe Roll Society 10 (1888), 59). Abbot Richard's constitution was witnessed by Payn, abbot of Sawtry, who is known to have succeeded his predecessor after September 1164. Richard was succeeded in his abbacy of Leicester in 14 Henry ii (December 1167 x December 1168) and Earl Robert ii died on 5 April 1168.

14. Robert ii, earl of Leicester   September 1162 x April 1168

Order to his son, Robert de Breteuil, to exchange the manor of Knighton, Leics. with the abbot.

> A = Original, now lost. B = BL Harley 782, f. 96r (summary in English of *c*. 1604 by Ralph Brooke) (from A). C = BL Cotton Julius c vii, f. 232 (*c*. 1611 by Nicholas Charles) (from A) then in the College of Arms 'the seale broken away'.
>
> Pd. Nichols, *Leicester*, i pt. 2, Appendix p. 55 (from C); Crouch, 'Earls and bishops', 20.

[C]

Robertus comes Legr[ecestrie] universis sancte matris ecclesiae filiis et fidelibus salutem. Sciatis quod volo et precipio Roberto filio meo etc. ut excambiat terram de Chenctinton' cum abbate Legr[ecestrie]. Test[ibus] Turstino abbate de Terondona. Roberto priore de Kinedeworth. Roberto capell[ano]. Willelmo Bassett. Roberto de Craft. Rogero de Cranford. Anschetillo Mallore.

> The best indication of the date of this act is the leading attestation of William Basset. This is an indication that it was issued while he was sheriff of Leicestershire (September 1162 x Easter 1170). Earl Robert II died on 5 April 1168.

15. William of Lancaster   1156 x 1170

Grant to the abbey and its men of Cockerham, Lancs. with the agreement of William his son and heir and Gundreda his wife, for the health of King Henry II, Queen Eleanor and their children, and for the souls of Gilbert his father and Goditha his mother, his son Jordan and Margaret, the countess's daughter, of free commons throughout all his lordship of Lonsdale and Amounderness. The canons and their men to have all their benefits and beasts in those places with no exactions and service payable to William and his heirs, in the same way as they have them in their own woodlands, which extend beween Cockerham and Thornton, as far as the stream of Flackesfleth *running down to* Crokispul *and so into the river Lune* (Loir').

> A = Original, now lost. B = TNA JUST1/1400, m. 238 (transcript of A, inspected at assize at Wigan dated 2 August 1330).
> Pd. *Lancashire Pipe Rolls and Early Lancashire Charters*, ed. Farrer, 392–3.

[B]

Vniuersis sancte dei ecclesie fidelibus Will[elmu]s de Lancastre salutem. Notum sit vniversitati vestre me consilio et assensu Will[elm]i filii mei et heredis et Gundree uxoris mee. et pro salute domini mei Henr[ici] regis Angl[ie]. et regine A[lienore]. et puerorum suorum et pro salute animarum nostrarum et pro animabus Gileb[er]ti patris mei et Godithe matris mee et Iordani filii mei et Margarete filie comitisse et pro animabus parentum et omnium antecessorum meorum. dedisse et concessisse et hac presenti carta confirmasse in puram et perpetuam elemosinam. deo et ecclesie sancte Marie de Prato Leirc[estrie]. et canonicis regularibus ibidem deo seruientibus et hominibus suis de Cokerheim totam communam liberam per totum feodum meum in Lonisdale et in Aumundernesse in bosco et plano in aquis et pasturis. in pascione et in omnibus aliis locis necessariis. et vt sint quieti et homines sui in predictis locis de pannagio. Quare volo et firmiter constituo vt predicti canonici et homines sui de Cokerheim habeant omnia aisiamenta sua et aueria eorum in predictis locis. libere et quiete ab omni seruitio et exactione seculari erga me et heredes meos. sicut habent in suo dominico nemore quod extenditur vsque ad diuisas inter Cokerheim et Thurnum. scilicet vsque ad aquam que vocatur Flackesfleth' que descendit in Crokispul. et sic in Loir'. Et prohibeo ne aliquis heredum vel seruientium meorum aliquod grauamen. seu dampnum. vel impedimentum predictis canonicis vel hominibus eorum inferat. quin libere et quiete predictam communam habeant et teneant imperpetuum. sicut hec carta mea testatur cum omnibus libertatibus et liberis consuetudinibus. quas ego in predicto manerio de Cokerheim habui dum illud in meo dominico tenui. Hiis testibus. Will[elm]o filio meo et herede. Gundr[eda] filia comitisse. Rob[er]to capellano. Will[elm]o capellano de Warton'. Rad[ulf]o filio Nich[ola]i. Rob[er]to le Heriz. Rob[er]to de Mundeguma. Will[elm]o filio Danielis. Rob[er]to Mustel. Rob[er]to camerario. Will[elm]o de Kair'. Thomas filio Will[elm]i. Math[e]o filio Will[elm]i Malest[er]mi. Rog[er]o Agulin. Will[em]o de Langeford'. Alb[er]to de Cardula. Math[e]o de Leuns et multis aliis.

> The date of this charter must be subsequent to the confirmation by Henry II which does not mention its grants (see no. 8). It might otherwise date to any time until William of Lancaster's death in 1170. I must thank Dr David Crook of the National Archives for his help in identifying this act.

16. Hugh of Arden   *c.* 1178 x 1184

Grant of the place called Berwood (in Curdworth) Warwicks. with its assarts and meadows for the souls of himself, his wife Adeliza, his elder brother Osbert, and his younger brother Henry. Confirmation also to the canons of part of his wood there between the course of the stream called Ebrok *and the course of the river Tame, with the island called* Wychesholm *up to the boundaries of Erdington, and the homage and service which Alan of Bromwich owed Hugh for land worth twelve pence in rent within those boundaries. The canons gave Hugh forty marks (£26 13s. 4d.) for this confirmation, giving also an ounce of gold to his wife, and a mark (13s. 4d.) each to his brothers, and giving twenty marks (£13 6s. 8d.) to Earl William of Warwick, for his confirmation.*

A = Original, now lost. B = Second Leicester Cartulary (from A). C = TNA E13/76 m. 71, copy dated 1351 (from A). D = Leicester Rental (digest from B, now lost). E = Bodl. Laud misc. 625, f. 22r (from D).

[C]

Vniuersis sancte matris ecclesie filiis Hugo de Arden', salutem. Sciant omnes tam posteri quam presentes quod ego Hugo pro salute anime mee et Adelicie vxoris mee et fratrum meorum et pro animabus patris et matris mee et antecessorum meorum assensu et concensu Osb[er]ti fratris mei senioris et Henr[ici] fratris mei iunioris dedi et presenti carta mea confirmaui deo et ecclesie sancte Marie de Prato Leircestr' et canonicis regularibus ibidem deo seruientibus locum de Berewde cum exartis et pratis et omnibus aliis locis in puram et perpetuam elemosinam. Preterea concessi et presenti carta mea confirmaui[a] prenominatis canonicis in Berewda totam illam partem nemoris mei que est inter filum aque de Ebrok' et filum aque de Tama cum insula de Wychesholm vsque ad divisas de Erdynton' et homagium et seruitium Alani de Bromwych' de tenemento quod de me tenuit infra predictas diuisas scilicet de duodecim deneratis[b] terre. ipse autem Alanus et heredes sui reddent illos duodecim denarios prefatis canonicis annuatim in vigilia Pasche sicut Alanus michi ante reddere solebat. Pro nemore autem predicto et homagio et seruitio predicti Alani dederunt michi prenominati canonici quadraginta marcas argenti et vxori mee vnam vnciam auri et Osberto fratri meo vnam marcam argenti et Henr[ico] fratri meo vnam marcam argenti et domino Will[elmo] comiti de Warewic' pro concessione et confirmatione sua viginti marcas argenti. Volo itaque et firmiter constituo vt prenominati canonici omnia que prenominata sunt habeant et teneant in perpetuam et liberam elemosinam bene et in pace libere et quiete ab omni seruitio et exactione seculari erga me et heredes meos et omnes homines quia ego et heredes mei erga omnes homines omnia que prenominata sunt adquietabimus. Ita scilicet quod infra predictas diuisas habeant omnia aisiamenta sua sicut viderint magis expedire sibi et eccelesia sue habeant eciam pannagium suum quietum et omnes libertates suas. ita quod nullus heredum vel hominum meorum infra predictas diuisas sine voluntate canonicorum prenominatorum aliquid de nemore ipsorum capiat. quia volo quod homines mei habeant aisiamenta sua in nemore meo quod ibi habeo. Hiis testibus Adelicia vxore mea Rog[er]o fil[io] com[itis] Leircestr'. Helia de Molinton' Will[elm]o de Widuilla Rog[er]o de Houma Rob[er]to capellano comit[is] Leircestr' magistro Ric[ard]o de Aisfordeby et Rad[ulf]o fratre suo Adam de Branteston' Alex[andr]o dispensatore Rad[ulfo] janitore et multis aliis in testimonium conuocatis.

[a] interlined C. [b] sic C.

Roger, son of the earl of Leicester, is the well-known cleric and son of Robert III, who became chancellor of Scotland in 1187 and was elected to the see of St Andrews in 1189. He was consecrated in 1198 and died in 1202 (*Fasti Ecclesiae Scoticanae medii aevi ad annum 1638*, ed. D. E. R. Watt and A. L. Murray (rev. edn Edinburgh 2003), 379). Roger is known to have been born around 1168 and it is unlikely that his *recordatio* would have been inserted in a charter before he was ten years old, but he was certainly still under age when it was issued, for he did not reach his majority till 1184. He is not noted here as a clerk, which confirms he was not yet old enough to receive ordination into the major orders. The charter must otherwise date to before 1184 and the death of Earl William of Warwick. Hugh was the son of Siward of Arden, who died in 1139.

17. Richard I, king of England   Westminster, 8 November 1189
Takes the abbey under his personal protection, as if it were one of his own houses, with exemption from all secular exactions and free passage on land and through his ports.

A = Original, now lost. B = TNA C52/22 (Cartae Antiquae Rolls), m. 23 (s. xiii in.) (from A). C = BL Harley 84, f. 272r–v (s. xvii) (from B). D = BL Harley 6748, f. 13v (s. xvii) (brief notice from B).
Pd. (in part), Nichols, *Leicester*, i pt. 2, Appendix p. 58 (from C).

[B]

Ric[ardus] dei gratia rex Angl[orum]. dux Norm[annorum] Aquit[annorum]. com[es] And[egauorum]. archiepiscopis. episcopis. comitibus. baronibus. baill[iuis]. ministris. et omnibus fidelibus suis. Franc[is] et Angl[is]. salutem. Sciatis nos recepisse in nostra propria manu et custodia et protectione sicut unam de propriis nostris elemosinis, ecclesiam sancte Marie Leirc[est]r[ie] de Prato. cum omnibus pertinentiis suis. Quare volumus et firmiter precipimus. quod canonici in predicta ecclesia deo seruientes. omnia tenementa sua teneant bene et in pace. et libere. et quiete. et integre. et plenarie. et honorifice. in bosco et plano. in pratis et pascuis. in aquis et mariscis. in piscariis. in toftis et croftis. in viis et semitis. et in omnibus locis. tam in burgo quam extra burgum. libera et quieta de geldis et danegeldis. et auxiliis. et wapentacis. et hundredis. et schiris et tenemannetale. et murdro. et scuagio. et assisis. et summonitionibus. et de omnibus placitis et querelis. et occasionibus. et consuetudinibus. et de omni terreno seruitio. et seculari exactione. cum saca et socha et toll et theam. et infangenetheof. et aliis omnibus consuetudinibus et libertatibus. Et uolumus ut predicti canonici et homines sui habeant saluum conductum nostrum et fuerint liberi et quieti a passagio et pontagio. et teloneo. et stallagio per omnes ciuitates nostras. et burgos. et uenderint et emant libere et quiete. Et uolumus ut sint quieti a trauerso per omnes portus nostros. et siquis uersus domum illam aliquid de possessionibus eius clamauerit prohibemus ne pro aliquo respondeant. nec in placitum ponantur, nisi per nos et in presentia nostra. T[estibus]. B. Cantuar[ensi] arch[iepiscopo]. H. Dunelm[ensi] episcopo. W. de Longo campo cancell[ario] nostro. et Elyen[si] electo. Rob[erto] de Witef[elda]. viii. die Nouembris. Apud Westm[onasterium].

Although the transcript omits the regnal year, the fact that William de Longchamp is elect of Ely locates it in the king's first year.

18. Thomas of Arden   Northampton, 3 September 1189 x June 1190

Confirmation of grants made at Berwood (in Curdworth), Warwicks. by his uncle Hugh and his father Henry, with the consent of Earl William of Warwick. Confirmation also of the church of Curdworth with lands and the tithe of pannage and mills there. Grant of an acre from woodland in his lordship in breadth along the north bank of the Ebroc and in length from the road called Berewdestrete up to the course of the river Tame. For this confirmation and grant the canons gave him five marks (£3 6s. 8d.).

A = Original, now lost. B = Second Leicester Cartulary (from A). C = TNA E13/76 m. 76, copy dated 1351 (from A). D = Leicester Rental (digest from B, now lost). E = Bodl. Laud misc. 625, f. 22v (from D).

[C]

Vniuersis sancte matris ecclesie filiis Thom[as] de Ardena, salutem. Sciant omnes tam posteri quam presentes quod ego Thom[as] de Ardena pro salute anime mee et vxoris mee et liberorum meorum et pro animabus patris et matris mee et pro anima Hug[onis] de Ardena aduunculi mei concedo et ratum habeo et hac mea carta in puram et perpetuam elemosinam confirmo omnes donationes et elemosinas quas fecit Hugo de Ardena aduunculus meus et Henr[icus] de Ardena pater meus cum consensu Will[elm]i comitis de Warewich' domini mei ecclesie sancte Marie Leyc[estrensis] de Prato et canonicis regularibus ibidem deo seruientibus scilicet locum de Berewda cum exartis et pratis et omnibus aliis pertinentiis suis in bosco et plano et in omnibus locis cum omnibus libertatibus suis. Et ex donatione Hug[onis] aduunculi mei ecclesiam de Creddewrth' cum terris et omnibus pertinentiis et libertatibus suis et decimam de toto pannagio meo ad predictam ecclesiam pertinentem et decimam de molendinis de Creddewrth'. Preterea concessi et presenti carta confirmaui predictis canonicis totam illam partem nemoris mei de Berewida que est inter filum aque de Ebrok' et filum aque de Thama cum insula de Wichisholm' vsque ad diuisas de Erdurth[intuna] et homagium et totum seruitium Alani de Bromwych et heredum suorum de tenemento quod de me tenuit infra predictas diuisas. Quare volo et firmiter constituo vt prenominati canonici omnia que prenominata sunt habeant imperpetuum et teneant bene et in pace libere et quiete ab omni seruitio et exactione seculari contra me et heredes meos et contra omnes homines. Quia ego et heredes mei contra omnes homines que prenominata sunt warantizabimus. Et etiam quod infra predictas diuisas habeant aisiamenta sua sicut viderint magis expedire sibi et ecclesie sue. Habeant etiam pannagium suum totum quietum et omnes libertates suas de predicto bosco suo. ita quod nullus heredum uel hominum meorum infra predictas diuisas sine voluntate canonicorum prenominatorum aliquid de nemore ipsorum capiat, quia volo quod homines mei habeant aisiamenta sua in nemore meo. Preterea accreui predictis canonicis et hac presenti carta mea confirmaui et in puram et perpetuam elemosinam dedi vnam acram in latitudinem de dominico nemore meo iuxta aquam de Ebroc versus aquilonarem partem, in longitudinem a via que dicitur Berewdestrete vsque ad filum aque de Thama. Pro hac autem augmentatione et donatione et confirmatione predicte acre nemoris mei dederunt michi predicti canonici quinque marcas argenti. Omnes vero alias donationes predictas in puram et perpetuam elemosinam eis concessi et confirmaui. Hiis testibus. Benedicto abbate de Burgo Hucb[erto] archid[iacono] Ebroic[ensi] Rad[ulf]o fil[io] Steph[an]i

Galfr[id]o filio Petri Mich[ael]e Belet Ric[ard]o de Pech' Ioh[ann]e le Kenteis tunc justic[iariis] domini regis coram quibus facta est ista confirmatio aput Norhamt[onam] in primo anno coronationis domini Ric[ard]i regis Angl[orum]. Steph[an]o de Pousend' Will[elm]o de Ardena Math[eo] de Dunt' Alano de Bromwych' Simon[e] de Becheston' magistro Will[elm]o Purmentin Henr[ico] clerico de Estona Ad[a] decano de Bulkynt[ona] Ioh[ann]e capellano de Creft Nich[ola]o clerico de Creddewrth' Will[elm]o filio Godefridi et multis aliis.

> The charter's date can be refined by a reference in a later act of Thomas (see below no. 29), which makes it clear that this transaction was carried out as he was preparing to leave for the Third Crusade, it is likely then that it dates to a time before July 1190, when King Richard's army finally got under way, heading south through Burgundy.

19. Robert III, earl of Leicester   1168 x 1190

Confirmation to the abbey of a rent of four shillings in Welton, Northants. granted to it by Roger of Cranford and Elena his wife, which Elena had as a gift from the earl's mother, Countess Amice. The grant was acknowledged in his presence by John of Cranford, their son and heir, who asked the earl to confirm it by the impression of his seal.

> A = Original, now lost. B = Second Leicester Cartulary (from A). C = Leicester Rental (from B, now lost). D = Bodl. Laud misc. 625, f. 143r (from C).

[D]

Robertus comes Leyc[estrie] omnibus sancte matris ecclesie filiis salutem. Sciatis quod donatio quam Rogerus de Cranford et Elena uxor eius fecerunt abbathie sancte Marie de Prato Leyc[estrie] scilicet redditum terre de Weltona quam mater mea Amicia comitissa iamdicte Elene donauerat, unde .iiij.^{or} solidos per annum recepit. Johannes Cranford eorum filius et heres recognouit coram me et concessit et in testimonium predicte donationis et concessionis per petitionem predicti Johannis sigillum meum apposui et predictum redditum predicte abathie confirmaui. Hiis testibus, etc.

> The date of this act cannot be fixed any closer than the tenure of the earldom by Robert III.

20. John, king of England   Rouen, 4 August 1199

Notification that he has taken the abbey under his protection as if it were a house in his own advocacy, with exemptions from taxation and attendance on courts; exemptions from all secular demands; with safe passage for the canons and their men, quit of all tolls in his cities and boroughs, and free passage through his ports; and with the privilege that they are only to be tried for any plea before the king himself.

> A = Original, now lost. B = TNA c53/1 (Charter Roll of 1 John), m.25 (from A).
> Pd. *Rotuli Chartarum in turri Londinensi asservati*, ed. T. D. Hardy, Publications of the Record Commission 25 (London 1837), 9.

[B]

Iohannes dei gratia etc. Sciatis nos suscepisse in nostra propria manu. et custodia et protectione sicut unam de propriis nostris elemosinis, ecclesiam sancte Marie Leic' de Prato cum omnibus pertinentiis suis. Quare volumus et firmiter precipimus quod canonici in predicta ecclesia deo seruientes omnis tenementa sua teneant bene et in pace. et libere. et quiete. et integre. et plenarie. et honorifice. in bosco et plano. et pratis. et pascuis. et aquis. et mariscis. in piscariis. in toftis et croftis. in viis et semitis. et in omnibus locis tam in burgo quam extra. libera et quieta de geldis et de danegeldis. et auxiliis. et wapentac'. et hundredis. et sirris. et tenemmentale. et murdro. et scuagio. et assisis. et sumonitionibus et de omnibus placitis et querelis. et occasionibus. et consuetudinibus. et de omni terreno seruitio et seculari exactione. cum sacca et socca. tol et them. et infengenthef. et aliis omnibus consuetudinibus et libertatibus. Et volumus ut predicti canonici et homines sui habeant saluum conductum nostrum. et sint quieti et liberi a passagio et pontagio. et theloneo. et stallagio. per omnes ciuitates nostras et burg[os]. et vendant et emant libere et quiete. Et volumus ut sint quieti a tranverso per omnes portus nostros. et si quis versus domum illam aliquid de possessionibus eius clamauerit, prohibemus ne pro aliquo respondeant nec in placit[o] ponantur nisi per nos et in presentia nostra. sicut carta H[enrici] regis patris nostri testatur. T[estibus]. R[ogero] de sancto Andrea episcopo. W[illelmo] maresc[allo] com[ite] de Penbroc, etc. Dat[um] per manum H[uberti] Cant[uarensis] arch[iepiscopi] cancell[arii] nostri. Apud Roth[omagum] .iiij. die Aug[usti] anno regni nostri primo.

21. Robert IV, earl of Leicester   1192 x 1204, perhaps 1195 x 1198

Grant to the abbey with the burial of his body of a rent of a hundred shillings in land, to be drawn from twenty-four virgates of land in the village of Anstey, Leics. of which seven are assarted from the woodland and the other seventeen are held in villein tenure, paying £4. 16s. 0d per annum. Grant also of four cottagers with their tofts in the same village paying four shillings per annum to make up the rent to a hundred shillings.

> A = Original, now lost. B = Leicester Cartulary (from A). C = Inspeximus of Edward III, king of England, now lost (from A). D = Leicester Rental (digest of charter from B, now lost). E = TNA c56/16 (Confirmation Roll of 3 Henry VII, pt. 3), m. 18, copy of 1487 (from C). F = Bodl. Laud misc. 625, ff. 7r, 12r (from D).

[E]

Vniuersis sancte matris ecclesie filiis ad quos presens scriptum peruenerit Rob[er]tus comes Leycestrie filius Rob[er]ti comitis et Petronille comitisse salutem in domino. Nouerit vniuersitas vestre me dedisse et hac presenti carta mea confirmasse cum corpore meo deo et ecclesie sancte Marie de Prato Leycestrie et canonicis regularibus ibidem deo seruientibus pro salute anime mee et Lorete vxoris mee et omnium antecessorum et successorum in liberam quietam et perpetuam elemosinam centum solidatas terre scilicet viginti ct quatuor virgatas terre in villa de Anesty cum hominibus et omnibus aliis pertinentiis suis vnde septem sunt de assartis et decem et septem de vilenagio. Reddendo annuatim quatuor libras et sexdecim solidos prefatis canonicis. Preterea dedi eis in predicta villa quatuor cotarios cum toftis suis. reddendo eis annuatim quatuor solidos[a] ad perficiendum predictos centum solidatos terre. Quare volo et firmiter constituo vt predicti canonici hanc meam elemosinam habeant et teneant bene et in pace in bosco et plano in pratis et pascuis et in omnibus aliis locis libere et quiete ab omni seruitio et exactione seculari erga me et heredes meos et erga omnes homines. Hiis testibus. magistro H. de Gileuile. Ric[ard]o cel[er]ario de Lira. Will[elm]o capellano comitis magistro Ioh[ann]e archid[iacono] Ph[ilipp]o de Aubeni Thoma de Estleia tunc senescallo comitis. Walt[er]o. Franco Trenchefele Will[elm]o de Seineuile Will[elm]o de Langeton' Will[elm]o de Belegraue Luca Rob[erto] Ph[ilipp]o Jordano clericis domini comitis Rob[erto] de Kerebi et multis aliis.

> [a] silidos E.

> The date of this act is within the tenure of the earldom by Robert IV, and after his return from the Middle East in 1192. The appearance in the witness list of an archdeacon called M. John might narrow the date to between 1195 and 1198. No archdeacon called John has been noted between 1190 and 1204 in the fasti of the diocese of Lincoln, but it is possible that – if he were an archdeacon of Leicester – he could have occupied the archdeaconry between M. Roger of Rolleston (who became dean of Lincoln in 1195) and M. Reimund, whose earliest appearance as archdeacon was in 1198. The only John known as archdeacon in the diocese in this generation was M. John of Tynemouth, who was archdeacon of Oxford in succession to Walter Map; but since he did not succeed till after 1208, he cannot possibly be the John of this deed.

22. Robert IV, earl of Leicester   November 1200 x August 1203

Grant to the abbey of land at Farthinghoe and Syresham, Northants. called Westcote, which his grandfather, Robert II, had given to the see of Lincoln in exchange for the manor of Knighton, Leics. and the bishop's suburb of Leicester. The earl makes this grant to the abbey as an exchange for its lands at Asfordby and Seagrave, Leics. which the earl had transferred to Lincoln as part of the process of making peace over the issue of Knighton and the suburb.

> A = Original, now lost. B = Second Leicester Cartulary (from A). C = TNA E13/76 m. 71 (copy of A dated 1351). D = Leicester Rental, digest of charter from B, now lost. E = Bodl. Laud misc. 625, f. 64r (from D).

[C]

Notum sit omnibus tam presentibus quam futuris quod ego Rob[er]tus comes Leicestrie fil[ius] Petronille comitisse dedi et concessi et hac presenti carta mea confirmaui deo et ecclesie sancte Marie Leicestrie de Prato et canonicis regularibus ibidem deo seruientibus in liberam et perpetuam elemosinam terras de Farnighou et de Sigresham scilicet Westcote cum omnibus pertinentiis suis quas Rob[er]tus comes auus meus dederat ecclesie Lincoln[iensi] in escambium pro manerio de Knichtetona et suburbio Leicestr[ie] et canonicis dedi pro terris suis de Esfordeby et de Segraue cum pertinentiis suis quas assensu eorum dedi ecclesie de Lincoln[ia] pro pace reformanda inter me et ipsam ecclesiam super predicto manerio de Knichteton' et suburbio Leicestr[ie] cum pertinentiis suis in quibus predicte ecclesie Leicestr[ie] et canonicis concessi quicquid in eis habuerunt sicut carte antecessorum meorum et mea testantur. Hiis testibus. Thoma de Estleg' tunc senescallo meo Ph[ilipp]o de Aubeni Steph[an]o de Longo campo Oliuero de Aubeni Gruell[o] le Flemeng' Will[elm]o capell[ano] Luca clerico Will[elm]o de Seneuill' Will[elm]o Furmentin Waltero de Estleg' Will[elm]o Trenchefuille Rob[er]to clerico Hamone clerico et multis aliis.

The date of this act is established by the documentation of the cause between Earl Robert and the see of Lincoln. The earl had moved against the see during the vacancy between 1200 and 1203 and persuaded its guardians to surrender all claim on Knighton and its suburban estate: note that the concord reported here mentions no bishop involved. In April 1204 (see below) the new bishop, William of Blois, was forced to accept this deal by King John. The most likely date for the above act is therefore in the vacancy between November 1200 and August 1203 (see Crouch, 'Earls and bishops', 16–18).

23. Richard son of Herbert 1190 X 1204

Grant to the abbey of two acres in the meadows of Thurmaston, Leics. next to the meadowland the canons already had there.

A = Original, now lost. B = TNA E13/76, m. 68d, copy of 1351 (from A).

[B]

Omnibus Christi fidelibus ad quos presens scriptum peruenerit, Ricardus fil[ius] Herb[erti], salutem. Noueritis me concessisse et dedisse et hac presenti carta mea confirmasse in puram et perpetuam elemosinam deo et ecclesie sancte Marie de Prato Legr[ecestrie] et canonicis regularibus ibidem deo seruientibus duas acras prati in prato de Thurmodeston' iuxta dominicum pratum abbatis et canonicorum de Legr[ecestria]. Tenendas libere et quiete et honorifice inperpetuum ab omni seruitio et exactione erga me et heredes meos et omnes homines. Hiis testibus Gilbe[erto] de Mineriis. Alano filio Rob[er]ti Ph[ilipp]o clerico comitis. Will[elm]o Tasche Will[elm]o Vldeuer. Nichol[ao] de Cestresham Waltero Golci et multis aliis.

Since the witness Philip was a clerk of Earl Robert IV, the charter must date from his tenure of the earldom.

24. Robert IV, earl of Leicester 1192 X 1204

Confirms to the abbey the grants made by his father and grandfather (see above). These include his father's grants of the right to collect three cartloads of wood daily in Leicester forest for the abbey fires; the right to pasture the abbey's pigs there with the earl's own; the grant of a stag on the feasts of the Assumption and the Nativity of the Virgin Mary; license to fish in the earl's great ponds at Groby, Leics. on the eve of the feasts of the Purification, the Annunciation, the Assumption and the Nativity of the Virgin Mary; pasture at Desford, Leics. for ten cows with their calves for two years, with the grant of two acres there in the alder groves between the road and M. Ralph of Ulverscroft's land.

A = BL Sloane charter xxxii 22, fig. 1 and p. 192, fig. 22. Endorsed: .ij.ᵃ in [cartis] fund[atorum] pro pastura in Desforde (s. xiv); Confirmatio Roberti comitis Leycestrie pro duobus ceruis et pro multis aliis (s. xv); 479 x 245 + 35mm.; seal and tongue missing.

[A]

Uniuersis sancte dei ecclesie fidelibus Robertus comes Leircestr[ie]. filius Petronelle comitisse eternam in domino salutem. Nouerint cuncti fideles tam posteri quam presentes quod ego Rob[ertus] comes Leirc[estrie] pro salute mea et Laurete uxoris et heredum meorum et pro animabus Rob[erti] comitis patris mei et Petronelle matris mee et Rob[erti] comitis aui mei et omnium antecessorum et successorum meorum concedo et confirmo ecclesie sancte Marie de Prato Leircestr[ie] quam Rob[ertus] auus meus fundauit et Rob[ertus] pater meus confirmauit ad opus canonicorum regularium omnes prebendas et possessiones que fuerunt canonicorum secularium ecclesie sancte Marie infra castellum quas .R[obertus]. auus meus per manum Alexandri Lincoln[iensis] episcopi transtulit et concessit et iure perpetuo confirmauit in usus canonicorum regularium. In primis videlicet concedo et confirmo eisdem canonicis regularibus prefatam ecclesiam sancte Marie cum tota possessione et parrochia sua. cum terris et decimis et pratis et omnibus aliis pertinentiis suis. cum omnibus libertatibus et quietudinibus quas .R[obertus]. comes Mellenti attauus meus predicte ecclesie ante concesserat. Item. concedo eis et confirmo extra portam de North eadem libertate .v. carrucatas terre. et viij.ᵗᵒ. mansiones hominum et in alia parte ciuitatis .iiij. virgatas. et .iiij. bouatas terre. et de redditibus Leircestr[ie] .vj. libras per annum. Ecclesias quoque omnes Leircestr[ie] tam infra muros quam extra que mee dicionis sunt cum domibus et mansuris. cum terris et decimis. et omnibus pertinentiis suis. Ecclesiam quoque de Lilleburna cum terris et decimis et omnibus pertinentiis suis et .lx.ᵗᵃ. solidos per annum de redditibus eiusdem ville. In Turmodesthona .iiij. carucatas et unam virgatam terre. Ex dono Ysabel comitisse attauie mee unam virgatam terre in Burthona.

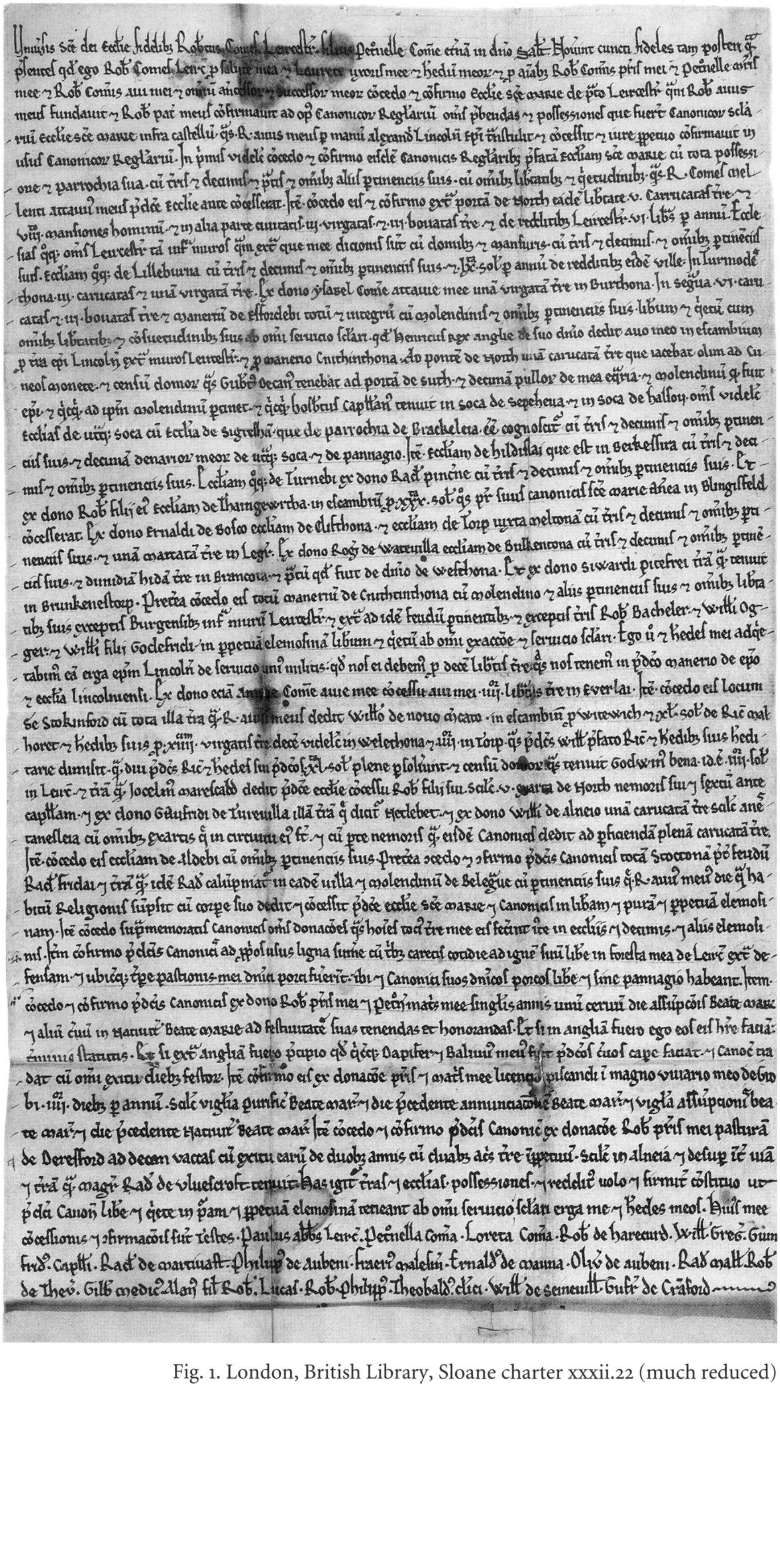

Fig. 1. London, British Library, Sloane charter xxxii.22 (much reduced)

In Segraua .vj. carucatas et .iij. bouatas terre et manerium de Esfordebi totum et integrum cum molendinis et omnibus pertinentiis suis. liberum et quietum cum omnibus libertatibus et consuetudinibus suis ab omni seruitio seculari. quod Henricus rex Anglie de suo dominio dedit auo meo in escambium pro terra episcopi Lincoln[ensis] extra muros Leircestr[ie] et pro manerio Cnithinthona. Ad pontem de North unam carucatam terre que iacebat olim ad cuneos monete. et censum domorum quas Gubertus decanus tenebat ad portam de Suth. et decimam pullorum de mea equaria. et molendinum quod fuit episcopi et quicquid ad ipsum molendinum pertinet et quicquid Hosbertus capellanus tenuit in soca de Sepeheua et in soca de Halsou. omnes videlicet ecclesias de utraque soca cum ecclesia de Sigresham. que de parrochia de Brackeleia esse cognoscitur. cum terris et decimis et omnibus pertinentiis suis et decimam denariorum meorum de utraque soca. et de pannagio. Item. ecclesiam de Hildislai que est in Berkessira cum terris et decimis et omnibus pertinentiis suis. Ecclesiam quoque de Turnebi ex dono Rad[ulfi] pincerne cum terris et decimis et omnibus pertinentiis suis. Et ex dono Rob[erti] filii eius ecclesiam de Thaingewrtha in escambium pro .xxx^{ta}. solidos. quos pater suus canonicis sancte Marie antea in Blingisfeld concesserat. Ex dono Ernaldi de Bosco ecclesiam de Clifthona. et ecclesiam de Torp iuxta Meltonam cum terris et decimis et omnibus pertinentiis suis. et unam marcatam terre in Legr[ecestria]. Ex dono Rogeri de Wateuilla ecclesiam de Bulkentona cum terris et decimis et omnibus pertinentiis suis. et dimidiam hidam terre in Brancota. et pratum quod fuit de dominio de Westhona. Et ex dono Siwardi Pitefrei terram quam tenuit in Brunkenestorp. Preterea concedo eis totum manerium de Cnithtinthona cum molendino et aliis pertinentiis suis et omnibus libertatibus suis exceptis burgensibus infra murum Leircestr[ie] et extra ad idem feudum pertinentibus. et exceptis terris Roberti Bacheler. et Willelmi Ogger. et Willelmi filii Godefridi, in perpetuam elemosinam liberum et quietum ab omni exactione et seruitio seculari. Ego uero et heredes mei adquietabimus eam erga episcopum Lincoln[iensem] de seruitio unius militis, quod nos ei debemus pro decem libratis terre. quas nos tenemus in predicto manerio de episcopo et ecclesia Lincolniensi. Ex dono etiam Amicie comitisse auie mee concessu aui mei .iiij^{or}. libratas terre in Everlai. Item, concedo eis locum de Stokinford cum tota illa terra quam R[obertus]. auus meus dedit Will[elm]o de Nouo mercato. in escambium pro Witewich et .xl. solidos de Ric[ardo] Malhoret et heredibus suis pro .xiiij^{cim}. virgatis terre, decem videlicet in Welethona et .iiij^{or}. in Torp. quas predictus Will[elmus] prefato Ric[ardo] et heredibus suis hereditarie dimisit. quamdiu predictus Ric[ardus] et heredes sui predictos .xl^{ta}. solidos plene persoluerint et censum domorum. quas tenuit Godwinus Bena. id est .iiij^{or}. solidos in Leirc[estria] et terram quam Jocelinus Marescald dedit predicte ecclesie concessu Rob[erti] filii sui. scilicet .v. exarta de North nemoris sui et sextam ante capellam. Et ex dono Gaufridi de Tureuilla illam terram que dicitur Netlebet. Et ex dono Will[elm]i de Alneio unam carucatam terre scilicet Anestanesleia cum omnibus exartis que in circuitu eius sunt. et cum parte nemoris quam eisdem canonicis dedit ad perficiendam plenam carucatam terre. Item. concedo eis ecclesiam de Aldebi cum omnibus pertinentiis suis. Preterea concedo et confirmo predictis canonicis totam Stoctonam preter feudum Rad[ulfi] Fridai et terram quam idem Rad[ulfus] calumpniatur in eadem uilla et molendinum de Belegraue cum pertinentiis suis que .R[obertus]. auus meus die quam habitum religionis sumpsit cum corpore suo dedit et concessit predicte ecclesie sancte Marie et canonicis in liberam et puram et perpetuam elemosinam. Item, concedo supramemoratis canonicis omnes donationes quas homines totius terre mee eis fecerint iuste in ecclesiis. et decimis. et aliis elemosinis. Item confirmo predictis canonicis ad proprios usus ligna sumere cum tribus carecis cotidie ad ignem suum libere in foresta mea de Leirc[estria] extra defensam. et ubicunque tempore pascionis. mei dominici porci fuerint, ibi et canonici suos dominicos porcos libere et sine pannagio habeant. Item. concedo et confirmo predictis canonicis ex dono Rob[erti] patris mei et Petron[ille] matris mee singulis annis unum ceruum die Assumptionis beate Marie et alium ceruum in Natiuitate beate Marie ad festiuitates suas tenendas et honorandas. Et si in Angliam fuero ego eos eis habere faciam, terminis statutis. Et si extra Angliam fuero precipio quod quicunque dapifer et baliuus meus fuerit predictos ceruos capere faciat. et canonicis^{a} tradat cum omni exitu diebus festorum. Item confirmo eis ex donatione patris et matris mee licenciam piscandi in magno uiuario meo de Grobi .iiij^{or}. diebus per annum. scilicet vigilia Purificationis beate Marie. et die precedente Annunciationem beate Marie. et vigilia Assumptionis beate Marie. et die precedente Natiuitatem beate Marie. Item concedo et confirmo predictis canonicis ex donatione Rob[erti] patris mei pasturam de Deresford' ad decem vaccas cum exitu earum de duobus annis cum duabus acris terre in perpetuum. scilicet in alneia et desuper inter uiam et terram quam magister Rad[ulfus] de Vluescroft. tenuit. Has igitur terras et ecclesias. possessiones. et redditus uolo et firmiter constituo ut predicti canonici libere et quiete in puram et perpetuam elemosinam teneant ab omni seruitio seculari erga me et heredes meos. Huius mee concessionis et confirmationis sunt testes. Paulus abbas Leirc[estrie]. Petronella comitissa. Loreta comitissa. Rob[ertus] de Harecurd. Will[elmus]. Greg[orius]. Gumfridus. capellani.[a] Rad[ulfus] de Martiuast. Philippus de Aubeni. Fraerius Malesin'. Ernaldus[b] de Mauna. Oliv[erus] de Aubeni. Rad[ulfus] Mall[ore]. Rob[ertus] de Thev'. Gilb[ertus] medicus. Alanus filius Rob[erti]. Lucas. Rob[ertus]. Philippus. Theobaldus. clerici. Will[elmus] de Seineuill'. G[a]ufr[idus] de Cranford'.

[a] canoc' A. [b] Ernaldo A.

The charter must date after the earl's return from crusade in 1192 and before his death in 1204. For an account of the scribal features of this charter see M. Gullick and T. Webber, 'Summary catalogue of surviving manuscripts from Leicester Abbey' above p. 192 (no. 25).

25. John, king of England   Wallingford, 20 April 1204

Notification that Earl Robert IV of Leicester has granted to William of Blois, bishop of Lincoln, the village of Asfordby, Leics. with the patronage of its church and its mills, along with six carrucates and three bovates of land in Seagrave, Leics. and the possessions of Leicester abbey there.

A = Original, now lost. B = TNA c53/5 (Charter Roll of 5 John), m. 7 (from A).
Pd. *Rotuli Chartarum*, ed. Hardy, 126.

[B]

Iohannes dei gratia etc. Sciatis Rob[ertus] comes Leirc[estrie] de consensu et voluntate P[auli] abbatis et conuentus Leirc[estrie]. coram nobis et coram domino H[uberti] Cant[uarensi] archiepiscopo. et multis aliis tam episcopis quam baronibus nostris. dedisse. et concessisse, et carta sua confirmasse. Will[elm]o episcopo Linc[olniensi]. et successoribus suis. et ecclesie Linc[olniensi] in perpetuum. totam villam de Essefordeby cum aduocatione ecclesie eiusdem ville. et cum molendinis et omnibus aliis pertinentiis suis. et sex carrucatas et tres bouatas terre in Segraue cum pertinentiis suis. et quicquid idem abbas et conuentus Leirc' tunc ibidem tenuerunt. Habenda et tenenda eidem episcopo. et successoribus suis. et ecclesie Linc[olniensi] in liberam. puram et perpetuam elemosinam. quieta ab omni seculari seruitio. Quare etc. quod predictus ep[iscopu]s Linc[olniensis]. et successores sui. et ecclesia Linc[olniensis] habeant et teneant omnia predicta tenementa cum omnibus pertinentiis suis inperpetuum. bene et in pace. libere. et quiete. et integre. in liberam. puram. et perpetuam elemosinam. sicut predictum est. T[estibus] G[aufrido] fil[io] Petri com[ite] Essex'. R[annulfo] com[ite] Cestr[ie]. Warin[o] fil[io] Ger[oldi]. Rob[erto] de Veteriponte. Petro de Stok'. Dat[um] per manum domini S[imonis] Cicestr[ensis] electi. Apud Waling' .xx. aprilis. anno etc. v[to].

26. John, king of England   Worcester, 24 March 1205

Confirmation of the grant to the abbey by its founder, Earl Robert II, of the manor of Knighton, Leics. with its mill and other belongings except the burgesses inside and outside the walls of Leicester who are attached to the fee and also except the lands of the earl's servants, Robert Bacheler, William son of Oger and William son of Godfrey, to hold in alms free of all exactions, except the service for Knighton of a knight towards the bishop of Lincoln. This the earls owe the bishop with ten pounds in rents which Robert II gave the diocese in Westcote, Northants. in return for Knighton and the suburb of Leicester.

A = Original, now lost. B = TNA c53/6 (Charter Roll of 6 John), m. 4 (from A).
Pd. Nichols, *Leicester*, i pt. 2, Appendix pp. 58–9 (copy from partial s.xvii transcript of B in BL Harley 84, f. 271v); *Rotuli Chartarum*, ed. Hardy, 145 (from B).

[B]

Iohannes dei gratia etc. Sciatis nos concessisse et presenti carta nostra confirmasse in liberam quietam et perpetuam elemosinam deo et ecclesie sancte Marie de Prato Leirc[estrie] et canonicis regulariter ibidem deo seruientibus. ex dono Roberti comitis Leirc[estrie] fundatoris eiusdem ecclesie. totum manerium de

Cnihtinton' quod eis dedit cum molendino et aliis pertinentiis. et omnibus libertatibus suis. exceptis burgensibus infra muros Leirc[estrie] et extra ad idem feodum pertinentibus. et exceptis terris seruientium suorum. scilicet Rob[erti] Bacheler. et Will[elm]i Oggeri. et Will[elm]i filii Godefridi. in perpetuam elemosinam. liberam et quietam ab omni exactione et seruitio seculari. ita quod heredes sui acquietabunt hanc elemosinam erga dominum episcopum Linc[olnie] de seruitio vnius militis, quod ei debent pro .x. libratis terre. quas tenuerunt in predicto manerio de episcopo et ecclesia Linc[olniensi]. Concessimus etiam et confirmauimus predictis canonicis in liberam et perpetuam elemosinam. ex dono Rob[erti] comitis Leirc[estrie] filius Petronille. terras de Farninghou et de Sigresham. scilicet Westcote. cum omnibus pertinentiis suis. quas Rob[ertus] comes auus eiusdem comitis dederat ecclesie Linc[olnensi]. in escambium pro predicto manerio de Cnihtinton' et suburbio Leirc[estrie] cum pertinentiis suis. quas etiam terras prefatus comes filius Petronille. assensu predicti episcopi et capituli Linc[olnie]. dedit predicte ecclesie et canonicis Leirc[estrie] pro terris suis de Esfordeby et de Segrave cum pertinentiis suis. quas assensu eorundem canonicorum dedit ecclesie Linc[olniensi] pro pace reformanda inter ipsos et ecclesiam Linc[olniensem] super predicto manerio de Cnihtinton' et suburbio Leirc[estrie] cum pertinentiis suis. in quo manerio et suburbio concessit predicte ecclesie et canonicis Leirc[estrie] quicquid in eis habuerunt. Preterea concessimus et confirmauimus eisdem canonicis Leirc[estrie] in liberam. quietam. et perpetuam elemosinam. ex dono predicti comitis filii Petronill[e] cum corpore suo .xxiiii.ᵒʳ virgatas terre in Anesty cum hominibus et aliis pertinentiis suis et .iiii.ᵒʳ cotarios cum toftis suis in eadem villa. et pasturam inter duas vias in defenso Leirc[estrie]. scilicet inter viam de Groby et viam de Anesty. ad aueria sua pascenda. et .i. carretatam ligni cotidie in foresta Leirc[estrie] inperpetuum ad focum domus infirmarie canonicorum Leirc[estrie]. cum aliis tribus carretatis suis quas ex donatione aui sui prius habuerunt. sicut carte predictorum donatorum quas inde habent rationabiliter testantur. Quare volumus etc. quod predicti canonici Leirc[estrie] habeant et teneant omnia predicta tenementa cum omnibus pertinentiis. in liberam et perpetuam elemosinam. sicut predictum est. bene et in pace. libere et quiete. integre et honorifice. in omnibus locis et rebus. cum omnibus libertatibus et liberis consuetudinibus. et quietantiis eis concessis tam per cartas regis H[enrici] patris nostri quam per alias cartas nostras quas habent. sicut carte ille testantur. T[estibus] G[alfrido] filio Petri comite Essex'. Henr[ico] de Buhun comite Hereford'. Will[elm]o de Braosa. Will[elm]o Briw[erre]. Petro de Stok'. Will[elm]o de Cantilup[o]. Sim[one] de Pateshill'. Iacob[o] de Poterna. Dat[um] per manum .I. de Well[es] apud Wigor[niam] .xxiiii. die marcii anno etc. viᵗᵒ.

27. Petronilla, countess of Leicester   1203 X 1212

Grant with the burial of her body to the abbey of her meadowland in Thurmaston, Leics. called Belholm *and her houses beyond the West Bridge in the suburb of Leicester, with their land and a garden, which Hugh the clerk once held.*

A = Original, now lost. B = Leicester Cartulary (from A). C = Inspeximus of Edward III, king of England, now lost (from A). D = Leicester Rental (digest of charter from B, now lost). E = TNA c56/16 (Confirmation Roll of 3 Henry VII, pt. 3), m. 18, copy of 1487 (from C). F = Bodl. Laud misc. 625, f. 5v, 12r (from D).

[E]

Vniuersis ad quos presens scriptum peruenerit Petronilla comitissa Leircestr[ie] salutem in domino. Nouerit vniuersitas vestra me dedisse et hac carta mea confirmasse cum corpore meo deo et ecclesie sancte Marie de Prato Leircestr' et canonicis regularibus ibidem deo seruientibus in liberam et perpetuam elemosinam totum pratum meum de Tormodeston' quod vocatur Belholm et domos meas in suburbio Leirc[estrie] cum terra et gardino vltra pontem de West que fuerunt Hug[onis] clerici. Tenendum et habendum imperpetuum sicut aliqua alia elemosina liberius et quietius dari poterit et teneri. Quod vt ratum et stabile perseueret imposterum presens scriptum sigilli mei munimine dignum duxi corroborare. Hiis testibus. A[dam] abbate Geroldon[e]. H. priore de War[ewico] Hugone de Marigny et Ric[ardo] de Marting[wast] Greg[orio] et Will[elm]o capell[an]is meis Simone et Will[elm]o filio Ylb[er]ti et Will[elm]o Luuell' et Ric[ardo] seruientibus meis et multis aliis.

The charter must date before the countess's death in 1212. The earlier limit is indicated by the presence of 'H' prior of Warwick, for his predecessor, M. Thomas, occurs in an act dated 1203 x 8. Similarly, Adam's predecessor as abbot of Garendon, Reginald, occurs in a fine dated 1202 x 3.

28. Thomas of Arden   *c.* 1185 x 1223

Grant of land lying between Pichesuben' *and the abbey's land, and between the path that runs above the mill pond and the road to Berwood (in Curdworth), Warwicks. Concession also of wood for making hedges around the canons' land.*

A = Original, now lost. B = TNA E13/76 m. 76, copy dated 1351 (from A).

[C]

Vniuersis sancte matris ecclesie fidelibus Thomas de Ardena, salutem. Nouerit vniuersitas vestra quod ego Thom[as] de Ardena diuini amoris intuitu et pro anima patris mei et matris mee et antecessorum meorum et successorum dedi concessi et hac presenti carta mea confirmaui deo et ecclesie sancte Marie de Prato Leyc[estrie] et canonicis regularibus ibidem deo seruientibus totam illam terram que iacet inter Pichesuben' et terra canonicorum et inter semitam que tendit super stagnum et viam que tendit Borewdiam in puram et perpetuam elemosinam ad tenendum de me et heredibus meis bene et in pace libere et quiete ab omni seculari exactione imperpetuum. Ego vero et heredes mei hanc terram predictis canonicis in omnibus et per omnia et contra canonicis in omnibus et per omnia et contra omnes homines warantizabimus. Preterea concessi predictis canonicis commutationem nemoris mei ad terram istam sepiendam. Hiis testibus Nich[ola]o sacerdote Ric[ard]o Marmiun Will[elm]o de Warewyk' Will[elm]o fil[io] Godefridi Horn'. Nich[ola]o clerico et multis aliis.

The identity of the Thomas here is assumed to be Thomas I of Arden, son of Henry. This is on the basis of the fact that the witnesses parallel that of the next act, which is undoubtedly that of the first Thomas, as it refers to his participation in the Third Crusade. Thomas I had succeeded his uncle Hugh in his lands by 1185 (see *The Langley Cartulary*, ed. P. R. Coss, Dugdale Society 32 (1980), 127), and he died at some time in or soon before 1223 (*Rotuli Litterarum Clausarum in turri Londinensi asservati 1204–1227*, ed. T. D. Hardy, 2 vols. (London 1833–44), i, 547) when Thomas II his son was in charge of his lands.

29. Thomas of Arden   1192 x 1223

Grant of part of his land with woodland with the following bounds. In length from the hump-backed oak standing on the acre belonging to the canons besides Old Sabroc' *(being that acre they bought from him before he left for Jerusalem) as far as the twisted alder, then by way of the crooked oak and Orm's ditch as far as the assart of William son of Geoffrey of Minworth. In breadth by the same bounds as far as the stream of the* Sabroc'. *The canons to pay him for life an annual rent of eighteen pence. After his death the canons are to pay his heirs the same rent for all his pieces of land and for the assarts which Orm held of him.*

A = Original, now lost. B = Second Leicester Cartulary (from A). C = TNA E13/76 mm. 76–76d, copy dated 1351 (from A). D = Leicester Rental (digest from B, now lost). E = Bodl. Laud misc. 625, f. 22r (from D).

[C]

Vniuersis sancte matris ecclesie fidelibus Thom[as] de Ardena salutem. Nouerit vniuersitas vestra quod ego Thom[as] de Ardena diuini amoris intuitu et pro animabus antecessorum et successorum meorum dedi et concessi et hac presenti carta mea confirmaui deo et ecclesie sancte Marie de Prato Leyc[estrie] et canonicis regularibus ibidem deo seruientibus illam partem terre mee cum nemore que est in longitudine a gibbosa[a] quercu stante in acra canonicorum Leyc[estrie] iuxta veterem Sabroc quam acram de me emerunt antequam iter Ierosolimitanum arripui vsque ad tortam aln[ea]m[b] et inde ad cructam quercum et sicut per fossatum Horm vsque ad assartum Will[elmi] fil[ii] Galfr[idi] de Mulneswythe et ab hiis diuisiis in latitudine [*m. 76d*] vsque ad aquam de Sabroc in puram et perpetuam elemosinam. Habend[am] et tenend[am] de me et de heredibus meis bene in pace honorifice libere et quiete ab omni seruitio et seculari exactione. Reddendo michi in vita mea annuatim .xviij. denarios pro omni seruitio ad festum sancti Michaelis. Post vero meum decessum prenominati canonici pro omnibus istis particulis terre mee et pro omnibus assartis quas Horm de me emit heredibus octodecim denarios ad predictum terminum reddent. Volo autem vt predicti canonici de ista predicta terra et de nemore quicquid eis melius visum fuerit et voluerint faciant. Ego vero et heredes mei memoratam terram sepedictis canonicis in omnibus et pro omnia et contra homines warantizabimus. Hiis testibus Will[elm]o de Warewyk' Nich[ola]o capell[ano] de Crudewrthe Ric[ard]o Marmyun. Henr[ico] de Ipeslea forestar[io] Ad[a] fil[io] Will[elm]i fil[ii] Godefr[idi].Rog[er]o forestar[io] et Eustach[io] fratre suo Hug[one] fil[io] Abbot Will[elm]o pistore Rog[er]o cognomine Petit et Will[elm]o coco et multis aliis.

^a gildosa C. orthography corrected from E.   ^b the reading of this boundary is very uncertain.

The date must be between the return of the bulk of the crusaders in 1192 and Thomas's death in or just before 1223.

30. Thomas of Arden   1192 X 1223

Grant of a stretch of his land with woodland which runs down from the old course of the Ebroc *beside* Hullesmor *up to the land of William son of Geoffrey of Minworth. Grant also of two small pieces of land, of which one is between* Bradenhet *and* Aldermaneseyhe, *and the other bounds are in length between the gate of* Mugehale *and the land of Nicholas of Minworth; the other piece is between the land of Henry of Minworth and that of Nicholas his brother. The canons to enjoy rights of taking wood for the hedging of the lands.*

> A = Original, now lost. B = Second Leicester Cartulary (from A). C = TNA E13/76 m. 76d, copy dated 1351 (from A). D = Leicester Rental (digest from B, now lost). E = Bodl. Laud misc. 625, f. 22r (from D).

[C]

Vniuersis sancte matris ecclesie fidelibus Thomas de Ardena salutem. Nouerit vniuersitas vestra quod ego Thom[as] de Ardena diuini amoris intuitu et pro anima patris mei et matris mee et antecessorum meorum et successorum dedi concessi et hac presenti carta mea confirmaui deo et ecclesie sancte Marie de Prato Leyc[estrie] et canonicis regularibus ibidem deo seruientibus totam illam lacam terre cum nemore que descendit ab antiqua Ebroc iuxta Hullesmor vsque ad terram Will[elm]i fil[ii] Galfr[idi] de Munnewrthe et duas particulas terre quarum vna est inter Bradenhet et Aldermanesleyhe et altera meta in longitudine inter ianuam de Mughale et terram Nich[ola]i de Munnewrth' et altera particula inter terram Henr[ici] de Munwrth' et terram Nich[ola]i fratris eiusdem cum tota alia terra sua quam tenent de me in puram et perpetuam elemosinam. Tenend[as] de me et heredibus meis bene et in pace libere et quiete ab omni seculari exactione imperpetuum. Ego vero et heredes mei predictas terras predictis canonicis in omnibus et per omnia et contra omnes homines warantizabimus. Ita vt de eisdem terris totam voluntatem suam faciant. Sciatis etiam pro vero quod ego T[homas]. concessi predictis canonicis commutationem nemoris mei ad predictas terras sepiendas. Hiis testibus. Math[e]o milite de Dunt' Nich[ola]o sacerdote Nich[ola]o clerico Math[e]o de Cruddewrth' Will[elm]o filio Godefridi Will[elm]o de Warewyk' Ric[ard]o Marmyun Henr[ico] de Ippesleye Hamun de Willac Galeb[er]t Ferrant Henr[ico] de Munnewrth'.

> The date limits must approximate those of the previous charter.

31. Reginald Basset of Wolvey   *c.* 1197 X 1224

Grant of a bovate of land in Lockington, Leics. which Seawin held of him from out of his demesne which lies amongst the fields of Lockington, also three plough strips which lie beside the house of Robert Blanchard' next to the land which William de Sainneville gave to the canon, also a toft which Robert Alfwin held outside Seawin's house.

> A = Original, now lost. B = TNA E13/76, m. 70d, copy dated 1351 (from A).

[B]

Notum sit omnibus hominibus tam presentibus quam futuris quod ego Reginaldus Basset pro salute anime mee et patris et matris mee dedi et hac presenti carta mea confirmaui deo et ecclesie beate Marie de Prato Leircestr[ie] et canonicis regularibus ibidem deo seruientibus in puram et perpetuam elemosinam vnam bouatam terre in villa de Lokynton'. illam scilicet quam Seawinus de me tenuit de dominico meo que iacet per culturas in campis de Lokynton' cum omnibus pertinentiis suis in villam et extra et tres selliones que iacent extra domum Rob[er]ti Blanchard' iuxta terram quam Will[elmu]s de Seineuil[la] dedit eisdem canonicis regularibus et vnum toftum quod Rob[er]tus Alfwin' tenuit extra domum Seawini memorati. Hanc autem elemosinam ego et heredes mei warantizabimus. Hiis testibus Will[elm]o de Dyua Will[elm]o de Charnel[lis] Will[elm]o Burdet magistro Rob[er]to de Barewell' Hug[one] de Butemunt' Reginaldo Pepin Waltero de Lokynton' et multis aliis.

> The abbey had several charters relating to estates at Lockington, Leics. which were once transcribed into its lost cartulary, including mid twelfth-century charters that proved that part of it was part of the barony Geoffrey Ridel held in the earldom of Leicester, which he conveyed to Ralph I, son of Richard Basset of Weldon, from whom it somehow came to Reginald son of Robert Basset of Wolvey, who might therefore have been Ralph I's grandson (see Bodl. Laud misc 625, f. 102r, and for Reginald, *Basset Charters c. 1120 to 1250,*

ed. W. T. Reedy, Pipe Roll Society 88 (1995), xxxi, 48). Reginald died in 1224, the suggested dates are those of his known independent political activity.

32. Reginald Basset of Wolvey   1220 x 1224

Grant of all the land he possessed in Lockington, Leics. for his burial at the abbey, saving only eighteen virgates which Bartholomew holds for service of a pound of cumin annually.

A = Original, now lost. B = TNA E13/76, m. 70d, copy dated 1351 (from A). C = TNA c56/16 (Confirmation Roll of 3 Henry VII), m. 18 (from A).

[B]

Omnibus Christi fidelibus presentibus et futuris, Reginaldus Basset de Wlueya salutem. Sciatis me in ligia potestate mea dedisse et concessisse et hac presenti carta mea confirmasse cum corpore meo deo et ecclesie sancte Marie de Pratis Leirc[estrie] et canonicis regularibus ibidem deo seruientibus pro salute anime mee et omnium antecessorum et successorum meorum totam terram quam habui in villa de Lokyntona cum omnibus pertinentiis suis infra villam et extra quietam et solutam de me et omnibus heredibus meis inperpetuum sine vllo retenemento videlicet decem et octo virgatas terre et vnam bouatam terre vnde Bartholomeus tenet duas virgatas terre per liberum seruitium vnius libre cymini per annum. Habendas et tenendas in puram et perpetuam elemosinam liberas et quietas ab omni seruitio et exactione seculari. Et ego Reginaldus et heredes mei warantizabimus totam dictam terram de Lokynton' cum omnibus pertinentiis suis iamdictis canonicis contra omnes homines et feminas. Vt autem hec mea donatio et concessio rata sit et stabilis, eam sigilli mei impressione roboraui. Hiis testibus Steph[an]o de Segraue Henr[ico] fratre eius Will[elm]o de Martiwast Ph[ilipp]o de Kyntona. Galfr[id]o le Nores Waltero de Lokynton' Rob[er]to de Yolgraue Ioh[ann]e de Parles.

For the date of Reginald's death, *Basset Charters*, ed. Reedy, xxxi. This charter must otherwise date from after 1220 due to the attestation of William de Martinwast and Stephen de Segrave (see nos. 38, 40). The solemn nature of the charter, its assertion of his free will in the matter, and the weight of the witnesses indicate that it accompanied Reginald's reception into the abbey in his last illness, which would put its date in or very soon before 1224.

33. William son of Ilbert of Kilby   s. xiii in.

Grant of three virgates in Kilby, Leics. two of which Hugh the priest held and the other Edward the priest owned and the widow Edith held, with a toft and four acres which William added from his own demesne. Two of the acres were upon Hoy *and two up against* Hunderissis, *with meadowland called the holm of* Attenrun. *For this the abbey has given William fourteen silver marks, eight shillings and eight pence.*

A = Original, now lost. B = TNA E13/76, mm. 67d–68, copy dated 1351 (from A).

[B]

Vniuersis sancte matris ecclesie filiis, Guill[elmu]s de Keleby filius Ileb[er]ti de Keleby, salutem. Notum sit vniuersitati vestre quod ego Guill[elmu]s pro salute anime mee et vxoris mee et puerorum meorum et antecessorum meorum dedi et presenti carta confirmaui in puram et perpetuam elemosinam ecclesie sancte Marie de Prato Leyrcestr[ie] et canonicis regularibus ibidem deo seruientibus tres virgatas terre in Keleby. Quarum duas Hugo presbiter tenuit et vnam quam Edwardus presbiter tenuit scilicet illam quam Editha vidua tenuit cum tofto ad eandem virgatam pertinente et cum quatuor acris terre quas eis accreui de dominio meo. duabus videlicet super Hoy et duabus contra Hunderissis et cum prato quod vocatur insula Attenrun liberas at quietas ab omni exactione et seruitio seculari erga me et heredes meos. Pro hac autem concessione mea, predicti canonici dederunt michi .xiiij. marcas argenti et octo solidos et octo denarios. Quare volo et firmiter constituo vt predicti canonici prenominatas virgatas terre et cum incrementis que eisdem accreui et omnibus aliis pertinentiis suis libere et quiete habeant et inperpetuum teneant. Hiis testibus. Rogero fratre meo de Kileby et Rodb[er]to Blund de la Leia Hugone et Edwardo presbiteriis Hugone sacerdote de omnibus sanctis. Reginaldo capellano Rob[er]to ianitore Simone coco. Simone de Aula Alexandro de Caldewelle Guill[elm]o de Salforde Rodberto de Alewoldestona et multis aliis.

The date of this act is difficult to assess, but the indications of the diplomatic, and notably the vocabulary applied to the priests named, indicates the first quarter of the thirteenth century, or possibly slightly earlier.

34. Henry III, king of England   Westminster, 16 March 1227
Confirmation to the abbey of the quittances and protection granted by his father, King John.

A = Original, now lost. B = TNA c53/18 (Charter Roll of 11 Henry III), m. 17 (from A). C = TNA c53/104 (Charter Roll of 11 Edward II) m. 4, copy dated 1318 (from A). D = TNA E13/76, m. 77d, copy dated 1351 (from C). E = BL Harley ms 84, f.9r (s. xvii), source unknown.

Pd. (in part), Nichols, *Leicester*, i pt. 2, Appendix p. 59 (partial copy from E); calendared, *Calendar of Charter Rolls, 1226–57*, 22 (from B).

[BC]

Henr[icus] *ªdei gratiaª* rex *ªAngl[orum]* dominus Hib[er]n[ie] dux Norm[annorum] Aquit[annorum] et comes Andeg[auorum]ª* archiepiscopis episcopis *ªabbatibus prioribus comitibus baronibus iusticiis vicecomitibus prepositis ministris et omnibus balliuis et fidelibus suis,ª* salutem. Sciatis nos recepisse in nostra propria manu et custodia et protectione sicut vnam de propriis elemosinis ecclesiam sancte Marie Leyc*'ᵇ* de Prato cum omnibus pertinentiis suis. Quare volumus et firmiter precipimus quod canonici in predicta ecclesia deo seruientes omnia tenementa sua teneant bene et in pace libere et quiete integre plenarie et honorifice in bosco et plano pratis et pascuis aquis et mariscis in piscariis in toftis et croftis in viis et semitis et in omnibus locis tam in burgo quam extra burgum libera et quieta de geldis et danegeld[is] et auxiliis et wapent[aciis]*ᶜ* et hundredis et shiris et tenemannetale et murdr[o] et scutag[io] et assisis et summonitionibus et de omnibus placitis et querelis et occasionibus et consuetudinibus et de omni terreno seruitio et seculari exactione cum soca et saca et tol et theam*ᵈ* et imfangenetheof*ᵉ* et omnibus aliis consuetudinibus et libertatibus. Et volumus vt predicti canonici et homines sui habeant saluum conductum nostrum et sint quieti et liberi a passagio pontagio et theloneo et stallagio per omnes ciuitates nostros et burgos et vendant et emant libere et quiete. Et volumus ut sint quieti a trauerso per omnes portus nostros sicut carte Henr[ici] regis aui nostri et domini Iohannis*ᶠ* regis patris nostri quas inde habent testantur. Si quis etiam versus domum illam aliquid de possessionibus eius clamauerit prohibemus ne pro aliquo respondeant nec in placitum ponantur nisi coram nobis vel coram capital[i] justic[iario] nostro aut per preceptum nostrum. Hiis testibus Eustach[io]*ᵍ* London[ensi] Petro Wynton[ensi]*ʰ* Iocelino*ⁱ* Bathon[ensi] Ric[ard]o Sar[esburiensi] episcopis. Hub[er]to de Burgo comite Canc[ie]*ʲ* justic[iario] nostro Rad[ulf]o fil[io] Nich[ola]i Ric[ard]o de Argenteem*ᵏ* senescall[is] nostris. Henr[ico] de Capella et aliis. Dat[um] per manum venerabilis patris Rad[ulf]i Cicestr[ensis] episcopi canc[ellarii] nostri. Apud Westm[onasterium] .xvjᵒ. die marcii anno regni nostri vndecimo*ˡ*.

ª⁻ª omitted in B. *ᵇ* Leic' B. *ᶜ* wapentacis B. *ᵈ* them B. *ᵉ* infangnethof B. *ᶠ* J[ohannis] B. *ᵍ* Eustachio B. *ʰ* Winton' B. *ⁱ* J[ocelino] B. *ʲ* Kanc' B. *ᵏ* Argentem B. *ˡ* .xjᵒ.

35. Agnes daughter of Ivo of Cossington   1220 X 1231
Grant of three rods of land in Barkby, Leics. of which one and a half is upon Waltydis *at the white stone; a rod is at* Helrumestub' *stretching as far as* Saltergathe; *and a half rod is at* Croftedice *lying next to* Norhenges. *Grant also of one and a half rods, and a quarter of a rod of meadowland also in Barkby, of which one rod is upon* Langedale; *a half rod at the stone, and the quarter rod in* Estmedwe *on the Beby side.*

A – Original, now lost. B = TNA E13/76, mm. 69d–70, copy dated 1351 (from A).

[B]

Vniuersis Christi fidelibus ad quos presens scriptum peruenerit, Agnes filia Yvonis de Cusynton' salutem. Nouerit vniuersitas vestra me pro salute anime mee et antecessorum et successorum meorum dedisse et concessisse et presenti carta mea confirmasse deo et ecclesie sancte Marie de Prato Leirc[estrie] et canonicis regularibus ibidem deo seruientibus in liberam puram et perpetuam elemosinam tres rodas terre in territorio de Barkeby quarum vna roda et dimidia est super Waltydis apud albam petram et vna roda apud Helrumestub' que se extendit versus Saltergathe et dimidia roda ad Croftdice que iacet versus Norhenges. Et vnam rodam et dimidiam et quartam partem vnius rode prati in eadem villa. Vnde vna roda est super Langedale et dimidia roda ad petram et quarta pars vnius rode in Estmedwe versus Beby. Quare volo quod dicti canonici hanc meam elemosinam libere honorifice habeant teneant et quiete ab omni seruitio et exactione seculari. Et ego Agnes et heredes mei predictas terras cum pratis memoratis warantizabimus predictis canonicis et defendemus contra omnes homines et feminas. Quod vt ratum in posterum perseueret et stabile, presenti scripto sigillum meum apposui. Hiis testibus, Petro de sancto Edwardo Will[elm]o de Martiwall' Briano forestar[io] Ioh[ann]e Fridai Will[elm]o filio Herb[er]ti Ioh[ann]e filio Ketelbern. Henr[ico] de Lilleburne. Waltero de Bristowe Petro clerico Ioh[ann]e de Parlis. et multis aliis.

> The date of this act is calculated as being after the succession of William de Martinwast to his father in 1220 (see no. 40), and before the death of Peter of St Edwards, which occurred in 1231, when the sheriff of Leicester was in charge of his lands and involved in a dispute about a deathbed grant of his to Holy Trinity Aldgate, *Close Rolls of the reign of Henry III, 1231–34*, 178.

36. Elias of Lindsey and Alice his wife   1235 X 1240
Grant of four virgates which they had of the grant of Richard son of William in Thurmaston, Leics. for their burial in the abbey.

A = Original, now lost. B = TNA E13/76, m. 68d, copy dated 1351 (from A).

[B]

Sciant presentes et futuri quod ego Helias de Lindish[eia] et Alicia vxor mea vnanimi vtriusque nostri assensu pro salute animarum nostrarum dedimus concessimus et hac presenti carta nostra confirmauimus cum corporibus nostris deo et ecclesie beate Marie de Prato Leirc[estrie] et canonicis regularibus ibidem deo seruientibus quatuor virgatas terre quas habuimus de dono Ric[ard]i filii Will[elm]i in vill[a] de Thurmodiston'. Habendas et tenendas inperpetuum cum omnibus pertinentiis suis et libertatibus in liberam puram et perpetuam elemosinam. sicut aliqua elemosina melius liberius et quietius dari vel possideri possit. Et ne aliquis in posterum aliquid iuris vel clamii sibi in dictis quatuor virgatis terre vendicare possit, ad maiorem eorum securitatem hoc scriptum sigillis nostris signatum eis fecimus et cartas Ric[ard]i filii Will[elm]i. et Margar[ete] comi[tiss]e Wynton[ie] quas inde habuimus cum toto iure nostro eis reddidimus. Hiis testibus Ioh[ann]e monacho tunc sen[escallo] domini comitis Wynton[ie] Henr[ico] Byset Briano forestar[io] Ioh[ann]e de Cranford. Rogero Buffe Henr[ico] de Anelep magistro Ric[ard]o de Meleford Rob[er]to de Wytebec. Will[elm]o Grym et multis aliis.

> The date of this act is calculated as being after the succession of Roger de Quincy to the earldom of Winchester on his mother's death in 1235. It features as witness his early seneschal, John le Moine, who served him in that capacity through the 1230s and had been succeeded by John of Cranford (who also attests) by September 1241 at the very latest, TNA E159/20, m. 16d, and see G. G. Simpson, 'The *Familia* of Roger de Quincy, Earl of Winchester and Constable of Scotland' in *Essays on the Nobility of Medieval Scotland*, ed. K. J. Stringer (Edinburgh 1985), 102–30 at 115.

37. Roger de Quincy, earl of Winchester   1235 X 1240
Grant of the homage and service of Elias of Lindsey and Alice his wife for four virgates of land which they held of the earl in Thurmaston, Leics.

A = Original, now lost. B = TNA c56/16 mm. 18–19, (Confirmation Roll of 3 Henry VII) (from A). C = TNA c56/27 m. 24 (Confirmation Roll of 1 Henry VIII) (from A).

[B]

Omnibus hanc cartam inspecturis vel audituris Rog[er]us de Quenc[i] comes Winton[ie] constab[ularius] Scott[ie] salutem. Noueritis nos dedisse concessisse et hac presenti carta nostra confirmasse pro nobis et heredibus nostris deo et beate Marie Leirc[estrie] et canonicis regularibus ibidem deo seruientibus homagium et seruitium Elye de Lindesey et Alicie vxoris sue de quatuor virgatis terre quas de nobis tenuit in villa de Thurmodeston' in liberam puram et perpetuam elemosinam cum omnibus aisiamentis libertatibus et liberis consuetudinibus ad dictam terram pertinentibus infra villam et extra. Ita vt dictis canonicis accrescat quicquid nobis vel heredibus nostris accrescere potuit in homagiis seruitiis et omnibus aliis eschaetis. Quare volumus et firmiter precipimus vt dicti canonici habeant et teneant hanc nostram elemosinam imperpetuum libere bene et honorifice absque omni exactione seculari consuetudine et demanda tam de francoplegio et forinseco seruitio. quam aliis secularibus demandis. Nos vero dictam elemosinam pro nobis et heredibus nostris prefatis canonicis contra omnes homines warantizabimus imperpetuum. Hiis testibus dominis Rob[erto] de Quenc[i] fratre nostro. Thomas de Alneto. Sah[er]o de sancto Andrea. Will[elm]o de Bosco. Ioh[ann]e le Moygne. Henr[ico] Byseth. Wil[elm]o de Chaumunt. militibus. Eustach[io] de Musteruilers capellano. Magistro Th[oma] de Mann'. Ioh[ann]e de Craunford. Briano forestario. Rog[er]o Buff'. Will[elm]o de Denton' clerico et multis aliis.

38. Thomas of Lincoln   *c. 1219 X 1240*

Grant of a carrucate in Hungarton, Leics. the same which the abbey previously held of him at farm.

   A = Original, now lost. B = TNA E13/76, m. 67d, copy dated 1351 (from A).

[B]

Sciant presentes et futuri quod ego Thomas de Lincoln' assensu et concensu Matild[is] vxoris mee et Petri filii et heredis mei dedi concessi et hac presenti carta mea confirmaui deo et ecclesie beati Marie de Prato Leicestr' et canonicis regularibus ibidem deo seruientibus vnam carucatam terre cum pertinentiis de dominico meo in territorio de Hung[ar]ton' illam scilicet quam predicti abbas et conuentus Leicestr' aliquando de me tenuerunt ad firmam. Habendam et tenendam dictis canonicis de me et heredibus meis libere quiete et honorifice in pratis pascuis viis et semitis cum omnibus libertatibus et esiamentis ad predictam terram pertinentibus in liberam puram et perpetuam elemosinam inperpetuum quietam et solutam ab omni seruitio et exactione seculari. Ego vero Thomas et heredes mei predictam carucatam terre cum pertinentiis predictis canonicis warantizabimus defendemus et acquietabimus contra omnes homines et feminas. Quod vt firmum sit et stabile huic scripto sigillum meum apposui. Hiis testibus. domino Steph[an]o de Segraue. Will[elm]o de Foleuill'. Hugone Barre. Petro filio meo et herede meo Rogero de Reresby. Rob[er]to de Yolegrave Thoma de Crec Rob[er]to de Wytebek Rob[er]to de Mountsorel Osberto de Arderna Waltero de Bristoliis et aliis.

   The presence of Stephen de Segrave here as a knight indicates a date between *c.* 1219, when he first appears as a knight and his death in 1241, see *ODNB, s.n.* Seagrave. As is clear from no. 43 below, Thomas himself had died in or soon before 1240.

39. Roger of Rearsby   *c. 1219 X 1240*

Grant of six virgates with their tofts and crofts and adjacent meadowland in Hungarton, Leics. namely the single virgates of Roger Sparhavec, William Patrich, Roger the clerk and Ralph of H . . . , the other two virgates being from Roger's own demesne; Roger adds to these two plough strips below Marchil with the barn he had there.

   A = Original, now lost. B = TNA E13/76, m. 73, copy dated 1351 (from A) (some damage along right side of membrane).

[B]

Sciant presentes et futuri quod ego Rog[er]us de Reresby dedi concessi et hac presenti carta mea confirmaui pro salute anime mee et antecessorum meorum deo et ecclesie beate Marie de Prato L[eycestrie] et canonicis regularibus ibidem deo seruientibus sex virgatas terre in territorio [de] Hung[er]ton' cum toftis et croftis et prato adiacente et omnibus aliis pertinentiis suis infra villam et extra. videlicet vnam virgatam terre quam Rog[er]us Sparh[auec] tenuit et vnam virgatam terre quam Will[elmu]s Patrich tenuit et vnam virgatam terre quam Rog[er]us clericus tenuit et vnam virgatam terre quam Rad[ulfu]s de H... tenuit et duas virgatas terre de dominico eiusdem ville. Habendas et tenendas in liberam et perpetuam elemosinam bene et in pace libere et quiete absque [omni] seruitio et exactione seculari ad me vel ad heredes meos pertinente saluo s... Preterea concessi et dedi et hac eadem carta mea confirmaui eisdem in auc[mentum] toftorum predictorum duas seliones sub Marchil cum grangia mea quam habui in predict[a villa] cum omnibus pertinentiis suis. Quare volo et firmiter constituo quod predicti canonici habeant et teneant omnia predicta cum omnibus suis pertinentiis imperpetuum sic[ut] predictum est. Ego vero et heredes mei hanc elemosinam contra omnes homines im[perpetuum] warantizabimus. In cuius rei testimonium huic scripto sigillum meum apposui. [Hiis] testibus domino Steph[an]o de Sedgraue Thom[a] de Lincoln' Henr[ico] de Sedgraue Will[elmo de] Martiwast Will[elm]o de Charneles Ric[ard]o de Curcun Will[elm]o de Kileby H[enrico] de Lilleburn' Rob[er]to de Muntsorel Ioh[ann]e de P[ar]les Hereb[er]to coco et aliis.

   For the date see no. 38.

40. Thomas of Lincoln   *c.* 1220 X 1240

Grant of six virgates of land in the village of Hungarton, Leics. those single virgates held by Roger Sperhavet and Osgot; the two held by William son of Herbert; and the other single virgates held by Walter son of Richard and Gervase, with the tofts and crofts attached to all six, their owners named. Confirmation also of two virgates in the same village which Walter son of Bence gave the abbey, which owed Thomas a half pound of cumin annually, a rent which Thomas now remits to the abbey.

A = Original, now lost. B = TNA E13/76, m. 67–67d, copy dated 1351 (from A).

[B]

Sciant posteri quam presentes quod ego Thom[as] de Lincoln' dedi et concessi et hac presenti carta mea confirmaui deo et ecclesie beate Marie de Pratis Leicestr[ie] et canonicis regularibus ibidem deo seruientibus in puram et quietam liberam et perpetuam elemosinam sex virgatas terre in villa de Hungurton'. cum toftis et croftis et omnibus pertinentiis suis infra villam et extra vnam scilicet virgatam terre quam Rog[erus] Sperhauet' tenuit. et virgatam terre quam Osegot tenuit cum toftis et croftis predictis duabus virgatis terre pertinentibus et duas virgatas terre quas Will[elmu]s filius Herberti tenuit. cum tofto et crofto que idem Will[elmu]s tenuit et cum alio tofto quod Hugo Joie tenuit. et cum dimidia acra terre in campo in aucmentum eiusdem tofti illam scilicet dimidiam acram terre que iacet iuxta croftum Gamell[i] super Dicfurlong et vnam virgatam terre quam Walterus filius Ric[ard]i tenuit. cum tofto et crofto que Rad[ulfu]s filius Hildi tenuit et vnam virgatam terre quam Geruasius tenuit cum tofto et crofto que Will[elmu]s le Westreis tenuit. Habendas et tenendas de me et heredibus meis in perpetuam elemosinam libere et quiete et honorifice absque omni forinseco seruitio et exactione seculari. Et ego Thom[as] de Lincoln et heredes mei warantizabimus iamdictis canonicis predictum tenementum cum omnibus pertinentiis suis infra villam et extra contra omnes homines et feminas et adquietabimus de omnibus seruitiis et demandis inperpetuum. Item confirmaui eisdem canonicis duas virgatas terre in eadem villa cum omnibus pertinentiis suis infra villam et extra in liberam puram et perpetuam elemosinam illas scilicet quas Walterus filius Bence eis dedit et carta sua confirmauit. de quibus duabus virgatis terre iamdicti canonici solebant reddere michi dimidiam libram cumini annuatim quam quidem ego eisdem pro me et heredibus meis remisi et quietam clamaui inperpetuum. Quare volo et firmiter constituo quod predicti canonici habeant et teneant predictas duas virgatas terre libere quiete plene et integre solutas et quietas ab omni seruitio et exactione seculari. Ego vero Thom[as] et heredes mei adquietabimus predictas duas virgatas terre de omnibus seruitiis et demandis et de forinseco seruitio erga omnes homines et feminas quod vt firmum sit et stabile presens scriptum sigilli mei inpressione roboraui. Hiis testibus Will[elm]o de Martiwaill' Rogero de Bray Petro de Ses Rad[ulf]o Arrabi Will[elm]o Daneth' Rogero de Reresby Roberto Walran Waltero de Bristol Roberto de Monte Sorel Ioh[ann]e de Parles Roberto de Aula et multis aliis.

The best indications of the date of this act is the career of the prominent witness, William de Martinwast of Noseley, who is known to have succeeded his father in 1220 and to have died in or soon before 1246, see *Rotuli Litterarum Clausaurum*, i, 420; TNA E159/23 m. 1; E159/25, m. 4d. However, it is likely from no. 43 that Thomas had been succeeded by his son, Peter by 1240.

41. Thomas of Lincoln   *c.* 1220 X 1240

Final concord between the abbey and its men of Northorp' in Thurmaston, Leics. and Thomas of Lincoln, lord of Barkby, by which Thomas acknowledged the abbey and its men had common of pasture in the wood of Barkby, Leics. for their domestic animals in Thurmaston annually from the ninth hour on 24 June to the 2 February following. Thomas also acknowledges they have free entry and exit to the common. The abbey in turn acknowledged the common rights of Thomas and his heirs in their woods in Thurmaston for his domestic animals, at the same term with free entry and exit. The abbey paid Thomas twenty–two shillings for the agreement.

A = Original, now lost. B = Leicester Rental (from A, now lost). C = Bodl. Laud misc. 625, f. 64r (from B).

[C]

Hec est concordia et conuentio facta inter abbatem et conuentum Leyc[estrie] et homines suos de Northorp' in Thurmeston ex vna parte et Thomam de Lyncoln' dominum de Barkeby ex altera. scilicet quod predictus Thomas de Linc[olnia] recognouit et concessit predicto abbati et conuentui et hominibus suis de Northorp' in Thurmeston' communem pasturam suam in haya sua de Barkeby ad aueria predicti abbatis et hominum predictorum de Northorp' pertinentem ad liberum tenementum predicti abbatis et hominum suorum de Northorp' in Thurmeston'. videlicet singulis annis ab hora nona die natalis sancti Ioh[ann]is baptiste vsque ad Purificationem beate Marie eodem anno. Predictus autem Thomas recognouit et concessit predicto abbati et conuentui et hominibus suis predictis liberum introitum et exitum ad communem pasturam suam inperpetuum ad finem predicte haye secundum quod mete fuerint site. Predictus abbas Leyc[estrie] et conuentus et homines sui de Northorp' in Thurmeston' recognouerunt et concesserunt predicto Thoma de Linc[olnia] et heredibus suis communam pasture sue in haya sua de Thurmeston' ad aueria sua propria de dominico suo pertinentem ad liberum tenementum suum in Barkeby scilicet singulis annis ab hora nona die natiuitatis sancti Ioh[ann]is baptiste vsque ad Purificationem beate Marie eodem anno cum libero introitu et exitu ad predictam pasturam. Predicte uero haye erunt in libero defenso singulis annis a Purificatione beate Marie vsque ad horam nonam die natiuitatis sancti Ioh[ann]is baptiste. vnusquisque autem alteri warentisabit communia predictarum pasturarum inperpetuum. Pro hac autem conuentionem et concessionem dederunt predicti abbas et conuentus et homines sui predicto Thoma de Lincoln' xxij solidos argenti. Vt autem hec conuentio rata sit et stabilis inposterum, predictus Thomas de Linco[lnia] huius partis cirographi sigillum suum apposuit etc vt in carta xxij.

42. Arnold VI du Bois   25 December 1239 x 31 December 1240

Confirmation of the grants of his ancestors, namely: the church of Clifton-upon-Dunsmore, Warwicks. with its chapels of Brownsover and Rugby; the churches of Evington and Humberstone, Leics. and the church of Bulkington, Warwicks. with two virgates of land; a carrucate of land in Barnacle, Warwicks. the one which Henry of Marston once held of Arnold (III); two virgates in Bramcote, Warwicks. which were Ranulf's, and meadowland once in the demesne of Weston-on-Avon, Warwicks.; six virgates in Bramcote which they had of the grant of Geoffrey L'Abbé; the mill of Bramcote, with its land, meadow and fishpond, namely Cresswell. Arnold concedes common pasture with his own men to the abbey's people as was traditional since the time of King Henry II. Confirmation also of the church of Thorpe Arnold near Melton Mowbray, Leics. with lands, tofts and crofts, with the site of a sheepfold and with ten acres of meadowland in the place called Redimwald, *between the meadow late of Alice Basset and his demesne meadowland, with common pasture for 120 sheep. Grant for the soul of himself and his wife Joan, and for the good standing of the church of Thorpe Arnold, of pasture for ten of the abbey's live- stock, namely eight oxen and two cows, in his own pastures with his own livestock, free of any charge except a pound of pepper annually on the feast of St Botolph as payment for the bovate of land Ralph the clerk held.*

A = Original, now lost. B = BL Additional 31826, ff. 270v–271r (s. xiv.)
Pd. (partially) Nichols, *Leicester*, i pt. 2, Appendix p. 57 ('Roper MS ex libro de placito 31 Edw I, penes Oliverum St John, f. 217').

[B]

Vniversis Christi fidelibus hoc presens scriptum uisuris uel audituris Ernaldus de Bosco salutem in domino. Nouerit vniuersitati uestra quod ego Ernaldus de Bosco concessi et in perpetuam elemosinam confirmaui omnes donationes et concessiones quas Ernaldus de Bosco attauus meus. et Ernaldus de Bosco auus meus. et Ernaldus de Bosco pater meus dederunt et concesserunt deo et ecclesie sancte Marie de Pratis Leycestrie et canonicis regularibus ibidem deo seruientibus. ecclesiam de Cliftona cum capellis de Wauere. et de Rokebi. et omnibus pertinentiis suis. ecclesias quoque similiter de Euinton' et de Humbirstan. cum omnibus pertinentiis suis et libertatibus. Item. ecclesiam de Bulkynton' cum duabus virgatis terre et omnibus aliis pertinentiis suis. Item vnam carucatam terre in Berhangil. illam scilicet quam Hanr(icus)[a] de Merston' aliquando de Ernaldo de Bosco auo meo tenuit. Item duas uirgatas terre in Bramkote que fuerunt Ranulfi et pratum quod fuit de dominico de Weston'. Item. sex virgatas terre in Bramkote quas habuerunt de dono Galfridi le Abbe. Item molendinum de Bramcota cum terra et prato et viuario scilicet Corsewalle. et cum omnibus ad ipsum molendinum pertinentibus. Et concessi ut homines predictorum canonicorum habeant communem pasturam cum hominibus meis vbique sicut umquam melius habuerunt tempore regis Henrici senioris. secundum tenorem cartarum predecessorum meorum. Item ecclesiam de Torp Ernald juxta Melton'. cum terris et toftis. et croftis cum situ bercarii eorum et omnibus pertinentiis suis cum decem acris prati in loco qui dicitur Redimwaldo. inter pratum quod fuit Alicie Bassett. et pratum de dominico meo. et communem pasturam ad sex vinginti[a] oues. Preterea dedi et concessi pro salute anime mee et Iohanne vxoris mee et omnium predecessorum meorum et successorum meorum ad*b* honorem dicte ecclesie de Thorpe ut sepedicti canonici inperpetuum habeant decem aueria scilicet .viii*to*. boues. et duas vaccas. in propria pastura mea cum propriis aueriis meis vbicumque pascantur. absque ullo grauamine. uel inquietatione mei uel successorum meorum. Quare uolo et firmiter constituo ut predicti canonici has omnes possessiones. donationes. et concessiones habeant et teneant. libere. bene. in pace. quiete. et honorifice. absque omni seruitio. et exactione. et seculari demanda erga me et heredes meos pertinentibus. in liberam puram et perpetuam elemosinam. salua mihi et heredibus meis. vna libra piperis. per annum ad festum sancti Botulfi solvenda pro bouata terre cum pertinentiis suis quam Radulfus clericus tenuit. Et ego dictus Ernardus *a* de Bosco et heredes mei hec omnia predicta dictis canonicis contra omnes gentes warantizabimus. Et confecta fuit hec carta. anno domini. M°.CC°.XL. ciclo lunari currente per sex. Hiis testibus. domino Rogero de Quinci comite Winton[ie] et constabulario Scocie. Thoma de Estleye. Serlon[e] de sancto Andrea. Ioh[ann]e de Herci. et Ricardo rectore de Thurkeliston. Radulfo de Arrebi. magistro Ric[ard]o de Meleforde. Will[elm]o Grim. et Will[elm]o filio Will[elm]i de Kelebi. Henrico de Lilleb[ur]ne. Simone clerico de Oseliston' et multis aliis.

a sic in B. *b* ad ad in B.

The highly unusual but not unprecedented dating clause is expressed in the lunar cycles of the Easter tables, and confirms that the year 1240 is intended, when the Golden Number for the calculation was 6 (for another example in this collection see no. 43). For the generations of the family of Du Bois (de Bosco) of Thorpe Arnold, see Crouch, *Beaumont twins*, 106–7, 109–11; R. Dace, 'Towards the banneret: studies in Midland society, 1150–1300', unpublished Leeds MPhil thesis, 1997), 112. My thanks to Professor Richard Sharpe and Leofranc Holford-Strevens for some very necessary help on the dating.

43. Peter of Lincoln son of Thomas of Lincoln *c.* 1240

Confirmation of six virgates in the estate of Hungerton, Leics. of his father's grant, those single virgates with tofts and crofts held by Roger Sparhavec and Osgot; the two virgates held by William son of Herbert, the tofts and crofts of which were held by William himself and Hugh Joye, with an additional half acre in the field next to the croft of Gamelin on Dicfurlang; the virgate held by Walter son of Richard with the toft and croft held by Ralph son of Hilda; and the virgate held by Gervase, with a toft and croft held by William Lewesfrey. Confirmation also of two virgates in the same village which Walter son of Bence gave the abbey, which owed his father Thomas a half pound of cumin annually, which Thomas now remitted to the abbey. Confirmation also of a carrucate of land which the canons held from his father's gift from his demesne in Hungerton. Confirmation also of six virgates in Hungerton which the canons had from the grant of Roger of Rearsby with tofts and crofts. Finally, quitclaim of a headland upon Brocfurlang against the walls which enclose the abbey's court at Barkby, Leics. over which there was a plea, and also of a ditch in Hungerton which the canons held of his fee and of which they were in seisin in the year 1239 (the year of the lunar cycle 5, 23 Henry III).

A = Original, now lost. B = TNA E13/76, m. 73, copy dated 1351 (from A).

[B]

Sciant presentes et futuri quod ego Petrus de Lincolnia filius Thome de Lincolnia concessi et hac presenti carta mea confirmaui deo et ecclesie beate Marie de Prato Leyc[estrie] et canonicis regularibus ibidem deo seruientibus in puram et perpetuam elemosinam sex virgatas terre in territorio de Hung[er]tona ex dono patris mei cum toftis et croftis et omnibus pertinentiis suis infra villam et extra vnam scilicet virgatam terre quam Rog[er]us Sparhauec tenuit et vnam virgatam terre quam Osgot tenuit cum toftis et croftis predictis duabus virgatis terre pertinentibus et duas virgatas terre quas Will[elm]us filius Herb[er]ti tenuit cum tofto et crofto que idem Will[elm]us tenuit et cum alio tofto quod Hugo Joye tenuit et cum dimidia acra terre in camp[o] in aucmentum eiusdem tofti, illam scilicet dimidiam acram terre que iacet iuxta croftum Gamelini super Dicfurlang et vnam virgatam terre quam Walt[er]us filius Ric[ard]i tenuit cum tofto et crofto que Radulphus filius Hilde tenuit. et vnam virgatam terre quam Geruasius tenuit cum tofto et crofto que Will[elm]us Lewesfrey tenuit. Item confirmaui eisdem canonicis duas virgatas terre in eodem territorio cum omnibus pertinentiis suis infra villam et extra in liberam puram et perpetuam elemosinam illas scilicet quas Walt[er]us filius Bence illis dedit et carta sua confirmauit de quibus duabus virgatis terre iamdicti canonici solebant reddere patri meo dimidiam libram cumini annuatim quam quidem ipse eisdem canonicis pro se et heredibus suis remisit et quietam clamauit imperpetuum. Item confirmaui eisdem canonicis vnam carucatam terre cum pertinentiis quam tenuerunt de dono patris mei de dominico suo in territorio de Hung[er]ton'. Habendas et tenendas dictis canonicis in liberam puram et perpetuam elemosinam. Item confirmaui eisdem canonicis sex virgatas terre in territorio de Hung[er]ton' quas scilicet prius habuerunt de dono Rog[er]i de Rerisby cum toftis et croftis et pratis adiacentibus et omnibus aliis pertinentiis suis infra villam et extra sicut aliqua elemosina melius et liberius et quiecius concedi potest et conferri. Habendas et tenendas eisdem canonicis in liberam et puram et perpetuam elemosinam bene et in pace libere et quiete ab omni seruitio et seculari demanda et ab omnibus exactionibus que de terra vel pro terra exigi possunt vel poterunt inperpetuum. Quare volo et firmiter constituo vt predicti canonici om[nia] predicta tenementa habeant et teneant libere et quiete in pace et honorifice [cum] omnibus libertatibus et aisiamentis ad predicta ten[ementa] pertinentibus quieta et soluta [de] omni seruitio et exactione seculari et demanda et eciam forinseco seruitio. Et ego Petrus de Lincoln[ia] et heredes mei hec omnia predicta dictis canonicis contra omnes homines et feminas warantizabimus acquietabimus et defendemus inperpetuum. Preterea ego Petrus de Lincoln[ia] et heredes mei omnes terras et possessiones infra villam et extra scilicet in vno forario in territorio de Barkeby super Brocfurlang in muris apud Barkeby circumeuntibus curiam dictorum canonicorum vnde clameum fuit et in fosseto in villa de Hung[er]tona quas dicti canonici tenuerunt de feodo meo et fuerunt in saisina anno regni regis Henr[ici] vicesimo tertio ci[clo] lunari quinto dictis canonicis contra omnes homines et feminas warantizabimus inperpetuum. Quod vt firmum sit et stabile presens scriptum sigilli mei munimine robora[ui]. Hiis testibus Eustagio de Foleuile milite magistro Ric[ard]o de Heleford' Hug[one] Ba[rre] Rob[er]to de Wytebec Nich[ola]o Pepin Will[elm]o Grim Elia de Lindeseya Mil[one] de Craxton' Will[elm]o filio Herb[er]ti de Barkeby Simone clerico et aliis.

> The reference to the abbey's seisin of land in Barkby and Hungerton in 1239 doubtless indicates the year that Peter succeeded his father. Apart from the attestation of Sir Eustace de Folleville of Ashby, who was murdered in 1274, there is no other close indication of date, but it was most likely drafted not long after 1239, as Elias of Lindsey seems to have been planning his departure from the world before that year. For the unusual use of the lunar cycle at Leicester Abbey to establish the year, see also no. 42.

44. Lawrence son of William son of Leofric   *c.* 1219 X 1241

Grant of two virgates in Walton, Leics. which William Thase gave to his daughter Leticia as a marriage portion, the abbey to pay a rent of two shillings to Richard of Sheavsby at two terms, the Purification of the Blessed Virgin Mary and Pentecost.

A = Original, now lost. B = TNA E13/76, m. 68, copy dated 1351 (from A).

[B]

Sciant presentes et futuri quod ego Laurentius filius Will[elmi] filii Leuerici dedi et concessi et hac presenti carta mea confirmaui deo et ecclesie sancte Marie de Pratis Leicestr[ie] et canonicis regularibus ibidem deo seruientibus pro anima patris mei et matris mee et pro anima Will[elm]i Thase et pro animabus omnium antecessorum et successorum meorum in perpetuam elemosinam duas virgatas terre in Waleton' cum omnibus pertinentiis suis infra villam et extra. illas videlicet quas Will[elmu]s Thase dedit Leticie filie sue in libero maritagio. Habendas et tenendas ipsis canonicis libere et quiete et plenarie in pratis et pascuis in communis et in omnibus libertatibus et esiamentis ad predictas duas virgatas terre pertinentibus infra villam et extra. Reddendo inde annuatim Ric[ard]o de Sheuisby et heredibus suis duos solidos ad duos anni terminos videlicet ad Purificationem beate Marie duodecim denarios et ad Pentecosten duodecim denarios pro omni seruitio ad predictam terram pertinente. Vt autem hec mea donatio et concessio robur optineat inperpetuum, sigillum meum apponi feci. Hiis testibus domino S. de Segraue Rog[er]o de Rerisby Henr[ico] de Lilleburn' Simone de Coleshull' Rob[er]to de Iolgraue Rob[er]to de Monsorel Rob[er]to de Wyzebech et multis aliis.

> The presence of Stephen de Segrave here as a knight indicates a date between *c.* 1219, when he first appears as a knight and his death in 1241, see *ODNB, s.n.* Seagrave.

45. Hugh de Loges   *c.* 1219 X 1241

Grant of the service of two virgates in Bramcote in the parish of Bulkington, Warwicks. from which he received two shillings annual rent from Henry son of William Lusse.

A = Original, now lost. B = TNA E13/76, m. 75d, copy dated 1351 (from A).

[B]

Sciant presentes et futuri quod ego Hugo de Logiis dedi concessi et hac presenti carta mea confirmaui deo et beate Marie et abbati et conuentui de Pratis Leyc[estrie] seruitium de duabus virgatis terre cum pertinentiis in Bramcote in parochia de Bulkynton' de quibus percipere solebam annuatim duos solidos per manum Henr[ici] filii Will[elm]i Lusse. Vnde volo quod idem abbas et conuentus Leyc[estrie] predictum seruitium in puram et perpetuam elemosinam libere et quiete inperpetuum habeant et possideant sicut aliqua elemosina melius et liberius alicui domui religiose conferri potest. Et vt hec mea donatio perpetue firmitatis robur optineat huic scripto sigilli mei munimen apposui. Hiis testibus. Stephano de Segraue Will[elm]o de Vernum Ph[ilipp]o de Kynton Henr[ico] de Segraue Ioh[ann]e filio Paui Henr[ico] de Lilleburne et multis aliis.

For date see preceding act.

46. Peter son of Thurstan of Barkby   s. xiii[1]

Grant of two plough strips in the fields of Barkby, Leics. one at Brodeshert *of two and a half rods, next to the abbot's strip, and the other on the hill of Queniborough of two and a half rods, next to the abbot's strips, with all his meadowland in* Estmedue.

A = Original, now lost. B = TNA E13/76, m. 70, copy dated 1351 (from A).

[B]

Omnibus ad quos presens scriptum peruenerit, Petrus filius Turstani de Barkeby, salutem. Nouerit vniuersitas vestra me concessisse et dedisse et hac presenti carta mea confirmasse in puram et perpetuam elemosinam deo et ecclesie beate Marie de Prato Leycestrie et canonicis regularibus ibidem deo seruientibus duos seleiones in campis de Barkeby vnum scilicet ad Brodeshert de duabus rodis et dimidiam iuxta sellionem abbatis et alium in monte de Quenibur' de duabus rodis et dimidiam iuxta selliones abbatis et totum pratum meum quod habeo in Estmedue. Quare volo et firmiter constituo vt predicti canonici hanc meam elemosinam habeant et teneant bene et in pace libere et quiete erga me et heredes meos et erga omnes homines. Quia ego et heredes mei hanc predictam terram predictis canonicis contra omnes homines warantizabimus. Et vt hec mea elemosina firma sit et stabilis, presens scriptum sigilli mei munimine roboraui. Hiis testibus domino Thoma de Lincoln' Will[elm]o capellano de Barkeby Gerold[o] Will[elm]o Herbert. Thoma seruiente Rob[er]to Gardin Willelmo Alger Hugone Alwyn Willelmo filio Roberti Reginaldo fabro Willelmo Winsun et multis aliis.

The presence of Sir Thomas Lincoln in the witness list firmly places this act in the first half of the thirteenth century, and probably before 1240.

47. Peter son of Thurstan of Barkby   s. xiii[1]

Grant of a half acre of land on Tungemare, *between the abbey's cultivated land in the field of Barkby, Leics.*

A = Original, now lost. B = TNA E13/76, m. 69d, copy dated 1351 (from A).

[B]

Sciant presentes et futuri quod ego Petrus filius Thurstani de Barkeby dedi et concessi et hac presenti carta mea confirmaui deo et ecclesie sancte Marie de Prato Leic[estrie] et canonicis ibidem deo seruientibus pro salute mea et antecessorum et successorum meorum dimidiam acram terre super Tungemare scilicet illam que iacet inter culturam abbatis Leic[estrie] in campo de Barkeby libere et quiete et honorifice in puram et perpetuam elemosinam sicut aliqua elemosina melius et liberius dari potest. Hiis testibus Will[elm]o sacerdote de Barkeby Rad[ulf]o Costein Will[elm]o filio Herberti Rad[ulf]o de Barkeby Alexandro filio sacerdotis Simone de Aula .P. clerico.

48. Peter son of Thurstan of Barkby   s. xiii[1]

Grant of two rods of land in the field of Barkby, Leics. of which one lies on Sandhil *and another stretches across* Redemora, *next to the land of his uncle Ralph, with grant also of meadowland on the other side of the path towards Syston, upon which meadow his father had been killed. Quitclaim also of his rights on a half-acre of land in* Dales *that he and his father had once held.*

A = Original, now lost. B = TNA E13/76, m. 75, copy dated 1351 (from A).

[B]

Vniuersis sancte matris ecclesie filiis ad quos presens scriptum peruenerit Petrus filius Thurstani de Barkeby, salutem. Nouerit vniuersitas vestra me dedisse et concessisse et hac presenti carta mea confirmasse pro salute anime mee et antecessorum et successorum meorum deo et ecclesie beate Marie de Prato Leyc[estrie] et canonicis regularibus ibidem deo seruientibus in puram liberam et perpetuam elemosinam duas rodas terre in campo de Barkeby quarum vna iacet super Sandhil et altera que se extendit in Redemoram iuxta terram Rad[ulf]i aduunculi mei et illud pratum quod se extendit vltra semitam versus Sideston' super quod pater meus occisus fuerat. Preterea quietum clamaui de me et heredibus meis imperpetuum predicte ecclesie et prenominatis canonicis omne ius quod habui in dimidia acra terre que iacet in Dales quam pater meus et ego Petrus aliquando tenuimus. Quare volo et firmiter constituo quod predicti canonici prefatam elemosinam habeant et teneant libere et quiete et honorifice absque omni seruitio et exactione seculari. Ego vero Petrus predictam elemosinam et heredes mei warantizabimus prenominatis canonicis contra omnes homines. Hiis testibus Will[elm]o capell[an]o de Barkeby Rad[ulf]o filio sacerdotis Will[elm]o filio H[er]eberti Gerardo de Barkeby Petro clerico Simon de Aula et aliis.

49. Robert Haliday of Barkby   s. xiii[1]

Grant of four plots of meadowland in the meadows of Barkby, Leics. attached to particular virgates: namely one plot in a place called Nesse; *another on the south side of the Wanlip bridge; a third in* Burnardeshull', *and the fourth in* Sutherdole. *For this the canons gave him three and a half silver marks.*

A = Original, now lost. B = TNA E13/76, m. 70, copy dated 1351 (from A).

[B]

Sciant presentes et futuri quod ego Rob[er]tus Haliday de Barkeby dedi concessi et hac presenti carta mea confirmaui deo et ecclesie beate Marie de Pratis Leircestr[ie] et canonicis regularibus ibidem deo seruientibus in liberam puram et perpetuam elemosinam quatuor placeas prati in prato de Barkeby scilicet vnam placeam prati iacentem in quodam loco qui vocatur Nesse pertinentem ad vnam virgatam terre. et vnam placeam prati pertinentem ad vnam virgatam terre iacentem ex parte australi iuxta pontem de Anlep'. et vnam placeam prati in Burnardeshull' pertinentem ad vnam virgatam terre. et vnam placeam prati in Suther dole pertinentem ad vnam virgatam terre cum pertinentiis. Habendas et tenendas predictis canonicis et eorum successoribus libere quiete pacifice pure et honorifice inperpetuum. Pro hac autem donatione concessione et presentis carte confirmatione dederunt michi predicti canonici tres marcas et dimidiam marcam argenti per manibus. Et ego predictus Rob[er]tus et heredes mei predictas quatuor placeas prati cum pertinentiis predictis canonicis et eorum successoribus sicut predictum est contra omnes gentes inperpetuum warantizabimus adquietabimus et defendemus. In cuius rei testimonium huic carte sigillum meum apposui. Hiis testibus Will[elm]o Poer de Thorp' iuxta Barkeby Waltero Geraud de eadem Will[elm]o de la Despense de eadem Will[elm]o Geraud de eadem Alano filio Christofori de Thurmodeston' Ioh[ann]e Ketelbern Ioh[ann]e le Machun de Thurmodeston' Rob[er]to clerico et aliis.

50. John le Wyte son of Walter le Wyte of Barkby   s. xiii[1]

Grant of a rod of land upon Branteclif' *[in Barkby, Leics.].*

A = Original, now lost. B = TNA E13/76, m. 74d, copy dated 1351 (from A).

[B]

Sciant presentes et futuri quod ego Ioh[ann]es le Wyte filius Walt[er]i le Wyte de Barkeby dedi concessi et hac presenti carta mea confirmaui deo et beate Marie de Pratis Leyc[estrie] et canonicis regularibus ibidem deo seruientibus vnam rodam terre super Branteclif' in puram et perpetuam elemosinam pro salute anime mee et patris mei et matris mee et antecessorum meorum. Habendam et tenendam libere quiete et honorifice bene et in pace pro omni seruitio seculari et demanda imperpetuum. Ego vero Ioh[ann]es et heredes mei predictam rodam terre contra omnes homines et feminas warantizabimus et acquietabimus. Vt autem hec mea donatio et concessio rata et stabilis imperpetuum permaneat presens scriptum sigilli mei inpressione roboraui. Hiis testibus Henr[ico] de Lilleburn' Rob[er]to de Wytebec Rob[er]to de Monte Sorello Galfr[id]o de Tychel' Will[elm]o Hereberd' Ioh[ann]e aurifabro et multis aliis.

51. Ralph son of the priest of Barkby   s. xiii[1]

Grant of two rods of land and a rod of meadow [in Barkby, Leics.], of which one is on Waltidis *at the white stone, another at* Hermescumb *running up to* Saltergate *and to the rod of meadow in* Langedale, *and the rod of meadow is at the stone.*

A = Original, now lost. B = TNA E13/76, m. 70, copy dated 1351 (from A).

[B]

Omnibus ad quos presens scriptum peruenerit, Rad[ulfu]s filius sacerdotis de Barkeby salutem. Notum sit omnibus vobis me pro salute anime mee et antecessorum et successorum meorum dedisse et concessisse et hac presenti carta mea confirmasse deo et ecclesie beate Marie de Prato Leyc[estrie] et canonicis regularibus ibidem deo seruientibus in puram liberam et perpetuam elemosinam duas rodas terre et vna roda prati. Quarum vna roda est super Waltidis apud albam petram et altera roda apud Hermescumb que se extendit vsque Saltergate et rodam prati ad petram. Quare volo et firmiter constituo quod predicti canonici hanc meam elemosinam habeant et teneant libere et quiete et honorifice absque omni seruitio et exactione seculari. Quia ego et heredes mei hanc elemosinam predictis canonicis contra omnes homines warantizabimus. Hiis testibus Will[elm]o capell[ano] de Barkeby Will[elm]o filio Herb[er]ti de Barkeby Petro filio Turstani de Barkeby magistro Simone de Aula et Matheo de Aula Rob[er]to de Lega Will[elm]o coco et multis aliis.

The witness list contains people who associate this act with the first half of the thirteenth century. There are some resemblances to places in act no. 35 above, which is dated 1220 x 31. Curiously the act fails to locate the grant in Barkby, although the place names confirm that this is where is meant.

52. William of Hungarton   s. xiii[1]

Grant of a croft in the estate of Hungarton, Leics. lying between the enclosure of the house of Hospitallers of Leicester on the east side and a plot running down from Lewynewell *on the other.*

A = Original, now lost. B = TNA E13/76, m. 67d, copy dated 1351 (from A).

[B]

Sciant presentes et futuri quod ego Will[elmu]s de Hungurton' dedi concessi et hac presenti carta mea confirmaui pro salute anime mee et predecessorum et successorum meorum deo et ecclesie sancte Marie de Prato Leicestr[ie] et canonicis regularibus ibidem deo seruientibus vnum croftum in territorio de Hungurton'. illud videlicet quod iacet inter curiam hospitalariorum Leicestr[ie] versus partem orientalem et sitam que descendit de Lewynewell'. Habendum et tenendum ipsis canonicis in liberam puram et perpetuam elemosinam. Quod vt firmum sit et stabile huic scripto sigillum meum apposui. Hiis testibus Thoma de Lincoln' Will[elm]o vicario de Barew Ioh[ann]e de Hingwareby Milon[e] de Crokeston' Rob[er]to de Hib[er]nia Petro de Hung[ur]ton' Rob[er]to de Iolegraue Rob[er]to de Munsorel Rob[er]to de Wytebec Hugone Peuerel Waltero de Bristoll' et multis aliis.

The date of this act must be roughly contemporary with those to the abbey of its first witness, Thomas of Lincoln, see above, nos. 41, 43.

53. Simon son of William son of Osmund of Thurmaston   s. xiii[1]

Grant of a plot of land in the village of Thurmaston, Leics. opposite Le Hov, *between land of the canons and the land Hugh Suarry used to hold. The canons to hold it for the benefit of their pittance, saving an annual ten pence rent which is to be put to the common uses of the abbey.*

A = Original, now lost. B = TNA E13/76, m. 68d, copy dated 1351 (from A).

[B]

Sciant presentes et futuri quod ego Simon filius Will[elm]i filii Osemundi de Thurmodeston dedi concessi et hac presenti carta mea confirmaui deo et ecclesie beate Marie de Pratis Leicestr[ie] et pietantie canonicorum regularium ibidem deo seruientium vnam placeam terre cum pertinentiis in villa de Thormediston' iacentem ex opposito le Hov inter terram predictorum canonicorum et terram quam Hugo Suarry aliquando tenuit. Habendam et tenendam predictis canonicis et eorum successoribus in puram et perpetuam elemosinam. Et ego predictus Simon et heredes mei predictam placeam terre cum pertinentiis sicut predictum est predictis canonicis et eorum successoribus contra omnes gentes warentizabimus aquietabimus et defendemus inperpetuum. In cuius rei testimonium presenti scripto sigillum meum apposui. Hiis testibus Alano filio Christofori de Thurmediston' Simone Glide Rob[er]to fabro Will[elm]o filio Petri Will[elm]o filio Laurencii et multis aliis.

The date of this act is argued on the basis of the occurrence of the witnesses in no. 49.

54. John son of Ketelbern of Thurmaston   s. xiii[1]
Grant of an acre of land on the other side of Barkehou *below the ditch; a rod of land in* Thormfurlong' *in* Weytholm, *alongside the other one he previously had given to the canons for making hay given instead of tithes; another rod in* Barthehouslad'; *two strips of ploughland which border on John's headland; a half acre lying in* Nesse *which belongs to a virgate of land, the half acre being sixty perches in length and in breadth at the upper end two and a half perches, and at the lower end two perches.*

A = Original, now lost. B = TNA E13/76, m. 74, copy dated 1351 (from A).

[B]

Sciant presentes et futuri quod ego Ioh[ann]es filius Ketelbern' de Thurmedeston' dedi concessi et hac presenti carta confirmaui deo et ecclesie beate Marie de Pratis Leyc[estrie] et canonicis regularibus ibidem deo seruientibus pro salute anime mee antecessorum et successorum meorum in puram et perpetuam elemosinam vnam acram terre citra Barkehou subtus fosse et vnam rodam terre in Thormfurlong' in Weytholm iuxta illam quam prius illis dederam pro factura feni dati pro decima et aliam rodam in Barthehouslad' et duas seliones que abuttant super foreriam Ioh[ann]is et dimidiam acram que iacet in Nesse que pertinet ad vnam virgatam terre que dimidia acra est in longitudine sexaginta perticarum et in latitudine ad capud superius duarum perticarum et dimidie et ad capud inferius durarum perticarum. Hec autem omnia predicta ego predictus Ioh[ann]es filius Ketelbern' et heredes mei dictis canonicis contra omnes homines warantizabimus acquietabimus et defendemus imperpetuum. Et vt hec mea donatio concessio confirmatio robur firmitatis optineat presens scriptum sigillo meo roboraui. Hiis testibus Gilb[er]to presbitero de Burstall' Rob[er]to filio Alani de Burstall' Simon[e] filio Yuonis de Belegraue. Will[elm]o filio Herebert de Barkeby et Walt[er]o filio eius et multis aliis.

The date of this act would seem to be somewhat earlier than the run of 1250s deeds of John Ketelbern, or John son of William Ketelbern, concerning Thurmaston, who may well be the same person as this grantor (taking his grandfather's name in his patronymic). In no. 57 below, dated 1253 x 1254, Walter son of William son of Herbert had then apparently succeeded his father, which again indicates an earlier date for this one.

55. Simon de Montfort, earl of Leicester   1239 x 1246, probably 1239 x 1240
Grant of three hundred acres of woodland, and twenty acres of mixed wood and open country bordering the rest in his forest called the Frith (Defensa) *next to Leicester, with bounds given as: from the Anstey road across to* Dalesike, *and* Dalesike *beyond* Sterkeshull *as far as* Oldefeld' *along the path from Cropston as it is defined by the boundaries, and from* Oldefeld *around the field of Belgrave and the canons' field back to the Anstey road. Grant also of all of* Cleyhegges *to be held in free alms, to be enclosed and ditched and cultivated or whatever the canons choose to do with it. The earl retains his right to hunt across the land, so that if his beasts should enter the canons' closes there, then the earl, his heirs and his bailiffs may enter the closes through the common gate and hunt and take the beasts, providing they do no damage to the canons' interests. If such damage by the earl's hunt does occur compensation is to be assessed by men of good standing.*

A = Original, now lost. B = TNA c53/45 (Charter Roll of 36 Henry III), m. 21 (from A).
Cal. *Calendar of Charter Rolls, 1226–57*, 408 (from B).

[B]

Vniuersis Christi fidelibus presens scriptum visuris uel audituris Simon de Monteforti com[es] Leyc[estrie] salutem in domino. Nouerit uniuersitas vestra nos pro salute anime nostre et animarum antecessorum et heredum nostrorum. dedisse. concessisse et presenti carta nostra confirmasse pro nobis et heredibus nostris inperpetuum deo et ecclesie sancte Marie de Prato Leyc[estrie] et canonicis regularibus ibidem deo seruientibus trescentas acras terre et bosci et viginti acras terre et bosci similiter cum pertinentiis contiguas trescentis acris predictis in foresta nostra que apellatur defensa iuxta Leyc[estriam] cum vestura et omnibus pertinentiis suis. et omni iure quod habuimus uel habere poterimus sine aliquo retenemento nobis et heredibus nostris. que videlicet omnes acre iacet a via de Anesty usque ad Dalesike in transuerso. et a Dalesik' ultra Sterkeshull'. usque ad Oldefeld' in transuerso supra semitam de Cropston' sicut per fines et bundas limitatus est et ab Oldefeld' in circuitu per campum de Belegreue et per campum dictorum canonicorum iterum ad iamdictam viam de Anesty. Dedimus etiam et concessimus dictis canonicis totum Cloyhegges cum vestura et omnibus pertinentiis suis integre sine aliquo retenemento habendum et tenendum dictis canonicis in liberam puram et perpetuam elemosinam. includendum et infossandum et in terram arabilem redigendum uel ad qualemcumque profectus eorum ut expedire prouiderint disponendum bene et in pace. libere et quiete. ab omni seruitio et exactione. et demanda sectis consuetudinibus et omnibus que de terra uel pro terra exigi possunt uel poterunt inperpetuum. sicut uero aliqua elemosina melius liberius et quietius alicui domui religionis potest confirmari et concedi. salua nobis et heredibus nostris venatione nostra. Ita tamen quod si fere nostre dictum cla[u]sum canonicorum intrauerint liceat nobis et heredibus uel balliuis nostris predictum cla[u]sum intrare per portam communem et easdem feras fugare et capere absque dampno uel detrimento dictorum canonicorum. Quod si aliquod dampnum uel detrimentum incurrerint per ingressum nostrum. eis incontinenti per visum bonorum et legalium virorum absque maliciosa dilatione satisfiet. Nos autem et heredibus nostri. predictas trescentas acras terre et bosci. cum viginti acris terre et bosci predictis. cum omnibus pertinentiis suis predictis et totum Cleyhegg' cum omnibus pertinentiis suis predictis predicte ecclesie sancte Marie et canonicis contra omnes gentes warantizabimus. defendemus et acquietabimus inperpetuum. vt igitur hec nostra donatio concessio et confirmatio perpetue firmitatis robur obtineat presens scriptum sigilli nostri munimine roborauimus. Hiis testibus. domino Steph[ano] de Segraue. domino Thom[a] de Meynill'. tunc sen[escallo] nostro. domino Ernald[o] de Bosco. domino Rad[ulf]o Basset. domino Will[elm]o de Vingnoles. domino Thoma de Estleya militibus. Nich[ol]ao de Marham. Will[el]mo le Faucun[er]. Will[el]mo de Seneuill'. Simone de Bruill'. Regin[aldo] tunc forestar[io]. Helia de Lindes[eia]. et aliis.

The earliest date limit is that of Simon de Montfort's investiture as earl in 1239. The witnesses help narrow it further. William (II) de Sainneville who attests here after the knights, appears in a Warwickshire deed of 1240 as a knight. He is known to have died in 1246 (for him see, *Descriptive catalogue of the charters and muniments in the possession of the Rt. Hon. Lord Fitzhardinge at Berkeley Castle*, ed. I. Jeayes (Bristol 1892), 48, 67–8, 87, 117; *Report on the manuscripts of the late Reginald Rawdon Hastings*, i, 98–9; TNA E326/3488; KB26/149, m. 9). As some support for this early date, Sir Thomas de Mesnil was one of Simon's earlier seneschals, representing his lord in Northamptonshire as early as June 1232 (TNA E159/12, m. 6). It is possible that this grant represents Simon's assertion of his new rights as advocate of the abbey after accession to the earldom. See also, A. Squires, 'The landscape of Leicester Abbey's home demesne lands to the Dissolution', above pp. 75–94.

56. Robert son of Henry of Bramcote   7 March 1249

Grant of the headland of his adjacent three plough strips for the extension and repair of the canons' fishpond at Cresswell, up as far as the ploughed ground.

A = Original, now lost. B = TNA E13/76, m. 75d, copy dated 1351 (from A).

[B]

Vniuersis Christi fidelibus hoc scriptum visuris vel audituris Rob[er]tus filius Henr[ici] de Bramcote salutem in domino. Nouerit vniuersitas vestra me dedisse concessisse et presenti carta mea confirmasse deo et ecclesie beate Marie de Pratis Leyc[estrie] et canonicis regularibus ibidem deo seruientibus in puram et perpetuam elemosinam ad dilatationem et emendationem uiuarii eorum de Cressewell' illam terram capitam trium selionum mearum que abuttant vsque in idem eorum viuariam vsque ad terram que fuit arabilem in dictis tribus selionibus meis tempore confectionis ista scripti, hanc autem meam donationem concessionem et confirmationem ego et heredes mei dictis canonicis Leyc[estrie]

warantizabimus acquietabimus et defendemus contra omnes gentes inperpetuum. In cuius rei
testimonium huic scripto sigillum meum apposui anno regni regis H[enrici] tricesimo tercio die
sanctarum Perpetue et Felicitatis. Hiis testibus. B. tunc vicar[io] de Bulkynton' Henrico Wyschard
Ioh[ann]e de M[er]ston' et Rob[er]to fratre suo Will[elmu]s Manyatin et aliis.

57. Walter son of William Herbert of Barkby   28 October 1253 x 27 October 1254
Confirmation of the grant by John le Wyte to the canons of a half bovate of land within the bounds of Barkby,
Leics.

> A = Original, now lost. B = TNA E13/76, m. 74d, copy dated 1351 (from A).

[B]

Sciant presentes et futuri quod ego Walt[er]us filius Will[elm]i Herbert de Barkeby dedi. concessi et hac
presenti carta mea confirmaui deo et ecclesie beate Marie de Pratis Leyc[estrie] et canonicis regularibus
ibidem deo seruientibus pro salute anime mee antecessorum et successorum meorum dimidiam bouatam
terre cum omnibus pertinentiis suis in territorio de Barkeby. illam scilicet quam Ioh[ann]es le Wyte eisdem
canonicis dedit et carta sua confirmauit. Habendam et tenendam dictis canonicis in liberam puram et
perpetuam elemosinam sicut aliqua elemosina melius liberius et quietius alicui domui religiose poterit
conferri vel concedi. Et ego predictus Walterus et heredes mei dictam dimidiam bouatam terre cum omnibus
pertinentiis suis dictis canonicis contra omnes homines et feminas warantizabimus et de omnibus wardis
castellorum auxiliis vicecomitum scutagiis et omnimodis aliis forinsecis acquietabimus et defendemus. Vt
autem hec mea donatio concessio ac presentis carte confirmatio roboris optineat firmitatem, presenti scripto
sigillum meum duxi apponendum. anno regni regis H[enrici] filii regis Ioh[ann]is tricesimo octauo. Hiis
testibus magistro Th[oma] de Luda Hug[one] vicario de Barkeby Henr[ico] Wyschard magistro Ric[ard]o
de Stapelton' Walt[er]o de Euinton' Will[elm]o Poer Ioh[ann]e Geraud' Walt[er]o Geraud Ioh[ann]e de
Cokerham Rog[er]o de Twyford' Simon[e] de Osulueston'. et aliis.

58. Simon de Montfort, earl of Leicester   London, 21 October 1255
Grant of a plot of woodland and open country called Doveland (Donelund') with its gate as it is presently
enclosed, with license for the canons to do with it as they wish. Grant also of another plot of woodland and open
country towards Anstey, called Olishawe (Osulueshawe) outside the enclosure of Leicester Frith with all the
pieces of wood and land between Olishawe and the road from Anstey outside the palisade of the Frith. Grant also
of a plot of arable land which William of Belgrave, a serjeant, once held, which lies next to the Frith and was once
part of it. The canons are also released from their obligation to pay suit of court that used to be exacted for a car-
rucate of land which Ranulf the doorkeeper once held. The earl reserves the right to hunt over the lands he has
granted.

> A = Original, now lost. B = Second Leicester Cartulary (from A). C = Leicester Rental (digest from B, now lost). D = TNA c56/16
> (Confirmation Roll of 3 Henry VII), m. 19 (from A). E = Bodl. Laud misc. 625, f. 5v (from C).

[D]

Vniuersis Christi fidelibus presens scriptum visuris vel audituris Simon de Monteforti comes Leyrcestr[ie]
salutem in domino sempiternam. Nouerit vniuersitas vestra nos pro salute anime nostre et anime Alienore
comitisse nostre et pro salute animarum antecessorum successorum et heredum nostrorum dedisse
concessisse et hac presenti carta nostra confirmasse pro nobis et heredibus nostris imperpetuum deo et
ecclesie beate Marie de Pratis Leyrcestr[ie] et canonicis regularibus idem deo seruientibus quandam
placiam terre et bosci que vocatur Donelund' cum apertura fossati sicut tempore confectionis presentium
includebatur. Ita tamen quod licebit predictis canonicis dictam placiam includere prout eis melius
viderint expedire. Dedimus etiam eisdem canonicis quandam placeam terre et bosci versus Anesty que
vocatur Osulueshawe extra paliciam defensi Leyrcestr[ie] cum omnibus angulis bosci et terre qui iacent
inter dictam placiam de Osulueshawe et viam de Anesty extra paliciam defensi memorati. Item dedimus
eisdem canonicis vnam placiam terre arabilis illam videlicet quam Will[elmu]s de Bellagraua seruiens
quondam tenuit. Que quidem placia terre dictorum canonicorum est contigua et aliquando fuit de
defenso. Hec omnia predicta predictis canonicis dedimus et concessimus. Habendas et tenendas in

liberam puram et perpetuam elemosinam ad includendum infossandum et in terram arabilem redigendum ad assartandum ad passendum et qualemcumque profectum eorum prout eis expedire viderint disponendum cum libero introitu et exitu ad cariandum et ad animalia sua fugandum bene et in pace libere et quiete ab omni seculari seruitio exactione et demandis sectis consuetudinibus et omnibus que de terra vel pro terra exigi possunt vel qualitercumque poterunt imperpetuum sicut aliqua elemosina melius liberius et quietius alicui domum religionis potest conferri vel concedi. salua nobis et heredibus nostris in dictis boscis omnimoda venatione ferarum vndecumque venerunt et qualitercumque ibidem intrauerunt. Relaxamus etiam eisdem canonicis pro nobis et heredibus nostris sectam curie nostre quam ab eisdem aliquando exigebamus occasione vnius carucate terre que quondam fuit Ranulfi ianitoris. Nos autem et heredes nostri omnia predicta predictis canonicis contra omnes homines et feminas warantizabimus acquietabimus et imperpetuum defendemus. In cuius rei testimonium sigilli nostri impressione roboramus presens scriptum. Hiis testibus dominis Petro de Monteforti. Ioh[ann]e de la Haye. Rad[ulf]o Basset de Sapecote. Thoma de Estleya. Ric[ardo] de Hauering et Will[elm]o Basset militibus. Petro filio Rog[er]i de Leycestr'. magistro Thoma de Luda. Bartholomeo iuueni. Waltero de Euinton'. Gerardo de Euinton' Rogero Beller. Rob[er]to de Burstall' et aliis. Dat[um] London[ias]. anno domini millesimo ducentesimo quinquagesimo quinto die iouis proxima post festum sancti Luce ewangeliste.

> For the identification of places in the text, see P. Courtney, 'Between two forests: the social and topographical evolution of medieval Anstey', *TLAHS* 77 (2003), 35–64 at 42.

59. Peter of Lincoln son of Thomas of Lincoln   1240 x 1259, possibly early 1250s

Confirmation of a toft Andrew Kidman once held in Hungarton, Leics. which William of Babbgrave had of Peter's grant, along with a plot of land opposite the toft across the road; a strip of ploughland just outside the plot within the toft; three more strips beyond Holewelledales; *a virgate Peter gave to Walter of Barford, rector of Hungarton; six butts belonging to that same virgate; the virgate which Richard Dreng of Babbgrave once held, which was previously William Herberd's, with the messuage Robert of Quenby once held of the brothers of the hospital of St John of Leicester which was previously Patrick's. To be held quit of all suits of court and view of frankpledge.*

> A = Original, now lost. B = TNA E13/76, m. 67d, copy dated 1351 (from A).

[B]

Sciant presentes et futuri quod ego Petrus de Lincolnia filius Thome de Lincolnia concessi et hac presenti carta mea confirmaui deo et ecclesie beate Marie de Pratis Leicest[rie] et canonicis regularibus ibidem deo seruientibus pro salute anime mee antecessorum et successorum meorum vnum toftum quod Andreas Kydeman aliquando tenuit. Quod toftum Will[elmu]s de Babbegraue habuit ex dono meo in villa de Hungarton cum placea ex altera parte vie eiusdem tofti et vnum sellionem extra placeam illam in tofto et tres selliones vltra Holewelledales cum omnibus pertinentiis suis et vnam virgatam terre quam dedi Waltero de Bereford rectori ecclesie de Hungurton et sex buttos ad eandem virgatam terre pertinentes. illam scilicet virgatam terre quam Ric[ard]us Dreng' de Babbegraue aliquando tenuit que fuit quondam Will[elm]i Herberd' cum omnibus pertinentiis suis et toftum et croftum cum mesuagio que scilicet Rob[ert]us de Quenby de fratribus hospitalis sancti Ioh[ann]is Leicest[rie] aliquando tenuit. quod etiam fuerunt Patricii cum omnibus pertinentiis suis. Habenda et tenenda dictis canonicis in liberam puram et perpetuam elemosinam et quietam de sectis ad visum franciplegii et omnimodis aliis sectis curie sicut aliqua elemosina alicui domui religiose melius quietius et liberius confirmari poterit vel concedi vel quocumque modo a quocumque seruitio quietum clamari. Et ego predictus Petrus de Linc[olnia] et heredes mei prefatos canonicos contra omnes homines et feminas de omnibus consuetudinibus et demandis et hac omnia subscripta pertinentibus acquietabimus et defendemus inperpetuum. Vt autem hec mea concessio et quietaclamacio et presentis carte mee confirmatio rata et stabilis inperpetuum permaneat, presens scriptum sigilli mei munimine roboraui. Hiis testibus magistro Thoma de Luda. magistro Ric[ard]o de Stapelton'. Waltero de Euinton' Ric[ard]o de Cley. Henr[ico] Wyschard Hugone de Neuilla Will[elm]o Cnotte de Role Ioh[ann]e de Cokerham Rog[er]o de Twyford' Simone de Osulueston' et aliis.

The coincidences of the witness list with that of no. 57 above, datable to 1253 x 54, gives a likely general date of the early 1250s. As is clear from no. 43 Peter succeeded his father in around 1240, so it must date after then. Similarly, Walter of Evington is known to have died in 1259, so it must date before then, for this see TNA JUST1/456, m. 13.

60. Iseult daughter of Peter son of Thurstan of Barkby   s. xiii med.

Grant in her widowhood for three and a half silver marks of three acres and a half rod of land in Barkby, Leics. which she had from her late father. Listed as a half rod at Byhow next to the land of William the turner; a rod and a half on the other side of Portgate next to the land Henry Cole once held; a rod and a half on Longeclif next to the land of William the turner; a rod and a half by Weston next to the land of Richard son of Thurstan; the half rod running from Queningburgate beside the land of William le Poer; a rod at Greneplot' next to the land of Walter Geroud; a rod on Dykfurlang next to the land of Richard son of Thurstan; a rod and a half on Esteresmereberewe next to the land of Richard son of Thurstan; a rod upon Longewold' next to the land of Richard fitz Thurstan; a half rod on Shortwold next to the land of Robert Haliday; a half rod beside Woldgate next to the land of William le Poer; and a patch of meadow on Hardemede next to the land of William the turner.

A = Original, now lost. B = TNA E13/76, m. 70–70d, copy dated 1351 (from A).

[B]

Sciant presentes et futuri quod ego Iseuda filia Petri filii Thurstani de Barkeby in mea libera viduitate dedi concessi et de me et de heredibus meis quietum clamaui deo et ecclesie beate Marie de Pratis Leircestr[ie] et canonicis regularibus ibidem deo seruientibus pro tribus marcis et dimidia argenti quas per manibus recepi. tres acras et vnam dimidiam rodam terre iacentes in territorio de Barkeby scilicet quas habui iure hereditario de tenemento quod fuit dicti Petri patris mei videlicet vnam dimidiam rodam ad Byhow iuxta terram Will[elm]i le Turnur. Et vnam rodam et dimidiam vltra Portgate iuxta terram quam Henr[icus] Cole aliquando tenuit. Et vnam rodam et dimidiam super Longeclif iuxta terram Will[elm]i le Turnur. Et vnam rodam et dimidiam by*a* Weston iuxta terram Ric[ard]i filii Turstani. Et vnam dimidiam rodam se extendentem vsque Queningburgate iuxta terram Will[elm]i le Poer. Et vnam rodam ad Greneplot' iuxta terram Waltero Geroud. Et vnam rodam super Dykfurlang iuxta terram Ric[ard]i filii Turstani. Et vnam rodam et dimidiam super Esteresmereberewe iuxta terram Ric[ard]i filii Turstani. Et vnam rodam super Longewold' iuxta terram Ric[ard]i filii Turstani. Et dimidiam rodam super Shortwold. iuxta terram Rob[er]ti Haliday. Et dimidiam rodam iuxta Woldgate iuxta terram Will[elm]i le Poer. Et vnam dolam in Hardemede iuxta terram Will[elm]i le Turnur cum toto prato ad predictas tres acras et dimidiam rodam terre pertinente et cum omnibus aliis pertinentiis suis in pratis pascuis pasturis et in quibuscumque aliis locis infra villam et extra. Habendas et tenendas memoratis canonicis in liberam puram et perpetuam elemosinam sicut aliqua elemosina liberius purius vel vberius dari poterit vel concedi. Et ne ego prefata Yseuda vel heredes mei in predictas tres acras et dimidiam rodam terre cum pertinentiis vel pratum prenominatum aliquid iuris vel clamii decetero habere possimus. Hiis testibus Waltero Geroud Walt[er]o Herb[er]t Ioh[ann]e Geroud Hugone Turstan Ric[ard]o Turstan Will[elm]o le Poer Simone ad crucem Rad[ulf]o summonitore Ric[ard]o Humfrey Will[elm]o Fipaud de Sizeton' et aliis.

a sic

61. Iseult daughter of Peter son of Thurstan of Barkby   1247 x 1270, probably s. xiii med.

Grant in her widowhood of an annual rent of 3½d rent from half a toft that Roger Wytecope held of him in Barkby, Leics. payable on 29 September. For this the abbey gives her three shillings.

A = Original, now lost. B = TNA E13/76, m. 75, copy dated 1351 (from A).

[B]

Omnibus Christi fidelibus hoc scriptum visuris vel audituris Iseolda filia Petri filii*a* Thurstani de Barkeby, salutem in domino. Noueritis me in libera viduitate mea dedisse concessisse et presenti carta mea confirmasse fratri Henr[ico] abbati ecclesie sancte Marie de Pratis Leyc[estrie] et eiusdem loci conuentui in puram et perpetuam elemosinam tres denarios et obolum annui redditus de medietate vnius tofti quam Rog[er]us Wytecope de me tenuit in Barkeby ad festum sancti Michaelis annuatim percipiendum cum quieta clamancia totius iuris et clamei quod ego vel heredes mei habuimus vel habere potuimus in medietate tofti predicta. Et ego Isold[a] et heredes mei predictos tres denarios et obolum annui redditus predictis abbati et conuentui et eorum successorum in forma predicta contra omnes gentes warantizabimus acquietabimus et defendemus imperpetuum. Pro hac autem donatione concessione et quieta clamancia dederunt michi predicti abbas et conuentus tres solidos argenti per manibus. In cuius rei testimonium presenti scripto sigillum meum feci apposui. Hiis testibus domino Hug[one] vicar[io] de Barkeby. Waltero Herbert de eadem Will[elmo] de Bittmeswell'de eadem Ioh[ann]e Ketelbern' de Thurmodeston' Mich[ael]e carpent[ario] de eadem et aliis.

> *ᵃ* Petri et fil' *in* B.

> The appearance of Abbot Henry gives a date in his abbacy (1247–70) and the witness list encourages the assumption of a date in the middle of the century.

62. Walter Herbert of Barkby   s. xiii med.
Grant of an annual rent of 2s. 6d. payable by William le Poer, from his land in Barkby, Leics.

> A = Original, now lost. B = TNA E13/76, m. 74d, copy dated 1351 (from A).

[B]

Sciant presentes et futuri quod ego Walt[er]us Herberd' de Barkeby dedi concessi et hac presenti carta mea confirmaui deo et ecclesie sancte Marie de Pratis Leyc[estrie] et canonicis regularibus ibidem deo seruientibus annuum redditum duorum solidorum et sex denariorum in villa de Barkeby quem quidem redditum percipere solebam de terra Will[elm]i le Poer ad tres terminos annui percipiendum scilicet ad Pentecost[en] decem denarios ad festum sancti Michaelis decem denarios et ad Purificationem beate Marie virginis decem denarios. Habendum et tenendum dictis canonicis in liberam puram et perpetuam elemosinam cum omnibus homagiis wardis releuiis escaetis et omnibus aliis pertinentiis tam infra villam de Barkeby quam extra. Ego vero dictus Walt[er]us et heredes mei dictum redditum cum homagiis wardiis et releuiis escaetis et omnibus aliis pertinentiis suis contra omnes gentes warantizabimus acquietabimus et defendemus inperpetuum. Vt autem hec mea donatio concessio et carta confirmationis rata et stabilis inperpetuum permaneat presenti carte sigillum meum apposui. Hiis testibus Hug[one] de Neyuill' Will[elm]o Cnotte Rob[erto] et Adam Cleu Rob[er]to le Fauconer Gerard[o] de Hemelton' Walt[er]o Gerard Henrico clerico et aliis.

63. John Ketelbern son of William Ketelbern of Thurmaston   s. xiii med.
Grant of six pence annual rent payable by Isabel of Glenfield, widow of Robert Pollard, for a bovate of land in the village of Thurmaston, Leics. at three terms, for the pittance of the canons.

> A = Original, now lost. B = TNA E13/76, m. 74, copy dated 1351 (from A).

[B]

Sciant presentes et futuri quod ego Ioh[ann]es Ketelbern filius Will[elm]i Ketelbern de Thurmodeston' dedi concessi et de me et heredibus meis imperpetuum quietum clamaui deo et ecclesie beate Marie de Pratis Leyc[estrie] et canonicis regularibus ibidem deo seruientibus sex denarios annui redditus percipiendos de Isabell[a] de Glenefeld' quondam vxoris Rob[ert]i Pollard' quos eadem Isabell[a] michi reddere solebat pro vna bouata terre cum pertinentiis in villa de Thurmedeston' videlicet ad festum sancti Mich[ael]is duos denarios et ad festum Purificationis beate Marie duos denarios et ad Pentecost[en] duos denarios. Habendum et tenendum dictis canonicis ad pietantiam conuentus in liberam puram et perpetuam elemosinam cum homagiis releuiis escaetis et cum omnibus aliis exitibus et fortunis que michi vel heredibus meis de predicto redditu aliquo modo prouenire possent imperpetuum. Et ego predictus Ioh[ann]es et heredes mei predictum redditum cum homagio seruitio et omnibus aliis exitibus inde prouenientibus sicut predictum est predictis canonicis contra omnes gentes warantizabimus acquietabimus et defendemus imperpetuum. Et vt hec mea donatio et concessio et quieta clamatio perpetue firmitatis robur optineant presentem cartam sigilli mei impressione roboraui. Hiis testibus magistro Ric[ard]o de Stapelton' magistro Alano de Wyteby Radulpho Friday Gerald[o] de Hamelton' Ad[a] Ketelb[er]n Iamis de Sum[er]uill' Rog[er]o clerico et aliis.

64. John Ketelbern of Thurmaston s. xiii med.

Grant of five rods of land held of him for a term of years at rent by Mathilda Dodeman lying in the fields of Thurmaston, Leics.: three upon Brodewong *and a half acre at* Le Gores.

A = Original, now lost. B = TNA E13/76, m. 68–68d, copy dated 1351 (from A).

[B]

Sciant presentes et futuri quod ego Ioh[ann]es Ketelbern de Thurmodeston' dedi concessi et hac presenti carta mea confirmaui deo et ecclesie beate Marie de Pratis Leirc[estrie] et canonicis regularibus ibidem deo seruientibus in liberam puram et perpetuam elemosinam quinque rodas terre iacentes in campis de Thurmod[estona] tres scilicet rodas super Brodewong' et dimidiam acra ad le Gores quas quidem quinque rodas Matild[is] Dodeman de me tenuit ad terminum. Habendas et tenendas predictis canonicis et eorum successoribus inperpetuum in liberam puram et perpetuam elemosinam cum omnibus libertatibus et aysiamentis ad predictam terram pertinentibus. Ego vero predictus Ioh[ann]es et heredes mei predictas quinque rodas terre cum pertinentiis suis predictis canonicis et eorum successoribus inperpetuum contra omnes homines warantizabimus adquietabimus et defendemus. In cuius rei testimonium huic presenti scripto sigillum meum apposui. Hiis testibus Ioh[ann]e le Masoun de Thurmod[estuna] Petro carp[e]nt[ario] de eadem Waltero fabro de eadem Thurstano de Galby Galfr[ido] de Lucteburgh' clerico Rob[er]to de Pecco clerico Hug[one] de la Breser' et aliis.

The date of this act is difficult to assess but is most likely in the middle of the thirteenth century in the light of John's datable act relating to Thurmaston (see no. 87).

65. John Ketelbern of Thurmaston s. xiii med.

Grant of the homage of William Alnath and his heirs with the service owed for a bovate of land he held of John in Thurmaston, Leics. namely a quarter pound of pepper and three silver halfpence rent payable annually on the feast of All Saints.

A = Original, now lost. B = TNA E13/76, m. 73d, copy dated 1351 (from A).

[B]

Sciant presentes et futuri quod ego Ioh[ann]es Ketelbern de Thurmodeston' dedi concessi et hac presenti carta mea confirmaui et omnino de me et heredibus [meis] imperpetuum quietum clamaui deo et ecclesie beate Marie de Pratis Leyc[estrie] et canonicis regularibus ibidem deo seruientibus in liberam puram et perpetuam elemosinam homagium Will[elm]i Alnath' et heredum suorum et totum seruitium quod ab eodem Will[elm]o annuatim recipere solebam seu recipere potui pro vna bouata terre cum pertinentiis quam de me tenuit in Thurmodeston' videlicet quartam partem vnius libre piperis et tres obolos argenti annuatim ad festum omnium sanctorum cum wardis releuiis maritagiis escaetis et omnimodis aliis comoditatibus et fortunis que michi de predicta terra qualitercumque possent accidere. Habendum et tenendum predictis canonicis et eorum successoribus in liberam puram et perpetuam elemosinam prout aliqua elemosina liberius et melius dari possit. Et ego predictus Ioh[ann]es et heredes mei et mei assignati predictum seruitium cum wardis releuiis maritagiis escaetis et omnimodis comoditatibus et fortunis predictis memoratis canonicis et eorum successoribus imperpetuum contra omnes homines warentizabimus adquietabimus et defendemus. In cuius rei testimonium presenti scripto sigillum meum apposui. Hiis testibus Gilb[er]to Wysman Rob[er]to Basil capell[an]is Alano Christofori Ioh[ann]e cementar[io] Rob[er]to fabro Petro carpentar[io] Galfr[id]o de Lutteburg' clerico.

66. John Ketelbern of Thurmaston s. xiii med.

Grant of an annual rent of two and a half pence payable by William son of Avice of Thurmaston payable at two terms, one and a half pence at Pentecost and one penny at the Purification (2 February), for six rods lying on Le Wong' *and a half acre of meadow in the meadowland on the* Anlip *side.*

A = Original, now lost. B = TNA E13/76, m. 73d, copy dated 1351 (from A).

[B]

Omnibus hoc scriptum visuris vel audituris Ioh[ann]es Ketilb[er]n de Thurmeston' salutem in domino. Noueritis me dedisse concessisse et presenti carta mea confirmasse deo et ecclesie beate Marie de Pratis Leyc[estrie] et canonicis regularibus ibidem deo seruientibus duos denarios et obolum annui redditus percipiendos singulis annis de Will[elm]o filio Auicie de Thurmeston' et de heredibus suis quos idem Will[elmu]s michi reddere solebat ad duos anni terminos videlicet ad Pentecost[en] vnum denarium et obolum et ad Pur[ificationem] beate Marie vnum denarium pro sex rodis terre que simul iacent in le Wong' et dimidiam acram prati in prato versus Anlep'. Habendos et tenendos dictis canonicis in liberam puram et perpetuam elemosinam cum homagio et seruitio dicti Will[elm]i et heredum suorum et cum toto iure et clamio quod habui vel habere potui in terra et prato predictis et cum omnibus que michi vel heredibus meis occasione dictorum terre et prati accidere vel accrescere possent. Et ego et heredes mei predictum redditum sicut predictum est contra omnes gentes prefatis canonicis warantizabimus acquietabimus et defendemus imperpetuum. In cuius rei testimonium huic scripto sigillum meum apposui. Hiis testibus Reginaldo fabro de Thurmeston' Thurstano de Galby de eadem Rob[er]to Wysman de eadem Rob[er]to de Stretton' de eadem Ioh[ann]e cementario Mich[ael]e carpentar[io] et aliis.

67. John Ketelbern of Thurmaston   s. xiii med.

Grant of the homage and service of William Sparewe of Thurmaston, Leics. for the tenement he held in the village with an annual rent of a penny payable from it at Pentecost.

  A = Original, now lost. B = TNA E13/76, m. 74, copy dated 1351 (from A).

[B]

Vniuersis Christi fidelibus presens scriptum visuris vel audituris Ioh[ann]es Ketelbern' de Tormedeston' salutem. Nouerit vniuersitas vestra me dedisse concessisse et hoc presenti scripto confirmasse deo et ecclesie beate Marie de Pratis Leyc[estrie] et canonicis regularibus ibidem deo seruientibus homagium et seruitium Will[elm]i Sparewe de Tormedeston' de tenemento quod idem Will[elmu]s de me tenuit in eadem villa et annuum redditum vnius denarii ad Pentecost[en] de eodem percipiendum pro tenemento prenominato. Habendum et tenendum dictis canonicis in liberam puram et perpetuam elemosinam. Ego vero dictus Ioh[anne]s et heredes mei dictum redditum cum homagio et seruitio dicti Will[elm]i et cum omnibus escaetis et fortunis de dicto tenemento prouenientibus contra omnes gentes warantizabimus acquietabimus et defendemus. In cuius rei testimonium huic presenti scripto sigillum meum apposui. Hiis testibus magistro Alano de Wyteby Reginaldo fabro Rob[ert]o Wysman Petro carpentar[io] Ioh[ann]e filio Lewyn et aliis.

68. John Ketelbern of Thurmaston   s. xiii med.

Grant of all the service he received from a bovate of land in Thurmaston. Leics. which John of Evington held of him, namely an annual rent of a penny and three farthings, an eighth part of a pound of pepper and an arrow flight at the feast of All Saints.

  A = Original, now lost. B = TNA E13/76, m. 74, copy dated 1351 (from A).

[B]

Sciant presentes et futuri quod ego Ioh[ann]es Ketilb[er]n dedi concessi et hac presenti carta mea confirmaui deo et ecclesie beate Marie de Pratis Leyc[estrie] et canonicis regularibus ibdiem deo seruientibus in puram et perpetuam elemosinam totum seruitium quod ego recipere solebam vel quocumque iure recipere possem de vna bouata terre in Thurmodeston' quam Ioh[ann]es de Euinton' de me tenuit, videlicet vnum denarium vnum obolum et vnum quadrantem annui redditus et octauam partem vnius libre piperis et vnam flettam annuatim de predicto tenemento ad festum omnium sanctorum percipiendum cum omni iure meo et omnibus euentibus et comodis que michi vel heredibus meis quocumque iure inde accidere potuissent. Et ego et heredes mei dictis canonicis et eorum successorum imperpetuum dicta seruitia cum omnibus euentibus et comodis prenotatis contra omnes homines warantizabimus acquietabimus et defendemus. In cuius

rei testimonium presenti scripto sigillum meum apposui. Hiis testibus Will[elm]o pistor[e] Alano filio
Christofori de Sytheston' Petro carpent[ario] de Thurmodeston' Mich[ael]e carpent[ario] de eadem
Will[elm]o Sparewe Will[elm]o filio presbiteri Will[elm]o Magot et aliis.

69. John Ketelbern   s. xiii med.

Grant of two ploughstrips [in exchange for] a rod and half of land in Thurmaston, Leics. upon Le Sutherdale
between the land held by Reginald Brun and that John Dodeman used to hold.

   A = Original, now lost. B = TNA E13/76, m. 74–74d, copy dated 1351 (from A).

[B]

Omnibus hominibus hominibus ad quorum notitiam presens scriptum peruenerit Ioh[ann]es Ketelbern'
salutem in domino. Nouerit vniuersitas vestra me dedisse concessisse et presenti scripto confirmasse et
omnino quietum clamasse de me et heredibus meis imperpetuum in puram et perpetuam elemosinam pro
salute anime mee et antecessorum et successorum meorum deo et ecclesie beate Marie de Pratis
Leyc[estrie] et canonicis regularibus ibidem deo seruientibus duos selliones iacentes [*a line apparently
omitted here in B in transcription*] pro vna roda et dimidia in territorio de Thurmed[estona] super le
Sutherdale inter terram quam Reginald[us] Brun tenuit ex parte vna et terram quam Ioh[ann]es Dodeman
aliquando tenuit ex altera. Habend[os] et tenend[os] predictis canonicis et eorum successoribus
imperpetuum in liberam puram et perpetuam elemosinam. Ego vero et heredes mei predictam terram
cum pertinentiis predictis canonicis et eorum successoribus imperpetuum contra omnes homines
warantizabimus acquietabimus et defendemus. In cuius rei testimonium presenti scripto sigillum meum
apposui. Hiis testibus Alano filio Christofori Ioh[ann]e le Mazun de Thurmod[estona] Petro
carpent[ario] de eadem Walt[er]o fabro de eadem Rob[er]to fabro de eadem Mich[ael]e carpent[ario] de
eadem. Galfr[id]o de Lutteburg' clerico et aliis.

70. John Ketelbern of Thurmaston   s. xiii med.

*Grant of an annual rent of one penny and a rose payable by William Osmund of Thurmaston, the penny at
Easter and the rose on 24 June. Grant also of a piece of meadowland in the meadows below* Languath', *as much as
belongs to a virgate.*

   A = Original, now lost. B = TNA E13/76, m. 74d, copy dated 1351 (from A).

[B]

Sciant presentes et futuri quod ego Ioh[ann]es Ketelbern' de Thurmodeston' dedi concessi et hac presenti
carta mea confirmaui deo et ecclesie beate Marie de Pratis Leyc[estrie] et canonicis regularibus ibidem deo
seruientibus annuum redditum vnius denarii et vnius floris rose annuatim percipiendum de Will[elm]o
Osmund de Thurmodeston' et de heredibus suis videlicet die Pasch[e] vnium denarium et die sancti
Ioh[ann]is baptiste vnum florem rose quos ego ad predictos terminos de dicto Will[elm]o percipere
consueui. Habendos et tenendos dictis canonicis in liberam puram et perpetuam elemosinam cum toto
iure et clamio quod ego habui vel habere potui in terris et tenementis quas vel que dictus Will[elmu]s de
patre meo seu de me tenuit et cum omnibus wardis releuiis fortunis escaetis que michi vel heredibus meis
de dictis terris aut tenementis aliquo modo accidere possent. Et ego et heredes mei dictum redditum cum
toto iure et aliis predictis prefatis canonicis contra omnes homines warantizabimus acquietabimus et
defendemus imperpetuum. Preterea dedi et de me et heredibus meis imperpetuum quietum clamaui deo
et ecclesie predicte et prefatis canonicis vnam dolam prati in prato ad vnam virgatam terre pertinet. Et vt
predicta mea donatio et quieta clamatio redditus iuris et prati perpetue firmitatis robur optineant presenti
scripto sigillum meum apposui. Hiis testibus Mich[ael]e carpentar[io] Ioh[ann]e cementar[io] Walt[er]o
fabro Rob[er]to filio Rog[er]i de Belegraue Alano filio Christofori et aliis.

71. Thurstan of Galby   s. xiii med.

*Grant of an annual rent of a halfpenny payable at Easter by Hugh the smith of Thurmaston for a half acre of
meadow which he held of Thurstan in Thurmaston, Leics. described as being cut in alternate years above and*

below the bridge, between the meadowland lately of Roger the reeve on the south side, and the meadowland of John of Stoughton on the north.

A = Original, now lost. B = TNA E13/76, m. 74, copy dated 1351 (from A).

[B]

Omnibus hoc scriptum visuris vel audituris Thurstanus de Galby salutem in domino. Noueritis me dedisse concessisse et presenti carta mea confirmasse deo et ecclesie beate Marie de Pratis Leyc[estrie] et canonicis regularibus ibidem deo seruientibus vnum obolum annui redditus percipiendum singulis annis die Pasche de Hug[one] fabro de Thurmedeston' quem ego percipere consueui annuatim de eodem Hug[one] pro vna dimidia acra prati quam de me tenuit in Thurmodeston' quequidem dimidiam acram prati singulis annis capiendum est vno videlicet anno supra pontem et altero anno infra pontem inter pratum quod Rog[er]us prepositus quondam tenuit ex parte australi et pratum quod Ioh[ann]es de Stocton' tenuit ex parte boriali. Habendum et tenendum. predictis canonicis in liberam puram et perpetuam elemosinam cum omni iure et clamio quod ego vel heredes mei in predicta dimidia acra prati exigere vel habere potuimus. Et ego Thurstanus et heredes mei predictum redditum cum toto iure et clamio nostro predicto prefatis canonicis contra omnes homines warantizabimus acquietabimus et defendemus imperpetuum. In cuius rei testimonium presenti scripto sigillum meum apposui. Hiis testibus Ioh[ann]e Ketelbern' de Thurmeston' Mich[ael]e carpentar[io] de eadem Rob[ert]o Wysman de eadem Will[elm]o de Barkeby Rog[er]o de Barkeby clerico et multis aliis.

72. Robert the Chaplain son of Thomas Prest   s. xiii med.

Grant of twenty-three strips of arable land and seven rods of meadowland in the fields of Thurmaston, Leics. The strips listed as one upon Stubfurlong *next to Robert's own land; one at* Shiredaicotes *next to the land Reginald the smith held; one upon* Clottilondis *also next to Reginald's land; one at* Holegrift, *next to Reginald's land; one opposite* Thornhow; *one upon* Ernothelond, *next to Reginald's land; one at* Blodhow, *next to Reginald's land; one upon* Coleby, *next to Reginald's land; one upon* Wetelondes *next to the land of Walter the smith with mead-owland lying next to it; one at the spring in* Estmede *with meadowland lying next to it; one upon* Tunhul, *next to Reginald's land; one above the church, next to Walter's land; one upon* Baddeston, *next to Reginald's land; one abutting upon* Shirhamdik' *next to the land of Robert of Holegate; one upon* Brademaris, *next to Robert of Holegate's land; one below* Galeberwe *next to Reginald's land; one at* Enedemaris, *next to Reginald's land; two strips lying together upon* Coleby, *next to Robert's own land; one in* Coleby Slade, *next to Reginald's land; one upon* Bruneshul *next to the land of John the Mason; one upon* Foxholes, *next to Reginald's land; one in* Banelondes *which reaches up to Robert's own land and lies next to the canons' land; a rod of meadowland at* Le Redeforn *next to* Pratelbi *which was Reginald the smith's; a rod in* Stonholm *next to Reginald's meadow; a rod at* Cokkiskomb *next to Walter the smith's meadow; a rod at* Thistlidoles *next to Reginald's meadowland; a rod at* Ouergong *next to Walter's meadowland; a rod at the bridge next to Robert's own meadows; half a rod at* Wylamwro *next to Reginald's land; a half rod at* Stoniford' *next to Reginald's meadowland; a small piece of meadowland next to the strip mentioned above lying at the spring in* Estmedwe; *all the pasture of one bovate of land in Thurmaston which Robert himself had along with all the lands and tenements he had from the grant of John son of Leofwin of Thurmaston.*

A = Original, now lost. B = TNA E13/76, m. 69, copy dated 1351 (from A).

[B]

Sciant presentes et futuri quod ego Rob[er]tus capellanus filius Thome Prest de Thurmodeston' dedi concessi et hac presenti carta mea confirmaui deo et ecclesie beate Marie de Pratis Leirc[estrie] et canonicis regularibus ibidem deo seruientibus viginti et tres selliones terre arabilis et septem rodas prati in campis de Thurmod[estona] videlicet vnum sellionem iacentem super Stubfurlong iuxta terram meam. et vnum sellionem ad Shiredaicotes iuxta terram quam Reginaldus faber tenuit. et vnum sellionem super Clottilondis iuxta terram quam predictus Reginaldus faber tenuit et vnum sellionem ad Holegrift. iuxta terram predicti Reginaldi et vnum sellionem ex opposito de Thornhow. et vnum sellionem super Ernothelond iuxta terram predicti Reginaldi et vnum sellionem ad Blodhow iuxta terram predicti

Regin[aldi] et vnum sellionem super Coleby iuxta terram predicti Regin[aldi]. et vnum sellionem super Wetelondes iuxta terram Walteri fabri cum prato adiacente et vnum sellionem ad fontem in Estmede iuxta terram predicti Regin[aldi] cum prato adiacente et vnum sellionem super Tunhul iuxta terram predicti Regin[aldi] et vnum sellionem supra ecclesiam iuxta terram Walteri fabri. et vnum sellionem super Baddeston iuxta terram predicti Regin[aldi] et vnum sellionem qui abbutat super Shirhamdik' iuxta terram que fuit Rob[er]ti de Holegate et vnum sellionem in Brademaris iuxta terram Rob[er]ti de Holegate et vnum sellionem sub Galeberwe iuxta terram predicti Reginaldi et vnum sellionem ad Enedemaris iuxta terram predicti Reginaldi et duos selliones simul iacentes super Coleby iuxta terram quam ego predictus Rob[er]tus tenui. et vnum sellionem in Coleby Slade iuxta terram predicti Regin[aldi] et vnum sellionem super Bruneshul iuxta terram quam Ioh[ann]es le Mazun tenuit et vnum sellionem super Foxholes iuxta terram predicti Regin[aldi]. et vnum sellionem in Banelondes qui se extendit super terram quam ego tenui et iacet iuxta terram predictorum canonicorum et vnam rodam prati ad le Redeforn iuxta Pratelbi quod fuit Regin[aldi] fabri et vnam rodam prati in Stonholm iuxta pratum predicti Reginaldi et vnam rodam prati ad Cokkiskomb iuxta pratum Walteri fabri et vnam rodam prati ad Thistlidoles iuxta pratum predicti Reginaldi. et vnam rodam prati ad Ouergong iuxta pratum Walteri fabri et vnam rodam prati ad pontem iuxta pratum quod ego predictus Rob[er]tus tenui. et dimidiam rodam prati ad Wylamwro iuxta terram predicti Regin[aldi] et dimidiam rodam prati ad Stoniford' iuxta pratum predicti Reginaldi et quandam particulam prati adiacentem ad illum sellionem superius nominatum qui iacet ad fontem in Estmedwe et totam pasturam vnius bouate terre in Thurmodeston' quam ego predictus Rob[er]tus habui vnam[a] omnibus terris et tenementis predictis de dono et feoffamento Ioh[ann]is filii Lewyne de Thurmodeston'. Habenda et tenenda predictis canonicis et eorum successoribus inperpetuum in liberam puram et perpetuam elemosinam prout aliqua elemosina liberius vel melius dari possit cum omnibus pertinentiis libertatibus et aysiamentis suis infra villam et extra. Et ego predictus Rob[er]tus et heredes mei predictos viginti et tres selliones terre et septem rodas prati et totam pasturam vnius bouate terre predictam cum omnibus pertinentiis suis predictis canonicis et eorum successoribus inperpetuum contra omnes homines warentizabimus adquietabimus et defendemus. In cuius rei testimonium, presenti scripto sigillum meum apposui. Hiis testibus. Will[elm]o pistore de Thurmodeston' Ioh[ann]e le Mazun Ioh[ann]e Ketelb[er]n Petro carpent[ario] Waltero fabro de eadem Will[elm]o castelein de Humberston Galfrido de Lutteburgh' clerico et aliis.

[a] *cum*, probably omitted here.

73. John son of William son of Avice of Thurmaston s. xiii med.

Grant of the toft in Thurmaston, Leics. late of Samuel of Thurmaston, lying between the tofts late of Reginald Schirteful and Robert Thom, next to the high road. The canons to hold it for the benefit of their pittance, saving an annual ten pence rent which is to be put to the common uses of the abbey.

A = Original, now lost. B = TNA E13/76, m. 68d, copy dated 1351 (from A).

[B]

Sciant presentes et futuri quod ego Ioh[ann]es filius Will[elm]i filii Auicie de Thurmodeston' pro salute anime mee et antecessorum meorum dedi concessi et hac presenti carta mea confirmaui deo et ecclesie beate Marie de Pratis Leyc[estrie] et canonicis regularibus ibidem deo seruientibus ad pietantiam conuentus ipsorum vnum toftum cum pertinentiis in Thurmodeston' illud scilicet quod quondam fuit Samuelis de Thurmodeston'. Et iacet inter toftum quod Reginaldus Schirteful aliquando tenuit et toftum quod Rob[er]tus Thom aliquando tenuit et se abbutat super altam viam. Habendum et tenendum dictis canonicis cum omnibus pertinentiis suis ad pietantiam predictam in liberam et perpetuam elemosinam. saluis eisdem canonicis decem denarios annuis ad vsus communes dicte ecclesie de predicto tofto debitis et consuetis. In cuius rei testimonium presenti scripto sigillum meum apposui. Hiis testibus Ioh[ann]e Ketelbern de Thurmod[estuna] Michaele carpent[ario] de eadem Ioh[ann]e cement[ario] de eadem Ioh[ann]e Loue de eadem Galfr[ido] de Lucteburgh' clerico et aliis.

74. John son of William son of Avice of Thurmaston   s. xiii[1]

Grant of one and a half acres of meadow in the meadowland of Thurmaston, Leics. below Wanlip, between the patch of meadow which was Robert son of Leofwin's on the one side and the patch of Roger son of Alexander on the other.

A = Original, now lost. B = TNA E13/76, m. 73d, copy dated 1351 (from A).

[B]

Sciant presentes et futuri quod ego Ioh[ann]es filius Will[elm]i filii Auicie de Thurmodeston' dedi concessi et hac presenti carta mea confirmaui deo et ecclesie beate Marie de Pratis Leyc[estrie] et canonicis regularibus ibidem deo seruientibus in liberam puram et perpetuam elemosinam vnam dimidiam acram prati cum pertinentiis iacentem in prato de Thurmodeston' sub Anlep inter dolam prati que fuit Rob[ert]i filii Lewini ex parte vna et dolam prati que fuit Rog[er]i filii Alexandri ex altera. Habendas et tenendas predictis canonicis et eorum successoribus inperpetuum in liberam puram et perpetuam elemosinam. Et ego predictus Ioh[ann]es et heredes mei predictam dimidiam acram prati cum pertinentiis predictis canonicis et eorum succcssoribus imperpetuum contra omnes homines warantizabimus acquietabimus et defendemus. In cuius rei testimonium presenti scripto sigillum meum apposui. Hiis testibus Mich[ael]e carp[e]nt[ario] de Thurmod[estona] Ioh[ann]e Ketelb[er]n de eadem Walt[er]o fabro de eadem Petro carpent[ario] de eadem Will[elm]o Magot de eadem Rob[er]to Tor de eadem Galfr[id]o de Lutteburg' clerico et aliis.

75. Thomas son of Richard of Sheavsby   s. xiii med.

Quitclaim of an annual rent of two shillings which he received from two virgates in Walton, Leics. which Lawrence son of William son of Leofric had previously given the abbey.

A = Original, now lost. B = TNA E13/76, m. 68, copy dated 1351 (from A).

[B]

Omnibus Christi fidelibus ad quos presens scriptum peruenerit, Thomas filius Ric[ardi] de Sheuesby salutem in domino. Nouerit vniuersitas vestra me remississe et inperpetuum de me et heredibus meis quietum clamasse deo et ecclesie beate Marie de Pratis Leircestr[ie] et canonicis regularibus ibidem deo seruientibus duos solidos annui redditus quos ab eisdem percipere consueui de duabus virgatis terre in villa de Waleton'. quas Laurenc[ius] filius Will[elm]i filii Leuerici eisdem dedit et carta sua confirmauit. Habendos et tenendos eisdem canonicis in liberam puram et perpetuam elemosinam. Et ne ego dictus Thom[as] nec heredes mei vel assignati aliquid iuris vel clamii in predicto redditu vel in predicta terra cum pertinentiis decetero habere possimus inperpetuum vel vendicare, hoc presens scriptum sigilli mei inpressione duxi roborandum. Hiis testibus magistris Rogero de Sadynton' Alano de Wyteby Thoma de Quappelade Hugone de de Neyuill' Rob[er]to de Oxindon' Ric[ard]o de Wauere Henr[ico] clerico et aliis.

This charter is a consequence of the grant by Lawrence son of William (above no. 44) which dates between 1220 and 1240. It is difficult to say how long after that it was transacted, but it seems to have been some years later, as by this time Thomas of Sheavsby had succeeded his father. The witnesses also indicate that the quitclaim was issued towards the middle of the century.

76. William of Galby   s. xiii med.

Grant of two and a half rods of land and a strip of ploughland in the estate of Thurmaston, Leics. of which one and a half rods are upon Hungerhull' *between the land of Walter Osmond and Ralph of Barrow, and the strip is situated at* Cherchesur Wasbech.

A = Original, now lost. B = TNA E13/76, m. 68d, copy dated 1351 (from A).

[B]

Sciant presentes et futuri quod ego Will[elmu]s de Galby dedi concessi et hac presenti carta mea confirmaui deo et ecclesie beate Marie de Pratis Leycestr[ie] et canonicis regularibus ibidem deo seruientibus duas rodas terre et dimidiam et vnum sellionem terre cum pertinentiis in territorio de Thurmodeston' scilicet vnam rodam et dimidiam super Hungerhull' que iacet inter terram Walteri

Osmond et terram Rad[ulf]i de Barue et vnum sellionem terre qui iacet super illum locum qui vocatur Cherchesur Wasbech. Habendas et tenendas dictis canonicis in liberam puram et perpetuam elemosinam cum omnibus libertatibus et esiamentis ad predictam terram pertinentibus infra predictam villam de Thurmodeston' et extra. Et ego predictus Will[elmu]s et heredes mei predictam terram cum pertinentiis predictis canonicis et eorum successoribus contra omnes gentes warentizabimus et defendemus in perpetuum. In cuius rei testimonium presentem cartam sigilli mei inpressione roboraui. Hiis testibus Will[elm]o Cnothe de Role Rob[er]to falconar[io] Ric[ard]o de Camped' Rob[er]to de Burstall' magistro Alano de Wyteby et aliis.

> The appearance of the witnesses William Cnothe and M. Alan of Whitby in this and other charters of this general period suggests a date around 1250.

77. William Alnath of Thurmaston   s. xiii med.

Grant of a rod of arable land in Thurmaston, Leics. lying in Le Ryefurlong *between the land of John of Stoughton and that of Isabel of Glenfield.*

> A = Original, now lost. B = TNA E13/76, m. 73d, copy dated 1351 (from A).

[B]

Sciant presentes et futuri quod ego Will[elmu]s Alnath de Thurmodeston' dedi concessi et hac presenti carta mea confirmaui et imperpetuum de me et heredibus meis omnino quietum clamaui deo et ecclesie beate Marie de Pratis Leyc[estrie] et canonicis regularibus ibidem deo seruientibus in liberam puram et perpetuam elemosinam vnam rodam terre arabilis cum pertinentiis in Thurmodeston' iacentem in le Ryefurlong' inter terram quam Ioh[ann]es de Stocton' tenuit ex parte vna et terram quam Isabell[a] de Clenefeld' tenuit ex altera. Habendam et tenendam predictis canonicis et eorum successorum imperpetuum in liberam puram et perpetuam elemosinam prout aliqua elemosina liberius et melius dari potest. Et ego predictus Will[elm]us et heredes mei et mei assignati predictam rodam terre cum pertinentiis predictis canonicis et eorum successoribus imperpetuum contra omnes homines warantizabimus acquietabimus et defendemus. In cuius rei testimonium presenti scripto sigillum meum apposui. Hiis testibus Rob[er]to Basil' capell[an]o Alano Christofori Ioh[ann]e cementar[io] Rob[er]to fabro Ioh[ann]e Ketelb[er]n Petro carpent[ario] Galfr[id]o de Lutteburg' et aliis.

78. Richard son of Bartholomew of Lockington   s. xiii med.

Grant of a virgate in Lockington, Leics. which the clerk, Walter of Sneinton, once held at farm from his father, Bartholomew, lying next to the land of Richard son of Alan in the fields of Lockington.

> A = Original, now lost. B = TNA E13/76, m. 70d, copy dated 1351 (from A).

[B]

Sciant presentes et futuri quod ego Ric[ardus] filius Barth[olome]i de Lokynton' dedi et concessi et hac presenti carta mea confirmaui deo et ecclesie beate Marie de Pratis Leyc[estrie] et canonicis regularibus ibidem deo seruientibus pro salute anime mee antecessorum et successorum meorum vnam virgatam terre cum omnibus pertinentiis suis in Lokynton. illam scilicet quam Walterus de Sneynton' clericus aliquando tenuit ad firmam de Barth[olome]o patre meo que quidem terra iacet proxima iuxta terram Ric[ard]i filii Alani in campis de Lokynton'. Habendam et tenendam dictis canonicis libere quiete pacifice integre et honorifice in pratis pascuis viis semitis et omnibus aliis locis infra villam et extra in liberam puram et perpetuam elemosinam sicut aliqua elemosina melius liberius et quietius alicui domui religiose poterit conferri vel concedi. Et ego Ric[ardu]s prenominatus et heredes mei dictam virgatam terre cum omnibus pertinentis suis sicut predictum est canonicis predictis contra omnes gentes warantizabimus adquietabimus et defendemus inperpetuum vt autem hec mea donatio et concessio rata et stabilis permaneat imperpetuum, presens scriptum sigilli mei inpressione roboraui. Hiis testibus Ioh[ann]e de Langeton' Galfr[id]o de Craumford' Ric[ard]o filio Alani de Lokynton' magistro Hugone Barre Adam de Yolegraue Simone mariscallo Ric[ard]o le Harpeur Thoma filio suo. Ioh[ann]e de Cokirham Simone de Osulueston' clerico et aliis.

79. Robert son of Henry of Bramcote   s. xiii med.

Grant of the homage and service of a furlong of land in Bramcote, Warwicks. which William the skinner of Coventry held for a rent of one penny a year payable at Easter.

A = Original, now lost. B = TNA E13/76, m. 75, copy dated 1351 (from A).

[B]

Vniuersis Christi fidelibus hoc scriptum visuris vel audituris Rob[er]tus filius Henr[ici] de Bramcote salutem. Nouerit vniuersitas vestra me pro salute anime mee et animarum antecessorum et successorum meorum dedisse concessisse et hac presenti carta mea confirmasse in liberam puram et perpetuam elemosinam deo et ecclesie beate Marie de Pratis Leyc[estrie] et canonicis regularibus ibidem deo seruientibus totum homagium et seruitium vnius quarterii terre cum pertinentiis in Bramcota quam Will[elmu]s parmentarius de Couentre de me tenuit videlicet vnum denarium red[ditus] annuatim ad Pascha soluendum. Et quicquid per predictum homagium et seruitium quocumque casu contingente michi vel heredibus meis poterit accidere. Habendum et tenendum libere integre et quiete ab omni seruitio consuetudine et demanda. Et ego prefatus Rob[er]tus et heredes mei prenominatum homagium et seruitium et quicquid de eisdem accidere poterit deo et ecclesie prefate et canonicis ibidem deo seruientibus contra omnes gentes imperpetuum warantizabimus et defendemus. In cuius rei testimonium presenti scripto sigillum meum apposui. Hiis testibus Henr[ico] Wyschard Ioh[ann]e de Wybetoft Hug[one] de Lilleburne Rob[er]to de Nuueray Ric[ard]o le chapeleyn de Ruthon' Rob[er]to de Ruthon' Rob[er]to de Wlfey Hug[one] de Syreford' Rob[ert]o Freman de Burnthon' Alano ad gardinum Rob[er]to de L[eycestria] clerico et aliis.

80. Robert son of Henry of Bramcote   s. xiii med.

Grant of the homage and service of a half virgate of land in Bramcote, Warwicks. which M. Robert of Hinckley held of him, that is, an annual rent of 1d. payable at Easter.

A = Original, now lost. B = TNA E13/76, m. 75, copy dated 1351 (from A).

[B]

Vniuersis Christi fidelibus hoc scriptum visuris vel audituris Rob[er]tus filius Henrici de Bramcote salutem. Nouerit vniuersitas vestra me pro salute anime mee et animarum antecessorum et successorum meorum dedisse concessisse et hac presenti carta mea confirmasse in liberam puram et perpetuam elemosinam deo et ecclesie beate Marie de Pratis Leyc[estrie] et canonicis ibidem deo seruientibus totum homagium et seruitium illius dimidie virgate terre cum pertinentiis in Bramcote quam magister Rob[er]tus de Hinkele de me tenuit videlicet vnum denarium redditus annuatim ad Pascha soluendum. et quicquid per predictum seruitium quocum[que] casu contingente michi vel heredibus meis poterit accidere. Habendum et tenendum libere et integre et quiete ab omni seruitio consuetudine et demanda. Et ego prefatus Robertus et heredes mei prenominatum homagium et seruitium et quicquid de eisdem accidere poterit deo et ecclesie prefate et canonicis ibidem deo seruientibus contra omnes gentes inperpetuum warantizabimus et defendemus. In cuius rei testimonium presenti scripto sigillum meum apposui. Hiis testibus. Hen[rico] Wyschard. Ioh[ann]e de Wybetoft. Hug[one] de Lilleburne Rob[ert]o de Nuu[er]ay Ric[ard]o le chapelein de Ruthon' Rob[er]to de Ruthon' Rob[er]to de Wlfeye Hug[one] de Syreford' Rob[ert]o Freman de Buruthon' Alano ad gardinum R[oberto] de Leyc[estria] clerico et aliis.

81. Robert son of Henry of Bramcote   s. xiii med.

Grant of a plot of land called Michelehowe, *and an acre of land in Bramcote, Warwicks.; the plot's dimensions are given as six perches and six feet in length and two perches and two feet in breadth. Of the acre, a half acre lies on* Flaxlond *between the land of Thomas le Bret and the land that William Curteys once held, and the other half acre is upon* Brocfurlang' *between the land of John Hubert and the land Robert le Bercher once held.*

A = Original, now lost. B = TNA E13/76, m. 75d, copy dated 1351 (from A).

[B]

Sciant presentes et futuri quod ego Rob[er]tus filius Henr[ici] de Bramcote dedi concessi et hac presenti carta mea confirmaui, deo et ecclesie beate Marie de Pratis Leyc[estrie] et canonicis ibidem deo seruientibus pro salute anime mee antecessorum et successorum meorum vnam placeam terre que vocatur Michelehow et vnam acram terre cum omnibus pertinentiis suis in territorio de Bramcote que quidem placea continet in se sex perticatas et sex pedes in longitudine et duas perticatas et duos pedes in latitudine et dimidia acra terre iacet super Flaxlond inter terram Thome le Bret et terram quam Will[elmu]s Curteys aliquando tenuit, et alia dimidia acra terre iacet super Brocfurlang' inter terram Iohannis Hubert et terram quam Rob[ertus] le Bercher aliquando tenuit. Habendas et tenendas dictis canonicis in liberam puram et perpetuam elemosinam. Et ego Rob[er]tus predictus et heredes mei dictam placeam et dictam acram terre cum omnibus pertinentiis suis dictis canonicis contra omnes homines et feminas warantizabimus acquietabimus et defendemus inperpetuum. Vt autem hec mea donatio et concessio rata sit et stabilis permaneat inperpetuum presens scriptum sigilli mei munimine roboraui. Hiis testibus Barth[olome]o vicar[io] de Bulkynton'. Ioh[ann]e de Couentre Rob[er]to Paramurs Ioh[ann]e de Hyda Rob[er]to le Mathuy de Merstun' Ad[a] de Yolegraue Ioh[ann]e de Cokirham Rog[er]o de Twyford' Regin[aldo] tunc marescallo abbatis Rog[er]o filio Will[elm]i Knotte de Ratheleye Simone clerico et aliis.

82. Robert son of Henry of Bramcote   s. xiii med., certainly before 1259

Grant of two acres of arable land and a half acre of meadow in the field of Bramcote, Warwicks. The two acres are located as follows: a half acre being in Werviland' *next to the land of Thomas le Brecce; another half acre upon* Lurtewalhil *next to Luke's land; a third on* Stonifurlong' *beside the road; the fourth half acre with the half acre of meadow lies on* Morefurlong' *next to the land of Adam the mercer. Further grant of a rent of six pence annually in Bramcote which Robert's sister Alice once held of him. Robert and his heirs or assigns to be free of any scutage on the said land, and the abbey to pay him fifteen shillings.*

A = Original, now lost. B = TNA E13/76, m. 75d, copy dated 1351 (from A).

[B]

Sciant presentes et futuri quod ego Rob[er]tus filius Henr[ici] de Bramcote dedi concessi et hac presenti carta mea confirmaui deo et ecclesie beate Marie de Pratis Leyc[estrie] et canonicis regularibus ibidem deo seruientibus in puram et perpetuam elemosinam duas acras terre et dimidiam acram prati in campo de Bramcote cum omnibus pertinentiis suis infra villam et extra in viis semitis aquis pratis pascuis et pasturiis, illas scilicet duas acras quarum vna dimidia acra iacet in Vueruiland' iuxta terram Thom[e] le Brecce, alia dimidia acra iacet super Lurtewalhil iuxta terram Luce, tercia dimidia acra iacet in Stonifurlong' iuxta viam et quarta dimidia acra cum dicto prato iacet in Morefurlong' iuxta terram Ade le Mercer. Preterea dedi et concessi predictis canonicis redditum sex denariorum in villa de Bramcote que Alicia soror mea aliquando tenuit de me tribus terminis anni soluendum, scilicet ad festum sancti Mich[ael]is duorum denariorum, ad Purificationem beate virginis duorum denariorum et ad Pentecosten duorum denariorum. Habendas et tenendas predictis canonicis in puram et perpetuam elemosinam libere quiete integre honorifice bene et in pace et hereditate. Et si contingat quod scuagium currat per Angliam ego Rob[er]tus et heredes mei siue assignati erimus liberati et soluti a scuagio ad predictam terram cum prato pertinente. Et pro ista donatio et concessione dederunt michi memorati canonici per manibus quindecim solidos. Ego vero Rob[er]tus et heredes mei siue assignati predictam terram cum prato et redditu contra omnes homines et feminas warantizabimus acquietabimus et defendemus. Et vt ista mea donatio et concessio rata sit et stabilis presenti scripto sigillum meum apposui. Hiis testibus magistro Hug[one] Barr' Walt[er]o de Euinton' Simon[e] de Osolueston' Ad[a] de Yolgraue Thoma le Harpur Regin[aldo] de Cokirham Henr[ico] de Lincoln' Rob[er]to Freman de Ritun Nich[ola]o filio Will[elm]i de Bulkyngton' Luca de Bramcote Rob[er]to filio Will[elm]i de Bramcote et aliis.

The attestation of Walter of Evington certainly dates the act before his death in 1259, TNA JUST1/456, m. 13.

83. Robert son of Henry of Bramcote

s. xiii med.

Grant of the service of a toft in Bramcote, Warwicks. that William Rude once held of him, which lies between the land of Alan de Gardino on one side and the land of the abbey on the other, that is, an annual rent of twelve pence at three terms

A = Original, now lost. B = TNA E13/76, m. 76, copy dated 1351 (from A).

[B]

Vniuersis Christi fidelibus hoc scriptum visuris vel audituris Rob[er]tus filius Henr[ici] de Bramcote salutem. Nouerit vniuersitas vestra me pro salute anime mee et animarum antecessorum et successorum meorum dedisse concessisse et hac presenti carta mea confirmasse in liberam puram et perpetuam elemosinam deo et ecclesie beate Marie de Pratis Leyc[estrie] et canonicis regularibus ibidem deo seruientibus totum seruitium illius tofti in Bramcote quod Will[elmu]s Rude aliquando de me tenuit quod iacet inter terram Alani de Gardino ex vna parte et terram dictorum abbatis et conuentus ex altera, videlicet duodecim denarios per annum ad festum sancti Mich[ael]is quatuor denarios, ad Purificationem quatuor denarios et ad Pentecosten quatuor denarios. Et quicquid de eodem tofto quocumque casu contingente michi vel meis accidere posset. Habendum et tenendum libere et quiete ab omni seculari seruitio consuetudine et demanda. Et ego et heredes mei dictum toftum vt predictum est sibi et eorum successorum contra omnes gentes warantizabimus acquietabimus et defendemus inperpetuum. In cuius rei testimonium presenti scripto sigillum meum apposui. Hiis testibus Henrico Wyschard Ioh[ann]e de Wybetoft Hug[one] de Lilleburne Rob[ert]o de Nueray Ric[ard]o le chapelein de Rutone Rob[er]to de Rutone Ad[a] de Yolgraue Rob[er]to de Trafford clerico et aliis.

84. Robert son of Henry of Bramcote

s. xiii med.

Grant of a quarter part of a virgate in Bramcote, Warwicks. which Agnes the daughter of William son of Lusce lately held.

A = Original, now lost. B = TNA E13/76, m. 76, copy dated 1351 (from A).

[B]

Sciant presentes et futuri quod ego Rob[er]tus filius Henr[ici] de Bramcote dedi concessi et hac presenti carta mea confirmaui, deo et ecclesie beate Marie de Pratis Leyc[estrie] et canonicis regularibus ibidem deo seruientibus quartam partem vnius virgate terre cum pertinentiis in territorio de Bromcote illam scilicet quam Agn[es] filia Will[elm]i filii Lusce quondam tenuit. Habendam et tenendam predictis canonicis et eorum successoribus in liberam puram et perpetuam elemosinam libere quiete bene et in pace cum omnibus pertinentiis et aysiamentis ad predictam terram infra villam de Bromcote et extra pertinentibus. Et ego Rob[er]tus et heredes mei predictam quartam partem vnius virgate terre cum pertinentiis sicut predictum est predictis canonicis et eorum successoribus contra omnes gentes warentizabimus acquietabimus et defendemus in perpetuum. Et vt hec mea donatio concessio et confirmatio perpetue firmitatis robur optineat in posterum, presenti scripto sigillum meum duxi apponendum. Hiis testibus Ric[ard]o chapelein de Ruyton' Ioh[ann]e de Hyda in Merston'. Rob[ert]o bercar[io] de Bromcote. Luca carpentar[io] et Ric[ard]o filio Alani de eadem magistro Ric[ard]o de Stapelton' Sewallo clerico et aliis.

85. Robert son of Isabel of Bramcote

s. xiii med.

Grant of an annual rent of twelve pence which he used to receive from his brother John from a toft and two acres of land in Bramcote, Warwicks. along with John's homage and that of his heirs.

A = Original, now lost. B = TNA E13/76, mm. 75d–76, copy dated 1351 (from A).

[B]

Sciant presentes et futuri quod ego Rob[er]tus filius Isabell[e] de Bramcote concessi dedi et de me et heredibus meis inperpetuum quietum clamaui deo et ecclesie sancte Marie de Pratis Leyc[estrie] et canonicis regularibus ibidem deo seruientibus duodecim denarios redditus quos de Ioh[ann]e fratre meo annuatim percipere consueui de quodam tofto et duabus acris terre quas de me tenuit in prefata villa de Bramcote cum homagio dicti Ioh[ann]is et heredum suorum wardis releuiis escaetis et omnibus aliis pertinentiis suis. Habendum et tenendum dictis canonicis in liberam puram et perpetuam elemosinam. Et ne ego dictus Rob[er]tus vel heredes mei in memoratis duodecim denarios redditus cum homagiis wardis releuiis escaetis et omnibus aliis pertinentiis de cetero aliquid iuris vel clamei habere valeamus, presens scriptum sigilli mei munimine roboraui. Hiis testibus Ric[ard]o chapelein Ric[ard]o Basset Rob[er]to ad Fraxinum Luca de Bramcote Rob[er]to filio Henr[ici] Rob[er]to de Leyc[estria] clerico Reginaldo marescallo Henr[ico] clerico et aliis.

86. Reginald Shirloc of Hinckley   s. xiii med.

Grant of an annual rent of two shillings and sixpence for a bovate of land in the village of Bramcote, Warwicks. payable by Ranulf Bret and his heirs and assigns according to the meaning of the charter which Ranulf has from M. Robert of Charley, of Hinckley, Leics. Reginald's predecessor in the property. The canons gave him two silver marks (26s. 8d.) for this grant.

A = Original, now lost. B = TNA E13/76, m. 75d, copy dated 1351 (from A).

[B]

Sciant presentes et futuri quod ego Reginaldus Shirloc' de Hinckelee dedi concessi et hac presenti carta mea confirmaui deo et ecclesie beate Marie de Pratis Leyc[estrie] et canonicis regularibus ibidem deo seruientibus quendam annuum redditum duorum solidorum et sex denariorum de vna bouata terre in villa de Bromcote per manus Ranulphi Bret et heredum vel assignatorum suorum percipiendum. Habendum et tenendum dictis canonicis et eorum successoribus cum wardis releuiis et escaetis et omnibus aliis fortunis que de predicta bouata terre cum pertinentiis aliquo modo accidere possunt secundum tenorem carte quam dictus Ranulphus habet de magistro Rob[er]to de Charlee de Hinckelee antecessore meo. Ego vero predictus Reginaldus et heredes mei et assignati mei predictum annuum redditum cum pertinentiis suis sicut predictum est contra omnes gentes warantizabimus acquietabimus et inperpetuum defendemus. Pro hac autem donatione concessione warantizatione et presentis carte confirmatione dederunt michi dicti canonici duas marcas argenti per manibus. In cuius rei testimonium presenti scripto sigillum apposui. Hiis testibus Ioh[ann]e de Couentre in Bulkenton' Rob[er]to de Bromcote Gilb[ert]o Lucas de Bromcote Rob[er]to Ysabel de eadem Rob[er]to filio Henr[ici] de eadem Will[elm]o de Hinkele clerico et aliis.

87. John Ketelbern   1247 x 1259

Grant of an annual rent of one penny he used to receive from Robert Wysman from a meadow lying within the confines of Thurmaston, Leics. at Nesse, containing in breadth at the northern end two and a half rods and at the southern end two rods.

A = Original, now lost. B = TNA E13/76, m. 73d, copy dated 1351 (from A).

[B]

Sciant presentes et futuri quod ego Ioh[ann]es Ketelbern dedi concessi et hac presenti carta mea confirmaui deo et beate Marie de Pratis Leyc[estrie] et fratri Henr[ico] abbati et eiusdem loci conuentui vnum denarium annui redditus que percipere consueui de Rob[er]to Wysman de vno prato quod iacet in territorio de Thurmedeston' scilicet in Nesse cum homagio dicti Rob[er]ti et heredum suorum, quodquidem pratum cont[inet] in latitudine ad caput versus aquilonem duas rodas et dimidiam et ad caput versus austrum duas rodas. Habendum et tenendum dictis abbati et conuentui et eorum successoribus in liberam puram et perpetuam elemosinam cum releuiis et escaetis et omnibus aliis que michi aut heredibus meis per predictum redditum possent accidero. In cuius rei testimonium presenti scripto sigillum meum apposui. Hiis testibus Ioh[ann]e Lewyne de Thurmedeston' Will[elm]o Osmund Regin[aldo] fabro Will[elm]o Poer de Barkeby Walt[er]o Herbert de eadem Rog[er]o de eadem clerico et aliis.

The date of this act has to be subsequent to the election of Abbot Henry in August 1247. John's son William succeeded him before the death of Walter of Evington in 1259.

88. Henry of Wanlip   1235 X 1259

Grant for his burial of two virgates with tofts and crofts which Robert son of Thurstan gave him, one belonging to the manor court and the other called Brethegerdelond'; *a bovate which Geoffrey son of Gilbert of Birstall once held of him, with a half virgate which Ralph son of Gilbert of Birstall gave him and a virgate which Robert son of Matthew of Birstall gave him; a halfpenny annual rent payable by Robert Wysman which he owed for four rods of land; and a penny annual rent from Samuel the miller for a plough strip next to his house; all in Thurmaston, Leics.*

A = Original, now lost. B = TNA E13/76, m. 69, copy dated 1351 (from A).

[B]

Sciant presentes et futuri quod ego Henr[icus] de Anlep' pro salute anime mee et animarum antecessorum et successorum meorum dedi et concessi et hac presenti carta mea confirmaui cum corpore meo deo et ecclesie beate Marie de Pratis Leyc[estrie] et canonicis regularibus ibidem deo seruientibus duas virgatas terre cum toftis et croftis et omnibus aliis pertinentiis suis in territorio de Thurmodeston'. illas scilicet quas Rob[er]tus filius Thurstani michi dedit et carta sua confirmauit quarum vna pertinet ad capitale mesuagium et altera vocatur Brethegerdelond' Item dedi et concessi et presenti carta mea confirmaui prefatis canonicis vnam bouatam terre in territorio de Thurmodeston' quam Galfr[idus] filius Gilb[er]ti de Burstall' aliquando de me tenuit cum omnibus pertinentiis suis libertatibus et esiamentis infra villam et extra et vnam dimidiam virgatam terre cum tofto et crofto in territorio de Thurmodeston' et cum omnibus aliis pertinentiis. libertatibus et eysiamentis suis infra villam et extra. illam scilicet quam Rad[ulfu]s filius Gilb[er]ti de Burstall' michi dedit et carta sua confirmauit. et vna virgata terre cum tofto et crofto et omnibus aliis pertinentiis suis in territorio de Thurmodeston' quam Rob[er]tus filius Math[ei] de Burstall' michi dedit et carta sua confirmauit. Preterea dedi et concessi et hac presenti carta mea confirmaui predictis canonicis vnum obolum redditus per annum percipiendum de Rob[er]to Wysman et heredibus suis vel suis assignatis quem michi reddere solebat pro quatuor rodis terre in territorio de Thurmodeston' cum releuiis wardis escaetis et omnibus exitibus de predicto redditu prouenientibus. Et de Samuele molendinario et heredibus suis vel suis assignatis vnum denarium redditus per annum quem michi reddere solebat pro quodam chenesco vnius sellionis iuxta mesuagium suum in territorio de Thurmodeston' cum releuiis wardis escaetis et omnibus exitibus de predicto redditu prouenientibus. Volo igitur et firmiter constituo quod prefati canonici predictas terras cum toftis et croftis prenominatis et cum omnibus libertatibus eysiamentis et aliis pertinentiis suis infra villam et extra et etiam redditus predictos cum exitibus inde prouenientibus sicut predictum est, habeant et teneant bene et in pace integre et plenarie in liberam puram et perpetuam elemosinam. Et vt hec mea donatio et concessio perpetue firmitatis robur optineant presentem cartam mei sigilli impressione roboraui. Hiis testibus magistris Hugone Barre Thoma de Luda Ric[ard]o de Stapelton' Waltero de Euenton' Simone de Osolueston' Henr[ico] filio Simonis de Wykyngeston' Waltero filio Will[elm]i de Cnicton' Ioh[ann]e de Anlep clerico Will[elm]o Ketelbern de Thurmodeston' Henr[ico] clerico abbatis Reginaldo de Cokerham et aliis.

The attestation of Walter of Evington dates the act before his death in 1259, TNA JUST1/456, m. 13 and in view of Earl Roger de Quincy's confirmation (no. 89) must date after 1235.

89. Roger de Quincy, earl of Winchester   1235 X 1259

Confirmation of four virgates of land in Thurmaston, Leics. which Henry of Wanlip gave the abbey for his burial there, with quitclaim of view of frankpledge and other suits of court for the canons and all dwelling on the said land.

A = Original, now lost. B = TNA C56/16 m. 19, (Confirmation Roll of 3 Henry VII) (from A). C = TNA C56/27 m. 24 (Confirmation Roll of 1 Henry VIII) (from A).

[B]

Omnibus Christi fidelibus presens scriptum visuris vel audituris Rog[er]us de Quency comes Winton[ie] constabular[ius] Scotie salutem in domino. Nouerit vniuersitas vestra me pro salute anime mee antecessorum et successorum meorum concessisse et hac presenti carta mea confirmasse deo et ecclesie beate Marie de Pratis Leyrcestr[ie] et canonicis regularibus ibidem deo seruientibus quatuor virgatas terre in territorio de Thurmodeston' quas Henr[icus] de Anlep' eisdem canonicis cum corpore suo dedit et carta sua confirmauit cum toftis et croftis et cum omnibus aliis pertinentiis suis infra villam de Thurmodeston' et extra cum redditibus possessionibus eysiamentis et omnibus aliis libertatibus et liberis consuetudinibus ad predictam terram vel redditum qualitercumque pertinentibus. sicut in carta feoffamenti a dicto Henr[ico] de Anlep' dictis canonicis confecta plenius continentur. Dedi et remisi et pro me et heredibus meis imperpetuum quietum clamaui eisdem canonicis et hominibus suis in predicta terra vel toftis manentibus visum franciplegii cum omnibus aliis sectis que de terra vel pro terra exigi possunt imperpetuum. Habendas et tenendas predictis canonicis in liberam puram et perpetuam elemosinam sicut aliqua elemosina liberius purius et quietius alicui domui religionis conferri potest vel concedi. In cuius rei testimonium presenti scripto sigillum meum apposui. Hiis testibus. dominis. Will[elm]o de Bosco. Ioh[ann]e Beckard et Rob[er]to de Hereford. militibus. Briano et Rob[er]to de Traford clericis. Ric[ardo] de Wykes Waltero de Euinton'. Rob[er]to falconario. Will[elm]o Cnotte de Roleya et aliis.

90. William son of John son of Ketelbern of Thurmaston   1247 X 1259
Grant and quitclaim of an annual rent of ten pence from a house site and seven rods of land which Henry the shepherd once held of him in the village of Thurmaston, Leics. Also grant and quitclaim of the homage and service that John Dudeman and William Morker once owed him for land and a house-site in the village and fields of Thurmaston.

> A = Original, now lost. B = TNA E13/76, m. 73–73d, copy dated 1351 (from A, slightly damaged).

[B]

Vniuersis Chr[isti fidelibus] hoc scriptum visuris vel audituris Will[elmu]s filius Ioh[ann]is filii Ketelberni de Thur[modestona] salutem in domino. Nouerit me dedisse et quietum clamasse deo et ecclesie [beate Marie] de Pratis Leyc[estrie] et canonicis regularibus ibidem deo seruientibus redditum decem d[enariorum] de vno mesuagio et septem rodis terre que Henr[icus] bercharius de me t[enuit] aliquando in villa de Thurmodeston'. Preterea concessi dedi et quietum clamaui predictis ecclesie et canonicis homagium et totum seruitium que Ioh[ann]es Dudeman et Will[elmu]s Morker michi aliquando facere consueuerunt de tota terra et mesuagio tam in villa quam in territorio de Thurmodeston'. Habenda et tenenda predictis canonicis in liberam puram et perpetuam elemosinam sicut aliqua elemosina liberius purius et quietius alicui domui religionis dari poterit vel concedi. Et ego dictus Will[elmu]s et heredes mei predictum redditum homagium et seruitium et omnia alia predictam terram contingentia contra omnes homines et feminas warantizabimus acquietabimus et defendemus inperpetuum. Et vt hec mea donatio et quieta clamatio rata sit et stabilis presentem cartam sigilli mei inpressione roboraui. Hiis testibus Walt[er]o de Euinton' Ric[ard]o filio Simon[is] de Bellagraua Rob[er]to de Borestall' Walt[er]o Herbert de Barkeby Rob[er]to Wysman de Thurmodeston' Ad[a] filio Ioh[ann]is filii Ketelb[erni] de eadem villa Henr[ico] de Anlep' et aliis.

> The attestation of Walter of Evington dates the act before his death in 1259, TNA JUST1/456, m. 13, and there is a certain coincidence of witnesses and characters with the charter of Henry of Wanlip (no. 88).

91. Roger de Quincy, earl of Winchester   1241 X 1264
Grant of a virgate of land in Whetstone, Leics. which Richard Kyrke held, with a concession of common rights of pasture for all their own animals throughout the earl's part of the forest of Leicester.

> A = Original, now lost. B = TNA C56/16 m. 19, (Confirmation Roll of 3 Henry VII) (from A). C = TNA C56/27 m. 24 (Confirmation Roll of 1 Henry VIII) (from A).

[B]

Sciant presentes et futuri quod ego Rog[erus] de Quenci comes Wynton[ie] constabular[ius] Scotie dedi concessi et hac presenti carta mea confirmaui deo et ecclesie beate Marie de Pratis Leyrc[estrie] et canonicis ibidem deo seruientibus in puram et perpetuam elemosinam vnam virgatam terre in Westan quam Ric[ardus] Kyrke tenuit. Concessi etiam eisdem communam liberam ad animalia sua propria pascenda omnimoda per totam forestam Leyrc[estrie] in purparte nostra eiusdem foreste in bosco et plano et aliis locis. Habendam et tenendam libere quiete bene et in pace predictam virgatam terre cum communia libera antedictis cum pertinentiis singulis absque omni contradictione vexatione et exactione seculari pro me et heredibus meis vel assignatis meis imperpetuum. Quare volo et firmiter precipio quod predicti canonici hanc meam elemosinam supradictam pacifice possideant imperpetuum. In cuius rei testimonium presenti scripto sigillum meum apposui. Hiis testibus. dominis. Gilb[er]to Kulewen'. Ioh[ann]e Becard'. Ioh[ann]e de Craunford' tunc senescallo. Ioh[ann]e Tuschet. Ph[ilipp]o de Chetewynd' militibus. Ric[ard]o Sweyn tunc seruiente de Groby. Rob[er]to Franceys et aliis.

> Sir John of Cranford appears here as the earl's seneschal, which dates this charter after his succession to John le Moine in the office in 1241. It must otherwise be earlier than the earl's death in 1264.

92. Roger de Quincy, earl of Winchester   1241 x 1264

Mandate to Sir Richard Chamberlain, his seneschal, that he is to put the abbey in full possession of rights to take wood for repairing hedges and houses in Shepshed, Leics. and to take timber for the repair and upkeep of its mill there, and also of its view of frankpledge.

> A = Original, now lost. B = Leicester Rental (from A, now lost). C = Bodl. Laud misc. 625, f. 22r (from B).
> Pd. Nichols, *Leicester*, i pt. 2, Appendix p. 56 (from C).

[C]

Rog[erus] de Quenci comes Wynt[onie] etc. dilecto et fideli suo domino R[adulfo] Chamburleyn senescallo suo salutem. Mandamus vobis firmiter precipientes quatinus ponatis abbatem et conuentum Leyc[estrie] in seysinam plenam de housbote et haybote in Schepished et de meremio ad emendationem et sustentationem molendini sui de Schepished et de visu franciplegii etc. vt in carta.

> It is difficult to date this act, although it is likely to be after 1241 and the tenure of the seneschalcy by John le Moine.

93. Roger of Coten   c. 1222 x 1265

Grant of a meadowland called Seggeholm *in the field of Lockington, Leics. which William de Sainneville had given Roger for his homage and service extending between* Toftes *and* Oldehe *according to its recognised bounds as far as* Stanforde. *The abbey to a pay a penny rent annually at Easter.*

> A = Original, now lost. B = TNA E13/76, mm. 72d–73, copy dated 1351 (from A).

[B]

Sciant presentes et futuri quod ego Rog[er]us de Cotun dedi et concessi et hac presenti carta mea confirmaui deo et ecclesie beate Marie de Pratis Leirc[estrie] et canonicis regularibus ibidem deo seruientibus pro salute anime mee antecessorum et successorum meorum quoddam pratum in campo de Lokintona. illud scilicet quod vocatur Seggeholm quod quidem pratum Will[elmu]s de Senevill[a] michi dedit pro homagio et seruitio meo et carta sua confirmauit et extendit de Toftes et Oldehe, sicut limitatum est per metas et bundas vsque in Stanforde cum omnibus pertinentiis suis infra villam et extra. Habendum et tenendum dictis canonicis de me et heredibus meis in perpetuum integre pacifice et honorifice in libertate et perpetuam elemosinam. Reddendo inde annuatim michi et heredibus meis vnum denarium ad Pascha pro omni seruitio exactione et demanda. Et ego Rog[er]us prenominatus et heredes mei dictum pratum cum omnibus pertinentiis suis sicut predictum est dictis canonicis contra omnes gentes warantizabimus acquietabimus et defendemus imperpetuum. Vt autem hec mea donatio et concessio rata sit et stabilis imperpetuum presens scriptum sigilli mei munimine roboraui. Hiis testibus Nich[ola]o de Marcham Ioh[ann]e de Cranford' Henrico Wiscard' Will[elm]o falconario Rob[er]to de Menil Rob[er]to de Beaumund Rob[er]to pincerna Galfr[id]o Orm de Blaby Ioh[ann]e de Reigad' de eadem. Will[elm]o Grim Simon[e] de Osiluiston' Ioh[ann]e de Kokerch' Thoma harpur Simon[e] marscall' Will[elm]o de Aula Will[elm]o de Keman Ranulpho de Bracin' Ioh[ann]e de Brichswrth' Rob[er]to scriptore et multis aliis.

> The best indication of the date is the presence of Sir John of Cranford, who came out of his minority in 1222 and had died by 1265 when his widow is mentioned, for which see TNA E368/4, m. 3; *Close Rolls of the reign of Henry III, 1264–68*, 110.

94. Roger of Barkby, clerk   1259 x 1278

Grant of an annual rent of 11s. 6d. drawn from the following listed properties: a virgate William le Poer held of him in Barkby, Leics. (4s.); a quarter virgate and a quarter bovate with toft and croft which the same William held of him in Barkby Thorpe, Leics. (4s. 6d.); a toft Alan of Thorpe held of him in Barkby Thorpe (2s.); and from a toft Ranulf of Radcliffe held for his life in Barkby Thorpe (12d.). The toft to revert to the canons after Ranulf's death, along with the homage and service of William and Alan, with suit of court and view of frankpledge.

A = Original, now lost. B = TNA E13/76, m. 74d, copy dated 1351 (from A).

[B]

Sciant presentes et futuri quod ego Rog[er]us de Barkeby clericus dedi concessi at hac presenti carta mea confirmaui deo et ecclesie beate Marie de Pratis Leyc[estrie] et canonicis regularibus ibidem deo seruientibus annuum redditum vndecim solidorum et sex denariorum argenti subscriptum videlicet quatuor solidos annuos de vna virgata terre quam Will[elmu]s le Poer de me tenuit in Barkeby et quatuor solidos sex denarios annuos de quarta parte vnius virgate terre et quarta parte vnius bouate terre cum tofto et crofto que idem Will[elmu]s de me tenuit in Thorp' iuxta Barkeby et duos solidos annuos de vno tofto quod Alanus de Thorp' de me tenuit in Thorp' prenominata et duodecim denarios annuos de vno tofto quod Ranulphus de Radecleue de me tenuit ad terminum vite ipsius Ranulphi in Thorp' sepedicta. Et illud idem toftum post decessum dicti Ranulphi cum homagio et seruitio dictorum Will[elm]i et Alani et heredum suorum et cum sectis curie et visu franciplegii eorundem ac Ranulphi predicti et cum omnibus wardis releuiis fortuniis et escactis et omnibusque michi vel heredibus meis de predictis terris aliquo modo accidere vel accrescere possent. Habendum et tenendum dictis canonicis in liberam puram et perpetuam elemosinam. Et ego Rog[er]us et heredes mei vel assignati mei predictum redditum cum homagio et seruitio et tofto et aliis omnibus predictis pertinentiis sicut predictum est prefatis canonicis contra omnes gentes warantizabimus acquietabimus et defendemus imperpetuum. In cuius rei testimonium presenti carte sigillum meum apposui. Hiis testibus. Gerardo de Hamelton' Ioh[ann]e le Falkener Rog[er]o Cnotte Ioh[ann]e de Euenton' de Humb[er]ston' Will[elm]o Casteline de eadem Rob[er]to filio Rog[er]I de Belegraue Will[elm]o de dispensa de Barkeby et aliis.

The presence of John Evinton of Humberstone indicates a date after his father's death in 1259. John Falconer of Thurcaston appears in deeds of the 1260s outside the knights in witness lists, but in the mid 1270s he had taken knighthood, so this deed must date before then, *Report on the manuscripts of the late Reginald Rawdon Hastings*, i, 69–70.

Bibliography

Airs, M. *The Tudor and Jacobean country house: a building history* (Stroud 1995)

Alexandre, J.-L., Grand, G. and Lanöe, G. *Bibliothèque municipale de Vendôme*, Reliures médiévales des bibliothèques de France (Paris 2000) with reviews by M. Gullick in *Manuscripta* 43/4 (1999–2000), 189–93, and N. Pickwoad in *The Library* 7th ser. 5 (2004), 80–2

———, and Maître, C. *Catalogue des reliures médiévales conservés à la Bibliothèque municipale d'Autun* (Paris 1997)

Allin, C. E. 'The ridge tiles' in Mellor and Pearce, ed. (1981), 52–70

Aston, M. *Monasteries in the landscape* (Stroud 2000)

Backhouse, J., Turner, D. H. and Webster, L. ed. *The golden age of Anglo-Saxon art 966–1066*, exh. cat. (British Museum: London 1984)

Bailey, T. *The processions of Sarum and the western Church* (Toronto 1971)

Barber, G. *Textile and embroidered bindings* (Oxford 1971)

Bartlett, R. ed. *Geoffrey of Burton: life and miracles of St Modwenna*, Oxford Medieval Texts (Oxford 2002)

Basset Charters c. 1120 to 1250, ed. W. T. Reedy, Pipe Roll Society 88 (London 1995)

Bateson, M. ed. *Records of the borough of Leicester*, 4 vols. (London 1899–1923)

Bearman, F. 'The origins and significance of two late medieval textile chemise bookbindings in the Walters Art Gallery', *Journal of the Walters Art Gallery* 54 (1996), 163–87

Beazeley, M. 'History of the chapter library of Canterbury Cathedral', *Transactions of the Bibliographical Society* 8 (1904–6), 113–85

Bedingfield, W. K. 'Presidential Address 1930–31', *Transactions of the Leicester Literary and Philosophical Society* 32 (1931), 5–24

Bernard, E. ed. *Catalogi manuscriptorum Angliae et Hiberniae* (Oxford 1697)

Biddle, M. ed. *Winchester in the early middle ages*, Winchester Studies 1 (Oxford 1976)

Billson, C. J. 'The open fields of Leicester', *TLAS* 14 (1925–6), 3–29

Binski, P. and Panayotova, S. ed. *The Cambridge illuminations: ten centuries of book production in the medieval west* (London and Turnhout 2005)

Bishop, T. A. M. 'Notes on Cambridge manuscripts, Part III', *Transactions of the Cambridge Bibliographical Society* 2 (1954–8), 192–9

Blair, J. and Sharpe, R. ed. *Pastoral care before the parish* (Leicester 1992)

Blake, H., Egan, G., Hurst, J. and New, E. 'From popular devotion to resistance and revival in England: the cult of the holy name of Jesus and the Reformation' in Gaimster and Gilchrist, ed. (2003), 175–203

Blanc Smith, G. le, *Haddon* (London 1906)

Book bindings at the Public Record Office (Kew 1999)

Bourne, J. *Understanding Leicestershire and Rutland place-names* (Loughborough 2003)

Brady, I. 'The rubrics of Peter Lombard's Sentences', *Pier Lombardo* 6.1–4 (1962), 5–25

Bremmer, R. H., Dekker, K. and Johnson, D. F. ed. *Rome and the North: the early reception of Gregory the Great in Germanic Europe* (Paris 2001)

Britton, D. 'Manuscripts associated with Kirby Bellars Priory', *Transactions of the Cambridge Bibliographical Society* 6 (1972–6), 267–84

Brown, C. and Robbins, R. H. *Index of Middle English verse* (New York 1943)

Brown, W. ed. *Cartularium prioratus de Gyseburne*, Surtees Society 86, 89 (Durham 1889–94)

Brownrigg, L. L. ed. *Medieval book production: assessing the evidence* (Los Altos Hills, CA, 1990)

Buckley, R. 'Abbey Park, Leicester: an archaeological desk-based assessment and survey', unpubl. ULAS Report 97/12 (1997)

———, and Butler, A. 'Leicester Abbey', *TLAHS* 75 (2001), 129–30

———, and Derrick, M. 'An archaeological evaluation at Leicester Abbey: first season, summer 2000', unpubl. ULAS Report 2001–074 (2001)

———, and George S. ed. 'Archaeology in Leicestershire and Rutland 2003', *TLAHS* 78 (2004), 143–78

Burtt, J. 'Contributions to the history of Leicester Abbey', *TLAAS* 4 (1878), 32–6

Butcher, A. 'Rent and the urban economy: Oxford and Canterbury in the later middle ages', *Southern History*, 1 (1979), 11–43

Butler, L. and Given-Wilson, C. *Medieval monasteries of Great Britain* (London 1979)

Calendar of Charter Rolls preserved in the Public Record Office, 1226–1516, 6 vols. (London 1903–27)

Calendar of Patent Rolls of Edward VI, 6 vols. (London 1924–9)

Calendar of Patent Rolls of Elizabeth 1558–82, 9 vols. (London 1939–)

Calendar of Patent Rolls of Philip and Mary, 4 vols. (London 1936–9)

Camfield, B. *A theological discourse of angels and their ministries* (London 1678)

Carley, J. P. and Tite, C. G. C. ed. *Books and collectors 1200–1700: essays presented to Andrew Watson* (London 1997)

Cartularium prioratus de Gyseburne, ed. W. Brown, Surtees Society 86, 89 (Durham 1889–94)

Cartulary of Cirencester Abbey, ed. C. D. Ross and M. Devine, 3 vols. (Oxford 1964–7)

Cartulary of Darley Abbey, ed. R. R. Darlington, 2 vols. (Kendal 1945)

Cartulary of the monastery of St Frideswide at Oxford, ed. S. R. Wigram, Oxford Historical Society 28, 31 (Oxford 1895–6)

Cartulary of Oseney Abbey, ed. H. H. Salter, Oxford Historical Society 89–91, 97–8, 101 (Oxford 1929–36)

Catalogi manuscriptorum Angliae et Hiberniae, ed. E. Bernard (Oxford 1697)

Chandler, J. *John Leland's itinerary: travels in Tudor England* (Stroud 1993)

Chapters of the Augustinian canons, ed. H. E. Salter, Canterbury and York Society 29 (London 1922)

Christian, P. *The history and practice of magic*, 2 vols. (London 1952)

Chronicon Henrici Knighton vel Cnitthon, monachi Leycestrensis, ed. J. R. Lumby, Rolls Series 92, 2 vols. (London 1889–95)

Clapham, A. W. *Thornton Abbey* (London 1956)

Clark, J. W. *The care of books* (Cambridge 1901)

———, 'On the work done to the library of Exeter Cathedral in 1412 and 1413', *Proceedings of the Cambridge Antiquarian Society* 10 (1904), 294–306

———, ed. *The observances in use at the Augustinian priory of S. Giles and S. Andrew at Barnwell, Cambridgeshire* (Cambridge 1897)

———, ed. *Liber memorandum ecclesie de Bernewell* (Cambridge 1907)

Clark, M. *The art of all colours: medieval recipe books for painters and illuminators* (London 2001)

Clarkson, C. 'English monastic bookbinding in the twelfth century' in Maniaci and Munafò, ed. (1993), ii, 181–200

Close Rolls of the reign of Henry III preserved in the Public Record Office, 14 vols. (London 1902–38)

Coates, A. *English medieval books: the Reading Abbey collections from foundation to dispersal* (Oxford 1999)

Codices Boethiani: a conspectus of manuscripts of the works of Boethius, ed. M. T. Gibson, L. Smith and M. Passalacqua, Warburg Institute surveys and texts 25, 27–8 (London 1995)

Colker, M. L. 'Richard of St Victor and the Anonymous of Bridlington', *Traditio* 18 (1962), 181–227

Compton, C. H. 'The Abbey of St Mary de Pratis, Leicester', *TLAAS* 9 (1904–5), 197–204

Connor, A. and Buckley, R. ed. *Roman and medieval occupation in Causeway Lane, Leicester*, Leicester Archaeology Monographs 5 (Leicester 1999)

Coppack, G. *Abbeys and priories* (London 1990)

Coss, P. R. ed. *The Langley Cartulary*, Dugdale Society 32 (1980)

Coulton, G. G. *Europe's apprenticeship: a survey of medieval Latin with examples* (London 1940)

Courtney, P. 'Leicester Abbey: historical background' in Buckley, ed. (1997), 13–25

———, 'Lord's Place, Leicester: an urban aristocratic house of the sixteenth century', *TLAHS* 74 (2000), 37–58

———, 'Between two forests: the social and topographical evolution of medieval Anstey', *TLAHS* 77 (2003), 35–64

Cox, B. *The place-names of Leicestershire. Pt. I: the Borough of Leicester*, English Place-Names Society 75 (Nottingham 1998)

Cross, C. *The puritan earl: the life of Henry Hastings, third Earl of Huntingdon 1536–1595* (London 1966)

———, 'Dynastic politics: the local and national importance of the Hastings family in the sixteenth century' in Palmer, ed. (1982), 16–34

Crouch, D. *The Beaumont twins: the roots and branches of power in the twelfth century* (Cambridge 1986)

———, 'The foundation of Leicester Abbey and other problems', *Midland History* 12 (1987), 1–13

———, *The image of aristocracy in Britain, 1000–1300* (London 1992)

———, 'Earls and bishops in twelfth-century Leicestershire', *Nottingham Medieval Studies* 37 (1993), 9–20

———, *The reign of King Stephen, 1135–54* (London 2000)

Cunningham, I. C. 'Latin classical manuscripts in the National Library of Scotland', *Scriptorium* 27 (1973), 64–90

———, 'Sir James Balfour's manuscript collection: the 1698 catalogue and other sources', *Edinburgh Bibliographical Society Transactions* 6/6 (2004), 191–255

Dace, R. 'Towards the banneret: studies in Midland society, 1150–1300', unpublished Leeds MPhil thesis (1997)

Dalton, P. 'Civil war and ecclesiastical peace in the reign of King Stephen', in Dunn, ed. (2000), 53–75

Darlington, R. R. ed. *The cartulary of Darley Abbey*, 2 vols. (Kendal 1945)

Davies, J. G. *Dictionary of liturgy and worship* (London 1972)

Davis, G. R. C. ed. *Medieval cartularies of Great Britain* (London 1958)

Davis, R. H. C. and Cronne, H. A. ed. *Regesta Regum Anglo-Normannorum 1066–1154*, 3 vols. (Oxford 1968)

Descriptive catalogue of the charters and muniments in the possession of the Rt. Hon. Lord Fitzhardinge at Berkeley Castle, ed. I. Jeayes (Bristol 1892)

Dickey, M. 'Some commentaries on the *De inventione* and *Ad Herennium* of the eleventh and early twelfth centuries', *Medieval and Renaissance Studies* 6 (1968), 1–41

Dickinson, J. C. *The origins of the Austin canons and their introduction into England* (London 1950)

Dictionary of medieval Latin from British sources, ed. R. E. Latham, et al. (Oxford 1975–)

Dix, B. ed. *Leicestershire and Rutland: report and proceedings of the 149th summer meeting of the Royal Archaeological Institute* (2003)

Dolbeau, F. 'Un nouveau catalogue des manuscrits de Lobbes aux XIe et XIIe siècles', *Recherches Augustiniennes* 13 (1978), 3–36

Douar, F., Petit, B. and Ehm, C. ed. *La France romane au temps des premiers Capétiens (987–1152)* (The Louvre: Paris 2005)

Doyle, A. I. 'Book production by the monastic orders in England (*c.* 1375–1530): assessing the evidence' in Brownrigg, ed. (1990), 1–19

Dugdale, W. ed. *Monasticon Anglicanum: a history of the abbies and other monasteries, hospitals, frieries and cathedral and collegiate churches*, ed. J. Caley, H. Ellis and B. Bandinel, 6 vols. in 8 (London 1830)

Duke Humfrey's library and the Divinity School 1488–1988, exh. cat. (Bodleian Library: Oxford 1988)

Dunn, D. ed. *War and society in medieval and early modern Britain* (Liverpool 2000)

Dyer, C. 'Towns and cottages in eleventh-century England' in Mayr-Harting and Moore, ed. (1985), 91–106

———, *Standards of living in the later middle ages* (Cambridge 1989)

Eames, E. S. 'Appendix 1: the decorated floor tiles' in Mayes and Scott, ed. (1984), 173–87

Emden, A. B. *A biographical register of the University of Oxford to A.D. 1500*, 3 vols. (Oxford 1957)

———, *A biographical register of the University of Oxford, A.D. 1501 to 1540* (Oxford 1974)

Evans, A. K. B. 'Historical evidence for the Anglo-Saxon church and medieval abbey' in Wilkinson and McWhirr, ed. (1998), 14–18

Evans, J. *Art in medieval France, 987–1498* (London 1948)

Eyton, R. W. *Court, household and itinerary of King Henry II* (London 1878)

Farley, A. and Ellis, H. ed. *Domesday Book seu liber censualis Willelmi primi regis Angliae*, 4 vols. (London 1783–1816)

Farrer, W. ed. *The Lancashire Pipe Rolls and early Lancashire charters* (Liverpool 1902)

Fasti Ecclesiae Anglicanae, 1066–1300, ed. D. E. Greenway, J. S. Barrow, and M. J. Pearson, 9 vols. (London 1968–)

Fasti Ecclesiae Scoticanae medii aevi ad annum 1638, ed. D. E. R. Watt and A. L. Murray, Scottish Record Society, new series 25 (rev. edn. Edinburgh 2003)

Fellows-Jensen, G. and Springborg, P. ed. *Care and conservation of manuscripts 7*, Proceedings of the seventh international seminar held at the Royal Library, Copenhagen 18–19 April 2002 Copenhagen 2003)

Fielding Johnson, T. *Glimpses of ancient Leicester* (Leicester 1906)

Fletcher, W. D. G. ed. 'Some unpublished documents relating to Leicestershire, preserved in the Public Record Office', *Associated Architectural Societies Reports and Papers* 23.1 (1895) 213–52

———, 'On the efforts made to convert arable land into pasture in Leicestershire in the fifteenth and sixteenth centuries', *TLAAS* 8 (1899), 308–13

Forde, S. 'Social outlook and preaching in a Wycliffite *Sermones dominicales* collection' in Wood and Loud, ed. (London 1991), 179–91

——, 'The educational organization of the Augustinian canons in England and Wales and their university life at Oxford, 1325–1448', *History of Universities* 13 (1994), 21–60

Foster, C. W. ed. *Lincoln episcopal records in the time of Thomas Cooper, S.T.P., Bishop of Lincoln A. D. 1571 to A. D. 1584*, Canterbury and York Society 11 (London 1948)

Fowkes, D. V. and Potter, G. R. ed. *William Senior's survey of estates of 1st and 2nd Earls of Devonshire c. 1600–1628*, Derbyshire Record Society 13 (Chesterfield 1988)

Fowler, K. *The King's Lieutenant: Henry of Grosmont, duke of Lancaster, 1310–1361* (London 1969)

Fowler, R. C. ed. *Registrum Radulphi Baldock*, Canterbury and York Society 7 (Woodbridge 1911)

Fox, L. *Leicester Abbey: history and description* (Leicester 1938, 2nd edn. 1949, 3rd edn. 1971)

——, and Russell, P. *Leicester Forest* (Leicester 1948)

Furnivall, F. J. ed. *Robert of Brunne's Handlyng Synne*, Roxburghe Club (London 1862)

Gaimster, D. and Gilchrist, R. ed. *The archaeology of Reformation 1480–1580*, Society for Post Medieval Archaeology, Monograph 1 (Leeds 2003)

Galbraith, V. H. ed. *The St Albans Chronicle 1406–20* (Oxford 1937)

——, 'The Chronicle of Henry Knighton' in *Fritz Saxl, 1890–1984: a volume of memorial essays from his friends in England*, ed. D. Gordon (London 1957), 136–48

Gameson, R. *The manuscripts of early Norman England (c. 1066–1130)* (Oxford 1999)

——, *The scribe speaks? Colophons in early English manuscripts*, H. M. Chadwick Memorial Lectures 12 (Cambridge 2001)

Gasnault, P. 'Observations paléographiques et codicologiques tirées de l'inventaire de la librarie pontificale de 1369', *Scriptorium* 34 (1980), 269–75

Gasparri, F. ed. *Le xiie siècle: tournant et renouveau 1120–1150* (Paris 1994)

Gauthier, M-M. 'La Collection de E. et M. Truniger', *Bulletin de la Société archéologique et historique du Limousin* 93 (Limoges 1966–8), 17–34

——, *Émaux du Moyen Âge occidental* (Fribourg 1972)

——, and François, G. *Medieval enamels: masterpieces from the Keir collection* (London 1981)

Geoffrey of Burton: life and miracles of St Modwenna, ed. R. Bartlett, Oxford Medieval Texts (Oxford 2002)

Geophysical Surveys of Bradford, 'Geophysical survey of Leicester Abbey', unpubl. report (1997)

Gibson, M. T. 'Priscian, *Institutiones grammaticae*: a handlist of manuscripts', *Scriptorium* 26 (1972), 105–24

——, Smith, L. and Passalacqua, M. ed. *Codices Boethiani: a conspectus of manuscripts of the works of Boethius*, Warburg Institute surveys and texts 25, 27–8 (London 1995)

Gillespie, V. *Syon Abbey with the libraries of the Carthusians, edited by A. I. Doyle*, CBMLC 9 (London 2001)

Girouard, M. *Robert Smythson and the Elizabethan country house* (New Haven and London 1983)

Goldschmidt, E. P. *Medieval texts and their first appearance in print*, Bibliographical Society (London 1943)

Goodman, A. *John of Gaunt: the exercise of princely power in fourteenth-century Europe* (Harlow 1992)

Gordon, D. ed. *Fritz Saxl, 1890–1984: a volume of memorial essays from his friends in England* (London 1957)

Greene, J. P. *Medieval monasteries* (Leicester, London and New York 1992)

Greenway, D. E., Barrow, J. S. and Pearson, M. J. ed. *Fasti Ecclesiae Anglicanae, 1066–1300*, 9 vols. (London 1968–)

Gullick, M. 'The bindings' in Mynors and Thomson, ed. (1993), xxvi–xxxii

——, *Extracts from the precentors' accounts concerning books and bookmaking of Ely Cathedral Priory* (Hitchin 1985)

——, 'From scribe to binder: quire tackets in twelfth-century European manuscripts' in Sharpe, ed. (1996), 240–59

——, 'A Romanesque blind-stamped binding' in Pearson, ed. (2000), 1–8

Hall, T. N. 'The early English manuscripts of Gregory the Great's *Homiliae in Evangelia* and *Homiliae in Hiezechihelem*: a preliminary survey' in Bremmer, Dekker and Johnson, ed. (2001), 115–36

Hamel, C. F. R. de *Glossed books of the Bible and the origins of the Paris booktrade* (Woodbridge 1984)

——, 'The dispersal of the library of Christ Church, Canterbury, from the fourteenth to the sixteenth century' in Carley and Tite, ed. (1997), 263–79

Hamer, R. *A manuscript index to the 'Index of Middle English verse'* (London 1995)

Hamilton Thompson, A. 'The monasteries of Leicestershire in the fifteenth century', *TLAAS* 11 (1913–14), 89–108

——, 'The Leicestershire Archaeological Society in the present century', *TLAS* 21 (1940–1), 122–48

——, *The Abbey of St Mary of the Meadows, Leicester* (Leicester 1949)

——, ed. *Records of visitations held by William Alnwick, bishop of Lincoln, Part 1, visitations of religious houses in the diocese of Lincoln*, Canterbury and York Society 24 (London 1919)

Hardman, P. ed. *Medieval and early modern literary miscellanies*, Yearbook of English Studies, special number 33 (2003)

Hardy, T. D. ed. *Rotuli Chartarum in turri Londinensi asservati 1199–1216*, Publications of the Record Commission 25 (London 1837)

——, ed. *Rotuli Litterarum Clausarum in turri Londinensi asservati 1204–1227*, 2 vols. (London 1833–44)

Hemmeon, W. M. de, *Burgage tenure in medieval England* (Cambridge, MA, 1914)

Heuser, W. ed. *Die Kildare Gedichte*, Bonner Beiträge zur Anglistik 14 (Bonn 1904)

Hilton, R. H. 'A thirteenth-century poem on disputed villein services', *English Historical Review* 56 (1941), 90–7, reprinted in his *Class conflict and the crisis of feudalism: essays in medieval social history* (London 1985), 108–13

——, *The economic development of some Leicestershire estates in the fourteenth and fifteenth centuries* (Oxford 1947)

Hockliffe, E. ed. *The diary of the Rev. Ralph Josselin 1616–1683*, Camden Society 3rd ser. 15 (London 1908)

Hofmann, G. 'La biblioteca scientifica del monastero di San Francesco a Candia nel medio evo', *Orientalia Christiana Periodica* 8 (1942), 317–60

Holt, R. and Rosser, G. ed. *The English medieval town: a reader in English urban history* (London 1990)

Hoskins, W. G. 'Seven deserted village sites in Leicestershire', *TLAHS* 33 (1956), 36–51

Howlett, D. R. 'Fifteenth-century manuscripts of St Albans Abbey and Gloucester College, Oxford' in de la Mare and Barker-Benfield, ed. (1980), 84–7

Hudson, A. *The premature reformation: Wycliffite texts and Lollard history* (Oxford 1988)

Hussey, A. 'Notice on an ancient engraved copper', *Sussex Archaeological Collections* 5 (1852), 105–10

Huws, D. 'Sir Thomas Mostyn and the Mostyn manuscripts' in Carley and Tite, ed. (1997) 451–72

Initia carminum ac versuum medii aevi posterioris latinorum, ed. H. Walther (Göttingen 1959)

Iohannis Saresberiensis episcopi Carnotensis Policratici, ed. C. C. I. Webb, 2 vols (Oxford 1909)

Jackson, W. 'History and description of Leicester Abbey', *Journal of the Royal Institute of British Architects*, 3rd ser. 1 (1894), 129–34 and 166–70

James, M. R. *The ancient libraries of Canterbury and Dover* (Cambridge 1903)

——, 'Catalogue of the library of Leicester Abbey', *TLAHS* 19 (1935–7), 118–61 and 378–440, and *ibid.* 21 (1939–41), 2–88

Jeayes, I. ed. *Descriptive catalogue of the charters and muniments in the possession of the Rt. Hon. Lord Fitzhardinge at Berkeley Castle* (Bristol 1892)

Jocqué, L. and Milis, L. ed. *Liber ordinis Sancti Victoris Parisiensis*, Corpus Christianorum Continuatio Medievalis 61 (Turnhout 1984)

Jones, S. and Buckley, R. 'Leicester Abbey' in Buckley and George, ed. (2004), 143

——, and Buckley, R. ed. 'An archaeological evaluation at Leicester Abbey: third season, summer 2002', unpubl. ULAS Report 2004–65 (2004a)

——, and Buckley, R. ed. 'An archaeological evaluation at Leicester Abbey: fourth season, summer 2003', unpubl. ULAS Report 2004–78 (2004b)

Keene, D. 'Suburban growth' in Holt and Rosser, ed. (London 1990), 97–119

Kenyon, K. M. *Excavations at the Jewry Wall site, Leicester* (Oxford 1948)

Ker, N. R. 'The migration of manuscripts from the English medieval libraries', *The Library*, 4th ser. 23 (1942–3), 1–11, repr. in his *Books, collectors and libraries*, ed. Watson (1985), 459–70

——, 'Salisbury Cathedral manuscripts and Patrick Young's catalogue', *Wiltshire Archaeological and Natural History Magazine* 53 (1949–50), 153–83, repr. in his *Books, collectors and libraries*, ed. Watson (1985), 175–208

——, 'Sir John Prise', *The Library* 5th ser. 10 (1955), 1–24, repr. in his *Books, collectors and libraries*, ed. Watson (1985), 471–95

——, *English manuscripts in the century after the Norman Conquest* (Oxford 1960)

——, *Medieval libraries of Great Britain*, 2nd edn (London 1964)

——, *Books, collectors and libraries: studies in the medieval heritage*, ed. A. G. Watson (London 1985)

——, and Piper, A. J. ed. *Medieval manuscripts in British libraries*, 5 vols. (Oxford 1969–2002)

Kieckhefer, R. *Forbidden rites* (Stroud 1997)

King, E. J. 'Mountsorrel and its region in King Stephen's reign', *Huntingdon Library Quarterly* 44 (1980), 1–10

Kittredge, G. L. *Witchcraft in Old and New England* (Cambridge, MA, 1929)

Knighton's Chronicle 1337–96, ed. G. H. Martin, Oxford Medieval Texts (Oxford 1995)

Knowles, D. *The religious orders in England*, II. *The end of the middle ages* (Cambridge 1955)

——, and Hadcock, R. N. *Medieval religious houses in England and Wales* (London 1971)

Laffitte, M.-P. 'Le vocabulaire médiéval de la reliure d'après les anciens inventaires' in Weijers, ed. (1989), 61–78

——, Valansot, O., de Reyer, D. and Novik, W. 'Trois reliures médiévales à elements de tissu', *Bulletin du Centre International d'Etude des Textiles Anciennes* 74 (1997), 50–63

Lancashire Pipe Rolls and Early Lancashire Charters, ed. W. Farrer (Liverpool 1902)

Lapidge, M. 'Surviving booklists from Anglo-Saxon England' in Lapidge and Gneuss, ed. (1985), 33–89

——, and Gneuss, H. ed. *Learning and literature in Anglo-Saxon England. Studies presented to Peter Clemoes on the occasion of his sixty-fifth birthday* (Cambridge 1985)

Langley Cartulary, ed. P. R. Coss, Dugdale Society 32 (1980)

Latham, R. E. *Revised medieval Latin word-list from British and Irish sources* (Oxford 1965)

——, et al. ed. *Dictionary of medieval Latin from British sources* (Oxford 1975–)

Legg, J. W. and St John Hope, W. H. *Inventories of Christ Church, Canterbury* (London 1902)

Lehmann, P. *Mittelalterliche Bibliothekskataloge Deutschlands und der Schweiz. I Band. Die Bistümer Konstanz und Chur* (Munich 1918)

Liber memorandum ecclesie de Bernewell, ed. J. W. Clark (Cambridge 1907)

Liber ordinis Sancti Victoris Parisiensis, ed. L. Jocqué and L. Milis, Corpus Christianorum Continuatio Medievalis 61 (Turnhout 1984)

Liddle, P. 'The abbeys and priories of Leicestershire and Rutland', *TLAHS* 69 (1995), 1–21

Lincoln Episcopal Records in the Time of Thomas Cooper, S.T.P., Bishop of Lincoln A.D. *1571 to* A.D. *1584*, ed. C. W. Foster, Canterbury and York Society 11 (London 1948)

List of documents relating to the Household and Wardrobe: John to Edward I, Public Record Office Handbooks 7 (London 1964)

Lives of the bishops of Exeter and a history of the Cathedral, ed. G. Oliver (Exeter 1861)

Long, E. ed. *Diary of the marches of the royal army during the Great Civil War kept by Richard Symonds*, Camden Society 74 (London 1859)

Luard, H. R. ed. *Matthaei Parisensis, monachi Sancti Albani Chronica majora*, Rolls Series 57, 7 vols. (London 1872–83)

Lucas, A. M. *Anglo-Irish poems of the middle ages* (Dublin 1995)

Lucas, J. ed. 'An excavation in the north-east quarter of Leicester: Elbow Lane 1977', *TLAHS* 63 (1989), 28–51

Lumby, J. R. ed. *Chronicon Henrici Knighton vel Cnitthon, monachi Leycestrensis*, Rolls Series 92, 2 vols. (London 1889–95)

Maniaci, M. and Munafò, P. F. ed. *Ancient and medieval book materials and techniques*, Studi e Testi 357–8 (1993)

Manly, J. M. and Rickert, E. *The text of the Canterbury Tales*, 8 vols. (Chicago 1940)

Mare, A. C. de la, and Barker-Benfield, B. C. ed. *Manuscripts at Oxford: an exhibition in memory of R. W. Hunt* (Oxford 1980)

Marsden, E. 'Minor domestic architecture of the Rutland district', unpubl. PhD thesis, University of Manchester (1953)

Martin, G. H. ed. *Knighton's Chronicle 1337–96*, Oxford Medieval Texts (Oxford 1995)

Marshall, W. *The rural economy of the Midland counties including the management of livestock in Leicestershire and its environs*, 2 vols. (London 1790)

Maryon, H. *Metalwork and enamelling* (Dover 1971)

Matthaei Parisensis, monachi Sancti Albani Chronica majora, ed. H. R. Luard, Rolls Series 57, 7 vols. (London 1872–83)

Mayes P. and Scott, K. ed. *Pottery kilns at Chilvers Coton, Nuneaton*, Society for Medieval Archaeology, Monograph Series 10 (London 1984)

Mayr-Harting, H. and Moore, R. I. ed. *Studies in medieval history presented to R. H. C. Davis* (London 1985)

McWhirr, A. 'Brickmaking in Leicestershire before 1710', *TLAHS* 71 (1997), 37–59

Meek, J. and Buckley, R. 'An archaeological evaluation at Leicester Abbey: second season, summer 2001', ULAS Report 2002–010 (2002)

——, and Buckley, R. 'Leicester Abbey' *TLAHS* 76 (2002), 81–5

Mellor, J. and Pearce, T. ed. *The Austin friars, Leicester*, Council of British Archaeology research report 35 (Leicester 1981)

Mérindol, C. de 'Couleurs des couvertures et continus des livres à la fin du Moyen Age', *Bulletin de la Société Nationale des Antiquaires de France* (1991), 212–26

Meyer, W. ed. '*Quondam fuit factus festus*, ein Gedicht in Spottlatein', *Nachrichten von der königlichen Gesellschaft der Wissenschaten zu Göttingen.* Philologisch-historische Klasse (Göttingen 1908)

Monckton, A. 'Charred plant remains from evaluative excavations at Leicester Abbey in 2002 and 2003 (A8.2000)' in Jones and Buckley, ed. (2004b) 28–30

Mooney, L. R. 'John Shirley's heirs' in Hardman, ed. (2003), 182–98

Monasticon Anglicanum: a history of the abbies and other monasteries, hospitals, fieries and cathedral and collegiate churches, ed. W. Dugdale, J. Caley, H. Ellis and B. Bandinel, 6 vols. in 8 (London 1830)

Munk Olsen, B. *L'Etude des auteurs classiques latins aux xie et xiie siècles*, 4 vols. in 3 (Paris 1982–9)

Mynors, R. A. B. and Thomson, R. M. *Catalogue of the manuscripts of Hereford Cathedral library* (Cambridge 1993)

Nebbiai Dalla Guarda, D. 'Les livres de l'infirmerie dans les monastères médiévaux', *Revue Mabillon* n.s. 5 (1994), 57–81

———, and Genest, J.-F. ed. *Du copiste au collectionneur. Mélanges d'histoire des textes et des bibliothèques en l'honneur d'André Vernet*, Bibliologia 18 (Turnhout 1998)

Nederman, C. J. ed. *Policraticus: of the frivolities of courtiers and the footprints of philosophers* (Cambridge 1990)

Nevill, G. 'William Byg alias Lech, a fifteenth-century wizard', *The Archaeological Journal* 13 (1856), 372–4

Nichols, J. *The history and antiquities of the county of Leicester*, 4 vols. in 8 (London 1795–1815)

Nicholson, R. 'Fish remains' in Connor and Buckley, ed. (1999), 333–7

Nixon, H. 'The binding of the Winton Domesday' in Biddle, ed. (1976), 526–40

North, T. ed. *Accounts of the churchwardens of St Martin's 1489–1844* (Leicester 1884)

Ogilvy, J. *Britannia, or an illustration of the kingdom of England and dominium of Wales* (London 1675)

Oliver, G. ed. *Lives of the bishops of Exeter and a history of the cathedral* (Exeter 1861)

Onan, C. 'English medieval base-metal church plate', *The Archaeological Journal* 119 (1962), 195–207

Ordnance Survey, *Geological map of England at scale one inch to the mile* (1892)

Palmer, M. ed. *The aristocratic estate: the Hastings in Leicestershire and south Derbyshire* (Loughborough 1982)

Parkes, M. B. and Watson, A. G. ed. *Medieval scribes, manuscripts and libraries: essays presented to N. R. Ker* (London 1978)

Pearson, D. ed. *'For the love of binding'. Studies in bookbinding history presented to Mirjam Foot* (London and Newcastle 2000)

Pickwoad, N. 'Tacketed bindings – a hundred years of European bookbinding' in Pearson, ed. (2000), 119–68

Piper, A. J. 'The libraries of the monks of Durham' in Parkes and Watson, ed. (1978), 213–49

Platt, C. *The abbeys and priories of medieval England* (London 1984)

Policraticus: of the frivolities of courtiers and the footprints of philosophers, ed. C. J. Nederman (Cambridge 1990)

Powick, F. M. *The medieval books of Merton College* (Oxford 1931)

Raby, F. J. E. *A history of secular Latin poetry in the middle ages*, 2 vols (Oxford 1957)

Rackham, O. *Ancient woodland* (Colvend 2003)

Raine, J. *The fabric rolls of York Minster*, Surtees Society 35 (1859)

Rawlinson, W. G. *The engraved works of J. M. W. Turner R.A.* 2 vols. (London 1908–13)

Records of the borough of Leicester, ed. M. Bateson, 3 vols. (London 1899–1905)

Records of visitations held by William Alnwick, bishop of Lincoln, Part 1, visitations of religious houses in the diocese of Lincoln, ed. A Hamilton Thompson, Canterbury and York Society 24 (London 1919)

Reedy, W. T. ed. *Basset Charters c. 1120 to 1250*, Pipe Roll Society 88 (London 1995)

Regemorter, B. van, 'La reliure des manuscrits à Clairmarais aux XIIe au XIIIe siècles', *Scriptorium* 5 (1951), 99–100

Regesta Regum Anglo-Normannorum 1066–1154, ed. R. H. C. Davis and H. A. Cronne, 3 vols. (Oxford 1968)

Registrum Radulphi Baldock, ed. R. C. Fowler, Canterbury and York Society 7 (Woodbridge 1911)

Report on the manuscripts of the late Reginald Rawdon Hastings, Esq., of the Manor House, Ashby de la Zouche, Historical Manuscripts Commission, 4 vols. (London 1928–47)

Rigg, A. G. *A Glastonbury miscellany of the fifteenth century: a descriptive index of Trinity College, Cambridge MS O.9.38* (Oxford 1968)

Robert of Brunne's Handlyng Synne, ed. F. J. Furnivall, Roxburghe Club (London 1862)

Robbins, R. H. *The encyclopaedia of witchcraft and demonology* (London 1970)

Robinson, D. M. *The geography of Augustinian settlements in medieval England and Wales*, 2 vols. British Archaeological Reports, British series 80 (London 1980)

———, 'Site changes of Augustinian communities in medieval England and Wales', *Mediaeval Studies* 43 (1981), 425–44

Robinson, P. R. 'The "Booklet", a self-contained unit in composite manuscripts', *Codicologica* 3 (1980), 46–69

———, and Zim, R. ed. *Of the making of books. Medieval manuscripts, their scribes and readers. Essays presented to M. B. Parkes* (Aldershot 1997)

Ross, C. D. and Devine, M. ed. *The cartulary of Cirencester Abbey*, 3 vols. (Oxford 1964–7)

Rosser, G. 'The cure of souls in English towns before 1000' in Blair and Sharpe, ed. (1992), 267–84

Rotuli Chartarum in turri Londinensi asservati 1199–1216, ed. T. D. Hardy, Publications of the Record Commission 25 (London 1837)

Rotuli Litterarum Clausarum in turri Londinensi asservati 1204–1227, ed. T. D. Hardy, 2 vols. (London 1833–44)

Round, J. H. ed. *Ancient charters, royal and private, prior to 1200*, Pipe Roll Society 10 (London 1888)

Rouse, R. H. and Rouse, M. A. *Henry of Kirkestede: Catalogue de libris autenticis et apocrifis*, CBMLC 11 (London 2004)

Salter, H. E. ed. *Chapters of the Augustinian canons*, Canterbury and York Society 29 (London 1922)

———, ed. *The cartulary of Oseney Abbey*, Oxford Historical Society 89–91, 97–8, 101 (Oxford 1929–36)

Sawday, D. 'The post-Roman pottery' in Lucas, ed. (1989), 28–51

———, 'The pottery and medieval floor and ridge tile from excavations at Leicester Abbey (season 4)' in Jones and Buckley, ed. (2004b), 16–24

Sayers, J. E. and Watkiss, L. ed. *Thomas of Marlborough: history of the Abbey of Evesham* Oxford Medieval Texts (Oxford 2003)

Schadla-Hall, R. T., Green, A. and Liddle, P. 'Launde Abbey' in Dix, ed. (2003), 234–71

Schmidt-Künsemüller, F. A. *Die abendländischen romanischen Blindstempeleinbände* (Stuttgart 1985)

Scholla, A. 'Early western limp bindings: report on a study' in Fellows-Jensen and Springborg (2003), 132–58

Seary, P. and Sturgess, J. 'Survey of the precinct walls of Leicester Abbey', unpubl. ULAS report 97–12 (1997)

Shailor, B. A. *The medieval book* (New Haven 1988)

Sharpe, J. L. ed. *Roger Powell: the compleat binder. Liber Amicorum*, Bibliologia 14 (Turnhout 1996)

Sharpe, R. 'Accession, classification, location: shelfmarks in medieval libraries', *Scriptorium* 50 (1996), 279–87

———, *A handlist of the Latin writers of Great Britain and Ireland before 1540* (Turnhout 1997)

———, 'Richard Barre's *Compendium Veteris et Noui Testamenti*', *Journal of Medieval Latin* 14 (2004), 1–16

Simpson, G. G. 'The *Familia* of Roger de Quincy, Earl of Winchester and Constable of Scotland', in Stringer, ed. (Edinburgh 1985), 102–30

Smith, D. 'Assessment of Cavendish House and outbuildings' in Buckley, ed. (1997), 41–65

Smith, T. P. *The medieval brickmaking industry in England 1400–1450* British Archaeological Reports, British series 138 (Oxford 1985)

Soden, I. *Coventry: the hidden history* (Stroud 2005)

Somers, J. ed. *A collection of scarce and valuable tracts*, 2nd edn. revised and enlarged by W. Scott, 13 vols. (London 1809–15)

Skeat, W. W. ed. *The Complete Works of Geoffrey Chaucer*, 7 vols. (Oxford 1899)

Squires, A. and Jeeves, M. *Leicestershire and Rutland woodlands past and present* (Newtown Linford 1994)

St Albans Chronicle 1406–20, ed. V. H. Galbraith (Oxford 1937)

Stirnemann, P. D. 'Où ont été fabriqués les livres de la glose ordinaire dans la première moitié du xiie siècle' in Gasparri, ed. (1994), 257–301

———, 'Historia tripartite: un inventaire des livres de Pierre Lombard, un exemplaire de ses *Sentences* et le destinataire du Psautier de Copenhagen' in Nebbiai Dalla Guarda and Genest, ed. (1998), 301–18

Stohlman, W. F. 'Assembling marks on Limoges champlevé enamels as a basis for classification', *Art Bulletin* 16 (1934), 14–18

Stoneman, W. P. *Dover Priory*, CBMLC 5 (London 1999)

Streeter, B. H. *The chained library* (London 1931)

Stringer, K. J. ed. *Essays on the nobility of medieval Scotland* (Edinburgh 1985)

Sweet, R. 'John Nichols and his circle', *TLAHS* 74 (2000), 1–20

Szirmai, J. A. *The archaeology of medieval bookbinding* (Aldershot 1999)

Taburet-Delahaye, E. 'La naissance de l'emallerie méridionale', in Douar, Petit and Ehm, ed. (2005), 370–7

Thomas of Marlborough: history of the Abbey of Evesham, ed. J. E. Sayers and L. Watkiss, Oxford Medieval Texts (Oxford 2003)

Thompson, A. Hamilton *see* Hamilton Thompson, A.

Thompson, J. 'Proceedings of the central committee', *JBAA* 1 (1846), 237–62

———, 'On Leicester Abbey and its ancient remains', *JBAA* 6 (1851), 116–22

———, *Leicester Abbey: a historical paper* (1855) ROLLR L726

Thomson, R. M. *Manuscripts from St Albans Abbey 1066–1235*, 2 vols. (Woodbridge 1982)

———, *Catalogue of the manuscripts of Lincoln Cathedral Chapter library* (Woodbridge 1989)

———, *A descriptive catalogue of the medieval manuscripts in Worcester Cathedral library* (Cambridge 2001)

Throsby, J. *Select views in Leicestershire* (Leicester 1789)

———, *The history and antiquities of the ancient town of Leicester* (Leicester 1791)

Trenholme, N. *The English monastic boroughs: a study in medieval history* (Columbia, MO, 1927)

Turcheck, J. P. 'A neglected manuscript of Peter Lombard's *Sententiarum* and Parisian illumination of the late twelfth century', *Journal of the Walters Art Gallery* 44 (1986), 48–69

Turner, R. *Ars Notoria: the notory art of Solomon* (London 1657)

Vaughan, R. *Matthew Paris* (Cambridge 1958)

Venn, J. and Venn, J. A. *Alumni Cantabrigienses. A biographical list of all known students, graduates and holders of office at the University of Cambridge, from the earliest times to 1751*, 4 vols. (Cambridge 1922–5)

Vezin, J. 'Une reliure carolingienne de cuir souple (Oxford, Bodleian Library, Marshall 19)', *Revue française d'histoire du livre* 36 (1982), 235–41

———, 'Une reliure souple en cuir souple estampé du xiiie siècle (Paris, Bibliothèque Nationale, lat. 6637A)', *Revue française d'histoire du livre* 36 (1982), 243–9

———, 'Le vocabulaire Latin de la reliure au moyen age' in Weijers, ed. (1989), 56–60

———, '"Quaderni simul ligati": Recherches sur les manuscrits en cahiers' in Robinson and Zim, ed. (1997), 64–70

Vincent, N. 'The early years of Keynsham Abbey', *Transactions of the Bristol and Gloucestershire Archaeological Society* 111 (1993), 95–113

Wager, S. J. *Woods, wolds and groves: the woodland of medieval Warwickshire*, British Archaeological Reports, British series 269 (Oxford 1998)

Walther, H. ed. *Initia carminum ac versuum medii aevi posterioris latinorum* (Göttingen 1959)

Ward, H. L. D. and Herbert, J. A. *Catalogue of romances in the department of manuscripts in the British Museum*, 3 vols. (London 1883–1910)

Watson, A. G. 'Thomas Allen of Oxford and his manuscripts' in Parkes and Watson, ed. (1978), 279–314

———, *Catalogue of dated and datable manuscripts c. 435–1600 in Oxford libraries*, 2 vols. (Oxford 1984)

———, 'The manuscript collection of Sir Walter Cope', *Bodleian Library Record* 12 (1985–8), 262–97

———, ed. *Medieval libraries of Great Britain, supplement* (London 1987)

Watt, D. E. R. and Murray, A. L. ed. *Fasti Ecclesiae Scoticanae medii aevi ad annum 1638*, Scottish Record Society, new series 25 (rev. edn. Edinburgh 2003)

Wattenbach, W. *Das Schriftwesen im Mittelalter* (3rd edn. Leipzig 1896)

Webb, C. C. I. ed. *Iohannis Saresberiensis episcopi Carnotensis Policratici*, 2 vols (Oxford 1909)

Webber, T. 'Latin devotional texts and the books of the Augustinian canons of Thurgarton Priory and Leicester Abbey in the late middle ages' in Carley and Tite, ed. (1997), 27–41

———, and Watson, A. G. *The libraries of the Augustinian canons*, CBMLC 6 (London 1998)

Weijers, O. ed. *Vocabulaire du livre et de l'écriture au Moyen Age* (Turnhout 1989)

Welding, J. D. ed. *Leicestershire in 1777: an edition of John Prior's map of Leicestershire*, Leicestershire Libraries and Information Service (Leicester 1984)

Whitcomb, N. R. *The medieval floor tiles of Leicestershire* (Leicester 1956)

White, W. *History, gazetteer and directory of Leicestershire and the small county of Rutland* (Sheffield 1846)

Wigram, S. R. ed. *The cartulary of the monastery of St Frideswide at Oxford*, Oxford Historical Society 28, 31 (Oxford 1895–6)

Wilkinson, D. and McWhirr, A. ed. *Cirencester Anglo-Saxon church and medieval abbey* (Cirencester 1998)

William Senior's survey of estates of 1st and 2nd Earls of Devonshire c. 1600–1628, ed. D. V. Fowkes and G. R. Potter, Derbyshire Record Society 13 (Chesterfield 1988)

Williamson, T. 'The history of Abbey Park' in 'Abbey Park Restoration Management Plan' III, Leicester City Council unpubl. report (1997), 1–33

Williman, D. and Corsano, K. 'Medieval Latin manuscripts in Scotland: some provenances', *Edinburgh Bibliographical Society Transactions* 6/5 (2002), 178–90

Willmott, H. *Early post-medieval vessel glass in England c. 1500–1650*, Council for British Archaeology, research report 132 (York 2002)

Wilton, A. *The life and works of J. M. W. Turner* (London 1979)

Winckley, S. T. 'Excursion to Houghton on the Hill, Ingarsby and Quenby', *TLAAS* 10 (1911–12), 254–6

Wood, I. N. and Loud, G. A. ed. *Church and chronicle in the middle ages: essays presented to John Taylor* (London 1991)

Wood, M. *The English medieval house* (London 1965, reprinted 1971)

Woodfield, P. 'Midland yellows', *West Midlands Pottery Research Group Newsletter* 2 (1984)

Wood-Jones, R. B. *Traditional domestic architecture in the Banbury region* (Manchester 1963)

Woodland, R. 'The pottery', in Mellor and Pearce, ed. (1981), 81–129

Wooley, R. M. *Catalogue of the manuscripts of Lincoln Cathedral Chapter library* (Oxford 1927)

Wormsley Library, exh. cat. (Pierpont Morgan Library: New York 1999)

Wright, C. E. *Fontes Harleiani* (London 1972)

Yoshitake, K. 'The arrest of the bishops in 1139 and its consequences', *Journal of Medieval History* 14 (1988) 97–114

Zarnecki, G., Holt, J. and Holland, T. *English Romanesque art 1066–1200* (The Hayward Gallery: London 1984)

Index of manuscripts

Cambridge, King's College 2: 134 (fig. 1), 145, 173–4

Cambridge, Queens' College 2: 134, 136, 146, 147, 169–70 (figs 4 and 5), 174-5 (figs 1 and 2)
———, 5: 146, 153
———, 6: 146, 153
———, 7: 146
———, 8: 134–6 (figs 3 and 5), 146, 147, 151, 168 (fig. 3), 169–70 (fig. 4), 174–5
———, 9: 146
———, 10: 146

Cambridge, Pembroke College 119: 159 (fig. 2)

Cambridge, St John's College E 29: 155, 172

Cambridge, Trinity College B.1.8: 137–8 (figs 6 and 7), 146, 176
———, B.2.16: 140, 143, 145, 178
———, B.2.22: 136, 146, 176–7 (figs 3–4)
———, B.3.27: 136, 146, 176, 178 (figs 5–6)
———, B.14.7: 135 (fig. 4), 140, 142–4, 146, 164, 178
———, B.14.30: colour plate E, 138 (fig. 8), 146, 149, 178–9 (fig. 7)
———, B.16.5: 136, 146, 149, 179–81 (figs 8–11)
———, O.2.40: 144–5
———, O.9.38: ix

Cambridge, University Library II.6.6: 187

Chatsworth, the Devonshire Collection, The William Senior Leicester Abbey Map: colour plate B, 14, 15, 17, 20, 21, 24, 25, 63, 75–7, 81–5, 89, 91–4

Derby Record Office D258/20/2/7: 98

Durham, Dean and Chapter Library C.iv.29: 189

Edinburgh, National Library of Scotland, Advocates 18.5.13 ff. 1–47: 134 (fig. 2), 146, 181

Hereford, Hereford Cathedral Library O.i.4: 154
———, P.iv.3: 153

Hereford, Dean and Chapter Archives 1448A: 153

Lincoln, Lincoln Cathedral Chapter Library 31: 153

Lincoln, Lincolnshire Archives, Visitation Book vj I: 219–20 (fig. 1)

London, British Library Add. 31826: 261
———, Add. 32050: 156

———, Add. 40165: 159
———, Add. 57533: 136, 145, 182
———, Add. 63077: 153
———, Cotton Claudius E iii: 120, 145, 183
———, Cotton Galba E iii, ff. 83–173: 145, 182, 185
———, Cotton Julius C vii: 243
———, Cotton Nero D x, ff. 140–97: 145, 182–3, 226
———, Cotton Tiberius C vii: 120–1 (fig. 1), 144, 145, 183, 228
———, Cotton Vitellius F xvii: 145, 183, 226, 234
———, Egerton 2900: 172
———, Harley 84: 241, 245. 252, 257
———, Harley 782: 243
———, Harley 913: x
———, Harley 3509: 187
———, Harley 6748: 241, 245
———, Harley 7333: 145–6, 189–90 (fig. 20)
———, Royal 2 C.viii: 165
———, Royal 15 A.vi: 157
———, Sloane ch. xxxii.22: 136, 192 (fig. 22), 225, 227, 249–50 (fig. 1)

London, Lambeth Palace Library 232: 172
———, 343: 165
———, 363: 187

London, Society of Antiquaries 154: 172

Munich, Bayerische Staatsbibliothek Clm 849: 222

New Haven, Yale University, Beinecke Library 494: 172
———, Marston 24: 158
———, Marston 262: 154

Oxford, Bodleian Library Bodley 57: x, 145, 190–1
———, Bodley 636: 191 (fig. 21)
———, Laud misc. 623: x, 127–33, 137, 139–40, 143, 145, 150, 182, 183–5 (fig. 12), 220
———, Laud misc. 625: x–xi, 76, 86, 134, 144, 145, 160, 183–4, 185–6 (fig. 13), 195, 197, 201, 225–6, 228, 231–2, 234, 236, 237, 239, 241, 241, 243, 245, 246, 247, 248, 254, 255, 260, 269, 286
———, Rawlinson A 445: 134, 145, 147, 186
———, Rawlinson C 153: 136, 146, 186–7 (figs 14–15)

Oxford, Corpus Christi College 206: 153

Oxford, Jesus College 6: 159
———, 18: 159

Record Office for Leicestershire, Leicester and Rutland 28D64/12: 90
———, CM28/7: 11, 13
———, DE2897/8: 22

————, DE5463/38: 101
————, DE6218/1: 10, 25, 59
————, DE6218/3: 10, 25
————, Flower sketchbook; 18, 20
————, Henton Collection: 18
————, L914.2 Cable Collection; 4, 5

Shrewsbury School xxxi: 187

Sotheby's 19.vi.2001 lot 3: 187

Stockholm, Kungliga Biblioteket Isl. perg. 4°15: 159

The National Archives (TNA), Augmentation office, 4 Edw VI,
    section 3: 15, 96
————, C 52/22: 241, 245
————, C 53/1: 247
————, C 53/5: 252
————, C 53/6: 252
————, C 53/18: 257
————, C 53/45: 267
————, C 53/104: 239, 257
————, C 53/123: 239
————, C 54/1361: 98
————, C 56: 227
————, C 56/16: 239, 248, 256, 258, 269, 284, 285
————, C 56/27; 239, 258, 284, 285
————, DL 42/7: 159
————, E 13/76: 227, 234, 236, 239, 242, 243, 245, 246, 248, 249, 254,
    255, 256, 257, 258, 259, 260, 262, 263, 264, 265, 266, 267, 268, 269,
    270, 271, 272, 273, 274, 275, 276, 277, 278, 279, 280, 281, 282, 283, 284,
    285, 286, 287
————, E 101/14/22: 156
————, E 101/368/27: 156, 158
————, E 159/12: 268
————, E 159/20: 258
————, E 159/23: 260
————, E 159/25: 260

————, E 164/9: 152
————, E 326/3488: 268
————, E 368/4: 286
————, KB 26/149: 268
————, JUST 1/456: 281
————, JUST 1/1400: 244
————, SC 12/10/11: 3, 67

Uppsala Universitetsbibliothek C 222: 153

Vatican City, Biblioteca Apostolica Vaticana, Borghese lat. 57: 189

Versailles, Archives départementales des Yvelines 24 h 9: 229

Washington, Library of Congress, Rosenwald 1: 172

Winchester, Winchester Cathedral Library xxB: 234

Worcester, Worcester Cathedral Library Q.7: 153
————, F.12: 153
————, F.40: 153
————, F.69: 172
————, F.70: 154
————, F.87: 172
————, F.111: 154
————, F.144: 154
————, Q.39: 155
————, Q.44: 156, 159
————, Q.52: 155
————, Q.75: 153
————, Q.78: 156
————, Q.78a: 156

Wormsley, J. P. Getty s.n.: 153

York, York Minster xvi.m.6: colour plate F, 134, 136, 146, 160, 187–8
    (figs 16–18)
————, xvi.m.7: 136, 146, 160, 189 (fig. 19)

Index of medieval people and places

Index personarum

Note: spelling follows the orthography of the texts. Sixteenth- and seventeenth-century names are included.

Abbé, Geoffrey l' 243
Abeus, son of Hugo de Bedeford 238
Adam, abbot of Garendon 253
Adam, deacon of Bulkington 247
Adam, son of William son of Godfrid 254
Adeliza, wife of Hugh of Arden 244, 245
Agnes, daughter of Yvo of Cossington 257
Agnes, daughter of William son of Lusce 282
Agulin, Roger 244
Alan 'ad gardinum' 280, 282
Alan, son of Christopher 265, 267, 273, 275, 279
   Christopher of Syston 275
Alan, son of Robert 249, 252
Alby, daughter of Henry 206
Aldith, William 204
Alexander, 'dispensator' 245
Alexander III, pope 241, 242
Alexander, bishop of Lincoln 230, 234, 235, 249
Alexander, son of Simon 'sacerdos' de Aula 264
Alfwin, Robert 255
Alger, William 264
Alice, sister of Robert son of Henry of Bramcote 281
Alice, wife of Elias de Lindsey 258
Allen, Thomas 145, 182
Allesley, Iuo de 242
Alnaia, Hugh de 240
Alnath, William 273, 279
Alneio, William de 251
Alneto, Thomas de, 'dominus' 'miles' 258
Alnwick, William, bishop of Lincoln 131, 141, 217, 218, 223, 224
Alpius, G. 73
Alwalton, Robert de 256
Alwyn, Hugh 264
Amice, countess of Leicester 83, 137, 235, 238, 238, 240, 243, 247, 251
Amphelys, Robert 201
Ancoats, Joan/John de 215
Ansty, Christine de 199, 211
Arabi, Robert 240
Arden, Henry of 246
Arden, Hugh of 226, 239, 240, 244, 245, 246
Arden, Osbert of 259
Arden, Siward of 245

Arden, Thomas I of 226, 246
Arden, Thomas II of 226, 254, 255
Arden, William of 247
Argenteem, Richard de 258
Armerer, Robert le 211
Arrabi, Ralph 260
   Arrebi, Ralph 262
Asfordby, Richard de 245
Asheby, John de 201
Asheby, William de 203
Asty, Canon Thomas 142, 218, 222, 223, 224
Attemaydnes, John 202
Atthall', Robert 214
   Atthalle 215
Attwater, William, bishop of Lincoln 72
Aubeni, Oliver de 248-9, 252
Aubeni, Philip de 248, 252
Aula, Mathew de 266
Aula, Robert de 260
Aula, Simon de 256, 264, 265, 266
Aula, William de 286
Aumblere, Robert 202
Auneia, William de 240
Aungerville, Sir Roger 140
Aurifaber, William 205
Aveline, wife of Robert 238
Avenel, William 232, 239, 240
Aveline, wife of Robert 238
Ayleston, William de 201

Baker, Walter 202
B., 'vicarius' of Bulkington 269
Bacheler, Robert 251, 252, 253
Baggrave, Richard Dreng de 270
Baggrave, William de 270
Baldewyne, Anselm 203
Baldewyne, William 202, 209
Baldock, Ralph, bishop of London 218
B[aldwin], archbishop of Canterbury 246
Balfour, Sir James 146
Balle, William 206
Banastre, William 223
Bangor, bishop of *see* Pexall
Bara, Richer de la 243
Barewell, Robert de 255
Barfoot, Arthur 2, 3
Barkby, Gerard de 265
Barkby, Henry de 205
Barkby, Hugh 'vicarius' de 269, 272
Barkby, John le Wyte son of Walter le Wyte, de 265

Barkby, John 133
Barkby, Ralph de 264
Barkby, Richard de 209
Barkby, Robert Haliday de 265, 271
Barkby, Roger de, 'clericus' 276, 283, 286-7
Barkby, Walter Herbert de 272, 283, 285
   Barkby, Walter son of William Herbert de 269
Barkby, William de 202
Barkby, William de 276
   'capellanus' 264, 265, 266
   'sacerdos' 264
Barkby, William 'de dispensa de' 287
Barkby Thorpe, Alan de 287
Barkby Thorpe, William Poer de 265, 269, 271, 272, 283, 286, 287
Barkby Thorpe, Walter Geraud de 265
Barkby Thorpe, William de la Despense de 265
Barkby Thorpe, William Geraud de 265, 269
Barker, Walter 202, 208, 209
Barkere, Geoffrey 209
Barkere, John son of Hugh le 207
Barnesby, Alice de 203
Barnwell, Agnes de 199, 211
Barre, Hugh, archdeacon of Leicester 137, 242, 259, 279
   'magister' 282, 284
Barre, Richard 137, 155, 190
Barre, William 239, 240
Barrow, Ralph de 279
Barrow, William, 'vicarius' of 266
Bartholomew 256
Bartholomew, 'iuvenis' 270
Barton, Ralph de 210
Barton, Rychardus 174
Basil, Robert, 'capellanus' 274, 279
Basset, Alice 261
Basset, Ralph, 'dominus', 'miles' 268
Basset, Richard 283
Basset, William, sheriff of Leicestershire 238, 244
Basset, William, 'dominus' 'miles' 270
Bath and Wells, bishop of *see* Jocelin
Bathe, Thomas 141
Bawdewyn, W. 202
Bayeux, bishop of *see* Philip
Baylli, Ralph le 204
Beaumont family 99
Beaumont, Robert de 286

Becheston, Simon de 247
Beckard, John, 'dominus' 'miles' 285
    Becard, 'dominus' 'miles' 286
Becket, Thomas, archbishop of Canterbury
    70
Bedford, Hugh de 238
Belet, Michael 247
Belgrave, Canon 223
Belgrave, Richard 89
Belgrave, Simon son of Ivo de 267
Belgrave, William de 248, 269
Belgrave, William de 207
Beller, Roger 270
Bena, Godwin 239, 240, 251
Bene, William le 213
Benedict, abbot of Peterborough 246
Benedict XII, pope 139
Bercher, Robert le 280, 281
Bernard, Edward 146
Bernard, 'magister' 238
Bernard, prior of Kiningeuurde
    (Kenilworth?) 235
Biset, Manesserus 241
Bitteswell, William de 272
Blaby, Geoffrey Orm de 286
Blaby, Hugh de 238
Blaby, John 132
Blaby, Ralph de 243
Blanchard, Nicholas 202
Blanchard, Robert 255
Blancharde, Cecily 201
Blisse, William 211
Blois, William of, bishop of Lincoln 248,
    249, 252
Blound, William 202, 204
Blynde, John 214
Blysse, Roger 206
Bois, Arnold III du 229, 230, 234
    Bosco, Ernaldus de 235, 238, 240, 242,
    251
Bois, Arnold VI du 261
    'dominus' 'miles' 268
Bokedene, John 142, 220
Bordigny, Reginald de 235, 238, 240
Bordigny, Roger de 240
Borer, Emma 199, 211
Boresworth, Henry de 208, 209
Borhog, Stephen 214
Bosco, William de, 'dominus' 'miles' 259,
    285
Bosworth, Robert of 239, 240
Bourchier, John, abbot of Leicester 95
Bracken, Ranulf de 286
Bramcote, Gilbert Lucas de 283
Bramcote, Luke de 281, 283
Bramcote, Robert de, 'bercarius' 282, 283
Bramdoon, Thomas de 211
Bramley, William de 213
Brandon 212
Branteston, Adam de 245
Brantiston', John de 202
Braosa, William de 253
Bray, Roger de 260
Brecce, Thomas le 281
Breser, Hugh de la 273
Bret, Ranulf 283
Bret, Thomas le 280, 281
Breteuil, Robert de 243, 244
Brian, 'forestarius' 258, 259

Bristol, Walter de 258, 259, 260, 266
Briwerre, William 253
Brixworth, John de 286
Bromwich, Alan de 244, 245, 247
Broughton, William de 205
Bruce, Christian 98
Bruill, Simon de 268
Brunne, Robert 21
Brun, Reginald 275
Bryde, Robert 206
Buck, brothers 31, 34, 38, 39, 93, 94, 98, 101,
    108, 110, 112, 115, 116, 117
Buffe, Roger 258, 259
Buhun, Henry de, earl of Hereford 253
Burdet, William, 'magister' 255
Burgey, Nicholas 205
Burgeys, John 207
Burgeys, N. 207
Burgh, Hubert de, earl of Kent 257
Burscena, William de 205
Burstall, Clement de 213
Burstall, Gilbert 'presbiter' de 267
Burstall, Henry de 211
Burstall, Robert de 270, 285
    Robert son of Allan 267
    'magister' 279
Burstall, Robert de 212
Burton Overy, Edith de 203
Burton Overy, Robert of 239, 240
Burton Overy, Robert Freman of 280
Busby, heirs of Walter de 204
Butemunt, Hugh de 255
Byg, William 219, 222
Byset, Henry 258
    Byseth 'dominus' 'miles' 259

Cagge, John 205
Camera, Hugh de 203
Camera, Simon de 203
Camfield, Benjamin 222
Campanar', Stephen 208
Camped, Richard de 279
Canterbury, archbishop of see Baldwin,
    Becket, Hubert
Cantilupo, William de 253
Capella, Henry de 257
Cardula, Albert de 244
Carpentar', Richard 210
Carte, Samuel 3
Carter, William 202
Castel, Robert 205
Catere, Thomas, 'miles' 215
Cave, Sir Francis 82, 91, 95, 96, 97
Cavendish family 1, 4, 9, 13, 14, 16, 17, 19,
    21, 27, 28, 35, 36, 38, 78, 82, 83, 85, 92,
    93, 98, 100, 101, 103, 104, 108, 109, 112,
    116, 117
Cavendish, William, first earl of
    Devonshire 14, 75, 96, 98, 99, 101
Cavendish, William, second earl of
    Devonshire 98
Cavendish, William, third earl of
    Devonshire 98
Chamburleyn, Ralph, 'senescallus' 286
Charles I, king 101
Charley, Robert de 283
Charley, William de 255, 259
Chartres, bishop of see Salisbury
Chartlett, Dr 3

Charyte, William, prior of Leicester 38, 84,
    86, 128, 129, 130, 132, 134, 141, 143, 144,
    145, 147, 149, 150, 156, 157, 159, 162, 163,
    164, 165, 181, 182, 183, 184, 185, 186, 197,
    220, 225, 226, 227, 228, 234
Chaucer, Geoffrey 189, 218, 220
Chaumunt, William de, 'dominus' 'miles'
    259
Chede, Richard 211
Chereby, William de 243
Chesham Bois, Nicholas de 249
Chesney, Robert de, bishop of Lincoln 238
Chetwynd, Philip de, 'dominus' 'miles' 286
Chichester, bishop of see Simon
Chiffrewast, Robert de 239, 240
Chiffrewast, William de 239, 240
Choloun, Walter 205
Cirre, Adam de 235
Clement, Henry 242
Cleu, Adam 272
Cleu, Robert 272
Cley, Richard de 270
Cloune, (Clowne) William, abbot of
    Leicester 15, 24, 38, 120, 139, 141
Clounham, William de 206
Cnotte, Roger 287
Cockerham, Adam de 199, 212, 213
Cockerham, John de 269, 270, 279, 281
Cockerham, Reginald de 284
Cockerham, William de 199, 213
Cockowh', William 209
Cocus, Herbert 259
Cocus, John 208
Cocus, Richard 205
Cocus, Simon 256
Cocus, William 254, 266
Cocus, William 208
Coddington, Roger de 211
Cokenbred, Richard 208
Cole, Henry 271
Coleshull, Simon de 263
Colstone, Thomas 219
Comyn, William 212
Cope, Walter 191
Cossby, Ralph 145
    Cosseby 174
Cossington, Richard de 202
Costein, Ralph 264
Coten, Roger de 286
Cotes, Robert of 239, 241
Cotton, Sir Robert 145
Coureyour', Simon 205
Coventry, John de 281, 283
Coventry, William de, 'parmentarius' 280
Cranford, Geoffrey de 252, 279
Cranford, John de, 'senescallus' 247, 258,
    259, 286
Cranford, Richard de 206
Cranford, Roger de 235, 243, 244, 247
Cranford, Roger de 201
Craxton, Milo de 266
Crayke, Thomas de 259
Creft, Anschetillus de 242
Creft, John de, 'capellanus' 247
Croft, Geoffrey de 235, 239, 240
Croft, Ralph de 243
Croft, Robert de 239, 242, 244
Cromber, Adam 213
Cromwell, Thomas 95

Cropston, William de 210
Crouchback, Edward 119
Curdworth, Mathew de 255
Curdworth, Nicholas de, 'clericus' 247
  'capellanus' 254
Curleuache, Geoffrey 203
Curteys, William 143, 280, 281
Cute, Roger, son of Roger of Bosworth
  239, 240

Dalby, Geoffrey of 239, 240
Daneth, William 260
Daubeney, William 201
Daventry, John de 206
Denton, William de, 'clericus' 259
Devonshire, countess of 2, 6
Diker', William le 207
Dodeman, John 275
  Dudeman 285
Dodeman, Matilda 273
Dole, Robert 207
Donington, William de 206
Doucepeper', William 203
Doveland, William de 210
Dunham, Hugo de 242
Dunmow, Matilda de 199, 214
Dunt', Mathew de, 'miles' 247, 255
Durham, bishop of see Puiset
Dyngelee, Helen de 199, 211
Dyua, William de 255

Eastleigh, Thomas de 248, 249, 262
  'dominus', 'miles' 268, 270
Eaton, Robert de 213
Edith, widow 205
Edmund, 'magister' 238
Edward II, king 120
Edward III, king 96, 120, 122, 123, 124, 197,
  201
Edward VI, king 174
Edward, 'presbiter' 256
Edward, the 'Black Prince' 120
Eleanor (of Aquitaine), queen 244
Elizabeth I, queen 83, 96, 97, 186
Elmete, Thomas 215
Ely, bishop of see Longchamps, Nigel
Emelot, Adam 201
Emma, wife of Geoffrey l'Abbé 243
Enderby, Christopher de 203
Enderby, John de 206
Enderby, Robert de 206
Envermeu, William de 239, 240
Ernaldus, Christian, 'de camera' 242
Ernaldus, 'iunior' 235
Essex, Henry of, 'constabularius' 241
Eugenius III, pope 235, 236
Eustace, bishop of London 257
Eustace, brother of Roger 'forestarius', son
  of Hugh 254
Evesham, Nicholas of 161, 166
Evington, Gerard de 270
Evington, John de 274
Evington, Walter de 269, 270, 281, 283, 284,
  285
Evington, wife of J. de 206

Faber, John 208
Falkener, John le 287
Fatte, John 211

Fauconer, Robert le 272
Faucuner, William le 268
Ferrant, Gilbert 255
Fischer, W. 205
Flandr', Simon 208
Fleming, Gruellus le 249
Fode, Ralph 203
Fole, W. 213
Foleville, Eustace de 259
  'miles' 263
Foleville, John de 204
Foleville, William de 259
Fouk', William 206
Fox, Euphemia 223
Fox, Richard 212
Foxton, William de 203
Franceys, Robert 286
Fraxinum, Robert ad 283
Freman 203
Freman, William le 208
Fremnel, Richard 235
Fridai, John 258
Friday, Ralph 239, 272
  Fridai 240, 251
Furmentin, William 249

Galby, Thurstan de 273, 274, 275-6
Galby, William de 278
Galeys. J. 204
Gamelin 262
Gamellus 260
Gardin, Robert 264
Gardiner', Richard de le 201
Gardiner', Robert le 201, 212
Gaule, John 221
Gaunt, John of, duke of Lancaster 1, 5, 6,
  7, 9, 119, 122, 123, 124, 125
Genus, William 284
Geoffrey, son of Gilbert of Burstall 284
Geoffrey, father of Robert of Croft 242
Geoffrey, son of Peter 247
Geoffrey, son of Peter, earl of Essex 252,
  253
Geoffrey, abbot, son of Ralph 'pincerna'
  235, 238
Geoffrey l'Abbé 243
Gerald 264
Gerard, Walter 272
Geraud, John 269
Geraud, Walter 269
Geroud, John 271
Geroud, Walter 271
Gervase 260, 262
Gervase, son of Robert 238
Gervase, son of Turgis 238
Geryn 195, 197, 201
Geryn, Helen 209
Geryn, Margaret 207
Geryn, William 209
Gilbert, father of William of Lancaster
  244
Gilbert, 'medicus' 252
Gileville, H. de, 'magister' 248
Gilofr' 202
Glenfield, Isabel de 272, 279
Glide, Roger 211
Glide, Simon 267
Glovere, Richard 214
Godehewer, Ralph 213

Goditha, mother of William of Lancaster
  244
Golci, Walter 249
Gold, John 211
Gower, John 189
Grandmesnil, Hugh de 228
Great Easton, Henry de, 'clericus' 247
Gregorius, 'capellanus' 252, 253
Gregori, William 210, 212
Grene, Robert 220
Grescote, William de 204
Grey, Lady Jane, queen 96
Grim, William 262, 263, 286
  Grym 258
Groby, Robert de 207
Grodye, Felicia 199, 212
Grosmont, Henry of, duke of Lancaster
  119, 122, 123, 124
Gryffyn 208
Gubert, dean of Leicester Abbey 229, 230,
  234, 235, 251
Guisborough, Walter of 120
Gumfredus, 'presbiter' 238
Gumfridus, 'capellanus' 252
Gundreda, wife of William of Lancaster
  237, 244

H[ugh] de Puiset, bishop of Durham 246
H., prior of Warwick 253
H., Ralph de 259
Haldenby, Alice de 208
Halom, Thomas 141
Haluemar', Helen 199, 211
Hamilton, Gerard de 272, 287
Hamo, 'clericus' 249
Hamwise, wife of John Faber 208
Harcurt, Ivo de 238
Harcurt, Robert de 252
Hardwick, Elizabeth, countess of
  Shrewsbury 98, 101
Harpeur, Richard le 279
Harpur, Thomas le 281, 286
Hasloe, John 3
Hastings family 1, 14, 83, 99, 101, 105, 108
Hastings, Sir Edward, Lord Loughborough
  83, 97, 98, 101
Hastings, Sir Edward, brother of earl of
  Huntingdon 98, 101
Hastings, Henry, earl of Huntingdon 83,
  97, 98, 101, 105
Hastings, Henry, son of Edward 98
Hastyng, Richard 138
Hathern, Agnes de 199, 215
Hatton, Sir Christopher 83, 91, 97, 117
Havering atte Bowe, Richard de, 'dominus'
  'miles' 270
Haye, John de la, 'dominus' 'miles' 270
Haywode, Nicholas de 212
Helen, wife of Roger of Cranford 247
Heloise, wife of Hugh de Launay 239, 240
Hendeman, Nicholas 204
Henry I, king 228, 229, 234
Henry II, king 83, 84, 231, 232, 237, 238,
  239, 241, 242, 243, 244, 247, 251, 253,
  261
Henry III, king 83, 119, 257, 263, 269
Henry IV (Bolingbroke), King 119, 124, 140,
  143, 145, 178
Henry VIII, king 91, 92, 96, 225

Henry, abbot of Leicester 271, 272, 283
Henry, brother of Hugh of Arden 244, 245
Henry, brother of Stephen of Seagrave 256
Henry, 'bercharius' 285
Henry, 'clericus' 272, 278, 283
   'clericus abbatis' 284
Henry, duke of Lancaster 87, 91
Henry, son of Simon de Wigginton 284
Henry, son of William Lusse 263, 264
Herberd, William 270
Herbert 264
Herbert, Walter 271
   Herberd 272
Herbert, William 264
Herci, John de 262
Hereberd, William 266
Hereford, Robert de, 'dominus' 'miles' 285
Heriz, Robert le 244
Herle, W., 'dominus' 205
Hexham, Walter 212
Higden, Ranulph 120
Hinckley, Reginald Shirloc de 283
Hinckley, Robert de, 'magister' 280
Hinckley, William de, 'clericus' 283
Hingwareby, John de 266
Hoccleve, Thomas 189
Holand, Sir Robert de, 'dominus' 201
Holgate, Robert de 276, 277
Houby, Emma de 206
Houchel, Henry 202
Houchl', Letice 205
Houchl', Robert son of Henry 205
Houma, Roger de 245
Howby, Richard de 206
Hubert, archbishop of Canterbury 247, 252
Hubert, John 280, 281
Hucbert, archdeacon of York 246
Hugh, 'aucupe' 238
Hugh, 'clericus' 253
Hugh, 'faber' 275, 276
Hugh, 'presbiter' 256
Hugh, 'sacerdos' 256
Hugh, son of Thurstan 271
Humberstone, John Eventon de 287
Humberstone, William Casteline de 287
Humez, Richard de, 'constabularius' 241
Humfrey, Richard 271
Hungarton, Peter de 266
Huscher, Richard le 201
Hyde, John de 281, 282

Inglod, Alice 206
Ingram, William 130
Innocent III, pope 4, 10, 72, 137, 182
Iohi, John de 235
Ipsley, Henry de, 'forestarius' 254, 255
Ireland, Robert of 266
Isabel, countess of Meulan 235
Iseult, daughter of Peter son of Thurstan
   of Barkby 271, 272
Ithell, Geoffrey 190

Jackson, Henry 145, 191
James I, king 98
Jekyll, Sir Joseph 187, 190
Joan, wife of Arnold vi du Bois 261
Joan, wife of Becke 206
Jocelin, bishop of Bath and Wells 257
John, king 83, 247, 248, 252

John 238
John, Archdeacon 248
John, 'aurifaber' 266
John, 'cementarius' 273, 274, 275, 279
John, 'homo' of the abbot of Leicester 243
John, 'monachus tunc senescallus' of the
   earl of Winchester 258
John, 'scriptor' 238
John, son of Paul 264
John, son of Ketelbern (see also Ketelbern,
   John) 258
   of Thurmaston 267
John, son of Lewyne of Thurmaston 276,
   277
John, brother of Robert son of Isabel of
   Bramcote 282
John, son of William son of Avice of
   Thurmaston 277, 278
Joie, Hugh 260, 262
Jordan, 'clericus comitis' 248
John, son of Lewyn 274
Jordan, son of William of Lancaster 244
Joscelin, 'marscaldus' 251
Josselin, Ralph 101

Kair, William de 244
Kegworth, R. 133
Kelyng, Henry 206
Kelyng, John 204
Kelyng, Robert 206
Keman, William de 286
Kendal, William of Lancaster, lord of 232
Kent 202
Kent, David de 208
Kenteis, John le 247
Kenton, Phillip de 256, 264
Ketelbern, Adam 272
   Adam son of John son of Ketelbern of
     Thurmaston 285
Ketelbern, John (see also John, son of
   Ketelbern) 265, 272, 273, 274, 275, 276,
   279, 283
   of Thurmaston 276, 277, 278
   son of William Ketelbern of
     Thurmaston 272
   Ketilbern 274
Ketelbern, William 284
   William son of John son of Ketelbern of
     Thurmaston 285
Kilby, Roger de 256
Kilby, William of 239, 240, 259
Kiningeuurde (Kenilworth?), Bernard prior
   of 235
Kinloss, Lord 98
Kirby, Robert de 248
Kirby, William of 239
Kirkham, Richard de 259
Kirkstead, Henry of 143
Knaptoft, Nicholas de 242
Knighton, Henry 89, 91, 119, 120, 122, 123,
   124, 125, 137, 139, 141, 144, 145, 183, 227
Knyttecotte, John 202
Kokerch, John de 286
Kulewen, Gilbert, 'dominus' 'miles' 286
Kydeman, Andrew 270
Kyrke, Richard 285
Labbé, Geoffrey 243
Labbé, Richard 239, 240, 241
Ladbroke, William de 239, 240

Ladde, Alice 199, 215
Lancaster, William de 237, 239, 241, 244
Langeford, William de 244
Langton, William de 248
Latoner, Richard le 214
Lauda, Helen de 199, 215
Lauda, Richard de 215
Launay, Hugh de 239, 240
Launay, William de 238, 240
Laurence, son of William, son of Leueric
   263, 278
Lavener, Gilbert 204
Lawrence, John 89
Lawrence, Steven 89
Leamington, Osbert of 239, 240
Leia, Rodbert Blund de la 256
Leicester, abbot of 197, 198, 199, 200
Leicester, earl of 195, 201
Leicester, Robert de, 'clericus' 280, 283
Leigh, Robert de 266
Leland, John 24, 76
Leticia, daughter of William Thase 263
Leuns, Mathew de 244
Leveriche, John 202
Lewesfrey, William 262
Lilbourne, Henry de 258, 259, 262, 263,
   264, 266
Lilbourne, Hugh de 280, 282
Lincoln, bishop of 195, 198, 219
   see also Alexander, Alnwick, Attwater,
     Blois, Chesney, Repyngdon, Robert,
     Wells
Lincoln, Henry de 281
Lincoln, Peter de, son of Thomas de
   Lincoln 262, 270
Lincoln, Thomas de 259, 260, 266
   'dominus' 264
Lindsey, Elias de 258, 263, 268
Lira, Richard de, 'cellerarius' 248
Loges, Hugh de 263, 264
Lokynton, Walter de 255, 256
London, bishop of 218
   see also Baldock, Eustace
Longchamps, Stephen de 248
Longchamps, William de, bishop of Ely
   246
Lord, William 202
Loreta, Countess 252
Loughborough, Geoffrey de 273, 279
   'clericus' 275, 277, 278
Loveman, Hugh 202
Lucy, Richard de 241
Luda, Thomas de, 'magister' 269, 270, 284
Luke, 'carpentarius' 282
Luke, 'clericus comitis' 248, 249, 252
Luuell', William, 'servus' 253
Lydgate 189

Macʒon, Ralph 203
Macʒon, William le 210, 213
Magot, William 275
   de Thurmaston 278
Makepays, J. 206
Malerba 238
Malesin, Fraerius 252
Malhoret, Richard 251
Mallore (Mallory), Anschetil 244
Mallore (Mallory), Radulf 252
Mallori (Mallory), Richard 240

Malthous, Robert de 214
Mann, Thomas de, 'magister' 259
Manners, Sir John 101
Manyatin, William 269
Map, Walter, archdeacon of Oxford 248
Marcham, Nicholas de 286
Marescald, Jocelinus 251
Mareshall, Henry 215
Mareshall', Robert 214
Margaret, countess of Winchester 258
Margaret, daughter of Gundreda 244
Margaret, granddaughter of Earl Robert III
    of Leicester 83
Marigny, Hugh de 253
Marmiun, Richard 254
    Marmyun 254, 255
Marshal, Joscelin 84, 238, 240
Marshal, William, earl of Pembroke 247
Marshall, William 145, 182
Marston, Henry de 261
Marston, John de 269
Marston, Robert le Mathuy de 281
Martival, Radulf de 240, 252
Martival, Richard de 239, 240, 253
Martival, William de 256, 258, 259, 260
Martyn, Thomas, 'capellanus' 203
Marwe, wife of John 203
Mary I, Queen 97
Mathew, 'capellanus' 242, 243
Mathew, son of William Malestermi 244
Matilda, wife of Thomas of Lincoln 259
Mauna, Ernaldus de 252
Maurice 220, 221, 222, 223, 224
Mazun, John le 275
Melbourne, Thomas de 201
Melford, Richard de 258, 262
Melton, John de 204
Menill, Robert de 286
Mercer, Adam le 281
Mercer, Ralph le 204
Meynill, Thomas de, 'dominus' 268
Mineriis, Gilbert de 249
Minworth, Henry of 255
Minworth, Nicholas of 255
Mitton, Arthur 219
Mollington, Elias de 245
Montfort, Peter de, 'dominus' 'miles' 270
Montfort, Simon de, earl of Leicester 83,
    84, 85, 86, 87, 89, 91, 227, 267, 268,
    269
Moore, John 186
Morker, William 285
Mostyn, Sir Thomas 182
Mountsorrel, Robert de 263, 266
Mowsley, Reginald of 239, 240
Moygne, John le, 'dominus' 'miles' 259
Moyses, Reginald 214
Mundeguma, Robert de 244
Musseburt, Sir William 205
Mustel, Robert 244
Musteruilers, Eustace de, 'capellanus' 259

Neubolt, John 164, 178
Neufmarché, William de 238, 240, 251
Neuilla , Hugh de 270,
    Neyuill' 272, 278
Neuton, John 164
Neuton', Jordan de 202
Newcastle upon Tyne, William de 205, 207

Newton, Letice de 202
Nicholas, 'clericus' 255
Nicholas, 'sacerdos' 254, 255
Nicholas, son of William of Bulkington 281
Nichols, John 3, 13, 15, 18, 19, 21, 23, 38, 39,
    40
Nigel, bishop of Ely 241
Nores, Geoffrey le 256
Northern, J. 208
Nottyng, Roger 214
Nuueray, Robert de 280, 282

Oadeby, Alice de 203
Oakham, Simon de 203
Oakham, Walter de 203
Oakham, William de 204
Ogger, William 251, 252, 253
Ogilvy 93
Olm, Ralph 206
Orm 254
    Horm 254
Osbert, 'capellanus' 230, 234, 235, 251
Osbert, brother of Hugh of Arden 245
Osberton, Geoffrey de 205
Osgot 260, 262
Osleston, Simon de, 'clericus' 262, 269,
    270, 279, 281, 284, 286
Osmond, Walter 278, 279
Osmund, William 283

Packyngton, Amice de 211
Packyngton, John de 211
Palmer, Robert 201
Palycere, William le 213
Paramurs, Robert 281
Parles, John de 259, 260,
Parlis 258
Parmentor', Reginald le 203
Parr, Catherine, queen 96
Parr, William, marquess of Northampton
    15, 83, 91, 96, 97, 100, 101
Passelewe, John 201
Pateshill, Simon de 253
Patrich, William 259
Patroc, Godfrey 239, 240
Paul, abbot of Leicester 21, 24, 252
Payn, abbot of Sawtry 243
Pecco, Alice de 199, 212
Pecco, John de 210
Pecco, Robert de, 'clericus' 273
Pecco, Richard de 247
Pecco, Thomas de 210
Peeke, Thomas 145, 186
Penny, abbot of Leicester 21, 24, 184, 189,
    191
Pepin, Nicholas 263
Pepin, Reginald 255
Pepyn, Richard 138
Pepyn, William, abbot of Leicester 138
Peronell, William 207
Pesceremne, Gilbert 242
Pestel, Roger 202
Pestel, Reginald 204
Petelyng', John de 201
Peter, bishop of Winchester 257
Peter, 'carpentarius' 273, 274, 275, 277, 279
    de Thurmaston 275
Peter, 'clericus' 258, 265
Peter, de Stok' 253

Peter, 'famulus abbatis' 238
Peter, son of Robert of Leicester 270
Peter, son of Thomas of Lincoln 259
Peter, son of Thurstan of Barkby 264, 265,
    266
Petit, Robert 209
Petit, Roger 254
Petronilla, countess of Leicester 40, 83,
    248, 249, 253
Peverel, Hugh 266
Pexall, Richard, bishop of Bangor 24
Philip, bishop of Bayeux (Normandy) 241
Philip, 'clericus comitis' 248, 249, 252
Pikeryng, R. 204
Pistor, William, abbot of Leicester 254
Pistor, John 203
Pitefrid, Siward 83, 234, 235
    Pitefrei, Siward 251
Plummer', Richard 208
Poher, Walter le 239, 240
Pollard, Robert 272
Pollesworth, Richard de 211, 215
Pomery, John 224
    Pomerey 142, 162
Popes see Alexander, Benedict, Eugenius,
    Innocent
Porter, Robert le 208
Poterna, Jacob de 253
Pousend', Stephen de 247
Priour, Simon 207
Proudfote 206
Puiset, H[ugh] de, bishop of Durham 246
Purmentin, William, 'magister' 247
Pyrye, William de 211

Quappelade, Thomas de 278
Quarreour, Simon le 207
Quenby, Robert de 270
Queniborough, Ralph de 239, 241
Quincy, Robert de, 'dominus' 'miles' 258
Quincy, Roger de, earl of Winchester 83,
    227, 232, 258, 262, 284, 285, 286
Quincy, Saer de, earl of Winchester 83

Rabbaz, Robert 239, 240
Radulf, brother of Richard of Asfordby 245
Radulf, son of Gillebertus 235
Radulf, son of Nicholas 244, 257
Radulf, son of Stephen 246
Ralph, bishop of Chichester 257
Ralph, 'clericus' 261, 262
Ralph, son of Gilbert of Burstall 284
Ralph, son of Hildi 260, 262
Ralph, son of a priest 265, 266
Ralph, son of Richard Basset of Weldon
    255
Ralph, son of Richard de Martinwast 239,
    240
Ralph, 'summonitor' 271
Ralph the butler 234, 235, 241, 251
Ralph, uncle of Peter son of Thurstan of
    Barkby 264, 265
Ranulf II, earl of Chester 231, 236, 237, 238,
    240, 252
Rannulf, 'pistor' 238
Ranulph, 'Ianitor/Portarius' 84, 238, 245
Rearsby, Roger de 259, 260, 262, 263, 264
Reginald, 'capellanus' 256
Reginald, earl of Cornwall 241

Reginald, 'faber' 264, 274, 276, 283
Reginald, 'forestarius' 268
Reginald, 'mariscallus abbatis' 281, 283
Reid, John 84
Reid, Lawrence 84
Reigate, John de 286
Repyngdon, Philip, abbot of Leicester,
    chancellor of Oxford University and
    bishop of Lincoln 123, 140, 141
Richard I, king 232, 245, 247
Richard II, king 122, 124
Richard, abbot of Leicester 228, 242, 243
Richard, bishop of Salisbury 257
Richard, 'camerarius' 235, 244
Richard, 'chapelein' 283
Richard, 'servus' 253
Richard, son of Alan of Bramcote,
    'magister' 282
Richard, son of Alan of Lockington,
    'magister' 279
Richard, son of Bartholomew of
    Lockington 279
Richard, son of Geoffrey l'Abbé 243
Richard, son of Herbert 249
Richard, son of Philip 239, 240
Richard, son of Simon of Belgrave 285
Richard, son of Thurstan 271
Richard, son of Walo 239, 240
Richard, son of William 258
Ridel, Geoffrey 255
Ritun, Robert Freman de 281
Robert, bishop of Lincoln 238, 241
Robert, brother of John of Marston 269
Robert, 'capellanus' 235, 242, 243, 244, 245
Robert, 'clericus' 249, 252, 265
    'clericus comitis' 248
Robert, 'faber' 267, 273
Robert, 'falconarius' 279, 285
Robert, 'ianitor' 256
Robert, 'pincerna' 286
Robert, prior of Kinedeworth (Kenilworth)
    244
Robert, 'scriptor' 286
Robert, son of Col 239, 240
Robert, son of Geoffrey of Craft 235
Robert, son of Henry 205, 206
Robert, son of Henry of Bramcote 268,
    280, 281, 282, 283
Robert, son of Isabel of Bramcote 282, 283
Robert, son of Jocelin Marescald 251
Robert, son of Lewyne of Thurmaston 278
Robert, son of Mathew of Burstall 284
Robert, son of Ralph 238, 239, 240, 251
    son of Ralph the butler 235
Robert, son of Robert son of Col 239, 240
Robert, son of Roger of Belgrave 275, 287
Robert, son of Suanus 238
Robert, son of Thurstan 284
Robert, son of William of Bramcote 281
Robert, son of William Preest, 'capellanus'
    276
Robert the alchemist 223
Robert I, count of Meulan 228, 229, 230,
    234, 235, 239, 249
Robert II, earl of Leicester 75, 83, 137, 153,
    229, 231, 232, 234, 236, 237, 238, 239,
    242, 243, 244, 248, 249, 252
Robert III, earl of Leicester 40, 83, 232, 245,
    247, 249

Robert IV, earl of Leicester 83, 227, 232,
    248, 249, 252
    son of Petronilla 227, 253
Rodyngton 208
Roger, archbishop of York 241
Roger, bishop of Salisbury 230
Roger, bishop of St Andrews 245, 247
Roger, 'clericus' 259, 272
Roger, earl of Warwick 231, 232, 237, 238,
    240
Roger, 'forestarius' 254
Roger, 'homo abbatis Legrecest' 243
Roger, 'prepositus' 276
Roger, son of Alexander 278
Roger, son of William Knotte de Rothley
    281
Roper', Agnes la 199, 213
Roper, Helen le 199, 213
Roper, Stephen le 213
Ropere, William le 213
Rotarius, Robert son of Alan 207
Rothley, Helen de 199, 210
Rothley, Henry of, abbot of Leicester
    233
Rothley, Magg' de 199, 215
Rothley, Matilda de 206
Rothley, Richard, abbot of Leicester 141
Rothley, William Cnotte de 270, 272, 285
    Cnothe 279
Rude, William 282
Russell', John 215
Russell', Margery 199, 208
Ruyton, Richard 'le chapeleyn' de 280, 282
Ruyton, Robert de 282
Rydyng, Hector 182

Saddington, Amory de 209
Saddington, John 142
Saddington, Roger de 278
Sadyngton (Saddington), William, abbot
    of Leicester 142, 217-24
Sainneville, William de 248, 249, 252, 255,
    268, 286
St Andrews, bishop of see Roger
St Andrews, Sahero de, 'dominus' 'miles'
    258-9
St Andrews, Serlon de 262
St Edward, Peter de 258
St Leonard's, master of 207, 210
St Leonard's, vicar of 209
Salford, William de 256
Salisbury, bishop of see Ralph, Richard,
    Roger
Salisbury, John of, bishop of Chartres 218
Sall, Richard de, 'magister' 242
Salow, Geoffrey 139, 141, 144, 155, 163
Sampson, Roger 239, 240
Sampson, William 205, 206
Samuel, 'molendinarius' 284
Sapcote, Ralph Basset de, 'dominus' 'miles'
    270
Sawer, Richard le 207
Scheperd, Henry le 214
Schirforde, John 203
Schirteful, Reginald 277
Scot, John 209
Scot, Reginald 213
Scott, Richard 138
Scriptor, William 207

Seagrave, Henry of 259, 264
Seagrave, Stephen of 233, 256, 263, 264
    'dominus' 259, 263 , 268
Seawin 255
Sées, Peter de 260
Seman, Laurence 204
Senior, William 14, 15, 17, 20, 21, 24, 25, 63,
    75, 76, 77, 82, 83, 84, 85, 89, 91, 92, 93,
    94, 96, 98, 99
Sewell, 'clericus' 282
Seynt, Amice 199, 215
Seyton, Ralph 139, 141
Shearsby, Richard de 263
Shelton, Richard de 203
Shepshed, Isabel de 207
Shepshed, John 142, 162
Shepshed, William de 215
Sibson, John de 209
Sibson, Roger de 207, 213
Sifrewast, Bartholomew de 242
Sileby, widow of Adam de 204
Sileby, William de 203
Simon 'ad crucem' 271
Simon, bishop elect of Chichester 252
Simon, canon of Kiningeuurda
    (Kenilworth?) 235
Simon, 'clericus' 263, 281
Simon, 'mariscallus' 279, 286
Simon, 'servus' 253
Simon, son of William son of Osmund of
    Thurmaston 266
Sire, Robert 206
Siston, William Fipaud de 271
Smythson, John 116
Smythson, Robert 116
Sneinton, Walter de, 'clericus' 279
Somers, Lord John 146, 187, 190
Sorel, Thomas 239, 240
Sparhavec, Roger 259, 262
    Sperhavet 260
Spicere, William le 205
Spick, Geoffrey 202
Squirt, Diana 199, 213
Stafford, Letice de 199, 215
Stafford, Sir Humphrey 117
Stake, Peter 201
Staleworth, Alice, wife of Roger 215
Stamford, Richard de 208
Stanton, Geoffrey de 207
Stapleton, Richard de, 'magister' 269, 270,
    272, 282, 284
Stephen, king 83, 119, 228, 229, 230, 231, 236
Steyne, Henry 215
Stiworman, William 204
Stockton, John de 212
Stockton, Robert de 212
Stockton, Roger de 214
Stoke Golding, Peter de 252
Stori, Roger 242
Stoughton, John de 279
Stoughton, William 189, 190
Stretford, Henry 139
Stretton, Robert de 274
Strippelyng, Geoffrey 212
Sturdy, Robert 204, 205
Suarry, Hugh 266, 267
Sumeruill, James de 272
Sutor, John 209
Swepstone, Richard de 207

Sweyn, Richard, 'servus de Groby' 286
Swinderby, William 125
Symonds, Richard 98, 101
Syreford, Hugh de 280

Tacker, John de 211
Tannator, John son of Hugh 208
Tannator, Walter 205, 208, 209
Tannour, John le 209
Tasche, William 249
Tayllour, Elias le 207
Taylour, Adam 213
Thase, William 263
Theobald, 'clericus' 252
Thev', Robert de 252
Thom, Robert 277
Thomas, 'cancellarius' 241
Thomas, earl of Lancaster 120
Thomas, prior of Warwick 253
Thomas, 'servus' 264
Thomas, son of Richard le Harpeur 279
Thomas, son of Richard of Sheavsby 278
Thomas, son of William 244
Thornton, Henry de 205
Thornton, William de 132
Thorp, Amphelis de 208
Thorpe, John, abbot of Wellow 139
Thorpe, Thomas 116, 186
Thringstone, J. de 202
Thurcaston, Ralph 164
Thurcaston, Richard rector of 262
Thurlston, Ralph 139, 140, 141, 142, 143, 144, 164, 178
Thurmaston, Alan son of Christopher, de 265, 267
Thurmaston, John de 207
Thurmaston, John Lewyne de 283
Thurmaston, John Loue de 277
Thurmaston, John le Machun de 265
    'cementarius' 277
    le Masoun 273
    le Mazun 275
Thurmaston, Matilda de 209
Thurmaston, Michael de, 'carpentarius' 272, 274, 275, 276, 277, 278
Thurmaston, Peter de, 'carpentarius' 273, 275, 278
Thurmaston, Reginald de, 'faber' 274
Thurmaston, Robert de, 'faber' 275
Thurmaston, Robert Tor de 278
Thurmaston, Robert Wysman de 274, 276
Thurmaston, Samuel de 277
Thurmaston, Thomas de 201
Thurmaston, Walter de, 'faber' 273, 275, 277, 278
Thurmaston, William Alnath de 279
Thurmaston, William Osmund de 275
Thurmaston, William de, 'pistor' 277
Thurmaston, William Sparewe de 274, 275
Thurstan see Turstin
Tourville, Geoffrey de 238, 240, 251
Tourville, Ralph de 239, 240

Trafford, Brian de 285
Trafford, Robert de, 'clericus' 282, 285
Trenchefuille, William 249
Triket, William 239, 240
Trompur, Henry 212
Trunchon, Richard 206
Turnour, William 206
Turnur, William le 271
Turstin (Thurstan), abbot of Garendon (Terondona) 244
Turveye, John 203
Tuschet, Henry 239, 240
Tuschet, John, 'dominus' 'miles' 286
Twyford, Roger de 269, 271, 281
Tychel, Geoffrey de 266
Tyndall, Francis 146, 174, 175
Tynemouth, John of, archdeacon of Oxford 248

Ulverscroft, Ralph de, 'magister' 252

Vatteville, Robert de 237, 238, 239, 240
Vatteville, Roger de 234, 235, 237, 238, 239, 240, 243
Vernham's Dean, William de 264
Vernon, Sir Richard de 232
Vescy, Thomas 208
Veteriponte, Robert de 252
Vignoles, William de, 'dominus', 'miles' 268
Vldeuer, William 249

Walcellinus 238
Waleran, count of Meulan and Worcester 229, 231, 234, 235, 236, 237
Waleran, earl of Warwick 226
Walran, Robert 260
Walter, 'medicus' 243
Walter, son of Bence 260, 262
Walter, son of Richard 260, 262
Walter, son of William son of Herbert 267, 269
Walter, son of William de Knighton 284
Wanlip, Henry de 284, 285
Wanlip, Henry de, 'magister' 258
Wanlip, John de, 'clericus' 284
Wantoun, Walter 202
Wareyn', William 202
Warin fitz Gerald 241, 252
Warton, William de, 'capellanus' 244
Warwick, William de 254, 255
Waryn, Amice, daughter of John 203
Wauere, Richard de 278
Waynhous, John le 205, 206
Wells, Hugh de, bishop of Lincoln 226
Welles, I. de 253
Weston, Hugh 186
Weston, Robert 186
Weston, William 186
Westreis, William le 260
Wetherby, Petronilla de 199, 214
Wetherby, Thomas de 213
Whatton, Henry 137, 138

Whetstone, John de 215
Whitbeck, Robert de 258, 263, 266
Whitby, Alan de 272, 274, 278, 279
Whiteby 212
Whitfield, Robert de 246
Whitfield, John 143
Wibtoft, John de 280, 282
Widuilla, William de 245
Willac, Hamun de 255
William, 'capellanus' 238, 248, 249, 252, 253
William, 'dispensator' 238
William, earl of Warwick 226, 245, 246
William, 'falconarius' 286
William, 'pistor' 275
William, 'scriptor' 238
William, son of Avicie de Thurmaston 273, 274
William, son of Daniel 244
William, son of Geoffrey of Minworth 254, 255
William, son of Godfrid 247, 251, 252, 253, 255
William, son of Godfrid Horn' 254
William, son of Herbert 258, 260, 263, 265, 266, 267
William, son of Ilbert of Kilby 256
William, son of Laurence 267
William, son of Peter 267
William, son of a priest 275
William, son of Robert 264
William, son of William of Kilby 262
William, son of William of Lancaster 237
William, son of Ylbertus, 'servus' 253
William I, king 228
Willis, Browne 3
Willmer, George 146, 176, 178, 179, 181
Willoughby, Roger de 204
Willoughby, Thomas de 203
Willscheyr, John 173
Winchester, bishop of see Peter
Winsun, William 264
Wolsey, Cardinal Thomas 3, 6, 13
Wolvey, Reginald Basset de 255
Wolvey, Robert de 280
Woodgate, Amice de 199, 214
Wyclif, John 123, 140
Wykes, Richard de 285
Wykyngston, Roger de 203
Wymondham, William 144, 145
Wyschard, Henry 269, 270, 280, 282
    Wiscard 286
Wysman, Gilbert, 'capellanus' 273
Wysman, Robert 283, 284
    de Thurmaston 285
Wyte, John le 269
Wytecope, Roger 271

York, archbishop of 219
    see also Roger
Youlgreave, Adam de 280, 281, 282
Youlgreave, Robert de 256, 259, 263, 266
Ysabel, countess of Leicester 249

Index locorum

Notes: the orthography used follows the that of the texts. Medieval names are identified wherever possible, and cross-references provided only for those that are markedly different to the modern name.

'Abbat Garden' //
'Abbat's Wood' 83
Abbey Gate, Leicester 90
Abbey Lane, Leicester 90
Abbot Guerne 21
Abbot Penny's Wall 21-4
Abbot's Stocking, Leics. 85
Adestok (Adstock, Bucks.) 240
Alcester Abbey, Warw. 235
Aldebi (Aldeby, Leics.) 240, 251
Aldermaneseyhe 255
Alewoldestuna (Alwalton, Cambs.) 256
Allespatha (Allesley, Warw.) 242
All Saints, church of, Leicester 173, 205, 208
All Saints, church of, Warwick 228
All Saints, parish of, Leicester 195, 197, 198, 205
Alnaia 240
Alneio 251
Alneto 258
Alnwick Tower, Old Palace, Lincoln 219
'Alta strata' (Highcross Street, Leicester) 205
Anecote (Ancoats, Lancs.) 215
Anelep 258
Anlep bridge (nr. Barkby, Leics.) 265
Anstey, Leics. 85, 86, 248
 Anestalesleia 240
 Anestanesleia 251
 Anesty 248, 253, 268, 269
 Ansty 199, 211
Anstey Lane, Leics. 79, 82, 86, 90, 91
Arden 226, 239, 244, 245
 Ardena 246, 247, 254, 255
 Arderna 259
 Hardena 240
Argenteem 257
Asfordby, Leics. 230, 234, 248, 252
 Aisfordeby 240, 245
 Asfordeby 235
 Esfordeby 249
 Essefordeby 252
Ashby (Ashby Folville, Leics.) 263
 Asheby 201, 203
Ashby de la Zouch Castle, Leics. 38, 108
Ash Close, Leics. 92
Asheclose Meadow, Leics. 96
Asseuella (Ashwell, Rutland) 240
Attenrun (meadow nr. Kilby, Leics.) 256
Aubeni 248, 249, 252

Aula 256, 260, 265, 266, 286
Aumundernesse (Amounderness, Lancs.) 244
Auneia (Launay) 240
Ayleston, Leics. 133, 201, 222
Aylestone Hall, Leics. 112

Baddeston (Thurmaston, Leics.) 276, 277
Baggrave, Leics. 96, 97
 Babbegrave 270
Baio[censis] (Bayeux, France) 241
Banelondes (Thurmaston, Leics.) 276, 277
Bangor 24, 189, 191
Bara 242
Barbican, Leicester Castle 201
 Bareswrth (Husband's Bosworth, Leics.) 240
 Barewswrth 240
Barewell (Barwell, Leics.) 256
Barkby, Leics. 133, 227, 228, 233, 239, 257, 260, 262, 263, 264, 265, 266, 269, 271, 272, 286, 287
 Barkeby 202, 205, 209, 240, 257, 260, 261, 263, 264, 265, 266, 267, 269, 271, 272, 276, 283, 285, 287
Barkehou (Thurmaston, Leics.) 267
Barlborough Hall, Derbys. 116
'Barley Close', Leics. 91, 92
'Barley Hill', Leics. 89, 92
'Barn(e) Close', Leics. 83, 85
Barnesby 203
Barnwell Priory, Cambridge 129, 150, 193
Barrow-on-Soar, Leics. 231, 239
 Barew 240, 266
 Barewa 240
 Barue 279
 Barwa 240
Barthehouslad (Thurmaston, Leics.) 267
Barton 210
Barwood, Warw. 239
Bathon (Bath, Somers.) 257
Batts Close, Leics. 85, 89, 90
Bavaria 222
Beaumont, Normandy, France 229
Beaumont Leys, Leics. 79, 82, 86, 90, 92, 93
 'Bealmont' 86
 Beaumund 286
Beaumont Leys Lane, Leics. 85, 88, 90

Beaumont Walk, Leics. 86
'Beaumont Wood', Leics. 82
Beby (nr. Barkby, Leics.) 257
Bec, abbey of, Normandy, France 229
Becheston 247
Bedeford (Bedford, Beds.) 238
Belgrave, Leics. 79, 82, 85, 86, 89, 90, 207, 231, 239, 268, 269
 Belegraua 240
 Belegraue 248, 251, 267, 275, 287
 Belegreue 268
 Bellagraua 269, 285
Belgravegate 208
Belholm (Thurmaston, Leics.) 253
Bereford (Barford) 270
Berewdestrete (Curdworth, Warw.) 246
Berhangil (Barnacle, Warw.) 261
Berchesira (Berks.) 235
 Berkesira 240
Berewda (Curdworth, Warw.) 245, 246
 Berewida 246
 Berewode 240
 Berwode 226
 Borewdia 254
Bermondsey, Surrey 148
Bernegate 201
Bernewell (Barnwell, Northants.) 199, 211
Billesdon, Leics. 239, 240
Billynges (Billing Magna, Northants.) 240
Birstall, Leics. 79, 82, 83, 86, 89
Bitteswell, Leics. 239
 Bitmeswella 240, 241
 Bittmeswell 272
Blaby, Leics. 239, 243, 287
 Blabi 238, 240
Blackbird Road 79, 82, 90
Blois, Maine et Loire, France 249, 252
Blynfield, Dorset 234
 Blingesfeld 235
 Blingisfeld 251
Bodleian Library, Oxford 191
Bondcroft 211
Bordigny 238
 Bordeni 240
 Bordeneius 235
Bordesley, Worcs., abbey of 229
Boresworth' (Husbands Bosworth, Leics.) 208

Bosco 235, 238, 240, 242, 251, 259, 261, 262, 268, 285
Bracin (Bracken, East Yorks.) 286
Brackley, Northants. 231, 234
    Brachaleya 235
    Brackeleia 240, 251
Brademaris (Thurmaston, Leics.) 276, 277
Bradenhet 255
Bradgate House, Leics. 24, 117
Bradsole 148, 157, 165, 166
Bramcote, Warw. 227, 233, 234, 238, 239, 240, 243, 261, 263, 264, 268, 280, 281, 282, 283
    Bramcota 261, 280
    Bramkote 261
    Bromcote 282, 283
    Brancota 235, 238, 251
    Brancothe 243
Bramdoon (Brandon) 211
Bramlcye (Bramley) 213
Branteclif (Barkby, Leics.) 266
Branteston (Branston, Leics.) 245
    Brantiston' 202
Brantingeby (Brentingby, Leics.) 240
Braosa 253
Bray, Berks. 260
Braundon (Brandon) 212
Brethegederlond (Thurmaston, Leics.) 284
Breteuil, L'Oise, France 243
Brichsworth (Brixworth, Northants.) 286
Brick Close, Leicester 24, 91, 92, 94
Bristol, Gloucs. 259, 260
    Bristowe 258
    Bristoliis 259
    Bristoll 266
Brocfurlang (Bramcote, Warw.) 262, 263, 280, 281
Brodeshert (nr. Barkby, Leics.) 264
Brodewong (Thurmaston, Leics.) 273
Broghton' (Upper Broughton, Leics. or Nether Broughton, Notts.) 205
'Brokkytt' wood, Leics. 89
Bromkinsthorpe, Leics. 79, 82, 83, 84, 85, 234
    Brunchenestorp 84, 235
    Brunkenestorp 251
Bromwich 244
    Bromwych 245, 246, 247
Bruill' 268
Bruneshul (Thurmaston, Leics.) 276, 277
Buckinghamshire 232
Bulkington, Warw. 234, 238, 261, 263
    Bulchintona 235
    Bulkentona 251
    Bulkinton 240
    Bulkyngton 281
    Bulkynton' 261, 264, 269, 281
    Bulkyntona 247
Burgo ('Burch', Peterborough, Cambs.) 246
Burnardeshull (nr. Barkby, Leics.) 265
Burscena 205
Burstall, Staffs. (or Birstall, Leics.) 267, 270, 279, 284
    Borestall 285
    Burstale 212
    Burstalle 211, 213
'Burstal More', Birstall, Leics. 83, 92

Burton Overy, Leics. 136, 145, 182, 186, 203, 234, 239, 240, 241
Burnthon 280
Burtona 235
Buruthon 280
Bury St Edmunds, Suffolk 143
Busseby (Busby) 204
Butemunt' 255
'Byggyng, le' 199, 213
Byhow (Barkby, Leics.) 271

Caldewelle (Caldwell, North Yorks.?) 256
'Calidus vicus' (Hot Gate, Leicester) 203
Calverhay, Leics. 86, 87, 89, 90
Cambridge University 96, 130, 152, 158, 171, 172
Camped' 279
Cancie (Kent) 257
Candia, Crete 148, 150, 152, 153, 157
Canterbury, Kent 73
    Cantuariensis 246, 247, 252
    Christ Church cathedral 130, 131, 148, 151, 154, 157
    Saint Augustine's abbey 128, 148, 157
Capella 257
Cardula 244
Carlisle, Cumbria 189, 191
Carlton Curlieu, Leics. 145
    Carleton Curle 186
Castile 123
Causeway Lane, Leicester 63
Cavendish House, Leicester 1, 4, 9, 13, 14, 16, 17, 19, 21, 27, 28, 29, 35, 36, 38, 78, 92, 93, 98, 100, 101, 103, 104, 108, 109, 112, 116, 117, 118
Chace (Royal Forest) of Leicester 76, 91
Charlee (Charley, Leics.) 283
    Charneles 259
    Charnellis 255
Charnwood Forest, Leics. 90
Chatsworth, Derbys. 75, 101
Chaumunt 259
Cherchesur Wasbech (Thurmaston, Leics.) 278, 279
Chereby 243
Chesham Bois, Bucks. 239
    Cestresham 240, 249
Chester 231, 236, 238, 252
    Cestrie 237, 240, 252
Chetewynd (Chetwynd, Salop.) 286
Chiffrewast 239
Christ Church cathedral, Canterbury 130, 131, 148, 151, 154, 157
Christchurch, Twynham 229
Cicestrensis (Chichester, Sussex) 252
Cirencester (abbey) 135, 172, 193
Cirre 235
Citeaux, Burgundy, France 161
Clairmarais 153
Clare College, Cambridge 158
Clay Hedges, Leics.
    Clay Egges 86
    Cleyhegg 268
    Cleyhegges 267
    Cloyhegges 85, 86, 14, 15
Cley, Norfolk 270
Clifton-upon-Dunsmoor, Warw. 229, 230, 234, 261
    Cliftona 235, 261

Clitheroe, Lancs. 123
Clottilondis (Thurmaston, Leics.) 276
Clounham 206
Cocis (Cotes, Leics.) 241
Cockerham, Lancs. 232, 237, 239, 244
    Cokerham 199, 212, 213, 241, 269, 270, 284
    Cokirham 279, 281
    Cokerheim 237, 244
    Kokerham 199, 210, 212
Coddington' 211
Cogweir 205
Cokkiskomb (Thurmaston, Leics.) 276, 277
Coleby (Thurmaston, Leics.) 276, 277
    Coleby Slade 276
Coleshull (Coleshill, Berks.) 263
College of Arms, London 146
Conkersbury, Derbys. 232, 239
    Cankersburia 240
'Copie, the', Leics. 92
Cornubie (Cornwall) 241
Corpus Christi College, Cambridge 148, 158
Corpus Christi College, Oxford 145, 191
Corsewalle (Cresswell, Derbys.) 261
Cossibi (Cosby, Leics.) 239
Cosyngton (Cossington, Leics.) 202
Cotun (Coten) 286
Countesthorpe (Torp), Leics. 240
Coventry 25
    Couentre 280, 281, 283
Cranford (Cranford St Andrew and St John, Northants.) 235, 242, 244, 247, 252, 258, 286
    Cramford 201
    Cramforth' 206
    Craumford 279
    Craunford 259, 286
Craxton 263
Crec (Crayke, North Yorks.) 259
Cressewall (Cresswell, Derbys.) 268
Crimblis (Crimbles, Lancs.) 237
Croft 238, 239, 242
    Craft 235, 244
    Cratfh 243
    Creft 240, 242, 247
    Crest 242
Crokeston (Croxton, Leics.) 266
Crokispul (Pool nr. Cockerham, Lancs.) 244
Cropston, Leics. 85, 86, 210, 267, 268
Curcun (?Kirkham, Lancs.?) 259
Curdworth, Warw. 226, 227, 239, 244, 246, 254 (see also Berwode)
    Creddewrth 246, 247
    Croddeworth 240
    Cruddewrth 255
    Crudewrthe 254
Cusynton (Cossington, Leics.) 257

Dalby (Old Dalby, Leics.) 238, 239, 240, 241
Dalesike, Leics. 85, 86, 267, 268
Darley Abbey, Derby 193
Dauentr' (Daventry, Northants.) 206
'Defensa' (Frith) (forest nr. Leicester) 85, 267
Denton 259
Derbyshire 98, 232

Desford 227, 249
  Deresford 251
  Desforde 227, 249
Devoncroft 210
Devonshire 98, 101
Dicfurlong (nr. Hungarton, Leics.) 260
  Dicfurlang 262
  Dykfurlang 271
Donelund (Doveland) 269
Donemowe (Great and Little Dunmow,
  Essex) 199, 214
Donyngton (Donington, Leics.) 206
Doveland(s), Bromkinsthorpe, Leics. 82,
  83, 85
  Doueland 210
Dover (Kent) 238, 241
Dover Priory 129, 143
Droitwich, Worcs. 231, 236, 237
  Wich 237
Dunham, Northants. 242
Dunstable (abbey) 193
Dunt' 247, 255
Durham, County Durham 148
  Dunelm 246
Dyngelee 199, 211
Dyua (Chester) 255

Earl Shilton, Leics. 79
East Gate, Leicester 198
Eboracum/Ebroicensis see York
Ebrok (stream) 244, 245, 246
  Ebroc 246, 255
Eindona (Eydon, Northants.) 240
Elhale (Cockerham, Lancs.) 237, 241
Elmete 215
Ely Cathedral, Cambs. 137
Elyiensis (Ely, Cambs.) 246
  Heliensis 241
Empingham, Rutland 239, 240
Enderby, Leics. 203, 206
Enedemaris (Thurmaston, Leics.) 276, 277
Envermeu 239
Erdesby (Harby, Leics.) 240
Erdington, Warw. 244
Erdurthintuna (nr. Curdworth, Warw.)
  246
Ernothelond (Thurmaston, Leics.) 276
Essex 96, 241, 252, 253
Estleg (Eastleigh, Hants.) 248, 249
  Estleia 248
  Estleya 268, 270
  Estleye 262
Esteresmereberewe 271
Estmede (Thurmaston, Leics.) 277
Estmedwe (Barkby, Leics.) 257, 276, 277
  Estmedue 264
Estona (Great Easton, Leics.) 247
Estwella (Eastwell, Leics.) 240
Ettona (Eaton, Leics.) 40
  Eton 213
Euermou (Envermeu) 240
Euinton' (Evington, Leics.) 240, 261, 269,
  270, 274, 281, 285
  Euenton 284, 287
  Euintona 240
  Evyngton 206
Eversley, Wilts. 231, 238
  Euerlais 240
  Everlai 251

Evesham, Worcs. 148, 161, 166
Exeter, Devon 90, 148, 150, 151, 154, 156
Exeter cathedral, Devon 127, 130, 132, 138,
  179

Farthinghoe, Northants. 248
  Farningehou 240
  Farninghou 253
Flackesfleth (stream nr. Cockerham,
  Lancs.) 244
Flandr' 208
Flaxley, Gloucs. 148
Flaxlond (Bramcote, Warw.) 280, 281
Folleville 263
  Foleuile 263
  Folleuill 259
  Follevile 204
Fontevrault, Maine et Loire, France 60
Fosseway 79, 82, 83, 89, 90
Foxholes (Thurmaston, Leics.) 276, 277
Foxton, Leics. 203
  Foxtona 239, 241
Freake's Ground, Leicester 85, 90
Frog Island, Leicester 84

Galby, Leics. 273, 274, 275, 276, 278
Galeberwe (Thurmaston, Leics.) 276, 277
Garendon, Leics., abbey of 75, 229, 253
  Geroldone 253
  Terondona 244
Gascony 122, 124
Ghent 123
Gileuile 248
Glastonbury Abbey, Somers. 39, 60, 61, 66,
  148, 150
Glenefeld (Glenfield, Leics.) 272
  Clenefeld 279
Gouteby (Goadby, Leics.) 240
Gores, Le (Thurmaston, Leics.) 273
Gotham, Notts. 226, 239
  Gaham 240
Grace Dieu, Leics. 99
'Great Stockins', Leics. 89-90
Greneplot 271
Grescote 204
Groby, Leics. 84, 207, 249, 253, 286
  Grobi 251
Groby Manor House, Leics. 38
Groby Road, Leicester 82, 84, 85, 90
Grosmont 199, 122, 123, 124
Guildhall, Leicester 38
Guildhall, London 98
Guisborough 120

Haddona (Haddon, Derbys.) 240
Haldenby 208
Halse, Leics. 228, 234
  Alsou 240
  Halsou 235, 251
Hanechestoft (Rothley, Leics.) 236, 237
Hatherne 199, 215
Heacham Drive, Leics. 86
Hemelton (Hamilton, Leics.) 272
  Hamelton 273, 287
Harcurt 238
  Harecurd 252
Hardemede 271
Hardwick House, Derbys. 116
Harpe Orchard, Leics. 96

Harran 221
Harston, Leics. 238, 239
  Arestona 238
  Harestan 240
Hastings house 1, 14
Hathern, Leics. 133
Hauering (Havering atte Bowe, Essex)
  270
Haywode 212
Heath Old Hall, Yorks. 116
Heleford (Helford, Cornwall) 263
Helrumestub (stream? nr. Barkby, Leics.)
  257
Herci 262
Hereford 253, 285
Hereswode, Leics. 79
Hermescumb (Barkby, Leics.) 266
Hexham (Northumb.) 212
Hibernia/Ireland 266
'High Parke', Leics. 85
Hildeslai see West Isley, Berks.
Hingwareby 266
Hinkele (Hinckley, Leics.) 280, 283
  Hinckelee 283
Holand (Holland, South Lincs.) 201
Holdenby, Northants. 108
Holegate (Holgate, West Yorks.) 276, 277
Holegrift (Thurmaston, Leics.) 276
Holewelledales (Holwell, Leics.) 270
Holy Trinity, church of, Aldgate, Leicester
  258
Honecote (Huncote, Leics.) 240
Houby 206
  Howby 206
Houghton on the Hill, Leics. 217
Houma 245
Hov, Le (Thurmaston, Leics.) 266, 267
Howden 139, 141
Hoy (stream? nr. Kilby, Leics.) 256
Hullesmor 255
Hulne, Northumb. 148, 150, 151, 152, 154
Humberstone, Leics. 239, 261, 287
  Humberston 277
  Humberstan 240
  Humbirstan 261
Humez 241
Huncote, Leics. 77
Hunderissis (stream? nr. Kilby, Leics.)
  256
Hungarton, Leics. 227, 239, 259, 260, 266,
  270
  Hungerton 262, 263
  Hungertona 240, 263
  Hungurton 260, 266, 270
Hungerhull (Thurmaston, Leics.) 278
Huntingdon, Cambs. 83, 97, 98, 101
Hyda in Merston (Marston) 282
  Hyda 281, 282

Ibstock, Leics. 133, 199
Ierosolimitanum (Jerusalem) 254
Ilmesdon 240
Indeslai see West Isley, Berks.
Ingarsby, Leics. 91, 127, 128, 140, 141, 217,
  218, 219, 220, 223, 224
  Yngwardby 131
Iohi 235
Ipeslea (Ipsley, Warw.) 254
  Ippesleye 255

Jerusalem 254
John's Headland (Thurmaston, Leics.) 267

Kair' 244
Kegworth, Leics. 133
Keman 286
Kendal 232
Kenilworth 230
    Kinedeworth 244
    Kiningeuurda? 235
Kent 202
Keuelingworth (North Kilworth, Leics.) 240
Kilby, Leics. 239, 256
    Kelebi 240, 262
    Keleby 256
    Kileby 256, 259
Kilworth see Keuelingworth, Westkyuelyngwrd'
Kinedeworth (Kenilworth) 244
Kingscliffe, Northants. 116
King's Hall, Cambridge 154
King's Lodging, Leicester Abbey 28, 39, 59
King's Norton 226
King's Tower, Leicester Abbey 60
Kiningeuurda (Kenilworth?) 235
Kirby Bellars, Leics. 144, 227, 239
    Kerebi 248
    Kereby 241
Kirby Hall, Northants. 116
Kirby Muxloe Castle, Leics. 24, 38
Knaptoft, Leics. 242
    Cnapetoft 240, 242
Knighton, Leics. 89, 119, 120, 122, 123, 124, 125, 137, 139, 141, 144, 145, 226, 227, 228, 230, 232, 234, 243, 248, 249, 252
    Cnenctinton 244
    Cnichtetona 235
    Cnicton 284
    Cnihtinthona 251
    Cnihtinton' 253
    Cnitthon 137
    Knyton 242
Knipton, Leics. 238, 239, 240
    Cnipeton 238
    Kniptona 240
Kokerch 286
Kynton (Kenton, Northumb.) 264
    Kyntona 256

Lancaster, Lancs. 87, 91, 119, 120, 122, 124, 232, 237, 239, 244
Langedale (stream? nr. Barkby, Leics.) 257, 258, 266
Langeford 244
Langley Priory 223
Langton, Leics. 238
    Langeton 240, 248, 280
Languath (Thurmaston, Leics.) 275
Lanthony priory, Gloucs. 135, 148, 149, 150, 157, 161, 165, 166
Lauda 211, 215
Launde Abbey, Leics. 99
Lementona (Leamington, Warw.) 240
Lega (Leigh) 266
Leicester, Leics. passim
Leicester Abbey passim

Leicester Abbey, parish of, Leicester 84
Leicester Castle 38, 119, 120, 122, 228, 229
Leicester forest 249
Leicester Frith 90
'Leicester Meadow' 83
Leicestershire 75, 79, 82, 86, 90, 115, 225, 227, 229 230, 231, 232, 233, 244
Lenton, Notts., abbey of 232
Leuns 244
Lewynewell (Hungarton, Leics.) 266, 277, 283
Lilbourne, Northants. 234, 239
    Lilleburn 259, 263, 266
    Lilleburna 235, 240, 241, 249
    Lilleburne 258, 264, 280, 282
Lincoln, Lincs. 76, 90, 123, 219, 230, 234, 235, 238, 241, 244, 248, 249, 251
Lincoln, cathedral of 228
Lincoln, diocese of 130, 140, 226, 232, 248, 248, 249, 251, 252, 259, 260, 261, 262, 263, 264, 266, 270, 281
Lindisheia (Lindsey, Lincs.) 258
    Lindeseia 268
    Lindesey 258
    Lindeseya 263
Lira 248
Lisieux Abbey, Normandy, France 137
'Litel Stocking', Leics. 86
Lockington, Leics. 255, 256, 279, 286
    Lokintona 286
    Lokynton' 255, 256, 279
    Lokyntona 256
Lodbrok' (Ladbroke) 240
Logiis (Loges) 264
Loir (river Lune, Lancs.) 244
Lomond Close, Leics. 86
London 98, 218, 227, 257, 269, 270
Longeclif (Barkby, Leics.) 271
    Longewold' 271
Longleat House 116
Longo campo (Longchamps) 246, 248
Lonsdale, Lancs. 244
    Lonisdale 244
Lord's Place, Leicester 98, 101
'Lowe Parke', Leics. 90, 91
Loughborough, Leics. 97, 101
    Lucteburgh 273, 277
    Lutteburg' 273, 275, 278, 279
    Lutteburgh' 277
Lucy 241
Luda 269, 270, 284
Lurtewalhil (Bramcote, Warw.) 281
Lyre, abbey, Normandy, France 229, 232

Malthous 214
Mann 259
Marcham, Berks. 286
Marchil (nr. Rearsby, Leics.) 259
Marham, Norfolk 268
Marigny 253
Market Harborough, Leics. 223
Martinwast (Martival, Leics.) 239, 256, 258, 260
    Martiuast 252
    Marting' 253
    Martiuall 240
    Martiwall 258
    Martiwaill 260
    Martiwast 256, 259

Mauna 252
Meadowplace, nr. Youlgreave, Derbys. 232
Melbourne, Derbys. 201
Meleford (Melford, Staffs.) 258, 262
Melton Mowbray, Leics. 204, 261
Merston (Marston) 261, 282
Merton College, Oxford 145, 182
Meryvale 21, 77
Meryvale Close, Leics. 96
Meulan, Yvelines, France 228, 229, 230, 234, 236
    Mellend 239
    Mellenti 235, 249
Meuse, river 71
Meynill' 268
    Menil 286
Michelehowe (Bramcote, Warw.) 280
Mineriis 249
Minworth, Warw. 254, 255
    Mulneswythe 254
    Munnewrthe 255
    Munwrth 255
Molinton (Mollington, Ches.) 245
Montfort 83, 84, 85, 86, 87, 89, 91, 227, 267, 268, 269
    Monteforti 268, 269, 270
Morefurlong (Bramcote, Warw.) 281
'Mortuus Vicus' (Dead Lane, Leicester) 204
Mottesfont abbey, Hants. 139, 164, 178
Mountsorrel, Leics. 231, 259
    Monsorel 264
    Monte Sorel 260
    Monte Sorello 266
    Mountsorel 259
    Munsorel 266
    Muntsorel 259
Mowmacre Estates, Leics. 82
Munich, Germany 222, 223
Muslai (Mowsley, Leics.) 240
Mugehale 255
Mundeguma 244
Musteruilers 259

Narborough, Leics. 231, 238
    Norburgh' 240
Naseby, battle of 101
Nesse (nr. Barkby, Leics.) 265, 267, 283
Nettlebed, Oxon. 238
    Netlebehd 240
    Netlebet 251
Neufmarché, Normandy, France 238
    Novo Mercato 240, 251
Neuilla 239
    Neyuill 272, 278
Newarke Gateway, Leicester 25
Newfoundpool, Leicester 85, 90
Newton 202
    Neuton' 202
Northampton, Northants. 83, 91, 96, 101
Northamptonshire 117
Norhenges (nr. Barkby, Leics.) 257
North Bridge, Leicester 76, 84, 90, 234
Northfolke (Norfolk) 202
North Gate, Leicester 84, 90, 195, 196, 198, 199, 201, 208, 228, 230, 234
North Kilworth, Leics. (Keuelingworth) 240

'North Meadow' 84
Northorp' (nr. Thurmaston, Leics.) 260
Nortona (Norton-by-Twycross, Leics.)
    240
Noseley, Leics. 260
Nottyng (Nottingham, Notts.) 214
Novo Castillo (Newcastle upon Tyne) 205,
    207
Nueray 282
    Nuueray 280
Nuneaton, Warw. 42, 86
Nuneaton nunnery, Warw. 137

Oadeby (Oadby, Leics.) 203
    Oudeby 203
Okam (Oakham, Rutland) 203
Old Dalby, Leics. 239
'Oldefield', Leics. 85
    Oldefeld 267, 268
Oldehc (Lockington, Leics.) 286
Old Gildhall 204
Orm's Ditch 254
Osberton' (Osberton, Notts.) 205
Oseliston (Osleston, Derbys.) 262
    Osiluiston 286
    Osolueston 281, 284
    Osulueston 269, 270, 279
Osney Abbey, Oxford 193, 196
Osulueshawe (nr. Ansty, Leics.) 269
'Otylsyke', Leics. 86
Ouergong (Thurmaston, Leics.) 276, 277
Over, Warw. 229
Oxford, Oxon. 130, 139, 140, 141, 142, 145
    19, 20, 23, 248
Oxford University 123, 164, 171, 172
Oxindon (Great and Little Oxendon,
    Northants.) 278

Packyngton (Packington, Leics.) 211
    Pakyngton 211
Parles 256, 259, 260
    Parlis 258
Pateshill (Patshull, Staffs.) 253
Pech' (Peak District, Derbys.) 247
    Pecco 199, 210, 212, 273
Penbroc (Pembroke) 247
Pershore, Worcs. 73
Peterborough, Cambs. (Burgo/'Burch')
    246
Petelyng 201
Pichesuben' (nr. Berwood, Warw.) 254
Pinders Close, Leicester 85, 90
Pineslade (Husbands Bosworth, Leics.)
    240
Pollesworth (Polesworth, Warw.) 211,
    215
Portgate (Leicester, Leics.) 271
Poterna 253
Pousend' 247
Pratelbi (Thurmaston, Leics.) 276, 277
Pyrye 211

Quappelade 278
Queens' College, Cambridge 136, 146, 174,
    175
Quenby, Leics. 217, 270
Queniborough, Leics. 239, 264
    Quenibur 264
    Queneburcht 241

Queningburgate, Leicester 271
Quincy, France 83
Quorndon, Leics. 238
    Querendona 240

Radclyff (Ratcliffe on Soar, Notts.) 182
Radecleue (Radcliffe on Trent, Notts.)
    287
Ramsey, Cambs. 96
Reading, Berks. 127, 148, 155
Redeforn, Le (Thurmaston, Leics.) 276,
    277
Redemora (Barkby, Leics.) 264, 265
Redimwald (nr. Thorp Arnold, Leics.)
    261
'Reedes Close' 84, 85
Reigad (Reigate, Surrey) 286
Reresby (Rearsby, Leics.) 259, 260
    Rerisby 263
Ritun (Ritton, Northumb.) 281
'Robert Dole's Dufhous' 207
Rochester, Medway 148, 161
Rokebi (Rugby, nr. Clifton-upon-
    Dunsmoor, Warw.) 240, 261
Rolueston (Rolleston, Leics.) 240
Rothley, Leics. 231, 233, 236, 237, 243
    Ratheleye 281
    Role 270, 279
    Roleia 237
    Roley 206
    Roleya 285
    Rothele 199, 210
    Rotheley 199, 215
    Ruelawa 243
Rottingdean, Sussex 73
Rouen, Normandy, France 241, 247
Roydene Crescent, Leics. 86, 91
    'Warldsend' 91
Rugby, Warw. 229, 230, 261
Rumburgh, Suffolk 148
Rusper priory, Sussex 73
Rutland 101, 117
Ruyton, Salop. 282
    Ruthon' 280
    Ruton 282
Ryefurlong (Thurmaston, Leics.) 279

Sabroc' (stream) 254
Sadynton' (Saddington, Leics.) 278
    Sadyngt' 209
St Alban Hall, Oxford 145, 182
St Alban's Abbey, Herts. 127, 136, 176
St Andrews, Scotland 245
    Sancto Andrea 247, 259, 262
Saint Augustine's abbey, Canterbury 128,
    148, 157
Saint-Claude, Jura, France 151
St Clement, parish of, Leicester 198
St Edward 258
Saint Gall, Switzerland 157
St Leonard, church of 210
St Leonard, hospital of 207, 210
St Leonard, parish of, Leicester 84, 195,
    198, 199, 209
St Margaret, church of, Leicester 16, 228
St Margaret, parish of, Leicester 195, 197,
    198, 208
St Margaret's Way, Leicester 90
St Martin, church of 98, 201, 204

St Martin, parish of, Leicester 195, 197, 198,
    201
St Mary de Castro, church of, Leicester 83,
    84, 85, 201, 228, 229, 234, 243
St Mary de Castro, parish of, Leicester 84,
    198
St Michael, church of 195, 205
St Michael, parish of, Leicester 195, 197,
    205
St Nicaise, Meulan, Normandy, France
    229
St Nicholas, parish of, Leicester 195, 197,
    202
St Peter, church of 204
St Peter, parish of, Leicester 195, 197, 204
St Victor, infirmary of, Paris 71, 129, 141,
    142
Sainneville, Seine-Maritime, France 255
    Scincuile 248
    Seneuil 249, 268
    Seineuill' 252
    Seneuilla 255
Salforde (Salford, Oxon.) 257
Salisbury, Wilts. 230
    Saresburiensis 257
Salisbury cathedral, Wilts. 131, 179
Sallau (Sall, Norfolk) 242
Saltergate (Barkby, Leics.) 266
    Saltergathe 257
Sandhil (Barkby, Leics.) 264, 265
Sapecote (Sapcote, Leics.) 270
Saturday Market 204
Savoy, London palace of John of Gaunt
    122
Schelton' (Shelton, Notts.) 203
Scotland 245, 258, 284, 285
Seagrave, Leics. 233, 234, 248, 252, 259,
    263
    Sedgraue 240, 259
    Segraue 248, 252, 256, 259, 264, 268
    Setgraua 235
Segeswold (Six Hills), Leics. 238, 240
Seggeholm (Lockington, Leics.) 286
Ses (Sées, France) 260
Sharnebrok (Sharnbrook, Beds.) 240
Sheavsby (Shearsby, Leics.) 263, 278
    Sheuesby 278
    Sheuisby 263
Shepshed, Leics. 133, 145, 174, 228, 234,
    286
    Sepeheua 235, 240, 251
    Schepeshed 199, 207, 215
    Schepisched 286
Shield Close, Leics. 92
Shiredaicotes (Thurmaston, Leics.) 276
Shirhamdik' (Thurmaston, Leics.) 276,
    277
Shortwold 271
Shrewsbury, Salop. 98
Sideston (Siston, Leics.) 265
    Sibbesdon' 209
    Sibbisdon 207
    Sizeton 271
    Sybbesdon 213
    Sytheston 275
Sifrewast 240, 242
Sileby, Leics. 203
    Syleby 204
Six Hills, Leics. 238, 240

Sleaford, Lincs. 230
Sneynton (Sneinton, Notts.) 280
Soar, river 75, 76, 78, 79, 82, 83, 84, 85, 89, 90, 92, 94
South Gate, Leicester 25, 195, 201, 234, 239
Stafford, Staffs. 199, 215
Stanforde (nr Lockington, Leics.) 286
   Staunford 208
Stanton on the Wolds, Notts. 207
   Stantona 240
Stapelton (Stapleton, Leics.) 269, 270, 272, 282, 284
'Stocking, the', Leics. 82, 83, 86, 89
   Stockinges' 83, 89
Stocking Closes, Leics. 77, 82, 83, 86, 92
Stocking Farm, Leics. 77, 82, 86
Stockingford, Warw. 86, 238
   Stockiford 240
   Stokinford 251
   Stockingforth 186
Stocking Hill, Leics. 86, 89
   Sterkeshull 267, 268
   'Sterkes Hull' 85, 86
Stocking Wood, Leics. 83, 86, 88, 89, 93
Stok' (Stoke Golding, Leics.) 240, 252, 253
Stoney Lane, Leics. 89, 90
Stonholm (Thurmaston, Leics.) 276, 277
Stoniford (Thurmaston, Leics.) 276, 277
Stonifurlong (Bramcote, Warw.) 281
Stoughton, Leics. 226, 231, 239, 276, 279
   Stocton 212, 214, 276, 279
   Stoctona 240, 251
   Stoucton 199, 212
Stretton, Leics. 274
Stubfurlong (Thurmaston, Leics.) 276
Sugkebergia (Shuckburgh, Warw.) 240
Sumeruill' 272
Surrey 98
Sutherdale, Le (Thurmaston, Leics.) 275
Sutton (Sutton Cheney, Leics.) 239, 240, 242
Syreford' 280
Syresham, Northants. 234, 239, 248
   Sigresham 235, 240, 248, 251, 253
Swepston' (Swepstone, Leics.) 207
Swinesmarket 204
Syon Abbey, Middlesex 128, 129, 132, 133

Tacker 211
Tame, river 245, 246
   Thama 246
Terondona (Garendon) 244
Theddingworth, Leics. 234, 239
   Tamgenuurd 235
   Tamgwrtth 240
   Thaingewrtha 251
   Themgworth 241
Thev' 252
Thewh, le (Sanvey Gate, Leicester) 212
Thistlidoles (Thurmaston, Leics.) 276, 277
Thormfurlong (Thurmaston, Leics.) 267
Thornton, Leics. 132
   Thorneton' 205
   Thorentona 240
Thorney, Cambs. 96
Thornhow (Thurmaston, Leics.) 276

Thornton Abbey, North Lincs. 31, 36, 37, 38, 39, 66
Thurnum (Thornton, Lancs.) 244
Thorentona (Thornton, Leics.) 240
Thorp, Leics. 208, 238
Thorp iuxta Barkeby (Barkby Thorpe, Leics.) 265, 287
Thorpe, Northants. 238
   Trop 240
Thorpe Arnold, Leics. 234, 261, 262
   Torp 240, 251
   Torp Ernald 261
   Torp iuxta Meltona 235, 251
   Torpe Ernalde 201
   Trop 240
Threngston (Thringstone, Leics.) 202
Thurcaston, Leics. 77, 79, 81, 82, 89
   Thurkeliston 262
Thurgarton, Norfolk 148
Thurmaston, Leics. 201, 207, 227, 233, 234, 249, 253, 258, 260, 266, 267, 272, 273, 274, 275, 276, 277, 278, 279, 283, 284, 285
   Thormediston 267
   Thurmedeston 267, 272, 276, 283
   Thurmedeston 267
   Thurmeston 209, 260, 261, 274, 276
   Thurmodeston 249, 258, 265, 266, 272, 273, 274, 275, 276, 277, 278, 279, 284, 285
   Thurmodestuna 273, 277
   Thurmodiston 258
   Tormodeston 253, 274
   Turmodesthona 249
   Turmodeston 240
   Turmodestona 240
Thurnby, Leics. 234
   Turnebi 240, 251
   Turneby 235
Tirlington, Leics. 238
   Turlinton 240
Titchfield, Hants. 148, 157, 165, 166
Toftes (nr Lockington, Leics.) 286
Toledo, Spain 221
Tooley Park, Leics. 79, 82
Torp (Countesthorpe, Leics.) 240
Tourville, France 238, 239
   Tureuilla 251
   Turuuilla 240
Trafford, Northants. 282
   Traford 285
Trinity College, Cambridge 146, 176, 178, 179, 181
Trop (Thorpe, Northants.) 238, 240
Tungemare (nr. Barkby, Leics.) 264
Tunhul (Thurmaston, Leics.) 276, 277
Turret Gateway, Leicester 25
Twyford, Leics. 269, 270, 281
Tychel (Titchwell, Norfolk) 266
Tynemouth 248

Ulverscroft, Leics. 249
   Vluescroft 252

Vatteville, Normandy, France 234, 236, 237, 239, 243
   Wateuilla 235, 238, 240, 243, 251
Venice, Italy 71, 73
Vernum (Vernham's Dean, Hants.) 264

Veteriponte 252
'Vicus parcamenti' ('Parchment Place') 203
Vingnoles (Vignoles, France) 268

Waleton (Walton, Leics.) 263, 278
Waling' (Wallingford, Berks.) 252
Waltydis (stream? nr. Barkby, Leics.) 257
   Waltidis 266
Wanlip, Leics. 239, 265, 278, 284, 285
   Anlep 240, 274, 278, 284, 285
   Anlep bridge (nr. Barkby, Leics.) 265
   Anelep 258
Wareham, Dorset 229
Warton, Warw. 244
Warwick, Warw. 226, 228, 231, 232, 237, 238, 245, 246, 253
   Warewic 245
   Warewich 246
   Warewyk' 254, 255
   Warrewych 240
Wauere (nr. Clifton-upon-Dunsmoor, Warw.) 240, 261, 278
Waynhous 205, 206
Welbeck Avenue, Leicester 90
Weldon, Northants. 256
Wellow Abbey, Lincs. 139
Wells, Somers. 226
   Welles 253
Welton, Northants. 238, 240, 247
   Welethona 240
   Weltona 247
Werviland' (Bramcote, Warw.) 281
Westan (Whetstone, Leics.) 286
West Bridge, Leicester 198, 253
Westcotes, Leicester 84, 85
West Gate, Leicester 25, 38, 84, 239
West Isley, Berks. 234
   Hildeslai 240
   Hildislai 251
   Indeslai 235
Westminster 148, 245
   Westmonasterium 257
Westcote (Syresham, Northants.) 248, 252, 253
Westkyuelyngwrd' (West Kilworth, Leics.) 242
Weston (Barkby, Leics.) 271
Weston-on-Avon, Warw. 234, 261
   Westhona 251
   Westona 235
Wetelondes (Thurmaston, Leics.) 276, 277
Wetherby, Yorks. 199, 213, 214
Weytholm (Thurmaston, Leics.) 267
Whetstan (Whetstone, Leics.) 240
   Wheston 215
Whiteby 212
Widuilla 245
Willac 255
Wilughby (Willoughby, Leics.) 203
   Wylughby 204
Winchester, Hants. 72, 83, 227, 232, 257, 258, 284, 285, 286
Wintonie 257, 258, 262, 284
Wiricestresira (Worcs.) 237
Wisbech, Cambs. (Wyzebech) 264
Witefelda (Whitfield, Northants.) 246
Witewich (Whitwick, Leics.) 240, 251

Wollaton Hall, Notts. 116
Wolvey, Warw. 255, 256
   Wlfey 280
   Wlfeye 280
   Wlueya 256
Wong, Le (Thurmaston, Leics.) 273, 274
Woodgate, Leicester 90
   Wodgate 210
   Wodegate 199, 214
   Woldgate 271
Wootton Lodge, Staffs. 116
Worcester, Worcs. 229, 237, 252
   Wigornia 253

Wychesholm (Curdworth, Warw.) 244, 245
   Wichisholm 246
Wye, river 239
Wylamwro (Thurmaston, Leics.) 276, 277
Wybetoft (Wibtoft, Warw.) 280, 282
Wykyngeston (Wigginton, Herts.) 284
   Wykes 285
   Wykyngston 203
Wymondham, Leics. 144, 145
   Womyndham 144
Wytebec (Whitbeck, Cumbria) 258, 263, 266
   Wytebek 259

Wyteby (Whitby) 273, 274, 278, 279
Wyzebech (Wisbech, Cambs.) 264

York 187, 189, 219
   Eboracum 241
   Ebroicensis 247
York Minster 146
Youlgreave, Derbys. 199, 232, 239
   Ialgraue 240
   Iolgraue 263
   Iolegraue 266
   Yolegraue 259, 279, 281
   Yolgraue 256, 281, 282

General index

Note: page numbers in *italics* refer to illustrations.

abbey church *see* churches
Abbey Grounds 3–13
  see also Abbey Park
Abbey House
  see also Cavendish House
  19th century 103
  main elements 104
  west range (Phase 4) 110, 112–15
Abbey Meadow 5–6
Abbey Park 77, *78*, 93
  creation 1, 5, 9, 75
  opening 65, 102–3
Abbot Penny's wall 21–4
abbots
  see also chair 46
  hall 24
  institution 228, 231
  lodgings 39, 43, 60, 99, 105
  park 90–1
  Sadyngton, William 217–34
accommodation *see* lodgings
acreages, post-Dissolution 82–3
administrative records 143–4, 145
All Saints parish 195, 197, 205–8
altars 13, 73, 74
animal bones 58, 63
arable land 91–2
arch, east range 45
archaeological investigations *see*
  excavations
archives 26, 122, 145, 160
assarting 81–2
astrology 220–1
astronomy 221
author catalogue 128, 129, 147, 163

banks, estate boundary 86, *87–8*
barbican 36–8
barns 1, 13, 99
Bathe rental (1408) 226
Beaumont Leys *81*, 86, 90, 93
  map (1656) colour plate C
Beaumont Wood 82
behaviour, Abbot Sadyngton 217–24
Belgrave Wood 79, 82, 89
bestiaries 150
Bible commentaries 171, 174–5, 176
bibles 138, 173–4
biblical studies 131, 137
biggin closes 83

binding descriptions 147–72
  abbreviated descriptions 161–2
  book sizes 149–50
  colours 152, 154, 156, 159–60
  earlier catalogues 162–5
  limp covers 156–9, 165–7
  miscellaneous 159–61
  overcovers 150–1, 170
  stiff-boards 151–4, 165–7, *168*, 169–70
  terminology 172
Birstall Wood 79, 82, 89
bishop's visit 217–18, 219–20, 223–4
blindstamped bindings 153, 154–5
book bindings *see* binding descriptions
book collections 127–46
  see also binding descriptions; catalogue
    of books; manuscripts
  12th and 13th centuries 135–8
  14th and 15th centuries 139–43
  15th century holdings 128–32
  acquired by Abbot Charyte 143–4, 149,
    163
  acquired by Abbot Sadyngton 220–1
  donations 132–5, 137, 162–3
  location 128, 129, 131–2
  loss and dispersal 145–6
  ownership 133–5, 137, 138, 145–6
  patterns of use 130
  production 135–7, 143–5
  shelf-order 128, 129, 131, 149, 171
  surviving 127, 133–6
  textbooks 129, 131, 137, 139–40, 142
Bordesley Abbey 229
boulder clay 77–9
boundaries, home demesne estate *81*
boys 217–19, 221, 222–4
Bradsole Abbey book catalogue 166
breviates 225–6
brick kilns 24
bricks
  gatehouse 4, 38–9
  hearth 63
  tank 65
  wall 21–4
brickwork patterns 22–3, *23*
Bromkinsthorpe lands 82–4, 85
building stone 95
burgage tenements 195, 196
burgesses 195, 198
burials 42, 46

business manuscripts 143–4

canons
  15th century 217
  Black Canons 193
  book donations 133, 139–42
  duties 119, 141
  Kenilworth 230
  Knighton, Henry 119–20
cartularies 149, 225–7
  see also charters
catalogue of books 119, 127–30
  see also book collections
  author catalogue 128, 129, 147, 163
  binding descriptions 147–72
  fair copy 162, 183
  function 130
  manuscript 183–5
  other British catalogues 165–6
  scripts 130
  subject catalogue 128, 129, 147
Cavendish House
  see also Abbey House; gatehouse
  Countess of Devonshire's residence 98,
    101
  evidence for interpretation 104
  farmhouse *103*
  fire damage 101, 104, 116
  kitchen block *102*, *109*, 110–12
  L-shaped form *109*, 117
  modifying features *102*, 115–18
  north façade 35–6, *100*, 105, *107*, 110, 117
  Phases 1 and 2 (medieval gatehouse)
    104
  Phase 3 (late 16th-century) 104–10
  Phase 4 (late 16th–17th century) *109*,
    110–18
  remains 9, 13, 28
  south range modifications 110–12
  south view *101*, *102*, *108*, 117
  view from river (1796) *78*
  west range 112–15, 117–18
cellars 45, 105–7
chained books 150, 155–6
champlevé enamelling 70
chapels
  abbey 40
  Ingarsby Grange 217, 218, 223
chapter house 46–7
  plan *41*

charcoal 53, 54, 63
charters xi, 225–87
see also cartularies; grants of land
foundation charter 227–8, 234–5
royal confirmation 231–2, 252–3, 257
texts 227, 234–87
Chartwary see cartularies
Charyte, William
book acquisitions 143–4, 149, 163
book catalogue 128, 147, 150, 164–5
cartulary 225–6, 234
rental 197, 198, 234
Chilvers Coton tile kilns 42
chimney breast 36, 102, 108–10, 112, 116–17
Chronicle of Henry Knighton xi, 119–25,
144, 183, 227–8
churches
see also chapels; parishes
abbey 13, 40, 67
book locations 128, 131–2
excavations 9–10
St Mary de Castro 83–5, 228–9, 243
Cistercian Ware 57
classical features 102, 115–16
claustral buildings 40–7, 67
chapter house 46–7
cloister 40–3
demolition 100
east range 44–9
plan of trenches (2000–5) 41
post-Dissolution 97
south range 43–4
west range 43
Clay Hedges 86
cloister 40–3
coal 94
coat of arms 23
cobbled yard 56–7, 61
coffins, stone 3, 10
coloured book coverings 152, 154, 156,
159–60
commercial life 91
communications 90
copper incense-boat cover 69–74
corner towers 15–16, 20, 31–5
costs of abbey foundation 230
courtyard 39
crenellation 16, 36, 38
Crown Commissioners' Survey (1538/9)
27–8, 31, 39, 67

Dalesike 85, 86, 87
Dane Hills sandstone 15, 105
dating
catalogue entries 164
foundation charter 227–8
de Pyn rental (1254) 225
debts 95
deer park 91, 93
defensive structures 24–5
demolition 95–7
devotional literature 141, 144, 191
diaper brickwork patterns 22–3, 23
dining chamber 59
Dissolution 2–3, 95–103
ditches, estate boundary 86, 87–8
divination 218–24
see also onychomancy; scrying
Domesday woodlands 79–82

domestic rubbish 53, 55, 58, 63
donations of books 132–5, 137, 162–3
dormitory 44–5, 46
double volume bindings 163
Doveland Wood 82–3, 85
drainage, natural 76
drains 8
cloisters 43
east range 44, 45
kitchen 49, 53, 55, 56
main 64
rainwater 57–9, 62
drinking poems ix–x

Earthenware 3 pottery 56
east range, monastery 44–9
east walls 17–21, 19, 24
east–west drains 57, 58, 62
economic affairs 125
embroidered vestment 10
enamelling
incense-boat cover 69–74
Limoges method 70–1, 73, 74
encaustic tiles 3, 4, 8
enclosures
northern 11, 12, 14–21
southern 12, 21–4
entrance 16
estate see home demesne estate
excavated remains 25–65
church and claustral buildings 40–7
gatehouse 28–39
infirmary 63–4
yard and kitchen 47–59
excavations
see also plans; trenches
17th century 2–3
19th century 3–6, 8
1923–7 6–9, 26
1929–32 1, 9–13, 25–7, 65
2000–5 xiii, 2, 104
claustral buildings 41
kitchen (monastic) 2002–5 48, 49, 51–3
mansion, south range 2004 111
exemplars 144–5

farm 7, 96
farm buildings 27, 39, 103
fire damage (1645) 101, 104, 116
fireplaces 49, 50, 52–3, 54, 59–60
fish remains 63
fishponds 13, 94, 99
floodplain 76–7
Fosseway 80–1, 83–4, 89, 90
foundation of the abbey 227–33
charter 227–8, 234–5
Earl Robert ii's influence 229–30, 231
endowments 230–1
grants 228–9, 231–2
royal confirmation 231–2, 236–7, 238–41,
252–3, 257
France, enamel work 71
frankincense 73, 222
Freake's Ground 80, 85
The Frith 79, 91

gables 102, 108
gardens 4, 14, 17, 20, 21, 27, 99
garderobe 19

gatehouse
see also Cavendish House
bricks 38–9
construction 24
detached kitchen 36, 39
dimensions and features 36–7
dwelling 1, 98
east gate hall turret 34–5
excavations 2000–4 28
internal walls 30
lodgings 31, 39
northern facade 35–6
Phase 1 (12th or 13th century) 28–31
Phase 2 (c. 1350–1500) 31–9
Phase 3 (late 16th-century mansion)
104–10
Phase 4 (late 16th–17th century) 14, 109,
110–18
plans 29, 37
porch 107–8, 109, 110
post-Dissolution 100
remodelling 105–7
south-east corner turret 35
south-western turret 32–4
west gate hall turret 32–3, 34, 38
gates 38
gateway, outer 14, 16–17, 16, 99
geology 77–9
Geryn's Rental 195, 201–15, 226, 228
glacial soils 77–9
glazed earthenware 8
gluttony ix–x
grain 94
granite 15, 34
grants of land
see also charters; patrons
1551 96
abbey foundation 83, 231–2
Belgrave family 89
post-Dissolution 82–3
St Mary de Castro 83–5
Simon de Montfort 85–9
gravel pit 30
graves 42, 46
great hall 39
Great Schism 123
guest facilities 47–8, 60, 99

halt-way walls 16–17, 24, 29
haymaking 92
Hereswode 79, 84
Heritage Lottery Fund 1
higher studies 129, 131, 137, 142
history
book collections 132–5
Henry Knighton's Chronicle 120–5
home demesne estate 75–94
abbot's park 90–1
communications 90
early grants 83–5
land use 91–2
post-Dissolution history 82–3
Stocking Hill boundary 81, 89–90
topography and geology 76, 77–9
western and northern boundary 81,
85–9
woodlands 79–82
horoscope 221
human skeletons 3, 8, 9

incantations 222
incense burning 73–4
incense-boat cover 69–74
    acquisition and use 71–3
    manufacture 70
    parallels 71, 72
income 75, 218
infirmary 17, 18, 27, 28, 63–4, 132
Ingarsby Grange chapel 217, 218, 223
inner court 39–40
interval towers 15, 18–19, 18

jambs 113–14, 117
jug handle 3

Kenilworth canons 230
kilns 24, 42
King's Lodging 28, 59
kitchen (gatehouse)
    chimney breast 36, 102, 108–10, 112,
      116–17
    detached 36, 37, 39
    post-Dissolution 100
kitchen (monastic)
    dimensions 50, 59–60
    excavations 2002–5 48, 49, 51–3
    external features 55–7
    internal features 52–5
    ovens 49, 53, 54, 60, 63, 100
    walls 49–51, 52
Knighton, Henry
    Chronicle ix, 119–25, 144, 183, 227–8
    economic affairs 125
    John of Gaunt's campaigns 122–3, 124
    Lollardy 123–4
    manuscript 183
    war with the French 122

land use 91–2
landscape 75–94
Lanthony Abbey book catalogue 165
'The Laundry' 3, 4
lavatorium 43
law textbooks 131, 137, 139
lead
    roofing 95–6, 97
    water pipes 49, 62–3
leasing 96
lecterns 128, 130–1, 171
Leicester, medieval layout and abbey xii
Leicester Cartulary 225, 226, 234
Leicester City Council 1–2, 6, 9, 65, 101–3
Leicester Navigation 77, 78
Leicester Rental 234
Leics. Archaeological and Historical
    Society xiii
libraria 119, 128–9, 130–1, 149, 166, 170–2
limestone 35
Limoges enamel, incense-boat cover 10,
    69–74, colour plate D
limp cover bindings 156–9, 165–7
liturgical books 132, 144, 149
liturgical vessels 72–3
livestock 93–4
location, outside borough xii, 193, 195,
    199
lodgings
    abbot's 31, 39, 43, 60, 99, 105
    king's 28, 59

Lollardy 123–4
loose quires 156, 157–8
lordship 196–7

magic 218–19
main drain 64
mansion house 27, 99, 100, 104
    see also Cavendish House
manufacture of books 135–7, 143–5
manuscripts colour plates E, F
    see also separate index
    acquisition 134
    single-sheet charter 192
    surviving 127, 133–6, 173–92
maps
    see also plans
    Beaumont Leys colour plate C
    medieval Leicester xii
    parishes 80
    rental sites 194
    survey of the site (1613) colour plate B
    William Senior (1613) 14, 75–6, 82, 84,
      89–93
market garden 27, 65
meadows 91–2
medical books 131, 139, 142
medieval Fosse 80–1, 83–4, 90
middle ages reconstruction colour plate A
Midland Blackware 55
Midland Yellow pottery 54
mills 17, 84, 94
mullions 112–13, 117
myrrh 73

narrative 120–5
necromancy 221, 222, 223
Newfoundpool 80, 85
niches see statue niches
nonae tax 197–8
North Bridge 76, 90
North Gate suburbs 198, 199, 200
North Meadow 84, colour plate B
north wall 15–16, 24
north-south drain 57–8, 62
northern enclosure 14–21
    reconstruction (1930) 11
novum Rentale xi, 26, 86, 183, 234

occupation post-Dissolution 100–1
onychomancy 218, 219–20, 221
orchard 14, 20, 21
oriel window 48
outbuildings 14
outer court 64–5
outer gateway 14, 16, 16, 99
ovens 49, 53, 54, 60, 63, 100
overcovers 150–1, 170
ownership
    books 133–5, 137, 138, 145–6
    Cavendish family 75, 82–3, 98, 101, 116
    grants 82–3
    Hastings family 83, 97–8, 105, 108
    Leicester City Council 6, 9, 65, 101–3
    Parr, William 96–7
    post-Dissolution 96–101

papal bulla 4, 10
parapet 102, 116
parchment bindings 157

parishes 84
    map 80
    rents 194, 195, 197, 201–15
parks 90–1
    see also Abbey Park
passageways 47, 55–6, 60–1
pasture 82, 91–3
patrons
    see also charters; grants of land
    Leicester, Earls of 229–32
    Quincy, Roger de 232
    Segrave, Stephen de 232–3
pedestrian access 37, 38
pedimented chimneys 116–17
perimeter walls 15
pipes 49, 62–3
plans
    see also maps
    1923–5 excavations 7, 26, 27
    1929–32 excavations 26, 27
    abbey reconstruction (1930) 11
    Cavendish House (17th century) 109
    chapter house 41, 47
    gatehouse 29, 37
    kitchen excavations (2002–5) 48
    northern enclosure (1930) 11, 12
    Phase 3 gatehouse 105
    restoration (1894) 5
    southern enclosure 12
    trenches, claustral ranges (2000–5) 41,
      44, 47
poetry ix–x
porch, gatehouse 107–8, 109, 110
post-Dissolution
    book loss and dispersal 145–6
    demesne estates 82–3
    demolition and sale 95–8
    estate identification 103–4
    Phase 3 mansion house 104–10
    Phase 4 mansion house 110–18
    secular estate 99–103
Potters Marston Ware 52, 56
pottery 8, 52, 54, 55, 56, 57
precentor 119, 129
precinct walls
    excavated remains 1, 13–24
    gatehouse relationship 30–1
    post-Dissolution 99–100, 113–14
property xiii, 75, 84
    see also rural property; suburban
      property; urban property
Protestantism 123, 124
pseudo-military features 19–21, 25
purlins 114–15
pyx 72

rainwater drains 57–9, 62
reconstructions
    abbey (1930) 11
    later middle ages colour plate A
    northern enclosure (1930) 11
    survey of the site (1613) colour plates B
      and C
refectory 44, 59
registers 149, 225–6
rentals
    Bathe (1408) 226
    Charyte, William 197, 198, 234
    de Pyn (1254) 225

Geryn (1341) 195, 197, 198, 201–15, 226,
    228
'Leicester Rental' 234
manuscripts 183–4, 185–6
'novum Rentale' xi, 26, 86, 183, 234
'Second Leicester Rental' 234
sites *194*
rents 195–7
    in fowl 196
    income 196, 197
    Osney Abbey comparison 193, 196
reredorter 45–6
rituals, divination 218–14
river gravels 77–9
robber trenches
    see also stone robbers
    chapter house 46
    church 13
    gatehouse 28–30, 31, 38
    kitchen 49–50
Roman finds 5, 6, 8
Roman Fosseway *80–1*, 90
roof timbers 114–15
routeways 90
royal confirmation 231–2, 236–7, 238–41,
    252–3, 257
royal patronage 119
ruins 9
    see also excavated remains
rural property 226

sacristy 69, 72
Sadyngton, William 217–34
St Leonard's parish *80*, 84, 195, 197,
    209–15
St Margaret's parish 195, 197, 208–9
St Martin's parish 195, 197, 202–4
St Mary of the Annunciation parish 195,
    201–2
St Mary de Castro church
    charter 243
    grant of lands 83–5
    origins 228–9
St Michael's parish 195, 197, 205
St Nicholas' parish 195, 197, 202
St Peter's parish 195, 197, 204–5
sale of abbey 95–8
sandstone 15, 34, 105
Scheduled Ancient Monument 2
schoolbooks 149, 166
scribes 162
scriptoria 128, 131, 149
scripts 130, 135, 137–8
scrying 218–19, 222
Second Leicester Cartulary 225, 226, 234
Second Leicester Rental 234
secundo folio references 129, 133, 147, 163
semi-limp and flexible bindings 172
Senior, William, map (1613) *14*, 75–6, 82,
    84, 89–93
sermons 131, 137, 139, 140, 144, 155, 176, 178,
    186
sheep 93
site description 13–24, 67
site geography 76–9, 193, 195, 199

skeletons 3, 8, 9
slate 8
slype 47
Smythsonian architecture 116
soakaway 56, 59
Soar, River 17, 76–7, *78*
soils 77–9
sorcery 217–18
south range
    abbey 43–4
    Abbey House *109*, 110–12
south walls 17–21
southern enclosure 21–4, 25
specularii 218
spinster clustering 199–200
stained glass 4
stair turrets
    Cavendish House 108, *109*, 110, *111*
    west range 112, 114, *114*, 115
staircases 108, *117*
statue niches 22–4, *22*, *23*
stiff-board bindings 151–4, 165–7, *168*,
    169–70
    overcovers 150–1, 170
stirrup 4
The Stocking 77, 82
Stocking Closes 82–3, 86, 89
Stocking Hill boundary *81*, 89–90
Stocking Wood 82–3, 86, *88*, 89, 92–3
stone coffins 3, 10
stone robbers 40, 43, 44, 46
    see also robber trenches
stone tank 42
stratified deposits 52, 62
sub-circular tower 20
subject catalogue 128, 147
suburban property 196, 198, 199, 200
Swithland slate 8

tanks 4–5, 42
tanned skin bindings 153, 154
tawed skin bindings 170
taxes 197–8
tenements xi, 195–6
terminology, book bindings 172
textbooks 129, 131, 137, 139–40, 142, 190–1
textile book coverings 160
texts of charters 227, 234–87
theft 218, 223
theological textbooks 131, 137, 140, 190–1
thumbnail divination 218, 219–20, 222
Thurcaston Wood 79–82, 89
thurifers 74
tiles 3, 4, 8, 40–2
Titchfield Abbey book catalogue 165–6
tomb, Cardinal Wolsey 3, 6
topography 76, 77–9
toponymic bynames 199
towers
    see also turrets
    interval 15, 18–19, *18*
    north-east corner 15–16
    outer gateway 16–17
    south-east corner 20
training in excavation 2, 65–6

trenches
    see also excavations; robber trenches
    1860s excavations 4
    1923 excavations 7–8
    2000–5 excavations *41*, *44*, 47
    gatehouse 29
turrets
    see also stair turrets; towers
    gatehouse 31–5, *32–3*, 38
    outer gateway 16–17, *16*

unbound books 157–8, 161
undercrofts 43, 44
university textbooks 131, 137, 139–40,
    142
urban immigration 199, 200
urban property 193–215
    cartulary 226
    immigration 199, 200
    income 196, 197
    map *194*
    rents 195–7
    value 193–5

Victorian bay windows *114*
visit of Bishop Alnwick 217–18, 219–20,
    223–4
visitation book *219*

walls
    see also precinct walls
    Abbot Penny's wall 21–4
    east 17–21, *19*, 24
    halt-way 16–17, 24, *29*
    kitchen (monastic) 49–51, *52*
    north 15–16, 24
    south 17–21
    west 15
warming house 44
waste land 89
water supply 49, 62–3
water tank 8
water-mill 96
wealth xiii
wells 49, 57, 61
west range
    Abbey House 112–15, 117–18
    monastery 43
west wall 15
white book coverings 151, 152, 156, 159
windows
    Abbey House 112–14, *113*, 115
    gatehouse 105–6, 110, *111*
    oriel 48
    stained glass 4
    Victorian period *114*
witchcraft 218–19
Wolsey, Cardinal 3, 6
women, tenants 199–200
wooden book boards 151, 153–4, 170
Woodgate 90
woodlands 79–82, 91–2

yard 48–9
York Minster 187–9

Compiled by *Indexing Specialists (UK) Ltd*, Regent House, Hove Street, Hove, East Sussex BN3 2DW